CLASSICS
An Investor's Anthology

CLASSICS
An Investor's Anthology

Edited by
Charles D. Ellis
Managing Partner
Greenwich Associates

with
James R. Vertin

BUSINESS ONE IRWIN

Homewood, Illinois 60430

The Institute of Chartered Financial Analysts is pleased to
have facilitated the publication of this volume, but neither
endorses nor rejects the philosophies and views expressed in the
articles.

This publication is designed to provide accurate and
authoritative information in regard to the subject matter
covered. It is sold with the understanding that neither the
author nor the publisher is engaged in rendering legal, accounting,
or other professional service. If legal advice or other expert
assistance is required, the services of a competent
professional person should be sought.

*From a Declaration of Principles jointly adopted by a Committee
of the American Bar Association and a Committee of Publishers.*

Managing editor: Merrily Mazza
Production manager: Stephen K. Emry
Jacket Design: Tim Kaage
Compositor: Publication Services, Inc.
Typeface: 11/13 Times Roman
Printer: R.R. Donnelley & Sons Company

LIBRARY OF CONGRESS
Library of Congress Cataloging-in-Publication Data

Classics : An Investor's Anthology / edited by Charles
    D. Ellis with James R. Vertin.
        p.   cm.
    ISBN 1-55623-098-2
    1. Investments.   2. Risk Management.   3. Stock exchange.
    I. Ellis, Charles D.   II. Vertin, James R.
    HG4522.C57 1989
    332.6'78 — dc19   88–17609
                                                                CIP

Printed in the United States of America
        8 0 DO 5 4 3 2

*To Dave Dodd and Ben Graham
with gratitude for their personal
friendship and professional wisdom.*

As an important part of the celebration of the 30th Anniversary of the CFA program and the founding of the Institute of Chartered Financial Analysts, *Classics I* and *II* are being sent to members of the Association for Investment Management and Research.

What better way to celebrate the 30th Anniversary of the ICFA — with its wonderfully successful commitment to developing a Body of Knowledge — than to share with the membership a collection of several centuries of thoughtful writings on the subject of investing.

Special thanks to AIMR, editors Ellis and Vertin, and Business One Irwin (Richard D. Irwin, Inc.) for their collective efforts in making *Classics I* and *II* available to our membership.

Darwin M. Bayston, CFA
President and CEO
Association for Investment
Management and Research

Introduction

The foundation for our profession was set more than 50 years ago by David Dodd and Benjamin Graham through their splendid textbook on investment analysis and decision-making formally titled *Security Analysis*, but widely admired as "Graham and Dodd." *Security Analysis* has been the most useful and influential book ever written in the field of investments, and the student (of whatever age) who returns to it is always rewarded.

A number of works on investing—including many of extraordinary value—have gone out of print and are difficult to find. Many others have never appeared in book form at all. This is a loss for all who love financial analysis, investing in securities, and managing portfolios, and all who enjoy being caught up in the continuing romance of this varied, dynamic, frustrating, and exciting endeavor.

This "investor's treasure chest" is offered in tribute to the many gifted thinkers and writers who have provided investors with insight, instruction, and entertainment. It is a storehouse of value to those who wish to reread familiar classics or experience firsthand the initial pleasure of reading the writings of great investors they do not yet know.

Preparing the volume has been a very happy experience for me. Who could feel otherwise after spending a Saturday reading Warren Buffett and the following Sunday reading Maynard Keynes? During the past five years, it has been my pleasure and privilege to read many documents I had always hoped to find time to read. The process of discovery has been delightful.

This project has introduced me to a community of interest and connection. For example, Warren Buffett studied with Ben Graham at Columbia—as did John Templeton—and says Phil Fisher had "quite an impact on him." Keynes reviewed Edgar Lawrence Smith's book in the *Adheneum*. Edwin LeFevre's book stimulated Mr. Johnson to leave Ropes Grey and the practice of law and to buy Fidelity Fund (when its total assets were just $3 million versus today's $80 *billion*). Buffett, Keynes, and Johnson were the heros in Adam Smith's *Money Game*. In a way, this collection invites us all to visit in their community.

Many investors generously helped make this collection possible and introduced me to documents that had been unfamiliar. Hopefully, the process of collecting can and will continue. All readers are invited to nominate articles, essays, chapters of books, speeches, and memoranda they would like to see in a future edition.

Note: For each selection, I have written a brief introduction, which appears at the beginning of the piece. In some cases, only certain parts of a selection were used; omission of text is noted by a series of five asterisks. All page numbers cited in footnotes refer to the original source rather than this volume.

I gratefully acknowledge the forbearance and perseverance of the following staff members of the Institute of Chartered Financial Analysts: Darwin Bayston, Katy Sherrerd, Susan Brennan, Nina Hutchinson, April Ford, and Ellen Goldlust.

I am especially grateful to my dear friend Jim Vertin for his wisdom, guidance, and insight in making this publication possible.

Charles D. Ellis
Greenwich, Connecticut

LIST OF CONTRIBUTORS

Peter Avenali, CFA

James Balog

Thomas Barry, CFA

Rex J. Bates, CFA

Charles M. Becker, CFA

Fischer Black

Douglas K. Blair, CFA

Edmund M. Bleich, CFA

Frank E. Block, CFA

A. William Bodine

John F. Bohmfalk, Jr., CFA

Thomas H. Broadus, Jr., CFA

Thomas B. Brown, CFA

Warren E. Buffett

Philip W. Burge, CFA

Thomas Burnett, CFA

Glenelg P. Caterer, CFA

George D. Clark, Jr., CFA

James B. Clinton, CFA

John M. Convery, CFA

Charles E. Coupal, CFA

M. Colyer Crum

Ted T. Dahl, CFA

John S. Dale, CFA

George M. DeVoe, Jr., CFA

Walter M. Dixon, Jr., CFA

David L. Dodd

Peter F. Drucker
M. Harvey Earp, CFA
John English
Daniel J. Forrestal III, CFA
Albert A. Fulton, CFA
J. Gordon Gibson, CFA
George J. W. Goodman
J. Parker Hall III, CFA
James R. Hamilton, CFA
Joseph S. Hancort
Donald M. Helton, CFA
John Hinkle, CFA
Bernhard Hoffman, CFA
Robert H. Jeffrey
H. Alden Johnson, Jr., CFA
Philip R. Keller, CFA
Donald H. Korn, CFA
Richard W. Lambourne, CFA
Peter Landau
Charles Larsen III, CFA
Dean LeBaron, CFA
Martin L. Leibowitz
Jay O. Light
Thomas N. Mathers, CFA
Edward J. Mathias
Gary F. J. McDonald, CFA
John G. McDonald
Peter M. McEntyre, CFA
Gary E. Mede, CFA
Edmund A. Mennis, CFA
William Miller, CFA
Peter L. Mitchelson, CFA
Charles H. Mott, CFA
Frederick L. Muller, CFA
John A. Nielsen

Harold Newman
Theodore M. Ohashi, CFA
Scott D. Opsal, CFA
J. Hunter Orr, Jr., CFA
Donvan J. Paul, CFA
W. Robert Perkins, CFA
H. Bradlee Perry, CFA
David R. Porter, CFA
Norton H. Reamer, CFA
James F. Rothenberg, CFA
Robert S. Salomon, Jr.
Edward A. Sawin, Jr., CFA
David N. Schaaf, CFA
Gerd E. Schaeffer, CFA
Richard R. Schmaltz
Sir David Scholey
John J. F. Sherrerd, CFA
Charles T. Silverson, Jr., CFA
Tyler J. Smith, CFA
Dewain A. Sparrgrove, CFA
George B. Springman, CFA
John M. Templeton, CFA
M. David Testa, CFA
Howard C. Tharsing, CFA
Theodore M. Theodore, CFA
M. Jay Trees, CFA
Donald I. Trott, CFA
James R. Vertin, CFA
James N. von Germeten, CFA
Charles C. Walden, CFA
Nelson S. Weller, CFA
William L. Wilke, CFA
Arthur Williams III, CFA
Allis Wolf, CFA
Arthur Zeikel

SOURCES

The following sources granted the editors permission to reprint the articles appearing in this book.

Permissions Director
Atlantic Monthly
8 Arlington Street
Boston, MA 02116

Permissions Director
Publications
David L. Babson & Co., Inc.
1 Memorial Drive
Cambridge, MA 02142-1300

Mr. Warren E. Buffett
Chairman
Berkshire Hathaway, Inc.
1440 Kiewit Plaza
Omaha, NE 68131

Permissions Director
The Syndics of the
Cambridge University Press
32 East 57th Street
New York, NY 10022

Permissions Director
Publications Department
CIGNA Corporation
Hartford, CT 06152

Citicorp
Investor Relations
399 Park Avenue, 31st Floor
New York, NY 10043

Permissions Director
Dean Witter & Co., Inc.
101 Barclay Street, 22nd Floor
New York, NY 10007

Permissions Director
Donaldson Lufkin & Jenrette
Securities, Inc.
140 Broadway
New York, NY 10005

Permissions Director
Doubleday & Co., Inc.
245 Park Avenue
New York, NY 10167

Permissions Director
Dow Jones & Company, Inc.
P.O. Box 300
Princeton, NJ 08540

Permissions Director
Dow Jones-Irwin, Inc.
1818 Ridge Road
Homewood, IL 60430

Permissions Director
E.P. Dutton
2 Park Avenue
New York, NY 10016

Permissions Director
Financial Analysts Journal
1633 Broadway
Suite 14402
New York, NY 10019

Permissions Director
Forbes
Forbes Building
60 Fifth Avenue
New York, NY 10011

Permissions Director
Publications Department
The Ford Foundation
320 East 43rd Street
New York, NY 10017

Permissions Director
Fortune
Time & Life Building
Rockefeller Center
New York, NY 10020

Permissions Director
Fraser Publishing Company
309 South Willard Street
Burlington, VT 05401

Permissions Director
Frederick Fell Publishers, Inc.
2131 Hollywood Boulevard
Hollywood, FL 33020

Mr. George H. Ross Goobey
Greystoke
19 Walton Road
Clevedon Avon
BS21 6AE
England

Permissions Director
Copyrights and Permissions Department
Harcourt Brace Jovanovich, Inc.
Orlando, FL 32887

Manager, Copyrights and Permissions
Harper & Row Publishers, Inc.
10 E. 53rd Street
New York, NY 10022

Permission Director
Harvard Business Review
Boston, MA 02163

Permissions Director
Holt, Rinehart & Winston, Inc.
6277 Sea Harbor Drive
Orlando, FL 32821

Permissions Director
Houghton Mifflin Company
1 Beacon Street
Boston, MA 02108

Permissions Director
Indicator Research Group, Inc.
451 Grand Avenue
Palisades Park, NJ 07650

Permissions Director
Institutional Investor, Inc.
488 Madison Avenue
New York, NY 10022

Mr. Richard Jenrette
Chairman
Donaldson Lufkin & Jenrette Securities, Inc.
140 Broadway
New York, NY 10005

Mr. Edward C. Johnson 3d
82 Devonshire Street
Boston, MA 02109

Permissions Director
The Journal of Finance
New York University
100 Trinity Place
New York, NY 10006

Permissions Director
The Journal of Portfolio Management
488 Madison Avenue
New York, NY 10022

Mr. Robert G. Kirby
Capital Guardian Trust Company
333 South Hope Street
52nd Floor
Los Angeles, CA 90071

Permissions Director
Liberty Fund, Inc.
7440 North Shadeland Avenue
Suite 100
Indianapolis, IN 46250

Permissions Director
Macmillan Publishing Company
866 Third Avenue
New York, NY 10022

Mr. David Mathey
c/o Mr. L.V. Sylvester, Jr.
Horizon Trust Company
76 Nassau Street
Princeton, NJ 08542

Mr. Dean Mathey
c/o Mr. James R. Cogan, Esq.
Walter, Conston, Alexander and Green
90 Park Avenue
New York, NY 10016

Permissions director
McGraw-Hill Book Company, Inc.
1221 Avenue of the Americas
New York, NY 10020

Mr. Paul F. Miller, Jr.
Miller, Anderson & Sherrerd
2 Bala-Cynwyd Plaza
Bala-Cynwyd, PA 19004

Permissions Director
The MIT Press
55 Hayward Street
Cambridge, MA 02142

Permissions Director
Publications Department
Morgan Stanley & Co., Inc.
1251 Avenue of the Americas
New York, NY 10020

Mr. Roy R. Neuberger
Neuberger and Berman
522 Fifth Avenue
New York, NY 10036

Permissions Director
Prentice-Hall, Inc.
Prentice-Hall Building
Englewood Cliffs, NJ 07632

Permissions Director
PSR Publications
301 Henrik Road
Woodside, CA 94062

Permissions Director
Random House, Inc.
201 East 50th Street
New York, NY 10022

Permissions Director
Publications Department
Salomon Brothers Inc.
One New York Plaza
New York, NY 10004

Permissions Director
Scudder, Stevens & Clark
345 Park Avenue
New York, NY 10154

Permissions Director
Simmons-Boardman Publishing Corp.
1908 Capital Avenue
Omaha, NE 68102

Permissions Director
Simon & Schuster, Inc.
1230 Avenue of the Americas
New York, NY 10020

Sterling Lord Literistic, Inc.
One Madison Avenue
New York, NY 10010

Permissions Director
T. Rowe Price Investment Services
100 East Pratt Street
Baltimore, MD 21202

Permissions Director
Teachers Insurance & Annuity
Association of America
730 Third Avenue
New York, NY 10017

Mr. John M. Templeton
Templeton, Galbraith & Hansberger, Ltd.
Suite 2100
Broward Financial Center
Fort Lauderdale, FL 33394

Permissions Director
Investment Office
University of Rochester
590 Mt. Hope Avenue
Rochester, NY 14620

Permissions Director
Unwin Hyman Limited
15-17 Broadwick Street
London W1V 1FP
England

Mr. Peter H. Vermilye
Baring America Asset Management
77 Franklin Street
Boston, MA 02110

Permission Directors
John Wiley & Sons
605 Third Avenue
New York, NY 10158

Mr. John Burr Williams
30 Lowen Road
Wellesley, MA 02181

CONTENTS

Memorandum
Dean Witter **157**

From Dean Witter & Co. Letterhead, New York, New York,
May 6, 1932, by permission of Dean Witter & Co., Inc.

PART 2   THE 1950s **163**

$12,000—Headline of the Week
Rip Van Winkle II Returns to Wall Street
David L. Babson **165**

From David L. Babson, *Weekly Staff Letter from David L. Babson & Co.,
Inc.* (Cambridge, Massachusetts, 1950, 1969), 1-4, 1-4 (respectively), by permission of David L. Babson & Co., Inc.

Is Growth Stock Investing Effective?
Some Guides to Successful
Lifetime Investing
David L. Babson and Thomas E. Babson **173**

Reprinted with permission of Macmillan Publishing Company from
Investing for a Successful Future by David L. Babson and Thomas
E. Babson. Copyright 1959 by Macmillan Publishing.

Growth Companies vs. Growth Stocks
Peter L. Bernstein **192**

Reprinted by permission of the *Harvard Business Review*. "Growth
Companies vs. Growth Stocks" by Peter L. Bernstein (September–
October 1956). Copyright 1956 by the President and Fellows of
Harvard College; all rights reserved.

Common Stock and Common Sense
*William H. Donaldson, Dan W. Lufkin, and
Richard H. Jenrette* **215**

From William H. Donaldson, Dan W. Lufkin and Richard H.
Jenrette, *Common Stock and Common Sense* (New
York, New York, 1959), 1-15, by permission of the authors.

CLASSICS
An Investor's Anthology

PART 1

PRE-WORLD WAR II

THE INVESTMENT TRUST

Paul C. Cabot

Paul Cabot's best-known success as an investor was in guiding Harvard's endowment into stocks prior to the great bull market that followed the Second World War. In the spring of 1929, he cautioned against the abuses then occurring in investment trusts.

I

Although there have been investment trusts in operation in this country for over forty years, they have not until recently enjoyed any prominence, nor have large amounts of capital been invested in them. The idea was really first developed in Great Britain and had already attained considerable proportions as early as 1880. The investment-trust plan as conceived by Mr. Robert Fleming, who is now possibly the most important English investment-trust manager, is more or less typical of the entire movement at that time. Coming from Dundee to New York as a mercantile clerk, Mr. Fleming was greatly impressed with the possibility of investing funds in this country, particularly in our then rapidly growing railroads. It was possible for him at that time to borrow money in England for as low as 3 per cent and then turn around and lend it to the American railroad companies, taking their first-mortgage bonds for

Reprinted from *Atlantic Monthly*, Vol. 143, March 1929, 401–408. Boston, Massachusetts: The Atlantic Monthly Company.

as high as 6, 7, and indeed 8 per cent. Obviously the profits for the promoters and common shareholders were very large, and the movement expanded rapidly. By 1888, eighteen of these trusts with a capital of over £23,000,000 were listed on the London Stock Exchange. By 1890 a trust "mania" was under way. For some years the British debt had been steadily reduced; capital had continued cheap and abundant; the investment trusts had been uniformly successful, paying large dividends, and there had been rapidly mounting quotations for their securities.

Referring to this "boom" in the investment-trust plan, the London *Economist* for April 6, 1889, remarks that "although successful with the public, the companies have not in some cases been able to make a very favorable start in business, for they have followed so fast upon each other's heels that they have experienced great difficulty in purchasing proper investments. The supply of really sound securities is in many directions so very limited that any decided increase in the demand at once causes a considerable advance in prices . . . indeed so rapid has been the advance that it is stated several of the new trusts have been unable to effect purchases and are rather doubtful as to the direction in which their money shall be invested."

These words have certain interesting applications to the present situation. As a result of the conditions described by the *Economist* a variety of abuses arose. The pyramiding process, or superimposing of one company on top of another, increased rapidly. For example, the Anglo-American Debenture Company was responsible for the creation of thirteen different but interconnected trusts at this time. This in itself might not have been objectionable had it not resulted in the manipulation of accounts, the creation of corners, and a great deal of general manoeuvring in order to sustain and increase the market value of the securities of the various trusts. In my opinion there is to-day in this country a large and well-known investment trust whose shares are selling for far more than their intrinsic or liquidating value, which has continually managed its portfolio so that it can show the greatest possible profits and thereby obtain the greatest market value for its shares, regardless of their real worth. Generally speaking, in this trust during the past year the good securities that have appreciated in value have been sold and the poorer ones retained or increased, simply to show profits.

The *Economist* tells us that this is exactly the game they were playing in England almost forty years ago. In 1890 the Baring crisis marked the beginning of a long period of difficulty for the investment trusts. It is interesting to note some of the expedients resorted to by the managers of the tottering trusts at this time. Mr. J. Edward Meeker, economist of the New York Stock Exchange, in an interesting paper on the subject, cites the following instance. "The 'Imperial and Foreign Investment and Agency Corporation,' with a 'strong board' of directors, saw fit to carry the valuations of their holdings at cost instead of at market prices, and on this basis to declare a dividend which absorbed £20,000 of their fictitious revenue balance of £32,409. The long-suffering auditor revolted and refused to shoulder further responsibility for the company's accounts." By April 1891 the ordinary and deferred shares of ten of the more important trusts had declined in the market on an average of 34 per cent. In February 1893 the *Economist* made the following commentary: "It may be said with truth that, having sown the wind they (the trusts) are now reaping the whirlwind. Week after week evidence accumulates proving only too forcibly that those responsible for the management of these trusts have based no inconsiderable part of their operations upon false principles, with the inevitable result that, after a more or less brief period of apparent prosperity, losses and difficulties have arisen." Scandal followed close on the heels of financial difficulty. It turned out that the banking house of Murietta and Company "had agreed to subscribe for 12,000 shares of the 'Imperial and Foreign Investment and Agency Corporation' provided the latter would purchase from it certain securities which it had been unable to sell elsewhere. These depreciated £114,358 while in the trust's possession. What stirred the ire of the shareholders was that despite their losses the trust, directors, and managers had made fortunes."[1]

It was not until 1896 that the *Economist* noted "the upward movement in prices of trust securities generally."

I have given at some length the history of the difficulties of the investment trusts in England because I strongly believe that unless we avoid these and other errors and false principles we shall inevitably go through a similar period of disaster and disgrace. If such a period should come, the well-run trusts will suffer with the bad as they did in England forty years ago. Of course, the honest and ably managed companies would emerge from the difficulties eventually. Even during the worst period in England "proof was afforded of the innate soundness of the investment-trust idea when properly administered." Of the thirty-one leading trusts of the time studied by the *Economist*, seven were able to make headway against the completely adverse current of conditions. In the hope and belief that we shall profit by the example of the older trusts and escape the worst of their difficulties, I shall now try to point out what in my opinion are some of the present dangers. Before doing so, however, I should like to emphasize the fact that the honesty and ability of the management are paramount and that good practices can be completely vitiated by dishonest and unsound investments.

II

Of the investment trusts of which I am speaking I propose to recognize two broad classes. First, those whose primary idea is the borrowing of money at a rate lower than that at which they can lend or invest it, and which in their investment programme follow a very wide diversification. Second, those that do not follow such wide diversification and that buy with the idea of appreciation, or that have attempted to buy securities which are cheap and will go up over a period of years. In England these two classes are generally differentiated as "trust companies" and "finance companies." In this country we have tended to group them all under the general category of investment trusts. Both types have advantages and disadvantages that appeal variously to different investors. The broadly diversified trust has relatively small holdings in a great many issues. It attempts to secure a cross section of the various securities of the United States or of the world. Its particular advantages are that it permits small investors to participate in the ownership of a widely diversified group of securities, thereby obtaining such benefits as go with wide diversification. By its very nature, however, it is attempting to secure a representative average; it cannot, therefore, hope to turn in more than an average performance. Now the primary objective of buying into an investment trust should be the desire to have expert and constant management which can do better than the average. As we have seen, however, a very broadly diversified portfolio means average results, and therefore the purchaser of the securities of such a trust cannot expect the full benefits of managerial ability. Of course, in fairness it should be said that poor management cannot do as much harm following wide diversification as otherwise.

There is a restriction in the by-laws of one investment trust which provides that as soon as the trust has $5,000,000 it shall have at least four hundred different issues. In contrast to this, the trust indenture of the Investment Managers Company of New York provides that it shall not have more than thirty issues. The first company has by its policy of diversification attempted to obtain security. The Investment Managers

Company by its opposite policy has, however, obtained greater security. No one can get an issue into the portfolio of the Investment Managers Company without proving to the directors that it is not only good, but better than one of the existing issues for which it is to be substituted.

In the other company almost any security will get by. The pet issue of each director and officer can find its way in. Director A passes director B's security, although he may not be very enthusiastic about it, so that director B will not blackball his issue. Another disadvantage to the highly diversified portfolio is either the inability of the management to follow closely so many issues or the expense of so doing. One of the worst of some of the present abuses is the ignorance and lack of attention of some investment managers. An investment-trust manager should know far more about the companies in which his money is invested than the average investor. This, I am afraid, is not always the case, and obviously it is far more expensive to follow closely and thoroughly a list of securities spread all over the face of the globe than a list restricted to a limited group of the best investments. I think it fair to say that the average highly diversified trust does not closely follow its list, but relies on its policy of diversification to save it, and, therefore, cannot produce more than an average showing.

In pointing out the difference between these two types of trust, I have already touched on one of the cardinal abuses—inattention. Of course, this evil may apply to the trust with a more limited and selected portfolio. I should also like to point out that it may apply to those trusts run by the big banks and brokerage houses. They may be honest and they may be able, but before their securities are bought one wants to be sure that they will continually apply and reapply that ability to the running of the trust into which one may be buying.

I think the worst cases of lack of attention come where the managerial control rests in rather numerous hands. Concentration of control with extensive powers is a feature of the utmost importance, avoiding the delay and lack of positive action that usually result when many individuals holding diverse opinions attempt to translate their ideas into action.

Some months ago I was asked by an investment house if I would consider running an investment trust that they had sold to the public some time before. During the course of the discussion I asked if I might see the portfolio. In examining this, I noted a very large block of the shares of a company which, as a banking house, they had recently acquired and sold to the public. I asked the gentleman with whom I was talking whether, if I were to advise them on their portfolio, and if I could convince the directors that the shares of another company in the same industry were a preferable investment, they would make the exchange. He replied, "No, not necessarily. This trust is part of our general machine, and if the selling of these shares adversely affected __ and Company we would not make the sale." And yet the securities of this trust were sold to the public, whose money was being used not for the best interests of the men and women who had supplied the funds, but for the best interests of __ and Company. This case brings up two common abuses to which the investment trust is now being put. First, that of being for ulterior motives and not primarily for the best interests of the shareholders; second, that of being used as a depositary for securities that might otherwise be unmarketable. There are, of course, certain trusts that have been formed with avowedly ulterior purposes. Such procedure is obviously beyond reproach. It is only when a trust says it is formed to accomplish one thing and then attempts to do another that it becomes an abuse.

The practice by which a house of issue sells a part of its own underwriting to its own trust, although not necessarily unethical and unsound, is extremely dangerous. Those trusts run by banks and brokers are particularly subject to this temptation. In my opinion such companies should have a provision or a firmly established policy that they will in no way deal with themselves as principals; that if they wish to acquire part of an issue in which they as a house may be interested they will have to acquire it from some entirely outside source.

III

Some months ago, in testifying before a committee of the New York Stock Exchange, I was asked to state briefly what were, in my opinion, the present abuses in the investment-trust movement. My reply was: (1) dishonesty; (2) inattention and inability; (3) greed.

It is of the last of these that I now wish to speak. You may be asked to subscribe to a trust that is both honestly and ably run, and yet find it inadvisable to do so simply because there is nothing in it for you. All the profits go to the promoters and managers.

There are an infinite number of ways whereby this unduly large slice of the spoils is kept by the insiders. They may own all or a very large percentage of the equity stock; they may have warrants and options; or, more rarely, they may be able to take out the money in the form of expenses or managerial fees of one sort or another. There certainly is no ethical objection to promoters and managers getting away with all they can in the way of profits. Free competition is bound to keep this down to a reasonable figure. The objection comes when the amount so to be taken is not clearly set forth. The most common method of accomplishing this result on the part of promoters is an exceedingly complicated capital structure. There are many investment-trust prospectuses in which it takes literally hours to figure out just how profits are to be divided. To those not trained in finance the task becomes impossible, and the promoters have accomplished their purpose. Certainly a clear statement of how the money is supplied and the profits divided, together with a simple, straightforward capital structure, is highly desirable.

Another danger, usually the result of greed, takes the form of a very large funded or floating debt or an excessive issue of preferred stocks. Very often the managers and promoters receive their compensation and profit in the form of common stock for which they have paid little or nothing. There is nothing to criticize in this procedure if it is clearly and simply stated so that all can easily understand. As is pointed out in such cases, the management receives nothing until it has earned and paid some fixed percentage on the senior securities. In other words, the compensation is dependent upon the success of the enterprise. But the difficulty is that the management or promoters have put up only a very small percentage of the total funds. If the enterprise is a complete failure, they have little or nothing to lose. It is natural, therefore, that they should take the attitude of "Let's either win big or win nothing." This they accomplish by a very heavy pyramiding process. I do not believe that there are many people who with only $1000 equity would, as a general practice, proceed to borrow and buy anywhere from $800 to $1000 worth of securities, and yet this is exactly what many investment trusts are doing to-day.

There is another difficulty to which pyramiding leads. With very heavy fixed charges and preferred dividends to meet, the management is under the constant necessity of producing a large dollar income the first and every succeeding year of operation with which to meet the relatively large fixed charges. This pressing necessity to produce immediate and constant income forces the investment of a large proportion of the funds in securities of a less desirable type.

A danger that I have already spoken of I should like to touch on again. There are a great many trust indentures, by-laws, and more or less formal policies that provide a variety of restrictions, the basic purpose of which seems to be to prevent, in the case of dishonest or incapable management, a complete dissipation of the funds.

Such a motive is praiseworthy, but all the restrictions in the world will not mitigate the evils of poor management, and about all they can do is to restrict the efforts of good management. Is it not probable that excess restrictions which we may place on the investment-trust manager during a period of rising prices may be entirely wrong for a changed period of declining prices? I believe that no principles and restrictions should be developed so rigidly that they may not be changed at any time in order to conform with the best judgment of the management.

There are a great many other dangers confronting the investment trusts, but there is only one other I wish to mention here, and that is the excessive market price to which, in my opinion, the shares of certain trusts have been bid. To say what is a fair price for such securities I find extremely difficult—indeed, I do not know. I do think, however, that there are a few principles which may aid us in this determination.

Where the assets of an investment trust are not grossly overvalued, I should say that its various securities are at least worth the net liquidating value, or what would be realized in actual liquidation. The difficulty comes in saying how much more than the liquidating value the securities may be worth. I can think of only two factors that might bring this out. The first is the factor of management, and the second is the ability of the trust to borrow money at low rates of interest. If, for example, the X Trust can borrow $5,000,000 at 5 per cent for twenty years, that ability undoubtedly has a present market worth. Similarly, the ability of the management to make money in excess of the current rate of return over a period of years also has a present value. When, however, I find the shares of a very large trust selling in the market for nearly three times their liquidating value, particularly when that liquidating value is figured from a grossly inflated portfolio value; when there is no possible value to be added through funds borrowed at a low rate; and when, on top of it all, the management has in my opinion demonstrated inability and possibly dishonesty, I am inclined to think the shares somewhat high.

IV

What can be done about these abuses? I should say that the remedies are publicity and education. Every industry has its abuses and dangers, and many industries present far more alarming hazards than the investment trust. Before touching on these remedies I should like very briefly to say a word about what purports to be remedial legislation. There has been much discussion of this topic, and many states have already gone far in setting laws on their statute books. Just as in the case of charter restrictions, about all these laws can do is to hamper able management and fail to protect the public against inability and dishonesty. No law can replace the necessity for investors to think intelligently and to investigate a situation before investing their money. We have had many examples of the evils of overregulation in other fields, and it would indeed be unfortunate to hamper by laws that cannot accomplish their purpose so valuable an instrument of finance as the investment trust. All that legislation should do is to require a degree of publicity that will enable any investor to form a sound opinion. It should not require publicity that would interfere with the honest and successful operation of the trusts.

For the publicity that not only should be required, but is good policy for the trust, I should suggest the following provisions. First, a clear statement should be made showing exactly where the control lies and who constitutes the active management. Second, it should be shown exactly how and in what proportion profits and losses are divided, particularly the existence of options, warrants, calls, and the like. Third, the investment policy of the managers should be made plain by figures giving the percentages invested in the various classes and types of securities.

There has been much discussion of the advisability of requiring that complete portfolio holdings be revealed. Arguments in favor of revealing them include the following points:

1. The trust cannot be called and ceases to be a blind pool.
2. Dishonest or mistaken investment policies are more quickly revealed.
3. Public confidence is increased; the trust is ashamed of nothing and has nothing to hide.
4. The security holders of the trust can better appraise the trust investment policies and attune the rest of their investment procedure accordingly.

Among the disadvantages of portfolio publication are these:

1. The results of the costly investment research paid for by the security holders of the trust are revealed to all, and an outsider by following the list can get the same benefits free of charge.

2. Where a trust is either selling or buying a security with a limited market, that market can be seriously interfered with to the detriment of the trust.
3. Investors may be misled. An investment that is good for a trust may not be good for an individual, particularly when the individual does not know and cannot follow the risks and hazards involved.
4. Publication of a list can seriously hamper the managers in their investment search.

Generally speaking, I should say that for trusts pursuing a very wide diversification the publication of the lists is advisable; whereas for that type which tends more to concentration and the selection of a few outstanding issues it is inadvisable. The best English practices have tended away from the publication of holdings.

Every trust should publish complete balance sheets and income accounts. The balance sheets, of course, should reveal all liabilities, contingent or otherwise; securities should be carried at cost, but their present market value should be clearly revealed. Such a policy permits anyone to determine exactly the liquidating value, which is essential in a determination of the value of the various securities. The income account should be detailed and reveal exactly from where the income was derived. It is essential that interest and dividends received should be clearly separated from profits from sales. Similarly, the expense account should be broken down, showing how much is paid in salaries and other overhead expenses. The compensation of management should be segregated.

If the investment trusts of the country pursue this policy of complete information, bad practices, simply by revelation, will be eliminated.

V

In pointing out some of the present abuses of the investment-trust movement, I have indicated by implication rather than directly what can be considered sound and constructive practice. It only remains briefly to suggest what can and has been accomplished in this field when these dangers and abuses are avoided. Without enlarging on the various possible benefits accruing to investors in this movement, I should merely like again to say that far and away the most important contribution that the investment trust can make is to supply honest, constant, expert, and unbiased management, and that if it pursues too extensive diversification it indicates that it will not or cannot supply that management. For investors to pay a heavy loading charge, in the form of management charges and sales commissions, to the managers and promoters of a "fixed trust," who by its very charter are restricted from using any judgment whatsoever, is in my opinion ridiculous and unjustifiable.

I am often asked what will happen to the investment trusts during a period of declining security prices. In my opinion it is during that period that the real value of the investment-trust movement can be demonstrated. The investment-trust manager should be a financial expert similar in his profession to the doctor of medicine. When we most need a medical doctor is when we are sick. Equally it should be, and I believe is, true that when the investing public most needs expert assistance is during a period of falling security prices. Almost anyone can make money during a period of rising prices, but it will take real skill to curtail losses when things are moving in the opposite direction. I should not go so far as to say that the well-run trusts will not lose money during a period of deflation, but certainly they should, and I believe will, lose less money than the average investor. With conservative capitalization, sound policies, and able management, the investment trusts will make more money than the average investor in good times and lose less in poor times. Such a performance not only justifies but ensures their existence and growth.

FOOTNOTES

1. "Some Notes on Investment Trusts," by J. Edward Meeker.

STOCKS VERSUS BONDS

Lawrence Chamberlain
George W. Edwards

Contemporary investors who are sure that stocks are superior to bonds
may find it interesting to see why the opposite view was considered sound
about half a century ago. Here is a chapter from Lawrence Chamberlain's
and George Edwards' book, *The Principles of Bond Investment*, originally
published in 1927, which explains the natural superiority of bonds—or,
if you prefer, the natural inferiority of common stocks, whose dividends
can so easily be cut—in the areas then thought to be of first importance:
security of principal and stability of income.

Since stocks are the typical speculative paper and bonds the typical
investment security, it is manifestly unfair to measure them both by
the investment standard to the predetermined disparagement of stocks.
But on the other hand stocks, as a class, are so generally thought of
as investments, and the distinction between investment and speculation
is so inadequately recognized, that a contrast of stocks with bonds as
channels for pure investment may be worthwhile, even if the conclusion
is foregone.

The comparison may well take the form of a test by the various
postulates of our ideal investment, beginning with Security of Principal.

This analysis should be confined to characteristics inherent in stocks and bonds, and irrespective of external influences arising out of the business cycle. . . .

Security of Principal. From which, stocks or bonds, is a man surer of recovering the funds he has once relinquished? This question of itself involves no matter of profit, or of income, but merely of recovery. The answer lies in the very nature of stocks and bonds. Legally, a share of stock is a certificate of ownership of a corporation. Unless otherwise stipulated, it represents a right to pro rata participation in control, in profits, and (if the corporation liquidates) in whatever assets are unattached. But although a share of stock represents part ownership in a corporation, and the right to participate in profits, it does not represent any property except this right.

Most people fail to comprehend the meagre property rights of stock, hence all the nonsense and farrago about stock watering,—as if there were or should be some inherent significance to the par value of stock; or that the par value should represent so many dollars paid in. The par value of bonds, even, does not signify any definite payment in purchase— or any definite amount received by the company in the first instance. Most people seem to think that a certificate of stock is, or should be, equivalent to a cashier's check, which certifies to a deposit of money equal in value to the face of the check, or to a warehouse receipt calling for the delivery of some commodity equal in weight or quantity to the amount of the receipt. There is nothing in the legal nature of stock to give the owner cause to look to the company's assets for the full recovery of his principal.

Except in bank stocks, recovery in liquidation seldom amounts to more than the merest fraction of the sum invested; for ordinarily corporations expire because of their very inability to do business at a profit; and the equitable interest in unprofitable property, which survives the prior demands of creditors, cannot, as a rule, amount to much, so long as corporations are financed largely by the sale of obligations, secured or unsecured. When, as nowadays, not only the rights, franchises, and physical properties, but even the very shares of the corporation, are pledged to secure borrowed money, the stockholder has little to expect under the hammer.

Security of principal in a stock investment is further lessened to the extent that the shares are subject to assessment.

The only resource for the recovery of principal in stock purchases is sale. Two questions then arise: is there a market for the stock; and will it sell for more or less than cost? Marketability of stock will be discussed in its turn. As to market prices, stocks, in keeping with their speculative character, fluctuate more widely than bonds.

If the stock is bought at an average price (assuming such a price), and its intrinsic worth remains undiminished, the investment can be recovered by sale a fair portion of the time. But if its intrinsic worth lessens or disappears, the possibility of sale at cost, or better, diminishes or vanishes, taking with it any element of security for the principal. So, in the last analysis, security of principal depends upon the permanency of equitable assets having a pro rata value equal to the cost of the stock.

Bonds, on the other hand, represent, in the majority of cases, an investment by the obligor of an amount at least equal to their cost. Not legally but in fact, they correspond with reasonable accuracy in the comparison to cashier's checks and warehouse receipts. Although the amount of debenture or unsecured obligations is growing rapidly, nevertheless it is small in comparison with the amount of bonds that have the backing of mortgage or collateral. The principal of bonds, therefore, is usually fortified by actual representative assets on which it has a prior claim, and the bondholders as a class are secured, or at least preferred creditors.

Stability of Income.   Just as a knowledge of the relative legal status of stocks and of bonds makes clear the superior security for bond principal, so an understanding of the economic nature of each makes clear the necessarily inferior stability of dividends as compared with interest payments.

Economically, stocks represent shares in the corporate risk. If shareholders have contributed all the capital, their dividends represent, in part, the return on *invested* capital, since a company doing business in good faith must have some assets realizable under any conditions. Even when shareholders have contributed all the capital, the returns are bound to vary from year to year and to show maxima and minima of net earnings. The difference between high and low earnings represents the reward to the *speculated* capital. The inevitableness of high and low tides of income often obtains recognition in the share capitalization, by the classifications, preferred and common stock, of "A" and "B" stock.

Whether the capitalization consists merely of the share liability, or of shares and funded debt, the twofold nature of the returns can be compared to the returns on capital invested in real property. A man may buy a piece of real estate with a mortgage for two-thirds of its value. The surplus income from the property, after payment of taxes, repairs, insurance, and interest on the mortgage, is his premium for the assumption of risk. He is entitled to greater return on his speculated capital than the mortgagee, who takes little or no risk.

In like manner it is easy to provide, in a spirit of conservatism, for the stability (i.e., not only for the security, but for the regularity and uniformity) of the interest charges of a company, when it is bonded, and when legal distinctions exist between the classes of its capitalization. But to the extent that earnings vary, the dividends may properly adjust themselves to preserve the integrity of the surplus, and for the disadvantages to which the shareholder is subjected by this adjustment, he should be recompensed by high returns upon his capital, if they are possible.

When the dividend rate is less than the interest rate of the same company, it is no sign that the shareholder is not being reimbursed as fully as the bondholder because the so-called par value of stock approximates less truly than the par value of bonds the amount of capital committed.

A table of comparisons will readily show how much more susceptible to unfavorable influences are the dividends of a corporation than the interest payments. We suppose a company capitalized with $700,000 outstanding bonds, $250,000 preferred stock, and $650,000 common. The ratios assumed in capitalization and earnings will not be thought unusual.

In good times each of the three classes of capital is paid something like a fair return upon par. If these three income accounts represent three consecutive years, it will be seen that funded debt has been paid

	Good Times	Normal Times	Hard Times
Net Earnings	$150,000	$100,000	$60,000
Bond Interest (5%)	$35,000	$35,000	$35,000
Pref'd Stock (6%)	15,000	15,000	(4%)10,000
Common Stock (8%)	52,000	(4%) 26,000	(—) —
	102,000	76,000	45,000
Balance for Surplus, etc.	$48,000	$24,000	$15,000

15 per cent, preferred stock 16 per cent, and common 12 per cent. If these three years were representative, the common might be considered unfortunately situated; but we must remember that a common stock subject to such fluctuations in return, or to such a low average of return, would probably cost less than par and would represent less than $100 per share of cash capital paid in; therefore the nominal annual return would be much less than the real.

In hard times, when earnings decline and the "margin of safety" narrows, and even bond interest is threatened, the equities in earnings, charged to dividends and balances, will be adjusted to preserve the integrity of the interest as long as possible. Interest must always be supported at the expense of dividends.

Although stability of interest has more to do with the economic than with the legal position of bonds, nevertheless the latter has its marked effect. In the trust agreement of bond issues, whether mortgage or debenture, precaution is usually taken to prevent the creation of future indebtedness that, in whole or in part, could become a lien prior to the obligations. In the nature of corporations there can be nothing to prevent the stockholders who are in control from imposing on the company obligations that shall be a charge upon revenues to be met before dividends are paid.

In considering securities by types and classes there is a natural tendency to have in mind the more prominent issues listed on the leading exchanges. Yet listed securities, but particularly listed stocks, are not thoroughly representative of their classes. Therefore if it is the common practice to lower the dividends on our best listed stocks, it is a fair inference (supported by the facts) that, in general, reserves are not sufficiently strong to relieve dividends of their natural office in the income account.

During the first nine months of business depression following the panic of 1907, the dividends of 80 large railroad and industrial corporations were passed or reduced. Sixteen railroads passed their dividends: among them the Missouri Pacific, the Cleveland, Cincinnati, Chicago, and St. Louis, the Southern Railway, the Erie, and the Lake Erie and Western. Ten prominent railroads reduced their dividends: including the Pennsylvania, New York Central, Atchison, Louisville and Nashville, Norfolk and Western, and Atlantic Coast Line. Twenty-six prominent industrial corporations omitted dividends entirely and twenty-nine radically reduced them.

Frequently dividends are passed, or cut, or the proper rate is not declared, to serve the ends of an irresponsible directorate. The minority shareholders have almost no voice in the matter while the courts would speedily find relief for a minority note- or bondholder who was being deprived of his return.

Fair Income Return.   Since the shareholder, not the bondholder, assumes the main hazard of corporate enterprise, his return in dividends, immediate or prospective, should, in general, exceed the interest returns by that ratio which fairly represents the relative risk to the two classes of capital. Any expression of opinion as to whether he does, in the long run, obtain this relatively fair return must, at present, be purely personal. Anyone with a taste for figures and ample leisure for investigation might ascertain the facts beyond cavil for listed securities; but to do so he must institute an elaborate system of constantly changing costs (or market prices) for stocks and bonds and corresponding net returns upon cost.

Marketability.   We have just stated that the superior marketability of listed stocks over listed bonds was part cause of the low average return upon the cost price shown by the stocks in the above table. But again, let it be remembered that listed securities in general are in the minority, and are by no means representative for illustration of investment principles. The tendency to use them is natural because board transactions are recorded and easily accessible for reference.

There is no statistical means of proving, among *unlisted* securities, the superior marketability of bonds over stocks, but it has been our experience that bonds are more easily sold than stocks. This, too, is the natural inference from the superior intrinsic worth of bonds, and from the fact that investment conditions are more uniform and can be more easily and generally recognized than speculative conditions. The article of superior and acknowledged merit will be the more readily disposed of.

The American bond market—that is, the bond market in Canada and the United States—is an institution without parallel in other countries. Although the discussion of this market comes more properly under other heads, such as *The Bond Houses* and *Listed Versus Unlisted Bonds*, it is fitting to state that the American bond market is the basis of a special business that encourages professional knowledge of values and seeks selling places for the multitudinous issues. The result is a broader and quicker response to bond offerings than the unlisted stock market furnishes for stocks.

Hypothecary Value. The value of any security as collateral depends mainly on its market and its worth. In general, a listed security is more acceptable as collateral than an unlisted, because current quotations are an easily accessible index of current values, and the frequency and volume of sales are an indication (although not always reliable) of the breadth and responsiveness of the market. The more actively dealt in a security is, the less necessary is a knowledge of its intrinsic worth as the basis of loan. For this reason listed bonds have no advantage over listed stocks. If, in general, the security and marketability of bonds are superior to that of stocks, it is the natural and correct inference that bonds, in general, are the more acceptable collateral.

Tax Exemption. As regards the burden of taxation very few people realize the great disadvantage under which bonds labor; for, although in no state are all bonds unequivocally free of tax, in 39 states and territories shares of stock may not be assessed against shareholders when the issuing corporation or its property is directly taxed.

Only Delaware, Georgia, Louisiana, and Washington assess shareholders quite irrespective of the corporation tax; but Maryland, the District of Columbia (in a measure), Alabama, and Iowa assess shareholders on that part of the value of their stock which represents the excess of its market value over the assessed value of the properties. The legal theory is that this excess represents otherwise untaxed good-will and other intangible property.

The fact that government bonds are free from tax to individuals within the country is of little avail because of their prohibitive price. However, the insular issues, the Philippines, Hawaiians, and Puerto Ricans, are tax exempt and sell on approximately an investment basis. The bonds of states are now very commonly exempt to holders within the given state, and the proportion of municipal bonds exempt under the same conditions is steadily growing. In fact the tendency to exempt both bonds and stocks seems as inevitable as it is welcome.

But as conditions now are, personal property taxes work greater hardship to bondholders than to stockholders, for the demand for tax-free bonds is greater than for tax-free stocks, since bonds are the staple investment of institutions and trustees whose holdings come under the cognizance of courts and state officials.

Freedom from Care. So far as the mere instruments are concerned, stocks and bonds are about on parity in regard to care. Loss of either security is, at the most, a matter of mere inconvenience. But a coupon bond is negotiable and passes by delivery. Therefore it should be guarded as carefully as currency.

As to freedom from care in the larger sense, ownership carries with it the major responsibility, and the degree of individual thought or anxiety should conform to a degree of investment risk.

Acceptable Duration. The test of acceptability in the duration, or life, of the investment cannot be applied in this comparison, since stocks, ordinarily, have no maturity. A discussion of duration must resolve itself into a question of marketability, on which we have already commented.

Acceptable Denomination. To the large majority, the possibility of having funds invested in small denominations is a great advantage. Occasionally a big investor or corporation objects to $500 pieces and eagerly seizes upon $5,000 bonds like the old Pennsylvania notes of 1910, so as "not to clutter up the safe deposit box." But registered bonds and stock certificates have another advantage in common, in that one certificate may serve for any denomination. Although whatever advantage there is lies with stocks, inelasticity of denomination is not so marked as in the case of mortgages, which, as channels of investment, suffer severely from this limitation.

Appreciation. The economic and legal positions of bonds and stocks, which throw the onus of risk on stocks and lessens their security of both principal and interest, will bring commensurate possibilities of appreciation. The very nature of a loan precludes great possibilities of advance in price, as we have noted and shall note elsewhere. An exception may be taken for loans which are convertible into stocks.

PRINCIPLES OF VALUATION

Arthur Stone Dewing

Since it was first published in 1919, Arthur Stone Dewing's great two-volume text, *The Financial Policy of Corporations*, has delighted students of business with its clean, direct prose, its extensive footnotes, and its references to the ancient Greek and Roman writers. Dewing was both a distinguished Harvard professor and a successful investor. Here he explains "value."

Underlying all practical problems in connection with the financial aspects of the corporation, there is the problem of value. It is fundamental to the promotion of a corporation, to the conduct of the business in which the corporation is engaged, to its fortunes as a successful expanding business or its failure to make a profit, and its final liquidation or reorganization. It may concern the business as a going enterprise; or it may concern the property employed in the business, both tangible and intangible. However phrased, further study of the financial operations of the business rests on an understanding of what we mean by the values of a business.

When we ask what is the value of a business or of its property, we are immediately confronted with a problem constantly recurring wherever the individual human being seeks to understand and to adjust himself to his environment. Throughout the ages, man's reflective consciousness has sought to find an ultimate sanction to which might be

From Arthur Stone Dewing, *The Financial Policy of Corporations* (New York, New York, 1941), 275–277 by permission of John Wiley and Sons, Inc.

referred all judgments and from which all human experiences, emotions, and actions might derive at once their relative significance and their relative importance. The state, God's will, a final moral law, the gradual unfolding of a supreme reality, even evolution from the simple to the complex, have appeared in succession and in various forms as ultimate sanctions of value. Not only is the demand for a definite criterion of value more than a task of mental gymnastics, but the necessity for such a criterion underlies all attempts to apply any theory of value to concrete and restricted ranges of human experience, no matter how narrow the field, or how trivial the apparent significance of the problems involved.

The modern world's greatest classic of reflective thinking began with this very simple statement: *"Dass alle unserer Erkenntnis mit der Erfahrung anfange, daran is gar kein Zweifel."* Yet experience is the beginning and not the end of reflective thinking; and it is in experience that we find two purposes linked together in any theory of value. Fundamentally there is the idea of human worthwhileness, the idea of an end to be achieved through action, or, when reduced to simple economic terms, an end useful to man. Coupled with the idea of human worthwhileness goes the idea of difficulty of attainment, of struggle for achievement, of sacrifice in terms of other things lost. Values are ideas or ideals or things desirable in themselves, yet for the attainment of which sacrifices of mind or body must be endured.

This analysis can be applied to the restricted field of economic experience. The first consideration of economic value is usefulness—the greater the utility, the greater the value. Yet even though useful, there may be no economic value attached to a thing or service unless some restriction to its desirability or its possession limits its availability. Air has the extreme value of maintaining life. It is the thing without which life may not be continued beyond a few seconds; yet it has no economic value unless conditions exist which make it hard to obtain. If some sacrifice is necessary to get air, its value will be measured by this sacrifice; if no sacrifice is required to get air, then it will have no economic value, notwithstanding its paramount importance for man's physical well-being. To constitute economic value, then, not only must a thing or a service be useful to man's well-being, but the obtaining of it must require the giving up of something else. Economic value is born of sacrifice.

In the field of economic values, there is, however, one important corollary. If the basis of economic value is human usefulness— usefulness to satisfy a want—this usefulness may be obtained by several means. When a human being finds that the same satisfaction can be secured through more than one channel, he will necessarily choose that means which entails the least personal sacrifice. Consequently, the value of any single economic thing or service is limited by the cost, in man's judgment, of the sacrifice entailed in obtaining other things or services that will meet his need equally well. No matter how great may be the usefulness to an individual of a single piece of food, its economic value is limited by the sacrifice or cost he must undergo to acquire another piece of food equally useful. Hence, when several services or commodities satisfy a human want equally well, the value of each one of them is determined not by the sacrifice necessary to obtain each, but rather by the sacrifice necessary to obtain the one most easily available, which may be substituted for any one of the others. This is always the one involving the least sacrifice. This conception of substitution value distinguishes economic values from all other human values—esthetic, moral, sexual, parental, political, social and religious.

The presumption of a substitution value involves the postulate of a common denominator of values—one economic value cannot be substituted for another unless the two can be put on a single plane. There must be a possible basis to balance the relative usefulness and the relative sacrifice of one thing or one service against another. In other words, the economic value of a thing or service at any one time to the single individual human being is the cost or sacrifice then and there of obtaining a substitute—the cost to be expressed in terms of some common or arbitrary unit.

Value is subjective; it is based on individual human experience. Hence, when the individual tries to find an objective standard or criterion for his own personal values, he is confronted with endless confusion. Value changes from hour to hour; value is different according to the standards of experience and the standards of judgment. Consequently, when attempts are made to set up legal postulates to control economic value—such postulates as original cost or the cost of reproduction—nothing but uncertainty and contradiction results. In the end the test of value is pragmatic—where does the judgment of most men meet? It is the composite of many judgments, not the reaching for an illusory fixed and unvarying basis of value on which the judgment of all people should agree.

* * * * *

A PERSISTENT DELUSION

Henry W. Dunn

Henry Dunn of Scudder, Stevens & Clark spoke out against what he called the Persistent Delusion that stock market forecasting could be done successfully, and urged his fellow investment counselors to insist on the separation of investing and stock market guessing. (Readers will also enjoy his graceful, long sentences.)

There is hardly anything more important to the future standing and usefulness of the investment counsel profession than that every reasonable effort should be made to disabuse the public mind, as far as possible, of the widespread belief or assumption, unwarranted and erroneous in fact, that competent investment management is largely a matter of anticipating stock market movements, and hence that the chief function of investment counsel is successful stock market guessing.

That statement, however, is altogether too condensed for all its implications to be immediately apparent. In attempting to deal with the situation to which I refer, it should, I believe, first of all be made clear, if means can be found to do that effectively, that investment counsel, properly so described, professes to be qualified to give advice on investment, and not on the quite different and much more adventurous activities of stock market trading—a fundamental distinction which, in my opinion, a large section of the public entirely fails to recognize or

Reprinted with permission of Scudder, Stevens & Clark.

appreciate. It is necessary to go further, however, in order to give that distinction practical importance in the public mind, and to make known as widely as possible what I regard as the plain truth: that, with all the effort which has been expended on attempts to discover or devise new and better methods of forecasting or to develop greater skill in the use of the old methods, guessing the next move of the stock market, with due reference to the two vital factors of direction and timing, still remains little more than a gamble. The importance to the profession of disseminating that knowledge, and incidentally, of refusing, in its relations with actual or prospective clients, to compromise with any mistaken ideas about it, is the point which I wish most of all to emphasize. As I see the situation, a true understanding by the public at large of the proper functions of investment counsel, and any general acceptance of a reasonable standard for valuing the results to be obtained through its services, are not likely to be attained, unless the profession can find effective means of combatting what I have chosen to call the persistent delusion: that coming moves of the stock market can be successfully guessed, bringing greater rewards to those relying on that procedure than are obtainable through the adoption of any other policy; and that the guessing is only a question of knowing the necessary technique, or perhaps of having mastered any one of various effective techniques—from which the popular assumption follows that anyone professing to be an expert on the handling of funds may reasonably be expected to know and successfully apply whatever technique is required, and thus to produce, with satisfactory regularity, handsome trading profits for his clients. . . .

If the distinction between investment and trading activities, which is generally recognized and accepted, more or less as a matter of course, in connection with dealings in bonds or real estate, sometimes appears, in the light of modern investment practice, rather less clear-cut as applied to common stock transactions, and perhaps calls for a little further analysis, it is largely, I think, because of certain situations likely to arise in the conduct of an investment program in which, in connection with common stock purchases, it is difficult to divorce entirely what I should describe as strictly investment considerations from what might be called the trading motive, or in other words, from some thought of the possibilities of substantial profits to be realized on subsequent resale. I believe it nevertheless to be a sound general statement, as applied either to common stocks or to other investment media, and one which will help us in clear thinking on these matters, that investment as such seeks its returns from the earnings of the capital invested, rather than from profits to be realized through buying and selling operations in a fluctuating market.

Here again I am conscious of a lack of precision in the terminology available for the statement of fundamental propositions in this field, from which it follows that no such brief statement as I have just made can be wholly clear without some further definition of terms; but I shall try not to spend too much time on mere verbal refinements. I would like you to note, however, that I placed the emphasis on the earnings of the capital invested as the source of investment returns, rather than on income exclusively. In the case of bonds or mortgages, representing capital loaned, I should not call the difference material, since I should regard the interest received as the earnings of the capital invested; but in the case of common stocks, there is more than one method of employing earnings to produce what I should recognize as investment returns. The application of earnings to the payment of dividends is, of course, the most obvious method; and though, in the choice of common stock investment, the immediate dividend return can undoubtedly be over-emphasized, I am very much inclined to add that, in the effort to avoid that error, it is easily possible to minimize too much the very tangible and definite advantages of income in hand. My attempted brief characterization of investment objectives, however, recognizes other possible methods of utilizing earnings to the ultimate advantage of the investor.

I have in mind, of course, that class of stocks which, in accordance with my understanding of the term, are properly described as "growth stocks," or, in other words, the stocks of companies showing, underneath any cyclical fluctuations to which the earnings may be subject, an underlying trend of growth in earnings per share, which is naturally reflected sooner or later in a more or less similar increase both in dividend payments and in market values. While other factors have sometimes contributed, generally for limited periods, the principal source of this sort of growth, other than the favorable industry conditions which must first be assumed, is the regular reinvestment of a substantial part of the earnings in the profitable expansion of the business. What that commonly means from an income standpoint is merely that earnings which might have been paid out immediately in dividends are employed instead in such a manner as to produce higher dividends later, and the typical investment reason for buying growth stocks would be the expectation of eventual rewards in the form of a more or less continuously increasing income. For many and perhaps most classes of investors, I should be disposed to class the accompanying appreciation as a mere incident, or, at most, a secondary advantage rather than a major objective, its chief importance being that if and when, as is likely to happen sooner or later, the company appeared to be approaching its limit of profitable growth, and a shift to another investment might appear advisable, the shift could probably be made on a basis to retain the advantage of the increase in income realized in the meanwhile.

Let us, however, look briefly at the special case of the investor not requiring immediate income, but interested in the building up of his fund for future requirements. If he were to buy either bonds or other investments with a fixed income return, or common stocks paying out most of their earnings in dividends, and build up his invested capital by himself reinvesting his income in additional bonds or stocks, we should certainly not describe that as anything but an investment procedure. However, I can see no essential difference if, with the same objective, he elects to invest in growth stocks and permit the companies to do a large part of the reinvesting for him. In both cases the resulting increase in the total capital value of the fund is brought about by the process of converting actual or potential income into additional capital. In the case, therefore, of any such use of growth stocks, my statement with respect to investment objectives does not exclude the recognition of capital appreciation resulting directly from the profitable reinvestment of earnings as a legitimate investment objective.

Obviously, however, that is something quite different from appreciation sought through active buying and selling operations in the effort to realize trading profits. . . .

I believe, however, that anyone pursuing the inquiry far enough will find ample evidence that the record of common stocks with respect to growth has differed very materially in different periods of our history, that underlying conditions characterizing the particular period studied have a great deal to do with the prevalence of growth characteristics among the common stocks of investment quality available in that period, and that the period. . . terminating in 1928, must be recognized as having been exceptionally favorable to the type of growth under discussion. I will add that various reasons lead me to doubt whether the investor looking for growth stocks, and particularly for those in which the probable growth is not already heavily discounted in the price, will find opportunities as numerous, or the rate of growth as favorable, in the period immediately before us. . . . At any rate, we have recently had a severe lesson with respect to the possibilities of cyclical interruption, continued for too long a period for its importance to be overlooked; and the developments of the past ten years have undoubtedly directed much more attention to cyclical factors in relation to common stock investment.

It is the current emphasis on such factors which gives special importance to the type of situation previously referred to, in which a possible combination of motives has tended to dull somewhat, as applied to common stock transactions, the sharp edge of the distinction, elsewhere readily recognized, between investment and trading activities or objectives. The underlying reason which gives rise to such situations may be found in what I should call the overviolent swings of the stock market. These excessive fluctuations are characteristic, not merely of the more speculative stocks, but also of sound stocks in strong companies, which, whether stable or cyclical in the matter of earnings and dividends, I should class as entirely suitable for investment holdings when reasonably priced on a long-term basis. In short, for all types of stocks, the fluctuations of stock market prices in the course of a full cycle are likely to be quite out of proportion to any accompanying changes in what might be called the long-term investment values of the stocks in question. . . .

It follows that the investor proceeding on strictly investment principles, who recognizes the important part which common stocks may play in a balanced investment program, is likely to find himself buying stocks when they appear to be either reasonably priced or under-valued on a long-term investment basis, and later selling the same stocks, under changed conditions, at substantially higher prices. This may be done either because they then appear to be definitely over-valued, meaning that other investments definitely promise better returns on the then market value, or because, as a result of price readjustment, their relative attractiveness in comparison with other available investment media is sufficiently reduced to call, not perhaps for the sale of all common stock holdings, but at least for a reduction in common stock proportions. This not only in-volves the realization of what might be called trading profits, but if such profits are successfully conserved, the contribution which they may make to long-term investment results can hardly be ignored. . . .

Lest this reference to possible or probable profits as incidental to a sound investment program should be interpreted too optimistically, I wish to insert parenthetically an expression of my conviction that, in this uncertain and rapidly changing world, the conduct of an investment program on the soundest investment principles, if sometimes permitting or promoting the realization of substantial profits, can hardly be expected to eliminate the necessity of accepting also some losses, and that the balance between the two is likely to depend, not merely on the excellence of the management, but also on whether the underlying conditions of the period in which the program has to be carried out prove to be favorable or unfavorable. . . .

Subject to some possible qualifications under rather exceptional conditions, my personal preference would be rather strongly for the investment approach to each common stock purchase and to each question later arising of sale or retention, with the realization of profits left out of consideration as far as practicable as a planned objective, and with any profits in fact resulting from action dictated by investment considerations to be accepted rather as a fortunate windfall, blown the investor's way by the gusty winds of over-violent stock market fluctuation. The only definite rule, however, which I would attempt to lay down for such transactions, would be that the contemplation of possible profits, even if frankly given some weight as a hoped-for objective, should not be permitted to induce either purchase or sale, or retention in place of sale, unless in each case the purchase, sale or retention could be fully justified on strictly investment grounds.

One obvious reason for the rule just stated is that insistence on investment merit at the time of the purchase is the only sound insurance of the hoped-for or expected profit; but the application of the rule to later questions of retention or sale is no less important. The temptation to keep on holding at excessive prices in the hope of a still larger profit, especially in what may appear to be a strongly rising market, should perhaps be particularly emphasized, lest the investor find himself merely speculating on how much more stocks will sell for than they are reasonably worth, with the hoped-for results depending on his outguessing other similar speculators in picking the time to unload. . . .

I am convinced by observation running back over a great many years, and by many bits of evidence that have come to my attention, that there is among the great American public a widespread belief, or in many cases perhaps a mixed hope and belief in all degrees of mixture, which has about the same practical effect, that the coming movements of the stock market can be either scientifically anticipated from economic statistics and business indices, or read from charts, or predicted, if not from any set formula, through an informed and discriminating judgment of the various factors recognized as controlling at the time, or forecast in some other way, or just plain guessed, perhaps not all the time or with 100 percent of accuracy, but enough of the time, and with a high enough percentage of accuracy, to make buying and selling stocks on such judgments the most profitable way to employ money.

For brevity, and perhaps influenced, as you might suspect, by a lack of sympathy with this widespread belief or assumption, I shall, as I have occasion to refer back to the procedure of endeavoring to forecast what the stock market is going to do next, by any of the various methods above referred to or any other, embrace them all under the short description of "stock market guessing". . . .

[M]y main thesis involves not only an assertion of the prevalence and persistence among the general public of an always wishful and more or less confident belief in the predictability by experts of coming stock market movements, but also the further assertion that this persistent belief, or mixture of hope and belief, is in fact a delusion.

To present definite records of factual research sufficient to prove beyond doubt or argument a negative proposition of that character would be an almost impossible task, and your evident response to one or two of the statements I have already made on this subject encourages me to think that you will not regard that as necessary. Enough is certainly known of the past failures of various forecasting methods so that I think the burden of proof may fairly be thrown on the man who seriously claims to have perfected the necessary technique. In other words, I propose to stand on the assertion I have made, and like the political orators, challenge successful contradiction.

If, however, there should be among my hearers any who still retain a good deal of confidence in their own forecasting ability, I will add for their benefit a word of caution and warning. In a field presenting as many difficult problems as the field of investment, in which there are many uncertainties besides those of stock market guessing—and a good many rules at one time generally accepted and successfully followed have had to be later modified or abandoned to meet changes in underlying conditions none too easily or promptly recognized—there seem to me to be some lessons taught by long and responsible investment experience which, I am almost tempted to say, are effectively taught in no other way. That would be going too far, but the maxim that experience is the best teacher refers very definitely to firsthand experience, and, in this field as in certain others, there appear to be some in every new generation, not lacking in either intelligence or sincerity, by whom the lessons of past experience have to be rather painfully relearned. I therefore feel safe in saying that the lessons of investment experience to which I have referred would be much more commonly known and understood if, among those currently devoting their attention to the study of investment problems, the disposition, the capacity and the necessary effort to profit fully by the experience of others were more generally and carefully cultivated.

The long-run unreliability of stock market predictions as a basis for either investment or trading policy is, I believe, one of the lessons taught by long and responsible experience, and nonetheless effectively because various systems may at times have appeared to work fairly well for periods just long enough to mislead the unwary. I am willing to rest my conclusions on this point on what I believe would be the overwhelming testimony of those whose experience has been sufficiently extended for an adequate test of ultimate results.

INTRODUCTION
THE SCOPE AND LIMITATIONS OF SECURITY ANALYSIS.
THE CONCEPT OF INTRINSIC VALUE
A PROPOSED DEFINITION OF INVESTMENT

Benjamin Graham
David L. Dodd

The Benjamin Graham/David Dodd collaboration that produced *Security Analysis* not only resulted in a justly famous textbook that has been admired for more than fifty years, but also launched a new profession. Whether seeking (as in the 3rd edition excerpt) to assess and understand the real meaning of the Great Depression, or (as in the excerpt from the 4th edition, coauthored with Sidney Cottle) proposing a definition of investment, the ideas, insights, and logic continue to shine with the brilliant light that has illuminated the path of virtually all present practitioners in the early years of their careers.

From Benjamin Graham and David L. Dodd, *Security Analysis* [New York, New York, 1951 (3rd Ed.), 1962 (4th Ed.); originally published in 1934], 1–23 (3rd Ed.), 48–52 (4th Ed.), by permission of McGraw-Hill Book Company, Inc.

INTRODUCTION

The Significance of Recent Financial History To the Investor and the Speculator

Distinctive Character of the 1927–1933 Period.
Economic events between 1927 and 1933 involved something more than a mere repetition of the familiar phenomena of business and stock-market cycles. A glance at the appended chart covering the movements of the Dow-Jones averages of industrial common stocks since 1897 will show how entirely unprecedented was the extent of both the recent advance and the ensuing collapse. They seem to differ from the series of preceding fluctuations as a tidal wave differs from ordinary billows and, as such, would undoubtedly be governed by special causes and produce unparalleled effects.

Any present examination into financial principles or methods must start with a recognition of the distinctive nature of our recent experiences, and it must face and answer the numerous new questions which these experiences inspire. For clarity of treatment we may classify these questions into four groups, as they relate respectively to:

I. Speculation.
II. Investment in:
   A. Bonds and preferred stocks.
   B. Common stocks.
III. The relations between investment banking houses and the public.
IV. The human nature factor in finance.

Speculation

It can hardly be said that the past six years have taught us anything about speculation that was not known before. Even though the last bull and bear markets have been unexampled in recent history as regards both magnitude and duration, at bottom the experience of speculators was no different from that in all previous market cycles. However distinctive was this period in other respects, from the speculator's standpoint it would justify applying to Wall Street the old French maxim that "the more it changes, the more it's the same thing." That enormous profits should have turned into still more colossal losses, that new theories should have been developed and later discredited, that unlimited optimism should have been succeeded by the deepest despair are all in

CHART A

The Dow-Jones Industrial Stock Averages—1897–1934 (Monthly High and Low of Closing Averages)

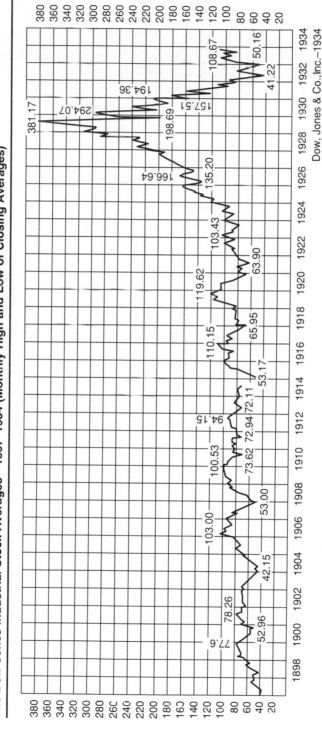

Dow, Jones & Co.,Inc.–1934

strict accord with age-old tradition. That out of the very intensity of the debacle there will arise new opportunities for large speculative gains appears almost axiomatic; and we seem to be on firm ground in repeating the old aphorisms that in speculation *when* to buy—and sell—is more important than *what* to buy, and also that almost by mathematical law more speculators must lose than can profit.

New and Disturbing Problems of Investment

But, in the field of investment, experience since 1927 inspires questions both new and disturbing. Of these the least troublesome arise from the misuse of the term "investment" to cover the crassest and most unrestrained speculation. If that were the only cause of our investment difficulties, it could readily be cured by readopting the old-time, reasonably clean-cut distinctions between speculation and investment. But the real problem goes deeper than that of definition. It is bound up not with the grotesque failure of speculation masquerading as investment but with the scarcely less calamitous failure of investment itself, conducted in accordance with time-honored rules. It is not the wild gyrations of the common-stock averages but the precipitate decline in the bond averages (see Chart B) that constitutes the really novel and arresting feature of recent financial history—at least from the standpoint of investment logic and practice. The heavy losses taken by conservative investors since 1928 warrant the serious question, Is there such a thing as sound and satisfactory investment? And also the secondary question, Can the investor rely upon the care and good faith of investment banking houses?

Unhappy Experience of the Bondholder Since 1914
It should be pointed out that the experience of bond investors as a class had been relatively unsatisfactory throughout the period since our entry into the World War, so that for years prior to 1928 there had been developing a realization that bonds did not afford sufficient protection against loss to compensate for the surrender of the profit element. The years 1917–1920 were marked by a tremendous decline in all bond prices as the result of war financing followed by the postwar inflation and collapse. The later recovery was not without its many individual disappointments, chiefly because the bulk of bond investment had previously been made in the railroad field and the credit of the carriers had on the whole been declining during most of the period in which numerous industrial companies had been showing extraordinary improvement. Even public-utility

CHART B
Dow-Jones Bond Averages

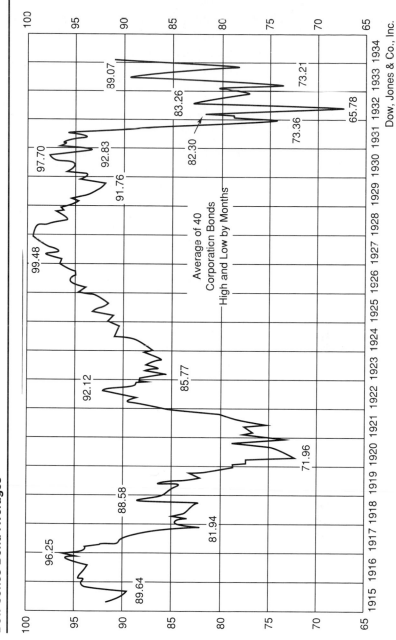

Average of 40
Corporation Bonds
High and Low by Months

Dow, Jones & Co., Inc.

bonds had been adversely affected from 1919 to 1922 by the postwar increase in operating costs, as against relatively inelastic rates. On the other hand, the resultant rapid broadening of the industrial bond list had not been without its disadvantages, because many issuing companies not only failed to participate in the general improvement but even fell into difficulties. Hence the purchaser of industrial bonds found himself in a precarious field, wherein he benefited but slightly, if at all, from the brilliant successes but suffered more or less severely from the frequent failures.

It was the natural disaffection with their experience as bond owners which predisposed investors to embrace the new doctrine of common stocks as the superior form of investment—a doctrine which had a real validity within a limited range of application, but which was inevitably misapplied, with consequences too harrowing to dilate upon. Today the doctrine of common stocks as long-term investments seems discredited, but this fact does not in itself restore the bond to its old estate as the sound investment *par excellence*, nor does it explain away the unhappy history of the bondholder in recent years.

If we were to regard the record of the bond list since 1927 as indicative of what the future has in store, the considered conclusion would be warranted that sound investment as formerly conceived—meaning generally the purchase of bonds at prices close to par—no longer exists. For while it is true that a good many bond issues have come through this period without alarming depreciation in either price or quality, their number is relatively too small—nor was their superiority sufficiently manifest in advance—to warrant the belief that careful selection would have restricted commitments to this group and protected the shrewd investor against the losses suffered by others. The decline in the general bond averages was caused in part by an unwarranted lack of confidence and in part also by the depressing influence of large sales by banks intent on maintaining liquidity at all costs. But besides these temporary and psychological factors, it has reflected an undeniable and disconcerting impairment of safety in many individual cases.

The theory that a sound bond will be unaffected by a period of depression has suffered a rude shock. Margins of safety considered ample to withstand any probable shrinkage in earnings have proved inadequate; and enterprises once regarded as depression-proof are having difficulty in meeting their fixed charges. Hence if our judgment were based primarily on recent experience, we should have to advise against all investment in securities of limited value (excepting possibly short-term government bonds) and voice the dictum that both bonds and stocks should be bought only as speculations, by people who know they are speculating and who can afford to take speculative risks.

1927–1933 Period an Extreme Laboratory Test

However, we do not accept the premise that 1927–1933 experience affords a proper norm by which to judge the future of investment. The swing of the speculative pendulum during this period was of such unprecedented amplitude as to warrant the belief that it will not recur in similar intensity for a long time to come. In other words, we should regard it more as an economic phenomenon akin to the South Sea Bubble and other isolated instances of abnormal gambling frenzy than as an indication of what the typical speculative cycle of the future will be. As a *speculative* experience, the recent cycle differed from previous ones in kind rather than in degree; but in its effects upon the *investment fabric* it had unique characteristics, seemingly of a nonrecurrent type.

We think, therefore, that from the standpoint of bond investment the last six years may be regarded as a sort of extreme laboratory test, involving degrees of stress not to be expected in the ordinary experience of the future. From this viewpoint, bond investment does not become a hopeless practice. By applying the lessons taught by this "laboratory test" to the selection of bonds, reasonably satisfactory results should be experienced in the years to come. These lessons would enjoin a more rigid insistence than heretofore upon the twofold assurances of safety—those arising from the inherent soundness and stability of the enterprise (as evidenced by the nature of the business, its relative size, its management and reputation, etc.) and equally those arising from generous margins of coverage shown by actual earnings over a sufficient period, as well as by the presence of an adequate junior equity. The strict application of these tests would no doubt result in a sharp diminution of the number of new issues which can qualify as sound investments, but it should still leave a restricted field in which bond investment can be satisfactorily practiced.

Education in Bond Selection Still Useful

To some this conclusion may appear unduly optimistic, yet whether it is so or not will probably not make so much practical difference as would at first appear. For even if bond investment, judged over a long period, were to prove inherently unprofitable, nevertheless investment houses will continue to sell bonds and the public will proceed to buy them—just as people have always persisted in speculating, although we know that most of them must lose money. Furthermore these bond buyers would very likely be wise to make their bond investments, even though they proved moderately unremunerative, rather than to run the risks of much larger loss implicit in stock speculation. Hence education in sound and careful bond selection should be useful to the public on any hypothesis, even the pessimistic one that some final net loss is inevitable.

As this introduction is being written, the investor in high-grade bonds is faced with a new and alarming hazard, viz., that inflation and consequent depreciation of the currency may impair the value of his interest and principal. However serious this danger may be, the problem it presents is essentially *temporary* in character. It relates not to the value of bonds as a channel for investing money but to the value of money itself; and it terminates as soon as the value of the monetary unit is again definitely established, whatever the new level may be. German inflation, for example, wiped out the prewar German bonds; but it had no permanent effect upon the theory of bond investment in Germany. A similar result followed the 80% depreciation of the franc. Bond investment was resumed as soon as the value of the currency was stabilized, and the principles and technique of selecting sound bonds remained exactly the same after the devaluation as before.

It is clearly preferable to own tangible property rather than money during a period when the value of money is depreciating, but this objection to money ceases the moment its value is stabilized. Exactly the same statement applies to high-grade bonds.

Common-Stock Theory a Sound Principle Misapplied

Investment in common stocks would seem to be in a still more question-able state than investment in bonds. Not only is the doctrine of common stocks as the best long-term investments in eclipse, but no less an author-ity than Lawrence Chamberlain has not hesitated to express the view that all stocks are by their nature essentially and unavoidably speculative.[1] Hence, to him the lesson of recent years is that the only sound invest-ment is a bond. The logic of this pronouncement will be examined in some detail in an early chapter on investment and speculation. Dealing here with the narrower question of what is signified by recent experi-ence, we repeat our former statement that the "common-stock insanity" was a monumental example of a *sound* principle grievously misapplied. Its history teaches us more about the nature of human beings than the nature of common stocks. Long before the "new-era" gospel was being preached, there were principles guiding the selection of common stocks for investment as distinguished from speculation. Broadly speaking, an investment stock was required to meet the same tests of safety and stability as were exacted of a bond. Common stocks passing these tests generally gave a good account of themselves as investments and in addition held possibilities of appreciation in value which were not shared by bonds.

Investment in Common Stocks Not Wholly Discredited

In our opinion, the pyrotechnics of 1928–1933 are less destructive of the logic of this position than in the case of investment bonds. They show, of course, that stocks apparently sound could suffer an unexpected disappearance of earning power, and that as between "sound bonds" and "sound stocks" the latter group was more severely affected by the depression.

But a rigid observance of old-time canons of common-stock investment would have dictated the sale of one's holdings at a substantial profit very early in the upswing and a heroic abstinence from further participation in the market until at some point after the 1929 collapse when prices were again attractive in relation to earnings and other analytical factors. No doubt this would have resulted in making repurchases too soon—as matters turned out—with consequent paper or actual losses. But whatever the net result, the fact remains that the common-stock investor, proceeding along old-time conservative lines, had opportunities of profit commensurate with any risks he ran—an advantage not possessed by the typical bond buyer. The chief weakness of these investment principles was the difficulty of adhering firmly to them in the speculative contagion of 1928 and 1929. Given a recurrence from present levels of the narrower market swings of former years, conservative diversified investment in common stocks based on careful analysis should again be productive of satisfactory results.

Lowered Standards of Investment Banking Houses

Our third question related to the status of investment banking houses and the attitude to be taken by the public toward them. Until recent years, the leading houses of issue were able successfully to combine the somewhat discordant functions of protecting their clients' interests and making money for themselves. The public was safeguarded as much for business as for ethical reasons, since a firm's reputation and continued existence depended on the soundness of the merchandise which it sold. Investment banking houses, therefore, were considered, and considered themselves, as occupying a semifiduciary relationship toward their customers. But in 1928 and 1929 there occurred a wholesale and disastrous relaxation of the standards of safety previously observed by the reputable houses of issue. This was shown in the sale of many new offerings of inferior grade, aided in part by questionable methods of presenting the facts to the public. The general collapse in values affected these unsound and unseasoned issues with particular severity, so that the losses suffered by investors in many of these flotations have been little short of appalling.

Causes of the Lowered Standards

This general lowering of standards by investment banking firms was due to two causes, the first being the ease with which all issues could be sold, and the second being the scarcity of sound investments to sell. The latter fact arose from the new vogue of financing through common-stock offerings, as the result of which the stronger corporations not only avoided additional bond issues but even retired large amounts of their funded debt.[2] Hence the supply of new bond issues complying with the former strict standards of investment quality was undergoing a sharp reduction at the very time that the volume of funds seeking investment reached record proportions. In previous years, when houses of issue had their choice between selling good bonds or poor ones, they habitually chose the good securities, even at some sacrifice of underwriting profit. But now they had to choose between selling poor investments or none at all—between making large profits or shutting up shop—and it was too much to expect from human nature that under such circumstances they would adequately protect their clients' interests.

Problem of Regaining Public Confidence

Investment banking houses seemingly face a difficult task in regaining the confidence of a public properly mistrustful of their motives and their methods. At the present time such firms are proceeding with the utmost caution in bringing out new investment issues—a policy dictated among other reasons by the impossibility of selling any but the highest grade of bonds in so poor an investment market, and by the new difficulties imposed by the Securities Act of 1933. But if past experience is any guide, the current critical attitude of the investor is not likely to persist; and in the next period of prosperity and plethora of funds for security purchases, the public will once again exhibit its ingrained tendency to forgive, and particularly to forget, the sins committed against it in the past. Its future protection is more likely to come not from its own discrimination but from the chastened attitude of the houses of issue, anxious to retain their slowly recovered prestige by avoiding a repetition of their recent errors.

Increased Need for Thorough Knowledge
of Investment Principles

But a serious obstacle to sound investment-house policies is likely to result from the relative scarcity of new bond issues which can meet the much more exacting requirements enjoined, as we suggested above, by the experience of the past 15 years. If a large popular demand for bonds should return, the difficulty of supplying really good issues in sufficient quantity will almost inevitably result once more in numerous offerings of inferior caliber and unsatisfactory performance. From this survey, we conclude that there is greater need than before of either a thoroughgoing knowledge of investment principles on the part of the individual bond buyer or else of recourse by him to advice which is both expert and disinterested.

The need for such knowledge or such expert advice is only slightly lessened by the passage of the Securities Act of 1933. This measure requires the submission of elaborate data in connection with new security issues, and it greatly extends the liability of bankers, directors, etc., for losses following misstatements or material omissions. These provisions do not ensure the soundness of the security but only that the facts will be adequately disclosed.[3] The questionable character of many speculative stock offerings made after the Securities Act was passed is a striking confirmation of this fact.

The Factor of Human Nature

One of the striking features of the past five years has been the domination of the financial scene by purely psychological elements. In previous bull markets the rise in stock prices remained in fairly close relationship with the improvement in business during the greater part of the cycle; it was only in its invariably short-lived culminating phase that quotations were forced to disproportionate heights by the unbridled optimism of the speculative contingent. But in the 1921–1933 cycle this "culminating phase" lasted for years instead of months, and it drew its support not from a group of speculators but from the entire financial community. The "new-era" doctrine–that "good" stocks (or "blue chips") were sound investments regardless of how high the price paid for them—was at bottom only a means of rationalizing under the title of "investment" the well-nigh universal capitulation to the gambling fever. We suggest that this psychological phenomenon is closely related to the dominant importance assumed in recent years by intangible factors of value, viz., good-will, management, expected earning power, etc. Such value factors, while undoubtedly real, are not susceptible to mathematical calculation; hence the standards by which they are measured are to a great extent arbitrary and can suffer the widest variations in accordance with the prevalent psychology. The investing class was the more easily led to ascribe reality to purely speculative valuations of these intangibles because it was dealing in good part with surplus wealth, to which it was not impelled by force of necessity to apply the old-established acid test that the principal value be justified by the income.

No Automatic Relationship between Value and Price
There are a number of other factors involving human nature in Wall Street to which recent experience should lead us to pay more serious attention than was previously accorded them. Investment theory should recognize that the merits of an issue reflect themselves in the market price not by any automatic response or mathematical relationship but through the minds and decisions of buyers and sellers. Furthermore, the investors' mental attitude not only affects the market price but is strongly affected by it, so that the success of a commitment—properly considered—must depend in some part on the subsequent maintenance of a satisfactory market price. Hence in selecting an investment, even one presumably purchased for income only, reasonable allowance must be made for such purely market-price elements as can be ascertained, in addition to the more primary consideration which is paid to factors of intrinsic value. (Institutions such as life insurance companies and savings banks are much less concerned, under ordinary conditions, with the question of the market price of their investments than are individuals. But a cataclysm of the amplitude of that of 1931–1932 made them rudely conscious of market valuations.)

Speculation Not a Satisfactory Substitute for Investment
If the field of sound investment has suffered a severe contraction, as we suggested above, it would seem natural to turn our attention to intelli-

gent speculation, on the theory that a good speculation is undoubtedly superior to a poor investment. But here again we must recognize that the psychology of the speculator militates strongly against his success. For, by relation of cause and effect, he is most optimistic when prices are highest and most despondent when they are at bottom. Hence, in the nature of things, only the exceptional speculator can prove consistently successful, and no one has a logical right to believe that he will succeed where most of his companions must fail. For this reason, training in speculation, however intelligent and thorough, is likely to prove a misfortune to the individual, since it may lead him into market activities which, starting in most cases with small successes, almost invariably end in major disaster.

If investment is likely to prove unsatisfactory and speculation is certain to be dangerous, to what may the intelligent student turn? Perhaps he would be well advised to devote his attention to the field of undervalued securities—issues, whether bonds or stocks, which are selling well below the levels apparently justified by a careful analysis of the relevant facts. The opportunities in this direction have always been numerous and varied. . . . It is true that bargain hunting in securities is not without its pitfalls, and in recent years especially it has been subject to many disadvantages and disappointments. Yet under more normal conditions it should yield satisfactory average results, and, most important of all, it promotes a fundamentally conservative point of view, which should constitute a valuable safeguard against speculative temptations.

* * * * *

THE SCOPE AND LIMITATIONS OF SECURITY ANALYSIS. THE CONCEPT OF INTRINSIC VALUE

Analysis connotes the careful study of available facts with the attempt to draw conclusions therefrom based on established principles and sound logic. It is part of the scientific method. But in applying analysis to the field of securities we encounter the serious obstacle that investment is by nature not an exact science. The same is true, however, of law and medicine, for here also both individual skill (art) and chance are important factors in determining success or failure. Nevertheless, in these professions analysis is not only useful but indispensable, so that the same should probably be true in the field of investment and possibly in that of speculation.

In the last three decades the prestige of security analysis in Wall Street has experienced both a brilliant rise and an ignominious fall—history-related but by no means parallel to the course of stock prices. The advance of security analysis proceeded uninterruptedly until about 1927, covering a long period in which increasing attention was paid on all sides to financial reports and statistical data. But the "new era" commencing in 1927 involved at bottom the abandonment of the analytical approach; and while emphasis was still seemingly placed on facts and figures, these were manipulated by a sort of pseudo-analysis to support the delusions of the period. The market collapse in October 1929 was no surprise to such analysts as had kept their heads, but the extent of the business collapse that later developed, with its devastating effects on established earning power, again threw their calculations out of gear. Hence the ultimate result was that serious analysis suffered a double discrediting: the first—prior to the crash—due to the persistence of imaginary values, and the second—after the crash—due to the disappearance of real values.

In the Introduction we expressed the view that the experiences of 1927–1933 should not be taken as a norm by which to judge the future of bond investment. The same holds true for analysis as well, and for the same reason, viz., that the extreme fluctuations and vicissitudes of that period are not likely to be duplicated soon again. Successful analysis, like successful investment, requires a fairly rational atmosphere to work *in* and at least some stability of values to work *with*.

Three Functions of Analysis:
1. Descriptive Function

The functions of security analysis may be described under three headings: descriptive, selective, and critical. In its more obvious form, descriptive analysis consists of marshalling the important facts relating to an issue and presenting them in a coherent, readily intelligible manner. This function is adequately performed for the entire range of marketable corporate securities by the various manuals, the Standard Statistics and Fitch services, and others. A more penetrating type of description seeks to reveal the strong and weak points in the position of an issue, compare its exhibit with that of others of similar character, and appraise the factors which are likely to influence its future performance. Analysis of this kind is applicable to almost every corporate issue, and it may be regarded as an adjunct not only to investment but also to intelligent speculation in that it provides an organized factual basis for the application of judgment for purposes of investment or speculation.

2. The Selective Function of Security Analysis

In its selective function, security analysis goes further and expresses specific judgments of its own. It seeks to determine whether a given issue should be bought, sold, retained, or exchanged for some other. What types of securities or situations lend themselves best to this more positive activity of the analyst, and to what handicaps or limitations is it subject? It may be well to start with a group of examples of analytical judgments, which could later serve as a basis for a more general inquiry.

Examples of Analytical Judgments: In 1928 the public was offered a large issue of 6% noncumulative stock of the St. Louis-San Francisco Railway Company priced at 100. The record showed that in no year in the company's history had earnings been equivalent to as much as 1 1/2 times the fixed charges and preferred dividends combined. The application of well-established standards of selection to the facts in this case would have led to the rejection of the issue as insufficiently protected.

A contrasting example: In June 1932 it was possible to purchase 5% bonds of Owens-Illinois Glass Company, due 1939, at 70, yielding 11% to maturity. The company's earnings were many times the interest requirements—not only on the average but even at that time of severe depression. The bond issue was amply covered by current assets alone, and it was followed by common and preferred stock with a very large aggregate market value, taking their lowest quotations. Here, analysis would have led to the recommendation of this issue as a strongly entrenched and attractively priced investment.

Let us take an example from the field of common stocks. In 1922, prior to the boom in aviation securities, Wright Aeronautical Corporation stock was selling on the New York Stock Exchange at only $8, although it was paying a $1 dividend, had for some time been earning over $2 a share, and showed more than $8 per share in cash assets in the treasury. In this case analysis would readily have established that the intrinsic value of the issue was substantially above the market price.

Again, consider the same issue in 1928 when it had advanced to $280 per share. It was then earning at the rate of $8 per share, as against

$3.77 in 1927. The dividend rate was $2; the net-asset value was less than $50 per share. A study of this picture must have shown conclusively that the market price represented for the most part the capitalization of entirely conjectural future prospects—in other words, that the intrinsic value was far less than the market quotation.

A third kind of analytical conclusion may be illustrated by a comparison of Interborough Rapid Transit Company First and Refunding 5s with the same company's Collateral 7% Notes, when both issues were selling at the same price (say 62) in 1933. The 7% notes were clearly worth considerably more than the 5s. Each $1,000 note was secured by deposit of $1,736 face amount of 5s; the principal of the notes had matured; they were entitled either to be paid off in full or to a sale of the collateral for their benefit. The annual interest received on the collateral was equal to about $87 on each 7% note (which amount was actually being distributed to the noteholders), so that the current income on the 7s was considerably greater than that on the 5s. Whatever technicalities might be invoked to prevent the noteholders from asserting their contractual rights promptly and completely, it was difficult to imagine conditions under which the 7s would not be intrinsically worth considerably more than the 5s.

Intrinsic Value vs. Price
From the foregoing examples it will be seen that the work of the securities analyst is not without concrete results of considerable practical value, and that it is applicable to a wide variety of situations. In all of these instances he appears to be concerned with the intrinsic value of the security and more particularly with the discovery of discrepancies between the intrinsic value and the market price. We must recognize, however, that intrinsic value is an elusive concept. In general terms it is understood to be that value which is justified by the facts, e.g., the assets, earnings, dividends, definite prospects, as distinct, let us say, from market quotations established by artificial manipulation or distorted by psychological excesses. But it is a great mistake to imagine that intrinsic value is as definite and as determinable as is the market price. Some time ago intrinsic value (in the case of a common stock) was thought to be about the same thing as "book value," i.e., it was equal to the net assets of the business, fairly priced. This view of intrinsic value was quite definite, but it proved almost worthless as a practical matter because neither the average earnings nor the average market price evinced any tendency to be governed by the book value.

Intrinsic Value and "Earning Power"

Hence this idea was superseded by a newer view, viz., that the intrinsic value of a business was determined by its earning power. But the phrase "earning power" must imply a fairly confident expectation of certain future results. It is not sufficient to know what the past earnings have averaged, or even that they disclose a definite line of growth or decline. There must be plausible grounds for believing that this average or this trend is a dependable guide to the future. Experience has shown only too forcibly that in many instances this is far from true. This means that the concept of "earning power," expressed as a definite figure, and the derived concept of intrinsic value, as something equally definite and ascertainable, cannot be safely accepted as a *general premise* of security analysis.

Example: To make this reasoning clearer, let us consider a concrete and typical example. What would we mean by the intrinsic value of J. I. Case Company common, as analyzed, say, early in 1933? The market price was $30; the asset value per share was $176; no dividend was being paid; the average earnings for ten years had been $9.50 per share; the results for 1932 had shown a deficit of $17 per share. If we followed a customary method of appraisal, we might take the average earnings per share of common for ten years, multiply this average by ten, and arrive at an intrinsic value of $95. But let us examine the individual figures which make up this ten-year average. They are as follows:

1932	$17.40(d)
1931	2.90(d)
1930	11.00
1929	20.40
1928	26.90
1927	26.00
1926	23.30
1925	15.30
1924	5.90(d)
1923	2.10(d)
Average	$ 9.50

(d) Deficit.

This average of $9.50 is obviously nothing more than an arithmetical resultant from ten unrelated figures. It can hardly be urged that this average is in any way representative of *typical* conditions in the past or representative of what may be expected in the future. Hence any figure of "real" or intrinsic value derived from this average must be characterized as equally accidental or artificial.

The Role of Intrinsic Value in the Work of the Analyst

Let us try to formulate a statement of the role of intrinsic value in the work of the analyst which will reconcile the rather conflicting implications of our various examples. The essential point is that security analysis does not seek to determine exactly what is the intrinsic value of a given security. It needs only to establish either that the value is *adequate*—e.g., to protect a bond or to justify a stock purchase—or else that the value is considerably higher or considerably lower than the market price. For such purposes an indefinite and approximate measure of the intrinsic value may be sufficient. To use a homely simile, it is quite possible to decide by inspection that a woman is old enough to vote without knowing her age, or that a man is heavier than he should be without knowing his exact weight.

This statement of the case may be made clearer by a brief return to our examples. The rejection of St. Louis-San Francisco Preferred did not require an exact calculation of the intrinsic value of this railroad system. It was enough to show, very simply from the earnings record, that the margin of value above the bondholders' and preferred stockholders' claims was too small to ensure safety. Exactly the opposite was true for the Owens-Illinois Glass 5s. In this instance, also, it would undoubtedly have been difficult to arrive at a fair valuation of the business; but it was quite easy to decide that this value in any event was far in excess of the company's debt.

In the Wright Aeronautical example, the earlier situation presented a set of facts which demonstrated that the business was worth substantially more than $8 per share, or $1,800,000. In the later year, the facts were equally conclusive that the business did not have a reasonable value of $280 per share, or $70,000,000 in all. It would have been difficult for the analyst to determine whether Wright Aeronautical was actually worth $20 or $40 a share in 1922—or actually worth $50 or $80 in 1929. But fortunately it was not necessary to decide these points in order to conclude that the shares were attractive at $8 and unattractive, intrinsically, at $280.

The J. I. Case example illustrates the far more typical common-stock situation, in which the analyst cannot reach a dependable conclusion as to the relation of intrinsic value to market price. But even here, *if the price had been low or high enough*, a conclusion might have been warranted. To express the uncertainty of the picture, we might say that it was difficult to determine in early 1933 whether the intrinsic value of Case common was nearer $30 or $130. Yet if the stock had been selling at as low as $10, the analyst would undoubtedly have been justified in declaring that it was worth more than the market price.

Flexibility of the Concept of Intrinsic Value
This should indicate how flexible is the concept of intrinsic value as applied to security analysis. Our notion of the intrinsic value may be more or less distinct, depending on the particular case. The degree of indistinctness may be expressed by a very hypothetical "range of approximate value," which would grow wider as the uncertainty of the picture increased, e.g., $20 to $40 for Wright Aeronautical in 1922 as against $30 to $130 for Case in 1933. It would follow that even a very indistinct idea of the intrinsic value may still justify a conclusion if the current price falls far outside either the maximum or minimum appraisal.

More Definite Concept in Special Cases
The Interborough Rapid Transit example permits a more precise line of reasoning than any of the others. Here a given market price for the 5% bonds results in a very definite valuation for the 7% notes. If it were certain that the collateral securing the notes would be acquired for and distributed to the note holders, then the mathematical relationship—viz., $1,736 of value for the 7s against $1,000 of value for the 5s—would eventually be established at this ratio in the market. But because of quasi-political complications in the picture, this normal procedure could not be expected with certainty. As a practical matter, therefore, it is not possible to say that the 7s are actually worth 74% more than the 5s, but it may be said with assurance that the 7s are worth *substantially more*—which is a very useful conclusion to arrive at when both issues are selling at the same price.

The Interborough issues are an example of a rather special group of situations in which analysis may reach more definite conclusions respecting intrinsic value than in the ordinary case. These situations may involve a liquidation or give rise to technical operations known as "arbitrage" or "hedging." While, viewed in the abstract, they are probably the most satisfactory field for the analyst's work, the fact that they are specialized in character and of infrequent occurrence makes them relatively unimportant from the broader standpoint of investment theory and practice.

Principal Obstacles to Success of the Analyst

a. *Inadequate or Incorrect Data.*   Needless to say, the analyst cannot be right all the time.   Furthermore a conclusion may be logically right but work out badly in practice.   The main obstacles to the success of the analyst's work are threefold, viz., (a) the inadequacy or incorrectness of the data, (b) the uncertainties of the future, and (c) the irrational behavior of the market. The first of these drawbacks, while serious, is the least important of the three.   Deliberate falsification of the data is rare; most of the misrepresentation flows from the use of accounting artifices which it is the function of the capable analyst to detect. Concealment is more common than misstatement. In the majority of cases the analyst's experience and skill should lead him to note the absence of information on an important point; but in some instances the concealment will elude detection and give rise to an incorrect conclusion.

b. *Uncertainties of the Future.*   Of much greater moment is the element of future change. A conclusion warranted by the facts and by the apparent prospects may be vitiated by new developments.   This raises the question of how far it is the function of security analysis to anticipate changed conditions. We shall defer consideration of this point until our discussion of various factors entering into the processes of analysis. It is manifest, however, that future changes are largely unpredictable, and that security analysis must ordinarily proceed on the assumption that the past record affords at least a rough guide to the future. The more questionable this assumption, the less valuable is the analysis. Hence this technique is more useful when applied to senior securities (which are protected against change) than to common stocks; more useful when applied to a business of inherently stable character than to one subject to wide variations; and, finally, more useful when carried on under fairly normal general conditions than in times of great uncertainty and radical change.

c. *The Irrational Behavior of the Market.* The third handicap to security analysis is found in the market itself. In a sense the market and the future present the same kind of difficulties. Neither can be predicted or controlled by the analyst, yet his success is largely dependent upon them both. The major activities of the investment analyst may be thought to have little or no concern with market prices. His typical function is the selection of high-grade, fixed-income-bearing bonds, which upon investigation he judges to be secure as to interest and principal. The purchaser is supposed to pay no attention to their subsequent market fluctuations, but to be interested solely in the question whether the bonds will continue to be sound investments. In our opinion this traditional view of the investor's attitude is inaccurate and somewhat hypocritical. Owners of securities, whatever their character, are interested in their market quotations. This fact is recognized by the emphasis always laid in investment practice upon *marketability*. If it is important that an issue be readily salable, it is still more important that it command a satisfactory price. While for obvious reasons the investor in high-grade bonds has a lesser concern with market fluctuations than has the speculator, they still have a strong psychological, if not financial, effect upon him. Even in this field, therefore, the analyst must take into account whatever influences may adversely govern the market price, as well as those which bear upon the basic safety of the issue.

In that portion of the analyst's activities which relates to the discovery of undervalued, and possibly of overvalued, securities, he is more directly concerned with market prices. For here the vindication of his judgment must be found largely in the ultimate market action of the issue. This field of analytical work may be said to rest upon a twofold assumption: first, that the market price is frequently out of line with the true value; and, second, that there is an inherent tendency for these disparities to correct themselves. As to the truth of the former statement, there can be very little doubt—even though Wall Street often speaks glibly of the "infallible judgment of the market" and asserts that "a stock is worth what you can sell it for—neither more nor less."

The Hazard of Tardy Adjustment of Price To Value
The second assumption is equally true in theory, but its working out in practice is often most unsatisfactory. Undervaluations caused by neglect or prejudice may persist for an inconveniently long time, and the same applies to inflated prices caused by overenthusiasm or artificial

stimulants. The particular danger to the analyst is that, because of such delay, new determining factors may supervene before the market price adjusts itself to the value as he found it. In other words, by the time the price finally does reflect the value, this value may have changed considerably and the facts and reasoning on which his decision was based may no longer be applicable.

The analyst must seek to guard himself against this danger as best he can: in part, by dealing with those situations preferably which are not subject to sudden change; in part, by favoring securities in which the popular interest is keen enough to promise a fairly swift response to value elements which he is the first to recognize; in part, by tempering his activities to the general financial situation—laying more emphasis on the discovery of undervalued securities when business and market conditions are on a fairly even keel, and proceeding with greater caution in times of abnormal stress and uncertainty.

The Relationship of Intrinsic Value To Market Price

The general question of the relation of intrinsic value to the market quotation may be made clearer by the appended chart, which traces the various steps culminating in the market price. It will be evident from the chart that the influence of what we call analytical factors over the market price is both *partial* and *indirect*—partial, because it frequently competes with purely speculative factors which influence the price in the opposite direction; and indirect, because it acts through the intermediary of people's sentiments and decisions. In other words, the market is not a *weighing machine*, on which the value of each issue is recorded by an exact and impersonal mechanism, in accordance with its specific qualities. Rather should we say that the market is a *voting machine*, whereon countless individuals register choices which are the product partly of reason and partly of emotion.

* * * * *

A PROPOSED DEFINITION OF INVESTMENT

Investment should be identified with safety, but the safety must be more than a mere expectation. The concept can be really useful only if it is based on something more tangible than the psychology of the purchaser. Safety must be ensured or at least strongly indicated by the application of definite and well-established standards.

CHART C
Relationship of Intrinsic Value Factors to Market Price

I. General market factors.

II. Individual factors.

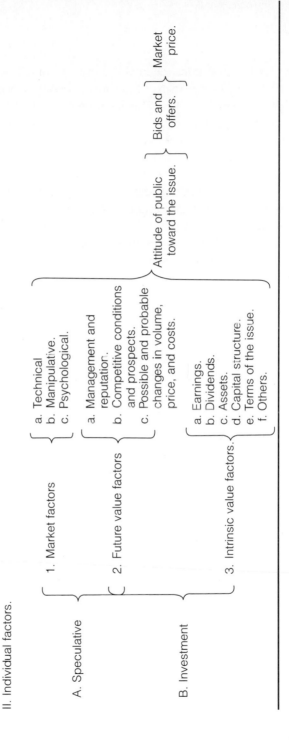

A. Speculative

1. Market factors
   - a. Technical
   - b. Manipulative.
   - c. Psychological.

2. Future value factors
   - a. Management and reputation.
   - b. Competitive conditions and prospects.
   - c. Possible and probable changes in volume, price, and costs.

B. Investment

3. Intrinsic value factors.
   - a. Earnings.
   - b. Dividends.
   - c. Assets.
   - d. Capital structure.
   - e. Terms of the issue.
   - f. Others.

Attitude of public toward the issue.

Bids and offers.

Market price.

Had this attitude been taken by the purchaser of common stocks in 1928–1929, the term "investment" would not have been the tragic misnomer which it was. But in proudly applying the designation "blue chips" to the high-priced issues chiefly favored, the public unconsciously revealed the gambling motive at the heart of its supposed investment selections. These differed from earlier common-stock investments in the one vital respect that the buyer did not determine, by the application of firmly established standards of value, that they were worth the price paid. The market made up new standards as it went along, by accepting the current price, however high, as the sole measure of value. Any idea of safety based on this uncritical approach was clearly illusory and replete with danger. Carried to its logical extreme, it meant that no price could possibly be too high for a good stock, and that such an issue was exactly as "safe" after it had advanced to 200 as it had been at 25.

We conclude, therefore, that expected safety must be based on study and standards. At the same time, investment does not necessarily require the existence of current income for the purchaser. The investor may at times legitimately base his purchase on a return which is accumulating to his credit and which will be realized by him after a longer or shorter wait. With these observations in mind, we suggest the following definition of investment as one in harmony with both the popular understanding of the term and the requirements of reasonable precision:

An investment operation is one which, upon thorough analysis, promises safety of principal and a satisfactory return. Operations not meeting these requirements are speculative.

Certain implications of this definition are worthy of further discussion. We speak of an "investment operation" rather than an issue or a purchase, for several reasons. It is unsound to think always of investment character as inhering in an issue per se. The price is frequently an essential element, so that a stock (and even a bond) may have investment merit at one price level but not at another. Furthermore, an investment might be justified in a group of issues, which would not be sufficiently safe if made in any one of them singly. In other words, diversification might be necessary to reduce the risk involved in the separate issues to the minimum consonant with the requirements of investment. (This would be true, in general, of purchases of common stocks for investment.)

In our view it is also proper to consider as investment operations certain types of arbitrage and hedging commitments which involve the sale of one security against the purchase of another. In these rather specialized operations the element of safety is provided by the combination of purchase and sale. This extension of the ordinary concept of investment appears to the writers to be entirely logical.

The phrases, "thorough analysis," "promises safety," and "satisfactory return" are all chargeable with indefiniteness, but the important point is that their meaning is clear enough to prevent serious misunderstanding. By "thorough analysis" we mean, of course, the study of the facts in the light of established standards of safety and value. An "analysis" made in 1959 that recommended investment in Thiokol Chemical common—or many similar issues—at a price forty times its current and a hundred times its average earnings, merely because of its excellent prospects, would be clearly ruled out, as devoid of all quality of thoroughness.

The "safety" sought in investment is not absolute or complete; the word means, rather, protection against loss under reasonably likely conditions or variations. A safe bond, for example, is one which would suffer default only under exceptional and highly improbable circumstances. Similarly, a safe stock is one which holds every prospect of being worth the price paid except under quite unlikely contingencies. Where study and experience indicate that an appreciable chance of loss must be recognized and allowed for, we have a speculative situation.[4]

"Satisfactory return" is a wider expression than "adequate income," since it allows for capital appreciation or profit as well as current interest or dividend yield. "Satisfactory" is a subjective term; it covers any rate or amount of return, however low, which the investor is willing to accept, provided he acts with reasonable intelligence.

It may be helpful to elaborate our definition from a somewhat different angle, which will stress the fact that investment must always consider the price as well as the quality of the security. Strictly speaking, there can be no such thing as an "investment issue" in the absolute sense, i.e., implying that it remains an investment regardless of price. In the case of high-grade bonds and preferred stocks, this point may not be important, for their prices are rarely so inflated as to introduce serious risk of loss of principal.[5] But in the common-stock field this risk may frequently be created by an undue advance in price—so much so, indeed, that in our opinion the great majority of common stocks of strong companies must be considered speculative a good part of the time after a bull market is well under way, simply because their price is too high to warrant safety of principal in any intelligible sense of the phrase. We must warn the reader that prevailing Wall Street opinion does not agree with us on this point; and he must make up his own mind which of us is wrong.

Nevertheless, we shall embody our principle in the following additional criterion of investment: *An investment operation is one that can be justified on **both** qualititative and quantitative grounds.*

Analysis and Speculation

It may be thought that sound analysis should produce successful results in any type of situation, including the confessedly speculative, i.e., those subject to substantial uncertainty and risk. If the selection of speculative issues is based on expert study of the companies' position, should not this approach give the purchaser a considerable advantage? Admitting future events to be uncertain, could we not count on the favorable and unfavorable developments to cancel out each other, more or less, so that the initial advantage afforded by sound analysis will carry through into an eventual average profit? This is a plausible argument but a deceptive one; and its overready acceptance has done much to lead analysts astray. It is worthwhile, therefore, to detail several valid arguments against placing chief reliance upon analysis in speculative situations.

In the first place, what may be called the mechanics of speculation (in the sense of active trading) involves serious handicaps to the speculator, which may outweigh the benefits conferred by analytical study. These disadvantages include the payment of commissions and interest charges, the so-called "turn of the market" (meaning the spread between the bid and asked price), and, most important of all, an inherent tendency for the average loss to exceed the average profit, unless a certain technique of trading is followed which is opposed to the analytical approach.

The second objection is that the underlying analytical factors in speculative situations are subject to swift and sudden revision. The danger, already referred to, that the intrinsic value may change before the market price reflects that value is therefore much more serious in speculative than in investment situations. A third difficulty arises from circumstances surrounding the unknown factors, which are necessarily left out of security analysis. Theoretically these unknown factors should have an equal chance of being favorable or unfavorable, and thus they should neutralize each other in the long run. For example, it is often easy to determine by comparative analysis that one company is selling much lower than another in the same field, in relation to earnings, although both apparently have similar prospects. But it may well be that the low price for the apparently attractive issue is due to certain important unfavorable factors which, though not disclosed, are known to those identified with the company—and vice versa for the issue seemingly selling above its relative value. In a speculative situation those "on the inside" often have an advantage of this kind, which nullifies the premise that good and bad changes in the picture should offset each other, and which loads the dice against the analyst working with some of the facts concealed from him.

The value of analysis diminishes as the element of chance increases. The final objection is based on more abstract ground, but, nevertheless, its practical importance is very great. Even if we grant that analysis can give the speculator a mathematical advantage, it does not ensure him a profit. His ventures remain hazardous; in any individual case a loss may be taken; and after the operation is concluded, it is difficult to determine whether the analyst's contribution has been a benefit or a detriment. Hence the latter's position in the speculative field is at best uncertain and somewhat lacking in professional dignity. It is as though the analyst and Dame Fortune were playing a duet on the speculative piano, with the fickle goddess calling all the tunes.

By another and less imaginative simile, we might more convincingly show why analysis is inherently better suited to investment than to speculative situations. In Monte Carlo the odds are weighted 19 to 18 in favor of the proprietor of the roulette wheel, so that on the average he wins $1 out of each $37 wagered by the public. This may suggest the odds against the untrained investor or speculator. Let us assume that, through some equivalent of analysis, a roulette player is able to reverse the odds for a limited number of wagers, so that they are now 19 to 18 in his favor. If he distributes his wagers evenly over all the numbers, then whichever one turns up he is certain to win a moderate amount. This operation may be likened to an investment program based upon sound analysis and carried on under propitious general conditions.

But if the player wagers all his money on a single number, the small odds in his favor are of slight importance compared with the crucial question whether chance will elect the number he has chosen. His "analysis" will enable him to win a little more if he is lucky; it will be of no value when luck is against him. This, in exaggerated form perhaps, describes the position of the analyst dealing with essentially speculative operations. Exactly the same mathematical advantage, which practically ensures good results in the investment field, may prove entirely ineffective where luck is the overshadowing influence.

It would seem prudent, therefore, to consider analysis as an adjunct or auxiliary rather than as a guide in speculation. It is only when chance plays a subordinate role that the analyst can properly speak in an authoritative voice and accept responsibility for the results of his judgments.

* * * * *

FOOTNOTES

1. See Chamberlain, Lawrence, and William W. Hay, *Investment and Specu-lation*, pp. xii, 8–11, 55–56, New York, 1931; especially the following from p. 55: "Common stocks, as such, are not superior to bonds as long-term investments, because primarily they are not investments at all. They are speculations."
2. See Appendix, Note 1, for supporting data.
3. "All the Act pretends to do is to require the 'truth about securities' at the time of issue, and to impose a penalty for failure to tell the truth. Once it is told, the matter is left to the investor." William O. Douglas and G. E. Bates, *The Federal Securities Act of 1933*, Yale Law Journal 171, December 1933.
4. For the relationship between "safety" and "market-price" fluctuations, see Chap. 16 of *The Intelligent Investor*, 2d rev. ed., by Benjamin Graham, Harper & Brothers, New York, 1959.
5. Yet the example of Atchison, Topeka and Santa Fe General 4s/1995 selling at 141 in 1946 (given in Chap. 3) might be said to illustrate a "serious risk" in a high-grade bond. It subsequently declined to 89.

THE COMPANY'S
INVESTMENT POLICY

R. W. Huntington

R. W. Huntington wrote this article about Connecticut General's investment policies in early 1929. It was reprinted by *Best's Insurance News* in 1933, at which time the editor noted, "We have never seen anywhere a better exposition of the principles underlying sound investment practice."

About twenty-five years ago I attempted to address a body of agents on the subject of life insurance company investments. Either I was unable to make the subject as interesting as I should have been able to make it or the agents, per se, were not interested in the subject of investments. I suspect my failure was due to both of these causes. At any rate, I have fought shy of talking about investments to the agents ever since.

The subject has, however, been invested, if I may so use the word, with considerable interest of late, partly because the War made us a nation of investors, and partly because a good many young people who have never seen stocks go down until very lately have made a good deal of money.

We might as well admit in the first place that for the last six years the prudent and experienced have not made on paper, at least had not two

From R. W. Huntington, *The Company's Investment Policy* (Hartford, Connecticut, 1929), by permission of CIGNA Corporation months ago, as much as the rash and inexperienced who had never seen hard times or severe recessions. We old fogies have been told time and again that we have entered a new era which we were incapable of understanding; that the past used to be the best guide for the future but that Patrick Henry's famous saying, "I have but one lamp by which my feet are guided and that is the lamp of experience. I know of no way of judging the future but by the past," was a back number, to be put with Washington's farewell address and other similar things, all right then but no good now. We have been told that the bulls of this country were the fellows who made the money, and it has been intimated that the sky was the only limit and that the old criteria of judging investments by present and past earnings were no good. What one thought they might earn three, four, ten years from now was the proper way of judging.

Now as our theory of investment had always been founded on a distrust in our ability to tell what was going to happen ten years from now, all this was a little disturbing. We remembered how in 1901 or thereabouts a pamphlet giving the opinions of twenty-five of the leading financiers of New York on the subject of the future rates of interest was published and circulated. Interest rates had been going down for twenty-five years and there was a singular unanimity of opinion that they were going to continue to do so and that from two to three per cent interest was all we could expect to ultimately realize on our assets. It clouded the horizon for the time being for me and I was doubtful whether we ought to stop making mortgage loans at five per cent temporary return and buy only long-term bonds at not more than four per cent return, or whether a five per cent temporary return was justifiable, especially if we could make some sort of a reserve out of the extra one per cent.

Just before this in 1898 and 1899 the Baltimore and Ohio Railroad had issued three different mortgage bonds bearing three and one-half per cent interest, all maturing in 1925. They were understood to have picked out this relatively short maturity because they expected to be able to refund the bonds at two and one-half or three per cent at the worst. They did the refunding at five per cent, but we didn't know then that they were going to have to.

While we were still revolving [*sic*] these things in our minds, along came Mr. Charlton Lewis and read to the Actuarial Society a learned and interesting paper which traced the rate of interest from the dark ages to the present time, showed, roughly perhaps, the variations and ended with the prediction that it was about time the rate of interest began to increase. As I look back on it now I am inclined to believe that when in 1901 leading financiers expressed the opinion that the rate of interest was going to drop, the rate had already begun to rise, but they hadn't perceived it.

Mr. P. H. Woodward, then vice president of the company, was our financial adviser. And a very wise one he was. He used to say to me, "When other people run, you walk" and "Remember that in financial matters you are justified in turning a somersault as often as the circumstances seem to demand it." He also taught us all how to read a financial statement. His great criterion for judging investment was earnings. Not earnings next year and the years to come—he didn't know what they were going to be as the public does now—but earnings last year and the year before. Then the character of the management of any concern influenced him. He wanted nothing to do with the speculators or the wreckers. He wanted to go with the builders. And he founded our investment policy, which I will try to further unfold.

We believe that what we need in our investments is the best combination of safety and yield that we can get: That circumstances may from time to time change our immediate investment program: That our investments ought at all times to be highly diversified so that the incidence of any depression in any particular line of business will not fall upon us too heavily. In following out this line we have invested, so far as the laws of the state allowed us, in railroad, public utility, and miscellaneous bonds, and in preferred stocks and common stocks of railways and public utilities and also in bank stocks. We have taken first mortgages on city real estate and on farm real estate.

What is the standard for investment in common stocks? They must show over a period of years earnings considerably greater than the dividend payments. The financial structure must be sound and not what is called top-heavy. That is, the stocks must not bear too small a ratio to the bonded indebtedness. The yield on the investment at the purchase price must be such that we are satisfied with it. There are possible exceptions to all rules, and as I write I can think of one or two [of] these, but they are immaterial to the general principles.

One can diversify to a certain extent in common stocks, but there is no doubt but that, taken by and large, the market values will vary more than bond values, and that however well picked, the income will vary more, both up and down, than the income from an equally well picked line of mortgage bonds. But what is in a name? Illinois Central

Railroad stock for instance has paid dividends without intermission since it began to do business and accumulate earnings, seventy or more years ago, while the bonds of the original corporations preceding many now equally prosperous roads, like Atchison, Topeka and Santa Fe and Union Pacific, have been in default and foreclosed.

We are told that common stocks are to be invested in because the value of the dollar has grown smaller and when we are paid the interest or principal of a fixed long-term investment, we are paid less because of this depreciation, and that common stocks don't come due and dividends do increase as the value of the dollar lessens. But because the value of the dollar has lessened on the whole since 1914, or even since 1896, is it going to keep on doing so?

So our attitude has been that a certain small proportion of our assets can well be invested in common stocks if we can find those that look satisfactory; but that, generally speaking, the investment should be made in times of general depression of business and discouragement on the part of the investors who are heavy borrowers. We should be disturbed if half or three-fifths of our assets were so invested, even at figures well below the present market.

The simple fact is that the insurance company investments ought to be made on the principle of hedging. Do we think that the value of the dollar is on the decrease and that common stocks are low? We are justified in proceeding on this basis and investing in common stocks. But we don't want to do it to so great an extent that if we are wrong, the company will be seriously hurt, so we had better invest in some long-time bonds as a hedge.

Do we think that the rate of interest is going to go down and we had better invest in long-time bonds to the exclusion of shorter time securities and mortgage loans? We can indulge ourselves in so investing, provided we do not do it to an extent which is going to hurt the company if we are wrong, and we had better keep on investing in mortgage loans and perhaps even now and then in short-time bonds, because even the wisest have gone astray on these long-time predictions.

If we knew that the farm loan situation was going to continue as it is at the present, we would drop out of the farm loan business entirely and liquidate our investments therein. The government has established the Federal Farm Loan Banks, and they can take care of the farmer better than we can because they can sell his obligations on a non-taxable basis to the rich. But we have a good organization for the care of farm loans and if we desert it entirely, it is going to desert us, and things may change.

Is the price of agricultural lands going to improve? We think it is, but if and when we get a reasonable offer for any of our foreclosed farms, we had better take it, because we may be mistaken.

There isn't any bet we can make in investment matters that we hadn't better hedge on, and we must always remember, in the words of Mr. Woodward, which I have quoted, that in financial matters we are justified in turning a somersault as often as the circumstances seem to demand it.

What is the object of those in charge of investing an insurance company's funds? First, last, and all the time, to keep the principal intact. Above everything we want to make our insurance sure; and the surest way of doing this from an investment standpoint is to so wisely invest our money that whatever happens to any one class of securities will not seriously affect the company unfavorably.

PERILS OF THE WILL
TO BELIEVE

Fred C. Kelly

Fred Kelly's warning against the "Perils of the Will to Believe" in his 1930 book, *Why You Win or Lose: The Psychology of Speculation*, calls to mind the later observation and advice of "Adam Smith": "The stock doesn't know you own it!"

After vanity and greed, perhaps the most malign influence to one trying to make money from the market is the *Will To Believe*. We think to be true whatever we *hope* is true. When a reputable doctor tells a man he has an incurable disease, the man is then quite likely to fall into the hands of a quack who says *he* can cure him. The patient wouldn't believe the quack ordinarily, but now if he doesn't believe his only hope in life is gone. Poor, pathetic sufferers who flock to the grave of a dead priest, expecting somehow to be benefited, wouldn't have such faith if they weren't desperately in need of it, having vainly tried everything else. Likewise, men pin their faith to poor stocks and expect these to advance 40 or 50 points, because here is their last hope of financial salvation. When a man declares confidently that a certain stock is going

---

From Fred C. Kelly, *Why You Win or Lose: The Psychology of Speculation* (Burlington, Vermont, 1930), 47–51, Fraser Publishing Company.

to advance, what he means is: "Oh, if it only *would!*" What sounds like an opinion, based on inside knowledge, is simply a hope, expressed from time to time, to bolster up one's courage.

I have seen men earnestly listening to the advice of a broker's . . . porter—because he was telling what they earnestly desired to think was true. The studious fellows who work over pages of figures in the backrooms of big brokerage houses could often give valuable advice, well mixed with caution. But customers seldom take the trouble to hunt them up, for they would rather listen to the chatty floor-men of charming personality who have little time for study but are sure that almost any stock is about to go up. They are prepared to tell what customers most wish to hear. I know just one man who saw the October panic coming and when he told his employers about it, what do you suppose they did? Discharged him! His story seemed too unpleasant to be true and they decided that he must be hopelessly unreliable.

A friend of mine made a small fortune in the last big bull market only to lose it, and along with it the savings of a lifetime. He at one time had a profit of about $20,000. In his imagination he had already spent the money, building a new home, buying a new car and sending his mother-in-law on a tour which would keep her away at least six months. One morning he discovered which instead of having $20,000, his profits had shrunk to $16,000. Now, even $16,000 dropped into one's lap out of the stock market is not to be sneezed at; but once having mentally spent his $20,000, he did not like the idea of slipping back to a mere $16,000. He said to himself, "Oh, well, the drop is only temporary. When it comes back I'll again have my $20,000. To be sure of this I'll buy more stock and then only a small advance will give me my original profit."

But instead of advancing again, prices continued to drop. He now found that he must have far more stock than before to gain $20,000 profit on an average upturn of only one or two points. The $20,000, though only on paper, had become as real to him as if it were in his pocket; and his imaginary expenditures, particularly those for pleasure, had become so much a part of his scheme of life that he thought he simply *had* to have that money. So he bought still more stock. The fact that prices had been dropping should have been indication enough that the peak had been reached and that the toboggan had started down the other side. But his paper profit had obscured his vision. His profits dwindled to a mere $2,000. Somebody suggested to him that instead of waiting for two or three points' gain in the next upward rally, he should buy a certain stock about to advance twenty-five points. In other words, he was lured into buying a highly speculative stock that could move downward as easily as upward. Ready to grab at straws, he quickly lost nearly all the money he had. Toward the last he believed any silly story he heard and he was lucky to get out of the market with the clothes on his back. He was a victim of the *Will To Believe*.

THE STATE OF LONG-TERM EXPECTATION

John Maynard Keynes

In this passage from his *General Theory of Employment Interest and Money*—full of insight, profundity, and wit—John Maynard Keynes elegantly explains the conversion from "real" investment to market-driven investment. Note in particular his concern about excessive attention to short-term market considerations rather than diligent pursuit of long-term business building—a concern others have come to share 50 years later.

A conventional valuation which is established as the outcome of the mass psychology of a large number of ignorant individuals is liable to change violently as the result of a sudden fluctuation of opinion due to factors which do not really make much difference to the prospective yield; since there will be no strong roots of conviction to hold it steady. In abnormal times in particular, when the hypothesis of an indefinite continuance of the existing state of affairs is less plausible than usual even though there are no express grounds to anticipate a definite change, the market will be subject to waves of optimistic and pessimistic sentiment, which are unreasoning and yet in a sense legitimate where no solid basis exists for a reasonable calculation.

But there is one feature in particular which deserves our attention. It might have been supposed that competition between expert professionals,

From John Maynard Keynes, *The General Theory of Employment Interest and Money* (New York, New York, 1936), 154–158, by permission of Harcourt Brace Jovanovich, Inc.

possessing judgment and knowledge beyond that of the average private investor, would correct the vagaries of the ignorant individual left to himself. It happens, however, that the energies and skill of the professional investor and speculator are mainly occupied otherwise. For most of these persons are, in fact, largely concerned, not with making superior long-term forecasts of the probable yield of an investment over its whole life, but with foreseeing changes in the conventional basis of valuation a short time ahead of the general public. They are concerned, not with what an investment is really worth to a man who buys it "for keeps," but with what the market will value it at, under the influence of mass psychology, three months or a year hence. Moreover, this behaviour is not the outcome of a wrong-headed propensity. It is an inevitable result of an investment market organised along the lines described. For it is not sensible to pay 25 for an investment of which you believe the prospective yield to justify a value of 30, if you also believe that the market will value it at 20 three months hence.

Thus the professional investor is forced to concern himself with the anticipation of impending changes, in the news or in the atmosphere, of the kind by which experience shows that the mass psychology of the market is most influenced. This is the inevitable result of investment markets organised with a view to so-called "liquidity". Of the maxims of orthodox finance none, surely, is more anti-social than the fetish of liquidity, the doctrine that it is a positive virtue on the part of investment institutions to concentrate their resources upon the holding of "liquid" securities. It forgets that there is no such thing as liquidity of investment for the community as a whole. The social object of skilled investment should be to defeat the dark forces of time and ignorance which envelop our future. The actual, private object of the most skilled investment to-day is "to beat the gun", as the Americans so well express it, to outwit the crowd, and to pass the bad, or depreciating, half-crown to the other fellow.

This battle of wits to anticipate the basis of conventional valuation a few months hence, rather than the prospective yield of an investment over a long term of years, does not even require gulls amongst the public to feed the maws of the professional—it can be played by professionals amongst themselves. Nor is it necessary that anyone should keep his simple faith in the conventional basis of valuation having any genuine long-term validity. For it is, so to speak, a game of Snap, of Old Maid, of Musical Chairs—a pastime in which he is victor who says *Snap* neither too soon nor too late, who passes the Old Maid to his neighbour before the game is over, who secures a chair for himself when the music stops. These games can be played with zest and enjoyment, though all the players know that it is the Old Maid which is circulating, or that when the music stops some of the players will find themselves unseated.

Or, to change the metaphor slightly, professional investment may be likened to those newspaper competitions in which the competitors have to pick out the six prettiest faces from a hundred photographs, the prize being awarded to the competitor whose choice most nearly corresponds to the average preferences of the competitors as a whole; so that each competitor has to pick, not those faces which he himself finds prettiest, but those which he thinks likeliest to catch the fancy of the other competitors, all of whom are looking at the problem from the same point of view. It is not a case of choosing those which, to the best of one's judgment, are really the prettiest, nor even those which average opinion genuinely thinks the prettiest. We have reached the third degree where we devote our intelligences to anticipating what average opinion expects the average opinion to be. And there are some, I believe, who practise the fourth, fifth and higher degrees.

If the reader interjects that there must surely be large profits to be gained from the other players in the long run by a skilled individual who, unperturbed by the prevailing pastime, continues to purchase investments on the best genuine long-term expectations he can frame, he must be answered, first of all, that there are, indeed, such serious-minded individuals and that it makes a vast difference to an investment market whether or not they predominate in their influence over the game-players. But we must also add that there are several factors which jeopardise the predominance of such individuals in modern investment markets. Investment based on genuine long-term expectation is so difficult to-day as to be scarcely practicable. He who attempts it must surely lead much more laborious days and run greater risks than he who tries to guess better than the crowd how the crowd will behave; and, given equal intelligence, he may make more disastrous mistakes. There is no clear evidence from experience that the investment policy which is socially advantageous coincides with that which is most profitable. It needs *more* intelligence to defeat the forces of time and our ignorance of the future than to beat the gun. Moreover, life is not long enough — human nature desires quick results, there is a peculiar zest in making money quickly, and remoter gains are discounted by the average man at a very high rate. The game of professional investment is intolerably boring and overexacting to anyone who is entirely exempt from the gambling instinct; whilst he who has it must pay to this propensity the appropriate toll. Furthermore, an investor who proposes to ignore near-term market fluctuations needs greater resources for safety and must not operate on so large a scale, if at all, with borrowed money—a further reason for the higher return from the pastime to a given stock of intelligence and resources. Finally it is the long-term investor, he who most promotes the public interest, who will in practice come in for most criticism, wherever investment funds are managed by committees or boards or banks.[1] For it is in the essence of his behaviour that he should be eccentric, unconventional and rash in the eyes of average opinion. If he is successful, that will only confirm the general belief in his rashness; and if in the short run he is unsuccessful, which is very likely, he will not receive much mercy. Worldly wisdom teaches that it is better for reputation to fail conventionally than to succeed unconventionally.

So far we have had chiefly in mind the state of confidence of the speculator or speculative investor himself and may have seemed to be tacitly assuming that, if he himself is satisfied with the prospects, he has unlimited command over money at the market rate of interest. This is, of course, not the case. Thus we must also take account of the other facet of the state of confidence, namely, the confidence of the lending institutions towards those who seek to borrow from them, sometimes described as the state of credit. A collapse in the price of equities, which has had disastrous reactions on the marginal efficiency of capital, may have been due to the weakening either of speculative confidence or of the state of credit. But whereas the weakening of either is enough to cause a collapse, recovery requires the revival of *both*. For whilst the weakening of credit is sufficient to bring about a collapse, its strengthening, though a necessary condition of recovery, is not a sufficient condition.

FOOTNOTES

1. The practice, usually considered prudent, by which an investment trust or an insurance office frequently calculates not only the income from its investment portfolio but also its capital valuation in the market, may also tend to direct too much attention to short-term fluctuations in the latter.

INVESTMENT POLICY
AND INSURANCE
KEYNES AS AN INVESTOR

John Maynard Keynes

An articulate advocate for a deliberately bold approach to investment management, John Maynard Keynes was active—and highly successful—in institutional investing. Keynes was Bursar of King's College, Cambridge, Chairman of the National Mutual Life Assurance Society (1921–38), director of Provincial Insurance, and a director of several investment trusts. The following excerpts of Keynes writings, spanning a period from 1924 through 1942, should be a source of pleasure for readers on investment.

INVESTMENT POLICY AND INSURANCE

In May 1924 *The Nation* published an Insurance Supplement. Keynes provided one signed article on investment policy and one unsigned one on bonuses.

From John Maynard Keynes, *The Collected Writings of John Maynard Keynes, Volume XII, Economic Articles and Correspondence: Investment and Editorial*, Donald Moggridge, ed. (New York, New York, 1983), 240–244, 37–40, 66–68, 70, 106–109, 81–83, by permission of The Syndics of the Cambridge University Press.

FROM *THE NATION AND ATHENAEUM*, **May 17, 1924**

Investment Policy for Insurance Companies

The question of investment policy for life insurance companies has been much under discussion in the last year or two. The issues which have been raised are the result, not so much of new ideas, as of new facts. The problem of wise investment, as it has presented itself since the War, is largely a new one, and the life insurance world has been slowly feeling its way to new principles suited to the new conditions.

What was the pre-war field of investment? Leaving aside real property and reversions, advances on policies, and the like, the chief categories were (1) mortgages, (2) a limited selection of trustee securities, of which Consols was the main British Government stock, (3) American dollar securities, and (4) the better-class bonds of certain foreign governments and railways. If companies were to keep up their average interest earnings to a satisfactory level, compatible with not placing too much capital outside the first two classes mentioned above, there was not a very wide scope for varying the proportions invested in the different classes; and within each class there was not much scope for gaining advantage from moving from one security to another. Some companies, however, were finding it difficult to keep up a satisfactory interest yield, which sometimes induced them to put a proportion of their resources into second-class bonds of various kinds—investments which on the average have not turned out well.

During the War there was, of course, a big movement, both on public and private grounds, into the various new types of British Government securities which were being issued. Many companies disposed of almost the whole of their dollar securities. Thus the end of the War found many companies with a far greater proportion of British Government securities in their hands than they had ever dreamt of holding in the past.

Not only is there now a much wider range of choice within the field of British trustee securities than there was before, but the comparative suitability of the pre-war classes of investment has greatly changed. The margin of yield between first-class mortgages and British Government securities has narrowed. The yield on American bonds no longer bears its old relation of superiority to the yield on sterling securities, apart from which doubts about the future course of exchange introduce a new and difficult factor. All our old ideas about the security of foreign government bonds have been entirely upset, and the element of political risk must now be given far greater weight than formerly. Even some British trustee stocks need a watchful eye, and doubts can reasonably be felt which before the war would have seemed unnecessary. Few investors, for example, care to hold a heavy amount of India stocks, and, as we have seen lately, circumstances can arise in which even colonial stocks do not seem perfectly safe.

Thus the question of security itself cannot be settled by the old rules of thumb which used to be deemed sufficient. The wise investor must now doubt all things, and constantly revise his ideas in accordance with changing events in the political world.

But not only do new risks require a more watchful eye. The range of choice within a given class of security gives new opportunities for obtaining an advantage through judicious transferences in accordance with the fluctuations which occur from time to time in relative prices. Above all, the choice between long- and short-dated British Government securities inevitably raises a problem of a constantly varying aspect. I suppose that in old days the choice between mortgages and Consols had to be determined on much the same principles as the choice today between long- and short-dated securities. Essentially it is an eternal problem. But the range of choice actually available for investment, the shortest and longest dated securities and those of almost every intermediate date being available in large quantities, makes it practicable to act promptly on any considered opinion which may be reached.

Most companies compromise to a certain extent and never back any opinion, however plausible and well-founded it may seem, up to the full extent. Nevertheless, it is very unlikely that the same proportionate division of assets between long- and short-dated securities can always be right. It is bound to change in accordance with the fluctuations of the business world. Insurance companies have a special opportunity to take advantage of these fluctuations, because it seldom happens that they are under any necessity to diminish their aggregate holdings. An industrial firm which holds a portion of its liquid resources in gilt-edged securities, in order to enable it to finance its affairs in particularly brisk times, is inevitably a seller from time to time. In the same way banks are bound to vary the volume of their gilt-edged investments to balance corresponding variations in the opposite direction in the amount of their advances to their customers. When insurance companies sell, it is always to buy something else instead, which fact puts them in an extremely strong position for benefiting from the fluctuating demands of the rest of the market.

Thus it comes about that the management of an insurance company is almost inevitably driven, whether it likes it or not, into what has been termed lately "an active investment policy;" which, after all, is merely another name for being alive to the fact that circumstances change. Unfortunately, it is not possible to make oneself permanently secure by any policy of inaction whatever. The idea which some people seem to entertain that an active policy involves taking more risks than an inactive policy is exactly the opposite of the truth. The inactive investor who takes up an obstinate attitude about his holdings and refuses to change his opinion merely because facts and circumstances have changed is the one who in the long run comes to grievous loss. Particularly in these days, no one is so wise that he can foresee the future far ahead. Anyone who obstinately takes up the view that over the next twenty years the rate of interest is bound to fall, or is bound to rise, is going beyond the evidence. If he is to be wisely guided he must take a shorter view and be prepared constantly to change it as the tide of events ebbs and flows.

It is equally false to believe that one form of investment involves taking a view and that another one does not. Every investment means committing oneself to one particular side of the market. The holder of long-dated securities lays himself open to losses, which may be very large, through the depreciation of his capital; whilst the holder of short-dated securities equally lays himself open to earn a lower rate of interest than that on which he has calculated. No one can get both security of capital and security of income; yet it is a great mistake to think that an insurance company, which depends on both, can neglect either. It was the neglect of these principles in the period which elapsed between the era of cheap money in 1896 and 1897 and the beginning of the Great War, which involved the companies in the serious capital losses which were then shown both in their annual accounts and in their valuation results. Capital depreciation is the great enemy of life assurance, and an "active" investment policy has for its object the avoidance of capital loss at least as much as the making of capital profits.

The ideal policy for an insurance company is to put itself, so far as it can, into a situation where it is earning a respectable rate of interest on its funds, while securing at the same time that its risk of really serious depreciation in capital value is at a minimum. This, of course, is obvious. But it must be equally obvious that there is no golden rule for this, no invariable method. And this itself is the reason why constant vigilance, constant revision of preconceived ideas, constant reaction to changes in the external situation, in short "an active investment policy," seems to some of us an essential condition, and at the same time the most difficult and important branch, of the sound management of the great insurance societies and corporations which now administer so considerable a proportion of the national savings.

KEYNES AS AN INVESTOR

Perhaps the most interesting of Keynes's letters on the National Mutual were written in the aftermath of the 1937–8 recession. When the accounts for 1937 revealed a capital loss of £641,000, F. N. Curzon, acting chairman in Keynes's absence, initiated a discussion of investment policy and urged further liquidations. Keynes was not at all happy with what followed and unsuccessfully tried in correspondence to restrain the board. On 13 March, Curzon sent Keynes a 14 page letter criticising the investment policy of previous months and suggesting further liquidations of doubtful shares. Keynes replied.

LETTER TO F. N. CURZON, MARCH 18, 1938

Dear Curzon,

Thank you for your very full letter. I was hoping to hear from you, and am glad to have this careful explanation of your general point of view. I admit that, being out of touch and not fully informed, some of my criticisms have been ill-directed.

My attitude is governed by the following general considerations, and I fancy that, whilst we do not see eye to eye, you do not disagree with some at least of these.

1. I do not believe that selling at very low prices is a remedy for having failed to sell at high ones. The criticism, if any, to which we are open is not having sold more prior to last August. In the light of after events, it would clearly have been advantageous to do so. But even now, looking back, I think it would have required abnormal foresight to act otherwise. In my own case, I was of the opinion that the prices of sterling securities were fully high in the spring. But I was prevented from taking advantage of this, first of all by the gold scare,[1] and then by the N.D.C.[2] scare, both of which I regarded as temporary influences for the wearing off of which one should wait. Then came the American collapse with a rapidity and on a scale which no one could possibly have foreseen, so that one had not got the time to act which one would have expected. However this may be, I don't feel that one is open to any criticism for not selling after the blow had fallen. As soon as prices had fallen below a reasonable estimate of intrinsic value and long-period probabilities, there was nothing more to be done. It was too late to remedy any defects in previous policy, and the right course was to stand pretty well where one was.

2. I feel no shame at being found still owning a share when the bottom of the market comes. I do not think it is the business, far less the duty, of an institutional or any other serious investor to be constantly considering whether he should cut and run on a falling market, or to feel himself open to blame if shares depreciate on his hands. I would go much further than that. I should say that it is from time to time the duty of a serious investor to accept the depreciation of his holdings with equanimity and without reproaching himself. Any other policy is antisocial, destructive of confidence, and incompatible with the working of the economic system. An investor is aiming, or should be aiming primarily at long-period results, and should be solely judged by these. The fact of holding shares which have fallen in a general decline of the market proves nothing and should not be a subject of reproach. It should certainly not be an argument for unloading when the market is least able to support such action. The idea that we should all be selling out to the other fellow and should all be finding ourselves with nothing but cash at the bottom of the market is not merely fantastic, but destructive of the whole system. I do not believe you differ from me on this. But I repeat it because it is profoundly the basis of my general attitude.

3. I do not agree that we have in fact done particularly badly. I have been carrying on for my own benefit a post mortem into results and making such comparison with other institutions as are open to me. Recknell, who has helped me with these investigations, would agree, I think, that, whilst we do not come out particularly well, we do not come out particularly badly. As far as I can judge, there is extremely little difference between our results and those of other people. If we take the Prudential, for example, with its very large holdings of ordinary shares, I should say that, though they may have done just a trifle better than we have, there is extremely little in it. Moreover, if our results are compared with those of the Index, for a period, they are extremely good. We have done a very great deal better than the Index, and have in that way shown power of management and have justified the capacity of insurance offices to undertake constructive investment. If we deal in equities, it is inevitable that there should be large fluctuations. Some part of paper profits is certain to disappear in bad times. Results must be judged by what one does on the round journey. On that test we have come out successfully. If, on the other hand, we do not hold equities, we must either be content with earning a definitely lower rate of interest, or we shall be tempted, in my judgment, into risks which, while they may be less apparent and take longer to mature, are really much more serious than those of equity holders.

As I began by saying, I think it is easy to exaggerate the extent of the divergences of our opinions. I feel sure that you agree with a great deal of the above, and on several occasions you have shown yourself a supporter in practice of a steady policy as against some other members of the Board. One main difference lies, I fancy, in your taking a less favourable view as to our experience over the whole swing of recent years. And I believe that, if full comparisons were available, you would find yourself greatly comforted.

* * * * *

MEMORANDUM FOR THE ESTATES COMMITTEE, KING'S COLLEGE, CAMBRIDGE, MAY 8, 1938

II

In fact the chief lesson I draw from the above results is the opposite of what I set out to show when, what is now nearly 20 years ago, I first persuaded the College to invest in ordinary shares. At that time I believed that profit could be made by what was called a credit cycle policy, namely by holding such shares in slumps and disposing of them in booms; and we purchased an industrial index including a small holding in an outstanding share in each leading industry. Since that time there may have been more numerous and more violent general fluctuations than at any previous period. We have indeed done well by purchasing particular shares at times when their prices were greatly depressed; but we have not proved able to take much advantage of a general systematic movement out of and into ordinary shares as a whole at different phases of the trade cycle. In the past nine years, for example, there have been two occasions when the whole body of our holding of such investments has depreciated by 20 to 25 per cent within a few months and we have not been able to escape the movement. Yet on both occasions I foresaw correctly to a certain extent what was ahead. Nevertheless these temporary severe losses and the inability to take substantial advantage of these fluctuations have not interfered with successful results.

As the result of these experiences I am clear that the idea of whole-sale shifts is for various reasons impracticable and indeed undesirable. Most of those who attempt it sell too late and buy too late, and do both too often, incurring heavy expenses and developing too unsettled and speculative a state of mind, which, if it is widespread, has besides the grave social disadvantage of aggravating the scale of the fluctuations. I believe now that successful investment depends on three principles:

1. a careful selection of a few investments (or a few types of investment) having regard to their cheapness in relation to their probable actual and potential *intrinsic* value over a period of years ahead and in relation to alternative investments at the time;

2. a steadfast holding of these in fairly large units through thick and thin, perhaps for several years, until either they have fulfilled their promise or it is evident that they were purchased on a mistake;

3. a *balanced* investment position, i.e., a variety of risks in spite of individual holdings being large, and if possible opposed risks (e.g., a holding of gold shares amongst other equities, since they are likely to move in opposite directions when there are general fluctuations).

On the other hand, it is a mistake to sell a £1 note for 15s. in the hope of buying it back for 12s. 6d., and a mistake to refuse to buy a £1 note for 15s. on the ground that it cannot really be a £1 note (for there is abundant experience that £1 notes *can* be bought for 15s. at a time when they are expected by many people to fall to 12s. 6d.).

Another important rule is the avoidance of second-class safe invest-ments, none of which can go up and a few of which are sure to go down. This is the main cause of the defeat of the average investor. The ideal investment portfolio is divided between the purchase of really secure future income (where future appreciation or depreciation will depend on the rate of interest) and equities which one believes to be capable of a *large* improvement to offset the fairly numerous cases which, with the best skill in the world, will go wrong.

The following is an illustration of how much more is to be made by picking the right shares than by wholesale shifts between market leaders and cash through a correct anticipation of the major swings. If the latter is aimed at then (if one is responsible altogether for a *large* body of investment) specialties which cannot be sold in quantity on a falling market must be avoided and the holding must be widely spread amongst the highly marketable leading shares, which means that the movements of the index numbers can be taken as a good guide to the actual movements of values relevant to such an investment policy. Now the index numbers . . . show (for Jan.1) two peaks in 1929 and 1937 and two bottoms in 1932 or 1933 and 1938. British shares fell from 100 to 50, rose again to 90 and fell to 74; Americans fell from 149 to 46, rose to 88 and then fell to 55. These figures from Jan.1 are, of course, not the absolute tops and bottoms; but anyone who managed to sell all his British shares at an average of 100, reinvesting his money at 50, sold again at 90 and reinvested at 74 (and similarly with his American shares selling at 149, reinvesting at 46, selling again at 88 and reinvesting at 55) would have shown almost superhuman skill in predicting credit cycle movements. Now if he held half his money in sterling and half in dollar securities, allowing for loss of interest at 5 per cent during the periods when he was liquid, he would have raised the value of his investments from 100 to 182 in the nine years. In fact the Chest investments were raised during this period from 100 to 262, so that the appreciation (162 per cent) was almost exactly double that earned by the credit cycle genius (82 per cent).

In the main, therefore, slumps are experiences to be lived through and survived with as much equanimity and patience as possible. Advantages can be taken of them more because individual securities fall out of their reasonable parity with other securities on such occasions, than by attempts at wholesale shifts into and out of equities as a whole. One must not allow one's attitude to securities which have a daily market quotation to be disturbed by this fact or lose one's sense of proportion. Some Bursars will buy without a tremor unquoted and unmarketable investments in real estate which, if they had a selling quotation for immediate cash available at each Audit, would turn their hair grey. The fact that you do not know how much its ready money quotation fluctuates does not, as is commonly supposed, make an investment a safe one. Until recently tithe was a much more dangerous investment than tin mines, and Worlaby-cum-Elsham has been, since we bought the property, a much more speculative as well as a much less profitable and more troublesome holding than the investments of the Chest in ordinary shares. But it is true, unfortunately, that the modern organisation of the capital market requires for the holder of quoted equities much more nerve, patience and fortitude than from the holder of wealth in other forms. Yet it is safer to be a speculator than an investor in the sense of the definition which I once gave the Committee that a speculator is one who runs risks of which he is aware and an investor is one who runs risks of which he is unaware. The management of stock exchange investments of any kind is a low pursuit, having very little social value and partaking (at its best) of the nature of a game of skill, from which it is a good thing for most members of our Society to be free; whereas the justification of Worlaby and Elsham lies in its being a constructive and socially beneficial enterprise, where we exercise a genuine entrepreneurial function, in which many of our body can be reasonably and usefully interested. I welcome the fact that the Estates Committee—to judge from their poker faces and imperturbable demeanour—do not take either gains or losses from the Stock Exchange too gravely—they are much more depressed or elated (as the case may be) by farming results. But it may be useful and wise nevertheless, to analyse from time to time what is being done and the principles of our policy.

* * * * *

LETTER TO F. C. SCOTT, JUNE 7, 1938

I

It is important in conducting a post mortem to be sure what is one's test of success. One important test is the avoidance of 'stumers' with which many investment lists are disfigured. I mean by this definite mistakes where the fall in value is due not merely to fluctuations, but to an intrinsic loss of capital. These are in an altogether different category from fluctuating securities, since there is no particular reason to expect a subsequent recovery. There is apt to be great confusion of mind between depreciation arising out of fluctuations and depreciation arising out of serious mistakes in the choice of individual securities.

On this test I think we can claim very good success. Our list includes a proportion of the above sort of mistake, but the amount of capital involved is not large. It is particularly useful for future guidance to make a list of these and remember how they arose. The following is my list, in which I have not attempted to include Americans since it is particularly difficult at the present time to analyse them accurately from this point of view: Omes; Petters Preference; British and Dominions Film; Carbo Plaster; Enfield Rolling Mills; Grand Union Canal; South African Torbanite; Universal Rubber Paviors; Mortgage Bank of Chile.

You will notice that these are practically all specialities and rather obscure concerns, mostly bought on private advice. Omes was due to Trouton; Carbo Plaster and South African Torbanite to Falk; Enfield Rolling Mills and Grand Union Canal to Brett. I am sure experience shows that private and personal recommendations of this class of security tend to turn out wrong in the long run. I am not quite sure whether Enfield Rolling Mills is justifiably included in that list, since it may succeed in getting over its preliminary difficulties. But perhaps our holding of Textiles bought on Hunter's advice ought also to be included, since one rather doubts whether they will recover fully, even when industry is again at a peak.

The other chief test must be, I would urge, against representative index numbers. A valuation at the bottom of the slump tends to bring out an unduly unfavourable result as against an investment policy which on the whole avoids equities; since it allows nothing for the nest egg in hand arising out of the fact that such a valuation is assuming in effect that one has purchased a large volume of equities at bottom prices. As long as you are beating the index number by a satisfactory percentage on the round journey there is, I am sure, not too much to worry about. For provided that you are avoiding stumers and beating the index number, you are bound to do brilliantly in the long run.

The modern habit of concentrating on calculations of appreciation and depreciation tends to interfere with what should be the proper habit of mind that the object of an investment policy is averaging through time. Insurance policy is, of course, doing that a little bit; but on the whole investment [insurance?] policy is averaging over a number of items which are in the same position in time, but in different positions in place. Investment policy which is successful in averaging through time will produce the same good results as insurance policy which is successful in averaging through place; and one must not be deflected from the sound principles of that kind of averaging any more than one must be deflected in an insurance policy by a heavy loss in a particular place.

II

I come next to the question of the percentage of aggregate funds which it is prudent to hold in different classes of investments. We certainly need minimum percentage in government securities and maximum percentage in ordinary shares. This is required partly for appearances; partly in the case of government securities to provide a satisfactory margin over our large volume of deposited securities, and in the case of ordinary shares to avoid the risk of excessive fluctuations exceeding our investment reserves.

But apart from these two general principles I am strongly opposed to rigidities in other respects. Fixed percentage—particularly within each group of industry, etc.—is surely altogether opposed to having an investment policy at all. The whole art is to vary the emphasis and the center of gravity of one's portfolio according to circumstances. Subject to a minimum in government securities and a maximum in ordinary shares I would strongly urge the desirability of the greatest possible flexibility.

Proceeding to details, I am in sympathy with your suggestion for some increase in our holding of British Government securities. At present we hold a rather larger percentage than the average of all the insurance companies measured as a percentage of total assets. (At the end of 1936 insurance companies as a whole held 23.1 per cent in British Government securities as against our holding of 24.82 at the end of 1937 and 26.44 in March 1938.) Since, however, other offices held a much larger percentage of non-Stock Exchange assets their percentage of British Government securities measured as a percentage of Stock Exchange assets was higher than ours. There is, I agree, a good deal to be said for raising our percentage to some figure as you propose— 33 per cent. An alternative way to look at it would be to include public boards and railway debentures and aim to 40 per cent in British Government securities, British public boards, municipal securities and railway debentures taken altogether.

As regards colonial government and foreign government securities, I should be quite ready to cut them out altogether as a normal policy, apart from investments made on quite special considerations and those required for the purpose of insurance deposits.

In the case of ordinary shares there ought to be a fairly wide margin of fluctuation in the percentage held: say between 20 and 30 per cent and without any fixed percentages as between different classes of ordinary shares. . . .

One final *caveat:* Compared with their predecessors, modern investors concentrate too much on annual, quarterly, or even monthly valuations of what they hold, and on capital appreciation and depreciation generally; and too little either on immediate yield or on future prospects and intrinsic worth.

* * * * *

LETTER TO F. C. SCOTT, FEBRUARY 6, 1942

There are very few investors, I should say, who eschew the attempt to snatch capital profits at an early date more than I do. I lay myself open to criticism because I am generally trying to look a long way ahead and am prepared to ignore immediate fluctuations, if I am satisfied that the assets and the earning power are there. My purpose is to buy securities where I am satisfied as to assets and ultimate earning power and where the market price seems cheap in relation to these. If I succeed in this, I shall simultaneously have achieved safety-first and capital profits. All stocks and shares go up and down so violently that a safety-first policy is practically certain, if it is successful, to result in capital profits. For when the safety, excellence and cheapness of a share is generally realised, its price is bound to go up. The Elder Dempster case is a very good example of this. I have no particular expectation of this share going up at any early date. I picked it because it seemed to me exceedingly safe and, apart from short-term fluctuations, unlikely to go down in the years ahead.

I am quite incapable of having adequate knowledge of more than a very limited range of investments. Time and opportunity do not allow more. Therefore, as the investible sums increase, the size of the unit must increase. I am in favour of having as large a unit as market conditions will allow and, apart from a small group of securities, this generally means a smaller unit than would be made necessary by the size of the investible fund.

As good examples of speculative attempts at capital profits I should instance South American shares and oil companies within the area of hostilities. I should not deny for a moment that such investments may result in capital profits. My objection is that I have no information on which to reach a good judgment, and the risks are clearly enormous. To suppose that safety-first consists in having a small gamble in a large number of different directions of the above kind, as compared with a substantial stake in a company where's one information is adequate, strikes me as a travesty of investment policy.

The units we actually work to in the Provincial represent a very expensive concession from what I personally think the counsel of perfection.

There has been an extremely good experimental test of this in a comparison of results in the accounts of the Provincial and King's over the last twenty years. The spread of the King's investments between gilt-edged and others is much the same. The arguments against undue risk and in favour of stability of income are at least as great for a college as for an insurance company. Since I have been so closely concerned with both, the leading shares purchased by both have been very much the same in both cases. Where one institution has held a large stake in a particular direction in almost every instance the other one has also.

Nevertheless, King's has done immeasurably better than the Provincial. I am quite sure the reason for this is that our unit of investment, which has been practically the same size as for the Provincial, though our investible funds are only about one-third as large, has been so much larger. We have been much more strictly limited to shares where I felt myself in a position to have a sound judgment. We have not lived up to this as much as we should. We should have done better still if we had lived up to it more. Looking back, I feel this applies particularly to purchases in the American market as distinct from the London market, though on the whole the American investments have worked out all right.

The other day we were looking at our back records with a view to conducting a little bit of a post mortem and to discover whence the satisfactory results came. The answer seemed to be that (with one or two minor exceptions in the American market) there had scarcely been a single case of any large-scale loss. There had been big fluctuations in market prices. But none of the main investments had, in the end, turned out otherwise than all right. Thus, against the profits which inevitably accumulate, there were comparatively few losses to offset. Virtually *all* our big holdings had come right.

Now that is what I call a safety-first policy as judged by results. Where King's has made profits the Provincial has nearly always made profits too. But they have not been an equally high proportion of the total invested funds.

* * * * *

FOOTNOTES

1. On rumours that the official American price of gold would be reduced.
2. The National Defence Contribution was introduced in the 1937 budget. It was later substantially modified. See *JMK*, vol. xxi, pp. 409–13.

GENERAL CHARACTERISTICS OF CROWDS— A PSYCHOLOGICAL LAW OF THEIR MENTAL UNITY

Gustave LeBon

"A Crowd," explained Gustave LeBon, "is like a savage; it is not prepared to admit that anything can come between its desire and the realization of that desire." Here he explains the "Law of Mental Unity of Crowds" and notes that the existence of a Crowd does "not always involve the simultaneous presence of a number of individuals on one spot."

What constitutes a crowd from the psychological point of view—A numerically strong agglomeration of individuals does not suffice to form a crowd—Special characteristics of psychological crowds—The turning in a fixed direction of the ideas and sentiments of individuals composing such a crowd, and the disappearance of their personality—The crowd is always dominated by considerations of which it is unconscious—The disappearance of brain activity and the predominance of medullar activity—The lowering of the intelligence and the complete transformation of the sentiments—The transformed sentiments may be better or worse than those of the individuals of which the crowd is composed—A crowd is as easily heroic as criminal.

From Gustave LeBon, *The Crowd: A Study of the Popular Mind* (London, England, 1977; originally published 1895), 23–34, by permission of Unwin Hyman Limited.

In its ordinary sense the word "crowd" means a gathering of individuals of whatever nationality, profession, or sex, and whatever be the chances that have brought them together. From the psychological point of view the expression "crowd" assumes quite a different signification. Under certain given circumstances, and only under those circumstances, an agglomeration of men presents new characteristics very different from those of the individuals composing it. The sentiments and ideas of all the persons in the gathering take one and the same direction, and their conscious personality vanishes. A collective mind is formed, doubtless transitory, but presenting very clearly defined characteristics. The gathering has thus become what, in the absence of a better expression, I will call an organised crowd, or, if the term is considered preferable, a psychological crowd. It forms a single being and is subjected to the *law of the mental unity of crowds*.

It is evident that it is not by the mere fact of a number of individuals finding themselves accidentally side by side that they acquire the character of an organised crowd. A thousand individuals accidentally gathered in a public place without any determined object in no way constitute a crowd from the psychological point of view. To acquire the special characteristics of such a crowd, the influence is necessary of certain predisposing causes of which we shall have to determine the nature.

The disappearance of conscious personality and the turning of feeling and thoughts in a different direction, which are the primary characteristics of a crowd about to become organised, do not always involve the simultaneous presence of a number of individuals on one spot. Thousands of isolated individuals may acquire at certain moments, and under the influence of certain violent emotions—such, for example, as a great national event—the characteristics of a psychological crowd. It will be sufficient in that case that a mere chance should bring them together for their acts to at once assume the characteristics peculiar to the acts of a crowd. At certain moments half a dozen men might constitute a psychological crowd, which may not happen in the case of hundreds of men gathered together by accident. On the other hand, an entire nation, though there may be no visible agglomeration, may become a crowd under the action of certain influences.

A psychological crowd once constituted, it acquires certain provisional but determinable general characteristics. To these general characteristics there are adjoined particular characteristics which vary according to the elements of which the crowd is composed, and may modify its mental constitution. Psychological crowds, then, are susceptible of classification; and when we come to occupy ourselves with this matter, we shall see that a heterogeneous crowd—that is, a crowd composed of dissimilar elements—presents certain characteristics in common with homogeneous crowds—that is, with crowds composed of elements more or less akin (sects, castes, and classes)—and side by side with these common characteristics particularities which permit of the two kinds of crowds being differentiated.

But before occupying ourselves with the different categories of crowds, we must first of all examine the characteristics common to them all. We shall set to work like the naturalist, who begins by describing the general characteristics common to all the members of a family, before concerning himself with the particular characteristics which allow the differentiation of the genera and species that the family includes.

It is not easy to describe the mind of crowds with exactness, because its organisation varies not only according to race and composition, but also according to the nature and intensity of the exciting causes to which crowds are subjected. The same difficulty, however, presents itself in the psychological study of an individual. It is only in novels that individuals are found to traverse their whole life with an unvarying character. It is only the uniformity of the environment that creates the apparent uniformity of characters. I have shown elsewhere that all mental constitutions contain possibilities of character which may be manifested in consequence of a sudden change of environment. This explains how it was that among the most savage members of the French Convention were to be found inoffensive citizens who, under ordinary circumstances, would have been peaceable notaries or virtuous magistrates. The storm past, they resumed their normal character of quiet, law-abiding citizens. Napoleon found amongst them his most docile servants.

It being impossible to study here all the successive degrees of organisation of crowds, we shall concern ourselves more especially with such crowds as have attained to the phase of complete organisation. In this way we shall see what crowds may become, but not what they invariably are. It is only in this advanced phase of organisation that certain new and special characteristics are superimposed on the unvarying and dominant character of the race; then takes place that turning already alluded to of all the feelings and thoughts of the collectivity in an identical direction. It is only under such circumstances, too, that what

I have called above the *psychological law of the mental unity of crowds comes into play*.

Among the psychological characteristics of crowds there are some that they may present in common with isolated individuals, and others, on the contrary, which are absolutely peculiar to them and are only to be met with in collectivities. It is these special characteristics that we shall study, first of all, in order to show their importance.

The most striking peculiarity presented by a psychological crowd is the following: Whoever be the individuals that compose it, however like or unlike be their mode of life, their occupations, their character, or their intelligence, the fact that they have been transformed into a crowd puts them in possession of a sort of collective mind which makes them feel, think, and act in a manner quite different from that in which each individual of them would feel, think, and act were he in a state of isolation. There are certain ideas and feelings which do not come into being, or do not transform themselves into acts, except in the case of individuals forming a crowd. The psychological crowd is a provisional being formed of heterogeneous elements, which for a moment are combined, exactly as the cells which constitute a living body form by their reunion a new being which displays characteristics very different from those possessed by each of the cells singly.

Contrary to an opinion which one is astonished to find coming from the pen of so acute a philosopher as Herbert Spencer, in the aggregate which constitutes a crowd there is in no sort a summing-up of or an average struck between its elements. What really takes place is a combination followed by the creation of new characteristics, just as in chemistry certain elements, when brought into contact—bases and acids, for example—combine to form a new body possessing properties quite different from those of the bodies that have served to form it.

It is easy to prove how much the individual forming part of a crowd differs from the isolated individual, but it is less easy to discover the causes of this difference.

To obtain at any rate a glimpse of them it is necessary in the first place to call to mind the truth established by modern psychology, that unconscious phenomena play an altogether preponderating part not only in organic life, but also in the operations of the intelligence. The conscious life of the mind is of small importance in comparison with its unconscious life. The most subtle analyst, the most acute observer, is scarcely successful in discovering more than a very small number of the unconscious motives that determine his conduct. Our conscious acts are the outcome of an unconscious substratum created in the mind in the main by hereditary influences. This substratum consists of the innumerable common characteristics handed down from generation to generation, which constitute the genius of a race. Behind the avowed causes of our acts there undoubtedly lie secret causes that we do not avow, but behind these secret causes there are many others more secret still which we ourselves ignore. The greater part of our daily actions are the result of hidden motives which escape our observation.

It is more especially with respect to those unconscious elements which constitute the genius of a race that all the individuals belonging to it resemble each other, while it is principally in respect to the conscious elements of their character—the fruit of education, and yet more of exceptional hereditary conditions—that they differ from each other. Men the most unlike in the matter of their intelligence possess instincts, passions, and feelings that are very similar. In the case of everything that belongs to the realm of sentiment—religion, politics, morality, the affections and antipathies, etc.—the most eminent men seldom surpass the standard of the most ordinary individuals. From the intellectual point of view an abyss may exist between a great mathematician and his bootmaker, but from the point of view of character the difference is most often slight or non-existent.

It is precisely these general qualities of character, governed by forces of which we are unconscious, and possessed by the majority of the normal individuals of a race in much the same degree—it is precisely these qualities, I say, that in crowds become common property. In the collective mind the intellectual aptitudes of the individuals, and in consequence their individuality, are weakened. The heterogeneous is swamped by the homogeneous, and the unconscious qualities obtain the upper hand.

This very fact that crowds possess in common ordinary qualities explains why they can never accomplish acts demanding a high degree of intelligence. The decisions affecting matters of general interest come to by an assembly of men of distinction, but specialists in different walks of life, are not sensibly superior to the decisions that would be adopted by a gathering of imbeciles. The truth is, they can only bring to bear in common on the work in hand those mediocre qualities which are the birthright of every average individual. In crowds it is stupidity and not mother-wit that is accumulated. It is not all the world, as is so often repeated, that has more wit than Voltaire, but assuredly Voltaire that has more wit than all the world, if by "all the world" crowds are to be understood.

If the individuals of a crowd confined themselves to putting in common the ordinary qualities of which each of them has his share, there would merely result the striking of an average, and not, as we have said is actually the case, the creation of new characteristics. How is it that these new characteristics are created? This is what we are now to investigate.

Different causes determine the appearance of these characteristics peculiar to crowds, and not possessed by isolated individuals. The first is that the individual forming part of a crowd acquires, solely from numerical considerations, a sentiment of invincible power which allows him to yield to instincts which, had he been alone, he would perforce have kept under restraint. He will be the less disposed to check himself from the consideration that, a crowd being anonymous, and in consequence irresponsible, the sentiment of responsibility which always controls individuals disappears entirely.

The second cause, which is contagion, also intervenes to determine the manifestation in crowds of their special characteristics, and at the same time the trend they are to take. Contagion is a phenomenon of which it is easy to establish the presence, but that it is not easy to explain. It must be classed among those phenomena of a hypnotic order, which we shall shortly study. In a crowd every sentiment and act is contagious, and contagious to such a degree that an individual readily sacrifices his personal interest to the collective interest. This is an aptitude very contrary to his nature, and of which a man is scarcely capable, except when he makes part of a crowd.

A third cause, and by far the most important, determines in the individuals of a crowd special characteristics which are quite contrary at times to those presented by the isolated individual. I allude to the suggestibility of which, moreover, the contagion mentioned above is neither more nor less than an effect.

To understand this phenomenon it is necessary to bear in mind certain recent physiological discoveries. We know to-day that by various processes an individual may be brought into such a condition that, having entirely lost his conscious personality, he obeys all the suggestions of the operator who has deprived him of it, and commits acts in utter contradiction with his character and habits. The most careful observations seem to prove that an individual immerged for some length of time in a crowd in action soon finds himself—either in consequence of the magnetic influence given out by the crowd, or from some other cause of which we are ignorant—in a special state, which much resembles the state of fascination in which the hypnotised individual finds himself in the hands of the hypnotiser. The activity of the brain being paralysed in the case of the hypnotised subject, the latter becomes the slave of all the unconscious activities of his spinal cord, which the hypnotiser directs at will. The conscious personality has entirely vanished; will and discernment are lost. All feelings and thoughts are bent in the direction determined by the hypnotiser.

Such also is approximately the state of the individual forming part of a psychological crowd. He is no longer conscious of his acts. In his case, as in the case of the hypnotised subject, at the same time that certain faculties are destroyed, others may be brought to a high degree of exaltation. Under the influence of a suggestion, he will undertake the accomplishment of certain acts with irresistible impetuosity. This impetuosity is the more irresistible in the case of crowds than in that of the hypnotised subject, from the fact that, the suggestion being the same for all the individuals of the crowd, it gains in strength by reciprocity. The individualities in the crowd who might possess a personality sufficiently strong to resist the suggestion are too few in number to struggle against the current. At the utmost, they may be able to attempt a diversion by means of different suggestions. It is in this way, for instance, that a happy expression, an image opportunely evoked, have occasionally deterred crowds from the most bloodthirsty acts.

We see, then, that the disappearance of the conscious personality, the predominance of the unconscious personality, the turning by means of suggestion and contagion of feelings and ideas in an identical direction, the tendency immediately to transform the suggested ideas into acts; these, we see, are the principal characteristics of the individual forming part of a crowd. He is no longer himself, but has become an automaton who has ceased to be guided by his will.

Moreover, by the mere fact that he forms part of an organised crowd, a man descends several rungs in the ladder of civilisation. Isolated, he may be a cultivated individual; in a crowd, he is a barbarian—that is, a creature acting by instinct. He possesses the spontaneity, the violence, the ferocity, and also the enthusiasm and heroism of primitive beings, whom he further tends to resemble by the facility with which he allows himself to be impressed by words and images—which would be entirely without action on each of the isolated individuals composing the crowd—and to be induced to commit acts contrary to his most obvious interests and his best-known habits. An individual in a crowd is a grain of sand amid other grains of sand, which the wind stirs up at will.

It is for these reasons that juries are seen to deliver verdicts of which each individual juror would disapprove, that parliamentary assemblies adopt laws and measures of which each of their members would disapprove in his own person. Taken separately, the men of the French Revolutionary Convention were enlightened citizens of peaceful habits. United in a crowd, they did not hesitate to give their adhesion to the most savage proposals, to guillotine individuals most clearly innocent, and, contrary to their interests, to renounce their inviolability and to decimate themselves.

It is not only by his acts that the individual in a crowd differs essentially from himself. Even before he has entirely lost his independence, his ideas and feelings have undergone a transformation, and the transformation is so profound as to change the miser into a spendthrift, the sceptic into a believer, the honest man into a criminal, and the coward into a hero. The renunciation of all its privileges which the French nobility voted in a moment of enthusiasm during the celebrated night of August 4, 1789, would certainly never have been consented to by any of its members taken singly.

The conclusion to be drawn from what precedes is that the crowd is always intellectually inferior to the isolated individual, but that, from the point of view of feelings and of the acts these feelings provoke, the crowd may, according to circumstances, be better or worse than the individual. All depends on the nature of the suggestion to which the crowd is exposed. This is the point that has been completely misunderstood by writers, who have only studied crowds from the criminal point of view. Doubtless a crowd is often criminal, but also it is often heroic. It is crowds rather than isolated individuals that may be induced to run the risk of death to secure the triumph of a creed or an idea, that may be fired with enthusiasm for glory and honour, that are led on—almost without bread and without arms, as in the age of the Crusades—to deliver the tomb of Christ from the infidel, or, as in '93, to defend the fatherland. Such heroism is without doubt somewhat unconscious, but it is of such heroism that history is made. Were peoples only to be credited with the great actions performed in cold blood, the annals of the world would register but few of them.

WHEN DOES A
STOCK ACT RIGHT?

Jesse L. Livermore

Jesse L. Livermore made — and lost — four stock market fortunes. In 1939, he wrote *How to Trade in Stocks*, explaining his formula. In 1940, he committed suicide at age 63. "Anyone," he said, "who is inclined to speculate should look at speculation as a business. . .and should determine to learn and understand it, to the best of their ability with the information and data available."

Stocks, like individuals, have character and personality. Some are high-strung, nervous, and jumpy: others are forthright, direct, logical. One comes to know and respect individual securities. Their action is predictable under varying sets of conditions.

Markets never stand still. They are very dull at times, but they are not resting at one price. They are either moving up or down a fraction. When a stock gets into a definite trend, it works automatically and consistently along certain lines throughout the progress of its move.

At the beginning of the move you will notice a very large volume of sales with gradually advancing prices for a few days. Then what I term a "Normal Reaction" will occur. On that reaction the sales volume will be much less than on the previous days of its advance. Now that little reaction is only normal. Never be afraid of the normal movement. But be very fearful of abnormal movements.

From Jesse L. Livermore, *How to Trade in Stocks* (1966; originally published 1940), 27–32, by permission of Indicator Research Group, Inc., Palisades Park, New Jersey 07650.

In a day or two activity will start again, and the volume will increase. If it is a real movement, in a short space of time the natural, normal reaction will have been recovered, and the stock will be selling in new high territory. That movement should continue strong for a few days with only minor daily reactions. Sooner or later it will reach a point where it is due for another normal reaction. When it occurs, it should be on the same lines as the first reaction, because that is the natural way any stock will act when it is in a definite trend. At the first part of a movement of this kind the distance above the previous high point to the next high point is not very great. But as time goes on you will notice that it is making much faster headway on the upside.

Let me illustrate: Take a stock that starts at 50. On the first leg of the movement it might gradually sell up to 54. A day or two of normal reaction might carry it back to 52 1/2 or so. Three days later it is on its way again. In that time it might go up to 59 or 60 before the normal reaction would occur. But instead of reacting, say, only a point or a point and one-half, a natural reaction from that level could easily be 3 points. When it resumes its advance again in a few days, you will notice that the volume of sales at that time is not nearly as large as it was at the beginning of the move. The stock is becoming harder to buy. That being the case, the next points in the movement will be much more rapid than before. The stock could easily go from the previous high of 60 to 68 or 70 without encountering a natural reaction. When that normal reaction does occur, it could be more severe. It could easily react down to 65 and still have only a normal decline. But assuming that the reaction was five points or thereabouts, it should not be many days before the advance would be resumed, and the stock should be selling at a brand new high price. And that is where the time element comes in.

Don't let the stock go stale on you. After attaining a goodly profit, you must have patience, but don't let patience create a frame of mind that ignores the danger signals.

The stock starts up again, and it has a rise of six or seven points in one day, followed the next day by perhaps eight to ten points—with great activity—but during the last hour of the day all of a sudden it has an abnormal break of seven or eight points. The next morning it extends its reaction another point or so, and then once more starts to advance, closing very strong. But the following day, for some reason, it does not carry through.

This is an immediate danger signal. All during the progress of the move it had nothing but natural and normal reactions. Then all of a sudden an abnormal reaction occurs—and by "abnormal" I mean a reaction *in one day* of six or more points from an extreme price made in that same day—something it has not had before, and when something happens abnormally stock-marketwise, it is flashing you a danger signal which must not be ignored.

You have had patience to stay with the stock all during its natural progress. Now have the courage and good sense to honor the danger signal and step aside.

I do not say that these danger signals are always correct because, as stated before, no rules applying to stock fluctuations are 100% right. But if you pay attention to them consistently, in the long run you will profit immensely.

A speculator of great genius once told me: "When I see a danger signal handed to me, I don't argue with it. I get out! A few days later, if everything looks all right, I can always go back in again. Thereby I have saved myself a lot of worry and money. I figure it out this way. If I were walking along a railroad track and saw an express train coming at me at sixty miles an hour, I would not be damned fool enough not to get off the track and let the train go by. After it had passed, I could always get back on the track again, if I desired." I have always remembered that as a graphic bit of speculative wisdom.

Every judicious speculator is on the alert for danger signals. Curiously, the trouble with most speculators is that something inside of them keeps them from mustering enough courage to close out their commitment when they should. They hesitate and during that period of hesitation they watch the market go many points against them. Then they say: "On the next rally I'll get out!" When the next rally comes, as it will eventually, they forget what they intended to do, because in their opinion the market is acting fine again. However, that rally was only a temporary swing which soon plays out, and then the market starts to go down in earnest. And they are in it—due to their hesitation. If they had been using a guide, it would have told them what to do, not only saving them a lot of money but eliminating their worries.

Again let me say, the human side of every person is the greatest enemy of the average investor or speculator. Why shouldn't a stock rally after it starts down from a big advance? Of course it will rally from some level. But why hope it is going to rally at just the time you want it to rally? Chances are it won't, and if it does, the vacillating type of speculator may not take advantage of it.

What I am trying to make clear to that part of the public which desires to regard speculation as a serious business, and I wish deliberately to reiterate it, is that wishful thinking must be banished; that one cannot be successful by speculating every day or every week; that there are only a few times a year, possibly four or five, when you should allow yourself to make any commitment at all. In the interims you are letting the market shape itself for the next big movement.

If you have timed the movement correctly, your first commitment will show you a profit at the start. From then on, all that is required of you is to be alert, watching for the appearance of the danger signal to tell you to step aside and convert paper profits into real money.

Remember this: When you are doing nothing, those speculators who feel they must trade day in and day out, are laying the foundation for your next venture. You will reap benefits from their mistakes.

Speculation is far too exciting. Most people who speculate hound the brokerage offices or receive frequent telephone calls, and after the business day they talk markets with friends at all gatherings. The ticker or translux is always on their minds. They are so engrossed with the minor ups and downs that they miss the big movements. Almost invariably the vast majority have commitments on the wrong side when the broad trend swings [get] under way. The speculator who insists on trying to profit from daily minor movements will never be in a position to take advantage of the next important change marketwise when it occurs.

Such weaknesses can be corrected by keeping and studying records of stock price movements and how they occur, and by taking the time element carefully into account.

Many years ago I heard of a remarkably successful speculator who lived in the California mountains and received quotations three days old. Two or three times a year he would call on his San Francisco broker and begin writing out orders to buy or sell, depending upon his market position. A friend of mine, who spent time in the broker's office, became curious and made inquiries. His astonishment mounted when he learned of the man's extreme detachment from market facilities, his rare visits, and, on occasions, his tremendous volume of trade. Finally he was introduced, and in the course of conversation inquired of this man from the mountains how he could keep track of the stock market at such an isolated distance.

"Well," he replied, "I make speculation a business. I would be a failure if I were in the confusion of things and let myself be distracted by minor changes. I like to be away where I can think. You see, I keep a record of what has happened, after it has happened, and it gives me a rather clear picture of what markets are doing. Real movements do not end the day they start. It takes time to complete the end of a genuine movement. By being up in the mountains I am in a position to give these movements all the time they need. But a day comes when I get some prices out of the paper and put them down in my records. I notice the prices I record are not conforming to the same pattern of movements that has been apparent for some time. Right then I make up my mind. I go to town and get busy."

That happened many years ago. Consistently, the man from the mountains, over a long period of time, drew funds abundantly from the stock market. He was something of an inspiration to me. I went to work harder than ever trying to blend the time element with all the other data I had compiled. By constant effort I was able to bring my records into co-ordination that aided me to a surprising degree in anticipating coming movements.

LETTER TO
GORDON S. RENTSCHLER, ESQ.

Dean Mathey

In September, 1942, Dean Mathey wrote a letter to his friend Gordon Rentschler, excerpted here. Mathey and Rentschler were both on Princeton's investment committee; investments for Princeton were the subject of the letter. At the time, Mathey was chairman of the Executive Committee of the Empire Trust Company and a leading investor.

It is all right to stick our chests out and say "we pursue a very conservative policy" and feel a little self-righteous in uttering these trite words. But what is a true conservative policy? Is it buying securities marked AAA by Moody's, Fitch, Standard Statistics, etc. whose statisticians may come from some brokerage house gone out of business? Is it buying only first-mortgage bonds? If so, look at most first-mortgage rails and real-estate bonds that not long ago were considered the last word in conservatism. Or is it even buying long-term government bonds with inflation staring us in the face? It is one thing to talk conservatism and another thing to recognize the underlying factors that make some loans good when they are merely debentures and others no good even if they are secured by a first mortgage. Some of the soundest moves we have made were unorthodox. For instance,

From a letter written by Dean Mathey to Gordon S. Rentschler, Esq., New York, New York, September 25, 1942, reprinted by permission of Dean Mathey, Jr. and David Mathey.

the sale of some of our railroad securities and switching the proceeds over to natural-gas bonds in 1933, 1934 and 1935 selling around 65 to 75 percent of par. These gas bonds have *all* been called, and yet at the time many would have said we were buying second-grade bonds. The purchase of Superior Oil and Celanese securities might also seem second-grade to many.

The only true test of conservatism is to be right in the future and it seems to me that we should all be as objective as we possibly can in striving to obtain this goal in our investments. The past low price of a bond has very little to do with its value in these swift-moving times, and because a long-term security sells on a 2 ¾% basis today is no reason definitely to assume its ultimate safety.

* * * * *

CHANGE—THE INVESTOR'S ONLY CERTAINTY

T. Rowe Price, Jr.

Unusually well informed and very rigorous in his thinking, T. Rowe Price pondered individual investing throughout his life. He also thought deeply about the overall concept, environment, and purpose of investing. In this insightful writing from 1937, he shares his conclusions about change and its products.

SOCIAL, POLITICAL AND ECONOMIC TRENDS

When the Czar of Russia was murdered, when Hitler became Dictator of Germany, when Franklin D. Roosevelt was elected President of the United States, it was front page news. People realized that important changes had taken place. Few people, however, recognized that these historic events were but outer evidences of political, social and economic forces which had been working for a long time. These forces are constantly at work, have a direct bearing on business trends and consequently influence property values and security prices.

1. Social—the gradual evolution of civilization, reaching vital importance in time of great depressions and given too little consideration by business men and investors.

From T. Rowe Price, Jr., *Change—The Investor's Only Certainty* (Baltimore, Maryland, 1937), 3–16, by permission of T. Rowe Price Investment Services.

2. Political—a greater influence on intermediate trends in business than on the long-term or major trends, and frequently over-emphasized by business interests.
3. Economic—the most important of the three in its influence upon security prices.

While there is a distinct relationship between these forces, each influencing the other, the economic trend has a greater influence upon politics (both national and international) than politics has upon economics.

Social Trend

The *social trend* over the centuries is reflected in the rise of the masses to power and influence. Ortega's book on "The Revolt of the Masses" gives a clear picture of this social trend in Europe, particularly as it concerns the demand of the masses for a greater share of rights and privileges without the obligations and responsibilities that accompany them. It is necessary to recognize that for centuries there has been a gradual liberation of the common people from slavery, social and economic, through the slow process of civilization and education. This social movement, for obvious reasons, takes different forms in different countries. The timing and velocity of the movements vary as do climatic conditions and racial characteristics. The thought that must be kept constantly in mind, if perspective is to be maintained, is that the common people are having and will continue to have a more important part in making the laws that govern social and political life, and will continue to acquire a larger share of economic wealth and power in the future.

Political Trend

The *political trend* is influenced by both the economic and social trends. Too frequently we place undue emphasis on the importance of politics as a factor making for prosperity or depression. The rise in social consciousness of the masses of common people gives expression through political action. The overthrow of monarchies and the decline in the power and influence of royalty are evidence of this trend.

It is often stated that democracies are on the way out; that the trend is toward Fascism or Bolshevism, or other forms of dictatorship.

This is merely an intermediate reaction in a major political trend from the rule of kings to the rule of the masses. The overthrow of royalty in Russia and Germany, for example, was too abrupt. The common people had insufficient education and experience in self-government to cope with the economic crises following the World War. Stalin and Hitler are in power because they are supported by public opinion. When the masses want a change of government these leaders must change or be overthrown. Russian and German politics are different because their social and economic backgrounds are different, but both nations are headed toward governments that give the common people a larger share in economic wealth and power.

Economic Trend

In order to get a clear perspective on the *economic trend,* consider that peoples are divided into two groups—the "Haves" and the "Have Nots." The "Haves" are those who have economic wealth and political power, and are usually spoken of as the conservatives. The "Have Nots" are those who are constantly fighting to acquire economic and political power, and are often termed liberals, progressives or radicals. This contest is continuous all over the world. If we think in terms of nations we group Germany, Italy and Japan as "Have Nots," scheming, plotting and fighting, if necessary, to gain a larger share of power from those nations which may be regarded as the "Haves" and are represented by Great Britain, France, the United States, and Russia. The natural tendency is for those nations with a common objective to ally themselves against their common enemy. The nations which are in power are constantly trying to keep their adversaries at odds, as they fear a united front on the part of the "Have Nots," particularly when they represent aggressive peoples.

It is simpler to give the proper weight to current events as they take place if we recognize these underlying trends in international politics. We should recognize that the nations grouped as "Have Nots" are going to acquire a larger share of the wealth and natural resources by one means or another. Italy's first step was the conquest of Ethiopia and Japan's was the conquest of Manchukuo. Germany will acquire territory, preferably through peaceful means, but unless the "Haves" make concessions it will be through military force. There may be some doubt as to the timing, but little doubt as to the final outcome.

Regardless of one's nationalistic or political prejudices, a better distribution of the world's natural resources is constructive if accomplished without war, and it is a step toward increased trade and world prosperity. Unbalanced purchasing power and maldistribution of wealth restrict trade.

So far this represents a sketchy outline of the social and political trends as they apply to the world in general. If we consider our own country we find that a similar social and political revolution has been taking place here, although very dissimilar in the external aspects. Our revolution is against what is called "privilege." As in other parts of the world, the economic and social status of our people is the motivating force behind politics. The "New Deal" is the result of this movement and not the cause. It is an attempt to correct maldistribution of economic wealth and political power that has been abused.

In the United States, a democratic nation, there has never been a political dictator, but during the past hundred years of rapid growth in industrial wealth, economic rulers, or financial dictators, came into power with the result that too large a share of the nation's wealth was controlled by too few men. The recent depression was the culmination of several generations of economic oppression. We did not experience a bloody revolution like Russia or Spain, but the "New Deal" is a social and economic revolution. The term "Economic Royalists" is unpopular, nevertheless it is very expressive of the situation which existed in the past decade.

We are now in the process of a great *change* in the kind of *capitalism*, rather than in the *overthrow of capitalism*. The movement has been hastened by the World War which brought millions of people from all over the world together in a common cause. It has been hastened by inventions which have made most of the people in the world neighbors. Rapid communications and transportation have increased the velocity of this change. A correct appraisal of these Social, Political and Economic changes is essential to the successful management of invested capital.

BASIC NEW DEAL CONCEPTS

At this point it might be helpful to outline and comment briefly on a few of the Basic New Deal Concepts, since we have entered a second four-year administration of New Deal policies:

1. *Greater centralization of power in Federal Government to impose a broad program of national economic planning.* Regardless of one's personal opinion about the increased power of the Federal Government, and of the difficulties which will be encountered in the attainment of this end, this is a natural trend in the social evolution hastened by rapid communication and transportation. States' rights and private ownership will gradually be subordinated to Federal control, both political and economic. Some of the results of this trend are the Securities and Exchange Commission controlling security underwriting, distribution and trading, the Public Utility Holding Company Act, designed to give the Federal Government greater control of public utilities, and the transfer of the control and management of our banking system from private to Federal control.

2. *Redistribution of Wealth.* Redistribution of wealth is going on all over the world, as it has done ever since the world began. Wealth breeds indolence and selfishness, and the possessors adopt conservative or defensive tactics. Gradually the more virile, aggressive people revolt and fight to obtain or regain a larger share.

In this country the redistribution is being conducted under the leadership of the Federal Government. We call it the "New Deal." It is actually a "Re-Deal of Wealth." The process seems to be a necessary one, although the method is most objectionable to the "Haves." Many debtors cannot pay their creditors in full—either in interest or principal. Interest rates on debts have been reduced by artificially cheap money rates. Not only is this true of farm loans and home loans, but in the case of corporation loans, interest rates are being reduced for weak companies through reorganization and for stronger companies, through refunding of $4\frac{1}{2}\%$ to 6% coupons with $2\frac{1}{2}\%$ to 4% coupons. This means a reduction of 30% to 40% in income of investors.

The Government, by increasing taxes on the wealthy, is taking away from the "Haves" and giving it to the "Have Nots" in one form or another—relief, bonuses, public works projects, agricultural payments, etc. At the same time the dollar has been devalued and prices are being inflated, with the result that the creditor is having his principal depreciated in purchasing power value. It is a long, complicated process, but in simple language it is an attempt to redistribute wealth by lawful means, taking it from the "Haves" and giving it to the "Have Nots." Ultimately, it will lead to more even distribution of wealth and increased trade until finally too large a share will again gravitate into the possession of a few and the whole process will start all over again. The only difference is that the game will be played with a different set of rules by a different set of people. The basic fundamentals will be the same and they can all be traced to the weaknesses and strength in the character and habits of human beings.

3. *More Equalization of Earning Power.* While many important financial powers will dispute this, one of the causes of the depression was the concentration of too much wealth in the hands of a few who could not spend it all, and thereby create demand for sufficient goods to keep the factory wheels turning.

The National Recovery Act was designed to correct this maladjustment, and while the Supreme Court declared the Act unconstitutional as originally passed, the underlying principle of higher wages for many industries and general equalization of earning power has merit and will reappear during the near future in a different form of legislation. Revision in wage scales will mean revision in security earnings and values in more than one industry.

4. *Smooth Out Business Cycles.* It may appear that the Government is being successful in this undertaking, but the success will only be temporary. The most that can be done is to defer the sharp upturns and downturns in the business cycles or lengthen the time preceding a boom or collapse.

Artificiality is not lasting. Nature eventually wins, and nature requires resting periods as well as growing periods. You may take a stimulant and conceal your fatigue temporarily, but eventually collapse, rest and recovery follow, whether plant life, animal life, human beings, or business which is conducted by human beings and influenced by nature. It is absurd to think business cycles can be smoothed out unless you think man can permanently overcome the laws of nature.

5. *Regulation by Taxation.* Which is just another way of redistributing wealth and power, taking it from the "Haves" and giving it to the "Have Nots."

ECONOMIC INDICES

Starting with the premise that unbalanced relationships cause depression, correction of these relationships should bring recovery. To gauge or measure the progress of these fundamental relationships leading toward recovery it is necessary to have indices to picture the trends. In order to "determine where we are and whither we are tending," the following trends should be observed over a period of years:

I. Stabilization of World Currencies.

II. Balanced Relationship between Domestic and World Prices of Export Commodities.

III. Balanced Relationship between Exports and Imports of Wealth, represented by

(1) Merchandise,

(2) Services,

(3) Money

    a. Tourists

    b. Emigrant Remittances

    c. Investments.

IV. Balanced Relationship between Farm Purchasing Power and Industrial Purchasing Power.

V. Balanced Relationship between Building Costs and Rentals.

I. *Stabilization of World Currencies.* The World War caused maldistribution of monetary wealth (gold and silver) among nations and upset currency relationships. The post-war decade intensified this maldistribution, notwithstanding certain revaluations of currency, such as in the case of Germany, France, Italy and Austria. The process of revising currency values continues. While de facto stabilization between the Sterling Bloc and the American dollar has temporarily helped foreign trade, this problem is still unsolved and will probably remain so for some time to come. Corrective measures will be tried, but the basic trouble today is the maldistribution of wealth throughout the world. This factor has a most important bearing on the future trend of foreign trade, and until the problem is nearer a solution we should not expect world trade to recover to 1929 levels. At the present writing it appears that the United States will have to distribute part of its monetary wealth in one form or another. This may be done through the extension of credit to nations in dire need of capital, but of course on a much sounder economic basis than was done in the 1920's, or it may be accomplished by buying more than we sell to foreign countries.

U.S. recovery to date has been largely a result of nationalistic or internal policies. It appears that the final stage of the recovery cycle or boom period will be deferred until stabilization of exchange permits further expansion of foreign trade.

II. *Balanced Relationship Between Domestic and World Prices of Export Commodities.* The world depression led to a nationalistic tendency on the part of most nations. This led to artificial prices for basic commodities, particularly foodstuffs. In the United States the Administration created fictitious values for wheat, cotton, hogs, copper, etc. These commodities were formerly exported in large amounts, but due to overproduction and the fall in the price level, methods were adopted which restricted production and created artificial price levels. This artificial increase in the domestic price level for basic export commodities helped to restrict our foreign trade. It became necessary, therefore, for our prices to decline or world prices to rise to the point where a natural relationship became restored so trade could be resumed. This latter development has taken place during the past three years, and today a better balanced relationship exists between domestic and world prices for those basic commodities which formerly contributed to foreign trade. However, this country is unlikely to be an important exporter of farm products in the future, with the exception of cotton, and that portion of our population directly dependent upon export surpluses will either have to be subsidized by the Government or shift to new pursuits. Thus, while the current outlook for agriculture is favorable, the longer term outlook for certain agricultural sections is unfavorable.

III. *Balanced Relationship Between Exports and Imports.* When considering Exports and Imports we must bear in mind that in addition to merchandise we must also take into consideration services rendered such as shipping charges, transfer of money in the form of tourists' expenditures, emigrant remittances, and income on investments.

An export balance for the United States is an unfavorable balance as long as we are a creditor nation and hoard such a large percentage of the world's gold. There was a marked decline during 1936 in the excess of merchandising exports over imports, indicating a trend in the right direction. From the beginning of the recovery period to date, exports of manufactured products have benefitted at the expense of agriculture. Today we are importing many agricultural products which we formerly exported, and the ratio of U.S. cotton exported to foreign consumption is the lowest on record. While the balanced relationship between exports and imports has had a favorable trend in the last several years, it seems improbable that our total foreign trade will recover to pre-depression levels until there is a further correction in the maldistribution of wealth, and until foreign nations change their present policy of national self-containment due to war preparedness. World production in 1936, according to National Industrial Conference Board figures, has exceeded 1929 levels, yet world foreign trade has been less than 50% of 1929 levels.

IV. *Balanced Relationship Between Farm Purchasing Power and Industrial Purchasing Power.* The purchasing power of a large percentage of our population is dependent upon the prices of basic commodities which they are engaged in producing. If the price relationship of farm products and industrial products becomes seriously unbalanced, one declining or rising too fast in relation to the other, the purchasing power of the nation is adversely affected. Two years of drought, plus the Government's artificial restrictions, have corrected the unbalanced relationship that existed during the early years of depression. At the present time this factor, from the standpoint of price structure, is most favorable.

V. *Balanced Relationship Between Building Costs and Rentals.* The low activity in the building and construction industries is probably the most important cause of the large number of unemployed at the present time. Unbalanced relationship between building costs and rents largely determines the rate of activity. Because of excess building in the twenties, rents declined much faster than the cost of building. There has been a gradual correction due to greater increase in rents than in construction costs, but while this relationship has improved, costs are still too high in relation to rents to justify a building boom.

Conclusions drawn from the above discussion of social, political and economic trends may differ widely in accordance with the reader's perspective. The writer believes that long-term forecasting over the next few years becomes extremely hazardous because of managed economics such as artificial money rates, control of production and restricted speculation in commodities and securities, but at the present time it appears that,

1. *Wealth* will be subjected to increased taxation. Corporations of great size and influence will be special targets and their profits will be restricted by various means.
2. *Labor* will receive a larger percentage of corporation income in the future than in the past.
3. Most of our great *basic industries*, which include transportation—steam, electric and motor; shipping; coal; steel; textile; public utility; food, such as dairies, bakeries, chain stores, meat packing, etc.; and probably the automobile manufacturing

industry, will be subjected to control or regulation by Federal Government to the extent that individual enterprise will be restricted and invested capital will become less profitable than heretofore.

4. The greatest opportunity for *profitable investment* will be in new and rapidly growing industries, employing relatively few people and less subject to Governmental interference.

5. The *agricultural problem* has not been solved. Artificial measures are only a temporary cure, and two years of ordinary weather conditions throughout the world may bring wheat and corn prices to the American farmer back to levels much lower than now prevailing should inflation be controlled. The United States, as a result of Government subsidies, has definitely lost its position as a great exporter of farm products.

6. *Foreign trade* is likely to be very slow in recovering to pre-depression levels.

7. A boom in the *building and construction industry* is likely to be deferred beyond 1937.

8. *Inflation* will cause the dollar's purchasing power to decline during the years ahead, with resultant rise in cost of living to a higher level than existed during the post-war era.

9. *Bond prices* have probably reached their peak levels for the current recovery cycle and are headed downward.

10. *Stock prices* will probably advance to higher levels before the major recovery cycle has been completed. An intermediate recession may occur at any time and selectivity is of far greater importance now than at any time during the past five years.

* * * * *

Interpretation of the trend should be regarded as an opinion of the present, subject to revision.

Change is the investor's only certainty.

PICKING "GROWTH" STOCKS

T. Rowe Price, Jr.

T. Rowe Price's case for viewing growth stock investing as the only way to outrun inflation's erosion of purchasing power was originally developed in a series of articles in *Barron's*. Here are several important excerpts from a reprint of those articles.

FOREWORD

About 15 years ago an investment philosophy was developed which became very popular in the pre-depression days. This philosophy was based on the premise that American industry had a long period of substantial growth ahead of it. As a result, the argument ran, the conservative investor could safely share in the industrial growth of his country by holding common stocks—specifically, the shares of leading corporations.

For a while this theory appeared to work, but those who followed it and held their common stocks, bought in the 1929 boom, straight through the following decade have found that considerable variation now exists among different corporations as respects the rate of their growth. Some have actually retrogressed.

From T. Rowe Price, *Picking "Growth" Stocks* (Princeton, New Jersey, 1939), 3–18. Reprinted by permission of *Barron's*, copyright Dow Jones & Company, Inc., 1939. All Rights Reserved.

To investors with a long-range point of view, the selection of securities in growing industries and companies is extremely important, but the difficulties of achieving such a selection have become increasingly great as the growth of industry in general has slowed down.

The author of this study began to work out a theory of investment, based on a recognition of the fact that corporations have life cycles similar to those of humans, nearly 10 years ago. Since 1934 he has tested the soundness of his theory by applying it to an actual fund. The results of this investment experience are strong evidence that the restriction of one's investments to "growth" stocks is sound in practice as well as in theory.

* * * * *

CORPORATIONS, LIKE PEOPLE, HAVE LIFE CYCLES—RISKS INCREASE WHEN MATURITY IS REACHED

In planning an investment program, it is extremely important that the investor, before purchasing any securities, should ask himself, "What is my objective?" He must realize that except over a long period of years no common stock investment can give him safety of capital and that there may be other mediums more likely to provide him with a liberal, steady income.

Conserving Assets, Income or Market Appreciation

The three major objectives of investors are: (1) *Capital conservation*, or stability of market value of invested principal; (2) *Liberal income* at a fixed rate; and (3) *Capital growth*. While all securities involve risk, the degree varies widely in accordance with the type of security. One type, such as short-term government bonds, might well serve as a medium for safety of principal, but certainly should not be expected to produce substantial profits.

Another type, such as the common stock of an aviation company, might produce substantial profits, but certainly should not be expected to provide safety of principal. Either security may be qualified to do one job well, but no one security possesses the qualifications to accomplish all three major objectives. The individual must, therefore, determine in advance what percentage of his total fund should be invested for capital conservation, how much for liberal income and how much for capital growth, and then select the type of security best qualified to accomplish each objective. . . .

[W]hen money is invested for capital conservation, both liberal income and opportunity for captial growth are sacrificed; when money is invested for liberal income at a fixed rate, both stability of market value and capital growth are sacrificed; and when money is invested for capital growth, the other two major objectives, capital conservation and liberal income, must be sacrificed.

The "life cycle theory of investing," which is the main subject of this study, is equally applicable to the purchase of securities for capital conservation and liberal income as it is to the selection of securities for capital growth. In the explanation which follows, however, the discussion has been concentrated on common stocks because, as a class, they usually involve greater risks than bonds and preferred stocks, and because they are more sensitive to changing business trends. The "life cycle theory of investing," as applied to common stocks alone, does not constitute a complete investment program, since it does not guarantee either safety of capital or the highest, steady income. So far as that portion of an investor's funds designed to achieve capital growth is concerned, it does, in the author's opinion, afford the maximum gain with the minimum risk.

Three Phases of the Corporate Life Cycle

Earnings of most corporations pass through a life cycle which, like the human life cycle, has three important phases—growth, maturity and decadence. Insurance companies know that a greater risk is involved in insuring the life of a man 50 years old than of a man 25, and that a much greater risk is involved in insuring a man of 75 than one of 50. They know, in other words, that risk increases as a man reaches maturity and starts to decline.

In very much the same way, common sense tells us that an investment in a business affords greater gain possibilities and involves less risk of loss while the long-term, or secular, earnings trend is still growing than after it has reached maturity and starts to decline. Once a business is well established, the greatest opportunity for gain is afforded during the period of growth in earning power. The risk factor increases when maturity is reached and decadence begins.

So much is fairly obvious. As long as American industry in general was in the growing phase, investors could choose almost blindly without great danger, although, of course, even then there were companies or industries which had already passed out of the growth phase. Now, however, the situation has changed. American industry in large part appears to have reached the phase of maturity, and careful search is necessary to determine the companies whose earnings are still in the growth phase and which, therefore, afford the maximum gain with the minimum risk of loss.

Because the economic or business cycle runs concurrently with a company's life cycle, it is difficult to determine in advance when earning power is on the decline. Research and an understanding of social, political and economic trends, however, should enable one to recognize the change in the long-term earnings trend of a business in time to withdraw his capital before it is seriously impaired.

A Fully Invested Fund, 1935–38

The best proof that it is possible to select the stocks of companies which are in the growth phase is the experience of an actual fund to which has been applied what the author calls "the life cycle theory of investing." This theory has been developed over a period of approximately 10 years. In 1934 a small experimental fund was created in order to test the soundness of the theory. Since that time the principles and methods which are described in this and the following chapters have been used in the management of this actual fund, with the following results:

Throughout the four-year period 1935–38 the fund has been fully invested—no attempt was made, in other words, to catch the swings of the market. Frequent changes were made, however, in the list of growth stocks. Radical legislation and sudden and far-reaching economic developments during the period have altered the long-term earnings trends of many corporations. When stocks appeared to have reached their maximum earning power they were liquidated and the proceeds reinvested in other growth stocks. Naturally, not every selection was a successful one.

The increase in principal of this experimental fund from Dec. 31, 1934, to Dec. 31, 1938, amounted to 76.3%. During that time the gain in the *Dow-Jones* composite average, which is made up of industrials, rails and utilities, was only 31.6%. The *Dow-Jones* average of 30 industrial stocks appreciated 48.7% during these four years. . . .

Growth of income on the experimental fund is also impressive when compared with that of the *Dow-Jones* averages. Income on the fund and averages is shown in the following table for each of the four years, the return being expressed as a percentage of the original principal.

	1935	1936	1937	1938	4 Yr. Avg.
Growth stock portfolio	2.6%	7.8%	9.0%	6.04%	6.36%
Dow-Jones comp. avg.	4.2	6.2	7.2	4.50	5.52
Dow-Jones indl. avg.	4.3	6.7	7.8	4.80	5.90

As can be seen, the higher return which was obtained on the averages during the first year was more than offset by the higher return on the growth stock portfolio in the past three years. From 1935 to 1938, the income on the supervised portfolio increased by 131%, while that on the stocks in the composite average was only 7% higher in 1938 than in 1935, and income on the industrial average increased 12%. In 1938 the income on the growth stock portfolio was 34% higher than the income on the stocks in the composite average and 26% higher than that on the industrials alone.

Maximum Gain with Minimum Risk

These figures of income and capital gain, which, it should be emphasized, are based on an *actual investment experience*, and not on a theoretical investment which might involve the use of hindsight, appear to furnish convincing evidence of the soundness of restricting holdings to corporations which are still in the earnings growth phase of their life cycle. Such a policy affords the maximum gain with the minimum risk. What is also important, the figures prove *it can be done*.

* * * * *

MEASURING INDUSTRIAL LIFE CYCLES—
THE FALLACY OF INVESTING FOR
HIGH CURRENT INCOME

The two best ways of measuring the life cycle of an industry are unit volume of sales and net earnings available for stockholders. It is important to consider both, for common stock investments should be confined to industries which are growing in both volume and earnings.

An excellent illustration of decadence in volume is afforded by the railroad industry. From 1902 to 1918 the average annual increase in ton miles of Class I railroads was 9.3%. During the after-war period from 1918 to 1926, average annual increase was only 1.3%. From 1926, the year railroads reached their peak volume, to 1929, business activity showed a further increase, but railroad ton miles declined 1.6%, indicating that the railroad industry had reached its maximum growth. The decline was greatly accentuated during the following depression years, and although there has been some recovery from the lows, ton miles in 1937 were still 19.7% under 1929 levels, thus definitely establishing a decadent long-term trend. . . .

When unit volume of an industry enters the decadent phase net earnings are likely to decline at a much faster rate than unit volume, as illustrated by the railroad industry. From 1929 (year of maximum earnings) to 1937, ton miles declined 19.7%, while net earnings declined 89%. The railroad industry obviously is decadent in both volume and earnings.

[The] effect of this circumstance on the prices of railroad stocks since 1926 is apparent, especially when they are compared with the progress of industrial stock prices. . . .

The risk of loss to the investor in railroad stocks, as measured by the *Dow-Jones* average, was 76.5%, compared with 14.8% for industrial stocks, or more than five times as great. The investor's opportunity to gain in a rising market was much greater in industrial stocks, which advanced 98% from the mean prices of 1932 to those of 1938. During the same period railroad stocks declined 3%. Even during the most favorable period of comparing railroad stocks with industrial stocks (1932–36) the opportunity for gain was 152% for industrials, compared with 84% for railroads.

Within the industrial division of common stocks, there are, of course, variations in rate growth. Many enterprises have long since reached maturity and are definitely decadent. Increased competition, new products, new inventions, new markets, consumer's preferences and many other factors are preventing many well-known corporations, popular among investors, from continuing their former spectacular growth and profits. . . .

"Growth stocks" can be defined as shares in business enterprises which have demonstrated favorable underlying long-term growth in earnings and which, after careful research study, give indications of continued secular growth in the future.

Secular, or underlying long-term growth, should not be confused with the cyclical recovery in earnings which takes place as business activity increases from a period of depression to a period of prosperity. Secular growth extends through several business cycles, with earnings reaching new high levels at the peak of each subsequent major business cycle. . . .

The fact that a stock is considered to be a growth stock is no assurance against a decline in income or market value during the downtrend of a business cycle, as growth stocks often depreciate as much as other groups. However, the prospects for recovery are more favorable for growth stocks than for matured and decadent stocks.

There are two major types of growth stocks—"cyclical growth" stocks and "stable growth" stocks. During periods of depression the earnings and dividends of most companies decline to a greater or lesser degree. The ones which fluctuate most widely with the ups and downs of the business cycles, like Chrysler, have been classified as "cyclical growth" stocks. The ones which have demonstrated relatively stable earnings and dividends during business depressions, like International Business Machines, have been classified as "stable growth" stocks.

Each of these two groups has different characteristics and qualifies for different investment purposes. A stable growth stock is more suitable for the investor requiring relatively stable income, while a cyclical growth stock is more suitable for the investor whose major objective is capital gain during a period of cyclical recovery. . . .

"Matured stocks" are shares in business enterprises which, after careful study, appear to have reached their maximum earnings. The five stocks selected for this group represent popular companies among investors today—American Can, American Tobacco, American Telephone, Continental Can and Reynolds Tobacco. The can and tobacco stocks were in the stable growth list until several years ago and there may be some question of the justification for now placing them in the matured group. There is no clear-cut line of demarcation and the change in trend is a matter of personal judgment until a definitely decadent trend of long-term earnings has been established. It is perfectly possible that one or more of these companies may report new high earnings a share at some future date.

"Decadent stocks" are defined as shares in business enterprises which are experiencing a long-term, or secular, decline in earnings. Five leading food stocks have been selected—Borden, General Foods[1], National Biscuit, National Dairy Products and Standard Brands—which showed impressive growth in earning power during the 1920's, but which have subsequently experienced a decline as a result of social, political and economic developments. In all probability, unless important new developments reverse the trend, they will be unable to register new high earnings a share in the future, although it is reasonable to expect some cyclical recovery from the low earnings of the past several years. . . .

Comparing the peak recovery year, 1937, with the boom year, 1929, we find the results were as follows:

	Earnings	Dividends	Market Value
Growth stocks	inc. 47.3%	inc. 148.4%	inc. 67.1%
Matured stocks	dec. 16.6%	inc. 18.3%	dec. 13.8%
Decadent stocks	dec. 56.5%	dec. 43.0%	dec. 61.0%

There are two sound reasons for investing in common stocks—growth of income and growth of principal. Many investors prefer common stocks from which a high current income can be obtained. This is a fallacious policy because in the majority of cases a common stock which affords a relatively high yield at the time of purchase possesses a greater risk of reduction of income and loss in market value in the future.

This point is illustrated in [the] chart. This chart is divided into two parts. The first part, 1929 through 1934, represents hindsight; the second part, 1934 through 1938, represents foresight, as it covers the period of practical application of the Life Cycle Theory.

Average income for the ten-year period, 1929–1938, was 4.5% on the matured group, 4.2% on the growth stocks and 3.2% on the decadent stocks. The higher income on the matured stock group, taking the ten years as a whole, was the result of the fact that four of the stocks in the

CHART
Yield on Investment Made at 1929 Mean Prices

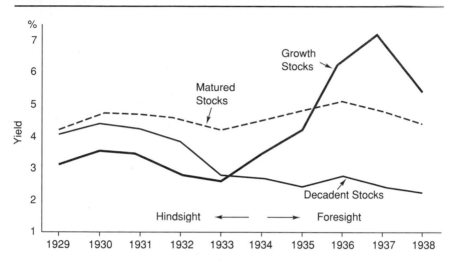

group continued to grow after 1929 and only reached maturity during the latter part of the decade under review. The growth stocks would compare more favorably if the comparison were limited to the past five years.

While stocks with matured and decadent earnings trends may yield more than growth stocks when purchased, over a period of several years growth stocks increase their dividends and, in the course of time, pay a better return on invested principal.

When the capital gain in the growth stocks is compared with the capital losses in the matured and decadent stocks, the results are even more convincing. One dollar invested in growth stocks in 1929 was worth, in 1938, twice as much as a dollar invested in matured stocks and five times as much as one dollar invested in decadent stocks.

Higher current income, it is evident, is obtained at the sacrifice of future income and the risk of loss of principal.

* * * * *

FOOTNOTES

1. General Foods has been mentioned in *Barron's* as a potential growth stock because of its Birdseye process, which is becoming increasingly popular. However, under Mr. Price's methods, the results of General Foods in recent years definitely class it as a "decadent" stock up to this point.

A FURTHER ANALYSIS OF INVESTMENT EXPERIENCE
THE FUTURE TREND OF COMMON STOCK VALUES
FUTURE OF THE INVESTOR'S PROBLEM

Dwight C. Rose

Dwight Rose of Scudder, Stevens & Clark based his book, *A Scientific Approach to Investment Management*, on a careful statistical study of the investment experience of insurance companies. This selection presents his conclusions.

A FURTHER ANALYSIS OF INVESTMENT EXPERIENCE

The preceding chapter presented a fair portrayal of the investment experience of the leading fire insurance companies in several major classes of investment. The fact, however, that one type of security has shown much better results for the last quarter century than another type does not necessarily mean that this condition will continue. We are interested not only in the experience of different classes of investment over the last quarter century, but also in the fundamental influences or inherent qualities responsible for the pronounced difference in results that we have seen. If we can isolate these fundamental influences or inherent qualities in certain types of investment experience, we must then ask ourselves whether or not they are of a permanent character that will be projected into the future. If we conclude that some of them will be projected into the future, we will want to know to what specific types of investment these permanent influences or inherent qualities are most definitely allied.

* * * * *

THE FUTURE TREND OF COMMON STOCK VALUES

The Long-Term Advantage of Industrial Common Stocks

From the long-term viewpoint we may conclude that industrial common stocks have shown an advantage over bonds approximating the extent that the ratio of earnings to selling price of the stocks has exceeded the yield on bonds; and that something more than changing commodity prices or changing interest rates will be required to interrupt the long-term upward trend of industrial stock values which has been fairly constant as far back as we can obtain reliable information.

But the experience of the past indicates that changes in the commodity price level and changes in interest rates may have a pronounced influence on, or may be primarily responsible for, temporary violent movements such as we observed during the war period and the deflation of 1920.

It should be emphasized, however, that our findings with respect to industrial common stocks are not dependent upon the last few years of extraordinary appreciation. In fact, if we had terminated our investment experience tables anywhere after the first 10 years (a period long enough to indicate a long-term trend) our studies would have supported substantially the same conclusions.

The compounding effect of reinvestment of excess earnings so much overshadows all other factors influencing the long-term trend of industrial stock values that it would appear that industrial stocks could be purchased with confidence in the continuance of this long-term upward trend so long as the industries supporting civilization move forward; so long as the dividends represent a conservative portion of total earnings; and so long as the major part[1] of excess earnings is not discounted in a greatly inflated market value.

* * * * *

FUTURE OF THE INVESTOR'S PROBLEM

The first essential for sound judgment in investment management is unprejudiced knowledge of past experience. Most of us have the brains and reasoning power to reach sound conclusions once the premises are accepted, and a few have sufficient imagination and insight to make adequate allowance for the introduction of new factors that are always complicating the issue by their unknown influences. But if all our reasoning and insight into the future are based upon an erroneous premise of past experience, our conclusions also are almost certain to be erroneous.

Unfortunately, many of our statistical or analytical studies in finance and investment have been carried on by students without practical investment experience, or by agencies that were not made to suffer keenly from the failure of their theories to work out in practice. Too frequently, perhaps, statisticians and forecasters, jealous of their reputations, have become more interested in interpreting current phenomena to justify previously announced theories than in recognizing the fallibility of the theories.

On the other hand, our large investors and financiers are naturally of the temperament that is primarily interested in applying their knowledge, inadequate as it may be, in a way that will be productive of real, practical results. The mental exercise of making judgments and acting on previously supplied data is more exhilarating and pleasant to the average intelligent man than spending a lifetime gathering the data wherewith others may derive the pleasurable exhilaration of reaching more scientific conclusions and acting thereon. The successful financier and executive is not mentally inclined toward statistical studies, and the average statistician does not have the practical knowledge and insight essential to guide him in such an undertaking.

Most laymen who elect to exchange their dollar surplus for investment securities have a working knowledge of the various types of stocks and bonds. Some investigate more carefully than others the management and earnings of the particular company in which they desire to place their funds, and a few are fortunate enough to be familiar with the general principles of corporation finance. It is, however, left for the investment specialist (the capitalist, and banker, and those who serve the public in purely advisory capacity) to discern the basic and subtle forces forever at work upon security prices.

THE INVESTMENT STUDENT'S CATECHISM

The investment student has already learned, for instance, that there is a close interrelation between the workings of our sensitive money civilization and the market values of stocks and bonds; he has learned that as our imperfect financial machinery operates, it often drives security prices materially above or below the levels of their intrinsic worth; that the market prices of securities are influenced not only by current interest rates (the going rental value of money), but also by the trend of commodity prices as evidenced by the varying purchasing power of the dollar; that whereas a large supply of idle funds resulting in a lowered interest rate will tend to raise the price of both bonds and stocks, "a contraction of credit is often the most conspicuous feature of crises as in the American panics of 1893 and 1897, while at other times credit contraction plays a minor role in comparison with the decline in volume of business as in the British Crisis of 1907";[2] that a continued surplus of gold or credit currency is likely to develop into inflation with higher security prices; that the latter stages of inflation are usually accompanied by illusory prosperity with an accelerated rise in stock prices but a fall in bond prices; and finally that the Federal Reserve Act, allowing for a more facile expansion and contraction of credit, may be expected to moderate violent fluctuations in the future course of the industrial cycle.

In addition, the investment student has learned that rising commodity prices result in a subtle transfer of wealth from those having fixed money incomes, such as bondholders and salaried men, to other members of society; that values change slowly and prices fast; that sentiment or crowd psychology often exerts a temporary yet powerful influence upon the course of security prices; that a rise in commodity and stock prices tends to generate a further rise in prices and continues to do so as long as the enterpriser's profits remain abnormally high; and, likewise, a fall in prices tends to generate a further fall in prices.

THE EXPERT AND THE APPRENTICE

There is nothing extraordinary in the fact that the investment specialist has learned through years of application and training to correlate with some degree of success the seething mass of forces operating incessantly to affect the market values of stocks and bonds. It is his business to interpret these multiple energies, estimating as accurately as possible the predominant tendencies resulting from their interplay. But the striking nonchalance and disregard of primary principles with which the layman seeks to invest his dollar surplus is remarkable. The great majority of the public have failed in signal fashion to evaluate the hazards attending the conservation[3] of wealth through the medium of stocks and bonds. Although successful investment is extremely difficult business, it is apparently the only field of endeavor in which the novice feels competent to engage without previous preparation or experience.

The bulk of the investor's information, knowledge, and advice finds its source with the investment banker. The banker with his prospectus and his influence on the corporate reports has, perhaps, done more than anyone else to give information to the investor. This information is given in good faith, but there is a fundamental suspicion which should attach to it from the investor's standpoint. The investor is interested in his own financial future. The investment banker is not primarily interested in the financial future of the investor, but in selling securities for the companies which he finances. The corporation wants to finance as cheaply as possible while the investor wants as much for his money as possible. Between the two stands the investment banker, not altogether as a disinterested judge, nor yet as a representative of one of the parties concerned. He has a third attitude and object: he is a merchant primarily interested in obtaining and selling marketable merchandise that will provide him with a fair profit.

Of course reputable merchants will insist upon handling good merchandise and the general integrity of individuals comprising the banking business in this country is probably higher than in any other commercial enterprise. Also, a more enlightened study of the investor's problem by the investor himself and a general mobilization of agencies operating in his interests during the last few years have forced the investment banker to give increasing recognition to the investor's welfare in order to maintain his clientele of customers. But at best there are two other interests frequently opposed to the investor's interests that have an equal claim to the banker's attention and support. These opposing or conflicting interests are:

1. Welfare of the financing corporation.
2. The banker's merchandising profit.

The time is now approaching when both corporations and investors are recognizing the losses they suffer through such a method of distribution. It is not unreasonable to assume that the investment banker will eventually become the representative solely of the financing corporation, and that the investor will retain his own expert representative. These two experts may then deal with each other on behalf of their respective clients.

DEVELOPMENTS IN THE INVESTOR'S INTERESTS

Two new enterprises that have been developing rapidly in this country since the war are fundamentally and exclusively concerned with the problem of the investor. They are the profession of investment counsel and the investment trust. They attract both the practical administrator with experience and judgment, and the theorist or student with the true zeal of the scientist. Proper recognition of the function of each type of man in these new enterprises serving the interests of the investor, and encouragement to investment students to proceed along more practical lines are essential in the development of a more scientific basis for investment management.

Although we may look to investment counsel and the management of investment trusts for a more scientific, or at least unprejudiced, analysis of some of the more urgent problems facing the investor, it should not be lost sight of that these recent entrants in the investment field also present a possible danger in that their growing popularity with the investor may encourage a general exploitation of the constructive economic service that they were designed to provide. We should realize that there is nothing magic about the words "investment counsel" or "investment trust" that can change security merchants into unbiased advisers or force an organization of questionable integrity to operate solely in the investor's interest. Investors should beware of organizations calling themselves investment counsel or investment trusts and offering their services free or for a nominal sum. Competent men in the field of investment expect fair remuneration for their time and effort. If the remuneration is not paid in the form of a fee, it will probably be obtained in some undisclosed manner which in many cases would render their advice or management detrimental rather than beneficial—in any event, it would become prejudiced.

During the formative period of these two agencies, the fundamental requirements of organization and operation which experience has shown to be essential to the investor's interests should be clearly understood. The writer would outline these requirements briefly as follows:

FUNDAMENTAL REQUIREMENTS OF INVESTMENT COUNSEL AND INVESTMENT TRUSTS

1. The executives should be men of integrity, ability, and experience.
2. In order that their judgment may be totally unbiased, they should be precluded from having any financial or brokerage interest in the securities sold and purchased; and equally important, their compensation should be based not on profit sharing—a basis which does not ensure the conservatism of judgment essential to safety—but on a fixed fee stated in advance and determined by the amount of capital placed under their supervision or management. Such a method assures not only the vigilant attention of the advisers or managers, but it also enables them to budget their expenses and provide a known fund for research.
3. The major part of fees received from clients or shareholders should be expended for intelligently directed investment research and the prospective client or shareholder is entitled to some concrete evidence of how the charges for supervision and management are expended in his interest.
4. The policy of investment should be fully defined in advance. In the case of investment counsel, this should involve a compre-

hensive report outlining the client's particular circumstances and objectives with the recommendation of a general long-term investment plan adapted to client's requirements. In the case of investment trusts, the policy of investment should be clearly stated in the indenture, which the prospective shareholder should read with care.

5. The clients of investment counsel should at all times keep their securities under their own control and be free to terminate the relationship at their option. Similarly, the shares of an investment trust should be redeemable at the shareholder's option, thus leaving him free at all times to terminate the contract of management and resume control of his property. If the shares of the trust are redeemable at the investor's option, he can at any time secure their actual value; if salable only, he must find a purchaser should he wish to sell his shares, and he has no assurance that he will receive their full value. Furthermore, if the shares are redeemable, the executives must continue to exert a vigilant supervision; for if the shareholders lose confidence, they will redeem their shares, and the compensation of the management will disappear.

We are today in a new world, struggling under old laws and practices. Our age has been one of unprecedented growth and startling transition. We have been rushed forward into new and varied realms of activity with such heartbreaking speed that in many ways our formulas do not fit or afford a proper interpretation of the existing facts. To use the apt phraseology of Woodrow Wilson in a discussion on our modern political and economic regimes, "We have not kept our practices adjusted to the facts of the case, and until we do, and unless we do, the facts of the case will always have the best of the argument." The investing public among others has failed to fit its practices to the facts, and the facts have had the best of the argument in the shape of losses to surplus totaling millions upon millions of dollars.

If our investment practices have failed to fit the facts in recent years, it behooves those responsible for investment management and advice to inquire more fully and scientifically into what the current investment facts actually are. In the practical yet highly involved business of investment management we must ever be ready to subordinate traditional theories evolved from the antiquated experience of former generations in order to adjust current practices to current facts. And when, as a result of intensive research and unprejudiced analysis, we have success-fully adjusted current practices to current facts, then it may truly be said that the pursuit of investment is emerging from the realm of vague and mysterious "dogma" into the realm of "practical science."

FOOTNOTES

1. If excess earnings were completely discounted in market price so that cash dividends paid plus reinvested earnings totaled no more than the current yield on high-grade bonds, we might still have the compounding influence of excess earnings, but this would only compensate for the sacrifice in current income. The situation would be comparable to a discount bond bought on a 5 per cent yield basis but paying out currently only 3 per cent on the purchase price. The compounding effect of the extra 2 per cent gradually accrues to the principal value of the bond. The bondholder has sacrificed income in favor of appreciation but has gained nothing over what he would have obtained by buying a 5 per cent bond at par, except the enforced saving and reinvestment of part of income.
2. Mitchell's *Business Cycles*, page 582.
3. Conservation here designates the retention of purchasing power in a money civilization where the value of the dollar is constantly fluctuating.

A PROFESSIONAL CHARGE
FOR INVESTMENT COUNSEL

Scudder, Stevens & Clark

Investment management is a relatively new profession. This 1927 pamphlet, distributed to the clients and prospective clients of Scudder, Stevens
& Clark, describes this new business in search of a way to charge for its
services.

When, in 1919, we initiated the work of Investment Counsel we had to
determine, without precedent to guide us, how to charge for our services.
We did not know what it would cost us to do this work, or what it would
be equitable for the investor to pay; we did not know whether to charge
an annual fee, or a fee for each transaction executed on our advice, and
whether this charge should be against principal or income. For nearly
two years, therefore, we conducted our work with a view to securing
data by which to solve these problems.

In regard to the basis of charge we reached the following conclusion:
that the fee for our services should be a charge against the investor's
principal and not against his income from that principal. A charge based
on income (the method unfortunately specified by law for trust funds)
tends to emphasize income at the expense of principal, with the result
that the principal may decline, involving permanent loss. If, however,

From a Scudder, Stevens & Clark memorandum, New York, New York, January 25, 1977
(Originally published 1927), reprinted by permission of Scudder, Stevens & Clark.

principal is protected and built up, income is not only safeguarded but gradually increased and its future integrity ensured. It was apparent to us, therefore, that we should place the emphasis on principal, and that our fee should be charged against principal.

What, however, should be the amount of that fee? It must be remembered that in our capacity as Investment Counsel we study the financial problem of the individual investor, we plan the investment structure which, in our opinion, is best calculated to promote his interests, and we constantly supervise his holdings so that he shall benefit rather than suffer from changes in economic conditions. To guess at a price for such services, and allow the character of our work to be determined by what we could afford to do for the price, was obviously undesirable. We must, in each case, be enabled to do as much work for the client as is to his advantage: that is, to do a thorough job. Accordingly, we tentatively adopted 1% of the principal involved in each purchase and each sale as the fee we should charge.

This method did not prove wholly satisfactory. Charges were subject to fluctuation, dependent as they were on the number of transfers of investment during the course of the year. There is no direct relation between the value and extent of our work and the number of transactions we may recommend. We give the same quality of supervision to each client. One estate may require many changes of investment during the course of the year; a no less careful supervision of another estate may show few desirable changes. We therefore reached the conclusion that our charge should be on an annual basis—that the client should pay us as counsel a definite annual fee, to be determined by the amount of principal under our supervision.

The idea was new. Would investors realize the value of unbiased professional advice? For generations men have fully recognized the importance of sound medical or legal advice, and will pay adequately for it. A precedent has there been established. We, however, have to prove that our services are worth paying for.

To demonstrate to the investor that it will be to his advantage to employ us as counsel, we undertake, upon his request, to make a report on his affairs. If he does not like our advice, he pays us nothing. If he accepts our report in substance, he pays us 1% of the sum involved in each purchase and each sale made on our advice. We agree, however, that for a trial period of two years the total of such charges—provided this total amounts to $1,000—shall not exceed 1% of the client's principal as shown by the appraisal in our original report. By this method we establish for this period of two years a maximum charge based on a rate of 1/2 of 1% per year, but no minimum.

This procedure has proved satisfactory both to our clients and to ourselves. The trial period enables the client to observe our work for two years, a time sufficient to estimate its merits. It enables us not only to prove the value of our services in the initial selection of securities but also to demonstrate the importance of the subsequent period of supervision.

At the end of this trial period, the client, now thoroughly familiar with the quality of our work, decides whether he wishes to continue his relation with us—at an annual fee of 1/2 of 1% of his principal as then appraised. Thereafter the client's capital is appraised annually. If the client adds new capital during the course of the year, the charge is pro rata from the date of the addition.

The client may regard our fee merely as an insurance premium paid by him for the safeguarding of his investments. In reality it is much more than that. As a charge against principal it has practically no effect on income or, eventually, upon principal itself. In return for each year of continuous professional service in his interest, the client pays us but 1/2 of 1% of the average dollar value of his capital. If during a year of depression we do no more than save that capital from a shrinkage of 1/2 of 1%, or in normal times increase it over and above that amount, our services cost nothing. In point of fact, during the last eight years the average annual gain to the client through investments made under our supervision has more than ten times exceeded the amount of our fee. We therefore believe this fee to be not only an equitable charge for our services but a profitable expenditure on the part of the client.

In the case of certain institutions, including charitable organizations, banks, and insurance companies, we have adopted a slightly different schedule of charge.

In conclusion we wish again to state our position as Investment Counsel. We study the investment field as a whole: existing conditions and probable tendencies, fields of industry and individual companies. We study the individual needs of each client. In return for our annual fee we give to each client expert professional counsel wholly unbiased by personal interest in the sale of securities. If we are to retain the confidence of the client—and our own position in our profession—this counsel must be sound.

INVERTED REASONING
AND ITS CONSEQUENCES
CONFUSING THE PRESENT WITH
THE FUTURE—DISCOUNTING

George C. Selden

In his 1912 book, *Psychology of the Stock Market*, George Selden presented some of the results of his early studies of human attitudes and behavior in the stock market. Many of his observations have a remarkably contemporary quality.

INVERTED REASONING AND ITS CONSEQUENCES

It is hard for the average man to oppose what appears to be the general drift of public opinion. In the stock market this is perhaps harder than elsewhere; for we all realize that the prices of stocks must, in the long run, be controlled by public opinion. The point we fail to remember is that public opinion in a speculative market is measured in dollars, not in population. One man controlling one million dollars has double the weight of five hundred men with one thousand dollars each. Dollars are the horsepower of the markets—the mere number of men does not signify.

From George C. Selden, *Psychology of the Stock Market* (Burlington, Vermont, 1965; originally published 1912), 21–29, 43–54, by permission of Fraser Publishing Company.

This is why the great body of opinion appears to be bullish at the top and bearish at the bottom. The multitude of small traders must be, as a plain necessity, long when prices are at the top, and short or out of the market at the bottom. The very fact that they *are* long at the top shows that they have been supplied with stocks from some source.

Again, the man with one million dollars is a silent individual. The time when it was necessary for him to talk is past—his money now does the talking. But the one thousand men who have one thousand dollars each are conversational, fluent, verbose to the last degree.

It will be observed that the above course of reasoning leads up to the conclusion that most of those who talk about the market are more likely to be wrong than right, at least so far as speculative fluctuations are concerned. This is not complimentary to the "moulders of public opinion," but most seasoned newspaper readers will agree that it is true. The daily press reflects, in a general way, the thoughts of the multitude, and in the stock market the multitude is necessarily, as a logical deduction from the facts of the case, likely to be bullish at high prices and bearish at low.

It has often been remarked that the average man is an optimist regarding his own enterprises and a pessimist regarding those of others. Certainly this is true of the professional trader in stocks. As a result of the reasoning outlined above, he comes habitually to expect that nearly every one else will be wrong, but is, as a rule, confident that his own analysis of the situation will prove correct. He values the opinion of a few persons whom he believes to be generally successful; but aside from these few, the greater the number of the bullish opinions he hears, the more doubtful he becomes about the wisdom of following the bull side.

This apparent contrariness of the market, although easily understood when its causes are analyzed, breeds in professional traders a peculiar sort of skepticism—leads them always to distrust the obvious and to apply a kind of inverted reasoning to almost all stock market problems. Often, in the minds of traders who are not naturally logical, this inverted reasoning assumes the most erratic and grotesque forms, and it accounts for many apparently absurd fluctuations in prices which are commonly charged to manipulation.

For example, a trader starts with this assumption: The market has had a good advance; all the small traders are bullish; somebody must have sold them stock which they are carrying; hence the big capitalists are probably sold out or short and ready for a reaction or perhaps for a bear market. Then if a strong item of bullish news comes out—one, let us say, that really makes an important change in the situation—he says, "Ah, so this is what they have been bulling the market on! It has been discounted by the previous rise." Or he may say, "They are putting out this bull news to sell stocks on." He proceeds to sell out any long stocks he may have or perhaps to sell short.

His reasoning may be correct or it may not; but at any rate his selling and that of others who reason in a similar way is likely to produce at least a temporary decline on the announcement of the good news. This decline looks absurd to the outsider and he falls back on the old explanation "All manipulation."

The same principle is often carried further. You will find professional traders reasoning that favorable figures on the steel industry, for example, have been concocted to enable insiders to sell their steel; or that gloomy reports are put in circulation to facilitate accumulation. Hence they may act in direct opposition to the news and carry the market with them, for the time at least.

The less the trader knows about the fundamentals of the financial situation the more likely he is to be led astray in conclusions of this character. If he has confidence in the general strength of conditions, he may be ready to accept as genuine and natural a piece of news which he would otherwise receive with cynical skepticism and use as a basis for short sales. If he knows that fundamental conditions are unsound, he will not be so likely to interpret bad news as issued to assist in accumulation of stocks.

The same reasoning is applied to large purchases through brokers known to be associated with capitalists. In fact, in this case we often hear a double inversion, as it were. Such buying may impress the observer in three ways:

1. The "rank outsider" takes it at face value, as bullish.

2. A more experienced trader may say, "If they really wished to get the stocks they would not buy through their own brokers, but would endeavor to conceal their buying by scattering it among other houses."

3. A still more suspicious professional may turn another mental somersault and say, "They are buying through their own brokers so as to throw us off the scent and make us think someone else is using their brokers as a blind." By this double somersault such a trader arrives at the same conclusion as the outsider.

The reasoning of traders becomes even more complicated when large buying or selling is done openly by a big professional who is known to trade in and out for small profits. If he buys 50,000 shares, other traders are quite willing to sell to him and their opinion of the market is little influenced, simply because they know he may sell 50,000 the next day or even the next hour. For this reason great capitalists sometimes buy or sell through such big professional traders in order to execute their orders easily and without arousing suspicion. Hence the play of subtle intellects around big trading of this kind often becomes very elaborate.

It is to be noticed that this inverted reasoning is useful chiefly at the top or bottom of a movement, when distribution or accumulation is taking place on a large scale. A market which repeatedly refuses to respond to good news after a considerable advance is likely to be "full of stocks." Likewise a market which will not go down on bad news is usually "bare of stock."

Between the extremes will be found long stretches in which capitalists have very little cause to conceal their position. Having accumulated their lines as low as possible, they are then willing to be known as the leaders of the upward movement and have every reason to be perfectly open in their buying. This condition continues until they are ready to sell. Likewise, having sold as much as they desire, they have no reason to conceal their position further, even though a subsequent decline may run for months or a year.

It is during a long upward movement that the "lamb" makes money, because he accepts facts as facts, while the professional trader is often found fighting the advance and losing heavily because of the over-development of cynicism and suspicion.

The successful trader eventually learns when to invert his natural mental processes and when to leave them in their usual position. Often he develops a sort of instinct which could scarcely be reduced to cold print. But in the hands of the tyro this form of reasoning is exceedingly dangerous, because it permits of putting an alternate construction on any event. Bull news either (1) is significant of a rising trend of prices, or (2) indicates that "they" are trying to make a market to sell on. Bad news may indicate either a genuinely bearish situation or a desire to accumulate stocks at low prices.

The inexperienced operator is therefore left very much at sea. He is playing with the professional's edged tools and is likely to cut himself. Of what use is it for him to try to apply his reason to stock market conditions when every event may be doubly interpreted?

Indeed, it is doubtful if the professional's distrust of the obvious is of much benefit to him in the long run. Most of us have met those deplorable mental wrecks, often found among the "chairwarmers" in brokers' offices, whose thinking machinery seems to have become permanently demoralized as a result of continued acrobatics. They are always seeking an "ulterior motive" in everything. They credit—or debit—Morgan and Rockefeller with the smallest and meanest trickery and ascribe to them the most awful duplicity in matters which those "high financiers" would not stoop to notice. The continual reversal of the mental engine sometimes deranges its mechanism.

Probably no better general rule can be laid down than the brief one, "Stick to common sense." Maintain a balanced, receptive mind and avoid abstruse deductions. A few further suggestions may, however, be offered:

If you already have a position in the market, do not attempt to bolster up your failing faith by resorting to intellectual subtleties in the interpretation of obvious facts. If you are long or short of the market, you are not an unprejudiced judge, and you will be greatly tempted to put such an interpretation upon current events as will coincide with your preconceived opinion. It is hardly too much to say that this is the greatest obstacle to success. The least you can do is to avoid inverted reasoning in support of your own position.

After a prolonged advance, do not call inverted reasoning to your aid in order to prove that prices are going still higher; likewise after a big break do not let your bearish deductions become too complicated. Be suspicious of bull news at high prices, and of bear news at low prices.

Bear in mind that an item of news usually causes but *one* considerable movement of prices. If the movement takes place before the news comes out, as a result of rumors and expectations, then it is not likely to be repeated after the announcement is made; but if the movement of prices has not preceded, then the news contributes to the general strength or weakness of the situation and a movement of prices may follow.

* * * * *

CONFUSING THE PRESENT WITH
THE FUTURE—DISCOUNTING

It is axiomatic that inexperienced traders and investors, and indeed a majority of the more experienced as well, are continually trying to speculate on past events. Suppose, for example, railroad earnings as published are showing constant large increases in net. The novice reasons, "Increased earnings mean increased amounts applicable to the payment of dividends. Prices should rise. I will buy."

Not at all. He should say, "Prices *have risen* to the extent represented by these increased earnings, unless this effect has been counterbalanced by other considerations. Now what next?"

It is a sort of automatic assumption of the human mind that present conditions will continue, and our whole scheme of life is necessarily based to a great degree on this assumption. When the price of wheat is high farmers increase their acreage because wheat-growing pays better; when it is low they plant less. I remember talking with a potato-raiser who claimed that he had made a good deal of money by simply reversing the above custom. When potatoes were low he had planted liberally; when high he had cut down his acreage—because he reasoned that other farmers would do just the opposite.

The average man is not blessed—or cursed, however you may look at it—with an analytical mind. We see "as through a glass darkly." Our ideas are always enveloped in a haze and our reasoning powers work in a rut from which we find it painful if not impossible to escape. Many of our emotions and some of our acts are merely automatic responses to external stimuli. Wonderful as is the development of the human brain, it originated as an enlarged ganglion, and its first response is still practically that of the ganglion.

A simple illustration of this is found in the enmity we all feel toward the alarm clock which arouses us in the morning. We have carefully set and wound that alarm and if it failed to go off it would perhaps put us to serious inconvenience; yet we reward the faithful clock with anathemas.

When a subway train is delayed nine-tenths of the people waiting on the platform are anxiously craning their necks to see if it is coming, while many persons on it who are in danger of missing an engagement are holding themselves tense, apparently in the effort to help the train along. As a rule we apply more well-meant, but to a great extent ineffective, energy, physical or nervous, to the accomplishment of an object, than to analysis or calculation.

When it comes to so complicated a matter as the price of stocks, our haziness increases in proportion to the difficulty of the subject and our ignorance of it. From reading, observation and conversation we imbibe a miscellaneous assortment of ideas from which we conclude that the situation is bullish or bearish. The very form of the expression "the situation is bullish"— not "the situation will soon become bullish"—

shows the extent to which we allow the present to obscure the future in the formation of our judgment.

Catch any trader and pin him down to it and he will readily admit that the logical moment for the highest prices is when the news is most bullish; yet you will find him buying stocks on this news after it comes out—if not at the moment, at any rate "on a reaction."

Most coming events cast their shadows before, and it is on this that intelligent speculation must be based. The movement of prices in anticipation of such an event is called "discounting," and this process of discounting is worthy of a little careful examination.

The first point to be borne in mind is that some events cannot be discounted, even by the supposed omniscience of the great banking interests—which is, in point of fact, more than half imaginary. The San Francisco earthquake is the standard example of an event which could not be foreseen and therefore could not be discounted; but an event does not have to be purely an "act of God" to be undiscountable. There can be no question that our great bankers have been as much in the dark in regard to some recent Supreme Court decisions as the smallest "piker" in the customer's room of an odd-lot brokerage house.

If the effect of an event does not make itself felt before the event takes place, it must come after. In all discussion of discounting we must bear this fact in mind in order that our subject may not run away with us.

On the other hand, an event may sometimes be over-discounted. If the dividend rate on a stock is to be raised from four to five per cent, earnest bulls, with an eye to their own commitments, may spread rumors of six or seven per cent, so that the actual declaration of five per cent may be received as disappointing and cause a decline.

Generally speaking, every event which is under the control of capitalists associated with the property, or any financial condition which is subject to the management of combined banking interests, is likely to be pretty thoroughly discounted before it occurs. There is rarely any lack of capital to take advantage of a sure thing, even though it may be known in advance to only a few persons.

The extent to which future business conditions are known to "insiders" is, however, usually overestimated. So much depends, especially in America, upon the size of the crops, the temper of the people, and the policies adopted by leading politicians, that the future of business becomes a very complicated problem. No power can drive the American people. Any control over their action has to be exercised by cajolery or by devious and circuitous methods.

Moreover, public opinion is becoming more volatile and changeable year by year, owing to the quicker spread of information and the rapid multiplication of the reading public. One can easily imagine that some of our older financiers must be saying to themselves, "If I only had my present capital in 1870, or else had the conditions of 1870 to work on today!"

A fair idea of when the discounting process will be completed may usually be formed by studying conditions from every angle. The great question is, when will the buying or selling become most general and urgent? In 1907, for example, the safest and best time to buy the sound dividend-paying stocks was on the Monday following the bank statement with showed the greatest decrease in reserves. The market opened down several points under pressure of liquidation, and many standard issues never sold so low afterward. The simple explanation was that conditions had become so bad that they could not get any worse without utter ruin, which all parties must and did unite to prevent.

Likewise in the Presidential campaign of 1900, the lowest prices were made on Bryan's nomination. Investors said at once, "He can't be elected." Therefore his nomination was the worst that could happen — the point of time where the political news became most intensely bearish. As the campaign developed his defeat became more and more certain, and prices continued to rise in accordance with the general economic and financial conditions of the period.

It is not the discounting of an event thus known in advance to capitalists that presents the greatest difficulties, but cases where considerable uncertainty exists, so that even the clearest mind and the most accurate information can result only in a balancing of probabilities, with the scale perhaps inclined to a greater or less degree in one direction or the other.

In some cases the uncertainty which precedes such an event is more depressing than the worst that can happen afterward. An example is a Supreme Court decision upon a previously undetermined public policy which has kept business men so much in the dark that they feared to go ahead with any important plans. This was the case at the time of the Northern Securities decision in 1904. "Big business" could easily enough adjust itself to either result. It was the uncertainty that was bearish. Hence the decision was practically discounted in advance, no matter what it might prove to be.

This was not true to the same extent of the Standard Oil and American Tobacco decisions of 1911, because those decisions were an earnest of more trouble to come. The decisions were greeted by a temporary spurt of activity, based on the theory that the removal of uncertainty was the important thing; but a sensational decline started soon after and was not checked until the announcement that the Government would prosecute the United States Steel Corporation. This was deemed the worst that could happen for some time to come, and was followed by a considerable advance.

More commonly, when an event is uncertain the market estimates the chances with considerable nicety. Each trader backs his own opinion, strongly if he feels confident, moderately if he still has a few doubts which he cannot down. The result of these opposing views may be stationary prices, or a market fluctuating nervously within a narrow range, or a movement in either direction, greater or smaller in proportion to the more or less emphatic preponderance of the buying or selling.

Of course it must always be remembered that it is the dollars that count, not the number of buyers or sellers. A few great capitalists having advance information which they regard as accurate may more than counterbalance thousands of small traders who hold an opposite opinion. In fact, this is the condition very frequently seen, as explained in a previous chapter.

Even the operations of an individual investor usually have an effect on prices pretty accurately adjusted to his opinions. When be believes prices are low and everything favors an upward movement, he will strain his resources in order to accumulate as heavy a load of securities as he can carry. After a fair advance, if he sees the development of some factor which *might* cause a decline—though he doesn't really believe it will—he thinks it wise to lighten his load somewhat and make sure of some of his accumulated profits. Later when he feels that prices are "high enough," he is a liberal seller; and if some danger appears while the level of quoted values continues high, he "cleans house," to be ready for whatever may come. Then if what he considers an unwarranted speculation carries prices still higher, he is very likely to sell a few hundred shares short by way of occupying his capital and his mind.

It is, however, the variation of opinion among different men that has the largest influence in making the market responsive to changing conditions. A development which causes one trader to lighten his line of stocks may be regarded as harmless or even beneficial by another, so that he maintains his position or perhaps buys more. Out of a world-wide mixture of varying ideas, personalities and information emerges the average level of prices—the true index number of investment conditions.

The necessary result of the above line of reasoning is that not only probabilities but even rather remote possibilities are reflected in the market. Hardly any event can happen of sufficient inportance to attract general attention which some other process of reasoning cannot construe as bullish and some other process interpret as bearish. Doubtless even our old friend of the news columns to the effect that "the necessary activities of a nation of one hundred million souls create and maintain a large volume of business," may influence some red-blooded optimist to buy 100 Union, but the grouchy pessimist who has eaten too many doughnuts for breakfast will accept the statement as an evidence of the scarcity of real bull news and will likely enough sell 100 Union short on the strength of it.

It is the overextended speculator who causes most of the fluctuations that look absurd to the sober observer. It does not take much to make a man buy when he is short of stocks "up to his neck." A bit of news which he would regard as insignificant at any other time will then assume an exaggerated importance in his eyes. His fears increase in geometrical proportion to the size of his line of stocks. Likewise the overloaded bull may begin to "throw his stocks" on some absurd story of a war between Honduras and Roumania [*sic*], without even stopping to look up the geographical location of the countries involved.

Fluctuations based on absurdities are always relatively small. They are due to an exaggerated fear of what "the other fellow" may do. Personally, you do not fear a war between Honduras and Roumania; but may not the rumor be seized upon by the bears as an excuse for a raid? And you have too many stocks to be comfortable if such a break should occur. Moreover, even if the bears do not raid the market, will there not be a considerable number of persons who, like yourself, will fear such a raid, and will therefore lighten their load of stocks, thus causing some decline?

The professional trader, following this line of reasoning to the limit, eventually comes to base all his operations for short turns in the market not on the facts but on what he believes the facts will cause others to do— or more accurately, perhaps, on what he *sees* that the news *is* causing others to do; for such a trader is likely to keep his fingers constantly on the pulse of buying and selling as it throbs on the floor of the Exchange or as recorded on the tape.

The non-professional, however, will do well not to let his mind stray too far into the unknown territory of what others may do. Like the "They" theory of values, it is dangerous ground in that it leads toward the abdication of common sense; and after all, others may not prove to be such fools as we think they are. While the market is likely to discount even a possibility, the chances are very much against *our* being able to discount the possibility profitably.

In this matter of discounting, as in connection with most other stock market phenomena, the most useful hint that can be given is to avoid all efforts to reduce the movement of prices to rules, measures, or similarities and to analyze each case by itself. Historical parallels are likely to be misleading. Every situation is new, though usually composed of familiar elements. Each element must be weighed by itself and the probable result of the combination estimated. In most cases the problem is by no means impossible, but the student must learn to look into the future and to consider the present only as a guide to the future. Extreme prices will come at the time when the news is most emphatic and most widely disseminated. When that point is passed the question must always be, "What next?"

THE MARKET AND PRICES

Adam Smith

"Value" was a concept that challenged early economists almost to distraction. How could something of such obvious necessity and great usefulness as water, for example, be "worth" next to nothing in terms of either its cost as a commodity or its purchasing power? Adam Smith elegantly explained this phenomenon—and, indirectly, introduced us to the fact that "value" and "price" need not be synonymous—more than 200 years ago.

The word value, it is to be observed, has two different meanings, and sometimes expresses the utility of some particular object, and sometimes the power of purchasing other goods which the possession of that objective conveys. The one may be called "value in use;" the other, "value in exchange." The things which have the greatest value in use have frequently little or no value in exchange; and, on the contrary, those which have the greatest value in exchange have frequently little or no value in use. Nothing is more useful than water: but it will purchase scarce anything; scarce anything can be had in exchange for it. A diamond, on the contrary, has scarce any value in use; but a very great quantity of other goods may frequently be had in exchange for it.

From *The Wisdom of Adam Smith*, Benjamin A. Rogge, ed. (Indianapolis, Indiana, 1976), 111–112, by permission of Liberty Fund, Inc.

BONDS AND THE DOLLAR COMPARISON BETWEEN COMMON STOCKS AND BONDS, 1901–1922
A NEW STOCK MARKET CHART, 1837–1923
TIME HAZARD IN THE PURCHASE OF COMMON STOCKS

Edgar L. Smith

Edgar Smith used extensive (and surely exhausting) original research on specific securities and their actual returns over many years to develop and support his conclusion that—in contrast to the prevailing judgment at that time—common stocks were better than bonds for long-term investment. Here are excerpts from his fascinating 1924 book, which some credited with providing the intellectual underpinnings to the bull market of the mid- and late-1920s. Note his emphasis on the importance of diversification and wise investment counsel.

From Edgar L. Smith, *Common Stocks as Long-Term Investments* (New York, New York, 1924), 3–5, 18–20, 68, 81–82, Macmillan Publishing Company.

BONDS AND THE DOLLAR

When the topic of conservative investment is under discussion, high grade bonds hold an unassailable position in the minds of most people, and the discussion usually resolves itself into weighing the relative merits of different issues of such bonds or how far it is safe to stray away from the most highly secured bonds in an effort to obtain a higher income return. Those who venture to suggest preferred stocks sometimes feel that they have gone as far as conservative opinion will support them. Common stocks are ordinarily left out of the discussion altogether.

Common Stocks are, in general, regarded as a medium for Speculation—not for Long Term Investment.

Bonds, on the other hand, are generally held to be the best medium for Long Term Investment—free from the hazards of Speculation.

Is this view sound? What are the facts?

A venerable tradition of conservatism has attached to first mortgages whether upon real estate or upon corporate property as the basis for an issue of bonds. This tradition was supported by experience up to 1897, when the purchasing power of the dollar reached its highest point. But the experience of investors in real estate mortgages and in mortgage bonds, with respect to a depreciating currency since 1897 and with respect to a rising interest rate since 1902, raises grave doubt as to the justification of this tradition with particular reference to personal as opposed to institutional investments.

Because common stocks are regarded as speculative, they are frequently omitted entirely from the lists of a great many investors. Is this omission based on a thorough study of the relative merits of bonds and stocks or is it based in part on prejudice? It is true that stocks fluctuate in price in response to many factors, some related to the industry they represent, some to general business conditions, some to the temporary market position of avowed speculators.

Is it not possible that the association of speculation with common stocks has somewhat influenced a majority of investors against them, and has exaggerated in their minds the danger of possible loss to those who buy them for long term investment?

Is it not possible that the definite weakness of otherwise perfectly safe bonds is overlooked—namely, that they cannot in any way participate in the growth and increasing activity of the country—that they are defenseless against a depreciating currency?

The fundamental difference between stocks and bonds is that—

Stocks represent ownership of property and processes; their value and income return fluctuating with the earning power of the property.

Bonds represent a promise to pay a certain number of dollars at a future date with a fixed rate of interest each year during the life of the loan.

The value of stocks, expressed in dollars, increases with the growth and prosperity of the country and of the industry represented. It also increases in proportion as dollars themselves decrease in purchasing power as expressed in a higher cost of living. Stocks are subject to temporary hazards of hard times, and may be destroyed in value by a radical change in the arts or by poor management.

The value of high grade bonds, expressed in dollars, changes far less because their value represents dollars and nothing but dollars.

The only commodity whose price in terms of dollars does not vary at all (except under most extraordinary conditions) is gold. That is because a dollar is, by definition, a certain weight of gold of a certain fineness. The price is legally fixed. The price at which bonds sell participates with gold in this legal, but to a certain degree fictitious, stabilization.

Such fluctuations as do occur in the dollar price of bonds result from—

1. Changes in the credit position of the issuing company—the prospects of its being able to pay interest and principal when due. This is largely influenced by its earning power in excess of current interest requirements.

2. Changes in the current demand and supply of liquid capital, in relation to the length of the unexpired term and the fixed interest rate of the bonds in question.

* * * * *

COMPARISON BETWEEN COMMON STOCKS AND BONDS, 1901–1922

In the tests that follow, the only principle of sound investment that has been applied to the selection of stocks is that of diversification. Without diversification, the purchase of common stocks cannot be considered.

It was necessary to eliminate any real judgment in the selection of particular stocks because of the danger of unconsciously basing this judgment upon facts which have become known subsequent to the supposed date of purchase.

Method of Selection

In each test an arbitrary method of selecting the stocks has been set up before the selection is made. The stocks are then taken according to this arbitrary method, thus eliminating every possibility that the knowledge of subsequent events has colored our choice. In fact, in one case at least, a stock which might well have fallen into the group chosen was eliminated because there was an element of doubt as to whether or not it would have come strictly within the formula established, and knowledge of the extraordinarily favorable experience that stockholders in this company have had made it unavailable for the test.

Research

The history of each stock selected as it appears in published records has been studied and tabulated. The working tables are too large to be included in this volume. They have been carefully checked, however, and the totals given herein are believed to be correct arithmetically. It is recognized that a few errors may have crept into the original tables because of uncertainties as to the exact meaning of some of the recorded data. When the doubt seemed likely to materially affect the result of the test, the stock has been sold out at current quotations. We have in no case changed our original list of stocks in a test, because of difficulty in determining the history of any stock. Occasionally we have been unable to find quotations for "rights," and have, therefore, failed to give full credit to income account.

The aim has been to favor stocks in no way, while every effort has been made to give all possible advantage to bonds in the comparison.

Importance of Tests

The importance of these tests lies in their cumulative force. No single test would have more than passing significance. But all of them together are strongly indicative of underlying factors which have been overlooked by too large a proportion of individual investors.

Each test assumes the investment of approximately $10,000 in ten diversified common stocks of large companies and an investment of an equal amount in high grade bonds. They cover the entire period from

1866 to date, and the supposed purchase of stocks is made without reference to the condition of the stock market at the time of purchase except in those tests where a peak in the market has been deliberately chosen (Tests 7 and 8).

Every test except one shows better results are obtained from common stocks than from bonds, as follows:

Period	Total Advantage of Stocks over Bonds
Test No. 1, 1901–1922 (22 years)	$16,400.94
Test No. 2, 1901–1922 (22 years)	9,242.26
Test No. 3, 1901–1922 (22 years)	21,954.72
Test No. 4, 1880–1899 (20 years)	11,982.04
Test No. 5, 1866–1885 (20 years)	2,966.85
Test No. 6, 1866–1885 (20 years)	−1,012.00
Test No. 7, 1892–1911 (20 years)	11,723.80
Test No. 8, 1906–1922 (17 years)	6,651.01
Test No. 8a, 1906–1922 (17 years)	4,938.08
Test No. 9, 1901–1922 (22 years), Railroads	13,734.72
Test No. 10, 1901–1922 (22 years), Railroads	3,329.72
Test No. 11, 1901–1922 (22 years), Railroads	17,140.25

The methods by which the stocks were selected are not recommended to an investor actually investing to-day, but they are important in judging the results of the tests. Sound investment counsel at the time purchases are made, and applied constantly to the holdings would, without any doubt, have greatly improved the showing made.

* * * * *

A NEW STOCK MARKET CHART, 1837–1923

These tests we have made are not in themselves conclusive, but cumulatively they tend to show that well-diversified lists of common stocks selected on simple and broad principles of diversification respond to some underlying factor which gives them a margin of advantage over high grade bonds for long term investment. But in view of the speculative attributes known to exist in common stocks we are hardly justified in accepting stocks as an alternative to high grade bonds for long-term investment unless we are able to isolate this underlying factor with a view to appraising its potency under varying conditions and the likelihood of its continued operation in the future.

$$* \quad * \quad * \quad * \quad *$$

TIME HAZARD IN THE PURCHASE OF COMMON STOCKS

We have found that there is a force at work in our common stock holdings which tends ever toward increasing their principal value in terms of dollars, a force resulting from the profitable reinvestment, by the companies involved, of their undistributed earnings. We have found that unless we have had the extreme misfortune to invest at the very peak of a noteworthy rise, those periods in which the average market value of our holdings remains less than the amount we paid for them are of comparatively short duration, and that even if we have bought at the very peak, there is definitely to be expected a period in which we may recover as many dollars as we have invested. Our hazard even in such extreme cases appears to be that of time alone.

In an attempt to measure the probability of this time element working against us, we have. . . asked ourselves for how many years immediately following the year of purchase these holdings would have shown a lower average market value than the price paid. There are 86 such years of assumed purchase (omitting 1923), and the result of our analysis of this time hazard may be summarized as follows:

			Cumulative Percentage
Number of times when the year succeeding the year of purchase shows no loss	54 times	63.0%	
Number of times when a loss in principal value lasts:			
1 year	13 times	15.1%	78.1%
2 years	8 times	9.3%	87.4%
3 years	2 times	2.3%	89.7%
4 years	4 times	4.7%	94.4%
6 years	2 times	2.3%	96.7%
7 years	1 time	1.1%	97.8%
10 years	1 time	1.1%	98.9%
15 years	1 time	1.1%	100.0%

These figures, which imply the total absence of any judgment in the selection of the *time* when purchases are made, suggest that in buying a well-diversified group of representative common stocks in essential industries, our chances of coming out even, or of making a profit in principal values, are within 1 year, 78 in 100; 2 years, 87 in 100; 4 years, 94 in 100.

There remain about six chances in one hundred that we should have to wait from six to fifteen years before having an opportunity to liquidate upon even terms. These are represented by five assumed purchases in the following years:

Year of Purchase	Number of Years of Lower Values, Immediately Succeeding Year of Purchase
1847	15 years
1853	10 years
1854	7 years
1873	6 years
1882	6 years

* * * * *

EVALUATION BY THE RULE
OF PRESENT WORTH

John Burr Williams

John Burr Williams is rightly credited with establishing the conceptual foundation upon which the formal discipline of investment management has been built. No mere theoretician, he was an active investor and a securities analyst. Here are the key steps in his exposition in *The Theory of Investment Value*, published in 1938.

Let us define the investment value of a stock as the present worth of all the dividends to be paid upon it. Likewise let us define the investment value of a bond as the present worth of its future coupons and principal. In both cases, dividends, or coupons and principal, must be adjusted for expected changes in the purchasing power of money. The purchase of a stock or bond, like other transactions which give rise to the phenomenon of interest, represents the exchange of present goods for future goods — dividends, or coupons and principal, in this case being the claim on future goods. To appraise the investment value, then, it is necessary to estimate the future payments. The annuity of payments, adjusted for changes in the value of money itself, may then be discounted at the pure interest rate demanded by the investor.

Most people will object at once to the foregoing formula for stocks

From John Burr Williams, *The Theory of Investment Value* (Cambridge, Massachusetts, 1938), 30, 542–543, by permission of the author.

by saying that it should use the present worth of future *earnings*, not future *dividends*. But should not earnings and dividends both give the same answer under the implicit assumptions of our critics? If earnings not paid out in dividends are all successfully reinvested at compound interest for the benefit of the stockholder, as the critics imply, then these earnings should produce dividends later; if not, then they are money lost. Furthermore, if these reinvested earnings will produce dividends, then our formula will take account of them when it takes account of all future dividends; but if they will not, then our formula will rightly refrain from including them in any discounted annuity of benefits.

Earnings are only a means to an end, and the means should not be mistaken for the end. Therefore we must say that a stock derives its value from its dividends, not its earnings. In short, a stock is worth only *what you can get out of it*. Even so spoke the old farmer to his son:

> A cow for her milk,
> A hen for her eggs,
> And a stock, by heck
> For her dividends.
>
> An orchard for fruit
> Bees for their honey,
> And stocks, besides,
> For their dividends.

The old man knew where milk and honey came from, but he made no such mistake as to tell his son to buy a cow for her cud or bees for their buzz.

In saying that dividends, not earnings, determine value, we seem to be reversing the usual rule that is drilled into every beginner's head when he starts to trade in the market; namely, that earnings, not dividends, make prices. The apparent contradiction is easily explained, however, for we are discussing permanent investment, not speculative trading, and dividends for years to come, not income for the moment only. Of course it is true that low earnings together with a high dividend for the time being should be looked at askance, but likewise it is true that these low earnings mean low dividends *in the long run*. On analysis, therefore, it will be seen that no contradiction really exists between our formula using dividends and the common precept regarding earnings.

How to estimate the future dividends for use in our formula is, of course, the difficulty. In later chapters ways of making an estimate will be given for such stocks as we now know how to deal with. In so doing, this book seeks to make its most important contribution to Investment Analysis.

* * * * *

Marketability, or salability, or liquidity, is an attribute of an investment to which many buyers of necessity attach great importance. Yet it would not be helpful to amend our definition of investment value in such a way as to make it take cognizance of marketability. Risk, to be sure, should be covered by the definition as done above, but not marketability, for the inclusion of marketability would only lead to confusion. Better to treat intrinsic value as one thing, salability as another. Then we can say, for instance, that a given investment is both cheap and liquid, not that it is cheap partly because it is liquid; the latter phraseology would only raise the question of how much of the cheapness was due to liquidity and how much to other factors. To divorce liquidity, or salability, or marketability from the concept of investment value is in conformity, moreover, with accepted usage outside the field of investment. In speaking of goods and services, for instance, one does not say that a pound of sugar is cheap at six cents because it is so "salable." Nothing of the sort; for the sugar is bought for consumption and not for resale. By the same token, why should one say that a bond is cheap because it is so salable? For if the bond is bought for investment, as by a life insurance company, it is not intended for resale at all, but for holding to maturity. Of course, if the buyer is a speculator, that is another matter, since investment value is only one of several things considered by a speculator. But even a speculator should not confuse salability with cheapness, any more than he should confuse popularity with cheapness. Just as market price determined by marginal opinion is one thing, and investment value determined by future dividends is another, so also salability is one thing and cheapness another.

Likewise *stability* is a thing distinct from investment value, and from marketability as well. While the expected stability of the price of a security in future years is a consideration of great importance to some investors, particularly banks, yet it is not a component of investment value as the latter term ought to be defined. Many individual investors who buy and hold for income do not need to concern themselves with stability any more than with liquidity; hence to include the concept of stability in the definition of investment value would only make investment value mean something different for each and every investor, according to his own personal need for stability as compared with other things.

In conclusion, therefore, it may be said that neither marketability nor stability should be permitted to enter into the meaning of the term *investment value*.

MEMORANDUM

Dean Witter

As he explained in this 1932 memorandum, Dean Witter had been worried by high stock prices in the spring of 1929. Three years later, he was trying to get investors to think about buying: "I wish to say emphatically that in a few years present prices will appear as ridiculously low as 1929 values already appear fantastically high."

A very interesting book could be written on mass psychology and the effect thereof. That everyone is influenced more or less by the opinion of others is obvious. There was no reason for the unwarranted heights which the market reached in 1929 except universal over-optimism— there is no excuse for the present market value of good bonds and stocks today except undue pessimism. In 1929 no pessimistic comment could survive. Today an expression of confidence in the future of the country is unpopular. Strangely, the peaks of 1929 and the low quotations of today are both due to the same cause, which is lack of intelligent and sound analysis. It is strange that such divergent conditions should come within such a short period and should be due to such identical factors.

We are no longer much interested in the fantastic heights of 1929 except that we marvel at our lack of sane judgment. We are keenly interested in the present, and until some time elapses and we can obtain a better perspective it is difficult to realize that present conditions and markets are just as abnormally low as 1929 conditions and markets were excessively high.

From Dean Witter & Co. Letterhead, New York, New York, May 6, 1932, with permission from Dean Witter & Co., Inc.

There are only two premises which are tenable as to the future. Either we are going to have chaos or else recovery. The former theory is foolish. If chaos ensues nothing will maintain value; neither bonds nor stocks nor bank deposits nor gold will remain valuable. Real estate will be a worthless asset because titles will be insecure. No policy can be based upon this impossible contingency. Policy must therefore be predicated upon the theory of recovery. The present is not the first depression; it may be the worst, but just as surely as conditions have righted themselves in the past and have gradually been readjusted to normal so this will again occur. The only uncertainty is when it will occur.

Everyone now seems to be indulging in the futile desire to buy at the bottom, just as everyone sought the very top in 1929. Most conservative people thought that values were much too high in 1928. Their judgment has since been fully vindicated in spite of the fact that values went much higher in 1929. Someone once said that they had made their fortune because they had never tried to buy at the bottom or sell at the top. This only means that they had not striven for the impossible but had been satisfied to buy when values were in general low and had been satisfied to sell when values were in general high, and without regard to peaks, which no one can identify and which, except by accident, are impossible to attain.

I think everyone must know that values are now abnormally low. In a few years and with a better perspective they will realize that they were low in 1931. In other words, they were even then way below normal. People are deterred from buying good stocks and bonds now only because of an unwarranted terror. Almost everyone says that prices are going still lower. All sorts of bugaboos are paraded to destroy the last vestige of confidence. Stories of disaster which are incredible and untrue are told to foolish and credulous listeners, who appear willing to believe the worst.

I wish to say definitely that values were low in the latter half of 1931 and that they are now ridiculous. To prove this one has only to take an average period of 10 to 20 years of earnings, which should provide a proper normal, and compare present values with the value which such normal earning power would adequately support. The stocks of many good companies which are faced with no ascertainable financial hazard are selling at only 2 or 3 times 10-year earnings, and at from 5% to 50% of sound book value, disregarding such valuable intangibles as good will, going concern value and trained intelligent organizations which it has taken years and the expenditure of vast sums of money to develop. I wish to say emphatically that in a few years present prices will appear as ridiculously low as 1929 values already appear fantastically high.

In 1929 one could only profit by selling. Many of us are instinctively reluctant to sell. There was the problem of reinvestment—there were taxes to be paid on profits. Today the situation is reversed. The present offers a splendid opportunity to the buyer. Great fortunes will be made out of securities bought today. There is no tax on buying and there is no sentimental deterrent. Only unwarranted fear or a futile desire to buy at the very bottom deters people from investment now. Most people who are buying at all are buying Treasury Certificates or the highest grade of municipals. Some are even putting money in their safe deposit boxes. None of these things are cheap. By comparison they are most expensive.

The time to have bought Treasury Certificates and the highest grade of short-term obligations was in 1928 and 1929 when values were high and in order to preserve the dollar intact. The present is the time to use the dollar in the purchase of good securities, whether they be greatly depreciated bonds or excessively deflated common stocks. All of our customers who have money must some day put that money to work, and into some type of revenue-producing investment. Why not invest it now when securities are cheap? Why leave it in cash or invest in Treasury Certificates which are dear? Some people say that they wish to await a clearer view of the future. When the future is again clear the present bargains will no longer be available. Does anyone think that present prices will continue when confidence has been fully restored? Such bargains exist only because of terror and distress. When the future is assured the dollar will long since have ceased to have its present buying power. If one holds either cash or the very highest grade of short-term bonds as a temporary medium of investment he will find that he has only permitted great investment opportunities in tremendously underpriced securities to escape him.

It requires courage to be optimistic as to the future of the country when nearly everyone is pessimistic. It is, however, cowardly to assume that the future of the country is in peril.

No successful policy can be established upon this unsound theory. It is easy to run with the crowd. The path of least resistance is to join in the wailings that are now so popular. The constructive policy, however, is to maintain your courage and your optimism, to have faith in the ultimate future of your country and to proclaim your faith and to recommend the purchase of good bonds and good stocks, which are inordinately depreciated. You will gain the respect of those people with whom you come in contact by such an attitude. If you can persuade them to evidence their confidence in the future of the country by the purchase of good securities now you will do them a great favor and they will be grateful to you later.

It is disconcerting to have recommended the purchase of securities in 1931 as they have gone much lower since. This shakes one's confidence in his own judgment. You were just as right, however, in 1931 as you are now in recommending investment in securities which were even then cheap. I can remember distinctly that I could find no justification for values which existed in 1928 and in many cases recommended sale or advised against purchase. I was decidedly wrong, as prices went much higher in 1929. I was only wrong, however, in that I failed to pick the very top of the market. It is true that values in 1928 were already inordinately high as judged by normal and average yardsticks.

On April 18, 1929, I dictated a memorandum which was published to the entire organization, copies of which are still available in the files. The subject matter of the memorandum was unpopular. It stated that people were buying stocks without regard to "value, earning power and dividends, present and prospective." It stated that people were buying stocks not because they were worth the price at which they were selling, but because they hoped they would go higher and could be sold at a profit. The memorandum stated that the average speculator who bought stocks upon that theory in the long run lost money. It compared the psychology which then existed (April, 1929) with the psychology of the Florida land boom, the commodity inflation of 1919 and other characteristic periods of inflation. It pointed out that one could not afford to buy stocks that earned less than 5% and paid less than 3% on market values then prevailing. It stated that "perhaps we are going to have the greatest era of prosperity in our history.

> Maybe we have already had this era. Perhaps we have nothing but increasing earnings and increasing dividends ahead of us. I hope so. If we have, present values are hardly justified; if we haven't they will decline. Many things can happen, most of them unforeseen—politics, wars, economic changes, European competition, money shortage, with-

drawal of foreign balances, adverse foreign trade balances, sudden with-drawal of large sums of bootleg money in the call market, Federal Reserve restrictions, interference by Congress or by the Government. These things probably won't happen but they might. If they don't present levels may be all right—if they do, the last holder will suffer and not the next to the last, but we can't all be next to the last.

The danger signals are waving—higher time money than we have ever known—more speculation than ever before—and tremendous brokers' loans, though this may be a proper and normal increase in a very rapidly growing country. Not only are the rich and intelligent speculating but many have their last dollar in the stock market on margin. $5,500,000,000 of record and a great deal more, unrecorded, is borrowed to carry stocks. People are paying 8 or 9% for this money and generally getting 3 or 4%. How long can this last? Can it last until the 3 or 4% catches up to the 8%? Probably not.

I am not a stock market prognosticator nor an analyst. I do not pretend to be a Moody, a Babson, or a Brookmire. I have been rather pessimistic about stock market prices for two years. If I had been an unqualified optimist I could have made a great fortune. I am not a pessimist—I think this country will prosper beyond conception in the next 20 years. I don't, however, believe in over-speculation. I don't believe in 9% money for 3% stocks. The former may be temporary—the latter is more or less permanent unless price levels change. I have been taught that a good stock should earn 10%, not 5%. Probably I am old-fashioned. In any event, this is not the prevailing custom today. I believe that people should speak honestly and not too guardedly. I would not want our brokerage department to be the means or vehicle of severe loss to people. It is hard to be patient with 3% stocks carried on 9% money. Will they stay at a level which produces a 3% return? John Moody and a great many other excellent authorities seem to think so. I don't know but I would not gamble on it."

PART 2

THE 1950s

$12,000—HEADLINE
OF THE WEEK
RIP VAN WINKLE II
RETURNS TO WALL STREET

David L. Babson

The Weekly Staff Letter of David L. Babson & Co. has won a wide audience among investment professionals because it is thoughtful, informative, and well written. Here are two letters written by David Babson himself, one arguing for investing in stocks in 1950 and the other questioning prices versus values in 1969.

"$12,000"—HEADLINE OF THE WEEK

While the State of the Union Message contained no surprises, the most eye-catching headline of the message was: "President Truman predicts average family income of $12,000 by the year 2000." If he had used a figure of $24,000 it might turn out to be more accurate than $12,000.

If you had told a Frenchman in 1913 that an American cigar, which then cost a franc, would cost 70 francs by the year 1950 he would have thought you were crazy. Yet the ravages of two World Wars and the

From David L. Babson, *Weekly Staff Letter from David L. Babson & Co., Inc.* (Cambridge, Massachusetts, 1950, 1969), 1-4, 1-4 (respectively), by permission of David L. Babson & Co., Inc.

shackles of socialistic experiments have dropped the value of the franc from 20 to the dollar to 286 to the dollar in the past three decades.

If we should experience a third world war, go into a chaotic depression, continue the 15-year trend toward greater and greater government deficits, the value of our dollar might drop further than President Truman's prediction indicates. The point is that it should not matter a whit what the average family income in dollars may be in the year 2000.

> If Mr. Truman had made some projections about how many pounds of beef, or how many pairs of shoes the average family would be able to buy, how many rooms in its home it would have for living space in 2000, they would have more meaning than a $12,000 or a $24,000 prediction.

The greatest asset that the modern politician has is the public's failure to recognize that it is not the number of dollars in the weekly pay envelope that counts but the pounds of food, pairs of shoes, etc. that those dollars will buy. Many voters whose incomes are $100 a week today vs. $50 in 1939, and whose living costs including taxes are also double, think the Administration has done a magnificent job in helping them.

Promising and artificially creating greater dollar income, thus forcing dollar living costs to increase, then blaming industry and trade for the higher price is a pretty tough political program to beat. No wonder Vice President Barkley had the courage to predict the Democrats would never lose control of Congress or the White House again!

It is not only the average voter who is fooled. Investors forget that it is their purchasing power and their living standards they should be conserving, not merely their dollar principal. Those people living on income from accumulated capital are in the poorest relative position compared to 1939 of all economic groups.

And among this group those who have concentrated a large portion of their assets in annuities, government bonds, etc. have suffered two-fold: (1) The buying power of their principal has declined even though its dollar value may be just as high, and (2) both the dollar amount and the buying power of their income has dropped.

Those, however, who have placed a large amount of their capital in *high-grade* common stocks have, to a large measure, offset the inflation—the dollar amount both of their income and principal has matched the decline in the buying power of the dollar.

If President Truman's prediction is entitled to thoughtful consideration, the conclusion to be drawn is that it will take three dollars in the year 2000 to buy what one dollar will buy in 1950, just as it takes about three dollars today to buy what one dollar bought in 1900.

So if your retirement plans hopefully include the year 2000, do not tie up the bulk of your capital in those forms of investment that cannot permit you to gain any offsetting benefits from the long-term decline in the buying power of the dollar which President Truman predicts will continue.

* * * * *

It is a peculiar thing but until the past few weeks we do not recall having seen "250–300 on the Dow Average" mentioned as a future possibility since 1946. With the Average breaking through 200 for the first time in four years, the number of the 250 forecasts is stepping up. What is peculiar is why no one talked about "250–300" when the Industrial Average was around 165–180 for the better part of three years. We do recall having seen several forecasts that the Dow Average was going to 125 during that period.

In these Staff Letters, we have gone on record time and again with our views on the long-term trend — that post-war industrial activity, corporate earnings and dividends should average double their pre-war levels and that common stock prices would reflect this condition sooner or later. If we double the yearly average (135) of the Dow Average in the 1935-39 period we get a post-war figure of 270. Thus the idea of the Dow Average reaching 250–300 should not startle clients.

* * * * *

We expect that the 1950 total of dividends paid by companies comprising the Dow Average will be higher than the 1949 payments of $12.60 per share even though earnings are likely to be moderately lower.

Past history shows that when the Dow Average is selling at 20 times or less its annual dividends, stocks have eventually turned out to be good values. Multiplying the present dividend total of $12.60 by 20 we get a figure of 252 for the Average. This checks out with our long-held view of "double the pre-war average." Hence, there seem to be honest reasons for eventually expecting prices to reach the 250 level.

However, we do not think the entire post-war adjustment is completed. We are expecting that a moderate business decline will set in this Spring which may bring unemployment up to the five million level. Under these circumstances and in view of the 25% rise in prices in recent months, we think it is best to be quite careful at the moment.

* * * * *

RIP VAN WINKLE II RETURNS TO WALL STREET

A bewildered Rip Van Winkle II returned to his Wall Street office this week after a twenty years' absence. Like his legendary ancestor of the Catskills, he had been presumed dead but actually had fallen into the same strange and prolonged sleep.

When our modern Rip awakened a few days ago, he headed back to Manhattan for the first time since he strolled off into the mountains on a beautiful spring day in 1949. He soon became even more befuddled than his forebear by how much everything had changed.

His first surprise was the way people looked and dressed. The young men with long, flowing locks of hair who crowded the streets — were they reenacting the resurrection? And why were so many bare-thighed office girls dressed for tennis in the heart of the city?

Suddenly hungry, Rip stopped in at a sandwich shop and ordered a quick hamburger and coffee. As he handed the cashier his customary 35 cents, he was startled to hear "Your check is $1.45". Next, though no one seemed to notice his shaggy appearance, he decided to get a haircut and shave. When the barber charged him $5 and asked for a tip, Rip was dumbfounded. The last day he was in town, he had paid only $1.50 for the same service.

He wondered if the financial community had undergone similar drastic changes. He recalled that before he fell asleep, nearly all his cronies at banks, mutual funds and brokerage houses were waiting for the big postwar depression. "Another 1929" was on everybody's mind. The main investment controversy was whether a "prudent man" should have as much as 25% of his portfolio in common stocks.

Rip remembered that his Wall Street buddies were chronically upset over the political trends. They could not understand why income taxes had not been reduced to prewar rates. But they said there was one natural law "not even the Democrats" could repeal and that was the law of supply and demand. They were positive that once the huge deferred needs created by the war were satisfied, "factories will be turning out so much stuff that you'll be able to buy all you want for half the price."

His friends were also convinced that the early postwar building boom was only a flash in the pan. They scoffed at all the veterans taking out 20-year mortgages at 3 1/2% to buy "cracker boxes." It would be much better for them to put their funds into savings accounts (at 1 1/2%) so they would have money when the housing market collapsed.

With all the coming economic adjustments, Rip's associates were limiting their new investments pretty much to bonds, which were selling to yield less than 3%. In fact, a lot of people claimed that the Victory 2 1/2's would never sell below "par."

Few of his investor friends were then interested in common stocks, which—as Rip recalled—were being appraised *at their lowest levels of the century*. General Motors and many other high-grade equities could be bought at dividend yields of 8–10%.

Rip remembered the amused contempt with which most portfolio managers looked upon the prices being paid by a few of their associates for "growth stocks"—a new-fangled idea that they did not understand. Why buy IBM or Minnesota Mining at a 3% yield, they asked, at a time when "good solid equities like Telephone give you almost 7%?"

As these memories rushed through his mind, Rip found himself in front of a familiar brokerage office. As he entered, he was appalled at the pandemonium inside—the deafening roar of voices, the constant jangle of telephones, the milling, carnival-like crowd. Could this be the same boardroom with its vast empty stillness—interrupted only by an occasional jiggle of the ticker—that he had visited, it seemed, only yesterday?

Glancing at the posted Averages, Rip could not believe his eyes. Ever since he had started out on the Street in the mid-1930's, the Dow had ranged between 100 and 200. On his last day of work in 1949, it was a lofty 176. What was this 900 figure? Had the Average been subjected to a "reverse split"?

Rip shouldered his way to the broad tape just in time to catch the latest bond quotes. One of his favorite issues was the bellwether Union Pacific 2 1/2s of 1991, which sold at 96 on that fateful day in 1949. Only 56? And Rip sensed that the 40-point drop must be only part of the real investment loss if the prices of hamburgers and haircuts were a measure of what had happened to the dollar's value.

Spying a life-long acquaintance at one of the desks, he started elbowing a path towards him. Old Wintergreen, Rip thought, still has that same knowing look about him. He sure never fell for all that "growth stock" malarkey. Better find out what's going on from him.

After the two friends exchanged greetings and Rip related the details of his misadventure, the conversation went something like this:

RIP:

> I can hardly believe the changes I've seen. What are you telling your customers to do these days?

WINTERGREEN:

> Well, as you know, Rip, I never buck the trend. The things to buy now are stocks with exciting futures–nursing home chains, highway franchisers, anti-pollution firms, computer services, oceanography.

RIP:

> I don't know what you are talking about, but I suppose these are the stocks that give the highest yields now. You were always keen on the big dividend-payers like Telephone and Big Steel.

WINTERGREEN:

> That idea is long dead. No one is interested in dividends any more. You do far better by going for capital growth. So you look for companies whose earnings are jumping 20%, 30%, even 50% a year.

RIP:

> I remember you once told me never to pay over 12 times earnings for *any* stock. I expect that a wise old bird like you is still picking them up for a song.

WINTERGREEN:

> Times have changed, Rip. You have to be aggressive today. People are paying 40, 60, even 100 times earnings but it's worth it to get into these dynamic new businesses.

RIP:

> You're confusing me. I thought you didn't believe in growth stocks.

WINTERGREEN:

> Well, I missed out on Eastman Kodak, Corning Glass and

Merck, but a few years ago I decided to catch up by buying tomorrow's growth stocks.

RIP:

But what about bonds? You used to say they would be the buy of a lifetime if yields got up over 3%.

WINTERGREEN:

You can pick up Treasuries at 6 1/2% and corporates at 7 1/2%. In fact, Transcontinental Gas Pipe Line is just bringing out a new debenture to yield well over 8%. But nobody wants bonds with inflation eating up income and principal at 4–5% a year.

RIP:

Then you've changed your mind about bonds, too?

WINTERGREEN:

Rip, you'd better get back to your office and let the boys over there bring you up to date.

Thoroughly flabbergasted by Wintergreen's words, Rip made his way to his firm's headquarters. He found they had been moved to the top floor of a new glass-like skyscraper. Someone showed him how to run the automatic elevator. As he entered the offices, he marvelled at the plush carpeting, the plant arrangements, the oil paintings—and the movie starlet at the reception desk. To his relief, he found that one of his old partners was still active.

As his partner's secretary guided him down the office corridor, almost all the men he noticed—even those in private offices with titles on the door—seemed to be in their 20's or early 30's. He recalled that back in the late 1940's, most of the people in the business were in their 50's and 60's, and almost no one was under 40.

His old associate was, of course, overjoyed to see him. After the strange tale was told, he was asked about his most immediate needs. "The first thing I want," Rip said, "is a summary-type report showing how the major economic and investment benchmarks have changed while I've been gone."

Within a couple of hours, he received a memorandum. As he picked it up, he thought if he could just find one basic aspect of the business which was still the same as he had known it, he might still be able to reorient himself.

Office Memo to Rip Van Winkle II

	March 1949	March 1969	% Change
Economic Yardsticks			
Population (mil.)	149	202	+ 36%
Gross National Product (bil.)	$259	$903	+248
Industrial Output (index)	66	170	+157
Value of the Dollar	$1.00	$0.67	− 33
Dow-Jones Industrial Average			
Price	176	917	+420
Earnings	$ 23	$ 60	+160
Dividends	$ 12	$ 31	+160
Investment Appraisals			
Common Stocks			
Price-Earnings Ratios*	8x	15x	+ 90
Dividend Yields*	6.8%	3.4%	− 50
Bond Yields			
Treasury Bills	1.00%	5.95%	+495
Long-Term Treasuries	2.40%	6.25%	+160
Single-A Corporates	2.90%	7.05%	+140
High-Grade Municipals	2.20%	5.35%	+140

*On Dow-Jones Industrials

As he studied the memo item by item, Rip was astonished at the enormous growth of the economy during his absence. The "consensus" of the late 1940's had certainly been dead wrong about the future. And the value of the dollar, far from increasing, had shrunk by a third.

What surprised him the most, however, was the complete turnabout of investment appraisals. He noted that while stocks yielded two-and-a-half times as much as bonds in 1949, bonds now yield over twice as much as stocks.

Even more amazing was how effective common stocks had been as investment during the 20-year span. The Dow Average had quintupled. True, half its advance was due to the increase in its price-earnings ratio. But the fact that its earnings and dividends had both risen by 160% was particularly impressive.

Rip also noted that the Dow was currently being appraised at 15 times earnings. This was in marked contrast to the fantastic multiples on "tomorrow's growth stocks" his friend Wintergreen thought were so attractive. Here at last was one thing that had not really changed much at all.

IS GROWTH STOCK INVESTING EFFECTIVE? SOME GUIDES TO SUCCESSFUL LIFETIME INVESTING

David L. Babson
Thomas E. Babson

David Babson and Thomas Babson wrote about growth stock investing in their 1959 book, *Investing for a Successful Future*. They focused on five key characteristics: (1) Industry sales growth is faster than the economy's; (2) a company's ability to translate increases in sales into a reasonably comparable rise in profits per share; (3) research-minded management; (4) low direct labor costs; and (5) consistently high margins. They then examined whether growth stock investing was effective. Finally, the brothers Babson provided a wise set of guidelines for lifetime investing.

IS GROWTH STOCK INVESTING EFFECTIVE?

Growth vs. Income Portfolios

There are of course no standard indexes of stocks by types as defined herein (growth, income, cyclical). Accordingly in September, 1951, the

---

authors drew up two sample portfolios that presupposed investment of $1,000 in each of ten growth stocks and an equal amount in each of ten income stocks at the mean between their high and low market prices for the year 1940.[1] Care was taken to select issues that in that year would have met the quality standards and suitability tests outlined [earlier in this book]. . . . The issues selected were:

Growth Portfolio	Income Portfolio
Abbott Laboratories	American Chicle
Celanese Corporation	American Telephone
Corning Glass Works	American Tobacco
Dow Chemical	Beneficial Finance
Eastman Kodak	Consolidated Edison
Gulf Oil	Corn Products Refining
Int'l Business Machines	General American Transport.
Minnesota Mining & Mfg.	General Foods
Standard Oil (New Jersey)	International Shoe
Union Carbide	Woolworth, F. W.

The figures on market values, dividends, income and yields of these two sample portfolios have been brought up to date from time to time. But as their purpose has been to serve as a continuous case study, no substitutions have been made in the companies since the lists were first compiled. At that time the figures (for the decade 1940–1950) stood as given in Table 58.

TABLE 58
Comparative Performance, Growth vs. Income Portfolios, 1940–1950

Performance Factors	Growth Portfolio	Income Portfolio
Value based on mean 1950 prices	$26,739	$11,445
Value based on mean 1940 prices	10,000	10,000
Gain in market value 1940–50	$16,739	$ 1,445
Dividend income mid-1940 to mid-1950	6,218	5,650
Gain in value plus dividends (decade)	$22,957	$ 7,095

Source: "How to Build a Retirement Fund," David L. Babson & Company, Inc., Boston, 1952.

The question arises as to whether the two portfolios continued to behave after 1950 in keeping with their respective characteristics. Table 59 indicates the changes from 1950 to 1956.

It will be seen that the differences in the nature of the two portfolios became even more evident on all counts in the period after their selection than in that preceding.

Performances of Some Individual Stocks

Out of the most carefully chosen list of stocks, one cannot expect all to do equally well over a long period of time. For example, between 1950 and 1956 the earnings and dividends of Celanese Corporation declined sharply and those of Abbott Laboratories made relatively little progress. In the income portfolio, both Beneficial Finance and General American Transportation registered above-average performance in contrast to the other income-type companies.

The lesson here is that in any intelligently compiled portfolio there will be wide differences in individual company performance over the years. In a list selected for income it is likely that about a fifth will do poorly, another fifth will turn in better-than-anticipated records and the balance will show about average results. In a portfolio carefully picked for growth the pattern may be expected to work out about as follows: 20 per cent will be disappointing, 40 per cent average, 20 per cent very good, and the remaining 20 per cent extraordinary.

The figures in Table 60, covering the two test portfolios for the

TABLE 59
Comparative Performance, Growth vs. Income Portfolios, 1950–1956

Performance Factors	Growth Portfolio	Income Portfolio
Value based on mean 1956 prices	$84,993	$17,760
Value based on mean 1945 prices	26,739	11,445
Gain in market value 1950–56	$58,254	$ 6,315
Dividend income mid-1950 to mid-1956	8,503	4,609
Gain in value plus dividends (6 years)	$66,757	$10,924

Source: Compiled by David L. Babson & Company, Inc.,

TABLE 60
Comparative Performance, Growth vs. Income Portfolios,
1940, 1950, and 1956

Performance Factors	1940		1950		1956	
	Growth	Income	Growth	Income	Growth	Income
Market Value (in dollars)	10,000	10,000	26,739	11,445	84,993	17,760
Annual Rate of income (in dollars)	390	618	1,199	663	1,789	893
Cumulative income (in dollars)	195	309	6,218	5,650	14,721	10,259
Yields at market (per cent)	3.9	6.2	4.5	5.8	2.1	5.0
Yields at 1940 cost (per cent)	3.9	6.2	12.0	6.6	17.9	8.9

entire 16-year period, show in detail how the growth list has answered the purposes for which it was selected.

Yields and Capital Gains

A surprisingly common fallacy of reasoning among many individuals subject to high personal tax rates is that they should seek as high a current yield as possible to offset the effect of taxes. A comparison of the results in the foregoing table will show that just the reverse is true.

The yields on the growth stocks in 1940 ranged between 1.9 per cent and 4.6 per cent. Thus none of these stocks would have appeared attractive to one who insisted on a yield of 5 per cent or more. The returns on the income stocks at the start of the period varied between 4.8 per cent and 9.2 per cent, and so all would have been acceptable for an average yield of about 5 per cent.

Annual dividends in 1940 from the growth portfolio would have been $390 versus $618 from the income list, a difference of $228 in favor of the latter. The question is: If a person had had his choice of these two lists of stocks in 1940, which one would have given him the better results over the 16 years in terms of both dividends and capital growth?

The record shows that $10,000 invested in the income list produced a total of $10,259 in dividends from 1940 to 1956, inclusive. The $10,000 invested in the growth stocks produced a 16-year income of $14,721, or $4,462 more. In the same period of years, higher market prices added $7,760 to the value of the income list, but they added $74,993 to the original $10,000 value of the growth portfolio. The $10,000 income account yielded a total of $18,019 in dividends and capital gains in the 16 years, while the growth portfolio produced combined dividends and capital gains of $89,714.

The most interesting point of all is that in the year 1956 the growth list was producing dividend income at the annual rate of $1,789, whereas the income portfolio was producing only $893. Thus, for an income sacrifice of $228 per year in 1940 over what he could have obtained from the income list, the investor who was willing to forego high current yield in favor of deferred income actually received more dividend dollars in the 16 years and ended with *twice* as much annual income on his initial investment.

Note also the after-tax consequences: the 50 per cent top-tax-bracket investor would have lost only $114 by sacrificing $228 dividends in the first year (1940), but in the final year (1956), by which time he might have retired and dropped to a much lower tax bracket, he would have received $896 more dividends from the growth than from the income list.

The growth portfolio may not outpace the income group by as wide a margin over the same number of ensuing years as in the period covered by our test. But the basic factors that account for the dissimilarity remain, i.e., the differences in the nature of the industries and the characteristics of the companies in the two lists. Therefore the results over the years ahead, although they may differ in degree, should continue to show the same general pattern.

Some General Principles

Based on the evidence presented in earlier chapters and illustrated by the above factual example, it appears fair to draw four conclusions:

1. Because of the great increase in taxes and living costs since prewar days, the methods of building capital that were sound up to the mid-1930's are now obsolete.

2. Investments for long-term purposes in the current era must meet three tests: a. capacity to furnish "deferred income;" b. potential for capital growth; and c. provision for relative safety of principal.

3. Among the various forms of investment reviewed, these qualifications are best met by the common stocks of strong, progressive companies in the fastest-growing industries.

4. The man who understands the long-term advantages of investing in such stocks has a far better chance of success in providing for his financial independence than the one who continues to rely largely on dollar savings (life insurance, bank accounts, government bonds) or the one who thinks investment success lies in trying to anticipate the short-term trend of stock prices.

* * * * *

SOME GUIDES TO SUCCESSFUL LIFETIME INVESTING

The investor who has been most successful over the years, in the observation of the authors, is one who has followed closely these principles and courses of action:

1. He has had a definite plan and program and has adhered to it faithfully.

2. He has not tried to forecast stock prices nor allowed himself to be influenced by those who think they can do so.

3. He has understood the differences in the characteristics of companies and has invested only in those suited to his long-term objectives.

4. He has bought only those stocks which, at the time of purchase, he could see no reason for ever wanting to sell.

5. He has diversified his holdings among various industries, not by following any mechanical formula but by analytical selection of those companies and fields of activity most likely to spearhead the long-range expansion of the American economy. That is, he has looked upon diversification not merely as a device for spreading risk but as a means of broadening opportunity for the progress of his investments. And he has avoided scattering his holdings among more companies than he could conscientiously follow.

6. Finally, and perhaps the most important of all, he has faced uncertainties in the business or market outlook with equanimity, not allowing himself to be distracted from his prescribed course by ominous predictions or tempting speculations.

Invest According To Plan

Having a sound long-range plan, and holding to it, is just as essential to building a list of suitable investments as it is to constructing a good house or winning a military campaign. Yet only a small percentage of people ever draw up a basic financial plan and follow it consistently over the years, through the recurrent periods of optimism and pessimism.

Among the thousands of portfolios that have been submitted to the authors for preliminary examination, it has been the exception to find an account that has been built according to a planned program based on long-term objectives. All too many investors are found to own mere "collections of securities" bought on tips, hearsay advice or casual comments of friends. And those few who have had some semblance of a plan more often than not have been following the financial thinking of a past era.

Lack of planning is particularly evident with respect to the types and quality of common stocks held. In many cases investors with substantial earned income, and therefore subject to very high personal tax rates, are found to own high-yielding income stocks. This not only aggravates their tax problems but involves assuming just as much risk as is inherent in growth stocks without enjoying the benefit of the growth factor. Many who rely heavily on their accumulated capital for income hold shares in new, unseasoned or highly cyclical companies, where dividends are uncertain or even absent. A large number of lists consist of illogical mixtures of securities of all kinds, scattered at random among industries having prospects for the future that are good, bad and indifferent.

Another indication of lack of planning is the large amounts of uninvested cash frequently accumulated by investors who cannot decide whether or when it is a good time to buy. Instead of continuing to invest regularly in the kind of stocks they should own for long-term progress, they hold off committing new cash in the speculative hope that tomorrow's buying opportunities will be better than those of today. By failing to keep such capital employed where it *can* grow, they handicap their long-range investment results.

Many retired persons and widows today are able to keep up their living standards because they, or others in their families, had the foresight to invest savings in sound common stocks and hold them through many years, ignoring price fluctuations and market "forecasts." However, for every investor who builds soundly in this way, there are literally hundreds who pursue the futile method of trying to buy low, sell high, and buy back lower.

A broad study of case histories clearly reveals the superior results obtained by the first of these two methods—that of acquiring part ownership in progressive companies with the intent of profiting from the long-range contributions to the growth of the American economy, rather than trading stock certificates in the hope of outwitting thousands of others engaged in the same game.

The vital fact to be borne in mind is that building up one's assets is, if not a lifetime project, one that usually spans a period of many years. If the stocks selected are those of strong companies expanding internally, history shows that the rewards from their development of new products, services and processes will be surprisingly large in the end.

New cash should be added to investment accounts as faithfully and regularly as life insurance premiums are paid, irrespective of the investor's own or someone else's guess as to the outlook for stock prices. Investors who have retired and are dependent on their portfolios for income should just as studiously avoid trying to anticipate changes in stock prices.

If new cash is regularly added to a fund, and if properly qualified stocks are purchased, the investor will have secured his combined commitments at fair *average* prices. What these securities may do pricewise in a week or a month or even over the next several years after their purchase is relatively unimportant. The true test of the soundness of selections will be how much their market values and their dividends have increased by the end of 10 or 20 years.

Avoid Trying To "Buy Low, Sell High"

Why is it that so many investors are interested in guesses about the future trend of stock prices—that they will pay attention to a prediction made by almost any self-labeled "authority" of whose record they know nothing? Several plausible reasons for this great preoccupation with forecasting come to mind.

One is that public interest in the economic cycle, generated by the 1929 experience, has led to the general impression that the trends of industrial activity and stock prices move closely together.

Another is that newspapers and mail-order advertisements with which some investment advisory firms continually bombard the public are so worded as to lead to the conclusion that calling the turn is necessary to investment success.

A third is that many investors seem to be completely unaware of the existence of any method of building an investment account other than by trying to buy low, sell high, buy back lower.

Stock Prices and Business Cycles
The stock market crash of 1929, perhaps more than any other one factor, is responsible for the almost universal concern of investors with the question, "What is the market going to do?" Following that event, economists and public commissions became active in investigating the forces that had brought about the 1929 and previous violent cycles of boom and panic.

In the course of these investigations, the cycle idea received wide publicity, and interest in it has persisted. An interesting study of cycles[2] was published in 1947 in which the authors detected different rhythms for various phases of the economy. Each of these rhythms was represented as having its own peculiar wave length, and it was indicated that all seemed to be headed for lows at about the same time in the 1951–1952 period, a coincidence that could occur mathematically only once in over 2,000 years.

That there must have been other not-yet-understood forces at work (a possibility that the authors frankly acknowledged) is made clear by observing what actually took place. The early 1950's completely failed to fulfill this disturbing prospect. Instead, new all-time high records were established for industrial production, national income, personal disposable income, real estate and building activity, corporate earnings and dividend payments.

The availability of more accurate and comprehensive statistics, and their more intelligent use, are improving the ability of analysts to look ahead. But those with good memories will agree with Dr. Geoffrey Moore[3] who, after reviewing the postwar predictions of many forecasting agencies both public and private, concluded that the record was "a dismal one."

While the business cycle itself is difficult enough to predict accurately, the popular idea that stock prices always move in close unison with the trend of industrial activity is not borne out by the record. In fact, during much of the time from 1939 to 1954 business activity and stock prices were moving in opposite directions.

In the first postwar decade there were a number of opportunities to buy the best stocks *at the lowest prices in relation to earnings and dividends in history*. Yet it is truly appalling how many investors missed their chances to acquire sound issues at those unprecedented levels because they were alarmed by the barrage of forecasts of "inevitable crashes" or otherwise preoccupied with their own or others' attempts to predict the immediate future of stock prices or business trends.

What About Market Forecasts?

As an example of the literature distributed by forecasters, consider the following "warning" from a broadside issued in 1954 when stocks were selling around 330 on the Dow-Jones Industrial Average:

> Will this major shake-up in America's wealth wipe out your savings and cripple your future? All the sweet talk from now to kingdom come can't save the shirts that are certain to be lost, Don't lose yours by sitting back and saying, "We'll never have another 1929."

Disturbing headline? But let's look back and see what this same agency said on previous occasions. Here are a few headlines and excerpts, together with the dates of the circulars, followed in each case by a record of the level of the Dow-Jones Average at that time (the Average, incidentally, stood at 450 early in 1957):

How to survive the coming breakdown in all markets
May, 1953—Dow Average 270–280

I look for a bust in common stocks, a decline that will be far more destructive than that of the 1929 crash.
November, 1952—Dow Average 270–283

Dear Reader: Don't fall for it—when they tell you, "Buy now! Prices are going higher!" Because prices are headed for one of the worst plunges you've ever seen!
December, 1951—Dow Average 262–269

Are you just "sitting tight" hoping against hope that this is merely a temporary slump? 1929 may be just around the corner.
October–November, 1949 — Dow Average 180–190

By implication, much of the advertising of the forecasting firms gives people who are not in a position to know the record of such agencies the impression that they have been successful in the past with their predictions. The authors of this book have not followed the records of all investment advisory or brokerage firms that base their policies on attempts to forecast the stock market, but they are familiar with those of many. *They know of no firm or individual investor who has been successful in predicting the market even as much as 50 per cent of the time.*

There is an even greater disservice to the investing public than the more obvious hocus-pocus put forth in this price guessing. It leads uninformed investors into believing that the one prerequisite of investment success is anticipating market movements. It encourages them to try to do what experience shows cannot be done, rather than to follow sound basic principles that have proved to be extremely effective over the years.

The case against the practice of basing investment decisions on the cycle theory has been well stated by Lucien Hooper, widely-known financial commentator, in the following words:

> Too much investment literature and investor thought is devoted to a cyclical approach toward common stocks. The existence of a bull or bear market never can be established beyond reasonable doubt until the trend is far progressed. Few people ever buy near the bottom or sell near the top; and the vast majority who try to do it obtain poorer net results than those realized by not trying too hard. . . .
>
> If a man owns a farm, store, apartment house, office building or a small manufacturing business, he seldom thinks whether what he holds is worth more today or less tomorrow but regards it in terms of earning power, growth or longer range value. If he owns shares in General Motors or General Electric, less risky and more substantial than the type of property just mentioned, he sees himself richer or poorer. The very marketability of a publicly owned stock, while a great asset, tends to make the owner overstress price.[4]

In addition to promoting the beat-the-stock-market idea, many agencies whose compensation depends on the volume of stock trading, or on sustaining interest in bulletin subscriptions, are constantly encouraging shareholders to speculate by trading from one stock to another. A short time ago, in a newspaper item, the partner of a large brokerage firm was reported to have said that an average holding period of 6 to 18 months (with a minimum of diversification) paid the greatest net return to one who was looking for above-average investment results.

If a large number of stockholders sell all of their securities every few months and buy others, a mountain of decisions must be made over the years. Most investors do not have the time, information or inclination to arrive at frequent buy-sell conclusions for themselves. And who that is truly endowed with the ability to make these ever recurring decisions correctly (if any such person exists) would need to earn his living by making them for other people or working for concerns who make them for others?

Those with the ability to do what these firms imply they can do could amass a fortune for themselves in short order. As an illustration of how quickly the correct anticipation of price swings can roll up capital, the authors made a study of the price changes in United States Steel, a typical leading industrial stock, over a period of 30 years.

If the shares were bought at the low of each year and sold at the high, beginning with $10,000 in 1927, the value would have built up to more than $1 million at the end of the first 10 years, to $56 million after 20 years and to over $1.3 billion at the end of 1956. Studies of other leading stocks would reveal similar results. It is obvious from this illustration that those with the rare talent to make these buy-sell decisions correctly over and over again would soon become multimillionaires and certainly would hardly want to spend their lifetimes advising others.

It is the author's observation, based on years close association with both new and experienced investors in all walks of life, that the majority are not interested in constant buying and selling or exposing themselves to the bookkeeping chores and distractions of mind that it involves. For inducing investors to believe that constant turnover of securities is the road to investment success, a large share of the blame must be attributed to the promotional bombardment to which they are continuously exposed.

The common stock investor should constantly bear in mind that while price is often affected by unpredictable emotional factors, value tends to fluctuate much less. Thus a stock may well sell at $50 today and drop to $40 or rise to $60 in a few weeks or months, with no essential change in asset value per share, earnings trend or fundamental position of the company. It has been said with some semblance of truth that as much as 25 per cent of the market price of the stock at any given time is accounted for by emotions rather than facts.

Of course securities should always be subjected to periodic reexamination. But anyone following the thesis that common stocks of acknowledged quality are intended primarily to be bought and sold like commodities exposes himself to unnecessary financial loss, fruitless buying and selling and needless worry.

But if one cannot hope to capture the secret of successful market forecasting, by what principles should he be guided in making his investment decisions?   There are two that have been proved to be especially sound in the past.

Buy for the Future

The first is to consider oneself a part owner of the companies whose stocks he has carefully selected, to plan to retain such ownership as long as he is satisfied they will progress at or above the rate of industry as a whole and to place his faith in the continuation of this country's dynamic growth, decade to decade.

Throughout its history the American economy has been healthy and expanding a much greater percentage of the time than it has been treading water or retreating. And each period of advance has carried far above the previous high point. This is the fundamental reason for having faith in the future progress of successful companies.

An exhaustive study[5] of the prices and dividends of all industrial common stocks listed on the New York Stock Exchange covering the period from 1871 to 1939 showed an average return of 8.1 per cent per year—5.3 per cent in dividends and 2.8 per cent in annual growth. From 1939 to 1956 the return averaged better than 12 per cent annually based on the Dow-Jones Industrial Average,[6] making an average of 9 per cent for the entire 86 years.

This period 1871–1956 has seen many different sets of conditions. There have been both liberal and conservative political administrations; nine periods of prosperity and depression; four major wars; cycles of rising and falling commodity prices; 43 years of no income taxes; 26 of low and 17 of high tax rates; decades of 3 per cent bond yields and decades of 6 per cent bond yields. But through this period of more than

80 years, the average return on industrial common stocks, capital growth and dividends combined, has been 9 per cent per annum.

It has not been necessary to engage in the hazardous and futile practice of stock-market forecasting to participate in this growth—only to buy and hold the shares of carefully selected companies.

Choosing the Right Stocks

The second of the two principles that past experience shows to be sound is that one should invest his money in a given company *not* because he thinks stock prices are going up but because he has faith in the future of the products manufactured or the services performed, the research done and the ability of the management of that specific company as compared with others.

The point is that if one is thorough in his analysis he has much *better* than a 50-50 chance of success in making the correct selection of industries and companies. By the law of averages, he should have a 50-50 chance of guessing the immediate trend of stock prices correctly, but experience shows that over the years the mistakes invariably outnumber the "right" decisions.

Another fact worth observing is that an investor does not buy an "average." He invests in a group of individual companies with distinct characteristics. His list will therefore not behave exactly the same pricewise as the various market indexes. The prices of the shares of the thousands of companies available for public ownership do not all go up or down precisely at the same time nor in the same degree. Differences in price behavior on a day-to-day basis are a function of supply of and demand for individual issues (often prompted by current news items). Long-term price trends, however, express the individual characteristics of the companies. . . .

While a well-chosen list of growth stocks will vary in market value in sympathy with the recurring periods of broad investment optimism or pessimism, over a period of years it should outperform the all-stock price average or any average based upon a group of stocks of mixed type and quality. . . .

Even with the most careful analysis prior to purchase, the investor is likely to find that some of his companies fail to make the progress anticipated. An occasional thorough analytical reappraisal of holding is therefore desirable. But before replacing a stock it will be wise for him to make sure the company's lack of advancement actually stems from a change in the fundamental factors that made it attractive in the first place, and not from obstacles that may prove to be temporary.

It is not to be expected that any group of companies—even those in the same industry—will display uniform progress in earnings or market value in any given period of time. Hence if one has been extremely thorough in his prepurchase appraisal, he should be all the more certain of his premises before making a replacement.

If one cannot safely put all his carefully selected stocks away and completely forget them, it is natural to inquire under what circumstances an occasional replacement should be made. We have several times emphasized that the characteristics of companies and industries do not change very much or very often. In instances where such changes do occur (and they are usually gradual) action may be in order.

For example, a company may, for some fundamental reason, fail to continue the progress that heretofore qualified its stock as a growth investment. As a case in point, consider F. W. Woolworth, which began with a new merchandising idea at the turn of the century. In its early years stockholders were rewarded with sharply rising earnings and dividends. But up to the time of this writing the price of the stock has never since 1929 even approached its high of that year. Earnings and dividends per share in 1956 were virtually unchanged from 25 years earlier.

The company originated the concept of the 5- and 10-cent store. Like any profitable innovation not capable of effective protection, it soon began to be widely imitated. Management, although highly able, came up with nothing radically new to replace it. (There were also other factors too involved to be detailed here). Woolworth's stock now fits the needs only of those investors who have retired or who for other reasons require a generous yield and steady return rather than long-range growth of capital and income.

Companies that are doing exceptionally well with one or a limited line of products or services may be vulnerable to such developments as patent expiration or intensified competition. There should be less reason for any long-term concern about those companies that combine the creative power of intensive research with the stabilizing advantage of a broad line of products.

Speculation Can Be Disastrous

On the surface, building up and holding a sound, well-planned portfolio of common stocks, each one of which fits the investor's basic plan and objectives, seems to be an easy assignment. In actual practice it is not. It requires great self-discipline to stick rigidly to the program originally laid down, and it calls for a more cold-blooded, unemotional attitude toward their capital than many people possess.

The best guarantee against being diverted from one's long-range investment plan is to buy only stocks he wants to keep. If this policy if faithfully followed, it automatically eliminates from consideration the risky "two-decision" stocks, i.e., those requiring a correct decision on *when to buy* and another correct decision on *when to sell*. It averts the danger of becoming involved with stocks of companies that friends or tipster services recommend be bought for a "quick turn" based on "inside information," or an anticipated temporary development, or the assumption that they are "behind the market" or other superficial reasons.

If the investor has successful results with a few such speculations, he soon becomes involved in further ventures. Then, little by little, he begins to forget his long-term program and to devote more of his attention to two-decision stocks. This process usually takes place in a period of rising public interest in speculation. As time goes on, instead of keeping his capital largely invested in a planned portfolio of shares of success-ful corporations in the most progressive industries, he accumulates an illogical collection of shares of unsuccessful companies that he thinks may become more successful, or marginal corporations in highly com-petitive industries or of new, unseasoned firms with inadequate finances but reputed to have "tremendous potential."

Then one day the investment background changes radically. Public interest in stocks evaporates. Only the professional investors (insurance companies, mutual funds, trust companies, and investment counselors) with a constant flow of new cash under their direction continue to buy stocks. But their selections are confined almost entirely to the types that are bought to keep.

Instead of profits on his accumulation of "special situations," the investor now shows book losses. He decides to hold for a rally in their prices. But the quotations drift lower and lower because there is no interest in this type of stock under the changed investment background. (Early in 1954, 80 per cent of all stocks listed on the New York Stock Exchange were still selling below their highs of the speculative 1946 market, whereas the Dow-Jones Industrial Average, consisting principally of better-grade stocks, had by then doubled its 1946 cyclical high.)   After a long period during which his speculations are quoted at prices far below his cost, the investor finally gives up hope and sells his list to establish a tax loss.

In a general way this has been the fate of millions of investors at one time or another over the years. Many learn from their bitter experience. But others never do; they keep right on trying to beat the market. Meanwhile, those who have held fast to the policy of buying only stocks they wanted to keep have had effective results with a minimum of risk and concern.

Where to Look for Sound Advice

It would be hard to find another field outside that of investing (unless it be health!) in which there is a broader range of opinion and prejudice, or more loose thinking and free advice, or more letters, bulletins and services—all too often feeding upon the human emotions of fear and greed. Some bulletin editors seem to adopt a deliberate policy of perennial optimism, a few of constant pessimism and alarm. One can only conclude that they do this in the belief that it will promote subscriptions. Much of this as yet is beyond the arm of the law or inadequately controlled.

Despite the fact that the field of investment is probably the most strictly regulated of all activities, the lay investor is faced with a real problem in trying to separate the wheat from the chaff. His best defense is a constant attitude of skepticism toward anything that savors of "something-for-nothing-quick" or prophesies either doom or the millennium; and not to send his dollars for lists of "10 stocks to switch" or "5 stocks to buy now."

Of all the qualifications for success in equity investing none is so important as a firm mind. The person who investigates thoroughly and intelligently before he buys a stock does not allow himself to be swayed hither and yon by every breeze and, having satisified himself as to the soundness and progressiveness of the companies of which he has become part owner, remains calm in periods of great uncertainty—he is the one likely to enjoy the most favorable lifetime results.

To know where to turn for the mass of information needed to make sound investment decisions, to develop talents for its analysis and especially to find the necessary time—these are the real problems of the investor who wishes to follow such a plan.

In his autobiography,[7] Bernard M. Baruch, pointing out that "the value of an investment can never be counted upon as absolute and unchanging," advises persons who cannot give full time to a study of securities "to seek out some trusted investment counselor," and adds: "The emergence of this new profession of disinterested investment analysts, who have no allegiance or alliances and whose only job is to judge a security on its merits, is one of the more constructive and healthy developments of the last half century." Since the emergence of professional investment counsel, to which Mr. Baruch alludes, is a development of relatively recent years, many are not aware of its availability and nature.

The Investment Advisors Act[8] provides for registration of persons or firms chiefly engaged in offering investment advice. It prohibits use of the designation "investment counsel" to describe the business of any such person (or firm) unless he is primarily engaged in rendering investment supervisory services. These services are defined as "the giving of continuous advice as to the investment of funds on the basis of the individual needs of each client."[9]

Mr. Baruch's reference to "this new profession of *disinterested* investment analysts" emphasizes its devotion to personal and continuous supervision of investments on the basis of the individual needs of each client rather than to activities such as actual purchase and sale of securities or issuing periodic bulletins of advice that are sent to all subscribers alike. Investment counsel firms receive compensation in the form of annual retainer fees which are in no way related to the number of transactions or degree of activity in their clients' accounts.

The services of investment counsel are particularly suited to the needs of professional men and business executives who do not have sufficient time for managing their own investments and for other owners of portfolios of moderate to substantial size who feel that their experience or knowledge of securities is inadequate.

The investor who is just beginning to accumulate a portfolio, or whose holdings are otherwise limited, has a large number of mutual funds from which he may choose if he feels incapable of supervising properly his own portfolio. Purchasers of mutual shares in effect pool their funds. These funds are then invested in a joint portfolio of securities by the sponsoring company under the direction of investment managers.

* * * * *

FOOTNOTES

1. "How to Build a Retirement Fund," David L. Babson & Company, Inc., Boston, 1952.
2. Edward R. Dewey and Edwin F. Dakin, *Cycles—The Science of Prediction*, New York: Henry Holt & Co., 1947.
3. Of the National Bureau of Economic Research, at a symposium on forecasting held in 1952.
4. Lucien O. Hooper, "Fallacy of Cyclical Approach," *Trusts and Estates*, July 1953, p. 500.
5. Cowles Commission for Research in Economics: Common Stock Indexes, 1939.
6. Computed by the authors.
7. Bernard M. Baruch, *My Own Story*. New York: Henry Holt & Co., 1957, p. 261.
8. House Report No. 768, 76th Congress, 34th Session, Chapter 686, H. R. 10065.
9. *Ibid.*, Section 202a (13), 203 and 208C.

GROWTH COMPANIES VS. GROWTH STOCKS

Peter L. Bernstein

Peter Bernstein has contributed an impressive share of the accumulated wisdom in investment management. A generation ago, he was teaching investors how to separate growth *companies* from growth *stocks*—a distinction we now know to be crucial in separating the leaders from the followers.

Growth companies have received so much attention in recent years that the term threatens to become our leading economic cliché. Whether it is management leadership, national importance, or simply prudent investment that one seeks to find, the method is always the same: look to the growth company.

But what is a growth company? Is it a company characterized by unusual technological activity and innovation? Is it merely a company whose sales and earnings have risen more rapidly than most? And what is a growth stock? Are all securities of "growth companies" *ipso facto* growth stocks?

The questions are deceptively simple—but tremendously important. If the phrase "growth company" is to blanket every company which does research or is doing more business this year than it did five or ten years ago, the term will be so broad as to be utterly useless. Only if we can pin it down to a practical, workable definition can we hope to distinguish it in a useful way from the concept of "growth stock."

The object of this article is not only to try to provide answers to these questions but also to demonstrate two rather heretical—but, I believe, constructive—points of view: (1) that growth companies constitute a very small and select rather than a broad and important roster of corporate enterprises; and (2) that growth stocks are a happy or haphazard category of investments which, curiously enough, have little or nothing to do with growth companies.

A STEP FORWARD

By getting away from our present muddled belief that growth companies and growth stocks are identical, we can take a long step toward a clearer understanding of the characteristics that set the creative, imaginative management groups in industry apart from other managements. By what signs shall we know them? We have often tended, it seems to me, to confuse leaders and followers. We have been inclined to use the label of "pioneer" indiscriminately, putting it on many a management that merely responds or reacts to its environment as well as on the true "growth company" that actually goes out and shapes economic trends and business conditions.

Better criteria for distinguishing between the two types of companies—and I am thinking here not only of qualitative standards but also of statistical measures of company performance—should be of practical interest to many business leaders, who are by and large a self-critical group of men, proud of the contribution which they make through their companies to the economy, and always eager to draw any valid comparisons between their firms and competitors.

Better criteria should also be of interest to the investor who seeks some way of comparing publicly owned corporations on the basis of the dynamism, the imagination, and the trail-blazing potentials of their managements—qualities which, needless to say, are significant in the investment picture.

It should be emphasized, however, that stocks of some companies which do not meet the criteria of growth used here may appreciate in value just as much as stocks of companies which do, and the stocks of some companies which do fulfill the criteria may turn out to do less well.

There are many accidental factors that can influence the results, not the least of which is concerted misjudgment by investors. But the point is that, by and large and over a period of time, the factors of true growth, being more fundamental, are more likely to be a reliable guide for the future than are past increases in market price or current evaluation by the market—or, at least, than either of these without the addition of the particular growth concept set forth here.

Later in this article I shall outline a new statistical method of analysis which demonstrates the soundness of this proposition and implements it for action.

TRUE GROWTH

Economic development or growth occurs in three different processes: in the increase of population, in the accumulation of capital, and in the technological progress which enables us to produce more things, better things, different things, or the same things more cheaply.

Each of these growth processes affects a business differently. As a businessman, the individual executive or owner can have no direct influence on the first of these three factors; his business may be affected *by* it, but he cannot have any effect *on* it. Not so with the other possibilities for growth, however; these are internally generated by business firms on their own initiative. This point is basic to the whole matter: *true growth is organic and comes from within.*

Since this is the crux of the argument, perhaps it will be helpful to use a homely metaphor to make it clear:

A man wears a larger suit of clothes than a boy, and a boy's clothes are larger than a baby's. Obviously, however, the increase in the size of the clothing is not growth but only a symptom or result of growth. The independent, dynamic force is the development of the child into the boy and then into the man. This is internally generated and is an active, not a passive, process.

Characteristics Illustrated

A good way to pinpoint the distinguishing characteristics of a growth company is to look at some cases which show what a growth company is *not*. Bear in mind that the crucial question is whether the firm's expansion is the result of internally determined conditions or simply a response to external events over which it has no control.

- A company which expands by acquiring other outfits is not a growth company. The acquisitions, once absorbed, may so change its character that it later becomes a growth company, but the process of expansion by acquisition *as such* is not growth in our terms here.
- Firms whose business increases simply because they serve growing markets are not growth companies, for they are not causing the market to grow but are only responding passively to outside events. Of course we must also resist being dazzled by an impressive earnings progression resulting largely from a company's ability to raise its prices in a sellers' market faster than its costs go up.

For example, it is fashionable to consider the oil companies in the growth class. Certainly their sales and earnings have expanded impressively. However, the growth in their operations has resulted primarily from a rising demand for oil which the oil companies themselves have capitalized on but did very little to create. Without the rising automobile population, the high volume of construction (which created the demand for space heating), and the growth of other industries, (like electric power) which use oil for fuel, there would have been very much less expansion in the oil industry.

- Most of the paper companies should probably be excluded from the growth company group, although they usually are included. The lines of demarcation are admittedly a little fuzzy here, for some of these companies have developed new products or found new uses for paper which did not exist in the past. Essentially, however, they have benefited from the burgeoning demand for paper for packaging, for newspapers and magazines, for paper towels, tissues, napkins, and so forth. This rising demand was a function of high industrial production, higher incomes, and increased population; the paper companies took advantage of these developments but had little to do with causing them to come about.
- Some observers have even gone so far as to call the steel industry a growth industry in recent years. It is true that the financial results of the big steel companies have been outstanding even when compared with the most successful growth companies, and it is also a fact that the per capita consumption of steel is rising persistently.

However, with modest exceptions, the steel companies are still selling to the same old markets (73% of steel consumption in 1955 was accounted for by automobiles, construction, machinery, and containers), and it is the growth of those markets which explains the rising demand for steel.

To be sure, new uses for steel have been developed, but either they have been worked out *in response to* a need first expressed by the customers, as in the case of certain stainless steels, or they do not make a significant contribution to the earnings of the big producers. Furthermore, the steel industry's earnings are unusually dependent on the maintenance of a highly inflated price structure, which has gone up more than twice as fast as the average of all nonagricultural commodities since the period 1947–1949 (as compared, for instance, with only a nominal increase in the price of chemicals). If steel prices were pushed back to 1947–1949 levels, all the steel companies would operate at substantial losses. This would not be the case with most true growth companies.

- As a general rule, it would seem that most raw material producers have to be excluded from the growth company category, partly because their growth is dependent on the demand for final products which they can have little influence on, and partly because substantial increases in earnings are basically the result of inflated prices. An obvious and significant exception to this statement is the aluminum industry. The demand for aluminum has grown and is growing phenomenally, not simply because the major consumers of aluminum are doing more business than they used to do but, perhaps more important, because the aluminum companies themselves have found so many new uses for the metal, and therefore so many new consumers of it. The aluminum industry is carving out its own market.

"Inner-Directed"

The ability to create its own market is the strategic, the dominating, and the single most distinguishing characteristic of a true growth company.
The reason for this is not simply that the development of new products, new processes, and new uses for old products leads to higher sales and bigger profits. More important is the fact that the *quality* of

a growth company's sales and earnings is fundamentally different from that of other companies.

A new product or a highly differentiated one is, for a brief period of time at least, unique; it has a virtual monopoly. There is only one Terramycin, one Dacron, one Univac, one Centravac; but the identical steel can be bought from Bethlehem or United States Steel, and the same copper from Kennecott or from Anaconda. Thus, growth company products tend to provide larger-than-average profit margins and to postpone or possibly even eliminate the danger of price competition. At the same time, the continuous development of new products and new markets offsets declining sales in old products and, perhaps most important of all, tends to insulate the company from many of the hazards of general economic trends.

In short, the real growth company is, to borrow sociologist David Riesman's phrase, "inner-directed" rather than "other-directed."[1] It is a nonconformist in economic society. It adapts the outside world to itself by creating something or a demand for something which did not exist before, instead of adapting itself to changes in the outside world. It does not necessarily grow faster than the economy as a whole, but it does grow faster than the markets in which its products are sold.

This is why so many (but by no means all) of the chemical, electrical equipment, and the electronic companies fall into the true growth company class. These companies are at the dynamic and technological frontiers of our society and are continuously developing new uses for old products, new products to replace old products, new products with new functions, and new processes for turning out goods and services of all types.

Creative Merchandising

But the creation of a market does not depend solely on the introduction of a new product or a new use for an old product. A market can be created in less glamorous industries, where dynamic merchandising creates such strong brand loyalty that consumers are convinced the product is unique and hence abandon other products in its favor. Growth, in other words, need not be the result of creating *new* demand; it can occur when a company wins a larger share of existing markets. For example:

Scott Paper Company has a fundamentally different character from most of the other paper companies and a far more successful earnings record. Of course, Scott Paper has developed new products or tangibly improved versions of old products, but in reality its merchandise is part of the stuff of everyday life. Yet Scott's merchandising methods to both the general public and to its important market among manufacturers and institutions have brought it unusually close to its customers and have created the feeling of assurance that its products *are* of superior quality.

As a result, Scott has more influence over its market than most other paper companies. Its success as an active rather than passive agent in the economy is dramatically illustrated by the way it persistently increased its earnings during the Great Depression and by the degree to which the growth in its earnings has markedly outpaced the rest of the industry in recent years.

Growth potentials can emerge where one least expects to find them, particularly where new markets are developed for old products. An intriguing development in this connection is the effort of the chewing gum manufacturers to take advantage of the salesmanship of the American GI in developing a taste for chewing gum in foreign countries during the war.

Perhaps my point can best be brought out by asking whether the successful automobile companies are growth companies. A good case can be made for the argument that they do not meet the criteria. The automobile is no longer a new product. A major share of the cars sold today are replacements rather than first purchases of a car. The expansion in the automobile market has largely been the result of a rising population and a higher level of personal incomes, and in this sense the automobile companies have been adapting to outside conditions rather than creating their own market.

Yet, when one studies what has happened in this industry in recent years, one wonders whether there is not another side to the question. Through dramatic and persistent changes in style and engineering, the automobile companies *have* created a new product and made old ones obsolete. Who can say whether the $3,000 car of 1956 with all its new gadgets is or is not more expensive than the same $2,000 brand in 1946? If the creation of new products has not been achieved, how else can we explain the fabulous success of the 1955 models, introduced during a recession and when most statistical tests indicated that the automobile market was well saturated? Does not the effort to sell a second car to every family open up a potentially enormous market? Thus, at least the leading companies in the industry would seem to come close to qualifying as growth companies.

Sharper Focus

As I am sure most readers are aware, there are many definitions of a growth company, and I do not claim that the one just outlined is the "last word." But it is, to my mind, a useful concept for the specific purpose of distinguishing the selected group of really dynamic, pioneering firms from the general run of well-managed firms. In particular, it should aid us in refining, building upon, and carrying a step further Robert W. Anderson's provocative analysis in the March–April 1955 issue of *HBR*, "Unrealized Potentials in Growth Stocks."

It will be remembered that Anderson would include as a growth company any firm which shows expansion, whether or not the impulse comes from within the organization itself. For example, in connection with his belief that growth companies are likely to turn up only in growth industries, he has this to say:

> Such an industry should be a basic element in the country's standard of living, and it should have existing products or services which have met with such increasing public acceptance that unit demand is rising at an average rate significantly greater than the average rate of unit growth of the economy as a whole, although not necessarily dramatic.

But within these terms—and this is the significant point—we could include the major elements of industries such as construction, food, fertilizer, and printing, where growth has been to a major extent a response to expanding demand rather than the creator of it, and where, furthermore, the financial results of the vast majority of companies have been mediocre to say the least and have been far from immune to the business cycle.

The remainder of Anderson's analysis establishes certain criteria, such as research programs, product and process planning, attitudes of management, and so on, which no growth company can be without. But are not these the characteristics which, by and large, one should seek in *any* well-managed company? Standard Oil of New Jersey, as a case in point, would probably meet Anderson's criteria every bit as well as, say, Scott Paper or Minnesota Mining and Manufacturing. However, if the emphasis is on the difference between active and passive growth, there can be no question that Scott and "3M" are growth companies, while there would be a substantial measure of doubt about Standard Oil of New Jersey in that regard.

FINANCIAL TEST

Now let us turn from the qualitative criteria of growth companies to the expression of those criteria in financial performance. A growth company's sales and earnings should be expected to show a rising trend, and the trend should climb more steeply than the average. "Results are what count."

For instance, the sheer size of appropriations for research and merchandising—sometimes used as a criterion—by itself means nothing. In fact, such expenses are "down the drain," since (a) they cannot justifiably be capitalized, (b) they cannot be turned off without running the risk that the company will lose its position, and (c) a large proportion of selling and research expense can only lay a foundation for future growth and does not bring in any immediate return. Activities of this sort can pay off only if they ultimately bring in substantial returns which will both recapture the money "down the drain" and provide a high return on capital; and the more expensive they are, the truer this is.

Actually, even a better-than-average uptrend in sales and earnings is not enough. A true growth company's financial results should meet the following criteria as well:

1. The uptrend in earnings should be relatively smooth. Earnings need not rise every single year, but they should increase in more years than they decrease, and they should show an increase in at least as many years as the "average" company's earnings increase.

2. What is true of earnings should also be true, in most cases, of dividends. There is little point in buying a stock yielding 2% or 3% unless over a reasonable period it pays out more than a fixed-income security or less "dynamic" stock.

3. Certainly, return on net worth should be maintained; and if the dividend payout is abnormally low, then return on net worth should actually be rising. In other words, the stockholder's money which is reinvested instead of paid out should earn at least as much as the old capital which produced these earnings. This ratio is indeed the most significant indicator of management's over-all ability and aggressiveness.

4. Increases in earnings and/or net worth should of course reflect an increase in the physical volume of output or at least a beneficial shift in product mix—rather than merely larger dollar results reflecting a rising price level.

33 Firms Analyzed

Now, financial performance has the added advantage of being readily subject to statistical measurement.

Exhibit 1 shows how a number of companies have met the foregoing test of financial performance. The sample includes Anderson's list of 25 "growth companies," plus 8 additional companies chosen to give deeper perspective to the yawning gap between the qualitative and quantitative characteristics of leading American corporations. (The additions are American Cyanamid, Bethlehem Steel, Corning Glass, General Motors, International Paper, National Lead, Scott Paper, and United States Steel.)

This is by no means an all-inclusive list of growth companies. Conversely, quite a few of the companies in the sample are not growth companies at all, at least in terms of our qualitative criteria. But this very make-up should help to sharpen the distinction between our concept of growth companies and the usual idea of growth stocks. The rationale for the table is as follows:

For the 33 companies, 1947–1949 average data are compared with 1953–1955 average data. The two periods are sufficiently separated in time to be revealing. Also, each includes a recession year, a reasonably good year, and a boom year.

Of course, it would be desirable to make the comparison over a longer period of time to avoid the effect of short-run influences. However, as we all recognize, the economy as a whole and many individual companies are basically different today from what they were in prewar days, so it would be more of a distortion to start with an earlier date. In any event, the comparison here is intended for purposes of general demonstration rather than for anything like selecting specific investment opportunities, so the effect of a few variations is not important.

All figures are expressed on a per-share basis, adjusted for stock splits and stock dividends—that is, they are expressed in terms of the number of shares outstanding at the end of 1955. (This applies to companies that pay regular as well as irregular stock dividends, which explains why the IBM and Dow Chemical figures may look a little unfamiliar to some readers.)

The figures in Exhibit 1 bear careful study. On the one hand, they largely confirm the ability of companies which do fulfill the qualitative

EXHIBIT I
Statistical Measures of Growth of 33 Corporations

Company	Number of Years in which Increase Occurred 1947–1955		Percentage increase, 1947–1949 to 1953–1955	
	Earnings	Dividends	Earnings	Dividends
American Cyanamid	5	5	67%	142%
Bethlehem Steel	5	4	85	149
Corning Glass	7	4	300	333
General Motors	7	6	86	100
International Paper	5	6	24	77
National Lead	7	7	174	269
Scott Paper	6	8	106	176
U.S. Steel	5	4	103	74
Johns-Manville	4	4	39	116
Minneapolis Honeywell	5	4	80	99
U.S. Gypsum	5	6	47	47
Du Pont	7	6	109	108
Dow Chemical	5	8	50	239
Hercules Powder	4	4	32	41
Monsanto Chemical	4	2	36	27
Union Carbide & Carbon	4	5	22	56
American Can	5	6	18	70
General Electric	7	6	68	139
Westinghouse Electric	6	3	0	67
Libbey-Owens-Ford	6	6	71	31
Owens Illinois	5	3	64	36
Hartford Fire Insurance	5	3	3	96
Insurance Company of North America	5	5	30	101
Eastman Kodak	5	7	37	78
IBM	7	8	59	53
Amerada	6	3	22	55
Continental Oil	5	5	4	61
Humble Oil	5	4	13	19
Standard Oil of California	7	7	55	78
Standard Oil of New Jersey	5	7	60	200
J.C. Penney	5	3	6	46
Sears, Roebuck	5	3	15	39
National Steel	4	6	20	109
Dow-Jones Industrial Average	6	7	40	65
Moody's Industrial Average	5	6	43	70

Percentage Increase in Price, 12/31/47–12/31/55	Return on Book Value		Ratio of Price to Earnings* 12/31/55	Ratio of Price to Increase-in-Earnings† 12/31/55
	1947–1949	1953–1955		
234%	14.2%	11.6%	20×	50×
382	12.4	13.9	11	24
760	15.5	23.0	28	38
395	30.9	26.8	15	31
528	20.4	14.5	18	92
664	13.9	20.7	26	41
535	18.2	14.8	30	59
346	7.6	11.0	13	25
120	13.5	12.4	14	51
363	28.0	18.4	28	63
195	17.1	16.9	16	51
402	20.2	21.0	32	61
427	16.9	11.4	39	116
160	20.1	17.2	25	104
142	18.8	11.6	28	124
244	20.4	16.2	29	159
146	13.2	10.8	17	116
382	19.5	18.1	26	65
106	13.7	9.1	15	—
244	22.6	22.8	17	40
86	11.3	13.3	19	49
213	11.9	6.7	17	640
240	10.6	6.0	18	77
190	17.3	15.0	23	84
404	26.2	18.2	37	99
279	31.0	20.5	28	161
284	20.0	13.8	23	550
186	22.0	15.0	24	210
246	16.4	15.0	14	39
325	15.9	15.0	16	42
136	26.5	18.5	19	382
176	21.4	14.7	19	144
166	16.6	11.1	12	75
160	13.6	12.4	15	53
210	16.4	14.5	16	54

*Average annual earnings per share 1953–1955, calculated on the number of shares outstanding on December 31, 1955.
†Increase in average annual earnings per share from 1947–1949 to 1953–1955, calculated on the number of shares outstanding on December 31, 1955.
Note: All data calculated on a per-share basis and on the number of shares outstanding on December 31, 1955.

criteria to meet the financial test as well. For instance, the five companies whose earnings show the greatest percentage increase between 1947–1949 and 1953–1955 include four clear examples of true growth companies (marked with asterisks), all but one of which, Scott Paper, increased the return on net worth:

Corning Glass*	up 300%
National Lead*	up 174%
Du Pont*	up 109%
Scott Paper*	up 106%
U.S. Steel	up 103%

On the other hand, the five companies whose earnings show the least increase over the period include only one which seems to fulfill our qualitative criteria of a growth company (marked with asterisk):

Westinghouse Electric*	up 0%
Hartford Fire Insurance	up 3%
Continental Oil	up 4%
J. C. Penney	up 6%
Humble Oil	up 13%

The same correspondence between increased earnings and growth criteria shows up throughout the whole list, though not quite to the same degree. With special or temporary circumstances always in the picture to alter or mask the financial results, there are bound to be some companies which have the qualitative requirements of a growth company but fail to meet the financial test (at least for the short run), and at the same time some companies which do not fulfill the qualitative criteria but show superior financial results (although it is a good question whether this superiority would persist through all economic vicissitudes).

Screening Tool

Of course, it must also be borne in mind that whether a company meets qualitative criteria or not is a matter of judgment. In the case of an oil company, for example, one might be justified in calling it a growth company because it was energetically increasing its holdings of oil lands for the future; or one might decide just the opposite. I also hesitate to single out company names for another reason; I do not wish to appear to be touting individual companies, and I certainly want to avoid damning other companies with faint praise. However, as a guide to the reader in following my train of thought, I do think that I can and should say this much:

1. There would probably be *general agreement* that Corning Glass, National Lead, Scott Paper, Du Pont, Dow Chemical, General Electric, and IBM come as close as any to meeting *all* the qualitative criteria *and* the items in the financial test.

2. *In my opinion* American Cyanamid, Minneapolis Honeywell, Libby-Owens-Ford, and Eastman Kodak also belong relatively high up on any list of true growth companies.

3. Beyond this there are certain *other companies* which undoubtedly qualify as growth companies too, but which neither I nor others could demonstrate to be such with the same degree of finality or faith.

I am afraid, in short, that readers will have to make their judgment of my judgment as I have just described it. But to the extent that they do accept it, then true growth characteristics as envisaged in this article are in fact usually expressed in superior financial results.

Accordingly, the items comprising our financial test do make an effective tool for screening out companies which fulfill the qualitative criteria we have established for true growth. If it works four times out of five, or anywhere near that much, that is a high rate of reliability, particularly when compared with the statistical basis of increased market value as used by Anderson. Indeed, the following facts raise the fundamental question whether any list selected like Anderson's 25 companies is representative of growth situations either in terms of company or of stock:

1. Only 10 of the 25 companies showed an increase in earnings over the 1947–1949 base which was better than the increase in earnings of the Dow-Jones Industrial Average. (Although the 30 companies in the Dow-Jones Industrial Average are used to represent the "average" company in this discussion, the Moody's Industrial Average of 125 companies would have resulted in only minor and insignificant differences in results.)

2. Only 13 of them raised their dividends by more than the increase in the dividend on the Dow-Jones Industrial Average.

3. Only 2 increased the rate of return on book value between 1947–1949, and 1953–1955. As a matter of fact, only 7 of the 33 companies in the table achieved this result. If we seek the number of companies which more or less maintained their rate of return, say, within two percentage points, then we can still add only 5 companies to this list.

4. The earnings on the Dow-Jones Industrial Average rose in three out of the five years 1947–1952 and in six out of the eight years 1947–1955. But 9 of the 25 companies failed to equal this result in the shorter period, and 14 of them failed to do so in the longer period.

5. The dividend on the Dow-Jones Industrial Average was increased four times during 1947–1952 and seven times during 1947–1955. But 15 of the 25 companies increased their dividends less than four times in the shorter period (9 of them increased their dividends less than three times) and 20 failed to do as well as the Dow-Jones Industrial Average in the longer period (11 failed to increase their dividends even five times).

Company vs. Industry

Exhibit 1 is revealing in another sense. It suggests that *superior financial results are apparently not the fortuitous outcome of being a member of a growth industry*. Instead, such results seem to reflect significant differences in management concepts, policies, and techniques. Wide variations in performance appear among companies in the same industry: for example, compare General Electric with Westinghouse, Bethlehem with National Steel, Du Pont with Union Carbide or Monsanto, Standard Oil of New Jersey with Continental Oil. Again, General Motors has an outstanding statistical record, but perhaps only one of its competitors would show up as well as does the average of the 33 companies in Exhibit 1; and the same is substantially the case with IBM and its competitors.

This is not to say that the stocks of all the companies which our table singles out as leaders are necessarily good buys for the future or, on the other hand, that the stocks of all the others can be expected to perform poorly in the years ahead. For instance, Hercules Powder appears lackluster in Exhibit 1, but actually it may have a growth potential today which few of the companies in the table can match.

The point here is simply that any broad generalizations drawn from statistical comparisons can be misleading when it comes to the selection of individual stocks for future appreciation. Qualitative analysis must also be brought to bear—to explore for special circumstances and, in particular, to determine to what extent the company exhibits the characteristics we have been discussing, i.e., whether it dynamically creates its own markets, has quasi-monopolistic features reflected in higher profit margins, is sufficiently inner-directed to be relatively immune to business fluctuations, and has turned in a consistent record of growth in earning power, dividends, and return on net worth.

Furthermore, one other dimension must be added—i.e., market price—before we have anything that can serve as a guide to investment opportunity. As a matter of fact, as I shall point out in the next section, the statistical method itself must be more refined before it can be really useful for the purposes under consideration.

THE INVESTOR'S PROBLEM

Now let us tackle the specific problem of what this all means to the investor who is looking for appreciation in value. The factors we have been discussing—particularly higher-than-average profit margins and superior growth in earning power, dividend payments, and return on net worth—obviously affect market values and are therefore of considerable interest to the investor. And, needless to say, the market effect is also of considerable importance to the growth company's management, for the investor's decisions influence the supply of equity capital. But do these factors dominate market value, or at least influence it to such an extent that growth companies are likely to be synonymous with growth stocks, and growth stocks with superior buys? That is the question.

Power of Glamor

One of the quickest and more forceful ways to answer this question is to turn again to Anderson's list of 25 corporations. This list, as we have already seen, includes a substantial group of companies that do not qualify as growth companies according to our criteria and which indeed have not returned as impressive financial results as the average of the 30 Dow-Jones Industrials. Now comparison of market prices in relation to earnings reveals that financial return such as would be consistent with true growth was not the main thing investors were interested in, anyway. In fact, it shows that they were apparently more interested in glamor than in growth.

Keeping in mind that the Dow-Jones Industrial Average at the end of 1955 was selling for 15.3 times the average of earnings in the 1953–1955 period, note that:

1. Only 3 of Anderson's 25 companies (National Steel, Johns-Manville, and Standard Oil of California) were selling at a price-earnings ratio lower than the Dow-Jones Average—proof of the upward pressure on prices exerted by investors. At the same time, while for a variety of reasons the three companies mentioned may have been low on glamor, as a group they showed average or better-than-average financial results!

2. General Motors, United States Steel, and Bethlehem Steel were also selling at less than 15 times 1953–1955 earnings at the end of 1955, although there is no question that the financial results of these 3 companies were outstandingly impressive.

3. Of Anderson's 25 companies, 12 were selling for more than 20 times 1953–1955 earnings, even though this group included companies with clearly subaverage financial results, such as Union Carbide & Carbon, Hercules Powder, and Continental Oil.

To be sure, there are cases where the market price of the stock in relation to earnings is in line with its true growth characteristics. Thus, Scott Paper, Du Pont, IBM, and Dow Chemical, which happen to be the most expensive companies of our list of 33, do appear well qualified for their exalted price-earnings ratio of more than 30 times 1953–1955 average earnings; they clearly meet our qualitative criteria, and their financial results are well above average by any standard of measurement. But in many other cases investors have pushed the price far above what is justified not only in terms of current earnings but in terms of growth potential as well.

From the mass of contradictory evidence available, is it possible for the investor to find some guide or bench mark in his search for "value"? How can he make a choice among a group of such outstanding companies with such widely dispersed price-earnings ratios? How can he decide whether General Motors at 14 times 1953–1955 earnings is a better buy than Dow Chemical at nearly 40 times, or whether it is worth paying nearly twice as much for a dollar's worth of General Electric's earnings as for a dollar's worth of Westinghouse's?

Valuing Earnings Growth

There is a possible basis for answering these questions, but it involves a rejection of the conventional ratio of price to earnings as a measure of value. While the method to be proposed, even if accepted by the investing public, would hardly go so far as to shift the main focus of market interest from growth stocks to growth companies, it might well be used by the managements of undervalued growth companies as an effective tool in gaining more recognition from investors.

There are two parts to this task of selecting stocks for future appreciation. The investor must satisfy himself (1) that the company is likely to continue to grow in earning power, and (2) that the stock is priced relatively low enough at time of purchase so the increase in earning power has a good chance to be reflected in greater value to the holder.

The first part we have of course already discussed in terms of qualitative analysis of the company (*not* the stock); a consistent upward trend in earnings and dividends, with the greatest possible potential based on dynamic management and supported by relative immunity to business fluctuations, should certainly indicate the prospects for continued growth in earning power.

The second part, which is our concern at this point, involves statistical analysis of the market price of the stock to determine whether it is a good buy in the sense of not being valued so high that in effect the results of future growth are already discounted (as so often happens when stocks become glamorized, particularly so-called growth stocks which do not have the characteristics of true growth to back them up).

But if the investor simply looks to see whether the stock is cheap or expensive on the basis of how many times earnings it is selling for, he ignores the primary consideration in his search—the discovery of growth. Earnings in any given period of time are a static concept. They are therefore only partly relevant to the valuation of growth companies. What the investor should look at is the *change* in earning power between two periods of time.

Accordingly, my suggestion is that the ratio of price to *increase*-in-earnings may be more significant than the conventional ratio of price to earnings. Investment requires a look into the future; intelligent appraisal of the future must be based on developing trends already in action and ascertainable; and this is one way of doing it. For example:

Let us take two fictional stocks, the Deadhead Company, selling for $20, and the Zoomar Company selling for $30. If they are both currently earning $2 a share, Deadhead is selling for 10 times earnings and certainly looks cheaper than Zoomar, which is selling for 15 times. But if five years ago Deadhead's earnings were $1.60 while Zoomar was earning only $1.00, Deadhead's price is 50 times its $0.40-a-share increase-in-earnings, while Zoomar's price is only 30 times its $1.00-a-share increase-in-earnings. Now Zoomar clearly seems like the better value.

If the investor believes that the two companies will continue to grow in the future at about the same rates they showed in the past, there is no question that Zoomar is cheaper. Five years hence Zoomar will again have doubled its earnings and will be making $4 a share; thus its present price of $30 is only 7.5 times its future earnings. Deadhead, on the other hand, will be earning only $2.50 five years from now, so its present price of $20 is 8 times its future earnings.

The ratio of price to increase-in-earnings makes some stocks look cheaper and some more expensive than the values indicated by the more conventional price/earnings measurement, as Exhibit II shows. (The figures are presented for illustrative purposes only. In any serious application of the method, it would naturally be wise to examine the increase-in-earnings records for any "windfalls"—large one-shot government contracts, and so forth—and make any adjustments deemed necessary.)

Indeed, Exhibit II shows clearly that the investor gets a wholly different "slant" on matters if he uses the ratio of price to increase-in-earnings rather than the more conventional ratio; the companies with superior financial results almost always appear to be more attractively

EXHIBIT II
Price/Earnings Increase Ratios of 10 Stocks

	End-of-1955 price as a multiple of	
	1953–1955 earnings	Increase-in-earnings 1947–1949 to 1953–1955
IBM	36.5×	99×
Du Pont	32.3	61
Scott Paper	30.4	59
National Lead	26.4	41
Corning Glass	28.4	38
Hartford Fire Insurance	17.3	640
Continental Oil	22.6	550
J.C. Penney	18.7	382
Humble Oil	24.2	210
Union Carbide	28.6	159
Dow-Jones Industrial Average	15.3	53

priced on the new basis—notably, for instance, National Lead and Corning Glass. But it is also worth noting that, as Exhibit III illustrates, some stocks were cheap at the end of 1955 by both standards of measurement— the explanation probably being that these are stocks where the glamor factor is relatively low, and thus the refinement of our method makes less difference.

In short, the price to increase-in-earnings ratio does serve to produce a different and presumably a truer, or at least more helpful, picture when the market is running ahead of growth in earning power, yet at the same time it causes no distortion when the opposite is the case.

Undervalued Stocks

Now, how effective in actual practice is the increase-in-earnings ratio as the second part of our method for selecting stocks for future appreciation—in other words, for determining whether the stock of a growth company is also a good buy for this purpose in terms of current market price?

A test based on data for our sample of 33 companies at the end of 1952 reveals rather impressive results. To give expression to the first part of our method, the sample was combed out to select those companies with the most consistent records of rising earnings and dividends and with the best record of maintaining or increasing return on net worth. From this group, the 5 companies with the lowest and the 5 companies with

EXHIBIT III

Stocks Undervalued on the Basis of Both Price/Earnings and Price/Earnings Increase Ratios

	12/31/55 price as a multiple of	
	1953–1955 earnings	Increase-in-earnings 1947–1949 to 1953–1955
Bethlehem Steel	11.0×	24×
U.S. Steel	12.9	25
General Motors	14.5	31
Standard Oil of California	13.5	39
Standard Oil of New Jersey	15.8	42
Johns-Manville	14.3	51
U.S. Gypsum	16.3	51

the highest ratios of price to increase-in-earnings—in other words, the 5 cheapest and 5 most expensive stocks—were chosen as if for purchase. What the results would have been as of the end of 1955 are compared in Exhibit IV (the companies are listed in ascending order of their price to increase-in-earnings ratios at the end of 1952).

Although this test is based on a relatively short time period with plenty of peculiarities, the results are highly consistent. It may be seen that as a group the cheapest companies in terms of the ratio of price to increase-in-earnings far outperformed the most expensive ones. It is also significant that all five of the cheapest companies went up by more than the Dow-Jones Industrials, while three of the expensive companies turned in very poor results.

Of course there also are a few stocks of companies on the list which fail to meet the qualitative criteria of growth and yet show appreciation like the stocks of the best growth companies. This simply emphasizes the fact that no statistical analysis is perfect or self-sufficient, and that inspection of the individual situation must always be brought into the decision to buy a stock. But at least this approach is far more fruitful

EXHIBIT IV
Price/Earnings Increase Ratios of 10 Stocks

	Percentage increase in price 12/31/52 to 12/31/59
Five cheapest companies in 1952	
Bethlehem Steel	221%
U.S. Steel	183
General Motors	108
Libbey-Owens-Ford	114
Standard Oil of New Jersey	96
Average	114
Five most expensive companies in 1952	
National Lead	160%
Westinghouse	25
Dow Chemical	45
Amerada	0
IBM	116
Average	69
Dow-Jones Industrial Average	65

than simply purchasing so-called growth stocks. Indeed, Anderson's own data prove this point. His 25 income stocks outperformed his 25 growth stocks from 1936 through 1945. For the entire period he reviews—1936 through 1954—his growth stocks were outperformed as a group by such "nongrowth" stocks as Goodyear, Bethlehem Steel, Beatrice Foods, and Truax-Traer Coal.

Here is one moral. In investing, nothing beats the discovery of an undervalued stock, no matter what the nature of its business or the past trend of its earnings. But simply purchasing so-called growth stocks tends to lead to the selection of overvalued stocks.

Furthermore, investors cannot wholly ignore the very low income return on most growth stocks—particularly institutional investors with little or no income tax to pay. The annual income on Anderson's 25 growth stocks did not catch up to that on his income stocks for 12 years or to the Dow-Jones Industrials for 14 years. By the end of 1954, the entire amount of income received on the growth stocks from the beginning of 1936 was still less than on the income stocks or the Dow-Jones Industrials.

Or look at it this way. In 1955, the dividend on the Dow-Jones Industrials was equal to 10.2% of the price at the end of 1947. On General Motors it was 23%, on Bethlehem Steel 24%, and on National Lead 26%. But on 17 of Anderson's 25 growth companies it was less than 10%, and 3 were actually yielding less than 6% on the 1947 price.

Thus, for those investors who can reinvest and compound income and for those who require a relatively high income, the very high premiums which some supposed growth stocks command may turn out to be less than worthwhile, even if satisfactory price appreciation results. For analysis proves that both appreciation *and* a large income can be realized with proper selection—i.e., selection of true growth companies with a relatively low ratio of price to increase-in-earnings.

CONCLUSION

The magic words "growth company" are high praise in the business world today. It is perfectly proper for the spotlight to focus on those companies which are either making a significant contribution to, or benefiting greatly from, the vigorous growth patterns of our modern economy. But in order to avoid dangerous oversimplifications and in order to apply the term "growth company" only where it has some useful meaning, the following considerations should be borne in mind:

1. Growth is a dynamic concept. The growth company can never be a passive beneficiary of economic change. Rather it must be an active agent at the technological or geographical frontiers of our society. Thus, it is not enough to be in, say, the chemical or electronic industries; a firm cannot become a growth company "by association." There may be more elements of growth—i.e., market creation—in a company like General Motors than in many chemical or electronic companies.

2. It is a mistake to believe that superior earning power is to be found only among growth companies, but it is a very decisive test for all such firms. Creativity and ambition in product development and merchandising alone are not enough; the ability to make money out of creativity is certainly at least as important.

3. The enchantment which some growth companies convey to the stock market lends a premium to their common stocks which is not always justified by the statistical background. An investor may do well with such stocks, but there is good reason to believe that he can do even better by giving the financial results—such as those shown by measures of increase-in-earnings power—a completely cold-blooded and objective analysis. No amount of study in this area can minimize the importance of trying to buy at a fair price; buying at any price and hoping that the future will take care of itself is a good short cut to disappointing results.

Indeed, perhaps the most important conclusion of this analysis is that the term "growth stock" is meaningless; a growth stock can be identified only with hindsight—it is simply a stock which went way up. But the concept of "growth company" can be used to identify the most creative, most imaginative management groups; and if, in addition, their stocks are valued at a reasonable ratio to their increase-in-earnings power over a period of time, the odds are favorable for appreciation in the future.

FOOTNOTES

1. For a critique of Reisman's views, see Theodore Levitt, "The Changing Character of Capitalism," *HBR*, July–August 1956, p. 37—the Editors.

COMMON STOCK AND COMMON SENSE

William H. Donaldson
Dan W. Lufkin
Richard H. Jenrette

William Donaldson, Dan Lufkin, and Richard Jenrette used a small brochure titled *Common Stocks and Common Sense* to introduce their new firm to institutional investors in 1959.

The record of remarkable capital gain performance by "blue chip" common stocks over the past ten years has fostered optimistic investor expectations of similar gain in the next ten years.

By any measure the performance of these leading U.S. industrial stocks during the post-war period has been remarkable. As of June, 1959, anyone who had invested equal amounts in each of the 30 stocks comprising the Dow-Jones Industrial Average at mean market prices prevailing in 1949 would have experienced nearly a five-fold increase in the market value of his securities. Similar outstanding results could have been obtained by investing in Vicker's "Favorite Fifty" stocks of institutional investors or Standard & Poor's 500 Industrial Stock Average.

In view of this performance, the great reliance placed by many investors and investment managers on the "blue chips" cannot be con-

From William H. Donaldson, Dan W. Lufkin and Richard H. Jenrette, *Common Stock and Common Sense* (New York, New York, 1959), 1–15, by permission of the authors.

sidered surprising. The normal tendency is to project such past gains into the future, with the result that a portfolio of leading U.S. industrial stocks is widely regarded as a relatively riskless route to large capital gain.

Are these expectations of future capital gain possibilities realistic? Can today's investor simply buy the "blue chips" and achieve general market appreciation on the order of the past ten years? While there is no intention here to say that some further gain will not be realized in the "blue chip" area, there are grounds for believing that expectations of future gain based on the record of the past decade are unrealistic.

The most significant change in the position of the 1959 investor *vis à vis* the 1949 investor is in the multiple of earnings reflected in common stock prices today. Today's "Favorite Fifty" stocks are selling at price-earnings ratios which average 21 times estimated 1959 earnings. Ten years ago these same stocks could have been purchased at prices averaging 7.7 times 1949 earnings.

The significant fact this marked widening of price-earnings ratios has tended to obscure is that corporate per share earnings have experienced no more than a relatively moderate growth in the past decade. Whereas today's "Favorite Fifty" *stocks* have appreciated in market value over six-fold from their mean average prices prevailing in 1947–49, *earnings* for these same companies on the average have only slightly more than doubled in this period.

The table [page 217] illustrates the much more rapid rate of growth in market values vs. per share earnings for Vicker's "Favorite Fifty."

The performance of certain so-called "growth" industries illustrates this fact even more dramatically. Two such industries are paper and rubber [See table on page 218].

In the case of these seven major paper equities, the price-earnings ratio has advanced from 5 times to 20 times estimated 1959 earnings. Using net profit before taxes, profits have roughly doubled. As a result, adjusting pretax profit figure for per share increase, the group as a whole has advanced nearly eight times in market price over these past ten years.

In the case of the five largest rubber equities, the price-earnings ratio has advanced from 4 times to 16 times estimated 1959 earnings (adjusting for depressed year earnings performance in 1949). Yet pretax earnings have only advanced 2 1/4 times. Adjusting pretax profit figures for per share increase, the group has advanced better than 8 1/2 times in market price from 1949 to 1959.

(Index 1947–49 = 100)

	1949	1950	1951	1952	1953	1954	1955	1956	1957	1958	1959 (E)
Mean Ave. Market Prices	102.0	135.8	182.7	202.7	202.7	269.4	357.3	436.9	447.9	495.3	613.8
Mean Ave. Earnings Per Share	100.5	135.2	129.1	127.1	140.0	130.2	202.7	206.7	206.7	189.0	222.4
Price × Earnings Ratio	7.7	7.9	10.8	12.3	11.4	13.3	14.2	15.8	16.3	20.2	21.0

Paper and Paper Products*
(Index 1947–49 = 100)

Average Sales Performance

1949	1950	1951	1952	1953	1954	1955	1956	1957	1958	1959–E
102	126	154	152	181	204	246	263	261	265	275

Average Profit Performance (Before Taxes)

1949	1950	1951	1952	1953	1954	1955	1956	1957	1958	1959–E
97	140	162	150	171	184	235	235	193	176	210

Stock Performance—(Average Price–Earnings Ratio)

1949	1950	1951	1952	1953	1954	1955	1956	1957	1958	1959–E
5.0x	5.7x	8.3x	9.3x	9.1x	12.5x	15.9x	16.8x	17.7x	23.1x	20x

*Includes Champion, Crown Zellerbach, International Paper, Kimberly-Clark, Rayonier, Scott Paper and West Virginia Pulp and Paper.

Rubber and Rubber Fabricators*
(Index 1947–49 = 100)

Average Sales Performance

1949	1950	1951	1952	1953	1954	1955	1956	1957	1958	1959–E
93	123	157	161	171	161	202	212	225	227	235

Average Profit Performance (Before Taxes)

1949	1950	1951	1952	1953	1954	1955	1956	1957	1958	1959–E
76	182	277	226	226	180	257	248	239	227	235

Stock Performance—(Average Price–Earnings Ratio)

1949	1950	1951	1952	1953	1954	1955	1956	1957	1958	1959–E
5.3x	3.6x	5.0x	6.6x	6.1x	9.2x	10.2x	11.6x	12.6x	16.2x	16x

*Includes Firestone, Goodyear, Goodrich, U.S. Rubber and General Tire.

There are a number of explanations for the willingness of investors to pay more per dollar of common stock earnings today. Fears of a serious post-World War II depression which were prevalent in the latter half of the 1940s have been replaced by expectations of continued inflation, with a consequent diminishing of the relative attractiveness of fixed income securities. Other factors often mentioned to justify the present level of stock prices relative to earnings include increased outlays for research and development, expanded cash flow through larger and accelerated depreciation, new stability in cyclical industries through lower break-even points, the gradual buildup of capacity which only now can be reflected in larger earnings, expectations of a marked upturn in sales and earnings flowing from the projected rise in family formations, increased real income, and expanding worldwide demand during the next decade, and finally the much discussed shortage of "blue chip" common stocks which are in greatest demand by investors.

It is not our purpose here to attempt to justify the current level of price-earnings ratios, but merely to point out the breakdown of gain in market value between actual earnings growth and growth in the price-earnings ratios, whether justified or not.

Assuming the existence of some practical ceiling on price-earnings ratios, however, one might expect future growth in overall stock values to be more nearly in line with growth in corporate earnings. While opinions vary as to whether the next ten years will witness some further widening of price-earnings ratios, or conversely an actual contraction, a repeat performance of the past decade in which average price-earnings ratios have nearly tripled seems unlikely. Such a performance would necessitate average multiples of 60 times earnings which few investors today would consider a realistic possibility.

Thus it seems unreasonable to assume that today's investor can expect a growth in multipliers from current levels to yield dramatic stock market performance for most of the large industry leaders with no more than an historical rate of earnings growth ahead of them. Certainly some industry groups will come into greater market favor and show good gain—such as the steels during 1958–59—but overall levels of even "unfavored" groups today are relatively high and multiplier gains of 3 times to 4 times for any group seem remote.

Today's investor seeking comparable gain in the 1960s will not be able to buy the "Favorite 50," the industry leaders, which have already been bid up to high earnings' multiples in the process of reaching the "charmed circle." Comparable gain in the 1960s will come primarily through identifying the "Future Favorite 50;" stocks of companies which will benefit from the two-pronged effect of first and foremost a large percentage earnings gain compounded in the company, and to a greater or lesser extent this gain compounded again by an increased price-earnings ratio in the market.

The problem of successfully identifying such companies breaks into two parts:

1. Where to look.
2. What to look for.

WHERE TO LOOK:

The most obvious place to look is where, for one reason or another, the majority of investors are not looking. This is usually in the over-the-counter or regional exchange markets. Most investors aren't looking here for a number of reasons:

- A greater element of capital risk is arbitrarily attached to this area by the investor group in general.
- Usually the limited number of shares available make large-scale investigative and selling efforts less lucrative for the majority of investment firms. Often the limited number of shares available precludes broad use of the stock in the accounts and/or recommendations of the larger investment firms.
- Limited demand and following, as well as investment house interest, affects immediate marketability. In addition, the immediate purchase or sale of large blocks is difficult except under special circumstances.
- Size, and sometimes local nature, of the company limits general investor knowledge.

All of these objections are legitimate to some varying degree, but as with most tenets in the investment field, there is no black and white. A number of the smaller companies traded in this area, with sales usually ranging between 5 to 50 million dollars and with well-established growth patterns, products, and markets carry a good deal less risk than size alone might imply, enjoy brisk if limited demand, can be purchased and sold in good volume in reasonable time and do enjoy some very sound and aggressive investment backing.

The very fact that people aren't generally looking in this area, however, frequently allows the stocks of such companies to be purchased at considerably lower earnings' multiples than their more widely known counterparts. In addition the larger percentage growth attainable on a smaller starting base often yields the superior sales and earnings performance desired, and such growth by definition soon moves the company into larger markets, expands the shares outstanding and available for trading, attracts investment interest and investors, begins to expand the multiplier, and tomorrow's "blue chip", institutional holding is discovered.

WHAT TO LOOK FOR:

The problem is to recognize a growth company at an early stage in development and to buy such a company at a reasonable multiple of earnings. First it is necessary to define a *growth company* and then a *reasonable* multiple of earnings.

. . . A Growth Company

To many people a growth company is any company whose stock goes up in price. As was pointed out above, however, in many cases this price rise has had little to do with actual company performance. What then is a growth company? There seem to be two general approaches to defining growth companies. For lack of better terms, we shall call these the *quantitative* and *qualitative* approaches, although the two more often than not overlap and the distinction is mostly one of degree. Samuel L. Stedman of Carl M. Loeb, Rhoades and Company defines a growth company as one which is showing a 12–15% growth in per share earnings compounded yearly. J. Eugene Banks of Brown Brothers, Harriman and Company calls a growth company one whose per share earnings are trending upward more rapidly than the per share earnings of the more widely used averages. William B. Harris, writing for *Fortune Magazine*, calls a minimum definition of a growth company "a corporation whose earnings per share have shown an annual rate of increase, over several years, of more than 4% (in constant dollars) or 6.5% (in current dollars) which is about the annual growth rate of the U.S. economy during the postwar period."[1] Perhaps the earliest definition of this quantitative measurement of growth was expressed by Fred Y. Presley writing in the Annual Report of *National Investors Corporation* in 1938:

> The studies by this organization, directed specifically toward improved procedure in selection, afford evidence that the common stocks of growth companies—that is, companies whose earnings move forward from cycle to cycle, and are only temporarily interrupted by periodic business depressions—offer the most effective medium of investment in the field of common stocks, either in terms of dividend return or longer term capital appreciation. We believe that this general conclusion can be demonstrated statistically and is supported by economic analysis and practical reasoning.

Although this group seems to lay major emphasis on compounded growth in earnings, qualitative analysis of the particular company in question also plays a part in the definition of a growth company. Mr. Harris, for example, lists a number of measurements to be applied to a potential growth company along with an emphasis on a particular growth rate. He includes the maturity of the industry, position in and type of markets served, dilution and dividend payout policies, company size in relation to its market, and alert management.

Philip Fisher, West Coast investment manager and author of *Common Stocks and Uncommon Profits*, lists 15 points to search for in a growth company.[2] Whereas Mr. Harris covers general areas in a company's internal and external operations, Mr. Fisher tends to go into much greater detail in the internal workings of a particular company, attempting to measure management determination at various levels of command, the type and quality of sales organization, labor and personnel policies, executive relations and depth, cost and accounting controls, incentives, individual product potentials, and effectiveness of R&D work, as well as some of Mr. Harris' broader measurements.

Peter Bernstein, writing in the *Harvard Business Review*, while measuring increase in earnings over a given period of time, also succinctly elaborates on the view that "true growth is organic, comes from within, and is reflected in the creation of the company's own market."[3] Mr. Bernstein would subscribe to a number of the characteristics outlined for a growth company, but in all probability would hold that these characteristics are typical in any well-managed company, and that they in themselves do not distinguish a growth company. (A good example of Mr. Bernstein's "internal growth and market development" concept might be Polaroid Corporation.)

Our own experience has directed an emphasis on four main points when defining a growth company:

1. A steadily improving record of sales (recognizing unit as well as dollar sales), per share earnings, and to a lesser extent, profit margins. (Two excellent examples of companies which fulfill this requirement are Henry Holt and Haloid Xerox.)

Any discussion of percentage or degree of improvement desired—the quantitative measurement—of necessity gets into price willing to be paid. The same can be said of the length of the record and the "quality" of the earnings; i.e., the durability and stability of such earnings. One cannot put arbitrary figures on such measurements except in the very broadest sense and then, as with so much in the analysis of growth companies, the rest must be left to individual investor judgment. To establish an arbitrary rate of growth as a criteria for a growth *company*, as distinguished from a growth *stock*, disregards price. Whereas a company at a 10–15% rate of growth compounded may have demonstrated growth characteristics, at 30 times earnings the characteristics of that company's stock would show perhaps a less than desired result. At this high multiplier, in itself carrying extra risk, the stock above would double in 5–8 years given no further rise from a higher price-earnings multiple.

Return on net worth is not included in the above group as so much depends on the individual company's situation that this factor in itself cannot be viewed as a hard and fast measurement. Even the trend must be looked at in the light of changing circumstances—for instance the introduction of the rental option *vs.* direct sale will play havoc with return on net worth.

2. A good record of new product or process development and/or old product or process improvement resulting in sales volume generated in new markets or through a steadily growing share of existing old markets. (Examples might be American Photocopy, Papercraft, and Beauty Counselors.)

In a limited way the share of total company sales enjoyed by products no more than, say, five years old gives some indication of a company's ability along these lines. Equally important, however, is the sales end—the merchandising—marketing skills of a particular company. Indeed an exceptional marketing organization lends stability to a growth trend well beyond the weight many investors attach to it. Usually these two attributes—product or process development and strong marketing—go hand in hand for the most successful growth companies.

3. Management. In some measure the companies which fulfill Points 1 and 2 above will of necessity have a well above average management. Yet the successful growth stock investor cannot rely solely on the past to judge the future. He must make judgments as to the policies management is pursuing to achieve comparable future growth. He must become thoroughly familiar with the industry and related industries as well as the particular company in question to cover this point adequately. This is one of the most important investment considerations, and there is no short-cut the investor can take. Yet the rewards are large, and the investor who can satisfy himself on a management's future policies, and ability to implement these policies, has as close to a "sure thing" as one can ever find in the investment field.

4. Operating in an area characterized by rapid development of new applications and new products within an expanding overall market. (Examples might be Haveg Industries, Indiana Steel Products and Heli-Coil Corporation.)

To a degree this is the external application of Point 2. Once an investor has satisfied himself as to the first three points above, then the most promising company is one which is operating within a climate favorable to continued long-term growth. (Such areas today might include plastics, electronics, light metals and so on.)

In addition, company size is an important factor in a growth company. Small size alone does not designate a growth company, but small size certainly should not arbitrarily disqualify a company from investment consideration. The relative size of a company must be measured against the background of the market and growth in the market served. (Point 4) Even more important the company itself should be measured first and foremost against the first three points outlined above.

It is a basic fallacy to assume automatically that a qualified smaller company cannot compete effectively with the larger companies in an industry. The flexibility and personal application that is more apt to be found in the smaller company in many cases far outweighs the greater resources of its larger competitors. The highly organized command levels, both staff and line, of some of our larger companies often slow the institution of new procedures, the creation, development and application of new ideas, and the implementation of new ways of approaching and solving problems. Given a strong nucleus of one to three capable men, personally involved through large stock ownership and initial creation, and concentrating on one particular area, a small company will out-perform and out-maneuver a good many of its larger, more diversified, many-tiered competitors.

Again the research and development work that can be accomplished by these smaller companies in direct competition with larger competitors, and larger resources, is too often overlooked in the market. One has only to view some of the recent developments of General Ceramics ($7 million sales), Epsco ($8 million sales), and H. I. Thompson ($11 million sales) to gain confidence in the research abilities of the qualified smaller company.

. . . A Reasonable Multiple of Earnings

Our second problem is that of defining a *reasonable* multiple of earnings. Basically a multiple of earnings reflects investor hopes for earnings' appreciation and dividend payout over a period of time. The multiple is also the market's appraisal of the degree of risk inherent in a particular investment—the durability and stability of earnings as well as projected earnings growth. Finally, the multiple of earnings reflects general investor confidence, or lack of confidence, in the economy as a whole.

The company whose stock is selling at a high price-earnings ratio is not *necessarily* overpriced. Indeed if Company A is growing at twice the rate of Company B then it might be argued that Company A is underpriced, other things being equal, if it is not selling at at least twice the price of Company B. Given a long-term rate of growth for Company A, there is no reason to assume that it should ever sell, again other things being equal, at less than double Company B's per share price. Yet this high price-earnings concept needs further examination.

There are a number of "formulas" which have been developed for appraising stock price outside of the conventional earnings multiplier approach. Among current favorites are the present worth concept of projected future earnings brought back to the present at a discount rate in proportion to judgment of risk involved or return desired, and the price [times] increase-in-earnings (past), or price [times] projected earnings (future) multiplier. Yet in applying all such formulas, a judgment must be made as to the rate of growth of *future* earnings and the degree of risk in these earnings. Above all else it is this judgment which is the key to a multiple of earnings. To justify a high multiple of earnings—over 20–25 times—one must have assured himself of the *four* points defining a growth company discussed above and must be able to see earnings compounding with little risk at an abnormal rate well into the future. Earnings must compound at an abnormal rate to realize the capital gain desired, for gain through an increase in multiplier has for the most part already occurred on the higher multiple stocks. A misjudgment of this future growth could not only fail to yield the desired gain but could result in some rather dramatic capital losses through a reduction in the multiplier. In addition, the risk involved with high multiple stocks may well lie beyond the investor's control. A general reversal of investor confidence usually tends to have a greater effect on those stocks which appear high on the basis of conventional multiplier analysis. This risk, however, is usually temporary in nature, and the investor who has done his homework well will come out satisfactorily over the longer term.

Yet it should be emphasized again that the high multiple stock must enjoy most of its future gain through a compounding of future earnings and not through an additional increase in the multiplier. Two similar companies—Haloid Xerox and American Photocopy—illustrate the importance of the multiplier for large capital gain investing. [On page 227] is a brief record of these two companies.

Earnings, sales and margin growth have been excellent in both companies (and incidentally these two companies qualify in other respects with our *four points* and are true growth companies). Yet during the 1958–59 period (the only comparison available as American Photocopy was first traded publicly in 1957) American Photocopy advanced from a low of 21 to a high of 151, or 7 times (readjusting for a 3–1 split), whereas Haloid Xerox advanced from a low of 47 bid to a high of 114 bid, or 2 1/2 times. As can be seen, Haloid's multiplier could advance only slightly from an already high level whereas American Photocopy was definitely "reasonable" and could enjoy the two-pronged effect of increased earnings in the company and an expanded multiplier in the market.

Apparently American Photocopy was initially judged by the market to hold an undue degree of risk. This could have reflected the fear of strong, larger company competition and/or the small size of American Photocopy. (Minnesota Mining, Eastman Kodak, and Sperry Rand all are in the single-copy reproduction field). Whatever the case, the degree

	American Photocopy				Haloid Xerox			
	Sales	Per Share Earnings	Pretax Margin	Average P–E Ratio	Sales	Per Share Earnings	Pretax Margin	Average P–E Ratio
1952	$ 2.5M	$ .25	16.5%	—	$14.8M	$ .78	10.2%	14.5
1953	5.3M	.59	19.3%	—	15.8M	.79	10.8%	15.0
1954	7.2M	1.08	25.0%	—	17.3M	1.08	12.2%	43.0
1955	9.3M	1.36	24.5%	—	21.4M	1.51	12.4%	33.0
1956	12.2M	1.90	27.0%	—	23.6M	1.61	12.4%	30.0
1957	14.9M	2.31	26.5%	15*	25.8M	1.83	13.2%	30.0
1958	17.5M	2.71	26.5%	18	27.6M	1.96	13.5%	34.0
1959(E)	23.0M	4.20**	29.0%	28***	30.0M	2.30	13.8%	36.0
								40.0***

*1st year of public market.

**On the basis of 825,000 shares outstanding before 3–1 split.

***January 1st, 1959–October 1st, 1959

of risk was misjudged by the market, and it was this misjudgment which allowed the astute investor to achieve such large capital gain.

Over the past year to 18 months a number of smaller, true growth companies have advanced in price to a point where one must seriously question the capital gain potential of their stock from present levels over the near to intermediate term. Over the longer term, however, the stock of these companies should yield the gain desired.

A few such seemingly high multiple companies are compounding earnings at such a rate, and with such a dramatic potential ahead of them for further growth with only limited risk, that their stock should show excellent capital gain even over the near to intermediate term.

CONCLUSION

The appreciation in average multipliers attached to the stocks of the larger "blue chip" companies over the past ten years has tended to obscure the more or less mediocre earnings growth in these companies. The price level of such stocks today would seem to rule out similar gain over the next ten-year period; indeed the multipliers attached to the "blue chips" in today's market could yield them quite vulnerable on the basis of only average projected earnings growth from an already large base.

For the most part investor misjudgment and lack of knowledge centers around the smaller companies, usually between $5 to $50 million annual sales, which frequently are traded over-the-counter or on a regional exchange. Primarily in this area are to be found the true growth companies—tomorrow's "blue chips" if-you-will—where dramatic capital appreciation can occur through compounded earnings on a relatively small base and advance in market stature as reflected by multipliers attached to such earnings. Here is where the astute capital gain investor can apply his theories of what constitutes a growth company and, with less risk than is generally realized, score excellent capital appreciation. And it is in this area that the tools of analysis and observation discussed above, the *four points*, can more readily be applied. If it is possible to fully understand and appraise an American Photocopy, the possibility of such an understanding and appraisal of an Eastman Kodak is a much more formidable task.

Mr. Thomas E. Brittingham, Jr. of Wilmington, Delaware, a

private investor who year in and year out has surpassed every published index of stock market performance, wrote a very fitting closing to this article more than twenty years ago:

> My own experience has proven conclusively that maximum results have been obtained through investing in growing companies, keeping these companies until they have completed their growth, and discarding them when the public fancy has changed them into "blue chips" and pushed them to fantastic heights where they are unattractive because of their ridiculously high price ratio to current earnings.
>
> A good horse can't go on winning races forever, and a good stock eventually passes its peak. Progress is the catch-word of today, so let's forget the old idea of what constitutes a conservative security and climb on the bandwagon with tomorrow's "blue chips".

FOOTNOTES

1. *Those Delicious Growth Stocks*; Fortune, April 1959.
2. *Common Stocks and Uncommon Profits*; Harper Bros., copyright 1958 by Philip Fisher.
3. *Growth Companies v. Growth Stocks*: *HBR*, September-October, 1956.

WHAT TO BUY—THE FIFTEEN POINTS TO LOOK FOR IN A COMMON STOCK WHEN TO SELL—AND WHEN NOT TO

Philip A. Fisher

Philip Fisher's *Common Stocks and Uncommon Profits* first appeared in 1958. In it, he presented the case for growth stock investing and explained the advantages of his "scuttlebutt" method for learning about companies by talking to competitors, suppliers, and, particularly, former employees. The book is full of practical Do's and Don'ts for individual investors. In these excerpts, Fisher explains what to look for in a prospective investment and identifies the only investment reasons ever to sell a stock.

WHAT TO BUY—THE FIFTEEN POINTS TO LOOK FOR IN A COMMON STOCK

There are fifteen points with which I believe the investor should concern himself. A company could well be an investment bonanza if it failed

From Philip A. Fisher, *Common Stocks and Uncommon Profits* (Woodside, California, 1984; originally published 1958), 15–51, 82–91. All rights reserved by PSR Publications, 301 Henrik Road, Woodside, California 94062. PSR Publications is a division of Fisher Investments, Inc.

fully to qualify on a very few of them. I do not think it could come up to my definition of a worthwhile investment if it failed to qualify on many. Some of these points are matters of company policy; others deal with how efficiently this policy is carried out. Some of these points concern matters which should largely be determined from information obtained from sources outside the company being studied, while others are best solved by direct inquiry from company personnel. These fifteen points are:

POINT 1. DOES THE COMPANY HAVE PRODUCTS OR SERVICES WITH SUFFICIENT MARKET POTENTIAL TO MAKE POSSIBLE A SIZABLE INCREASE IN SALES FOR AT LEAST SEVERAL YEARS?

It is by no means impossible to make a fair one-time profit from companies with a stationary or even a declining sales curve. Operating economies resulting from better control of costs can at times create enough improvement in net income to produce an increase in the market price of a company's shares. This sort of one-time profit is eagerly sought by many speculators and bargain hunters. It does not offer the degree of opportunity, however, that should interest those desiring to make the greatest possible gains from their investment funds.

Neither does another type of situation which sometimes offers a considerably larger degree of profit. Such a situation occurs when a changed condition opens up a large increase in sales for a period of a very few years, after which sales stop growing. A large-scale example of this is what happened to the many radio set manufacturers with the commercial development of television. A huge increase in sales occurred for several years. Now that nearly 90 per cent of U.S. homes that are wired for electricity have television sets, the sales curve is again static. In the case of a great many companies in the industry, a large profit was made by those who bought early enough. Then as the sales curve leveled out, so did the attractiveness of many of these stocks.

Not even the most outstanding growth companies need necessarily be expected to show sales for every single year larger than those of the year before. In another chapter I will attempt to show why the normal intricacies of commercial research and the problems of marketing new products tend to cause such sales increases to come in an irregular series of uneven spurts rather than in a smooth year-by-year progression. The vagaries of the business cycle will also have a major influence on year-to-year comparisons. Therefore growth should not be judged on an annual basis but, say, by taking units of several years each. Certain companies give promise of greater than normal growth not only for the next several-year period, but also for a considerable time beyond that.

Those companies which decade by decade have consistently shown spectacular growth might be divided into two groups. For lack of better terms I will call one group those that happen to be both "fortunate and able" and the other group those that are "fortunate because they are able." A high order of management ability is a must for both groups. No company grows for a long period of years just because it is lucky. It must have and continue to keep a high order of business skill, otherwise it will not be able to capitalize on its good fortune and to defend its competitive position from the inroads of others.

The Aluminum Company of America is an example of the "fortunate and able" group. The founders of this company were men with great vision. They correctly foresaw important commercial uses for their new product. However, neither they nor anyone else at that time could foresee anything like the full size of the market for aluminum products that was to develop over the next seventy years. A combination of technical developments and economies, of which the company was far more the beneficiary than the instigator, was to bring this about. Alcoa has and continues to show a high order of skill in encouraging and taking advantage of these trends. However, if background conditions, such as the perfecting of airborne transportation, had not caused influences completely beyond Alcoa's control to open up extensive new markets, the company would still have grown—but at a slower rate. . . .

Now let us take Du Pont as an example of the other group of growth stocks—those which I have described as "fortunate because they are able." This company was not originally in the business of making nylon, cellophane, lucite, neoprene, orlon, milar, or any of the many other glamorous products with which it is frequently associated in the public mind and which have proven so spectacularly profitable to the investor. For many years Du Pont made blasting powder. In time of peace its growth would largely have paralleled that of the mining industry. In recent years, it might have grown a little more rapidly than this as additional sales volume accompanied increased activity in road building. None of this would have been more than an insignificant fraction of the volume of business that has developed, however, as the company's brilliant business and financial judgment teamed up with superb technical skill to attain a sales volume that is now exceeding two billion dollars each year. Applying the skills and knowledge learned in its original powder business, the company has successfully launched product after product to make one of the great success stories of American industry. . . .

Correctly judging the long-range sales curve of a company is of extreme importance to the investor. Superficial judgment can lead to wrong conclusions. For example, I have already mentioned radio-television stocks as an instance where instead of continued long-range growth there was one major spurt as the homes of the nation acquired television sets. . . .

One potential development, color television, has possibly been overdiscounted by the general public. Another is a direct result of transistor development and printed circuitry. It is a screen-type television with sets that would be little different in size and shape from the larger pictures we now have on our walls. . . .

If a company's management is outstanding and the industry is one subject to technological change and development research, the shrewd investor should stay alert to the possibility that management might handle company affairs so as to produce in the future exactly the type of sales curve that is the first step to consider in choosing an outstanding investment. . . .

When the investor is alert to this type of opportunity, how profitable may it be? Let us take an actual example from the industry we have just been discussing. In 1947 a friend of mine in Wall Street was making a survey of the infant television industry. He studied approximately a dozen of the principal set producers over the better part of a year. His conclusion was that the business was going to be competitive, that there were going to be major shifts in position between the leading concerns, and that certain stocks in the industry had speculative appeal. However, in the process of this survey it developed that one of the great shortages was the glass bulb for the picture tube. The most successful producer appeared to be Corning Glass Works. After further examination of the technical and research aspects of Corning Glass Works it became apparent that this company was unusually well qualified to produce these glass bulbs for the television industry. Estimates of the possible market indicated that this would be a major source of new business for the company. Since prospects for other product lines seemed generally favorable, this analyst recommended the stock for both individual and institutional investment. The stock at that time was selling at about 20. It has since been split 2½-for-1 and ten years after his purchase was selling at over 100, which was the equivalent of a price of 250 on the old stock.

POINT 2. DOES THE MANAGEMENT HAVE A DETERMINATION TO CONTINUE TO DEVELOP PRODUCTS OR PROCESSES THAT WILL STILL FURTHER INCREASE TOTAL SALES POTENTIALS WHEN THE GROWTH POTENTIALS OF CURRENTLY ATTRACTIVE PRODUCT LINES HAVE LARGELY BEEN EXPLOITED?

Companies which have a significant growth prospect for the next few years because of new demand for existing lines, but which have neither policies nor plans to provide for further developments beyond this may provide a vehicle for a nice one-time profit. They are not apt to provide the means for the consistent gains over ten or twenty-five years that are the surest route to financial success. It is at this point that scientific research and development engineering begin to enter the picture. It is largely through these means that companies improve old products and develop new ones. This is the usual route by which a management not content with one isolated spurt of growth sees that growth occurs in a series of more or less continuous spurts.

The investor usually obtains the best results in companies whose engineering or research is to a considerable extent devoted to products having some business relationship to those already within the scope of company activities. This does not mean that a desirable company may not have a number of divisions, some of which have product lines quite different from others. It does mean that a company with research centered around each of these divisions, like a cluster of trees each growing additional branches from its own trunk, will usually do much better than a company working on a number of unrelated new products which, if successful, will land it in several new industries unrelated to its existing business.

At first glance Point 2 may appear to be a mere repetition of Point 1. This is not the case. Point 1 is a matter of fact, appraising the degree of potential sales growth that now exists for a company's product. Point 2 is a matter of management attitude. Does the company now recognize that in time it will almost certainly have grown up to the potential of its present market and that to continue to grow it may have to develop further new markets at some future time? It is the company that has both a good rating on the first point and an affirmative attitude on the second that is likely to be of the greatest investment interest.

POINT 3. HOW EFFECTIVE ARE THE COMPANY'S RESEARCH AND DEVELOPMENT EFFORTS IN RELATION TO ITS SIZE?

For a large number of publicly owned companies it is not too difficult to get a figure showing the number of dollars being spent each year on research and development. Since virtually all such companies report their annual sales total, it is only a matter of the simplest mathematics to divide the research figure by total sales and so learn the per cent of each sales dollar that a company is devoting to this type of activity. Many professional investment analysts like to compare this research figure for one company with that of others in the same general field. Sometimes they compare it with the average of the industry, by averaging the figures of many somewhat similar companies. From this, conclusions are drawn both as to the importance of a company's research effort in relation to competition and the amount of research per share of stock that the investor is getting in a particular company.

Figures of this sort can prove a crude yardstick that may give a worthwhile hint that one company is doing an abnormal amount of research or another not nearly enough. But unless a great deal of further knowledge is obtained, such figures can be misleading. One reason for this is that companies vary enormously in what they include or exclude as research and development expense. One company will include a type of engineering expense that most authorities would not consider genuine research at all, since it is really tailoring an existing product to a particular order—in other words, sales engineering. Conversely, another company will charge the expense of operating a pilot plant on a completely new product to production rather than research. Most experts would call this a pure research function, since it is directly related to obtaining the know-how to make a new product. If all companies were to report research on a comparable accounting basis, the relative figures on the amount of research done by various well-known companies might look quite different from those frequently used in financial circles.

In no other major subdivision of business activity are to be found such great variations from one company to another between what goes in as expense and what comes out in benefits as occurs in research. Even among the best-managed companies this variation seems to run in a ratio of as much as two to one. By this is meant some well-run companies will get as much as twice the ultimate gain for each research dollar spent as will others. If averagely run companies are included, this variation between the best and the mediocre is still greater. This is largely because the big strides in the way of new products and processes are no longer the work of a single genius. They come from teams of highly trained men, each with a different specialty. One may be a chemist, another a solid state physicist, a third a metallurgist and a fourth a mathematician. The degree of skill of each of these experts is only part of what is needed to produce outstanding results. It is also necessary to have leaders who can coordinate the work of people of such diverse backgrounds and keep them driving toward a common goal. Consequently, the number or prestige of research workers in one company may be overshadowed by the effectiveness with which they are being helped to work as a team in another. . . .

POINT 4. DOES THE COMPANY HAVE AN ABOVE-AVERAGE SALES ORGANIZATION?

In this competitive age, the products or services of few companies are so outstanding that they will sell to their maximum potentialities if they are not expertly merchandised. It is the making of a sale that is the most basic single activity of any business. Without sales, survival is impossible. It is the making of repeat sales to satisfied customers that is the first benchmark of success. Yet, strange as it seems, the relative efficiency of a company's sales, advertising, and distributive organizations receives far less attention from most investors, even the careful ones, than do production, research, finance, or other major subdivisions of corporate activity.

There is probably a reason for this. It is relatively easy to construct simple mathematical ratios that will provide some sort of guide to the attractiveness of a company's production costs, research activity, or financial structure in comparison with its competitors. It is a great deal harder to make ratios that have even a semblance of meaning in regard to sales and distribution efficiency. . . . Because sales effort does not readily lend itself to this type of formulae, many investors fail to appraise it at all in spite of its basic importance in determining real investment worth.

Again, the way out of this dilemma lies in the use of the "scuttlebutt" technique. Of all the phases of a company's activity, none is easier to learn about from sources outside the company than the relative efficiency of a sales organization. Both competitors and customers know the answers. Equally important, they are seldom hesitant to express their views. The time spent by the careful investor in inquiring into this subject is usually richly rewarded.

I am devoting less space to this matter of relative sales ability than I did to the matter of relative research ability. This does not mean that I consider it less important. In today's competitive world, many things are important to corporate success. However, outstanding production, sales, and research may be considered the three main columns upon which

An Indication of Magnificent Research
Hewlett Packard Co., Palo Alto, California

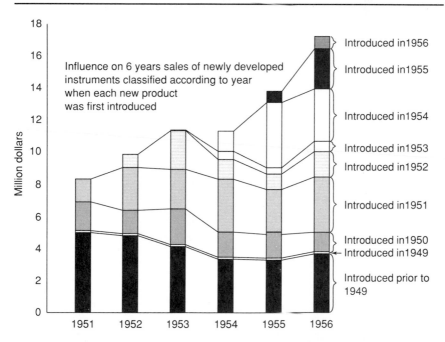

Influence on 6 years sales of newly developed instruments classified according to year when each new product was first introduced

such success is based. Saying that one is more important than another is like saying that the heart, the lungs, or the digestive tract is the most important single organ for the proper functioning of the body. All are needed for survival, and all must function well for vigorous health. Look around you at the companies that have proven outstanding investments. Try to find some that do not have both aggressive distribution and a constantly improving sales organization. . . .

POINT 5. DOES THE COMPANY HAVE A WORTHWHILE PROFIT MARGIN?

Here at last is a subject of importance which properly lends itself to the type of mathematical analysis which so many financial people feel is the backbone of sound investment decisions. From the standpoint of the investor, sales are only of value when and if they lead to increased profits. All the sales growth in the world won't produce the right type of investment vehicle if, over the years, profits do not grow correspondingly. The first step in examining profits is to study a company's profit margin, that is, to determine the number of cents of each dollar of sales that is brought down to operating profit. The wide variation between different companies, even those in the same industry, will immediately become apparent. Such a study should be made, not for a single year, but for a series of years. It then becomes evident that nearly all companies have broader profit margins—as well as greater total dollar profits—in years when an industry is unusually prosperous. However, it also becomes clear that the marginal companies—that is, those with the smaller profit margins—nearly always increase their profit margins by a considerably greater percentage in the good years than do the lower-cost companies, whose profit margins also get better but not to so great a degree. This usually causes the weaker companies to show a greater percentage increase in earnings in a year of abnormally good business than do the stronger companies in the same field. However, it should also be remembered that these earnings will decline correspondingly more rapidly when the business tide turns.

For this reason I believe that the greatest long-range investment profits are never obtained by investing in marginal companies. The only reason for considering a long-range investment in a company with an abnormally low profit margin is that there might be strong indications that a fundamental change is taking place within the company. . . .

POINT 6. WHAT IS THE COMPANY DOING TO MAINTAIN OR IMPROVE PROFIT MARGINS?

The success of a stock purchase does not depend on what is generally known about a company at the time the purchase is made. Rather it depends upon what gets to be known about it after the stock has been bought. Therefore it is not the profit margins of the past but those of the future that are basically important to the investor. . . .

POINT 7. DOES THE COMPANY HAVE OUTSTANDING LABOR AND PERSONNEL RELATIONS?

Most investors may not fully appreciate the profits from good labor relations. Few of them fail to recognize the impact of bad labor relations. The effect on production of frequent and prolonged strikes is obvious to anyone making even the most cursory review of corporate financial statements.

However, the difference in the degree of profitability between a company with good personnel relations and one with mediocre personnel relations is far greater than the direct cost of strikes. If workers feel that they are fairly treated by their employer, a background has been laid wherein efficient leadership can accomplish much in increasing productivity per worker. Furthermore, there is always considerable cost in training each new worker. Those companies with an abnormal labor turnover have therefore an element of unnecessary expense avoided by better-managed enterprises. . . .

POINT 8. DOES THE COMPANY HAVE OUTSTANDING EXECUTIVE RELATIONS?

If having good relations with lower-echelon personnel is important, creating the right atmosphere among executive personnel is vital. These are the men whose judgment, ingenuity, and teamwork will in time make or break any venture. Because the stakes for which they play are high, the tension on the job is frequently great. So is the chance that friction or resentment might create conditions whereby top executive talent either does not stay with a company or does not produce to its maximum ability if it does stay.

The company offering greatest investment opportunities will be one in which there is a good executive climate. . . .

POINT 9. DOES THE COMPANY HAVE DEPTH TO ITS MANAGEMENT?

. . . Those organizations where the top brass personally interfere with and try to handle routine day-to-day operating matters seldom turn out to be the most attractive type of investments. Cutting across the lines of authority which they themselves have set up frequently results in well-meaning executives significantly detracting from the investment caliber of the companies they run. No matter how able one or two bosses may be in handling all this detail, once a corporation reaches a certain size executives of this type will get in trouble on two fronts. Too much detail will have arisen for them to handle. Capable people just are not being developed to handle the still further growth that should lie ahead.

Another matter is worthy of the investor's attention in judging whether a company has suitable depth in management. Does top management welcome and evaluate suggestions from personnel even if, at times, those suggestions carry with them adverse criticism of current management practices? So competitive is today's business world and so great the need for improvement and change that if pride or indifference prevent top management from exploring what has frequently been found to be a veritable gold mine of worthwhile ideas, the investment climate that results probably will not be the most suitable one for the investor. Neither is it likely to be one in which increasing numbers of vitally needed younger executives are going to develop.

POINT 10. HOW GOOD ARE THE COMPANY'S COST ANALYSIS AND ACCOUNTING CONTROLS?

No company is going to continue to have outstanding success for a long period of time if it cannot break down its over-all costs with sufficient accuracy and detail to show the cost of each small step in its operation. Only in this way will management know what most needs its attention. Only in this way can management judge whether it is properly solving each problem that does need its attention. Furthermore, most successful companies make not one but a vast series of products. If the management does not have a precise knowledge of the true cost of each product in relation to the others, it is under an extreme handicap. It becomes almost impossible to establish pricing policies that will ensure the maximum obtainable over-all profit consistent with discouraging undue competition. There is no way of knowing which products are worthy of special sales effort and promotion. Worst of all, some apparently successful activities may actually be operating at a loss and, unknown to management, may be decreasing rather than swelling the total of over-all profits. Intelligent planning becomes almost impossible.

In spite of the investment importance of accounting controls, it is usually only in instances of extreme inefficiency that the careful investor will get a clear picture of the status of cost accounting and related activities in a company in which he is contemplating investment. In this sphere, the "scuttlebutt" method will sometimes reveal companies that are really deficient. It will seldom tell much more than this. Direct inquiry of company personnel will usually elicit a completely sincere reply that the cost data are entirely adequate. Detailed cost sheets will often be shown in support of the statement. However, it is not so much the existence of detailed figures as their relative accuracy which is important. The best that the careful investor usually can do in this field is to recognize both the importance of the subject and his own limitations in making a worthwhile appraisal of it. Within these limits he usually can only fall back on the general conclusion that a company well above average in most other aspects of business skill will probably be above average in this field, too, as long as top management understands the basic importance of expert accounting controls and cost analysis.

POINT 11. ARE THERE OTHER ASPECTS OF THE BUSINESS, SOMEWHAT PECULIAR TO THE INDUSTRY INVOLVED, WHICH WILL GIVE THE INVESTOR IMPORTANT CLUES AS TO HOW OUTSTANDING THE COMPANY MAY BE IN RELATION TO ITS COMPETITION?

By definition, this is somewhat of a catch-all point of inquiry. This is because matters of this sort are bound to differ considerably from each other—those which are of great importance in some lines of business can, at times, be of little or no importance in others. For example, in most important operations involving retailing, the degree of skill a company has in handling real estate matters—the quality of its leases, for instance—is of great significance. In many other lines of business, a high degree of skill in this field is less important. Similarly, the relative skill with which a company handles its credits is of great significance to some companies, of minor or no importance to others. For both these matters, our old friend the "scuttlebutt" method will usually furnish the investor with a pretty clear picture. Frequently his conclusions can be checked against mathematical ratios such as comparative leasing costs per dollar of sales, or ratio of credit loss, if the point is of sufficient importance to warrant careful study. . . .

POINT 12. DOES THE COMPANY HAVE A SHORT-RANGE OR LONG-RANGE OUTLOOK IN REGARD TO PROFITS?

Some companies will conduct their affairs so as to gain the greatest possible profit right now. Others will deliberately curtail maximum immediate profits to build up good will and thereby gain greater over-all profits over a period of years. Treatment of customers and vendors gives frequent examples of this. One company will constantly make the sharpest possible deals with suppliers. Another will at times pay above contract price to a vendor who has had unexpected expense in making delivery, because it wants to be sure of having a dependable source of needed raw materials or high-quality components available when the market has turned and supplies may be desperately needed. The difference in treatment of customers is equally noticeable. The company that will go to special trouble and expense to take care of the needs of a regular customer caught in an unexpected jam may show lower profits on the particular transaction, but far greater profits over the years.

The "scuttlebutt" method usually reflects these differences in policies quite clearly. The investor wanting maximum results should favor companies with a truly long-range outlook concerning profits.

POINT 13. IN THE FORESEEABLE FUTURE WILL THE GROWTH OF THE COMPANY REQUIRE SUFFICIENT EQUITY FINANCING SO THAT THE LARGER NUMBER OF SHARES THEN OUTSTANDING WILL LARGELY CANCEL THE EXISTING STOCKHOLDERS' BENEFIT FROM THIS ANTICIPATED GROWTH?

The typical book on investment devotes so much space to a discussion on the corporation's cash position, corporate structure, percentage of capitalization in various classes of securities, etc. that it may well be asked why these purely financial aspects should not be given more than the amount of space devoted to this one point out of a total of fifteen. The reason is that it is the basic contention of this book that the intelligent investor should not buy common stocks simply because they are cheap but only if they give promise of major gain to him.

Only a small percentage of all companies can qualify with a high rating for all or nearly all of the other fourteen points listed in this discussion. Any company which can so qualify could easily borrow money, at prevailing rates for its size company, up to the accepted top percentage of debt for that kind of business. If such a company needed more cash once this top debt limit has been reached—always assuming of course that it qualifies at or near the top in regard to further sales growth, profit margins, management, research, and the various other points we are now considering—it could still raise equity money at some price, since investors are always eager to participate in ventures of this sort.

Therefore, if investment is limited to outstanding situations, what really matters is whether the company's cash plus further borrowing ability is sufficient to take care of the capital needed to exploit the prospects of the next several years. If it is, and if the company is willing to borrow to the limit of prudence, the common stock investor need have no concern as to the more distant future. If the investor has properly appraised the situation, any equity financing that might be done some years ahead will be at prices so much higher than present levels that he need not be concerned. This is because the near-term financing will have produced enough increase in earnings, by the time still further financing is needed some years hence, to have brought the stock to a substantially higher price level. . . .

POINT 14. DOES THE MANAGEMENT TALK FREELY TO INVESTORS ABOUT ITS AFFAIRS WHEN THINGS ARE GOING WELL BUT "CLAM UP" WHEN TROUBLES AND DISAPPOINTMENTS OCCUR?

It is the nature of business that in even the best-run companies unexpected difficulties, profit squeezes, and unfavorable shifts in demand for their products will at times occur. Furthermore, the companies into which the investor should be buying if greatest gains are to occur are companies which over the years will constantly, through the efforts of technical research, be trying to produce and sell new products and new processes. By the law of averages, some of these are bound to be costly failures. Others will have unexpected delays and heartbreaking expenses during the early period of plant shake-down. For months on end, such extra and unbudgeted costs will spoil the most carefully laid profit forecasts for the business as a whole. Such disappointments are an inevitable part of even the most successful business. If met forthrightly and with good judgment, they are merely one of the costs of eventual success. They are frequently a sign of strength rather than weakness in a company.

How a management reacts to such matters can be a valuable clue to the investor. The management that does not report as freely when things are going badly as when they are going well usually "clams up" in this way for one of several rather significant reasons. It may not have a program worked out to solve the unanticipated difficulty. It may have become panicky. It may not have an adequate sense of responsibility to its stockholders, seeing no reason why it should report more than what may seem expedient at the moment. In any event, the investor will do well to exclude from investment any company that withholds or tries to hide bad news.

POINT 15. DOES THE COMPANY HAVE A MANAGEMENT OF UNQUESTIONABLE INTEGRITY?

The management of a company is always far closer to its assets than is the stockholder. Without breaking any laws, the number of ways in which those in control can benefit themselves and their families at the expense of the ordinary stockholder is almost infinite. One way is to put themselves—to say nothing of their relatives or in-laws—on the payroll at salaries far above the normal worth of the work performed. Another is to own properties they sell or rent to the corporation at above market rates. Among small corporations this is sometimes hard to detect, since controlling families or key officers at times buy and lease real estate to such companies, not for purposes of unfair gain but in a sincere desire to free limited working capital for other corporate purposes. . . .

There is only one real protection against abuses like these. This is to confine investments to companies the managements of which have a highly developed sense of trusteeship and moral responsibility to their stockholders. This is a point concerning which the "scuttlebutt" method can be very helpful. Any investment may still be considered interesting if it falls down in regard to almost any other one of the fifteen points which have now been covered, but rates an unusually high score in regard to all the rest. Regardless of how high the rating may be in all other matters, however, if there is a serious question of the lack of a strong management sense of trusteeship for stockholders, the investor should never seriously consider participating in such an enterprise.

* * * * *

WHEN TO SELL—AND WHEN NOT TO

There are many good reasons why an investor might decide to sell common stocks. He may want to build a new home or finance his son in a business. Any one of a number of similar reasons can, from the standpoint of happy living, make selling common stocks sensible. This type of selling, however, is personal rather than financial in its motive. As such it is well beyond the scope of this book. These comments are only designed to cover that type of selling that is motivated by a single objective—obtaining the greatest total dollar benefit from the investment dollars available.

I believe there are three reasons, and three reasons only, for the sale of any common stock which has been originally selected according to the investment principles already discussed. The first of these reasons should be obvious to anyone. This is when a mistake has been made in the original purchase and it becomes increasingly clear that the factual background of the particular company is, by a significant margin, less favorable than originally believed. The proper handling of this type of situation is largely a matter of emotional self-control. To some degree it also depends upon the investor's ability to be honest with himself.

Two of the important characteristics of common stock investment are the large profits that can come with proper handling, and the high degree of skill, knowledge, and judgment required for such proper handling. Since the process of obtaining these almost fantastic profits is so complex, it is not surprising that a certain percentage of errors in purchasing are sure to occur. Fortunately the long-range profits from really good common stocks should more than balance the losses from a normal percentage of such mistakes. They should leave a tremendous margin of gain as well. This is particularly true if the mistake is recognized quickly. When this happens, losses, if any, should be far smaller than if the stock bought in error had been held for a long period of time. Even more important, the funds tied up in the undesirable situation are freed to be used for something else which, if properly selected, should produce substantial gains.

However, there is a complicating factor that makes the handling of investment mistakes more difficult. This is the ego in each of us. None of us likes to admit to himself that he has been wrong. If we have made a mistake in buying a stock but can sell the stock at a small profit, we have somehow lost any sense of having been foolish. On the other hand, if we sell at a small loss we are quite unhappy about the whole matter. This reaction, while completely natural and normal, is probably one of the most dangerous in which we can indulge ourselves in the entire investment process. More money has probably been lost by investors holding a stock they really did not want until they could "at least come out even" than from any other single reason. If to these actual losses are added the profits that might have been made through the proper reinvestment of these funds if such reinvestment had been made when the mistake was first realized, the cost of self-indulgence becomes truly tremendous.

Furthermore this dislike of taking a loss, even a small loss, is just as illogical as it is natural. If the real object of common stock investment is the making of a gain of a great many hundreds per cent over a period of years, the difference between, say, a 20 per cent loss or a 5 per cent profit becomes a comparatively insignificant matter. What matters is not whether a loss occasionally occurs. What does matter is whether worthwhile profits so often fail to materialize that the skill of the investor or his advisor in handling investments must be questioned.

While losses should never cause strong self-disgust or emotional upset, neither should they be passed over lightly. They should always be reviewed with care so that a lesson is learned from each of them. If the particular elements which caused a misjudgment on a common stock purchase are thoroughly understood, it is unlikely that another poor purchase will be made through misjudging the same investment factors.

We come now to the second reason why sale should be made of a common stock. . . . Sales should always be made of the stock of a company which, because of changes resulting from the passage of time, no longer qualifies . . . to about the same degree it qualified at the time of purchase. This is why investors should be constantly on their guard. It explains why it is of such importance to keep at all times in close contact with the affairs of companies whose shares are held.

When companies deteriorate in this way they usually do so for one of two reasons. Either there has been a deterioration of management, or the company no longer has the prospect of increasing the markets for its product in the way it formerly did. Sometimes management deteriorates because success has affected one or more key executives. Smugness, complacency, or inertia replace the former drive and ingenuity. More often it occurs because a new set of top executives do not measure up to the standard of performance set by their predecessors. Either they no longer hold to the policies that have made the company outstandingly successful, or they do not have the ability to continue to carry out such policies. When any of these things happen the affected stock should be sold at once, regardless of how good the general market may look or how big the capital gains tax may be.

Similarly it sometimes happens that after growing spectacularly for many years, a company will reach a stage where the growth prospects of its markets are exhausted. From this time on it will only do about as well as [the] industry as a whole. It will only progress at about the same rate as the national economy does. This change may not be due to any deterioration of the management. Many managements show great skill in developing related or allied products to take advantage of growth in their immediate field. They recognize, however, that they do not have any particular advantage if they go into unrelated spheres of activity. Hence, if after years of being experts in a young and growing industry, times change and the company has pretty well exhausted the growth prospects of its market, its shares have deteriorated in an important way from the standards outlined under our frequently mentioned fifteen points. Such a stock should then be sold.

In this instance, selling might take place at a more leisurely pace than if management deterioration had set in. Possibly part of the holding might be kept until a more suitable investment could be found. However, in any event, the company should be recognized as no longer suitable for worthwhile investment. The amount of capital gains tax, no matter how large, should seldom prevent the switching of such funds into some other situation which, in the years ahead, may grow in a manner similar to the way in which this investment formerly grew.

There is a good test as to whether companies no longer adequately qualify in regard to this matter of expected further growth. This is for the investor to ask himself whether at the next peak of a business cycle, regardless of what may happen in the meantime, the comparative per-share earnings (after allowances for stock dividends and stock splits but not for new shares issued for additional capital) will probably show at least as great an increase from present levels as the present levels show from the last known peak of general business activity. If the answer is in the affirmative, the stock probably should be held. If in the negative, it should probably be sold.

For those who follow the right principles in making their original purchases, the third reason why a stock might be sold seldom arises, and should be acted upon only if an investor is very sure of his ground. It arises from the fact that opportunities for attractive investment are extremely hard to find. From a timing standpoint, they are seldom found just when investment funds happen to be available. If an investor has had funds for investment for quite a period of time and found few attractive situations into which to place these funds, he may well place some or all of them in a well-run company which he believes has definite growth prospects. However, these growth prospects may be at a slower average annual rate than may appear to be the case for some other seemingly more attractive situation that is found later. The already-owned company may in some other important aspects appear to be less attractive as well.

If the evidence is clear-cut and the investor feels quite sure of his ground, it will, even after paying capital gains taxes, probably pay him handsomely to switch into the situation with seemingly better prospects. The company that can show an average annual increase of 12 per cent for a long period of years should be a source of considerable financial satisfaction to its owners. However, the difference between these results and those that could occur from a company showing a 20 per cent average annual gain would be well worth the additional trouble and capital gains taxes that might be involved.

A word of caution may not be amiss, however, in regard to too readily selling a common stock in the hope of switching these funds into a still better one. There is always the risk that some major element in the picture has been misjudged. If this happens, the investment probably will not turn out nearly as well as anticipated. In contrast, an alert investor who has held a good stock for some time usually gets to know its less desirable as well as its more desirable characteristics. Therefore, before selling a rather satisfactory holding in order to get a still better one, there is need of the greatest care in trying to appraise accurately all elements of the situation.

At this point the critical reader has probably discerned a basic investment principle which by and large seems only to be understood by a small minority of successful investors. This is that once a stock has been properly selected and has borne the test of time, it is only occasionally that there is any reason for selling it at all. However, recommendations and comments continue to pour out of the financial community giving other types of reasons for selling outstanding common stocks. What about the validity of such reasons?

Most frequently given of such reasons is the conviction that a general stock market decline of some proportion is somewhere in the offing. . . . [P]ostponing an attractive purchase because of fear of what the general market might do will, over the years, prove very costly. This is because the investor is ignoring a powerful influence about which he has positive knowledge through fear of a less powerful force about which, in the present state of human knowledge, he and everyone else is largely guessing. If the argument is valid that the purchase of attractive common stocks should not be unduly influenced by fear of ordinary bear markets, the argument against selling outstanding stocks because of these fears is even more impressive. . . . Furthermore, the chance of the investor being right in making such sales is still further diminished by the factor of the capital gains tax. Because of the very large profits such outstanding stocks should be showing if they have been held for a period of years, this capital gains tax can still further accentuate the cost of making such sales.

There is another and even more costly reason why an investor should never sell out of an outstanding situation because of the possibility that an ordinary bear market may be about to occur. If the company is really a right one, the next bull market should see the stock making a new peak well above those so far attained. How is the investor to know when to buy back? Theoretically it should be after the coming decline. However, this presupposes that the investor will know when the decline will end. I have seen many investors dispose of a holding that was to show stupendous gain in the years ahead because of this fear of a coming bear market. Frequently the bear market never came and the stock went right on up. When a bear market has come, I have not seen one time in ten when the investor actually got back into the same shares before they had gone up above his selling price. Usually he either waited for them to go far lower than they actually dropped, or, when they were way down, fear of something else happening still prevented their reinstatement.

This brings us to another line of reasoning so often used to cause well-intentioned but unsophisticated investors to miss huge future profits. This is the argument that an outstanding stock has become overpriced and therefore should be sold. What is more logical than this? If a stock is overpriced, why not sell it rather than keep it?

Before reaching hasty conclusions, let us look a little bit below the surface. Just what is overpriced? What are we trying to accomplish? Any really good stock will sell and should sell at a higher ratio to current earnings than a stock with a stable rather than an expanding earning power. After all, this probability of participating in continued growth is obviously worth something. When we say that the stock is overpriced, we may mean that it is selling at an even higher ratio in relation to this expected earning power than we believe it should be. Possibly we may mean that it is selling at an even higher ratio than are other comparible stocks with similar prospects of materially increasing their future earnings.

All of this is trying to measure something with a greater degree of preciseness than is possible. The investor cannot pinpoint just how much per share a particular company will earn two years from now. He can at best judge this within such general and non-mathematical limits as "about the same," "up moderately," "up a lot," or "up tremendously." As a matter of fact, the company's top management cannot come a great deal closer than this. Either they or the investor should come pretty close in judging whether a sizable increase in average earnings is likely to occur a few years from now. But just how much increase, or the exact year in which it will occur, usually involves guessing on enough variables to make precise predictions impossible.

Under these circumstances, how can anyone say with even moderate precision just what is overpriced for an outstanding company with an unusually rapid growth rate? Suppose that instead of selling at twenty-five times earnings, as usually happens, the stock is now at thirty-five times earnings. Perhaps there are new products in the immediate future, the real economic importance of which the financial community has not yet grasped. Perhaps there are not any such products. If the growth rate is so good that in another ten years the company might well have quadrupled, is it really of such great concern whether at the moment the stock might or might not be 35 per cent overpriced? That which really matters is not to disturb a position that is going to be worth a great deal later.

Again our old friend the capital gains tax adds its bit to these conclusions. Growth stocks which are recommended for sale because they are supposedly overpriced nearly always will cost their owners a sizable capital gains tax if they are sold. Therefore, in addition to the risk of losing a permanent position in a company which over the years should continue to show unusual further gains, we also incur a sizable tax liability. Isn't it safer and cheaper simply to make up our minds that momentarily the stock may be somewhat ahead of itself? We already have a sizable profit in it. If for a while the stock loses, say, 35 per cent of its current market quotation, is this really such a serious matter? Again, isn't the maintaining of our position rather than the possibility of temporarily losing a small part of our capital gain the matter which is really important?

There is still one other argument investors sometimes use to separate themselves from the profits they would otherwise make. This one is the most ridiculous of all. It is that the stock they own has had a huge advance. Therefore, just because it has gone up, it has probably used up most of its potential. Consequently they should sell it and buy something that hasn't gone up yet. Outstanding companies, the only type which I believe the investor should buy, just don't function this way. How they do function might best be understood by considering the following somewhat fanciful analogy:

Suppose it is the day you were graduated from college. If you did not go to college, consider it to be the day of your high school graduation; from the standpoint of our example it will make no difference whatsoever. Now suppose that on this day each of your male classmates had an urgent need of immediate cash. Each offered you the same deal. If you would give them a sum of money equivalent to ten times whatever they might earn during the first twelve months after they had gone to work, that classmate would for the balance of his life turn over to you one quarter of each year's earnings! Finally let us suppose that, while you thought this was an excellent proposition, you only had spare cash on hand sufficient to make such a deal with three of your classmates.

At this point, your reasoning would closely resemble that of the investor using sound investment principles in selecting common stocks. You would immediately start analyzing your classmates, not from the standpoint of how pleasant they might be or even how talented they might be in other ways, but solely to determine how much money they might make. If you were part of a large class, you would probably eliminate quite a number solely on the ground of not knowing them sufficiently well to be able to pass worthwhile judgment on just how financially proficient they actually would get to be. Here again, the analogy with intelligent common stock buying runs very close.

Eventually you would pick the three classmates you felt would have the greatest future earning power. You would make your deal with them. Ten years have passed. One of your three has done sensationally. Going to work for a large corporation, he has won promotion after promotion. Already insiders in the company are saying that the president has his eye on him and that in another ten years he will probably take the top job. He will be in line for the large compensation, stock options, and pension benefits that go with that job.

Under these circumstances, what would even the writers of stock market reports who urge taking profits on superb stocks that "have gotten ahead of the market" think of your selling out your contract with this former classmate, just because someone has offered you 600 per cent on your original investment? You would think that anyone would need to have his head examined if he were to advise you to sell this contract and replace it with one with another former classmate whose annual earnings still were about the same as when he left school ten years before. The argument that your successful classmate had had his advance while the advance of your (financially) unsuccessful classmate still lay ahead of him would probably sound rather silly. If you know your common stocks equally well, many of the arguments commonly heard for selling the good one sound equally silly.

You may be thinking all this sounds fine, but actually classmates are not common stocks. To be sure, there is one major difference. That difference increases rather than decreases the reason for never selling the outstanding common stock just because it has had a huge rise and may be temporarily overpriced. This difference is that the classmate is finite, may die soon and is sure to die eventually. There is no similar life span for the common stock. The company behind the common stock can have a practice of selecting management talent in depth and training such talent in company policies, methods, and techniques in a way which will retain and pass on the corporate vigor for generations. Look at Du Pont in its second century of corporate existence. Look at Dow years after the death of its brilliant founder. In this era of unlimited human wants and incredible markets, there is no limitation to corporate growth such as the life span places upon the individual.

Perhaps the thoughts behind this chapter might be put into a single sentence: If the job has been correctly done when a common stock is purchased, the time to sell it is—almost never.

PENSION FUND INVESTMENT POLICY REVIEW OF INVESTMENT POLICY FOR THE PENSION FUND

G. H. Ross Goobey

G. H. Ross Goobey, trained as an actuary but devoted to investing, persuaded his employers, Britain's Imperial Tobacco Company, to make two bold and enormously productive decisions shortly after the Second World War: (1) Sale of Daltons (the 2 1/2 percent perpetual consols which were then at 85 and destined to lose three quarters of their value) and, (2) investment—up to a remarkable 100 percent—in a broadly diversified portfolio of common stocks. A great rugby player with a forceful, engaging personality, he is, in this private memorandum, defending that policy during the period of severe investor anxiety occasioned by Britain's drive toward socialism. Of particular note are his perceptions concerning inflation and the need for "spread" in the equity portfolios.

PENSION FUND INVESTMENT POLICY

[T]he motto for the investment policy is "The best possible result" and this is likely to be achieved by investment in equities as opposed to fixed interest securities because of the inflationary tendencies.

From two memoranda, August 30, 1955, and June 4, 1957 (London, England), by permission of the author.

Another point made is that we are alone in the field of Trust Funds to contemplate a 100% equity investment policy or even to have as much as 70% (by market value) in equities. This may well be so but there is a growing tendency in this direction and there is no doubt that our investment policy has been watched with interest and has encouraged others to consider it seriously. There seems little logic, however, in accepting equities at all for inclusion in investment portfolios without being prepared to agree on a policy of 100%. If one is convinced that they are worth including for the obvious advantages which they possess, then there seems to be no reason why one should not have all one's investments in the most attractive class. Indeed the whole policy being based on spread, the larger the amount invested in equities the more likely the policy is to work out satisfactorily.

Let us have the courage to do what all the facts point that we should do in spite of the traditions to the contrary.

REVIEW OF INVESTMENT POLICY FOR THE PENSION FUND

Eighteen months ago the decision was taken that the investment policy for the Pension Fund should be 100% in equities.

One of the principal reasons why this decision was taken was that in considering investment policy for a Pension Fund such as ours, one could afford to take a very long view

a. because the individual liabilities are in any case of long duration

b. there seems every indication that our Fund will continue to grow for very many years, even if we get no more inflation.

My own view on this last item is that we will always have a measure of inflation in the long term (even if there may be a periodic flattening out of the curve, or even a downward trend for a time), in which case Pension Funds will continue to grow in terms of pounds sterling.

In the memorandum dated 30th August 1955, which was prepared to enable the Committee to arrive at this momentous and perhaps revolutionary decision, the rather obvious platitude was made "one of the essentials of sound investment policy is that it can be altered at short notice to meet changed cirumstances." I submit that the circumstances have not changed to any material extent since this vital policy decision was taken eighteen months ago. If it is considered that they have, then I regard it as a severe reflection on the consideration which led up to that decision. I know that we are eighteen months nearer to the next Socialist Government, but the decision to go 100% into equities was not taken because we considered that we had a respite before that calamity befell us again.

In my memorandum of August 1955 I endeavoured to deal with the misfortunes most likely to fall upon the Pension Fund investment arising from the possible implementation of Socialist principles, and they are of such importance that I will repeat them.

DIVIDEND LIMITATION

When we are considering the relative merits of fixed interest securities and equities it strikes me as absurd that we get worried about the effect of *possible* dividend limitation on some equities some time in the future when there has always been, and always will be, "dividend limitation" on fixed interest securities. True, part of the attraction of equities will be removed (even so perhaps only temporarily) but in this case the additional undistributed profits will still redound to the benefit of the companies (and therefore to the shareholders) by providing additional funds for expansion out of the companies' own resources or by building up reserves and carry forwards. In the latter case these additional profits will no doubt be released again in due course, for one cannot rule out the probability of a Conservative Government returning to power again in due course to rescue the country from the mess the Socialists invariably get us into, in which case we may again see the dividend spurt which we saw from 1952 to 1955, which was partly the aftermath of the dividend restraint imposed by the previous Socialist Government.

The yields on equities as a whole are greater than those on fixed interest securities, and one would surely prefer to be limited to this higher return than to that obtainable on fixed interest securities. . . .

In the implementation of our policy we have rather eschewed the low-yielding Stocks (generally regarded as *the* growth Stocks) so that we probably stand to suffer less than some equity holders who have been working on the basis of "jam tomorrow." There is no doubt, of course, that if dividend limitation does come this will produce a setback in market prices as a reflection of the taking away (or a deferment) of the attraction of possible dividend increases. Here again this setback would no doubt be more particularly severe on the low-yielding shares. But this is a factor we can afford to ignore. Market prices at any particular moment are of no particular significance to a Pension Fund, (except, of course, in so far as they are a reflection of future prospects), or if it is intended to realise, which is not a likely event in our Fund. . . .

I have been accused of "being only interested in yield," the implication being that the higher the conventionally quoted yield is the more I am attracted to a Stock. This is true to a certain extent, especially when dealing with a Pension Fund, the income of which is free of tax, but I am of course aware that the conventionally quoted yield is based on last year's dividend only, and that the realised yield (and this alone is the yield with which we are concerned) depends on the dividends received in the future. Therefore, with each investment which we make there is a mental appraisal of the chances of last year's dividend being maintained or increased. We do not, for instance, invest in Greyhound company shares on a 15% yield basis because we appreciate that there is quite a probability of last year's dividend not being continued.

NATIONALISATION

Nationalisation has always been regarded as something to be feared and yet to my mind this fear emphasises the advantage of equities over fixed interest securities, particularly gilt-edged securities. Hitherto nationalisation has not been on confiscatory terms and I do not fear that it will be in the future. The more that pension funds, which after all are an accumulation of the workers' savings, acquire Ordinary Stocks and Shares the less likely is the Labour Party, whose support comes from those workers, to confiscate these savings. The experience of our Fund in the past has been quite satisfactory, especially as we did not retain the Government Stock which was given as compensation but sold it and re-invested in other equities. Indeed a concomitant of further nationalisation is the further reduction in the number of free enterprise Ordinary shares available giving them enhanced scarcity value. . . .

I have perhaps dwelt too early in this memorandum on the particular rather than the general, and perhaps I should recapitulate to a certain extent the general basis of the previous memorandum.

At the outset the objects of Pension Fund investment were adumbrated and the long-term nature of the liabilities was undeniably established. The special suitability of investment in Ordinary shares to fit in with such a picture was therefore advocated.

Next there were set out the fundamental differences between investing for a Pension Fund and for a Life Assurance company, and I think these differences are so important that I venture to set them out again. . . .

1. The liabilities of Pension Funds are generally geared to inflation inasmuch as the pension benefits are expressed as some function of the final salary or wage. . . . Life Assurance contracts, on the other hand, are money contracts and . . . need pay no attention to the changing purchasing power of the pound. It is preferable, therefore, that the assets of Pension Funds should be invested in securities which provide an opportunity of growth arising from genuine expansion or from inflation.

2. The liabilities of Life Assurance Funds are, generally speaking, of much shorter duration than the liabilities of a Pension Fund. Life Funds, by reason of their growing amount of Endowment Assurance business and the fact that the average age at entry is certainly higher than Pension Funds, have a much shorter average duration for their liabilities.

3. Even in the more traditional investment policy followed by Assurance Companies and with the safety-first methods pursued by Banks, depreciation of capital and realised losses has certainly not been unknown. It is fallaciously held in some quarters that with investment in Ordinary shares the risk of loss of capital is increased, but this risk can be reduced or eliminated by having a large "spread" of investments. Moreover, part of the additional income which is received on this type of investment could be used as a Sinking Fund against those occasional investments in this class where the capital is lost or depreciates. Pension Funds have a considerable advantage over Life Assurance Funds in this respect, since such a Sinking Fund could be set up out of "excess" income which is not subject to tax. In addition, statistical evidence can be produced to show that in the long run equities have proved to be a far safer investment, both as regards capital and income, than fixed interest securities. . . .

4. One of the reasons why Life Assurance Companies may have refrained from holding a large proportion of equity investment is the question of presentation of accounts. Under the Insurance Companies' Act, the Insurance Companies' Balance Sheets are required to show a state of solvency with the assets appearing

at not greater than their market value. It is perhaps thought that with a larger proportion of equity shares, whose prices might possibly fluctuate rather more than dated gilts, the difficulties on presentation of the Balance Sheet would be increased. Pension Funds are under no statutory obligation to show each year a state of complete solvency based on market values and therefore have a considerable advantage over Life Assurance Funds in this respect.

5. Pension Funds are not yet at a stage when they are so vast that investment in gilt-edged are almost essential to keep up with the amount of funds available for investment. This is no doubt another contributory reason for some Life Assurance Companies having a large percentage invested in gilt-edged.

6. A Life Assurance policy-holder can surrender his policy for cash at any time and the Company may feel that it must keep a proportion of its fund in readily marketable securities in order to avoid embarrassment if it has to meet abnormally heavy surrenders. Pension Fund membership is inevitably bound up with employment, and even in the most advanced state of mobility of labour it is unlikely that a Fund would have to deal with an unexpectedly large number of withdrawals. Any major reduction in members should be foreseeable by the Company in time for an allowance to be made in the Pension Fund investment policy.

I might also include in this memorandum a few obvious differences in approach between investing for a Pension Fund and for a private investor.

1. *The tax position.* Income and capital appreciation are equally valuable in a Pension Fund, as both are free of tax. To a private individual capital appreciation is free of tax whereas income is subject to income tax and surtax at whatever rate he happens to pay, and not unnaturally, therefore, he is far more interested in capital profits. I often think, however, that many private investors go the wrong way about achieving it because they imagine that they will get capital appreciation if they avoid income and they therefore choose the very low-yielding Stocks in the hope that they will appreciate in value as the increases in dividends which have been anticipated are received. Even Stocks which show higher yields do increase their dividends, and they have a chance of achieving a higher status (by coming down

to a lower yield basis) which automatically means an increase in market value. The private investor also is inclined to waste part of his capital appreciation by selling good Stocks when the expected appreciation has occurred and merely putting it into some other Stock which is perhaps no better or even worse.

2. The size of a private investor's portfolio may not be sufficient to enable him to get a good "spread," which is essential in pursuing a policy of equity investments. Assuming one accepts the general thesis of the advantages of equity shares as a whole, it may happen that the choice of a few shares might produce results very much below the average because of the unfortunate inclusion of a few losers amongst those shares.

3. The private investor is not always an all time investor and it may so happen that he might be forced to realise at an unfortunate moment. . . .

The Economist Intelligence Unit has also produced some rather staggering figures showing the comparative results of investing £1,000,000 on the 1st January 1919 in equities, and alternatively in 2 1/2% Consols. If the gross income is similarly re-invested at the end of each year the equity fund by the 1st January 1957 would have amounted to £28,072,000 whereas the gilt-edged fund would have amounted to £3,696,000!

On the assumption that £1,000,000 is invested *each year* on the 1st January and gross income is re-invested at the end of each year the respective size of the funds in 1957 is £283,360,000 and £70,020,000. If the income is not accumulated the respective figures are, in the case of the single investment of £1,000,000 in 1919, £4,134,000 and £886,000 respectively, and in the case of the investment of £1,000,000 each year, £80,950,000 and £31,340,000 respectively. . . .

* * * * *

INFLATION AND PENSIONS

William C. Greenough

William Greenough provided intellectual leadership in the area of retirement income for college and university educators when he prepared the analysis, excerpted here, that led to the establishment of the College Retirement Equities Fund (CREF)—an equity-linked companion to the annuities set up under Teachers Insurance and Annuity Association (TIAA). Prior to the period of the publication of this analysis, educational pension investments were almost entirely confined to bonds.

The rapid and far-reaching economic changes during recent decades have served to emphasize the difficulties of making adequate income provision for old age. Prior to this century very little had been done about retirement plans; the problem was scarcely recognized in an expanding but still predominantly rural economy.

When Andrew Carnegie gave ten million dollars in 1905 to establish free pensions for college professors, he provided a strong impetus to retirement planning not only for teachers but for other groups as well. In 1918 the Carnegie Foundation for the Advancement of Teaching and the Carnegie Corporation of New York established a broader and more enduring concept of contributory annuity benefits for educators through the establishment of Teachers Insurance and Annuity Association of America (TIAA). At that time the United States was just emerging

From William C. Greenough, *A New Approach to Retirement Income* (New York, New York, 1951), 7–15, by permission of the Teachers Insurance and Annuity Association of America.

from the first World War. No one then foresaw the violent economic fluctuations that were to follow, including those caused by the deepest depression in history, a second World War, and a long period of heavy expenditures for defense.

When planning for old-age income the educator, or for that matter anyone, must seek a method which has the best hope of affording him real security when he can no longer rely on his own efforts to provide a livable income. Security in retirement poses a difficult problem when it means providing not only a sufficient annuity income in dollars but also a reasonable income in current purchasing power. Traditional methods of saving for retirement have been effective in providing the dollar income; they have fallen short of the goal of providing a suitable purchasing power income. During the low prices prevailing in the 1930s, annuitants and others living on fixed incomes were receiving a larger "real" or purchasing power income than they might have expected; in 1950 their real income was seriously reduced. There is little in the present situation to assure us that the purchasing power of the dollar in the year 1960, 1970 or 2000 will be the same as it is today. This suggests that an effort be made to provide more dollars as retirement income when prices are high even though that may mean reducing the number of dollars when prices are low.

Eminent authorities believe that our economic system is now "replete with built-in inflationary bias," especially in periods of war or international tension accompanied by heavy expenditures for defense. They point to the tax structure, escalator wage clauses, parity prices, budget deficits, government borrowing from commercial banks, low rates of interest, cost-plus contracts, subsidies and the like. Some point to Keynesian economics, emphasis on full employment, the public welfare state, disinclination to return to the gold standard.

The "new era" philosophy has been with us on previous occasions, sometimes strongest just before a major turn. There is abundant evidence that the law of supply and demand has not been repealed. There are strains and stresses in the economy that could lead to a major depression sometime in the future. Although the hope of world peace looks visionary, it is by no means inconceivable that a long period of world peace could occur. It could be accompanied in America by constantly increasing productivity, higher standards of living, and declining prices.

At any one time the forces of inflation or the forces of deflation seem to be stronger. But planning for retirement income is a very long-range process. Transitory shifts in the economy are relatively unimportant; the objective must be to provide reasonable security for the retired person regardless of the direction in which the American economy moves.

The difficulty is that there seems to be no perfect protection against inflation. However, there is good reason to believe that retirement security can be substantially enhanced by broadening the scope and diversification of the investment of funds saved during working years. . . .

CONTRAST WITH USUAL INVESTMENT METHODS

Frequently the individual investor in common stocks purchases a single block of stock on a particular day, holds it until a later date and then sells it. He thereby does not obtain adequate diversification either among issues or over time. Most studies of common stock performance take a given list of stocks at one point in time and follow the experience through to another point. When this method of purchasing and selling stocks is used, the starting and ending dates are all-important.

The advent of the investment companies, especially the open-end mutual funds, offered the individual a chance to choose a fund that provided adequate diversification *among issues*. The individual can in some funds invest small sums periodically, thereby gaining diversification *over time* as well as among issues, unless he fails to stay with his long-range program. However, if the individual cashes out his entire fund at one point, the market prices of common stocks at that point assume great importance.

The method of investing planned for the College Retirement Equities Fund combines a number of well-known principles into a broad new pattern. The principle of *diversification among issues* of equity investments would be obtained through pooling a portion of the annuity savings of many employers and individuals into a substantial fund invested in a great many companies in a number of industries. The principle of *diversification over time* would be obtained by accepting small payments, month by month and year by year, over a major portion of each participant's working lifetime. These payments would be directly related to salary and therefore would continue at all levels of common stock prices. Effective use would be made of the principle of *dollar cost averaging* whereby more shares of stock are purchased by a given premium at low prices than at high. Even though salaries were reduced in many instances in the early 1930s, annuity premium income on existing policies proved more stable than payments into other investment media.

Perhaps the most interesting innovation is the *unit annuity*. Few individuals can expect to accumulate enough by retirement time to live entirely on the earnings from investments. Under ordinary conditions the retired individual dares not dip too deeply into principal because he has no way of knowing how long he and his wife will live. Some people die soon after retirement; others live 30 years or longer. Through a life annuity an individual can, with safety, use up capital as well as interest earnings and thereby obtain a substantially higher income throughout the remainder of his life.

The unit, or variable, annuity directly applies the annuity principle to a new area of investment, common stocks, allowing the individual the assurance again that he can use up both capital and dividend payments without danger of outliving his income.

GENERAL CONCLUSIONS FROM THE DATA

This economic study is, of course, based on historical data. There are cogent reasons why equities may not do as well in the future as they have in the past; there are reasons why they may do better. Not all of the inflationary forces previously mentioned would be reflected in increasing common stock prices and dividends; some are adverse to common stocks. Likewise, not all the influences toward a stable or declining price level would mean reduced performance of common stocks.

The conclusions to be drawn from the historical data will be stated with full realization that they are not necessarily a preview of the future. However, periods of inflation and deflation are included, as are periods of good and poor common stock performance, so that an indication may be gained of possible experience under varying economic conditions.

The comparisons in the study are drawn from general averages of all life insurance companies, where possible, and the large majority of common stocks. Therefore the study and the data behind it, while directly related to retirement plans in the field of higher education, of course have broader applicability for long-range investment programs and the channeling of retirement savings into productive enterprise.

The general conclusions are given at this point for the convenience of the reader and so that he may test them against the data as he proceeds.

The conclusions of course were reached after studying a much larger volume of data than deemed practical to include in this report.

1. It is unwise to commit *all* of one's retirement savings to dollar obligations, since decreases in the purchasing power of the dollar can seriously reduce the value of a fixed income annuity. Increases in the purchasing power of the dollar, on the other hand, improve the status of the owner of a fixed income annuity.

2. It is equally unwise to commit *all* of one's retirement savings to equity investments, since variations in prices of common stocks are much too pronounced to permit full reliance on them for the stable income needed during retirement. Changes in the value of common stocks and other equities are by no means perfectly correlated with cost of living changes, but they have provided a considerably better protection against inflation than have debt obligations.

3. Contributions to a retirement plan that are invested partly in debt obligations and partly in common stocks through an Equities Fund providing lifetime unit annuities offer promise of supplying retirement income that is at once reasonably free from violent fluctuations in amount and from serious depreciation through price level changes.

4. The Equities Fund should make no dollar guarantees. Its liabilities should always be valued directly in terms of its assets. This is a cardinal point of the suggested arrangement for two principal reasons:

> a. It ensures that the Equities Fund is "failure proof" in the technical sense and cannot be forced into liquidation of its assets at a low point in the market. Whether the market be high or low, the Equities Fund obligations are automatically limited to the then market value of its assets. Typical pension plans whose liabilities are expressed in dollar guarantees and whose assets are partially in fluctuating securities, such as common stocks, are vulnerable in this connection.

> b. It ensures the individual participant his full pro rata share in any rise in the net asset value of the Equities Fund. Under typical pension plans invested partially in common stocks, the employer gives a fixed dollar pension assurance to his employees. Any appreciation in common stock values is normally used to reduce the employer's cost or to create reserves, whereas it is needed in a period of rising prices as an increased benefit for the employees. Through a common stock fund free from the confinements of dollar promises, a participant can have a wider opportunity to share in the development of the American economy with part of his savings. Obviously, this opportunity to share in rises must be accompanied by a willingness to share in falls of the net asset values.

5. Common stock investments obtained through purchases month by month, at low prices as well as high, would have provided a very effective method of investing a portion of retirement funds. Most of the difficulties in individual investing in equities arise from lack of diversification both *among shares* and *over time*. So long as the period of regular payments into a fund invested in common stocks was reasonably long, so long as each person owned a portion of a large, well-diversified fund and so long as there were no substantial shifts either into or out of equities at a particular moment, the experience was normally considerably better than that of a fund invested wholly or principally in debt obligations.

* * * * *

IS THERE AN IDEAL INVESTMENT?
SOME "DON'TS" IN SECURITY PROGRAMS
WHAT TO BUY—AND WHEN
DIVERSIFICATION OF INVESTMENTS

Gerald M. Loeb

Gerald Loeb was for many years one of Wall Street's favorite observers, and his book *The Battle for Investment Survival* an enduring favorite. Here are four chapters—each as short and direct as Loeb himself always was.

IS THERE AN IDEAL INVESTMENT?

Discarding all theory I think the average "investor" is looking for a permanent medium to place a given number of dollars where it will return a reasonable income, and the original number of dollars will always be

---

From Gerald M. Loeb, *The Battle for Investment Survival* (Burlington, Vermont 1935–37, 1943, 1952–57, 1965), 20–22, 41–43, 52–55, 135–138, by permission of Fraser Publishing Company.

quickly obtainable in case of desire or need. This might be termed the standard or goal of orthodox investing. It is not to be found today, at least as far as I know, because all the possible investment mediums fail in one or more particulars.

Unfortunately, even if such an "ideal" permanent investment medium were to be had, it would fall short in another and most important particular. That other factor is, of course, the ability to get income and principal repaid in units of the same purchasing power as originally invested. There is nothing unreasonable in this desire. Please note, the only demand is to return what is invested plus the rental of profits secured from its use. It is not like buying a "gold clause" bond with a check on a bank and demanding repayment in the actual gold. The layman will usually argue that "a dollar is a dollar," but despite this he will at a later date see the point if the shoe happens to pinch. At least as far as my experience goes, this totally ideal "investment" is as totally non-existent.

It is not hard to see why it should be merely a theoretical formula. Nothing is safe; nothing is sure in any field of life. Specifically the wealth of the world does not increase fast enough to allow payment of compound interest or pyramiding of profits on existing "invested capital." Every so often adjustments are made partly through bankruptcies and other scaling down of obligations and partly through currency depreciation. And it's all as old as the hills.

In my opinion, all this is natural and normal, though I regret the impossible representation of complete safety and security held out by channels dealing in all types of "investments" including not only securities but also to an even greater extent "insurance," "real estate," "savings and loan," etc.

For years the tide has been swinging back and forth, and as the advantage has swung too far towards the debtor class, a cry for "deflation," usually popularly noted in objection to the "high cost of living," has generally grown until something was done about it, and then as the edge went to the creditor, "inflation" or, in other words, general complaint as to commodity prices being too low and money too scarce, dominated the public mind.

Thus it logically follows that in order to attempt even to approximate our definition of what the public really thinks it is getting when it buys a "safe investment," it is necessary to "speculate."

By speculate I mean principally to try to foresee these tides and, from an elementary standpoint, to attempt conservation of purchasing power through purchase or retention of fixed interest and principal obligations (including "cash"—a form of government promise to pay) only during cycles of deflation, and various forms of equity holdings only in cycles of inflation.

Thus it is really necessary at the start to admit and expect that the great majority are not going to be able successfully to invest or speculate, or whatever one calls their handling of their capital, any more than the majority succeed in the first place in securing their proportion of existing wealth or, for that matter, of existing happiness.

Successful preservation of capital must also overcome the increasing handicaps imposed by modern popular and socialistic governments, supposedly to help the masses.

Obviously, our ideas will sound wrong to most people. Any investment policy followed by all naturally defeats itself. Thus the first step for the individual really trying to secure or preserve capital is to detach himself from the crowd.

It is necessary to think in individualistic terms. One has to consider what seems best for one's own preservation. The masses always have, individually, an average of next to nothing per capita, contrasted to the minority of successful individuals. Thus they are always trying to wrest away the possessions of the few for what they believe their own advantage. It is surprising how much they can appropriate without much resistance. But after a while the industrious and the thrifty finally are worn down, and they begin to turn for protection to imagined "anti-social" devices.

In the history of the world we find the record of savings really saved through buying gold, hoarding precious stones, and other forms of "hard wealth" privately secreted. In the future history of America most of us will, in my opinion, learn this lesson too late. Currently this is a personal matter for each individual to decide and execute for himself without consultation.

Curiously, it is those of slight wealth who need this sort of protection rather than those of great means, who can really suffer large depreciation without really feeling the loss. And it is usually the latter who are best fitted to cope with the problem.

As to capital not so hoarded or employed in regular business channels but available for "investment" in the popular sense, the out-standing requirement is the specialized understanding that will discern trends correctly and analyze values essential to the constant shifting of funds necessary to success.

If not able to do this, one must have at least the insight to select honest and capable expert guidance. Such guidance is rare, but it can be found. Yet, rare as it is, even fewer have the psychological ability to recognize it or the confidence to follow it through.

* * * * *

SOME "DONT'S" IN SECURITY PROGRAMS

Readers should not expect to obtain here an infallible formula for the preservation of capital in spite of the obstacles cited in previous chap-ters—the changing purchasing power of money, politics, war, public sentiment and the vicissitudes of individual securities. The contention that investment is a battle for financial survival would disprove itself if the difficulties could be explained away so easily.

The object of these discussions is to influence the investment think-ing of readers in the direction of improving the results they may expect to attain. This is an attainable and worthwhile aim.

We have already sketched the fundamental necessity of having a thorough understanding of the difficulties and of keeping the objectives clearly in mind.

The basic practical working policy is never to invest unless the possibilities of the chosen stock seem very great. Investing solely for "income," investing merely "to keep capital employed," and investing simply "to hedge against inflation" are all entirely out of the ques-tion.

No security of any kind should under any circumstances be bought or retained, under this policy, unless in the investor's well and deeply considered judgment the profit possibilities are large and greatly out-weigh the visible risks. And the latter must be counted with detailed care.

When an investment is made, its prospects must be so good that placing a rather large proportion of one's total funds in such a single situation will not seem excessively risky. At the same time, the potential gain must be so large that only a moderate portion of total capital need be invested to get the desired percentage appreciation on total funds.

Expressing the matter in a different way, this means that once you attain competency, diversification is undesirable. One or two, or at most three or four, securities should be bought. And they should be so well selected, their purchase so expertly timed and their profit possibilities so large that it will never be necessary to risk in any of them a large proportion of available capital.

Under this policy, only the best is bought at the best possible time. Risks are reduced in two ways—first, by the care used in selection, and second, by the maintenance of a large cash reserve. Concentration of investments in a minimum of stocks insures that enough time will be given to the choice of each so that every important detail about them will be known.

This policy involves not only avoiding diversification but also at times holding one's capital uninvested for long periods of time. The bargains which must be sought to raise investment performance out of the average class, in which net losses occur, into the exclusive class of those who make and keep profits are not available except occasionally. It should be recognized also that such opportunities will inevitably be available principally when the majority of buyers of securities refuse, because of fear, to take advantage of low prices. Just as inevitably, the opportunities will not be available when securities are generally popular and eagerly bought. It should be axiomatic that the successful investor will keep his capital idle in times of popular over-investment and over-confidence. He will be sorely tried at times when profits and income are seemingly easy to procure.

Any program which involves complete investment of all capital at all times is not apt to be the most successful one. It should always pay in both dollars and cents and peace of mind not to be overcommitted. Unpredictable news developments can change the complexion of things without warning.

It is true that cash has lost purchasing power in this country but fortunately in our lifetime at a very slow rate compared to the rapid depreciation that can be suffered in a real stock market decline.

Buying on margin does not come into this discussion at all, as it is mainly the concern of traders in the strictest sense of that term.

Another concept essential to success in the battle for investment survival is that the investor must learn to think in terms of ultimate rather than current results. It is impossible to obtain 100% of the theoretical gain in each major movement of an individual stock or of stocks as a group. Efforts to do so inevitably lead to failure of the entire investment program. It is a real achievement if through judicious investment at intermittent times a satisfactory average profit over good years and bad is actually gained.

This whole thesis, which may at first sight seem extremely speculative, will in actual practice prove many times more conservative and safer than the policy followed by most investors.

* * * * *

WHAT TO BUY—AND WHEN

When and under what conditions should an investment actually be made by one who follows the theory of buying only securities which seem to have great potentialities for profit?   In the preceding chapters it was pointed out that this system involves remaining completely uninvested for long periods.

For practical reasons one necessarily has to make compromises. The factors that make an ideal investment are never all present at the same time. Even if such an opportunity actually did exist, it would be almost impossible for anyone to recognize its existence. Nevertheless, describing such conditions should be helpful. There are times when a majority of them might occur.

In the first place, the general background should be favorable, which means that popular sentiment should be bearish and the securities market well liquidated. Business conditions should be poor, or the general expectation should be that they will become poor.

The security itself should always be either a common stock, or a bond or preferred stock whose position is thought by the investing public at large to be so weak that it sells at low prices and is given generally low ratings. The company selected should be operating at a deficit, or its earnings should be abnormally low. Or, if earnings are currently satisfactory, the popular expectation must be that they are headed downwards. The stock should be paying no dividends, or the dividend should be lower than normal, or general opinion must lack faith in the continuance of a reasonable dividend.

The price of the stock must reflect a majority view that conditions affecting the company are bad, or soon will be bad, or will continue bad. At the same time, the buyer must hold an opinion contrary to these surface indications, and his opinion must be backed by sound judgment and access to reliable sources of information.

The importance of full consideration of popular sentiment, expectations and opinion—and their effect on the price of the security—cannot be overstressed. Major buying points often occur without a full-scale actual business depression. At such times the fear of a depression exists. Earnings and dividends can be normal, and yet the shares in question may be very attractive as misguided popular fears as to the future drive the price down to a level that might at other times represent a period of deficits. And vice versa, the expectation of favorable conditions to come might cause a speculatively high price to be put on shares when actual results of the company's operations are still considerably below normal.

Thus it is the earnings discounted *in the price* which are the determining factor, and not always the earnings level actually existing at the time of proposed purchase. There is little to be expected marketwise, for instance, in buying the shares of a company with a strong growth trend if the current price places a liberal valuation on that growth for several years to come.

It is important to stick to issues which in past times of bullish enthusiasm have had active markets and which can be expected to have active markets again. However, at the time of purchase they must be low-rated and unpopular, with their prices down and discouragement about their prospects quite general.

At long intervals even the highest grade shares become depressed, and then the opportunities are especially great. That happens only once or twice in a business lifetime. The objective is always buy that which the majority thinks is speculative and sell it when the majority believes the quality has reached investment grade. It is in this policy that both safety and profits exist. As price is the all-important consideration, the type of corporation and its characteristics are of relatively minor consequences.

The complete opposite of the thoughts expressed above is the theory held by people who wish to invest surplus cash as soon as it becomes available—that is, who desire to make investments at regular monthly or quarterly intervals. I never did approve of this point of view. Certainly those who want to follow it should buy the strongest and most stable companies. Companies in the consumer class are much to be favored. The products or services sold should not be great public necessities, as the latter become targets for political interference. Labor costs should be low, and the ability to finance expansion out of earnings should be present. Also, the actual cash income should be larger than the amount reported as earnings.

However, these considerations are not essential for buyers following the policy described in these chapters. In fact, such ideal investments are not often available at a price discount sufficient to make them attractive. More often and more profitably the purchase may be made in a company that still has considerable debt and in which ownership by the management may be small. If one can gauge trends correctly, the very reason for the purchase may be that debt will be reduced, perhaps eventually eliminated, and that management, seeing the improvement ahead, will increase its ownership substantially.

Except in cases of panic or near panic prices, the fact that a stock is widely held by investment trusts is not a good reason for buying, as such stocks are generally of the high-grade kind difficult to buy cheap. Since the aim is rather to buy an issue which is unpopular, the hope is, on the contrary, that while the investment companies do not hold much or any now, they will later, at a higher price, become interested and add it to their portfolios. The distinction of being the stock most frequently listed in published institutional holdings simply means not only that the price is probably high rather than low but also that there is a large number of potential sellers should the situation take a turn for the worse.

Willingness and ability to hold funds uninvested while awaiting real opportunities is a key to success in the battle for investment survival. Market valuations of most securities change in a single period of a very few months by an amount equivalent to many years of dividends or interest coupons. Therefore such changes in value are much more worth while seeking than is straight investment return.

I said at the start of this chapter that the theoretical idea is rarely encountered in practice. Nor is it readily recognized.

I feel that the simple equation of weighing what you think are the possibilities for profit vs. the risks for loss is really the soundest way to go about it.

* * * * *

DIVERSIFICATION OF INVESTMENTS

I think most accounts have entirely too much diversification of the wrong sort and not enough of the right. I can see no point at all to a distribution of so much per cent in oils, so much in motors, so much in rails, etc., nor do I see the point of dividing a fund from a quality angle of so much in "governments," and so on down the list to that so called very awful, speculative, non-dividend-paying common stock. Some geographical diversification might be justified for large funds.

This sort of thing might be necessary when capital reaches an unwieldy total, or it might be necessary where no intelligent supervision is likely. Otherwise, it is an admission of not knowing what to do and an effort to strike an average.

The intelligent and safe way to handle capital is to concentrate. If things are not clear, do nothing. When something comes up, follow it *to the limit*, subject to the method of procedure that follows. If it's not worth following to the limit, it is not worth following at all. My thought, of course, is always start with a large cash reserve; next, begin in one issue in a small way. If it does not develop, close out and get back to cash. But if it does do what is expected of it, expand your position in this one issue on a scale up. After, but not before, it has safely drawn away from your highest purchase price, then you might consider a second issue.

The greatest safety lies in putting all your eggs in one basket and watching the basket. You simply cannot afford to be careless or wrong. Hence, you act with much more deliberation. Of course, no thinking person will buy more of something than the market will take if he wants to sell, and here again, the practical test will force one into the listed leaders where one belongs. A smart trader isn't going to put all his capital into poor collateral, either.

In the old days when broker's loans were at fantastic heights, the banks used to get a quick idea of the finances of the brokers by the makeup of their loans. If the collateral was all bundles of big active leaders, the bank's opinion was high. But if it was a mixture of new, untried specialties, then the expression was, "So and so is getting to the bottom of his box." Why buy securities that your broker will try to hide in the bottom of his box if his finances permit? Diversification is a balm to many who don't mind taking a chance on something a little sour in a mixed list, figuring on the better ones to pull it out and make a good average.

So buy only staples in securities; the kind that are "not included in this sale." I am thinking now of men's clothing in which all sort of fancy ties, suitings and shirtings are sold at abnormal mark-ups early in the season and for what they are really worth at the close. But certain solid colored ties, white shirts, plain blue and grey suits, conservatively cut, are practically always excluded from the sale. Securities are not so different, and it is important to deal only in those that always, because of their nature or distribution, have a certain amount of residual interest. Be careful that in "diversifying" you are not supplying the bid for varying groups of narrow market issues that are the style for the moment because there is a special profit in trying to make them so.

Of course, we always have to remember that "one man's meat is another man's poison." The greatest safety for the capable, I might say, lies in putting all one's eggs in one basket and watching the basket. The beginner and those that simply find their investment efforts unsuccessful must resort to orthodox diversification.

I always feel that the less active a stock and the further distant the market, the more potential profit I need to see in it to make it worth buying. If one thinks he sees a potential profit of 100% in an active New York Stock Exchange leader, certainly one would have to expect more to go to a regional exchange or over-the-counter or to a foreign market. This is a fundamental and logical principle.

Another angle of diversification nowadays is the fear of atom bombing and what it might do to property. Investors have looked to geographical diversification because of these fears whereas in more normal times, purely profit motives made for concentration. It is purely a personal matter whether an investor feels that efforts at safety from bombing are more important than trying to get the maximum out of investing.

There is a further diversification which I've never seen mentioned and which is important to consider. This is diversification as between the position of varying companies in their business cycle or as between their shares in their market price cycle. This is a very important consideration because dividing one's funds between three or four different situations which happen all to be in the same sector of their cycle can often be discouraging or dangerous. After all, the final determinant of investment success or failure is market price. For example, industries which are in the final stages of a boom with rapidly increasing earnings, dividends and possibly split-ups, often offer shares high in price but apparently rapidly going higher. There is a sound justification for an investor who knows what he is doing to buy into such a situation, especially for short-term gains, but it would be quite dangerous for him to put all of his funds in three or four such situations. Taken the other way, naturally we all seek deflated and cheap bargains, but very often shares like this will lie on the bottom much longer than we anticipate and if every share we own is in this same category, we may do very badly in a relatively good market.

PORTFOLIO SELECTION

Harry Markowitz

In this article, Harry Markowitz "fired the shot heard 'round the world," starting the intellectual campaign that led to modern portfolio theory and brought technology to investing.

The process of selecting a portfolio may be divided into two stages. The first stage starts with observation and experience and ends with beliefs about the future performances of available securities. The second stage starts with the relevant beliefs about future performances and ends with the choice of portfolio. This paper is concerned with the second stage. We first consider the rule that the investor does (or should) maximize discounted expected, or anticipated, returns. This rule is rejected both as a hypothesis to explain, and as a maxim to guide investment behavior. We next consider the rule that the investor does (or should) consider expected return a desirable thing and variance of return an undesirable thing. This rule has many sound points, both as a maxim for, and hypothesis about, investment behavior. We illustrate geometrically relations between beliefs and choice of portfolio according to the "expected returns–variance of returns" rule.

One type of rule concerning choice of portfolio is that the investor

Reprinted from *The Journal of Finance*, Vol. 7, No. 1, March 1952, 77–91. New York, New York: American Finance Association.

does (or should) maximize the discounted (or capitalized) value of future returns.[1] Since the future is not known with certainty, it must be "expected" or "anticipated" returns which we discount. Variations of this type of rule can be suggested. Following Hicks, we could let "anticipated" returns include an allowance for risk.[2] Or, we could let the rate at which we capitalize the returns from particular securities vary with risk.

The hypothesis (or maxim) that the investor does (or should) maximize discounted return must be rejected. If we ignore market imperfections the foregoing rule never implies that there is a diversified portfolio which is preferable to all non-diversified portfolios. Diversification is both observed and sensible; a rule of behavior which does not imply the superiority of diversification must be rejected both as a hypothesis and as a maxim.

The foregoing rule fails to imply diversification no matter how the anticipated returns are formed; whether the same or different discount rates are used for different securities; no matter how these discount rates are decided upon or how they vary over time.[3] The hypothesis implies that the investor places all his funds in the security with the greatest discounted value. If two or more securities have the same value, then any of these or any combination of these is as good as any other.

We can see this analytically: suppose there are N securities; let r_{it} be the anticipated return (however decided upon) at time t per dollar invested in security i; let d_{it} be the rate at which the return on the ith security at time t is discounted back to the present; let X_i be the relative amount invested in security i. We exclude short sales, thus $X_i \geq 0$ for all i. Then the discounted anticipated return of the portfolio is

$$R = \sum_{t=1}^{\infty} \sum_{i=1}^{N} d_{it} r_{it} X$$

$$= \sum_{i=1}^{N} X_i \left(\sum_{t=1}^{\infty} d_{it} r_{it} \right)$$

$$R_i = \sum_{t=1}^{\infty} d_{it} r_{it}$$

is the discounted return of the ith security, therefore $R = \Sigma X_i R_i$ where R_i is independent of X_i. Since $X_i \geq 0$ for all i and $\Sigma X_i = 1$, R is a weighted average of R_i with the X_i as non-negative weights. To maximize R, we let $X_i = 1$ for i with maximum R_i. If several Ra_a, $a = 1, \ldots, K$ are maximum then any allocation with

$$\sum_{a=1}^{K} Xa_a = 1$$

maximizes R. In no case is a diversified portfolio preferred to all non-diversified portfolios.[4]

It will be convenient at this point to consider a static model. Instead of speaking of the time series of returns from the ith security $(r_{i1}, r_{i2}, \ldots, r_{it}, \ldots)$ we will speak of "the flow of returns" (r_i) from the ith security. The flow of returns from the portfolio as a whole is $R = \Sigma X_i r_i$. As in the dynamic case if the investor wished to maximize "anticipated" return from the portfolio he would place all his funds in that security with maximum anticipated returns.

There is a rule which implies both that the investor should diversify and that he should maximize expected return. The rule states that the investor does (or should) diversify his funds among all those securities which give maximum expected return. The law of large numbers will insure that the actual yield of the portfolio will be almost the same as the expected yield.[5] This rule is a special case of the expected returns–variance of returns rule (to be presented below). It assumes that there is a portfolio which gives both maximum expected return and minimum variance, and it commends this portfolio to the investor.

This presumption, that the law of large numbers applies to a portfolio of securities, cannot be accepted. The returns from securities are too intercorrelated. Diversification cannot eliminate all variance.

The portfolio with maximum expected return is not necessarily the one with minimum variance. There is a rate at which the investor can gain expected return by taking on variance, or reduce variance by giving up expected return.

We saw that the expected returns or anticipated returns rule is inadequate. Let us now consider the expected returns–variance of returns $(E\text{-}V)$ rule. It will be necessary to first present a few elementary concepts and results of mathematical statistics. We will then show some implications of the $E\text{-}V$ rule. After this we will discuss its plausibility.

In our presentation we try to avoid complicated mathematical statements and proofs. As a consequence a price is paid in terms of rigor and generality. The chief limitations from this source are (1) we do not derive our results analytically for the n-security case; instead, we present them geometrically for the 3 and 4 security cases; (2) we assume static probability beliefs. In a general presentation we must recognize that the probability distribution of yields of the various securities is a function of time. The writer intends to present, in the future, the general, mathematical treatment which removes these limitations.

We will need the following elementary concepts and results of mathematical statistics:

Let Y be a random variable, i.e., a variable whose value is decided by chance. Suppose, for simplicity of exposition, that Y can take on a finite number of values $y_1, y_2, \ldots, y_N$. Let the probability that $Y = y_1$ be p_1; that $Y = y_2$ be p_2 etc. The expected value (or mean) of Y is defined to be

$$E = p_1 y_1 + p_2 y_2 + \ldots + p_N y_N$$

The variance of Y is defined to be

$$V = p_1(y_1 - E)^2 + p_2(y_2 - E)^2 + \ldots + p_n(y_n - E)^2.$$

V is the average squared deviation of Y from its expected value. V is a commonly used measure of dispersion. Other measures of dispersion, closely related to V are the standard deviation, $\sigma = \sqrt{V}$, and the coefficient of variation, σ/E.

Suppose we have a number of random variables: $R_1, \ldots, R_n$. If R is a weighted sum (linear combination) of the R_i

$$R = a_1 R_1 + a_2 R_2 + \ldots + a_n R_n$$

then R is also a random variable. (For example R_1, may be the number which turns up on one die; R_2, that of another die, and R the sum of these numbers. In this case $n = 2$, $a_1 = a_2 = 1$.)

It will be important for us to know how the expected value and variance of the weighted sum (R) are related to the probability distribution of the $R_1, \ldots, R_n$. We state these relations below; we refer the reader to any standard text for proof.[6]

The expected value of a weighted sum is the weighted sum of the expected values. I.e., $E(R) = a_1 E(R_1) + a_2 E(R_2) + \ldots + a_n E(R_n)$.

The variance of a weighted sum is not as simple. To express it we must define "covariance." The covariance of R_1 and R_2 is

$$\sigma_{12} = E\{[R_1 - E(R_1)][R_2 - E(R_2)]\}$$

i.e., the expected value of [(the deviation of R_1 from its mean) times (the deviation of R_2 from its mean)]. In general we define the covariance between R_i and R_j as

$$\sigma_{ij} = E\{[R_i - E(R_i)][R_i - E(R_j)]\}$$

σ_{ij} may be expressed in terms of the familiar correlation coefficient ρ_{ij}. The covariance between R_i and R_j is equal to [(their correlation) times (the standard deviation of R_i) times (the standard deviation of R_j)]:

$$\sigma_{ij} = \rho_{ij}\sigma_i\sigma_j$$

The variance of a weighted sum is

$$V(R) = \sum_{i=1}^{N} a_i^2 V(X_i) + 2\sum_{i=1}^{N}\sum_{i>1}^{N} a_i a_j \sigma_{ij}$$

If we use the fact that the variance of R_i is σ_{ii} then

$$V(R) = \sum_{i=1}^{N}\sum_{j=1}^{N} a_i a_j \sigma_{ij}$$

Let R_i be the return on the ith security. Let μ_i be the expected value of R_i, σ_{ij} be the covariance between R_i and R_j (thus σ_{ii} is the variance of R_i). Let X_i be the percentage of the investor's assets which are allocated to the ith security. The yield (R) on the portfolio as a whole is

$$R = \sum R_i X_i$$

The R_i (and consequently R) are considered to be random variables.[7] The X_i are not random variables, but are fixed by the investor. Since the X_i are percentages we have $\Sigma X k_i = 1$. In our analysis we will exclude negative values of the X_i (i.e., short sales); therefore $X_i \geq 0$ for all i.

The return (R) on the portfolio as a whole is a weighted sum of random variables (where the investor can choose the weights). From our discussion of such weighted sums we see that the expected return E from the portfolio as a whole is

$$E = \sum_{i=1}^{N} X_i \mu_i$$

and the variance is

$$V = \sum_{i=1}^{N} \sum_{j=1}^{N} \sigma_{ij} X_i X$$

For fixed probability beliefs (μ_i, σ_{ij}) the investor has a choice of various combinations of E and V depending on his choice of portfolio $X_1, \ldots, X_N$. Suppose that the set of all obtainable (E, V) combinations were as in Figure 1. The E-V rule states that the investor would (or should) want to select one of those portfolios which give rise to the (E, V) combinations indicated as efficient in the figure; i.e., those with minimum V for given E or more and maximum E for given V or less.

FIGURE 1

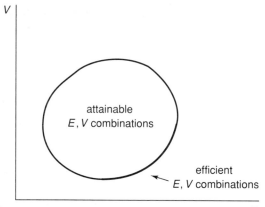

There are techniques by which we can compute the set of efficient portfolios and efficient (E, V) combinations associated with given μ_i and σ_{ij}. We will not present these techniques here. We will, however, illustrate geometrically the nature of the efficient surfaces for cases in which N (the number of available securities) is small.

The calculation of efficient surfaces might possibly be of practical use. Perhaps there are ways, by combining statistical techniques and the judgment of experts, to form reasonable probability beliefs (μ_i, σ_{ij}). We could use these beliefs to compute the attainable efficient combinations of (E, V). The investor, being informed of what (E, V) combinations were attainable, could state which he desired. We could then find the portfolio which gave this desired combination.

Two conditions—at least—must be satisfied before it would be practical to use efficient surfaces in the manner described above. First, the investor must desire to act according to the E-V maxim. Second, we must be able to arrive at reasonable μ_i and σ_{ij}. We will return to these matters later.

Let us consider the case of three securities. In the three security case our model reduces to

1) $$E = \sum_{i=1}^{3} X_i \mu_i$$

2) $$V = \sum_{i=1}^{3} \sum_{j=1}^{3} X_i X_j \sigma_{ij}$$

3) $$\sum_{i=1}^{3} X_i = 1$$

4) $$X_i \geq 0 \qquad \text{for } i = 1, 2, 3.$$

From (3) we get

$$3') \ X_3 = 1 - X_1 - X_2$$

If we substitute (3′) in equation (1) and (2) we get E and V as functions of X_1 and X_2. For example we find

1′) $$E = \mu_3 + X_1(\mu_1 - \mu_3) + X_2(\mu_2 - \mu_3)$$

The exact formulas are not too important here (that of V is given below)[8]. We can simply write

$$a)\ E = E(X_1, X_2)$$

$$b)\ V = V(X_1, X_2)$$

$$c)\ X_1 \geq 0, X_2 \geq 0, 1 - X_1 - X_2 \geq 0$$

By using relations (a), (b), (c), we can work with two dimensional geometry.

The attainable set of portfolios consists of all portfolios which satisfy constraints (c) and (3') (or equivalently (3) and (4)). The attainable combinations of X_1, X_2 are represented by the triangle abc in Figure 2. Any point to the left of the X_2 axis is not attainable because it violates the condition that $X_1 \geq 0$. Any point below the X_1 axis is not attainable because it violates the condition that $X_2 \geq 0$. Any point above the line $(1 - X_1 - X_2 = 0)$ is not attainable because it violates the condition that $X_3 = 1 - X_1 - X_2 \geq 0$.

We define an *isomean* curve to be the set of all points (portfolios)

FIGURE 2

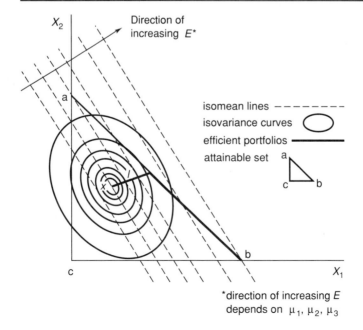

with a given expected return. Similarly an *isovariance* line is defined to be the set of all points (portfolios) with a given variance of return.

An examination of the formulae for E and V tells us the shares of the isomean and isovariance curves. Specifically they tell us that typically[9] the isomean curves are a system of parallel straight lines; the isovariance curves are a system of concentric ellipses (see Fig. 2). For example, if $\mu_2 \neq \mu_3$ equation 1' can be written in the familiar form $X_2 = a + bX_1$; specifically (1)

$$X_2 = \frac{E - \mu_3}{\mu_2 - \mu_3} - \frac{\mu_1 - \mu_3}{\mu_2 - \mu_3} X_1,$$

Thus the slope of the isomean line associated with $E = E_0$ is $-(\mu_1 - \mu_3)/(\mu_2 - \mu_3)$ its intercept is $(E_0 - \mu_3)/(\mu_2 - \mu_3)$. If we change E we change the intercept but not the slope of the isomean line. This confirms the contention that the isomean lines form a system of parallel lines.

Similarly, by a somewhat less simple application of analytic geometry, we can confirm the contention that the isovariance lines form a family of concentric ellipses. The "center" of the system is the point which minimizes V. We will label this point X. Its expected return and variance we will label E and V. Variance increases as you move away from X. More precisely, if one isovariance curve, C_1 lies closer to X than another, C_2 then C_1 is associated with a smaller variance than C_2.

With the aid of the foregoing geometric apparatus let us seek the efficient sets.

X, the center of the system of isovariance ellipses, may fall either inside or outside the attainable set. Figure 4 illustrates a case in which X falls inside the attainable set. In this case: X is efficient. For no other portfolio has a V as low as X; therefore no portfolio can have either smaller V (with the same or greater E) or greater E with the same or smaller V. No point (portfolio) with expected return E less than E is efficient. For we have $E > E$ and $V > V$.

Consider all points with a given expected return E; i.e., all points on the isomean line associated with E. The point of the isomean line at which V takes on its least value is the point at which the isomean line is tangent to an isovariance curve. We call this point $\hat{X}(E)$. If we let E vary, $\hat{X}(E)$ traces out a curve.

Algebraic considerations (which we omit here) show us that this

FIGURE 3

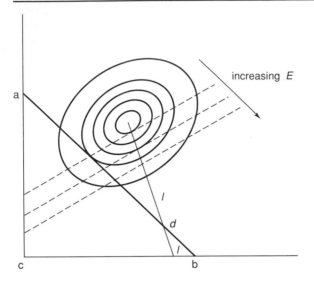

curve is a straight line. We will call it the critical line *l*. The critical line passes through *X* for this point minimizes *V* for all points with $E(X_1, X_2) = E$. As we go along *l* in either direction from *X*, *V* increases. The segment of the critical line from *X* to the point where the critical line crosses the boundary of the attainable set is part of the efficient set. The rest of the efficient set is (in the case illustrated) the segment of the $\overline{ab}$ line from *d* to *b*. *b* is the point of maximum attainable *E*. In Figure 3, *X* lies outside the admissible area but the critical line cuts the admissible area. The efficient line begins at the attainable point with minimum variance (in this case on the $\overline{ab}$ line). It moves toward *b* until it intersects the critical line, moves along the critical line until it intersects a boundary and finally moves along the boundary to *b*. The reader may wish to construct and examine the following other cases: (1) *X* lies outside the attainable set and the critical line does not cut the attainable set. In this case there is a security which does not enter into any efficient portfolio. (2) Two securities have the same μ_i. In this case the isomean lines are parallel to a boundary line. It may happen that the efficient portfolio with maximum *E* is a diversified portfolio. (3) A case wherein only one portfolio is efficient.

FIGURE 4

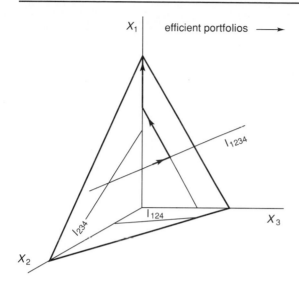

The efficient set in the 4 security case is, as in the 3 security and also the N security case, a series of connected line segments. At one end of the efficient set is the point of minimum variance; at the other end is a point of maximum expected return[10] (see Fig. 4).

Now that we have seen the nature of the set of efficient portfolios, it is not difficult to see the nature of the set of efficient (E, V) combinations. In the three security case $E = a_0 + a_1X_1 + a_2X_2$ is a plane; $V = b_0 + b_1X_1 + b_2X_2 + b_{12}X_1X_2 + b_{11}X_1^2 + b_{22}X_2^2$ is a paraboloid.[11] As shown in Figure 5, the section of the E-plane over the efficient portfolio set is a series of connected line segments. The section of the V-paraboloid over the efficient portfolio set is a series of connected parabola segments. If we plotted V against E for efficient portfolios we would again get a series of connected parabola segments (see Fig. 6). This result obtains for any number of securities.

Various reasons recommend the use of the expected return-variance of return rule, both as a hypothesis to explain well-established investment behavior and as a maxim to guide one's own action. The rule serves better, we will see, as an explanation of, and guide to, "investment" as distinguished from "speculative" behavior.

FIGURE 5

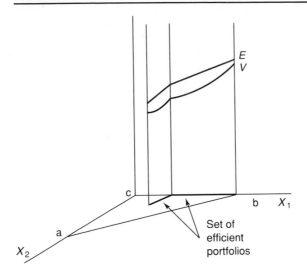

FIGURE 6

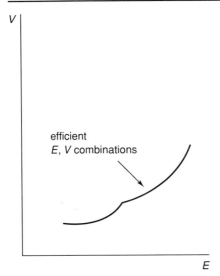

Earlier we rejected the expected returns rule on the grounds that it never implied the superiority of diversification. The expected return-variance of return rule, on the other hand, implies diversification for a wide range of μ_i, σ_{ij}. This does not mean that the E-V rule never implies the superiority of an undiversified portfolio. It is conceivable that one security might have an extremely higher yield and lower variance than all other securities; so much so that one particular undiversified portfolio would give maximum E and minimum V. But for a large, presumably representative range of μ_i, σ_{ij} the E-V rule leads to efficient portfolios almost all of which are diversified.

Not only does the E-V hypothesis imply diversification, it implies the "right kind" of diversification for the "right reason." The adequacy of diversification is not thought by investors to depend solely on the number of different securities held. A portfolio with sixty different railway securities, for example, would not be as well diversified as the same size portfolio with some railroad, some public utility, mining, various sorts of manufacturing, etc. The reason is that it is generally more likely for firms within the same industry to do poorly at the same time than for firms in dissimilar industries.

Similarly in trying to make variance small it is not enough to invest in many securities. It is necessary to avoid investing in securities with high covariances among themselves. We should diversify across industries because firms in different industries, especially industries with different economic characteristics, have lower covariances than firms within an industry.

The concepts "yield" and "risk" appear frequently in financial writings. Usually if the term "yield" were replaced by "expected yield" or "expected return," and "risk" by "variance of return," little change of apparent meaning would result.

Variance is a well-known measure of dispersion about the expected. If instead of variance the investor was concerned with standard error, $\sigma = \sqrt{V}$, or with the coefficient of dispersion, σ/E, his choice would still lie in the set of efficient portfolios.

Suppose an investor diversifies between two portfolios (i.e., if he puts some of his money in one portfolio, the rest of his money in the other. An example of diversifying among portfolios is the buying of the shares of two different investment companies). If the two original portfolios have *equal* variance then typically[12] the variance of the resulting (compound) portfolio will be less than the variance of either original portfolio. This is illustrated by Figure 7. To interpret Figure 7 we note that a portfolio (P) which is built out of two portfolios $P' = (X'_1, X'_2)$ and $P'' = (X''_1, X''_2)$ is of the form $P = \lambda P' + (1 - \lambda)P'' = (\lambda X'_1 + (1 - \lambda) X''_1, \lambda X'_2 + (1 - \lambda)X''_2)$. P is on the straight line connecting P' and P''.

The E-V principle is more plausible as a rule for investment behavior as distinguished from speculative behavior. The third moment[13] M_3 of the probability distribution of returns from the portfolio may be connected with a propensity to gamble. For example if the investor maximizes utility (U) which depends on E and $V(U = U(E, V), \delta U/\delta E > 0, \delta U/\delta E < 0)$ he will never accept an actuarially fair bet.[14] But if $U = U(E, V, M_3)$ and $\delta U/\delta M_3 \neq 0$ then there are some fair bets which would be accepted.

Perhaps—for a great variety of investing institutions which consider yield to be a good thing; risk, a bad thing; gambling, to be avoided— E, V efficiency is reasonable as a working hypothesis and a working maxim.

Two uses of the E-V principle suggest themselves. We might use it in theoretical analyses or we might use it in the actual selection of portfolios.

FIGURE 7

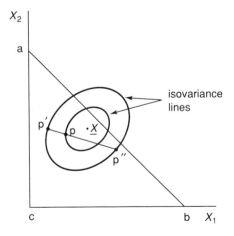

In theoretical analysis we might inquire, for example, about the various effects of a change in the beliefs generally held about a firm, or a general change in preference as to expected return versus variance of return, or a change in the supply of a security. In our analyses the X_i might represent individual securities or they might represent aggregates such as, say, bonds, stocks and real estate.[15]

To use the E-V rule in the selection of securities we must have procedures for finding reasonable μ_i and σ_{ij}. These procedures, I believe, should combine statistical techniques and the judgment of practical men. My feeling is that the statistical computations should be used to arrive at a tentative set of μ_i and σ_{ij}. Judgment should then be used in increasing or decreasing some of these μ_i and σ_{ij} on the basis of factors or nuances not taken into account by the formal computations. Using this revised set of μ_i and σ_{ij}, the set of efficient E, V combinations could be computed, the investor could select the combination he preferred, and the portfolio which gave rise to this E, V combination could be found.

One suggestion as to tentative μ_i, σ_{ij} is to use the observed μ_i, σ_{ij} for some period of the past. I believe that better methods, which take into account more information, can be found. I believe that what is needed is essentially a "probabilistic" reformulation of security analysis. I will not pursue this subject here, for this is "another story." It is a story of which I have read only the first page of the first chapter.

In this paper we have considered the second stage in the process of selecting a portfolio. This stage starts with the relevant beliefs about the securities involved and ends with the selection of a portfolio. We have not considered the first stage: the formation of the relevant beliefs on the basis of observation.

FOOTNOTES

1. See, for example, J.B. Williams, *The Theory of Investment Value* (Cambridge, Mass.: Harvard University Press, 1938), pp. 55–75.
2. J.R. Hicks, *Value and Capital* (New York: Oxford University Press, 1939), p. 126. Hicks applies the rule to a firm rather than a portfolio.
3. The results depend on the asssumption that the anticipated returns and discount rates are independent of the particular investor's portfolio.

4. If short sales were allowed, an infinite amount of money would be placed in the security with highest r.

5. Williams, *op. cit.*, pp. 68, 69.

6. E.g., J. V. Uspensky, *Introduction to Mathematical Probability* (New York: McGraw-Hill, 1937), chapter 9, pp. 161–81.

7. I.e., we assume that the investor does (and should) act as if he had probability beliefs concerning these variables. In general we would expect that the investor could tell us, for any two events (A and B), whether he personally considered A more likely than B, B more likely than A, or both equally likely. If the investor were consistent in his opinions on such matters, he would possess a system of probability beliefs. We cannot expect the investor to be consistent in every detail. We can, however, expect his probability beliefs to be roughly consistent on important matters that have been carefully considered. We should also expect that he will base his actions upon these probability beliefs—even though they be in part subjective.

This paper does not consider the difficult question of how investors do (or should) form their probability beliefs.

8. $$V = X_i^2(\sigma_{11} - 2\sigma_{13} + \sigma_{33}) + X_2^2(\sigma_{22} - 2\sigma_{23} + \sigma_{33})$$
$$+ 2X_1X_2(\sigma_{12} - \sigma_{13} - \sigma_{23} + \sigma_{33}) + 2X_1(\sigma_{13} - \sigma_{33})$$
$$+ 2X_2(\sigma_{23} - \sigma_{33}) + \sigma_{33}$$

9. The isomean "curves" are described above except when $\mu_1 = \mu_2 = \mu_3$. In the latter case all portfolios have the same expected return and the investor chooses the one with minimum variance. As to the assumptions implicit in our description of the isovariance curves see footnote 12.

10. Just as we used the equation $\sum_{i=1}^{4} X_i = 1$ to reduce the dimensionality in the three security case, we can use it to represent the four security case in 3 dimensional space. Eliminating X_4 we get $E = E(X_1, X_2, X_3)$, $V = V(X_1, X_2, X_3)$. The attainable set is represented, in three-space, by the tetrahedron with vertices $(0,0,0)$, $(0,0,1)$, $(0,1,0)$, $(1,0,0)$, representing portfolios with, respectively, $X_4 = 1$, $X_3 = 1$, $X_2 = 1$, $X_1 = 1$.

Let s_{123} be the subspace consisting of all points with $X_4 = 0$. Similarly we can define $s_{a_1}, \ldots, a_a$ to be the subspace consisting of all points with $X_i = 0$, $i \neq a_1, \ldots, a_a$. For each subspace $s_{a_1}, \ldots, a_a$ we can define a *critical line* $la_1, \ldots, a_a$. This line is the locus of points P where P minimizes V for all points in $s_{a_1}, \ldots, a_a$ with the same E as P. If a point is in $s_{a_1}, \ldots, a_a$ and is efficient it must be on $la_1, \ldots, a_a$. The efficient set may be traced out by starting at the point of minimum available variance, moving continuously along various $la_1, \ldots, a_a$ according to definite rules, ending in a point which gives maximum E. As in the two dimensional case the point with minimum available variance may be in the interior of the available set or on one of its boundaries. Typically we proceed along a given critical line until either this line intersects one of a larger subspace or meets a boundary (and simultaneously the critical line of a lower dimensional subspace). In either of these cases the efficient line turns and continues along the new line. The efficient line terminates when a point with maximum E is reached.

11. See footnote 8.

12. In no case will variance be increased. The only case in which variance will not be decreased is if the returns from both portfolios are perfectly correlated. To draw the isovariance curves as ellipses it is both necessary and sufficient to assume that no two distinct portfolios have perfectly correlated terms.

13. If R is a random variable that takes on a finite number of values $r_1, \ldots, r_n$ with probabilities $p_1, \ldots, p_n$ respectively, and expected value E, then

$$M_3 = \sum_{i=1}^{n} p_i (r_i - E)^3.$$

14. One in which the amount gained by winning the bet times the probability of winning is equal to the amount lost by losing the bet, times the probability of losing.

15. Care must be used in using and interpreting relations among aggregates. We cannot deal here with the problems and pitfalls of aggregation.

OUR INVESTMENT PHILOSOPHY

T. Rowe Price

Few men in any profession could hope to look back on their thoughts of a half-century earlier and find them as agreeably durable as did T. Rowe Price, founder of T. Rowe Price and Associates. As far back as 1937, he had developed a strong case for growth stocks—particularly because they produced greater dividend income over time—and, after World War II, wrote out his growth stock philosophy of investing. (At the risk of losing the charm of his detailed documentation of how well it had worked over two decades, this 1950 exposition has been somewhat abridged.)

An investment philosophy is a system of general beliefs about how investment funds should be managed. Unfortunately, most people have no clearly thought out investment philosophy and do not follow any plan. They buy the securities that are popular at the time they have funds available, regardless of whether these are best suited for their needs. When they sell, they usually dispose of the securities that show them a profit and hold on to the ones that show them a loss, regardless of the fact that the former may be better long term investments.

* * * * *

From T. Rowe Price, *Our Investment Philosophy* (Baltimore, Maryland, 1950), 3–12, 18–22, by permission of T. Rowe Price Investment Services.

Our investment philosophy aims to maintain the purchasing power of both income and principal with the minimum risk of loss of principal and reduction of income during periods of adversity. To accomplish this aim, both dollar income and market value of principal must increase over a period of years in order to keep pace with the rise in the cost of living.

Our investment philosophy combines some of the advantages of the formula and business cycle systems with three distinctive features of our own. We believe common stock holdings should be decreased as prices of individual issues rise above sound investment values, but do not think a certain percentage should be sold just because a stock index reaches some pre-determined figure. We also advocate the increase of common stock holdings during periods of business depression when stocks are selling at extremely low prices.

The three distinctive features of our investment philosophy are:

1. The formulation of an investment program which states each investor's ultimate objective and how it is to be attained.
2. The classification and selection of securities best qualified to provide Capital Conservation, Liberal Income, and Capital Growth.
3. The life cycle principle of investing.

1. FORMULATING AN INVESTMENT PROGRAM

It is amazing how few investors, including managers of big estates and trust funds, have sufficiently crystallized their thinking to write a sound and workable investment program. Still fewer adhere to a well conceived plan once it is agreed upon. Yet these same investors would not think of building a house without preparing blue-prints and following them carefully. As a result of the lack of planning, most security portfolios are unbalanced and contain numerous securities which are not suited for the particular fund.

The first step in the application of our investment philosophy is to determine the investor's objectives. Is it safeguarding his principal so that it can be turned into cash with little or no loss at any time regardless of whether markets for bonds and stocks are up or down? Is it safety of income at a fixed rate to meet current expenses? Is it profit or growth in market value of invested principal and higher income for the future? Oftentimes the investor has all three objectives.

After the objectives have been determined, a program should be drawn up which states what portion of the total fund should be invested for each purpose. This should not be taken to mean a permanent allocation of funds, as the program should be flexible so that the percentage of funds placed in each type of investment can be adjusted upward or downward with changes in the business cycle. Whenever the purchase or sale of a security is under consideration, reference should be made to the program to see if the change is in accordance with the over-all plan.

As the yields on common stocks decline, due to a prolonged rise in market values, or when unfavorable business prospects indicate a decline in earnings and dividends, the percentage of the over-all fund invested in this type of security is reduced. Conversely, during periods of low market prices for common stocks, a portion of the funds invested in capital conservation and liberal income securities is transferred to common stock commitments. Such a plan automatically reduces the risk factor during periods of excessively high prices and prepares for opportunities to buy common stocks during periods of low prices.

Investors should recognize that they can not make opportunities, nor can they often foresee them far in advance, but they can be prepared to take advantage of them as they occur. During periods of inflation, it is not always possible to increase both income and principal each year and thus keep pace with the rise in the cost of living. For illustration, excess profits taxes, price ceilings and other restrictions deferred, in many instances, the payment of higher dividends during the war period. During other periods, when investor sentiment is pessimistic, stock prices may decline even though earnings and dividends increase, thus preventing a consistent year to year increase in the market value of invested principal. This was the case in the period 1939-1942, and again in the period from May, 1946 to June, 1949. It is necessary, therefore, to have an investment program which prepares investors for opportunities, both buying and selling, as they often occur at unpredictable intervals.

2. CLASSIFICATION OF SECURITIES ACCORDING TO OBJECTIVE

The Three-Point Objective Defined

Investors have three objectives when buying securities: (1) safety of principal; (2) high current income; and (3) profit. Therefore, we classify all investments under three main headings: (1) Capital Conservation; (2) Liberal Income; and (3) Capital Growth.

This is contrary to the usual practice of classifying them as bonds, preferred stocks, and common stocks. Bonds may be gilt edged, medium grade or speculative, but even bonds with AAA ratings will not furnish stability in market value, as is illustrated by the 10% to 15% decline in long term municipals and the 5% to 10% decline in long term governments from the spring of 1946 to the fall of 1948. Preferred and common stocks also vary greatly in their characteristics. It is more practical, therefore, to group them according to their function rather than according to nomenclature.

Capital Conservation, Liberal Income and Capital Growth Defined

Capital Conservation—The primary purpose of investing for Capital Conservation is *safety of principal*. This portion of the investment portfolio consists of cash, savings bank deposits, United States Savings Bonds, and high grade, short term (one to five year maturities) bonds. The inclusion of short term municipals rather than short term taxable securities depends upon the income tax bracket of each individual. The uses of this portion of the fund vary with the objective and requirements of each investor but include the following: Provision for business expenditures, estate and other taxes, and reserves for future purchases of bonds, stocks, real estate and other investments.

Liberal Income—The primary purpose is *fixed income at a more liberal rate than is obtainable upon Capital Conservation funds*. This portion of the investment portfolio consists of (1) long term bonds and preferred stocks of high quality, which are subject to wide fluctuations in market value due to change in interest rates, and (2) lower quality bonds and preferred stocks paying a relatively high rate of income, but subject to wider fluctuations in market value as a result of changes in the cyclical earnings trends of the various companies, as well as changes in interest rates. These investments furnish higher current income, but do not afford stability in market value.

Capital Growth—The primary purpose is *long term growth of income and principal*. This portion of the investment portfolio consists of common stocks, with preference given to "Growth Stocks." A characteristic of "Growth Stocks" is that they usually sell at lower yields than other common stocks because a larger percentage of the companies' earnings is reinvested in the expanding business to provide higher earnings and dividends in the future.

Securities Possess Different Characteristics

No one security possesses the qualifications to accomplish all three of these major objectives. Therefore, securities best qualified to accomplish one objective well should be selected for each part of the portfolio. Securities, like carpenters' tools, vary greatly in their characteristics and uses. A saw will cut a board better than a hatchet; a hammer will drive a nail better than a screwdriver; a brace and bit will bore a hole better than a chisel.

A short term government bond will provide greater stability in market value than a long term bond. A high grade preferred stock will provide fixed income better than a common stock whose earnings are subject to wide fluctuations. A common stock in a growing enterprise will provide a better opportunity for capital gain than a share in a business that has no growth. Each security in a portfolio should have a functional objective and should be bought with that objective in mind.

Risk and Income Vary with Type of Security

While all securities involve risk, the degree varies widely in accordance with the type of investment. Investments which qualify for Capital Conservation possess the minimum of risk, but currently their yield averages less than 2%, and they afford little or no opportunity for profit. Most bonds and preferred stocks qualifying for Liberal Income currently yield 2 3/4% to 6%, but involve a higher degree of market risk. Common stocks provide the best medium for capital gains but they rarely furnish stability of income and market value. Their risk factor is the highest.

* * * * *

Companies Having the Best Growth Factor
Should Be Selected

After it has been determined that an industry is experiencing growth in both volume and earnings, the next step is to select those companies having the most capable managements and which are operating in those fields having the greatest opportunities for expansion.

Too much emphasis can not be placed on management. If the affairs of the business are being directed by capable men, important factors such as sound financial condition, intelligent research, and efficient operations will be taken care of.

The benefits to be gained by selecting the right companies are illustrated by comparing earnings of six chemical stocks on our approved list with Moody's group of 22 chemical companies. During the period 1929–1949, earnings of our six selected companies increased 313.1%, while earnings of Moody's group showed an increase of 191.1%.

"Growth Stock" Defined

The term "Growth Stock" means different things to different people. Some think in terms of expanding sales. But, as we have pointed out above, expanding sales do not necessarily mean greater profits for the stockholder.

In the past, we defined a "Growth Stock" as a "share in a business enterprise which has demonstrated long term growth in earnings and which, after careful research study, gives indications of continuing such growth in the future, reaching new high earnings per share at the peak of each subsequent major business cycle."

Due to the inflation that has already taken place in our economy, and the probability of further inflation during the next ten years, the definition of a "Growth Stock" has been revised to read as follows: "A share in a business enterprise which has demonstrated long term growth of earnings, reaching a new high level per share at the peak of each subsequent major business cycle and which, after careful research, gives indications of continuing growth, from one business cycle to the next, at a rate faster than the rise in the cost of living."

While frequently there is a delay between growth of earnings and increase in dividends and market value, the earnings factor, in the long run, determines the investment value of a share in a business.

"Growth Stocks" Afford Maximum Gain with Minimum Risk

As long as a company remains in the *earnings growth* phase of its life cycle, it is probable that the owner of the stock will have an opportunity to sell advantageously at a later date. This does not mean that a "Growth Stock" will not show a cyclical decline during a depression period; but it does mean that if the holder misses an opportunity to sell in one bull market he will, in all probability, have an opportunity to sell at a still higher level in a subsequent bull market.

The investor who buys or owns a share in a business which has reached *maturity* in earnings has much less assurance that he will be afforded an opportunity to sell at a profit. As more and more people realize that a company has ceased to grow, demand for its shares will decline and the selling pressure will increase, thereby preventing market prices from recovering to previous high levels during periods of business prosperity.

The investor who buys or owns a share in a business which is in the third or *declining* phase of its earnings life cycle assumes the greatest risk. Selling pressure increases as earnings and dividends decline, with the result that the market value reaches new lows during bear markets and fails to recover to previous highs during bull markets. This type of stock may afford the *speculator* an opportunity to make a quick profit, as a share in such a business usually declines to a very low level during a depression and subsequently recovers rapidly percentagewise during a bull market, based on the hopes of the uninformed that earning power may be restored to former levels. It should be avoided by the long term investor.

"Growth Stocks" Require Continuous Supervision as Their Status Changes

"Growth Stocks" require continuous supervision to detect changes in the prospective fortunes of the various business enterprises. There is a close analogy between the human life cycle and the corporation in that each is subject to unpredictable influences which accelerate or retard development. Increased competition, new inventions, expired patents, court decisions, new legislation, inflation and new management are some of the many factors which cause a change in the trend of earnings.

Public utility equities, for illustration, were included in our Growth List through 1937, but were removed in 1938 because of several adverse factors which led us to believe that the industry had reached the second phase (maturity) in the life cycle and that common stocks of these companies should be classified as matured. Some of the developments which led to this decision were: (a) the re-election of Roosevelt and the continuation of the Administration's persecution of the power and light industry; (b) adverse decisions handed down by Federal courts relative to rate cases; and (c) further socialization of the industry. In 1948, when earnings prospects for public utilities again appeared quite favorable, they were included, for the first time in ten years, in the list of common stocks recommended for purchase, although they were not classified as "Growth Stocks."

ADVANTAGES AND DISADVANTAGES OF OUR INVESTMENT PHILOSOPHY

Our investment philosophy, through the use of a flexible program and adherence to the life cycle principle of investing, combines the three objectives of the average investor, namely, safety of principal, liberal current income, and capital growth, weighting them in accordance with the requirements of the individual investor.

Like all other investment philosophies, it has certain disadvantages. For example, during the later stages of a bull market when the public is most profit-conscious, those who follow our system will be in the unhappy position of seeing some stocks which they have sold continue to rise to higher levels. This is why our philosophy is not suitable for all types of investors. It is not recommended to the short term speculator or the person who expects to buy at the bottom and sell at the top, or to the investor who wants to own stocks in every industry which is popular at the moment and expects every investment to be profitable.

Perfection is difficult to attain, and we do not promise that our philosophy will produce perfect results. We do believe that it is the soundest and safest plan for the average investor who aims to maintain the purchasing power of his income and principal with the minimum of risk. It is particularly adaptable for endowment funds and trust estates which buy for long term holding and desire to make the minimum of changes.

PART 3

THE 1960s

COMMENTS

David L. Babson

As the phenomenon of the "gunslinger" spread across the land, David Babson spoke directly and bluntly to the professional money managers assembled for the first Institutional Investor Conference in 1968.

What I am going to say won't sound very much like what the last speaker said. I feel a little bit lonely up here with three outstanding advocates of performance investing, but I am perfectly willing to make my position clear at the outset.

I firmly believe that those of you who have joined this performance cult, first, are responsible indirectly, if you aren't responsible directly, for the speculative orgy which is sweeping the country, particularly among unknowledgeable investors.

And, second, you are following a policy that may disrupt the whole economy and which is sure to win no Brownie points for institutional investors in the long run.

The program brochure describes me as "one of the outspoken critics of the techniques that characterize investment performance." I am glad that it doesn't describe me as an outspoken critic of good investment performance. To help you place what I am going to say in perspective, I would like to point out that my firm is not a newcomer to the principle of seeking good investment results. We have advocated 100 percent stock ownership as a sound policy for most people—during not just

From the transcript of the First Annual Institutional Investor Conference, January 31, 1968, reprinted by permission of Institutional Investor, Inc.

the past 5 or 10 years, but all of the past 20 years. We were among the first, if not the first, firm to describe, define, and recommend growth stocks back in the late 1940's.

That was when the revolution in money management, about which we are talking today, really began.

So we agree wholeheartedly that professional investors should always be striving for excellent results. But where we differ with the investment performance approach is in the method of seeking effective results.

Jerry Goodman says investment performance is usually defined as (1) a heavy concentration rather than a broad diversification of assets and, (2) a high portfolio turnover. So what we are really talking about, according to this definition, is at best trading performance and at worst outright gambling with other people's money.

When, on average, mutual funds churn their holdings at an annual rate of 40 percent and some turn them two or three or four times faster than the average, when even pension funds shift their assets at 20 percent a year, can anyone seriously call this investing? In plain language, the securities markets are being turned into a gigantic crap game. Yet, here we are, hundreds of experienced and responsible portfolio managers, euphemistically discussing what is going on as investment performance.

Now there are six points about this phenomenon and its potential danger.

First, as Ralph Saul, president of the American Stock Exchange, said last Friday, the security markets are having difficulty in coping with the huge chunks of capital that the institutions are constantly moving around. The daily price swings are getting to be a little short of fantastic. When even a strong favorite runs into a temporary problem, restless holders try to hit the exits all at once. And the unsophisticated followers of these fast-moving institutional investors get royally whip-sawed in the process.

I would like to ask the following questions: Should an involuntary transfer payment taken in this manner from the pocket of some little investor out in Pocatello, Idaho, and added to the assets of a major endowment fund be a source of any satisfaction to its trustees? Does it add anything to the gross national product? Is it likely to bolster public enthusiasm for the free enterprise system?

Second, if today's dice table approach continues, it seems obvious to me the government will have to take a hand. As someone said in Washington not long ago:

When smart speculators unload on less smart speculators, that becomes a problem. In other areas, we do not let professionals deal with amateurs. We do not allow a professional boxer to fight an amateur because that would be slaughter.

And when the smart speculators have hundreds of millions at their command to run the markets up and down, the dice are even more heavily loaded in their favor. The effects of what is going on today are not much different than those created by the old-time pools of the 1920's.

Third, today's speculative fever is badly distorting the expectations of investors, particularly the less informed. Here is a quote from an unsolicited letter that our firm recently received:

> The $50,000 I started with ten years ago has increased 152 percent. I am not at all pleased with this result. I am looking for a 40–60 average annual growth until I retire 20 years from now.

If this investor were to realize his objective of 20 years hence, his portfolio would be $100 million at a 40 percent rate and $1.5 billion at the 60 percent rate.

Nevertheless, with salesmen running around with tables showing how much X Fund went up last quarter and what Y Fund did last month, this unrealistic kind of thinking is infecting everyone.

Fourth, there is a big difference between an aggressive, imaginative investment program that uses promising growth stocks and a frenzied trading program that jumps in and out of stocks from week-to-week or month-to-month on a let's-outsmart-the-other-fellow basis.

Our firm was one of the first to use Honeywell, Corning, 3M, Merck, Polaroid and those kind of stocks. And our clients have stayed with these stocks as investments. As a result, they have done well.

But with the spotlight now focused on this daily numbers game, few people are thinking in terms such as the following:

> Here is a strong company in an industry which should continue to grow faster than the overall economy; its management is competent; its products are essential; its record is excellent; and its stock is selling at a reasonable appraisal of its value. I'd like to buy an ownership in that company and to share in the growth of its business, earnings and dividends over the years ahead.

These days, this kind of approach is looked upon as simple-minded, unsophisticated, even Neanderthal, thinking. But the fact is that almost no one in history has made a fortune and kept it by trading or speculating in the stock market.

My fifth point is that performance contains the seeds of its own destruction. As more and more institutions get into the act, the more likely it becomes that performance will go the way of all previous investment fads. The first practitioners at least were trading in and out of high-grade, readily marketable, seasoned growth companies. As others joined the parade, the emphasis moved along to secondary securities. Now, with everybody jumping on the bandwagon, the trend is toward highly speculative issues of fledgling companies with very limited marketability. With many of these stocks selling at 50 to 100 times earnings and 10 to 15 times sales, performance may already be running out its string.

My sixth and final point is that there is a silver lining in every cloud, and there is one in this fad, too. It is that performance seekers create wonderful opportunities for those willing to use a little courage and patience to work against them.

As just one example, look at the opportunities in the fall of 1966 when the performance people were dumping good growth stocks to build up cash. And right now, they are neglecting some of our best equities. Some well-established companies with large resources and perfectly satisfactory records, are selling at such low appraisals that they entail almost no risk.

Remember, it is very easy to measure your performance, but it isn't easy to measure the risks you take in seeking that performance. As professional investors, you and I have some idea of the risks being accepted, but most of the people whose capital we are managing have little or no conception of the dangers involved. When we seek spectacular short-term profits by performance methods, we run the risk of having disastrous long-term results. And I think this is ridiculous when we can have excellent long-term results taking hardly any risk at all.

CHARACTERISTICS
FOR SUCCESS AS
AGGRESSIVE INVESTORS

Douglas H. Bellemore

Douglas Bellemore taught investment for 40 years at New York University's night school. After 50 years of investing savings from Navy pay and teaching—and investment counseling—he put his money where his mouth was, investing all he had in General Motors at $32–34 (on a scale) because it met all of his tests for a superior investment. It then more than doubled. Here, he identifies the characteristics required for success as an aggressive investor.

Not all investors have the innate or acquired personal characteristics that are mandatory to succeed in building a portfolio of common stocks that will significantly outperform the market over the years.

What are these traits required for success as aggressive investors? Basically they are five:

1. Patience. The aggressive investor should not expect quick results although occasionally this occurs. Success depends, in large measure, on the ability to select undervalued situations not presently recognized by the majority of investors and to wait for expected developments to

From Douglas H. Bellemore, *The Strategic Investor* (Omaha, Nebraska, 1963), 23–25, by permission of Simmons-Boardman Publishing Corp.

provide capital gains which may only come after several years. After the investment commitment has been made, he must calmly hold common stocks, perhaps five to eight years. Individual investment in this sense is not unlike corporate investment, in which management must wait in order to reap benefits of new investment programs. Results cannot be expected to come quickly. In fact, many of the personal qualities for successful business management are the same as those for an aggressive investor.

2. Courage. The investor must have solid convictions and the courage and confidence emanating from them—that is, courage, at times, to ignore those who disagree. Resembling the courage displayed by top corporate management, it is tantamount to willingness to make and to accept responsibility for difficult decisions. Decision-making ability, which is the key to success in business, is vital to success in investing. Although not all decisions will be correct, a high majority must be.

Decisions should be made only after careful analysis of facts and consideration of recommendations of others. The final decision may be at variance with such recommendations. But it is this willingness to differ and to accept responsibility that distinguishes the top executive and the top investor, assuming, of course, judgments are right more often than wrong.

3. Intelligence. To realize success, the aggressive investor must possess average intelligence, but by no means does he need to be a genius. Intelligence alone, however, is by no means the only requisite for success. Common sense—impossible to test except by experience—is equally important in judgment decisions. Many highly intelligent investors have had poor investment records because they lacked common sense, i.e., the down-to-earth, practical ability to evaluate a situation.

4. Emotional stability. Although akin to patience this trait is broader in scope. Initially, it is needed to prevent the investor from being engulfed in waves of optimism and pessimism that periodically sweep over Wall Street. Moreover, it is required to separate the facts from the entangled web of human emotions. Bernard Baruch said once that most facts reach Wall Street through "a curtain of human emotions," and even sophisticated professionals in Wall Street find difficulty in distinguishing fact from emotion.

5. Hard work. To be successful an aggressive investor must do thorough research which requires considerable time and effort. He must be knowledgeable about the company in which he considers making an investment, the industry, the position of the company in the industry, and the place and future of that industry in the economy as a whole. Furthermore, he must do considerable financial analysis for which he must have some general knowledge of statements. Although not on the advanced level of a professional security analyst, he must adequately determine relative financial strength and earning power and project future earnings. The fundamentals of accounting and corporation finance can readily be self-taught for these purposes.

Brokers, of course, through the services of their research departments are a great help in stock analysis and will do much of the work of ferreting out facts; nevertheless, the investor can never escape judging the facts himself, and this takes knowledge.

6. Willingness to sacrifice the investment protection of diversification. Diversification based on the insurance principle can considerably reduce investment risks, although it cannot be achieved haphazardly. Nor can diversification be substituted for a certain amount of investment judgment, although a portfolio large enough to be distributed rather evenly among New York Stock Exchange stocks or all major industrial stocks would, for all practical purposes, reduce risk to that inherent in common stocks as a group. But diversification, say, among 20 or 30 stocks, cannot substitute for investment judgment.

While the conservative investor relies extensively upon diversification to minimize risks, his aggressive counterpart must sacrifice wide diversification if his portfolio is significantly to outperform the general market. Although wide diversification reduces risks by offsetting mediocre selections with good ones, it also reduces substantially the profit or capital gain potential of a portfolio. Just as no speculator ever amassed a fortune while following the principle of diversification, no investor who expects his portfolio to outperform the averages significantly and to provide major capital gains can practice broad diversification.

Finally, each investor must ask himself whether he meets all the qualifications that have been discussed for successful investing. Failure to meet any of these makes it probable that by following an aggressive approach to investment, the investor will have a poorer record than if he adhered to the tenets held by the conservative investor. Should the investor decide to become conservative, he will at least have the satisfaction of knowing he should do considerably better than the unqualified investor who attempts to pursue aggressive tactics.

There are no short cuts to successful investment for aggressive investors. To earn really sizable capital gains requires substantially more effort, patience, courage, and intelligence than that required of the conservative investor.

It requires much more on all of these counts. As in other fields, the investor cannot get something for nothing. Once the investor has selected his own investment classification, he must pursue adamantly the principles of his particular group.

OBSERVATIONS ON PERFORMANCE

Warren E. Buffett

Warren Buffett has taken the time to write out lessons on investing for his investors. This passage is from his January 1965 letter to the Buffett Partnership. It was preceded by a table showing that institutional investors were underperforming the Dow Jones Industrial Average. (The partnership was doing twice as well as the Dow Jones Industrial Average.)

The repetition of these tables [showing underperformance] has caused partners to ask: "Why in the world does this happen to very intelligent managements working with (1) bright, energetic staff people, (2) virtually unlimited resources, (3) the most extensive business contacts, and (4) literally centuries of aggregate investment experience?" (The latter qualification brings to mind the fellow who applied for a job and stated he had twenty years of experience—which was corrected by the former employer to read "one year's experience—twenty times.")

This question is of enormous importance, and you would expect it to be the subject of considerable study by investment managers and substantial investors. After all, each percentage point on $30 billion is $300 million per year.

From a letter to the Buffett Partnership, Omaha, Nebraska, January 1965, with permission from Warren Buffett.

Curiously enough, there is practically nothing in the literature of Wall Street attacking this problem, and discussion of it is virtually absent at security analyst society meetings, conventions, seminars, etc. My opinion is that the first job of any investment management organization is to analyze its own techniques and results before pronouncing judgment on the managerial abilities and performance of the major corporate entities of the United States.

In the great majority of cases the lack of performance exceeding or even matching an unmanaged index in no way reflects lack of either intellectual capacity or integrity. I think it is much more the product of: (1) group decisions—my perhaps jaundiced view is that it is close to impossible for outstanding investment management to come from a group of any size with all parties really participating in decisions; (2) a desire to conform to the policies and (to an extent) the portfolios of other large well-regarded organizations; (3) an institutional framework whereby average is "safe" and the personal rewards for independent action are in no way commensurate with the general risk attached to such action; (4) an adherence to certain diversification practices which are irrational; and finally and importantly, (5) inertia.

Perhaps the above comments are unjust. Perhaps even our statistical comparisons are unjust. Both our portfolio and method of operation differ substantially from the investment companies in the table. However, I believe both our partners and their stockholders feel their managements are seeking the same goal—the maximum long-term average return on capital obtainable with the minimum risk of permanent loss consistent with a program of continuous investment in equities.

* * * * *

In looking at the table of investment company performance, the question might be asked: "Yes, but aren't those companies run more conservatively than the Partnership?" If you asked that question of the investment company managements, they, in absolute honesty, would say they were more conservative. If you asked the first hundred security analysts you met, I am sure that a very large majority of them also would answer for the investment companies. I would disagree. I have over 90% of my net worth in BPL, and most of the family have percentages in that area, but of course, that only demonstrates the sincerity of my view — not the validity of it.

It is unquestionably true that the investment companies have their money more conventionally invested than we do. To many people conventionality is indistinguishable from conservatism. In my view, this represents erroneous thinking. Neither a conventional nor an unconventional approach, per se, is conservative.

Truly conservative actions arise from intelligent hypotheses, correct facts and sound reasoning. These qualities may lead to conventional acts, but there have been many times when they have led to unorthodoxy. In some corner of the world they are probably still holding regular meetings of the Flat Earth Society.

We derive no comfort because important people, vocal people, or great numbers of people agree with us. Nor do we derive comfort if they don't. A public opinion poll is no substitute for thought. When we really sit back with a smile on our face is when we run into a situation we can understand, where the facts are ascertainable and clear, and the course of action obvious. In that case—whether conventional or unconventional–whether others agree or disagree—we feel we are progressing in a conservative manner.

The above may seem highly subjective. It is. You should prefer an objective approach to the question. I do. My suggestion as to one rational way to evaluate the conservativeness of past policies is to study performance in declining markets. We have only three years of declining markets in our table and unfortunately (for purposes of this test only) they were all moderate declines. In all three of these years we achieved appreciably better investment results than any of the more conventional portfolios.

Specifically, if those three years had occurred in sequence, the cumulative results would have been:

Tri-Continental Corp.	− 0.7%
Dow	−20.6
Mass. Investors Trust	−20.9
Lehman Corp.	−22.3
Investors Stock Fund	−24.6
Limited Partners	+45.0

We don't think this comparison is all important, but we do think it has some relevance. We certainly think it makes more sense than saying

"We own (regardless of price) A.T. & T., General Electric, IBM and General Motors and are therefore conservative." In any event, evaluation of the conservatism of any investment program or management (including self-management) should be based upon rational objective standards, and I suggest performance in declining markets to be at least one meaningful test.

THE MEANING OF INCOME

William L. Cary
Craig B. Bright

William Cary and Craig Bright conducted a thoughtful analysis of the real (versus "assumed") constraints imposed by law on endowment funds—and found more room for choice than had been expected. This introductory section sets the tone for their report, *The Law and the Lore of Endowment Funds*.

While the explosive increase in costs has been the primary reason for the comparative decline in the importance of the contribution of endowment funds, it has not been the only reason. The portfolios of many endowment funds have been far too heavily laden with fixed-income securities to resist the relentless erosion of inflation. In a decade when the average price of common stocks has risen seven times as fast as the cost of living, and dividends on common stocks have risen three and a half times as fast,[1] many endowments have been exceedingly hard pressed even to keep abreast.

To some extent this has been the result of a conscious choice on the part of endowment fund managers. As a group they are conservative,[2]

From William L. Cary and Craig B. Bright, *The Law and the Lore of Endowment Funds* (New York, New York, 1969), 5–8, by permission of the Ford Foundation.

and some of them have insisted that their only duty is to safeguard the original dollar value of the funds entrusted to their care. Like the cautious servant in the parable of the talents, they have been well pleased to bury their funds, complacent in the belief that if their talents cannot multiply under their supervision at least they will not be lost.[3] But their talents have been lost, a little each year, as surely as if they were squandered or thrown away. Instead of safeguarding the legacy of tomorrow's students such managers have sacrificed it to fiscal "conservatism."

The great majority of endowment fund managers, however, are well aware that it is no longer "conservative" or prudent to ignore possibilities for long-term growth in formulating their investment policies.[4] In choosing between a high current yield of dividends and interest on the one hand, and long-term growth of principal on the other, they strive conscientiously to strike a balance between the demands of today and those of tomorrow. But too often the desperate need of some institutions for funds to meet current operating expenses has led their managers, contrary to their best long-term judgment, to forego investments with favorable growth prospects if they have a low current yield.[5]

It has been suggested that it would be far wiser to take capital gains as well as dividends and interest into account in investing for the highest overall return consistent with the safety and preservation of the funds invested. If the current return is insufficient for the institution's needs, the difference between that return and what it would have been under a more restrictive policy can be made up by the use of a prudent portion of capital gains. This suggestion has repeatedly been met with the response that as a matter of law the capital gains of endowment funds may not be expended, because the principal of endowment funds must be maintained intact and in perpetuity and capital gains are part of that principal.[6]

The sections of this report which immediately follow are devoted in large measure to an analysis of the validity and effects of that response.

* * * * *

It should be stressed at the outset that the purpose of this report is not to advocate either the expenditure or the preservation of capital gains. We do not presume to chart the "proper course" for all institutions, regardless of circumstances. The object of our inquiry is merely to determine whether the directors of an educational institution are circumscribed by the law or are free to adopt the investment policy they regard as soundest for their institution, unhampered by legal impediments, prohibitions or restrictions.

There is strong and vehement objection in some academic circles to any discussion of the proper allocation to principal or income of the realized gains of endowment funds, because for some persons the issue is a moral or ethical one which is not open to reasoned debate. Such persons argue that educational institutions are charged with the duty and responsibility of maintaining the principal of their endowment inviolate, and that principal "necessarily" includes realized appreciation. Many of them fail or are unwilling to recognize the latter part of that argument as nothing more than an assumption, the validity of which may be questioned. As was noted at a seminar on the financial problems of higher education:

> We may be in a period in which the mores regarding these matters are gradually shifting. Fifty years ago most trustees would have argued that it was immoral to purchase common stocks with endowment funds. At present nearly half of college endowment funds are in common stocks, and a similar shift with respect to the [utilization of] capital gains may be occurring.[7]

It should be clear to any legal scholar that there is nothing inherently sacrosanct about traditional views of principal and income, even as they apply to private trusts. Many of the views which are prevalent today in the trust field became so quite recently, after many years of debate between proponents of a number of competing treatments, and there is no evidence that the evolutionary process has ceased. It should be remembered that the strength of our system of jurisprudence has historically been its ability to adapt and change in response to the evolving needs of society. As the Supreme Court of Pennsylvania said in a recent case:

> Due process does not mandate that prior decisions or rules remain effective and controlling forever. Thus, it is settled that there is no vested interest in a definition or method of ascertaining income.[8]

There are those who insist that capital gains of endowment funds must be treated as principal, whether or not the law requires such treatment. They argue that any other treatment would thwart the intent of the donors of the funds.[9] But as Professor Scott has observed in this connection:

> The great difficulty with any argument based upon the intention of the settlor is that he generally fails to state his intention. The reason why he does not do so may be and generally is that the question never occurs to him. Ordinarily, therefore, the question is not what he intended or probably intended but what he would probably have intended if he had ever considered the matter. All that can be said with any confidence is that he would have intended whatever is fair and just, and we have already seen how difficult it is to determine what is fair and just. . . .[10,11]

Even if the donor had intended one accounting treatment in a given set of circumstances, would it be reasonable to assume that he intended that treatment to be applied through all eternity, regardless of changes in the financial and investment community? John Stuart Mill commented on such a position some time ago:

> Under the guise of fulfilling a bequest, this is making a dead man's intentions for a single day a rule for subsequent centuries, when we know not whether he himself would have made it a rule even for the morrow. . . . No reasonable man, who gave his money, when living, for the benefit of the community, would have desired that his mode of benefiting the community should be adhered to when a better could be found.[12]

Proponents of the theory that capital gains must be treated as principal, regardless of the requirements of the law, argue that failure to follow their mandate will lead to a decline in gifts to charity, because donors can no longer rely on their wishes being enforced.[13] Again, this argument is based on the questionable assumption that those wishes have been properly interpreted by the proponents of the argument. But even if it were granted, *arguendo*, that the intent of donors in this matter of administration could accurately be divined, the words of Professor Scott from half a century ago in his article entitled "Education and the Dead Hand" seem apropos:

> It may be suggested that unless donors can rely upon the strict observance of all their directions they will be dissuaded from making gifts for charitable purposes. But experience in England shows the fact to be otherwise. Charitable gifts were never more common in England than in

the early days of the Reformation, when the fact that Henry VIII had defeated the intentions of many a founder of religious institutions was fresh in the minds of every Englishman. Bequests to the English universities actually increased after Parliament had authorized them to depart from the directions of their founders and benefactors. It would seem rather that the charitably minded would be discouraged by the sight of charitable institutions gradually ceasing to accomplish the high purposes for which they were created.[14]

FOOTNOTES

1. *Bruere v. Cook*, 63 N.J. Eq. 624, 52 A. 1001 (Ch. 1902), *aff'd mem.*, 67 N.J. Eq. 724, 63 A. 1118 (E. & A. 1903); *Mason's Ex'rs v. Trustees of the Methodist Episcopal Church*, 27 N.J. Eq. 47. (Ch. 1876). *See also White v. Mayor & Common Council*, 89 N.J. Eq. 5, 103 A. 1042 (Ch. 1918).

2. *Brittenbaker v. Buck*, 58 Cal. App. 738, 209 P. 264 (1st Dist. 1922).

3. *Estate of McDole*, 215 Cal. 328, 334, 10 P.2d 75, 77 (1932).

4. *Crawfordsville Trust Co. v. Elston Bank & Trust Co.*, 216 Ind. 596, 610, 25 N.E.2d 626, 631 (1940).

5. For purposes of this report we polled all institutions of higher learning in the United States with investment portfolios having a market value of $3,000,000 or more as of June 30, 1967. Approximately 300 institutions were questioned, of which 186 furnished information about their investment practices. Eighty-five per cent of the responding institutions stated that their choice of investments is influenced at least to some extent by a desire for a high current return of dividends and interest, and 11% stated that their choice is influenced to a great extent by that desire. Conversely, 67% stated that a low current return of dividends and interest sometimes dissuades them from making investments with "unusually attractive long-term growth prospects." For 8% of the institutions a low current return is usually sufficient to block such an investment.

6. Of the institutions which responded to the questionnaire described in the preceding footnote, 50% stated that their investment portfolios would be changed to include more growth stocks if they were legally free to spend the capital gains of their endowment funds. Ten per cent of the institutions would purchase many more such stocks.

7. *Bible Inst. Colportage Ass'n v. St. Joseph's B. & T. Co.*, 118 Ind. App. 592, 75 N.E.2d 666 (1947).

8. *Stockton v. Northwestern Branch Missionary Soc'y,* 127 Ind. App. 193, 133 N.E.2d 875 (1956).
9. *In re Los Angeles Pioneer Soc'y,* 40 Cal.2d 852, 257 P.2d 1, *cert. den.,* 346 U.S. 888 (1953); *Ashton v. Dashaway Ass'n,* 84 Cal. 61, 22 P. 660, *aff'd mem. in banc,* 23 P. 1091 (1890); *Sherman v. Richmond Hose Co. No. 2,* 230 N.Y. 462, 130 N.E. 613 (1921); *Commonwealth v. Pauline Home,* 141 Pa. 537, 21 A. 661 (1891); *Humane Fire Co.'s Appeal,* 88 Pa. 389 (1879); *Mayer v. Society,* 2 Brewst. 385 (Pa. Sup. Ct. 1868); *Thomas v. Ellmaker,* 1 Pars. 98 (Pa. Ct. C.P. 1844); *accord, Lynch v. Spilman,* 67 Cal. 2d 247, 431 P.2d 636, 62 Cal. Rptr. 12 (1967). *But see Cone v. Wold,* 85 Minn. 302, 88 N.S. 977 (1902) (donations held on a resulting trust in favor of the donors).
10. *Hobbs v. Board of Ed.,* 126 Neb. 416, 253 N.W. 627 (1934); *Crane v. Morristown School Fnd.,* 120 N.J. Eq. 583, 187 A. 632 (E. & A. 1936); *Mills v. Davison,* 54 N.J. Eq. 659, 35 A. 1072 (E. & A. 1896).
11. As we point out later, donors very seldom give the slightest indication of how they want the capital gains of their gifts to be treated. Further, judicial interpretations of the presumed intent of donors in this respect are almost non-existent. An example is a decision of the Orphan's Court in Pennsylvania, which was asked to interpret a testamentary trust which required "interest and income" to be paid to named charities in perpetuity. The court held that the donor had intended "income" to include both realized and unrealized appreciation. Otherwise such gains would be accumulated to pass eventually to charities completely unknown to the testator, through the application of the doctrine of cy pres, upon the dissolution of the charities he intended to favor. (*See, e.g. Fordyce v. Woman's Christian Nat's Library Ass'n,* 79 Ark. 550, 96 S.W. 155 (1906); *St. Mary's Academy v. Solomon,* 77 Colo. 463, 238 P. 22 (1925).

    We have found no case in which a court was asked to determine whether the capital gains of the endowment funds of a charitable corporation, held by the corporation itself, should be classified as principal or as income.
12. *See, e.g., Parker v. Port Huron Hosp.,* 361 Mich. 1, 105 N.W.2d (1960), *overruling Downes v. Harper Hosp.,* 101 Mich. 555, 60 N.W. 42 (1894). *See also* CHAMBERS, COLLEGES AND THE COURTS:1936–40, 91 (1941).
13. *Loeffler v. Sheppard-Pratt Hosp.,* 130 Md. 265, 100 A. 301 (1917); *Perry v. House of Refuge,* 63 Md. 20 (1885); *Downes v. Harper Hosp.,* 101 Mich. 555, 60 N.W. 42 (1894) (deeds in trust to found hospital), *overruled, Parker v. Port Huron Hosp.,* 361 Mich. 1, 105 N.W.2d 1 (1960).
14. *Franklin v. Hastings,* 253 Ill. 46, 97 N.E. 265 (1912); *accord, Jansen v. Godair,* 292 Ill. 364, 127 N.E. 97 (1920); *Crerar v. Williams,* 145 Ill. 625, 34 N.E. 467 (1893).

AN INVESTMENT PHILOSOPHY

Henry G. Davis

Henry Davis is one of the remarkably few people who have made substantial fortunes from investments in common stocks. During the 1930s, he analyzed the experiences of other investors and developed—and then implemented—a long-term, fundamental philosophy of investment. The following are excerpts from a 1962 speech in which he presented some of his ideas.

Over the years countless systems have been devised to make money in the stock market. Tested against known conditions of the past, many of them seem to promise to work successfully in the future. Unfortunately, they never do so for long. Back in the 1930's the Cowles Institution made a study of the results of the systems which were then in vogue and concluded that the fruits of success in all but one were no better than could have been obtained through tossing a coin. The exception was an approach based on the assumption that what had been happening was more likely to continue than change. Unfortunately, such an approach necessarily involves suffering a substantial depreciation before there is definite confirmation that the longer term tide has changed either in the case of the market as a whole or of a particular company.

But a few investors do make money, as is evident when we see "the

---

Reprinted with permission from a speech given during the summer of 1962.

big houses on the hill." When we analyze the sources of this wealth we find that it almost never has been derived from mathematical or statistical techniques which are the basis of all systems. As will be brought out later, success seems to have come either from long holding of an interest in a successful enterprise or from having adequate cash when bargains were available.

To follow the philosophy I am proposing to you, which is long term and incidentally is based principally on informed common sense, you, as an investor, will have to abandon three almost universally accepted beliefs—(1) that anyone can guess the market's future behavior with sufficient accuracy to time one's moves in and out, (2) that, with rare exceptions, anything good is [n]ever cheap, and (3) that anyone can be successful if he stresses high present income.

Since the Cowles study of twenty-five years ago, many new systems have been invented to call the turns in the market and old ones have been refined and corrected to avoid the errors apparent in 1929 and 1937. But I wonder if an unbiased study of their success in anticipating this year's severe decline would show any better results than the old ones at past major turns. The Dow Theory identifies the present trend as a typical bear market, but it did so also in 1957 and then had to eat its words for the predicted decline lasted only another day or so longer. The theory that the small trader is always wrong has been confounded by a high proportion of odd lot sales lasting fully a year prior to the recent decline. Now the advocates of this system say that a preponderance of odd lot sales is not to be relied upon; instead we have to watch the volume of odd lot short selling. Proponents of Col. Leonard Ayres' breadth theory in recent years have missed the boat time after time. Reliance on Barron's Confidence Index has been no more consistent. The interpreters of the complicated Elliott Wave Theory have told us that we were on the final "5th wave of the 5th wave" but were assuring us that the market had to exceed its old highs by 10 to 20% before this last sub-wave would be completed. Now they are not so sure whether the predicted 150 to 300 point advance in the Dow Jones is still ahead or whether they should read the 735 top in December 1961 as the completion of this advance even though it exceeded the former one by only ten points. Those who rely on the banking figures to analyze money trends insist we have never had a recession while bank investments were still rising. The future still could prove them right but a 27% jolt in stock prices is a severe penalty to overlook.

What makes the timing problem double difficult is that for it to be successful it involves being twice right—for stocks sold must be repurchased later at cheaper prices or nothing has been gained. If the chances are one in two, as Cowles says, for the first successful timing, they become one in four for two correct moves in succession. Realizing these difficulties, and the additional problems involved in relying on a committee's action compared to the chances of one individual, many prominent institutions have adopted formula plans to lighten stockholdings automatically as prices advance and increase them as they fall. There are many such formulae—the original Vassar College plan, the Yale, the one used by the First National City Bank, etc. They have in common the assumption that no Investment Committee, no matter how able, will come up with as good average results.

The second approach you will have to abandon if you want to follow the unglamourous investment philosophy which has been responsible for most past fortunes is "cheap" vehicles. Common sense will tell you that in a free market nothing is ever cheap unless its value is to be affected by factors as yet unknown except to a very few. There are thousands of experts daily assessing values of individual stocks; if any security were really cheap today, it wouldn't be a week hence. Cheapness indicates inferior quality or defectiveness somewhere. Everyone accepts this when he is thinking in terms of furniture, paintings, shoes or automobiles, but somehow he rejects this logic as he remembers a Control Data which sold at 35 cents a share five years ago. But the odds of finding these are not much more favorable than unearthing a Picasso selling for $100. That has happened too, but along with acumen it involves also a quantity of luck we cannot count as our due.

When the elder J. P. Morgan decided he was going to collect paintings, he relied for his advice, I believe, on Mr. Duveen, the world's foremost authority on old Masters. Thanks to his guidance, he bought the world's best paintings but he was roundly criticized for paying "unheard of" prices. People said anyone could do that but only a man to whom money meant nothing would. The popular path only an exceptional man would have avoided was to search out unknown artists who a generation hence could be another Monet, Matisse or Cezanne. A generation later the Morgan collection had soared to values undreamed and kudos are awarded to Mr. Morgan's acumen for buying the best with price a very secondary condition. The man who buys the cheapest second-hand car of the make and year he seeks will usually later rue his temporary saving of a few hundred dollars. One can safely accept the tenet that you almost always get what you pay for whether you are buying paintings, cars, shoes, or stocks.

The smart operator in cheap stocks does not rely on the assumption that everyone else is wrong in his appraisal of known facts. He, like everyone else, sees the disease in a corporation and it is because of this sickness he wants control so as to have the power to perform the necessary operations to restore normal health or to use his control to liquidate the undervalued assets and so return him a profit.

The third idea you will have to abandon is that success will come from buying high income because this road probably has caused more unfortunate investment results over the longer term than any other approach, yet we all tend to succumb to its allure. Give a client, or even ourself, choice of a group of stocks from which to select a purchase, almost invariably it will be the one with the highest yield, whereas time usually will prove that the lowest yielding stock on the list would later turn out to be the most remunerative. You can prove mathematically that it is not possible to buy a good investment with a high yield. High yield necessarily means a low price in terms of earnings and thus an unpopular issue or its price-earnings ratio would be higher. Moreover, a high yield also means a large payout of available earnings in the form of dividends—which is only possible in the case of a mature company not needing to generate funds internally to finance its expected growth.

Twenty years ago when we were collecting evidence to support the philosophy of investment which seemed to have produced the bulk of the successes in the past, we analyzed the performance of specialized accounts which had stressed high income. The Keystone Custodian Group were merchandizing a number of packages designed to fit anyone's taste. In bonds you could buy funds specializing in quality, in high income, in railroad reorganizations, etc., you could buy preferred stock funds selected for high income, for quality, where dividends were in arrears, etc.; in common stocks you could get almost any specialization desired—growth, electronics, income, speculative, etc. In each section the relative performance over a ten year period was the poorest where high income had been the objective even though the dividends or interest received was added into the accumulated benefits.

OUR INITIATION TO THE PHILOSOPHY

Between September 1937 and March 1938 stock values were cut in half and in the following year earnings on the Dow Jones Industrials fell from $12.26 to $6.01. It is not surprising that any particular advisory group missed foreseeing the possibility of such a decline, but our group was hurt more than that for in the previous year we had increased our exposure to loss in our conclusion that the good stocks already had recovered sufficiently and it behooved us therefore to trade down our clients' portfolios to the second and third grades so as to enjoy their delayed recovery from the depression. We were right in this surmise for a year but at what turned out later to be a very heavy cost.

What is surprising is that almost none of the security experts saw the blow coming, or to express it more accurately, took any steps to shorten sails in advance. This was true then, as it is again today, whether you looked at banks, investment counsel, private foundations or insurance companies. Among the more highly regarded firms there was one exception, a leading investment counsel, who had sold 15% of their client's stocks in the summer of 1937. The story of how they came to do it is an object lesson for all of us who deal with a committee form of government. One of the seven men on this firm's policy committee became worried about the outlook as he saw it and continuously cajoled his associates to sell until in exasperation the committee agreed to recommend sale of one-seventh of their clients' stockholdings (his share of total vote) provided he would cease arguing further about the question and so leave time for the committee's other responsibilities. It is amusing today to hear that this firm still boasts about its prescience in 1937. Incidentally, the minority member of the committee later became this firm's president.

In 1938 our group was faced with a major job of rehabilitation to reinstill confidence in our staff and to stem the flow of cancellations from our clients. The staff was as able a group of individuals as could be found; however, we know that they could not be sold again on trusting to the intuition of any man or committee. Previously one man "of genius" at the top of our company, who acquired his following by fortuitous selling from 1929 to 1933, had to be replaced by a man of experience and reputation who realized that buying was again in order in 1935. Since the ability of our personnel was obvious, surely some way must exist for it to produce better than the average results. Thus, it became incumbent on us who owned the company to produce something which would restore our men's faith in their ability and which would guide the overall policy. We knew it had to be a logical method visible to all rather than a secret device or the intricate workings of another human's brain. Brokers had done such a poor job with their clients in 1929 that the ground was fertile for the growth of the investment counsel profession in the Thirties—investor faith was transferred to them as they had nothing to sell but their advice. Eight years later investment counsel had proved no more clairvoyant than the broker. Yet, over the years people had amassed fortunes from their investment; perhaps we would find the clues we needed to guide us in the methods they used. So, instead of trying to give birth to a new technique, we decided to start with the results which had been successful and work back to an analysis of the methods used. Our staff was asked to list the names of everyone they knew who had wealth and then describe briefly how it had been acquired. Hundreds of examples were turned in. It was soon obvious that if we did not count the cases where wealth had been acquired through marriage or inheritance, the others would fall into two categories. Nine out of ten of the rich had made their fortune because they had been long term stockholders in a successful enterprise; the small balance because they had ample buying power at the rare but repetitive times when bargains were available. Obviously these two groups had separately found a correct answer to the two questions we are always asked: "What to buy and when to buy?"

The larger group included not only the names of most of the American fortunes—the Du Ponts, Fords, Rockefellers, Hartfords, Harknesses, Vanderbilts, Dukes, Armours, Phipps, McCormicks, etc.—but in the small towns the owners of successful local enterprises. We already knew this but what was revealing was the concentration of these fortunes and the long continuity of their holdings. These people did not try to sell when their shares looked overpriced in the hope of buying them back later with fewer dollars. Perhaps because they were on the inside and knew of coming promising developments they had the courage to hold on through discouraging periods; perhaps it was the capital gains tax which fortuitously locked them into something good. But it was because they were locked into something good more or less permanently that they had become rich. In the future we planned to copy them in this by avoiding

investments particularly pointed to take advantage of temporarily beneficial condition we thought might lie ahead. We decided to look at our
"buy" recommendations as if we were acquiring a business which could
not be resold. We would only modify the approach we were trying to
emulate by diversifying in a representative selection of such opportunities instead of confining ourselves to the control of one, although we
realized, of course, that concentration was the way fortunes had been
made. Some diversification, so long as it could be accomplished within
the accepted standards, seemed the safer way to keep it.

In the small group who had concentrated on the "when" we were
surprised to find so few individuals who attained wealth because they
sold in 1929 or had gone short in bear markets. There were only one
or two who had been individually lucky enough to make money both
ways by alternating between bullish and bearish positions. This is to be
expected for an individual is basically inclined to be either optimistic or
pessimistic and only performs well when his character is in tune with the
atmosphere. The successful examples, the Rothschilds, Baruchs, etc.,
were people who had accumulated buying power long before the bargains
presented themselves. These people had sold when they felt prices were
fair without waiting for their holdings to be obviously overvalued. The
French Rothschilds bought the Paris-Orleans Railway in bankruptcy—
reorganized it—waited for earnings under brighter skies—and then resold
the company to the public. Examples of such acumen are not uncommon
but in this case three successive generations of Rothschilds repeated this
procedure three times with the same railway and later reconstituted their
cash resources for the next such opportunity.

It impressed us that the successful proponents of timing had also
been very long term in their concept. . . . One canny Scotsman at the turn
of the century discovered a clue to warn him when a cash position was
indicated. R. T. Wilson had been the purchasing agent in England for
the Confederacy during the Civil War and since his government was not
recognized abroad, he had to bank the funds under his own name. After
the war the Confederacy no longer existed so he pocketed the balances.
He moved to New York, married his four daughters to a Goelet, an
Astor, a Vanderbilt and a rich English Lord, and built a summer home
at Newport. In those days there were no Federal Reserve Index, no GNP,
or any of the mass of statistics available today but cannily he found a
substitute. His train ride from New York to Newport took him through

the then industrial heart of the U.S. When he saw the factories burning their lights at night, he sold stocks and then patiently waited to rebuy them until the factories were shut down or grass was growing in their yards.

Back in 1938 we thought we could borrow these tools which had proven a successful guide to Mr. Wilson's timing. We realized each cyclical peak probably would look so different from the past that it would again fool all but the occasionally lucky. We set up statistics to show us how close to capacity or past peaks the key industries were operating and resolved to be continuing sellers whenever three-quarters of them were operating at rates which had only been exceeded one-tenth of the time in the past. Unfortunately, we had no opportunity to test this system for this was 1938 and within a year war broke out and capacity operations were thus guaranteed almost everywhere for the duration and for some time after to supply the deferred demand. Then the Employment Act of 1946 made it incumbent on the Government to stimulate the economy by deficit spending whenever slack appeared. It is still too soon to be sure that the built-in stabilizers will always be successful but they certainly should take out of the economy the big swings with which past generations had to contend and of which the smart timer could hope to take advantage.

Accordingly we set the course of our investment philosophy within these two guides—both long term in concept. Any conversion of stocks into cash was not to be timed by a committee's enlightened judgment but became a matter of a slow but continuous process whenever activity in most areas of the economy was at levels which had rarely been exceeded in the past. We hoped we should be able to persuade clients to wait the years which might be necessary before funds so derived were reinvested in stocks. Second, we determined that any stocks we did buy should be sought as permanent possessions, to be held at least so long as their performance continued satisfactory due to the more favorable factors affecting the areas in which they were operating. Current price, therefore, was only a minor consideration in our selection or in our decisions. We had learned in 1937 the eventual cost from trading down into less desirable groups to obtain lower prices at such times as the individual prices of the desirable stocks looked too high because they were discounting their future too far in advance. We resolved instead to postpone buying at these times but not sell the "overpriced" unless we were reducing stocks as a whole due to skepticism that business activity could long continue its abnormal pace. Before we sold the best, even if they looked overpriced, we resolved to make sure that there were no poorer ones which could be disposed of to provide the cash for a cutback.

RELATIVE POTENTIAL OF TWO METHODS

Although most people focus their efforts on the probable course of the market, it can be clearly demonstrated that over a longer term of years selection has far greater influence on the investment results obtained than has timing. Moreover, we know from past experience how few can show a successful record of timing. That is why ten times as many of the "big houses on the hill" were built by selection as by timing.

* * * * *

Of course, many will wish they could do both simultaneously; however, looking at past records that hope seems out of reach. . . . (Y)our emphasis should be on selection rather than guessing the market, not only because it is more possible to be successful, but also because it has much greater potential.

HOW TO USE THE "WHEN" APPROACH

As indicated earlier, the essential is to have cash when bargains become available. The successful practitioners have been those who are in the habit of maintaining a fairly liquid position most of the time or ones who acquire it early and can keep it ready for long periods. The successful here are a breed quite different from the average investor and so we cannot copy their methods except for such brief periods that success is not apt to fall our way except through luck. . . . What the sophisticated American investor does today, particularly the Trustee, is to compromise and hold some bonds in an account, which he thinks of as a hedge against error but which also provide his buying power for bargains if they appear unexpectedly. The average American accepts these more or less permanent bond holdings for a portion of his portfolio more equably than a European for he has not felt the cost of currency inflation and because of the unique feature here of tax exempt bonds which greatly enhances the income he has to spend on his enjoyment of life.

Back in 1938 I learned that no group could be expected to sell ahead of a large market decline. After our very recent experience I am more sure of this than ever despite the additional statistics available, the competent economists now at our elbows and the lessons of the past to teach us that the "impossible" might re-occur. I do not think we can ever expect such difficult decisions from a group when it involves guessing the future. This is true not only of investment and business groups but government as well. We read now the histories of Cabinet meetings of many countries prior to both World Wars and find possibly one man out of a large group in each country who was reasonably close in his estimates of what lay ahead. Those who foresaw a long war, for example, were later termed lucky and acting on hunches rather than having conclusions reached by deductive reasoning. Consequently, are we justified in setting up our procedures so as to leave such difficult decisions to a majority vote?

HOW TO USE THE "WHAT" APPROACH

Unless you are a nimble professional like a floor specialist, I urge that any stock you buy pass three tests:

1. the sales of the product or service which the company sells must be growing and seem likely to continue to do so;
2. the company's profit margin must have been maintained so that this growth of sales will come through to profits. We should also check simultaneously on the return obtained from its expanding plant to obtain an indication of the probable course of future profit margins;
3. the response of the public must be in agreement with the above trends of sales and profits; in other words, if the price of the company's stock is not reflecting these trends we should re-analyze our conclusions carefully to see if something is being discounted in the future which has not yet been disclosed by statistics.

A useful method to determine the public's degree of acceptance of past facts is through relative charts, comparing the price of a security to an accepted Average periodically over an extended period of time. Growth in sales and earnings will be reflected here unless the market is discounting either greater advantages or troubles ahead, which it often has done many more years in advance than one would think possible. The relative price trend of a stock is an important tool available to the professional for in price is reflected almost every factor affecting a company's future—the ability of management, the safety of the capital structure, competitive conditions, the likelihood of corrosive legislation, the possibility of new products, the threat of too greedy labor, etc., etc. Changes in the market's appraisal of any of these factors are quickly reflected in it.

* * * * *

[A long] warning of troubles ahead was afforded in the railroad industry. Their growth in relative stock prices stopped in 1904, although it was not until 1925 that traffic began to decline nor until 1929 before total freight volume began to pay toll to competitors. Public rejection in the stock market had begun more than twenty years in advance of the sales or earnings figures. What put the spot-light in 1904 on future troubles was the creation of the Interstate Commerce Commission and the undertaking of the Panama Canal, which would eat into the rails' very profitable transcontinental traffic.

Since our clients' payoff comes in common stock prices and since these can reflect so many years ahead the environment which will affect earnings and dividends, the relative behavior of individual stock prices must be scrutinized. Where it does not confirm the behavior of sales and earnings be as suspicious as a doctor who finds a patient reacting abnormally to a standard test.

THE TREND OF DEMAND DETERMINES SALES

Having computed the relative price trends of more than a thousand companies here and abroad covering long periods back to 1919, one can't help but be impressed by the consistency of long term trends, which is particularly true on the down side. Looking at past performances where you have the benefit of the help of someone who knows a particular company intimately, the explanation for any behavior becomes clearly apparent. We have tried to correlate relative price movements with those of relative earnings but could not do so on any practical basis because individual stock prices are discounting *future* earnings and the degree of anticipation can vary from a few months to twenty or more years, depending how far it is possible to see ahead for any particular company's prospects.

One thing we found out was that there is a very definite correlation over the longer term between the demand for the product or service which a company sells and the performance of its stock—of course also with varying leads. We also know that this correlation will be disrupted if there are factors present which prevent the growth in sales from being reflected in profits. These neutralizers will be discussed later as they constitute our second test and explain why sales' growth doesn't always mean profits' growth. It can be stated categorically, however, that a company cannot long remain prosperous without growing volume; in fact, growth in sales is probably a more important determinant of success than any other factor. One often hears that it is the ability of management but company histories eloquently point out that in a young industry enjoying dynamic growth, all participants fare well and the influence of management only becomes obvious when the competitive road becomes rougher. A third-rate management in a dynamic industry will show a better performance than a top management in a declining one; a poor swimmer moving with current makes more progress than an expert swimming against the tide.

A successful investor must therefore limit his buying to areas of consistently growing demand, which demand seems likely to continue to grow in the future. . . .

* * * * *

[T]he performance of any portfolio I have ever heard boasted about by the parties responsible, whether it has been operated here, Switzerland, Great Britain or Holland, when dissected as to how the results were obtained inevitably pointed to the continuous long holding of one, two or three situations whose price had multiplied many-fold. What had been done in the balance of the portfolio did not matter much so long as these jewels continued to be held. A Xerox, an I.B.M., a Hoffmann-La Roche has covered up countless errors the same manager might have made.

It is much more important to hold on to winners than to weed out the losers. Supposing we start with an equal amount invested in two companies—let the mistake lose 90% of its relative price and the jewel multiply its own an equivalent ten-fold. After that price change, you will find the latter makes up 99% of the portfolio's value while the loser's influence has shrunk to 1%—provided only that the owner does not reap his profits from time to time from the rising stock and keep buying more of the poorer to average his costs, as is ever a very common human tendency but disastrous to good long-term results. It is important to learn early in life that money lost does not have to be regained in the same vehicle which lost it; it is usually easier to recoup in a fresh choice or even by increasing your holdings in the same stocks which have been yielding the most profits to you. . . .

I wrote . . . that losers had increasingly less influence on a portfolio than winners if both were maintained provided one did not stray into the fateful error of cutting back the size of the successful holding or buying more of the declining one to lower his costs. This does not mean, however, that good results are not greatly enhanced by frequent weeding, which is just as necessary as to the success of a garden. Losses can be huge and come much more suddenly in these days when portfolio managers are inclined to dump. A stock which drops 80% in value, and many have in the past year, nullifies a rise of 80% in another of equal weight. This is one time definitely not to be stubborn. We are all going to make many mistakes, do not compound the original one by adding to it. . . .

WHAT TO AVOID

When an investor has identified the areas where sales are apt to grow most rapidly, his job is only a part done for many factors can prevent this growth from reaching profits or can severely limit the number of prosperous years ahead. To name a few of the factors which can nullify this growth:

1. I know that when one makes a positive statement in the field of investment, he should realize that he might have to eat his words the next day for there are always exceptions and no sure rules to follow. One axiom, however, which still seems to withstand the variances of time is that it pays to avoid *"areas of overcapacity."* Where they exist, the stockholder almost always has fared badly. Such areas exist today almost everywhere—for practically all extracted commodities, for aluminum, plywood, steel, gypsum, fiberglass, paper, most chemicals, etc., etc. This statement does not, of course, apply to an industry like the public utility, where the excess capacity does not press on the price structure.

One constantly hears the argument that the growth in demand for this or that commodity is such that the excess will be eliminated automatically in a few years so it is advantageous to buy now when prices are depressed. As a matter of fact, I do not know of one instance where overcapacity has been removed for long by a natural growth of demand. Before it can come about some participant in the industry or some newcomer attracted to a lush field decides to build a new plant. Where oversupply has been eliminated it has come as the result of extraneous forces, of which three of the best known examples were in the oil, cement and paper industries. . . .

2. It is not only the participants in an industry which can ruin its prospects by overexpansion but often the *ingress of newcomers* in what looks like lush fields of growth. . . .

3. Beware of a *slowing growth in demand* for it will shrink profit margins. . . .

4. *Competition from foreign sources* is a new worry to plague many businesses because hourly wage costs abroad are but a third of those here. Despite tariffs, very sizeable proportions of our glass, oil, barbed wire, reinforcing steel bars, cement, bicycles, radios, cameras, etc., come from abroad. The list is sure to grow as overcapacity is built abroad or if the internal demand there slackens. The effect of profitability here can be the same as if we overbuilt ourselves.

5. The growth of many companies comes purely from geographical expansion and a point of *saturation* will some day be reached. . . .

6. *Government regulation* has done few industries good except momentarily. . . .

7. *Excessive debt* can kill the prospects for profit of an industry for stockholders except, of course, in utilities, whose earnings are limited to an overall percentage on their entire valuation. . . .

8. Due to the power of labor today, it is logical to avoid industries with high and *rigid labor costs*, such as railroads and maritime shipping. . . .

9. It also has usually been wise to avoid *industries where capital requirements are small* and needed skills are minor, for prosperity there grows participants like mushrooms. . . .

10. The last of the important things which can nullify the benefits of growing sales is *poor management*, resulting in poor control of costs. . . .

SUMMARY

. . . I realize that these three tests to apply before buying are not all practical for the amateur. He, however, can obtain some feel of (a) the probable demand for the product or service sold; for example, every time he recommends a new product to a friend like Metrecal or, as I was lucky enough to do years ago, Scotch Tape, he could ask questions about the company making it. But unless he has access to the studies of a fairly large research group the amateur could know nothing of (b) the trend of profit margins, and (c) the stock's relative price performance. There is one way, however, by which an amateur can come up with quite a good list. Let him go to any well informed professional and ask for the ten stocks he should buy if every stock in the market had the same earnings, paid the same dividend and sold at the same price. The result would be a list of stocks which very probably would fit closely into the investment philosophy outlined in this paper. Having bought these, he could probably improve the performance of his portfolio if each year he disposed of the poorest actor and reinvested the proceeds in the best; however, never reducing the list below five names. If he does this, however, I warn him never to disclose to his professional friend the use he is going to make of such a list for he would be sure to hear a hundred unanswerable arguments why this approach won't work, in addition to the unspoken one that it won't produce much brokerage commissions.

* * * * *

[One final caution: do] not expect changes in trend as the odds are that what has been happening is more likely to continue than reverse. Naturally, trends will change some day but don't let too high a price make you bet on it until the change is apparent otherwise. You alone don't set prices; they are the judgment of the world. Remember in every case there is someone with fuller knowledge to set a particular company's value than you.

* * * * *

Finally, if you want to follow the philosophy which has yielded many examples of success over the years, remember that in picking the securities for any sale, choose the poorest. If the selling proves ill-timed, you may not lose much, for they will likely be left behind in the market rise ahead. If instead you sell your best, even if it does go down, the chances are that you will never repurchase it even if you are lucky enough to be twice right in your timing, and so you will downgrade your portfolio. If you are going to buy, your safest choice is the best company serving the desired area even though it means paying the highest price and obtaining the lowest present yield.

FINANCIAL GOALS: MANAGEMENT VS. STOCKHOLDERS

Gordon Donaldson

Here, with clarity, candor, and concrete illustrations of the problem, Gordon Donaldson describes the "conflict of objectives" inherent in "managing the business" versus "maximizing shareholder interests." Writing 25 years ago, he clearly delineated the essence of today's debate concerning "corporate raiders" and the legitimacy of their activities.

Divergence of attitude toward corporate profits may lead to differences in major policy decisions.

Despite the widening gulf which separates ownership and management in our larger business corporations today, the assumption of a common viewpoint in business decisions shows remarkable vitality. To say that management and the shareholder have much in common is only to state the obvious. So do management and the labor force, consumers, or any other group having a vested interest in the corporate entity. But to extend this by saying that management, in pursuing corporate objectives as it sees them, necessarily serves the best interests of the stockholders, in either the short or long run, misstates the facts in certain important respects. It also leads to confusion in the misinterpretation of financial policy.

In this article I intend to consider some of the issues over which a conflict of interest may arise. I do so in the belief that a free and frank discussion of differences—differences commonly glossed over in statements to stockholders by those managements which equate stockholder relations with public relations—will lead to a better understanding of what each group can realistically expect to achieve from its participation in the corporation.

Questions & Issues

The evolution of a group of professional managers as the primary decision-making body in the modern large-scale corporation is now a well-known and well-documented characteristic of American business life. A number of noted observers of the business scene have attempted to interpret the implications of this for the future of our capitalistic society.[1] They note the separation of the ownership group from the center of influence in the corporation and the emergence of the investor as an external force acting on the professional manager. They raise questions as to (a) the probable effects of all this on the corporation as a legal institution, (b) the strength and vitality of competitive restraints, and (c) the continued efficacy of the profit motive as a stimulus to maximum efficiency. The debate continues as to whether this trend is a "good" or a "bad" thing, and whether its effects should be resisted, welcomed, or merely submitted to.

At the same time we have seen a parallel development in the professionalization of the shareholder group—the growing concentration of the investment decision in the hands of career security analysts representing individuals and financial institutions. This, too, has been well documented by observers of business trends. Though investment in corporate securities is still far from a science, investors are increasingly objective in the way they select, diversify, and manage a portfolio of common stock issues. And the financial officers of widely held companies are well aware of the steady increase in the probing for factual information by roving professional analysts. Large holdings of stock are still owned by individuals, but they too are strongly influenced by professional counsel in the decision as to what they hold and for how long.

Previous discussion of the legal, economic, and social implications of the separation of ownership and decision making in large corporations has recognized a possible divergence of attitude toward corporate profits on the part of the professional manager and the professional shareholder leading to differences of opinion on major policy decisions. By and large, however, the consideration of corporate financial goals, including profit maximization, has remained on a highly generalized level. As a result, there is a distinct need to deal with the problem at the more specific level of financial policy.

For this purpose I have selected a number of concrete issues which are significant areas of potential conflict in objectives. I intend to show that the pursuit of divergent objectives leads to different management "decision rules" of the kind which become embedded in the day-to-day decision-making process and which managers may employ without fully realizing their ultimate effects. The question raised by this discussion is not whether management today is deliberately frustrating the objectives of the shareholder. It is, rather, whether or not professional management, in the pursuit of the best interests of the corporation *as it sees them*, will be led to the same standards for financial decisions as would be proposed by an informed professional investor seeking the best interests of corporate ownership.

PART 1. CONTRASTING VIEWS

Before dealing with these issues, however, it will be necessary to examine what is implied by the distinction between a managerial and a stockholder point of view on financial decisions. As we shall see, the managerial viewpoint can be identified with the emerging concepts of professionalism and "trusteeship" in business policy formation. The stockholder, on the other hand, can be identified with the objectives which lie behind a diversified portfolio of corporate securities. Let us consider the stockholder first.

The Professional Owner

It should be said right at the outset that if there is a conflict in financial policy between management and the stockholder, most of the writers on the subject are on the side of the stockholder.

In fact, the preponderance of financial literature takes rather literally the legal concept of corporate ownership and the property rights of the holders of ownership certificates. The financial objectives of the corporation, in the judgment of these writers, are, or at least should be, focused on maximizing (or "optimizing") the financial interests of stock owners. The absolute priority of the stockholder interest is rarely challenged when financial policies of the individual firm are under discussion, particularly when the subject concerns "the way the world ought to be."

Thus, the debate moves quickly past the question of possible alternative viewpoints and goes on to the intellectually challenging questions of defining the stockholder interest in objective terms and measuring achievement toward the most beneficial financial position. Here the stockholder is viewed as an informed and rational investor in the organized securities market pursuing with great singleness of purpose his personal financial gain via dividends and/or capital gains. He is assumed to have access to a variety of investment opportunities and to take advantage of this through a diversified portfolio of common stocks (as well as, perhaps, a variety of fixed-income securities).

When it comes to the question of the most beneficial investment policy and the financial policies of individual companies which best serve the growth in investment value of their common stocks, there is, as one might expect, a great deal of disagreement. A variety of theories are being developed which are designed to link corporate financial policy with the market value of common stock.[2] In particular, there is the problem of the relationship between earnings, dividends, and market price. However, despite the sharp differences of evidence, opinion on evidence, and the underlying complexity of market value, there is a common thread running through all these viewpoints: corporate financial policy is seen through the unemotional eyes of a mobile, diversified investor seeking to maximize his personal financial objectives via ownership of common stock.

The Professional Manager

Without doubt, many professional managers would accept the foregoing description of the typical stockholder and would resent the inference that they may not be serving his best interests. Few corporate officers have been disposed (or have dared) to make an open break with the historic posture of ultimate allegiance to the owner group—a posture reflected in corporate law and organization as well as in the conventions of financial reporting. They are apt to argue that their primary duty and intent is to "make money for the stockholder" and that in the long run what is best for the corporation and for management is also best for the stockholder. This is all in the time-honored tradition of a society in which private ownership of the means of production has been regarded as a powerful motivating force toward maximum economic growth.

Whatever the real feelings of professional managers are in this regard (I know from private and public expressions that they are decidedly mixed), the fact is that the objectives of the stockholder as just described may conflict with the objectives of professional management, both in regard to the latter's own personal or selfish interests and in the broader context of management's responsibility to the corporate identity. It all depends, of course, on how one describes the management viewpoint. A considerable range of choice exists; so let us look at the possibilities.

Identification With Owners
Under one view, management voluntarily adopts, or by one device or another has imposed on it, an identification with the objectives of the professional stockholder. Supposedly the device of stock options works in this direction. If this is so, then it may be expected that the pressures of other groups involved in corporate activity—union members, white-collar workers, customers, the government, the general public, competitors—would be resisted and their interests subordinated to the stockholder interest.

Of course, it is recognized that full maximization of the stockholder interest is a theoretical extreme which is not attained in practice, and could not be even if the goals and related standards of performance were crystal clear (which they are not). However, it can still be an operational concept if the supremacy of the stockholder interest is accepted by management, in which case the idea of maximization is in reality a statement of tendency only or of the direction of thrust of financial policy.

Regardless of any misgivings about the desirability or practicality of this view, two things may be said in its favor: (1) it is consistent with the legal traditions of the corporation and the institution of private ownership; and (2) it is relatively simple, objective, and understandable as an operating guide.

Concept of Trusteeship

There has been growing support among professional managers for a second, quite different concept often referred to as "management trusteeship." In part, this concept reflects an emphasis on the professional view of management and on the responsibilities of management (with strong support from professional schools of business). More significantly, it has been interpreted as a recognition of the plurality of responsibility in the modern corporation and of the need for an arbitration role for management in balancing conflicting interests. Under the concept of trusteeship in its extreme form the stockholder interest is merely one of several coequal vested interests to be considered when corporate policy is formulated.

This approach is, it seems to me, a natural and predictable evolutionary step in the development of the larger scale corporate enterprise in today's society, though undoubtedly it has not yet reached the extreme form just suggested. If there is such a trend, then it is desirable to try to anticipate the effect on decisions in the area of financial policy. If the supremecy of the stockholder interest is abandoned, what takes its place?

Using Relative Priorities. One possibility, representing a moderate revision of the historic supremacy of ownership, may be described in terms of the legal concept of relative priority which was developed in regard to corporate reorganization. In reorganizing a bankrupt company it is often determined by the courts that although certain creditors have the legal right to all the residual asset values, the plight of other vested interests must be considered—including that of the former common stockholders. Thus, the creditors come to have a dominant, but by no means exclusive, claim on the assets and earnings of the newly formed company, and this in spite of prior ironclad legal contracts to the contrary.

This concept of relative priority may be employed by professional management in relating the conflicting interests of stockholders, employees, customers, the general public, government, and so on to each other.

Having abandoned the idea of *absolute* priority of the stockholder interest which existed only when management and ownership were one (and perhaps not even then), management continues to attach more weight to its responsibility to owners than to any other vested interest. This means, of course, that where a conflict of interest develops, management must determine how much of the stockholder interest will be sacrificed in order to behave "more responsibly" toward other interests such as the labor union or the customer. It does not mean, however, that either the direction of financial policy or the criterion by which achievement is measured has changed—only that the rate of the progress in improving the rewards to the stockholder has been retarded in response to a greater awareness of other interests.

More Extreme Approach. The logical extreme of the trusteeship concept is that, having no sense of primary allegiance to any single group, professional management will attempt to pursue those financial goals which are common to all interests, including its own. The one thing which all groups have in common is, of course, the corporation itself as a legal, economic, and human entity. It may be assumed, then, that the overriding consideration will be the economic and financial strength, continuity, and growth of this particular enterprise. The interests of other groups, including the stockholders, if in conflict with this, will be given secondary consideration. In general, it may be assumed that when they are in conflict, the interests of the special group will be catered to only to the extent necessary to get its cooperation.

In this respect there would seem to be no essential difference between stockholders and, say, the labor force. Management needs the continued support of both in order to pursue the corporate objectives. At the time of contract negotiations management will ultimately concede to the union whatsoever increases in wages and benefits are considered essential to gain the cooperation of the workers for a further contract period. Normally, however, the increase will be postponed as long as possible and, when it comes, it will be as small as possible so that the drain on the corporate cash position will be minimized.

Viewed in the cold light of economic considerations, the stockholder group presents the same kind of problem for management. The stockholder provides something which management needs: (1) personal freedom of action and continuity in office and, possibly

(2) new capital. For the large and mature corporation the second of these may not be a vital consideration; many such companies do not give serious consideration to new stock issues as a source of cash for growth, finding that internally generated funds, net of the customary dividends, very adequately supply the needed growth in the equity base.

Consequently, the primary thing which management requires of the stockholder is to be left alone to do its job, free of harassments from individual champions of the stockholder interest and free of the threat of raids which would unseat existing management. For this, management must pay a price which in real terms boils down to the cash outflows for dividend payments. Since this also erodes the cash reserves needed in furthering corporate interests, it is to be expected that management will keep the outflow as low as possible, minimizing increases and postponing them as long as possible. It gets a substantial assist in this regard from income tax law, which tends to transfer the stockholders' attention to capital gains and shifts the source of their gain from the company itself to the capital market.

The assertion that there is *no* essential difference between the influence or claims of the stockholder and the labor groups is admittedly extreme. It would be pure speculation to suggest where the majority of professional managers stand today between this concept of the stockholder and the other extreme—that of complete allegiance to the stockholder interest. There is little doubt, however, that the trusteeship concept represents a trend away from complete allegiance and is being accepted by increasing numbers of executives in those corporations where the voice of the individual stockholder is no longer heard in the councils of management.

It is therefore useful and important to explore the contrast between the two extremes of viewpoint.

PART II. AREAS OF DECISION

In order to deal with the issue as specifically as possible, I have chosen four aspects of financial decision making and will deal with each of them in turn:

1. By what yardsticks will financial performances be measured?

EXHIBIT 1

Different Yardsticks Used by Management and Stockholders

Types of Decisions	Management's Yardsticks	Stockholder's Yardsticks	Sample Areas of Possible Conflict
Measuring Financial Performance	Anticipated changes in specific cash flows in the foreseeable future–amount, certainty, and timing	Anticipated changes in property values as measured by trends in earnings per share (E.P.S.) and dividends	Ranking of investment alternatives; depreciation policy; stock options; acquisition of subsidiaries
Investment Proposals	Internal rate of return which existing management is capable of achieving –as indicated by past performance	External as well as internal investment opportunity rates, including competing business organizations of comparable risk	The cutoff rate on acceptable investment opportunities and amounts committed to perpetuate existing investments
Sources of Funds	Preference for (A) retained earnings, (B) long-term debt, and (C) new common stock – in that order	Preference likely to be for (A) debt, (B) retained earnings, and (C) new common stock – in that order	The extent of use of these sources in financing growth
Assumption of Voluntary Risk	Risk standard in terms of preserving the individual corporate entity and management's goals	Risk standard in terms of a portfolio of investments over many companies	Diversification of products and markets; debt/equity proportions

2. How shall be the limits of the capital investment in the business be determined?

3. On what basis will priorities be assigned among potential sources of funds?

4. What shall be the company's position with respect to avoidable financial risks such as that imposed by long-term debt contracts?

The discussion that follows has been summarized in Exhibit 1.

Measuring Performance

The question of the units of measurement to be used in analyzing financial problems and evaluating financial results is fundamental to the whole policy area. It obviously makes a great deal of difference whether the units of importance to top management are sales dollars, cash receipts, earnings per share, growth in market price of the common stock, percentage return on investment, or any one of the several alternatives. More importantly, behind each criterion there is a point of view—an identification with some goal toward which corporate effort is being directed. The criteria represent significant differences in corporate goals and viewpoints.

Cash-Flow Yardstick
It may be helpful to begin by reviewing certain obvious facts:

1. The professional manager is employed by only one corporate entity at a time. It is to his corporation that he owes his entire allegiance and on whose behalf he expends his entire energies. Although he may change allegiance during his lifetime, he normally behaves as if at any given point in time his entire career is bound up in the fortunes of a single business enterprise.

2. This identification with a limited corporate identity is an identification with two basic elements: (a) a specific group of people and (b) a specific body of physical and financial resources. We are primarily concerned here with management's attitudes and behavior toward the latter.

3. The basic role of management—the power to make decisions on company policy and to act on these decisions—rests heavily on its control over the physical and financial resources. To be

more precise, its capacity to influence or change the course
of corporate affairs depends in large measure on its financial
flexibility; and this in turn is determined by the availability of
resources which either are in liquid form (cash or near-cash) or
are readily convertible into liquid form. The power to enlarge
research, step up an advertising campaign, modernize a plant,
acquire a new subsidiary, or merely add more inventory or extend
more credit, all comes back to the current cash position of the
company.

Thus, the primary focus of interest of professional management
so far as financial affairs are concerned is necessarily with *cash flow*,
because it provides management with the power to do things differently.
It follows that the primary concern in a financial decision will be with
the question: How will cash flows be changed? This will include
a concern for the certainty and timing of cash flows as well as for
the amount. Furthermore, the interest in expected change will tend
to focus on that which will occur within the planning horizon of manage ment, which means, for industrial corporations, one to five years
hence.

Now, how does this approach differ from the stockholder view?

Earnings-per-Share Measure

The professional common stockholder stands to benefit from his association with a corporation in one or, more probably, a combination of
two ways: (a) dividend income, (b) capital gains through the sale of his
shares on the stock market. In general, we may assume that whatever
the preferred mix for any given stockholder, he will desire the maximum total gain possible over some future time period, short or long (for
some predetermined risk level). While factors making for improvement
in market price are many and their effects are rather obscure, it will be
generally agreed that the most central quantitative ratio by which anticipated change is measured is earnings per share (E.P.S.). The same is
true for dividends since most dividend-paying companies tend to adjust
payments according to some standard relationship to earnings.

We can assume, therefore, that in pondering investment decisions
the stockholder will focus on the anticipated effect on E.P.S. This view
is actively encouraged by the way in which both the stock market and
the corporation itself report information to the stockholder. The term

"earnings" means, of course, growth in the value of assets as defined by accepted accrual accounting principals and practices. Inevitably this means some sort of *normalized* return on investment after an accounting allocation of the original investment over its anticipated life as an earning asset. The deliberate objective of the conventional reporting of income is to smooth out short-term irregularities caused by the discontinuity and arbitrary timing of investment decisions and to present a long-run average of earning performance.

Thus, there exists a contrast between (a) the interests of management, which quite naturally relate to the specifics of near-term movements in cash inflow and outflow, with all their inevitable irregularities from one period to another; and (b) the interests of the stockholder, which relate to earnings per share as a predictor of long-term growth in property values.

Where Differences Show Up

Is this distinction a "red herring"? Are cash flow and earnings essentially the same, or do they at least move together, so that the ranking of financial alternatives would be the same in either case? I do not think so. To see how differently a financial problem can appear when viewed from a cash rather than from an earnings viewpoint, let us look at some examples:

Ranking investment alternatives in order of desirability—There are several methods for analyzing investment alternatives. Some of these methods have become rather complex. The leaders in the area of capital budgeting now look with some disdain at the simple decision rules of an earlier period, which are considered too crude to be useful. One of these is the payback period, viz., the length of time it is expected the new investment will take to return the cash originally invested in it.

It is a fact, however, that the simple payback period is still the most widely used criterion in business investment decisions. The reason, I believe, is not that management is unaware of more sophisticated approaches but, rather, that the payback approach tells management what it wants to know: How long will it have to wait before the cash to be committed to the investment will be available for reinvestment? Management can then make a judgment as to the acceptability of the risks over that period and the competing demands on cash.

The pressure for abandoning the payback approach came largely from those who had more of an earnings (shareholder) point of view, arguing that the investment decision be based on the expected earnings over its entire useful life. Thus, the emphasis shifted to the longer term earnings performance as a rate of return on the dollars invested. But— and this is important—the so-called unadjusted rate of return has now been replaced by a more complicated formula which also analyzes the investment over its financially productive life but does so in terms of the time-adjusted cash flows. The expected cash inflows are related to the initial cash outflows in terms of a compound interest rate which diminishes the present value of future inflows as the waiting period increases.

The effect of this latest approach is to give priority to those investment proposals which yield high cash inflows *early in the productive life*. Once again the method tends to be in accord with a managerial point of view. Whether it is also in accord with a shareholder point of view depends entirely on whether the assumptions of the method fit the company circumstances and, in particular, on what is done with the cash when it flows in. Under some circumstances an alternative investment which generates cash at a more regular rate over its productive life may ultimately produce higher earnings per share, since cash inflows do not always return immediately into income-generating employment and may be used to reduce the uncertainties for management rather than to increase earnings for the shareholder.

My main point here is simply that management can become preoccupied with near-term cash flows to the detriment of earnings performance, and that modern capital-budgeting techniques tend to encourage this preoccupation.

Accelerated depreciation—Another example of conflicting viewpoints is the current emphasis on accelerated methods of depreciation. This is in part a result of the almost universal dedication of businessmen to minimizing the government's take of corporate earnings (a dedication at times bordering on the irrational). It is also a result of management's desire to improve the company's near-term cash position by reducing cash outflows for any purpose as much as possible.

The fact is, however, that in doing so—i.e., in writing off as much as possible of those depreciable assets as soon as possible— earnings performance is correspondingly depressed since the tax saving is at most one-half of the increased depreciation charge. Thus, near-term earnings per share suffer, and the stockholder, also interested in the near term, may be adversely affected. The obvious answer is, of course, to use accelerated depreciation for tax purposes and straight-line depreciation when reporting income to shareholders and the stock market. This answer, however, is not one which is generally approved by the accounting profession.[3] There are problems which center around the inevitable distortion of tax liability over time and the inconsistency between reported earnings and the tax liability.

The conclusion to be reached here is *not* that a cash-flow frame-work necessarily produces the wrong decisions from the shareholder point of view, nor that it cannot be modified to reflect more accurately the actual circumstances under which investments are made. It is, rather, that in selecting the relevant considerations which will form a part of the methodology of investment decisions, a point of view will inevitably be built in. When the methodology of financial decisions becomes estab-lished and a matter of routine, the implicit point of view is rarely re-examined.

The stock option—To the extent that stock options represent a direct substitution for incentive cash payments to executives, they are "cost free" to the corporate entity and an expense only to the shareholder (in dilution of E.P.S. and market price growth). The cash position of the cor-poration goes untouched, but not the property values of the stockholder. It is little wonder that professional management enthusiastically supports the stock option.

While on this point I cannot resist adding some fuel to the fire of debate on the use of stock options.[4] One of the key arguments for the stock option is that it serves to identify the professional manager with the interests of the stockholder and thus helps to restore the his-toric identity of ownership and management. This is a misconception. As previously emphasized, the stockholder is a diversified investor with a multicompany viewpoint and a loyalty which persists only as long as superior investment performance persists. This can never be manage-ment's viewpoint. A stock option merely serves to give added strength to the ties which already bind an executive firmly to a single corporate entity and its unique future. The one thing that can be said for a stock option in this regard is that it reminds management that E.P.S. and market price are important considerations. It is unlikely, however, to overcome a primary allegiance to near-term cash flows.

Acquisition of subsidiaries—An exchange of common stock in an acquisition is also a "cost free" transaction in a cash sense as far as the corporate entity is concerned. Again, however, it obviously is not "cost free" from an E.P.S. and market-price viewpoint. I would like to stress the fact that I am not arguing here or elsewhere that professional management is necessarily insensitive to the effects of its actions on earnings and E.P.S. What I am arguing is that these "book earnings" are not the natural, primary concern of the corporate entity to which professional management is primarily responsible. The stockholder's interest in its property values, reflected in E.P.S. and market price, is likely to be considered primarily because he is able to exert pressure on management to serve his goals in some degree.

Limits of Investment

Having considered the problem of measuring financial performance and ranking investment alternatives, we now turn to another major problem— the so-called cutoff criterion or minimum acceptable rate of return which will separate acceptable from unacceptable investment proposals.

In this regard it is highly desirable to distinguish between the now-or-never kind of choice and the now-or-later kind. The average business enterprise does not have an inexhaustible supply of available investment opportunities, nor do they come in an even flow over time. The aim is to achieve the highest possible return on the investment over time, given a past record of performance, a finite set of present opportunities, and an unknown stream of opportunities in the future.

In general, the role of the minimum return standards found in corporate capital budgeting manuals is to prevent an excessive commitment of funds to low-yield opportunities currently available, thus enabling the company to take advantage of future opportunities offering the higher return which experience says may reasonably be expected. In setting a cutoff standard that will keep capital fully employed at the highest possible rate of return, professional management will normally confine its attention to those investments over which it can exercise some sort of direct managerial control.

These internal investment opportunities are not necessarily confined to the preservation and expansion of established products and markets;

but some managements may choose to do this, and it is also likely that the familiar will be given priority over the unfamiliar. There is the further significant limitation that the expected rate of return is that which *existing management is capable of achieving*. In practice there may be something of a target-rate approach to new opportunities—seeking to induce various levels of management to reach for higher returns—but this must somehow be related to reality or it will fail as a genuine incentive.

Past Performance as Guide

If these are the facts, they point rather naturally to the historical record of investment performance within the company as the primary guide to the accept-reject standard. This is likely to take the form of a percentage relationship between net earnings and dollars invested to date, averaged over the last, say, five years. This measure of what the company has been able to earn becomes the most important piece of evidence as to what may be expected in the future.

To be most useful the standard is likely to be broken down by major investment categories which reflect the basic mix of opportunities open to the company and the related differences in risk. It should also reflect an awareness of trends and a realistic appraisal of growth possibilities. The primary emphasis, however, must be *proven* earning capacity with *this* company and under *this* management.

It will be apparent that this standard may not be too helpful in appraising opportunities which lie outside the traditional mix of investments; a totally new product presents a different problem from any analyzed before. However, when management moves into unfamiliar areas, there is a natural tendency to relate the desired minimum return on investment to that which is expected on familiar investments, doing this in terms of assumed differences in risk.

Invariably the unfamiliar proposal involving a new product or new market must hurdle a substantially higher rate than must [sic] proposals which maintain existing production and marketing capacity.

Accordingly, the basic reference point is, once again, established performance. When experience in the new product area has been built up, actual achievable performance in that area will be substituted for what is, at the outset, largely a subjective measure of adequate compensation for the assumed risk involved.

Full Utilization

Of course there is a much simpler approach to the cutoff point on new investment proposals which may appeal to the professional manager, and that is to approve the list of proposals ranked in order of desirability down to the point where available funds are exhausted. However, this approach does not provide for the uneven and unpredictable timing of the better opportunities and would not provide for any accumulation of investable funds from year to year as would the historical standard. Hence the two approaches are likely to be used in combination, with the longer run goal being to keep available resources fully employed. If the historical standard is too high and there is an unusual buildup of liquid resources over time, it may be assumed that management will revise its standard or put new emphasis behind the search for new opportunities. If it is too low and unusual opportunities are missed because of lack of funds, it will be revised upward.

This brings out the point that the key characteristic of a cutoff standard based on the demonstrated record of management's achievement is that it may be expected to be adjusted *downward* as well as upward in such manner as to keep available resources fully employed. This follows automatically in part from a moving historical average of earnings if these earnings are trending downward. It follows also from a natural inclination to avoid excessive accumulations of idle or low-return capital. A question worth pondering is: At what point is the role of management in contributing to such a downward trend called to account?

Capital-Cost Criterion

The stockholder brings another significant dimension to the investment decision. In committing funds to investment, management is primarily concerned with the question: Now or later? To this question the stockholder adds: Here or elsewhere? We must remember that the professional stockholder has an investment in many businesses simultaneously and is constantly engaged in shifting resources among these and other opportunities. There is a complete absence of the sort of identification with a single company which management feels. The concept of "loyalty," if it can be used in this context, is loyalty to superior financial performance (past and/or expected) and to nothing else. Consequently, the shareholder is very willing to consider the question that management is emotionally incapable of asking: Is there another company and another management which can make better use of the available funds?

This question may be critical in setting the accept-reject standard for new investment proposals. The literature on the subject of capital budgeting has been strongly influenced by the stockholder viewpoint in this regard. In this literature the recommended standard is almost universally expressed in terms of what is called the cost of capital. The general line of reasoning is that a company will be willing to add to its investments as long as the return is in excess of the cost of the funds required to finance the project (with due allowance for risk differentials). It will reject proposals which fall short of the company's cost of capital. This line of reasoning is one with which management may agree in principle.

But what should be considered as "cost"? Here is where the professional manager and shareholder may again part company:

- Management will tend to consider two kinds of costs: (a) out-of-pocket costs in the accounting sense; (b) out-of-pocket costs in the cash sense. If the focus is on E.P.S., the relevant costs are bond interest and preferred dividends. If the focus is on cash, common dividends and sinking funds will come into the picture.
- In contrast, the shareholder will want the cost to reflect what could be done with the money outside the company—even in such alternatives as the company's most successful competitor. Thus, retained earnings as well as new common stock offerings would bear an inputed cost based on an estimate of what that money would do for the shareholder in other businesses having comparable risk characteristics. This is sometimes called an "opportunity cost." The direct implication of such a standard is that if internal investment opportunities cannot match the externally derived standard, over time liquid reserves will accumulate and will eventually be withdrawn from the corporation by the stockholder to be invested elsewhere (perhaps strengthening successful competitors). And this, after all, is what society has assumed would happen under a competitive free enterprise system.

Fortunately for some managements the differential between the capital gains and the personal income tax gives the company that generates equity capital through earnings a substantial advantage over external alternatives as far as the use of that capital is concerned. However, this will vary with the shareholder tax bracket, and in any case the advantage cannot be interpreted as meaning that the investment of such earnings is the exclusive prerogative of salaried management—or so, at least, the stockholder may be expected to argue.

Sources of Funds

In considering the preference for various sources of long-term funds for the corporation, we will focus attention on the three which are dominant in most businesses: retained earnings (adjusted for depreciation and other noncash charges), long-term debt, and issues of new common stock.[5]

Retained Earnings

From the point of view of the corporate treasurer there are a number of considerations which will have a bearing on the matter. Among these considerations are dependability, ease of access to the source, flexibility in use, restraints on management, risk, and cost. On virtually all counts internally generated funds are far more superior to other sources. Indeed, it is an almost automatic response for management to assume that all internally generated funds over and above the customary dividend will be used for investment requirements before any other source is given serious consideration.

What is the cost of using retained earnings? As previously mentioned, the word "cost," so far as management is concerned, means (a) an expense which reduces earnings on the income statement and/or (b) a cash expenditure. The reinvestment of after-tax earnings is completely free of cost in either of these contexts. Thus, any investment which is financed by retained earnings and yields anything above a zero return will make a net contribution to earnings. For instance, an investment of $100,000 which earns only 2% is contributing $2,000 to corporate net earnings and making a positive addition to E.P.S.

In view of the fact that most companies are consistently retaining in the neighborhood of 50% of their earnings and doing most of their financing by this no-cost source, it is a small wonder that E.P.S. is showing growth over the years.

There is, however, a limited sense in which retained earnings do represent a cost for management:

If a company follows a policy of a target-payout ratio for growth in earnings, then rising earnings resulting from the investments will ultimately mean rising dividends and a cost in a cash outflow sense. However, since the payout is flexible and a fraction of the earnings generated, there is little chance of having the "cost" exceed the return from the investment.

Another sense in which retained earnings may have a cost is when the amount retained cuts into an established dividend payment. Here management will probably be sensitive since a cut in the cash dividend may create problems with the stockholders, particularly if rapid growth or serious deterioration (the usual excuses for a cut in the dividend) are not apparent to the stockholder. If the customary dividend policy is undisturbed, however, management is not likely to be challenged on the use of the remaining earnings for whatever purposes it sees fit to pursue.

New Equity & Debt

In contrast, new equity capital raised via a new stock issue is a much more expensive proposition for these reasons:

1. The additional dividends on the new shares (paid out of after-tax dollars) add directly to the outflow of cash.
2. The increase in the number of shares results in a permanent drag on growth in E.P.S. To the extent that management feels a need to respond to the stockholder interest or is concerned about its own stock options, this will be a significant consideration.

It is apparent that management will prefer to fill its need for new equity money internally and will only go outside through new stock issues when it has misjudged the magnitude of these needs or is growing so fast that internal sources are inadequate.

For most businesses long-term debt in modest proportions is to be preferred over new stock issues (but *not* over retained earnings). The only cost in an accounting sense is the interest charge, and on an after-tax basis this is very small compared with common dividends on a comparable sum of money. There is likely to be an additional cash outflow "cost" for sinking fund payments, but, of course, this does not affect stated earnings and when matched up with after-tax interest may still be substantially less than common dividend payments. The primary concern with debt is usually with risk and loss of flexibility rather than with cost; this risk is normally handled by setting relatively strict limits on the maximum amount of debt that management can incur.

Thus, management's normal preference for sources of funds would be in this order:

1. Retained earnings.
2. Long-term debt.
3. New common stock.

It may be expected that, as each source is exhausted in turn, management will re-examine the urgency of its remaining needs before tapping the next source, and may in the process raise the "hurdle rate of return" on new investment, particularly before going into a new stock issue. It may also be noted that long-term debt is often used as a means of anticipating future earnings—tiding the company over an unusual peak of need until internally generated funds are again adequate and the debt can be retired.

Stockholders' Priorities

Are the professional stockholders' priorities as to sources of funds different from management's? I suggest that they are in one important respect: the stockholder reverses the ranking of retained earnings and long-term debt, putting the latter first on the list. For example:

Assume that a company needs $1,000,000 and may obtain this via retained earnings or via a long-term loan bearing 4% interest. Assume further that if debt is used, $1,000,000 of earnings then will not be needed for investment and will be paid out to the shareholders, and that their average tax bracket is such that they will pay 50% of the dividend to the Internal Revenue Service. If debt is used, after-tax earnings, as reflected in E.P.S., will be reduced by $20,000 a year. The shareholders would have to earn only 4% on their after-tax dividend income when invested elsewhere to match this reduction in earnings. (This figure is obtained by dividing $20,000—the after-tax reduction in earnings caused by debt—by $500,000, which is what would be left after taxes if the $1,000,000 were paid out.) Normally they could take the $500,000 and earn *more* than 4% on it by investing it somewhere else.

Thus, in view of the fact that for the established company long-term debt in modest proportions is available at a very low after-tax cost to the corporation, the stockholder may be expected to prefer, up to a point, its use as a substitute for equity funds. Beyond that point—to be discussed later—retained earnings will be preferred to new stock issues as long as the investments so financed earn more than what could be earned by the shareholder externally (as previously discussed). Another alternative would be to have the money paid out in dividends and then return what is left after taxes to the company by purchasing more stock; but this, of course, would not make good sense.

In short, the stockholder may be expected to push for more debt and for a more continuous use of debt than management prefers. This is likely to be particularly true where the corporate rate of investment more or less matches the rate of internal generation of funds, so that retained earnings appear to be a sufficient source over the long run. When this happens, there is reason to wonder whether management is deliberately "pacing" growth so as to avoid the use of external sources.

Attitudes Toward Risk

The subject of risk is a highly complex one and does not lend itself to easy generalization. There are, however, two major decision areas which have important implications for financial risk where the manager and the stockholder may hold conflicting views. These concern:

- The diversification of product and market for the purpose of stabilizing revenues (cash inflows).
- The balance of debt and equity in the capital structure which affects the proportion of the fixed cash outflows.

Seeking a Balance
In considering uncertainty we must distinguish between the objective side—the relative magnitude of the risk—and the subjective side—the attitude toward risk bearing on the part of those who have to make the decision and live with it. Remember that, when a company hires a top executive, it hires not only his knowledge and skills as a manager but also his built-in attitudes as well, attitudes which at the usual age of top management change slowly or not at all. To illustrate the importance of these attitudes, take the decision areas just mentioned:

- Companies that find themselves with a heavy concentration in an unstable industry or with a potentially unstable customer (e.g., the federal government) often seek to expand their line so as (a) to develop greater stability of earnings and cash flows over time and (b) to reduce the threat to the corporate entity posed by errors of judgment or occurrence of an unpredictable or unpredicted adverse event. At stake here is the survival of the corporate identity, its financial strength and future potential, and, no doubt, the kind of business environment within which management prefers to operate. We have today a number of corporate giants which have implemented the diversification principle to such an extreme degree that the distinction between their structure and that of an investment company or trust begins to blur. The effect of merging high-risk-and-return companies with low-risk-and-return companies is, of course, to move in the direction of average risk and return over all.

In view of the fact that management of the large corporation with widespread ownership has little evidence by which to identify the group attitude of its stockholders toward such risks, it undoubtedly must rely heavily on its own attitudes. Since the professional manager finds his own present and future immediately bound up with that of the corporation, any desire to reduce the riskiness of his own position must be accomplished by changing the specific corporate environment he works in.

Obviously no business can operate without risk. We are concerned here only with avoidable risk and with whether management seeks to exploit it or to minimize it. A policy of product and market diversification would generally be interpreted as a move to minimize the risk which derives from unstable cash inflows and errors of judgment.

- Another type of decision involving risk is limiting the amount of debt and lease obligations in the corporate capital structure below what is available from lending and leasing institutions. Here there is a dual concern for the threat to the cash position existing in long-term fixed commitments and for the reduced financial flexibility resulting from high utilization of these more reliable and readily available sources. Here there is an even more apparent trade-off between income and risk, and an even higher opportunity for management to interpose its own risk preference in making the decision. Unquestionably management will have the corporation as well as itself in mind when making the decision since the threat, if it exists, is a threat to both.

View From the Portfolio

The essential and important difference between management and the stockholder on the question of risk lies in the fact that the latter sees the circumstances of the individual corporation in the context of a portfolio decision. Here both diversification and debt leverage are treated, quite properly, on the basis of the portfolio as a whole.

If the ABC Corporation is heavily concentrated in highly cyclical capital goods or unpredictable war contracts, the shareholder in ABC need not wait on management to reduce its vulnerability; he merely maintains a modest position in ABC and balances it with a position in other progressive noncyclical consumer-goods companies. Indeed, he may well *prefer* to see ABC stay in its narrow line if he believes this is what it can do best. The more investment-trust-type corporations we get, the more difficult it becomes for the stockholder to select the desired emphasis of riskiness or stability in his portfolio.

In the same way the extent of leverage in a given company will be taken into account by the knowledgeable stockholder in the mix of securities in his portfolio. Companies which are highly "leveraged" will be recognized as more risky for that reason, and other common stocks like or unlike them will be chosen depending on whether the stockholder wishes to accentuate or minimize the potential gains and related hazards. Again, there may be no desire at all on the part of the stockholder to see high debt leverage reduced in an individual company even though he has a personal preference for a less risky debt-equity posture. Diversity in this respect among corporations gives a better chance to tailor a portfolio more precisely to individual shareholder preferences.

It is of interest in this connection to note that some recent financial theory[6] argues that the stockholder, being in a position where he can leverage his own investment program by personal borrowing, is not going to pay any premium whatever for leverage in the corporate capital structure. Thus, increased E.P.S. due to debt leverage will be directly offset by an adjustment in the price/earnings ratio for the increased risk so that the market price will remain the same.

While I am not prepared to accept this thesis as being valid except at the extremes of debt policy, it does bring out quite sharply the distinctly different contexts within which the management and the shareholder view risk—even disregarding differences in personal risk preferences. A company's management is bound to see both different advantages and different risks associated with diversification and capital structure policy.

Summing Up

Having reviewed four areas in which important financial decisions are made, we see that there can be important differences in the ways in which professional management and professional stockholders are inclined to approach a solution. Various criteria commonly used for decision making reflect these conflicting viewpoints. The viewpoint or bias which is embedded in these apparently objective criteria is not always evident to those who use and are affected by them. In particular I have argued that:

1. Management tends to focus on the effects of various actions on cash flows, particularly those in the immediate future. While this is not *necessarily* in conflict with the stockholders' interest in their personal share of corporate property values, there are circumstances where an increase in corporate cash flows retained for internal use may be obtained only at some sacrifice of growth in the property values as measured by dividends, earnings per share, and market price.

2. The stockholder, as a diversified investor, is inclined to impose investment standards leading to an increased cash outflow to him when the internal return on investment does not match external opportunities. It is, however, unrealistic to expect professional management to accept the implications for such a decision rule, which amounts to an open admission of inferior ability.

3. The potential conflict over investment standards is related to decisions on sources of funds, where management will always give top priority to retained earnings, thus implying that internally generated funds are automatically committed to internal investment opportunities. Though tax law favors the management position here, the stockholder is not likely to go along as a universal rule. A related preference of management is to minimize the cash flow to the stockholder in the form of dividends, though not to the point where an aroused stockholder group poses a threat to management.

4. Investment and fund-acquisition decisions are made by management in the light of risks to the individual corporate entity and executives' own personal risk preferences, and not in the context of the stockholders' portfolio risks (where diversification does much to modify risk magnitudes).

Owner Interest Subordinated

The common thread which runs through the kind of thinking I have ascribed to professional management is the absolute priority of the corporate interest—its continuity and growth—over the financial objectives of ownership. Only if one assumes that the individual stockholder is as completely and permanently committed to a given corporate entity as is its management does this reverse of the historical relationship between ownership and the thing owned cease to be a matter of potential conflict of interest. I believe that what management is wishfully thinking about when it speaks of stockholder loyalty is this identification with an individual business which would make the stockholder insensitive to competing investment opportunities.

On the other hand, such a view of the stockholder is quite contrary to the trend evidenced by the professionalization of investment in corporate securities.

Does the subordination of the stockholder interest to the corporate interest represent a serious loss to the stockholder? It is likely to be argued in defense of management that "in the long run" what is good for the company and its management is good for the stockholder. In answer to this, the real danger appears to lie in the capacity of weak management to perpetuate itself—in its inefficiency, its errors of judgment, and its conservatism beyond what would be permitted by stockholder-oriented decision rules. As long as things are going well—as long as the company can match or better the performance of comparable business entities—the decisions of professional management are likely to be very close to those which would be recommended by an informed professional stockholder. But this is not always the case in fact.

The continued supremacy of the corporate interest *can* lead to a wastage of the stockholders' property values in a defensive effort to preserve the corporate entity for those, including management, who are more closely tied to its future than are the stockholders themselves. New funds will be pumped in and stock values diluted in efforts to shore up sagging sales and profits, develop product or market diversification, and so on when from the viewpoint of stockholders (and the economy as a whole) the funds might be better diverted to other, more promising investment opportunities. Investment standards will be lowered when they should be raised, dividends will be reduced when they should be increased, stock will be used in acquiring new businesses to extend the rule of inefficiency or incompetence, and defensive conservatism will thwart bold moves which are essential to survival.

It will be argued by some that this is as it should be—that the large-scale corporate entity is much more than a vehicle for the shareholders' financial gain and cannot be abandoned merely because the shareholder finds greener pastures elsewhere. It is also argued with increasing frequency by management that because of his unusual mobility the stockholder in the large corporation can leave the company any time he does not like its policies or performance. The fact remains, however, that if these policies or this performance are not what they should be, the shareholder cannot leave without some financial loss.

Dominating Viewpoint

Thus the potential conflict between the professional manager and the professional stockholder is the latent problem, if not an active one, in every large-scale business. Every indication points to the emergence of the management (corporate identity) viewpoint as the dominant one in the long run. I mentioned at the outset that most academic writers have been on the side of the stockholder interest in discussions of how businesses ought to be run. My guess is that it will be financial theory and not management practice that will have to change if the two are to continue to have a valid relationship to each other.

FOOTNOTES

1. See, for example, Adolph A. Berle, Jr., *Power Without Property* (New York, Harcourt, Brace & Co., 1959): Edward J. Mason, *The Corporation in Modern Society* (Cambridge, Harvard University Press, 1959).
2. See John Litner, "Dividends, Earnings, Leverage, Stock Prices and the Supply of Capital to Corporations," *The Review of Economics and Statistics*, August 1962, pp. 243–269.
3. See, for example, Willard J. Graham, "Income Tax Allocation," *The Accounting Review*, January 1959, pp. 14–27.
4. See *HBR*'s "Stock Options Series."—*The Editors*
5. For a more detailed discussion of this subject, see my article, "In Defense of Preferred Stock" *HBR* July–August 1962, pp. 131–136.
6. See Franco Modigliani and Merton H. Miller, "The Cost of Capital Corporation Finance and the Theory of Investment," *The American Economic Review*, June 1958, pp. 261–297.

THE PROBLEM
THE APPROACH

Ford Foundation

Setting the agenda by asking relevant and uncomfortable questions has always been a respected function among investment professionals. The 1968 "Barker Report" captured center stage and stimulated discussion and debate on investment policy, a subject too long dormant. An expression of the policy guideline of the University of Rochester, referred to in this Ford Foundation analysis, appears later in this volume.

The record of most American colleges and universities in increasing the value of their endowments through investment management has not been good. The table below summarizes the recent investment appreciation

TABLE 1
1959–68 Total Return

	Cumulative	Annual Average
Fifteen educational institutions—average	134%	8.7%
Twenty-one balanced funds—average	143	9.2
The University of Rochester	283	14.4
Ten large general growth funds—average	295	14.6

Note: Total return includes both (i) appreciation and (ii) interest and dividends, which are assumed to have been reinvested.

From The Ford Foundation, *Managing Educational Endowments* (New York, New York, 1968), 3–7, by permission of The Ford Foundation.

and income of fifteen important educational institutions whose data have been made available to the Ford Foundation. Also shown are corresponding figures for the University of Rochester, whose endowment has been unusually well managed, and for two groups of mutual funds.

What is the explanation for so striking a contrast? We believe the fundamental reason is that trustees of most educational institutions, because of their semipublic character, have applied a special standard of prudence to endowment management which places primary emphasis on avoiding losses and maximizing present income. Thus, the possibility that other goals might be reasonable — and perhaps even preferable — has hardly been considered until the last few years, even though investment management shares with most other human activities the simple requirements that an objective be established before it can be achieved. If long-term growth through investment management is what is wanted for an endowment, that central fact must be recognized and planned for in advance.

* * * * *

In this report we trace the adverse consequences of the failure to establish the clear-cut objective of maximum long-term return, which we believe should be the primary endowment objective of every Board of Trustees. The report indicates the resulting constraints on endowment management and their heavy cost in years gone by. It also presents suggestions for organizing to achieve improved total return in the future.

When trustees consider their goals, there is sometimes an initial reluctance to concentrate on maximum long-term total return because of concern that such an objective may somehow entail greater risks. Full discussion of objectives and risk must wait . . . in order to permit drawing together the insights and conclusions of the preceding analysis. Let us make clear, however, that setting the objective is not the same as determining the kind of securities to be held. We are not recommending a policy of concentrating on securities with the largest appreciation possibilities. Neither are we recommending the degree of risk exposure to be accepted. What we are discussing is the goal the investment manager should have as he continuously weighs the potential risks and potential rewards of every investment and selects a portfolio based on the best relationship he can find between the two. Given the objective of maximum long-term total return, the manager has just as much incentive to avoid losses as to realize gains. It is our conviction that enhanced growth, greater safety, and increased support for operations are mutually compatible once that objective is adopted.

Objections to the approach in this report might include the following: (a) all we have done is use hindsight in selecting those policies that happened to produce the best results—a fallacious method of analysis; (b) foresight could not in the past and cannot now identify beforehand what policies will succeed in the future; (c) the environment is changing so rapidly that events of the past can be dangerously misleading for the future; and (d) if the recommended policies were universally followed, they would no longer be successful. In the four paragraphs that follow we address ourselves to these criticisms.

First, the essence of investment management is the frustrating but fascinating art of forecasting the future, and until the future becomes past there is no way of knowing how good the forecasting has been. It is only with hindsight that one can ever prove the merit or lack thereof of any investment approach or of any portfolio.

Second, as long as twenty years ago many investment managers recognized the vital importance of establishing long-term growth of capital as their central objective. They selected their portfolios accordingly. There also were formed new mutual funds concentrating on growth. The subsequent superior performance of those funds compared to the balanced funds was, in our opinion, primarily the result of the establishment of that objective rather than of good luck. Moreover, although all the educational institutions analyzed here maintained substantial positions in fixed-income securities throughout the period, we believe the remarkable investment success of the University of Rochester compared to the others was due largely to the fact that the University set for itself a growth objective for the balance of its endowment.

Third, as to the future relevance of the policies and principles enunciated here, we recognize that conditions in the American economy may be very different from those we have known in the past. Our frame of reference in this report must inevitably be historical, but the importance of the analysis lies not in its economic interpretations or investment conclusions about the past—all of which may be swept away by change— but in the principles for improving the management of endowment funds that are suggested thereby. These principles, we believe, are likely to have permanent value even though their specific applications may shift.

Fourth, it is obviously true in the abstract that, if every portfolio manager were to pursue the objective of maximum total return and if each were to perform with perfection in that pursuit, all investment performances would be the same and the opportunity to achieve better-than-average results would disappear. It seems equally obvious, however, that such a notion is completely theoretical. As more and more portfolio managers seek maximum total return, improvement should occur in average portfolio performance. It is also possible that better-than-average results may become somewhat harder to accomplish. However, perfection remains so completely beyond human approach that the need will continue undiminished for every portfolio manager to aim for maximum total return.

* * * * *

YOU ONLY HAVE
TO GET RICH ONCE

Walter K. Gutman

Starting in 1949, Walter Gutman wrote one of the first and most popular Wall Street "letters." This excerpt is from his 1961 book *You Only Have to Get Rich Once*.

When computers are as familiar as cash registers, I.B.M. will sell at a much less romantic value—you wait and see.

There is a particular moment when the value of mystery is at its greatest. When most investors are completely ignorant, they don't pay much for mystery—many of these stocks could have been bought at very reasonable prices in 1957. There is a special moment when everyone sees that something amazing is coming out of mystery and then they will pay a lot more to know more about this strange new thing. Later on, when mystery has given birth, when they know more, they will pay less. Thus most of the electronic stocks which boomed in 1959–61 will be selling for less in 1965, and all of them, I feel sure, will be selling for less in relation to their earnings. In other words, those companies which fulfill the vision of 1959 will be much better known to investors by 1965, and their stocks will be given a rating of knowledge rather than of mystery.

For most of us our greatest richness always has been and still remains in dreams. It may be in dreams about our future accomplishments, it may be in dreams about how wonderful it would be to meet that girl on the diving raft, it may be in dreams of our children, or dreams of the past recalled, or of revenge and future justice, or of religion and another world. We cannot hope for economic riches which are really greater than our dreams, but it is also true that economic riches can help our dreams. . . .

Because no wealth you will ever have—even if you are the richest man in the world—will equal your dreams, stocks go to particularly high levels when a lot of people think they might equal their dreams. Those stocks which are called growth stocks might better be called dream stocks. But dreams are real—we have them every day. It's a big mistake to think that dreams are unreal and what is called real life is real. If dreams were unreal, it would be possible for you to feel richer than your dreams if you were the richest man in the world. When the dream of a new industry comes true, then the dream ends and the stocks sell more conservatively, relating to what is real rather than to what was dreamed.

* * * * *

EQUITIES IN PERSPECTIVE

Robert L. Hoguet, Jr.

Robert Hoguet was one of the early conceptual advocates of equity investments for institutional portfolios. Here he makes his case.

This title permits me to expound my favorite investment thesis, to wit: he who would be a successful trustee or pension trust manager should concentrate on the selection of equities and not be overly concerned with timing problems and the general level of the market at any one moment in history.

When I am asked what I think of the market, I often parry by saying that my investment philosophy for a fifteen year old son is 100% common stocks, and it would still be that even if the Dow goes to 1090 in the near future, while my investment philosophy for my eighty-three year old mother is to the extent possible taxwise 100% fixed income securities, and it would still be that even if the Dow goes to 500 in the near future. It is virtually a truism to say that over a reasonably long period carefully selected common stocks will show substantial increases in earnings which will naturally be reflected in price. Of course there will always be substantial intermediate market fluctuations.

Over the eighteen or nineteen year post-war period the 1000 largest corporations in America earned an average return of 10% or more on their net worth. This fact alone to me makes correctly selected stocks an

---

Reprinted from an address given at the Correspondent Bank Forum, February 1, 1964.

ever attractive medium of investment. The difficulty, of course, is that
to share in this nice 10% plus investment return one has to put one's hard
earned savings at risk in the marketplace. Short term, it is a big risk.
Long term it should be almost no risk if the stocks are properly selected.
On the short term side nobody knows what untoward political event will
take place tomorrow in today's small world. What will market reaction
be to such unforeseen events? We all lived through 1932. Perhaps we
could have another such depression, but I doubt it would be so severe.
The important thing is that we always recover in this country and go on
to greater growth and wider prosperity. Naturally, like everyone else I
would rather buy stocks on the reaction than buy them at the top of an
upswing in price, but of even greater importance to me is whether I own
them at all, not when I bought them. I find an astonishing correlation
between increase in values and the length of time a portfolio or account
has been in existence. Of course, at times some of these portfolios were
worth less than cost but ultimately that is not very important. . . .

There is a feeling on the part of many competent observers that the
market is "high" today. On a short term frame of reference I think it very
probably is "high." It is no doubt quite vulnerable to the unexpected
political incident, and once there is a slackoff in overall economic
activity, which has to come sometime, there will very probably be
correction. However, this is not having any appreciable effect on my
appetite to buy stocks today. I would rather own and have paid for
in our accounts a stock costing $150 a share which short term market
considerations may force to a price of $75, than run the risk of not
owning at all, of course, on the assumption that its continued growth
in earnings is such as to make it sell one day at substantially more
than the $150 we paid for it. I appreciate, and I underscore this point,
that the stocks that are perhaps now most attractive from a long term
point of view, and the ones we ought therefore to be buying, are those
most vulnerable and sensitive on the down side to market upsets. My
confreres on the board of a charitable fund on which I serve decided in
the middle of 1957, when the Dow Jones averages were around 525,
that they wished to cut back the amount of common stocks we owned.
Their rationale was that the market was "high." I sought counsel of Joe
Morris, then senior investment officer in our organization. He said, "The
market is definitely high. I think it may well go off 100 points or so in
the near future, but I would strongly urge you not to cut back because
I doubt you will ever have the nerve to reinstate the percentage." I

followed his advice and voted against cutting back. I was out-voted. We sold a substantial amount of stocks, the market promptly went off 100 points. Of course, my confreres said to me, "We told you so." But that was the short term point of view. Long term, the passage of time proved Joe Morris and my resultant vote quite correct because we have never had the courage to buy back what we sold. . . .

When someone talks yield to me, I say I am more interested in what is happening to that portion of the earnings which is not paid to me than I am in the dividend. What are those reinvested earnings going to earn for me the next year. Our standards give us latitude to buy some exciting stocks. For example, we have bought substantial quantities of such names as Xerox, Control Data, Avon Products, and IBM at prices mostly lower than those prevailing today but at multiples which in some cases have been substantially higher than those prevailing today. . . .We are not afraid of high multiples if we have good reason to believe a strong underlying growth trend will continue. . . .

On the subject of diversification—I think one of the biggest mistakes we have made . . . in the postwar years is in over-application of the principle of diversification. It is abundantly evident to me that we have done better where we have had less rather than more extreme diversification. I am very grateful for the fact that on an overall basis ten good stocks account for 35 to 40% of our equity holdings.

HOW (NOT) TO EXPLAIN THE BOND MARKET TO YOUR WIFE

Sidney Homer

Sidney Homer's scholarly works on interest rates and the bond markets were balanced by his gentle good humor concerning the foibles of his fellows. This excerpt from his engaging book on the trials and tribulations of bond buyers will illustrate the point. Of course today, the explanation could just as easily be given by a bond buyer to (her husband) George.

We all know that if bond yields go up, bond prices go down and vice versa. And we are right. But, can we explain why?—especially to a woman who doubts?

The obvious is sometimes very hard to explain. You know how to walk. It's easy. But, can you explain how to walk to somebody who never has walked? It's hard.

It was close to your dinner hour and you found yourself at home with your wife, Florence. Each was poised on the brink of a martini. You were stroking the chilly side of your glass. She was dipping her little finger into the clear liquid and then tasting it—a trick her mother taught her. The conversation proceeded as follows:

THE FIRST MARTINI

SHE:

How was the bond market today, George?

From Sidney Homer, *The Bond Buyer's Primer* (New York, New York, 1968), 47–53, by permission of Salomon Brothers and Hutzler.

YOU:

Down again.

SHE:

Goodness, again? Hasn't it been going down for a long time? I hope that isn't bad for you.

YOU:

Bad and good. Of course, prices are down and we have some losses but the interest rates on bonds are getting better and better—they are really going through the roof—haven't been so high in thirty years.

pause

SHE:

Now, George, I just don't understand and I wish you would explain. You say that bond prices are going down and at the same time that the interest rates bonds pay are going up. That doesn't make sense. If they pay more interest certainly they would go up in price; at least that couldn't possibly put them down. Don't people want more interest? Of course, they do. I am sure I keep misunderstanding you. I wish you would explain.

There, you have it. Easy? Elementary? Just try.

YOU:

Very well, Florence, I'm glad to have you so interested in my work. The thing is that the rates bonds pay don't ever go up—or down—

SHE:

George! You keep say—

YOU:

Yes, I know, the rates bond buyers get are almost always going up or down, but the rate a bond pays never changes.

SHE:

George, how is that possible? If somebody gets more interest, somebody else pays more interest and if somebody gets less interest, somebody else pays less interest. And if somebody pays more interest, I am sure the buyer would pay a higher price than if they didn't. Why did you raise your interest rates at the bank last month? You said to get more deposits away from the Clayton. If those 4% bonds you bought me last year begin paying 5%, would that make them go down in price? I'll never believe it.

YOU:

Of course you are right, Florence. But those bonds won't ever pay a cent more or less than 4%. That's just it. It is not the rate they pay that changes, it's their yield that keeps changing.

SHE:

Yield . . . what is that?

YOU:

That is the rate of interest the buyer gets from the bonds. If the price goes down, naturally the yield goes up.

SHE:

George, don't just keep saying that! It makes you sound so foolish. I don't like to think of you that way. If the rate of interest the buyer gets goes up, why in the world does the price go down? Men aren't that dumb. I know Mr. Cortley doesn't know much about bonds, but . . .

YOU:

Flo, please don't bring Felix into this. I know he doesn't like bonds, but he is a wonderful president and he knows that when bond yields go up bond prices go down.

SHE:

I will ask him why.

YOU:

Please don't. That is my job. I'll start all over again in just a minute.

THE SECOND MARTINI

YOU:

> I still think that nail polish will poison you some day. Anyway, let's take a 4% bond, any 4% bond, and let's suppose it is selling at 100. You buy it at 100, or you sell it at 100, either way it yields 4%—are you with me?

SHE:

> Yes, George, I am. Am I buying it or am I selling it?

YOU:

> Either . . .

SHE:

> You mean I get the same interest whether I buy it or sell it? George, why should I ever buy it?

YOU:

> All right, you're right, to get the interest you have to buy it.

SHE:

> I thought so. I knew you were mixed up. So, I buy a 4% bond for $100?

YOU:

> Yes—No. It will really cost you $1,000.

SHE:

> Well, that's different! Why didn't you say so? Why should anybody ever pay $1,000 for a bond selling at $100? Do you?

YOU:

> Of course not. That's just the way bonds are quoted. 100 is not what you pay for a bond; it is the price it is selling at.

SHE:

> Georgie, say that again. I know the Government has laws about stocks and bonds, but I never realized . . .

YOU:

No, Flo, I am not talking about monkey business. I am talking about par value. Almost all bonds are $1,000 par value.

SHE:

Oh, yes, I know about par value. That is what goes down when they split. I am beginning to understand.

YOU:

No, Flo, they don't split bonds.

SHE:

Why not?

YOU:

Why should they? Nobody would gain anything; 10 bonds of $100 par would sell at exactly the same price as 1 bond of $1,000 par.

SHE:

Oh, no! Take my AT&T. I've worked it all out. Just let me show you.

YOU:

Flo, bonds are different: They are more mathematical and logical. They never split. Par value is always $1,000. The price they sell at is a ratio to par determined scientifically by the interest rate they pay which we call the coupon and which is also a percentage of par, and the market rate of interest for all bonds of that kind which we call the yield. If the rate they pay is low, of course, the bonds have to sell at a lower price, but if . . .

SHE:

Georgie, that's just what I said. If the rate goes down, the bonds go down.

YOU:

No, Fluff, the rate never changes, but on some bonds it's low and on other bonds it's high. Just let me give you my example and you'll understand everything. Take a 4% bond selling at 100. That means a $1,000 par value bond paying $40 a year and selling at $1,000. The price is the only thing that changes; the $40 never changes, and the bond will be paid off at maturity for $1,000 exactly. Suppose the bond is due to be paid off at $1,000 in exactly one year. So you buy it for $1,000 and you get in one year $1,040 and you have made $40 interest which is just 4% on your investment. How am I doing?

SHE:

I think that is all right, Georgie, but just go ahead.

YOU:

Okay. Now suppose the bond goes down to 99. That means it is selling at $990 for a $1,000 bond, due in one year. All right. So you get $40 interest plus the $10 profit. Add those up and you get $50 which is just a little over 5% on a price of $990. So you see Fluff if the price goes down from 100 to 99, the yield goes up from 4% to over 5%. There we have it, Flo. How about a dividend?

THE THIRD MARTINI

SHE:

Georgie dear, I don't like to be a pest and perhaps we'd better talk about this another time. The trouble is—well—the trouble is that you're wrong.

YOU:

But, Fluff—

SHE:

You said the bond goes down from 100 to 99.

YOU:

Yes, from a dollar price of $1,000 to $990.

SHE:

And it still pays the same old $40.

YOU:

Yes, dear.

SHE:

All right then, I see you still get the $40 but at 99 you've lost $10 and so you must take the $10 away from the $40. Your mistake was you added it. $40 interest less $10 loss is $30, not $50. That is just what I suspected all along. Of course, the more the market goes down the less you get.

YOU:

But dearest, you're not selling it at 99; you're buying it at 99.

SHE:

But Georgie, you said the yield was all the same at a price whether I bought or sold. I am sure you did.

YOU:

Fluffie, tomorrow I will bring you home some bond offering sheets and a yield book. Right now I am just a little bit hungry. Perhaps you'd better—

* * * * *

PORTFOLIO MANAGEMENT: SEVEN WAYS TO IMPROVE PERFORMANCE

Richard H. Jenrette

Portfolio management was, in Dick Jenrette's view, a neglected subject when, in 1966, he gave this talk to the New York Society of Security Analysts. His early identification of the future importance of performance measurement in the pension area was prescient in this speech.

WHY PORTFOLIO MANAGEMENT DESERVES MORE ATTENTION

Portfolio management is probably the most neglected phase of the investing process. Little has been written on the subject, and at our industry's study groups and seminars we typically concentrate either on economics or on industry and company analysis. Little attention is given to how these portfolio components fit into a logical whole.

Aside from the fact that portfolio management is a neglected subject, two new factors suggest that increasing attention should be given to the portfolio management function. First is the growing size of funds under institutional management. The sheer size of these funds precludes

Reprinted from the transcript of an address given to the New York Society of Security Analysts, October 19, 1966, with permission of Richard H. Jenrette.

relying on so-called "hot" investment ideas for portfolio performance. Increasingly, strategy becomes the over-all key determinant of success or failure. I refer to broad decisions affecting the equity ratio of the fund and decisions as to the kinds of industries and companies to be included in the portfolio and their weighting in the portfolio, as opposed to company selection. Today we have attempted to focus our comments on the development of investment strategy rather than individual company selection.

The second reason for giving greater attention to the portfolio management function is the increasing interest of clients in the subject of "performance measurement." First to feel these competitive pressures have been the mutual funds. The success of such funds as Fidelity and Dreyfus has challenged the entire mutual fund industry. In addition, many institutions which heretofore were relatively immune to pressures for performance are being affected. I refer particularly to the banks with large pension fund management responsibilities. The impetus comes from the corporate treasurer, who today is giving increasing attention to the performance of his company's pension fund. The size and rapid growth of pension funds and the cost of employee benefits in the U.S. today suggest that these pressures will accelerate, if anything.

Many observers of the current investment scene feel that the current emphasis on performance measurement has led to a dangerous short-term orientation, excessive risk-taking, and is directly responsible for a number of bad mistakes in investment judgment over the past year. I will agree that these charges and fears have considerable validity. Nevertheless, I believe it would be naive to believe that performance-measurement, once discovered by clients, will go away. The stakes are simply too high. If anything, bad investment results this year will accelerate the use of performance measures. Accordingly, our challenge as investment managers is to learn to live with the new performance-measurement, not being carried away by short-term results, but educating our clients on the intelligent use of performance-measurement and explaining some of its limitations—in general, turning performance-measurement into a tool for improving results as well as client satisfaction with results.

In summary, the portfolio manager today faces increasing pressures to improve investment performance. These pressures come at a time when his task of obtaining what are considered good results is becoming increasingly difficult, reflecting the huge size of assets under institutional management, the growing sophistication of professional managers generally and hence the competition between managers, and, of course, the challenge of the market itself.

Given the pressures to improve performance, what are some of the ways to improve results? I would like to outline seven steps which we believe are essential to superior investment results.

Step 1. Set Your Bogey—Define and Analyze What You Are Trying to Beat

The first step toward improving investment results is to gain agreement with the client as to what you are trying to accomplish. This, of course, usually involves agreement at the outset as to what funds, if any, are going to be set aside, more or less permanently, as fixed income holdings and what percentage of funds are eligible for equity-type investments with a less predictable return.

For the equity portion, we see a growing use of the popular market averages—Standard & Poor or Dow Jones Industrial—as a benchmark for measuring performance. The objective or account bogey increasingly assigned the portfolio manager is to do better than the market, as represented by one of the averages. The University of Chicago studies, showing a 7–8% average annual return from common stock over long periods of time suggest that "beating the market" is indeed a worthwhile goal. Particularly for the large institution whose own buying and selling of securities has a sharp market impact, and whose cash flow frequently reaches its peak simultaneously with the market, equalling the market is a very good performance. For the smaller and more flexible fund, a stated return above the market might be appropriate. In any case, for the equity portion of a portfolio, a bogey relative to the market is more realistic, in my judgment, than one put in terms of absolute percentage gains.

If doing better than the "market" is the account objective, and increasingly it seems to be, the logical first step is to examine in detail the thing that you are trying to beat. At DLJ, we obtain a monthly updated industry diversification for the Standard & Poor 500 index, which we use as a measure of the market. We prefer the S & P because it offers a finer analytical tool for portfolio composition than averages such as the Dow Jones which uses a far smaller and unweighted number of stocks. With the S & P we have full and accurately-weighted industry representation (except for banks and insurance companies). Currently, this breakdown of the S & P average shows, for example, that chemicals account for about 10% of the total; autos, 7%, etc.

The S & P average is nothing more than a starting point—but at least it is that. Common sense suggests that if you are favorably disposed toward a certain industry, and if your objective is to do better than the S & P average, then you should seriously consider giving the particular industry a greater weight in your portfolio than is found in the S & P. For example, about six months ago our firm became quite optimistic over prospects for the oil industry. When we mentioned this fact to many of our institutional clients, they agreed but replied they already had a large position in oils. On examination, we found that this usually meant 8–10% of the common stock portfolio. Yet at that time, the S & P average actually contained a 16% weight for oils. Holding a lower percentage in oils actually implied a negative judgment of the industry's prospects.

Applying the S & P point of reference generally, you might say that the investor whose objective is to equal the performance of these averages probably should not stray too far from the industry diversification of these averages in constructing his own portfolio. Similarly, if your objective is to do substantially better than the averages, you should see to it that your portfolio does differ—in the right way, of course—from the market averages' weighting.

Many of our clients have questioned the use of the S & P as an account bogey on the very valid grounds that (1) you can't invest in the averages, and (2) this is a "no-decision" bogey, and comparisons should be made with "decision" alternatives such as other mutual funds, common trusts of banks, privately managed pension funds, etc. In general, I am in agreement with this line of reasoning. There is a practical problem, however, in deciding what is a comparable fund for purposes of comparison. Moreover, the nature of the capital one is managing may preclude some of the investment practices of some of the swifter mutual funds.

Nevertheless, the practice of comparing one's performance with decision alternatives (as opposed to the no-decision S & P) does have considerable merit and may gain increasing acceptance. To the extent one does find himself compared to certain mutual funds, one can still follow the approach outlined in analyzing the composition of the S & P. We do this through quarterly breakdowns of institutional portfolios along the lines of the S & P industry diversification. Such an analysis, for example, recently disclosed a below-average market weighting in oils (less than the S & P 16%) for most of the aggressive funds. In view of our favorable view of oil industry prospects, this suggested a substantial accumulation of oil industry shares by the funds potentially was in the offing. These same funds also had 10% plus in airlines, suggesting no room for further accumulation. All this is a part of knowing what your competition is and deciding when and where you are going to differ from the competition, if at all.

Step 2. Know Your Limitations

Knowing your limitations is an important prerequisite to determining how you are going to manage the portfolio. How flexible can you be? Some funds have a portfolio turnover rate which would not be acceptable to many investors or trustees. Do you have discretion over the account, or do you have to go before a committee and then call up or write 500 clients, and then sweat out a painful buying and selling process in the order room? Does the character of the capital you manage prohibit certain types of investments or make them meaningless to overall performance?

Unless you have discretion and the ability to act quickly, you may as well forget about "fashion investing"—buying stocks currently in vogue but which may drop from favor quickly. At the other end of the spectrum, you may also be constrained from such "contrary opinion" approaches as buying depressed stocks or turn-arounds—if your limitations preclude flexibility. Turn-arounds often backfire and depressed stocks often keep going down for fundamental reasons not at first apparent.

In short, if you lack flexibility perhaps you are limited to fairly orthodox, middle-of-the-road quality companies, with a diversification weighting that resembles the market averages or your leading competitors, such as other funds. Moreover, if you lack flexibility, you had better operate on a considerably longer time span than many institutions currently appear to be.

Step 3. Have an Investment Philosophy

Most of us have an investment philosophy—usually reflected in the kind of company we are most comfortable buying. Some investors, for example, have an inherent bias toward small growth companies, some are most disposed toward turn-arounds, some like to "play" the business cycle, some buy strong fundamentals without regard to price or price/ earnings ratio, others avoid all investments that have a trace of cyclicality.

While we believe everyone should have an investment philosophy, we see certain dangers in a rigid approach, such as all the foregoing imply. At DLJ we have evolved a fairly simple investment philosophy which we believe is flexible to meet changing circumstances. It has led us to a variety of investments over the last seven years.

Rule No. 1: Buy relative earnings growth. By this, I refer to companies whose earnings are growing faster than overall corporate profits—for the time span in which we are making the investment. The concept of investing in relative earnings growth rests simply on the belief that the market will always show greatest interest in those companies showing the largest earnings gains—relative to overall corporate profits. The time span in which you choose to look for relative earnings growth relates back to step No. 2 above (how flexible can you be) and will vary from one investor to the next. We have usually used a time span of 1–3 years in which we look for relative earnings growth. Some institutions with a high degree of flexibility are operating on a shorter time span. Others, with little flexibility, might be well advised to use longer than a three-year span. It is surprising how short a time span many institutional investors are operating on today, which creates unusual opportunities for the investor willing to look just a little bit into the future. The important point is to concentrate the weight of your portfolio in companies showing much more rapid gains in earnings than the economy as a whole—during the time span in which you can operate.

Rule No. 2: At a reasonable relative price-earnings ratio. Here again one must apply the relative test. How does the stock's current multiple look relative to its historical relationship to the market's multiple? Under these guidelines, the ideal investment is a company whose earnings not only have been and are still moving up relative to corporate profits generally but also with a price/earnings ratio which has been moving down relative to the market—despite the above-average earnings growth. A vulnerable pattern would be declining or level relative earnings and an increasing relative multiple. Stocks demonstrating this pattern usually soon begin to lag the market, assuming, of course, that there is no reason to expect a reversal of the downward relative earnings trend. Stocks like Sears Roebuck and General Foods showed this pattern from early 1963 to early 1966.

As a guide to implementing this philosophy of concentrating the portfolio in companies and industries experiencing relative earnings growth, we use Standard & Poor computer tapes to compute relative price, earnings, price/earnings and yields for roughly 900 companies and 80 industry groups on a quarterly basis. The charts derived from this data have proved a valuable tool in identifying relative earnings trends which have not been reflected in price/earnings ratios. There is usually a sufficient lag between the emergence of relative earnings growth and price to permit accumulation of a substantial position.

The chief advantage of this rather simple philosophy of investing in relatively growing earnings at a reasonable relative multiple is its adaptability. The search for relative earnings growth might lead one to stress cyclical stocks at a given time (such as was appropriate in the 1962–66 period of rapid industrial expansion) or high growth rate stocks, or in another environment the moderate but predictable growth industries such as utilities, foods, etc. (suitable in the 1955–60 hiatus in corporate profits growth in the U.S.).

1966 provided a new challenge to investing in relatively increasing earnings. Recognition that bond yields would increase significantly in 1966 might have helped put the expected large corporate earnings increase in 1966 in perspective. As things turned out, the yield available to investors on high grade bonds at their peak had increased by about 25% over year-end 1965. This compares with an earnings increase of 10–15% for corporate profits. Corporate earnings thus declined relative to the increase in bond yields in 1966. The subsequent result was a considerable reduction in the total market price/earnings ratio.

Step 4. Develop an Investment Strategy

Having an investment strategy is essential to implementation of the investment philosophy just described. The strategy selected must encompass the time span for which you are investing. It grows out of your assessment of the *character* of the economy over this span. I place particular stress on the word character since we believe directional change and the general economic environment are far more important in developing investment strategy than is a detailed, specific forecast of GNP.

For example, is the economy likely to be characterized by price inflation or are deflationary pressures at work? Are wage increases running ahead of productivity gains as appears to be the case now? What is the net effect on profit margins? What segments of the economy are most vigorous? Capital goods, government, or consumer spending? In effect, you are trying to decide which stream to be fishing in, and the answers to these questions will provide a set of criteria which can be used to test existing or proposed commitments.

Out of your assessment of the character of the economy comes a strategy. Should the portfolio be weighted toward economy-oriented areas such as capital goods and other cyclical industries, or should it be skewed away from business cycle exposure, with heavy weighting in such groups as utilities, insurance, food, other consumer non-durables? Should one avoid labor-intensive industries, such as the current environment suggests? Should one stick to "quality" companies (such as in the early stages of market recovery) or are some of the "second-line" companies likely to be the main beneficiaries of the environment you foresee? What attitude should be taken toward high multiple growth stocks?

Evolving an appropriate strategy for changing economic and market conditions is admittedly difficult but absolutely essential to superior results.

Step 5. Concentrate the Portfolio

You may be right in your choice of strategy and have brilliant company selection, but if the portfolio manager lacks courage to implement the program the good effort will be subverted.

Over-diversification is probably the greatest enemy of portfolio performance. Most of the portfolios we look at have too many names. As a result, the impact of a good idea is negligible. Moreover, the greater the number of companies in the portfolio the more difficult it is for the fund manager to stay on top of developments affecting these companies. In our opinion, 25–30 companies is enough diversification even for a fund of $100 million. For a $1 million portfolio seeking to outperform the market, we believe the number of holdings might be as low as 10–15. We have yet to find an institutional investor who had more than 10–15 investment ideas that he really liked at a given time.

Limiting the number of names in the portfolio also forces an automatic weeding process since an existing holding usually must be sold to raise funds to purchase what appears to be a more attractive new name.

The chief roadblock to portfolio concentration in taxable funds is reluctance to take capital gains. While we could discourse at length on this subject, in our judgment the penalties involved in realizing capital gains from time to time are more than offset by the benefits of flexible management, which inherently involves change.

It is surprising that this reluctance to realize capital gains is also quite often found in tax-free funds. In all honesty, many of us as portfolio managers are reluctant to eliminate a holding with a big gain—which stands as a reminder of past wisdom! As focus increasingly shifts to over-all investment performance under some of the new measurement systems, I fear we may be far less comfortable holding securities with large unrealized gains if their potential no longer justifies retention.

Step 6. Flexibility

This brings us to the next key element in superior portfolio management, and this is flexibility. Nothing is more certain than change, and it seems rather obvious that flexibility is needed to meet changing circumstances. Yet most of us yearn for some sort of panacea which will carry us through without having to make change. Some portfolio managers seem to fear that making a change in the portfolio is tantamount to admitting a mistake. This fear is based on the mistaken view that there are "stocks for all seasons." Few companies are appropriate to all environments.

If flexibility is a key element in portfolio performance, it is surprising how few of us have structured our own organizations to respond to change. The rigidities built into most investment organizations are staggering. It is hardly surprising so few changes are made considering the red tape involved in implementing change. Because of this red tape, the relatively few organizations that have organized to act quickly enjoy a significant and growing competitive advantage over their more encumbered competitors.

Chiefly responsible for this inflexibility is our industry's reluctance to accept discretionary power over client funds—or to insist on it. It seems to us that the investment manager is going to be judged on results—regardless of whether the client concurs. We may as well face this responsibility and accept capital only on terms which permit us to do a first-rate management job.

Step 7. Keep Score

Buttressed by a 30-year bull market, the investment community, at least until recently, has seldom found it necessary to report results to its clients. Elaborate client appraisals give all sorts of information, but we rarely see one that reports the most important single piece of information in which the client should be interested, namely the performance of the fund. Even rarer are references to other published indices such as the market averages, which might be used for comparison purposes. If it is understandable why investment managers have not wished to make their clients more performance-oriented, it is nonetheless surprising how few of us bother to keep score for our own edification as professional investment managers. Interesting possibilities exist to go behind performance measurement figures to analyze why the account did better or worse than its objective.

In closing, I would like to say again that performance measurement is here to stay, whether we welcome it with open arms or not. The result is a much more competitive environment, stressing the need to turn performance measurement into an aid to better performance in line with objectives.

CONTRARY OPINION IN STOCK MARKET TECHNIQUES

Edward C. Johnson, II

Mr. Johnson—or, more formally, Edward C. Johnson, II—devoted his career to the Fidelity Funds, taking control in the early 1940s when assets under management were less than $5 million. Assets now exceed $80 billion. Mr. Johnson's approach to investing was informal to the point of appearing rumpled and was extraordinarily eclectic: he knew a lot about many things and was interested in all of them.

It's a great pleasure and privilege to be able to talk briefly with you fellow contrarians. I hope you'll forgive my bad habit of often waiting till just before speaking to put my thoughts together. It's a purely instinctive procedure. I suppose many of us need the spur of necessity to do things that can be put off. So I began thinking about what I'd talk about yesterday afternoon and I thought you had been told a great deal about stock markets this morning, in the most charming and informative way; it was really an education to listen to Mr. Wallace. I began to think maybe I would talk a little about Contrary Opinion itself and take a look at it. So I fortified myself with a can of Metrecal last evening, curled myself up, and went to work. . . .

I thought about this matter of Contrary Opinion. Maybe now I should tell you where I sit, because I think that it is important in eval-

Reprinted from a transcript of the First Annual Contrary Opinion Foliage Forum (Manchester, Vermont, 1963), by permission of Edward C. Johnson, II.

uating what anyone says to you. What is his angle? I am connected with a company that manages a group of investment companies ranging in size from $400 million down to $3 million. We have a semi-speculative fund, an income fund, an old line investment company—something for every taste. The only reason I mention this is that there is a different point of view that comes from the speculative angle, from the orthodox approach, and from the approach that the mutual fund industry has somewhat originated. You see it is a very new industry. It didn't really start until about 20 years ago. So this involved techniques and approaches that differ from the orthodox investment approaches.

We approach the problem of investment first and foremost from a money-making point of view. We are not interested in fancy ideas and theories; we are interested in things that work. You might call us empirical pragmatists. Those are almost too heavy words for anyone to swallow, but I hope they convey a picture. Our almost religion is that we believe strongly in analysis of the present. The past is dead. We can learn from it, trying not to indulge in the "backward" successes we might have made. The future is a dream. That may be as may be. If you come to think of it, the present (I talk like a Zen Buddhist now) the present is really the only thing that anybody can actually use. So many people spend their lives thinking about the future ahead that they are hardly conscious of the present. Now there is not much you can do with the future. You can't love it, you can't taste it, you can only dream about it. This is our actual approach; we don't try to forecast. We can't buy or sell securities a month from now; we can only do it today. So what do we do today? That is enough for us to know.

The present we try to use, however, is not a static affair. It is dynamic, full of motion. It is the analysis of these dynamics and motion that is completely vital. To analyze correctly in this way the present. . .is to take advantage of the future without the desperate chances inherent in successful forecasting.

We approach the practical investing problem from two angles. First is so-called fundamental research. Let's now look at Contrary Opinion itself. I got to considering it last night. I began to wonder what made Contrary Opinion useful and what was the kind of Contrary Opinion we were interested in. For example: The sun rises tomorrow. I suppose that the general opinion is that the sun will rise tomorrow and it is obvious that here is not an opinion that we wish to be contrary to. Same way with opinions about the weather. Why? Because the opinion itself has no effect on the fact. The general opinion that the sun is going to rise, of course, has no effect on the sun rising, nor has the opinion on the state of the weather any effect on the weather. So may we not say that the test for usefulness of Contrary Opinion is the extent to which the opinion affects the fact under consideration. For example, in contrast to the sun and weather let us look at the stock market. Obviously the general opinion on whether the stock market is going up or down has a profound effect on the action of the market itself. The more unanimous the opinion, the greater the what might be called inverse effect on prices will be.

All right, let's take that rule; let's look at so-called fundamental research. What do we do? We send men out all over the country and they talk to company officials and others, and with competitors particularly. Now so far as fundamental research is concerned I can't see that Contrary Opinion is too important. What people think IBM is going to do in the way of earnings and dividends has probably relatively little effect on what IBM does accomplish—yes, some effect—because if people have a good opinion of you maybe you are apt to do things that you wouldn't do so well if they had a poor opinion of you. But it is not a large factor. Again, one thing we do in particular; our men go around to competitors which is the first place you go to find out about a given company. We get the general opinion that a particular company is able, well run, and so forth and so on. We don't go contrary to that; we use it in [reaching] our conclusions. So Contrary Opinion probably wouldn't be useful there, either.

Next I'd like to discuss a rather subtle application of the principle of Contrary Opinion. Let us look at a certain kind of what might be called emotional involvement. Emotional involvement is a very broad thing—it comes up constantly in many forms. For example, an analyst gets emotionally involved with a company he goes to see, a psychiatrist gets emotionally involved with his patient, and the sexes get emotionally involved with each other (to put it mildly). This is something we have to allow for. When we find an analyst is getting that way—and you can tell almost by the tone of his voice and the way he looks when he talks about a company that this is happening—we cannot afford to satisfy the deep human instinct of faithfulness and trust which underlie emotional involvement. Because of the very nature of our business we have to follow the "love 'em and leave 'em" principle.

When troubles loom ahead for a company, what is one's natural instinct? You want to take off your coat and get out with management to tackle and solve the difficulties. But unfortunately that isn't our business, which is to keep investment dollars working in the most productive media. The men running the company involved of course stay with it through thick and thin, but our question always has to be whether other pastures may not be greener. We have the ability to change businesses which the ordinary man in a particular business does not. This is one of the things that makes our business so unnatural, but also, strangely, very satisfying too. So fascinating is our business that we have difficulty holding very good men because a man who can fairly consistently on balance make substantial money in securities is rare and he is coveted by the whole world. One of the things that may hold him, I think, is the fascination of the business of investing and the universality of it. The stock market represents everything that anybody has ever hoped, feared, hated, or loved. It is all of life. You leave that and you go to the XYZ Bottling Co. and the rest of your life is bottles.

Now, this emotional involvement is, I think, one of the things we combat by being contrary. This is, we go contrary to the deep instinct in everybody which wants to stand by the ship and fight through to the finish, so to speak. To paraphrase a famous statesman talking about nations, we have no loyalties or friends, only interests. Maybe this contrary element in our business contributes to its fascination, and it's often tough on the families at home because we in the business love it so much that we are apt to work unreasonably long hours.

Back to Contrary Opinion: Why does it pay to be contrary? Let's take the 1920's as an extreme example of how it works in the stock market. In 1929 nearly everybody who could had bought all the stocks he and his borrowing power could absorb, and in those days there were lots of 5% margins around. You had probably a very extreme example of a universal opinion that stocks were going up. Therefore, you had a nation jammed with potential sellers. The buying had all for the moment been done and way overdone. The panic of 1929 was a natural result. Again that shows how Contrary Opinion works. Crowds, when they carry often sound ideas to foolish extremes, tend to commit suicide. Ideally stock market prices should express average opinion of a fair estimate of probabilities and generally this is so. In other words, every price in itself is a healthy exercise of a kind of Contrary Opinion. I am referring to that part of the stock exchange transactions which you might call voluntary, not the necessity kind. Every transaction represents an opinion by the buyer that the price is wrong, it ought to be or become higher. And by the seller that the price is wrong, it ought to be or become lower. You go on beyond that and you get opinions of stock by the general public and you get a new element coming in. The crowd tends to suck others in its train so that A thinks thus because B does and B because C and so on. A body of general opinion tends to work on itself and create other similar opinions like a thunderstorm creating its own wind. A mass opinion tends to grow on itself, and here I believe is the heart and soul of the Contrary Opinion doctrine. It is this artificially engendered superheated general opinion that it pays to "copper" because it isn't really an opinion at all—it's a crowd psychology phenomenon. Now, all of us have inside of us a part of the crowd. I have always wondered about Humphrey and just how he gets his dope on what general opinions are. I never have to go outside the confines of my own room. Every one of us has a tuning fork inside of himself that vibrates to a greater or lesser extent along with the crowd. It works so uniformly that when sometimes I talk to salesmen of mutual funds I give them a rule, which is this: That the more it hurts them and the more they have to fight themselves to make a sale, the better it will be for the customer and also for the salesman himself. And that just means going contra to his inborn crowd segment.

That is the thing you get in the kind of area where you have superheated opinions—where the thing builds itself up. Another analogy is the chain letter effect. Are there any of you who are old enough to remember the chain letter? They were a great, great fad. There was a little fellow named Ponzi down my way who went on the same principle. In other words, the idea of the game is fine so long as you get new suckers to keep coming and bail the old ones out. The later Imrie deVegh called it the Bigger Fool Theory. You buy at a foolish price, but you hope you will get a bigger fool to pay you a bigger price later on. Dickson Watts was a famous cotton speculator, I think, and he laid down some principles for trading. He put it this way: "Against the crowd act boldly. With the crowd act cautiously. It may at any time turn and rend you." I think in very few words he has expressed in another way the principle involved in this kind of thing.

Actually, operation in securities is not mainly a matter of reasoning at all. The talented operators I know don't really reason things out (although they often pretend to). They just do it instinctively by experience. As a man plays golf or rides a horse. Our nation is a remarkable phenomenon, for we Americans are a very interesting group of people as seen in the light of history. We are essentially men of action. Do something about it! We are also men of science—tremendous men of science. But when we turn to art we find that it is not reasoning and not scientific; it is basically a matter of individual emotion and feeling for universality, channeled into a particular mode of expression such as painting, music, or philosophy as the latter involves understanding of the human soul. It is really an instinctive sense of things that exist but are too complicated to reason out. Here Americans appear deficient, somewhat as the Romans were. Thus you take a psychiatrist today—here you have an example of the attempt to apply the scientific method to the human mind. And it just plain doesn't work, because the conscious and subconscious human mind is so vast—the stock market, by the way, is just a bunch of minds—that there is no science, no IBM machine, no anything of that sort, that can tame it. What this means to us in practical affairs is that if we are able to do the thing that Americans find very hard to do—that is, understand ourselves (and consequently others) to some degree—we have really a chance of becoming effective stock operators. That is a hard thing and a rare thing.

Now coming down from these theoretical heights, let's look at the so-called technical aspect of markets. I suppose that word is a good one. The technical side of the stock market is an attempt to understand the demand-supply situation in securities as distinct from the fundamental which, of course, is the thing I was telling you about: going to see companies and checking industries and facts. There are a great number of "technical indicators." There is nothing secret about any of them (that are worth using). There is nothing very complicated. You can't get complicated anywhere in this business without being lost; each complication begets ten others, and so on.

You have these various tools: We have a number of test tubes that we experiment with and look at—such as the simplest of all, moving averages of stock prices. Take for example, say, a 12-month moving average of [the] Dow Jones Industrial Average. If any one of you people wanted to close your mind to everything else—never mind about all the forecasts—just the moving average, and use a few simple techniques, that moving average would get you into all big bull markets and would keep you out of all big bear markets. It would be far from perfect, but workable. Did you ever hear of anyone who ever did this in practical operation? I never did.

For light here let's look at the ancient Greeks. The Greeks were always great favorites of mine and, as you know, they used to have many gods and goddesses; and it was a trick to know which god or goddess to back. You remember Paris had a choice to make, for he had a golden apple to be given to the fairest goddess, and here were three leading goddesses standing in front of him—to whom should he give the apple? Foolishly he gave it to Venus. If he had given it to Athene or even Hera it would have been far better for everyone, including himself, because he already had a devoted girl friend who was far from ugly or ill favored. But he chose Venus and so destroyed his whole family and his whole city and nation because of it. You see, any choosing among gods or goddesses isn't easy. To choose one was to antagonize another. The Hebrews, on the other hand, looked to a single God, just one, and that did make life simpler at the cost of what one may learn or gain or lose through choosing for himself.

There's no one god in the investment world, so how are you going to decide which one of these indicators you are going to pick? . . . I wonder if, in the realm of art, too much thinking may not often be more responsible for trouble than too little thinking. If you will make the thinking that you do so simple as to choose some one "god" among all these technical things—then you have a chance. Remember the words: "Your God is a jealous God," and that is especially true in this kind of work. Various services put much stress on looking at many indicators and [g]oing along with a weighted majority. I submit to you that there's no mathematical way of averaging or weighing your indicators for practical stock market operation.

A violin to me is just wood and a bunch of strings. It takes an artist to play on it. These technical things are nothing but tools—nothing but the violin. They are no good without the player. Now this means that we don't want an orthodox investment approach. [A]n orthodox investment approach, handling as it does stupendous amounts of investment funds, more or less has to obtain average investment results. There isn't any other way of doing it. Unusual results in securities, as I say, have to be looked for in the basically artistic camp, which is relatively small in number as are all artistic groups.

INSTITUTIONAL SERVICE REPORT MONTHLY REVIEW

Paul F. Miller, Jr.

Paul Miller led the research department at Drexel & Co. (later Drexel, Harriman, Ripley) to institutional prominence before organizing the firm of Miller, Anderson, & Sherrerd with Jay Sherrerd and Clay Anderson. At Drexel, Paul studied the important advantages of low P/E stocks. Here is one of his several memoranda on the subject.

It's time again to review the results of our "bet" that the Dow-Jones Industrial Average could continue to be outperformed by the simple method of indiscriminate purchase of the 10 lowest price-earnings ratio stocks within the Dow.

The results shown in this report indicate that the year ended 6/30/64 was no exception to the pattern of the last twenty-eight years. In twenty-two of the twenty-eight years since 1936, the lowest 10 price-earnings stocks have out-performed the 30-stock Average, or a hefty 78.5% of the time. On the other hand, the 10 highest price-earnings stocks have outperformed the Average in only four out of twenty-eight years, or 17.9% of the time. Even more impressive is the record of the low 10 versus the high 10, which now totals twenty-four out of twenty-eight years in favor of the low 10.

Reprinted from Drexel & Co. Letterhead, Philadelphia, Pennsylvania, July 1964, by permission of the author.

For the computation of the historical P/E's, we have used June 30 prices and calendar year earnings (as more fully described in our original work on the subject in our *Monthly Reviews* of February and April 1963).

However, for the period 6/30/63 to 6/30/64 we categorized the list on two different bases:

1. Using the actual estimates of our research staff as of 6/30/63 for calendar 1963 earnings.
2. Using actual reported figures for 1963.

As might be expected, the use of the actual reported earnings slightly increases the edge of the low 10 over the high 10. In other words, some stocks (actually two—U.S. Steel and Standard Oil, New Jersey) turned out to be in the low 10, whereas using our 6/30/63 estimates they were in the middle 10, and Bethlehem Steel proved to be in the middle 10 instead of the low 10. The effect of this was to raise the performance of the low P/E group by two percentage points.

TABLE I
Dow-Jones-Industrials—Performance by P/E Categories 6/30/63–6/30/64

P/E's Based on Earnings Estimates as of 6/30/63		
	P/E	*Performance*
High 10		
Allied Chemical	20.2	+12.63
Alcoa	28.5	+11.70
duPont	27.2	+16.16
Eastman Kodak	26.7	+27.58
General Electric	25.1	+ 0.95
General Foods	24.8	+ 7.01
International Paper	20.3	+ 4.10
Owens-Illinois	21.1	+20.21
Procter & Gamble	27.5	+ 9.24
Sears, Roebuck	26.6	+32.07
		Average +14.17%
Middle 10		
American Can	16.6	+ 1.35
AT&T	20.2	+21.87
Goodyear	16.1	+23.83
International Nickel	18.9	+28.05
Johns Manville	16.1	+21.00
Standard Oil, New Jersey	16.7	+27.24
Texaco	17.6	+12.77
Union Carbide	19.3	+23.99
U.S. Steel	17.5	+20.05
Westinghouse	20.1	−13.17
		Average +16.70%
Low 10		
American Tobacco	12.2	+10.96
Anaconda	10.1	−11.44
Bethlehem Steel	14.0	+19.11
Chrysler	10.5	+54.37
General Motors	14.1	+24.91
International Harvester	13.4	+41.99
Standard of California	13.8	+ 4.67
Swift	12.0	+36.08
United Aircraft	15.3	+ 7.34
Woolworth	13.2	+28.96
		Average +21.70%

TABLE II
Dow-Jones-Industrials — Performance by P/E Categories 6/30/63 – 6/30/64

P/E's Based on Reported 1963 Earnings		
	P/E	Performance
High 10		
Alcoa	28.2	+11.70
AT&T	19.9	+21.87
duPont	24.4	+16.16
Eastman Kodak	29.2	+27.58
General Electric	26.3	+ 0.95
General Foods	24.6	+ 7.01
International Paper	19.3	+ 4.10
Procter & Gamble	27.5	+ 9.24
Sears, Roebuck	25.9	+32.07
Westinghouse	27.4	− 13.17
		Average +11.75%
Middle 10		
Allied Chemical	17.5	+12.63
American Can	18.1	+ 1.35
Bethlehem Steel	14.6	+19.11
Goodyear	14.9	+23.83
International Nickel	17.1	+28.05
Johns Manville	14.7	+21.00
Owens-Illinois	18.9	+20.21
Texaco	16.4	+12.77
Union Carbide	19.2	+23.99
United Aircraft	14.7	+ 7.34
		Average +17.03%
Low 10		
American Tobacco	11.4	+10.96
Anaconda	12.1	− 11.44
Chrysler	7.2	+54.37
General Motors	12.6	+24.91
International Harvester	12.6	+41.99
Standard Oil, California	14.3	+ 4.67
Standard Oil, New Jersey	14.4	+27.24
Swift	13.9	+36.08
U.S. Steel	14.5	+20.05
Woolworth	13.1	+28.96
		Average +23.78%

TABLE III
Dow-Jones Industrial Average and Three Component Groups Annual Change in Price

Years (June to June)	% Change in Year Dow-Jones	% Change in Year Low 10	% Change in Year Middle 10	% Change in Year High 10
1936–37	+ 7.4	+ 18.3	+ 15.3	+ 7.8
1937–38	− 20.9	− 30.5	− 10.8	− 24.0
1938–39	− 2.4	+ 4.1	− 4.2	− 11.8
1939–40	− 6.7	− 6.0	− 6.8	− 13.0
1940–41	+ 1.0	+ 9.3	+ 3.7	− 1.6
1941–42	− 16.1	− 8.6	− 12.3	− 17.6
1942–43	+ 38.8	+ 52.4	+ 48.6	+ 32.5
1943–44	+ 3.5	+ 1.5	+ 8.1	+ 0.9
1944–45	+ 11.4	+ 16.5	+ 12.6	+ 7.3
1945–46	+ 24.4	+ 32.0	+ 23.5	+ 15.8
1946–47	− 13.8	− 15.5	− 16.5	− 14.8
1947–48	+ 6.9	+ 20.1	+ 5.2	− 2.3
1948–49	− 11.6	− 19.4	− 10.8	− 6.4
1949–50	+ 24.9	+ 38.4	+ 19.1	+ 19.8
1950–51	+ 16.1	+ 25.8	+ 22.0	+ 4.2
1951–52	+ 13.0	+ 18.7	+ 6.0	+ 7.5
1952–53	− 2.2	− 4.9	+ 2.8	− 4.3
1953–54	+ 24.3	+ 26.4	+ 24.7	+ 26.0
1954–55	+ 35.3	+ 61.1	+ 25.8	+ 23.1
1955–56	+ 9.2	+ 13.0	+ 11.0	+ 1.2
1956–57	+ 2.1	+ 9.1	+ 0.4	+ 3.9
1957–58	− 5.0	+ 8.1	− 1.6	− 12.2
1958–59	+ 34.5	+ 35.7	+ 30.1	+ 30.7
1959–60	− 0.5	− 1.5	+ 8.9	− 8.2
1960–61	+ 6.8	+ 16.1	+ 13.7	− 2.2
1961–62	− 17.9	− 7.3	− 17.6	− 24.6
1962–63	+ 25.9	+ 40.5	+ 15.0	+ 22.4
1963–64	+ 17.8	+ 21.7	+ 16.7	+ 14.2

By now we're sure curiosity has gotten the best of the reader. He must know what the component groups were on 6/30/64. Here they are:

TABLE IV
P/E's Based on 6/30/64 Prices and
Est. 1964 Earnings

	P/E
High 10	
Alcoa	22.4
AT&T	26.2
duPont	23.0
Eastman Kodak	33.3
General Electric	28.0
General Foods	25.1
Procter & Gamble	27.6
Sears, Roebuck	27.1
Westinghouse	21.0
Union Carbide	21.5
Middle 10	
Allied Chemical	18.2
American Can	17.1
Goodyear	16.5
International Nickel	18.8
International Paper	16.7
Johns Manville	15.6
Owens-Illinois	20.8
Standard Oil, New Jersey	17.1
Texaco	17.1
Woolworth	16.4
Low 10	
American Tobacco	12.9
Anaconda	8.1
Bethlehem Steel	12.2
Chrysler	9.1
General Motors	13.5
International Harvester	13.1
Standard Oil, California	13.8
Swift	14.7
United Aircraft	13.2
U.S. Steel	13.4

THE ENIGMA OF INVESTMENT MANAGEMENT

Ragnar D. Naess

Ragnar Naess developed Naess and Thomas into a very successful investment counseling firm, principally serving individual investors. Here he
reflects on the lessons he learned over a 30-year period of market and
client involvement, commencing with the observation that "doing better
than the DJIA" is a difficult task.

A career in Wall Street should offer an opportunity, not available in
other professions, to accumulate capital over a period of time by judicious trading or investment in stocks. Those concerned with the investment of funds by the public and by institutions are supposedly able to
render sound and profitable advice regarding individual securities and
investment policy, and Wall Street does, in fact, render a valuable service to the average investor, a service which has improved greatly over
the last quarter of a century. Yet the record of advice, as shown by
analysis of opinions expressed over a long period of years and by the
results obtained when publicly available, indicates that it is difficult to
do much better than the Dow Jones Industrial Average. Few individuals
engaged in the investment field are able to accumulate capital by taking
advantage of the opportunities that are continuously available to them.

    In this article I will analyze the reasons for success and the obstacles

From *Readings in Financial Analysis and Investment Management* (Homewood, Illinois, 1963),
16–20, 25–26 by permission of Dow Jones-Irwin.

that have to be overcome in order to show a consistent and favorable record of investment advice by those engaged in our interesting and attractive profession.

I believe that it is possible to divide the basic problem of investment management into two main but related categories: They are those arising from human or psychological factors and those concerned with analytical skill, knowledge, and experience. Both are important, but I will consider first the problems that arise from human or psychological factors.

Maintaining Firm Point of View

First, there is the difficulty of firmly maintaining a point of view without being too easily swayed. Anyone engaged in research work, in formulating investment policy, or in dealing with investors runs up against human emotions including fear and anxiety, greed, impatience, and stubbornness. Many mistakes result from the purely psychological impact of events on the judgment and analysis of the individual. Wall Street is a highly emotional place and is a sounding board for new ideas, good or bad. Current developments become exaggerated far beyond their real significance. This necessarily affects every individual and influences his emotions to a greater or lesser degree. A sound and correct investment policy may have been established in ample time, and yet the emotional impact of the subsequent events may be so great that the right policy is not executed.

It is, therefore, easier to establish a correct policy than to execute it. A friend of mine, with whom I happened to be associated during 1929, mentioned recently that he will never forget my bearish views expressed at a luncheon with him in the summer of 1929. Despite my views at the time, the psychological impact of the general environment had done its damage, and the break in late 1929 left me with a lot of headaches. During early 1932, after I had maintained a bearish view for two years, economic trends suggested that a turn might take place within a few months. The psychological impact of the devastating crisis during the summer of that year impaired the usefulness of the correct investment policy that had been established and had worked out months before. The same psychological problem was present during other crucial periods such as 1937, 1938, 1942, and 1946. When stock prices are low and ready for an important long term advance, the principal difficulty in executing a correct policy is to overcome the fear of losing capital. When stock prices are high and ready for an important downward readjustment, the psychological obstacle is one of overcoming stubbornness and greed for a few more capital gains.

Disregarding Majority Opinion

Beyond these difficulties, which are formidable, there is the serious obstacle of overcoming or disregarding the opinions held by the majority, both among the public and among professionals. To think and act contrary to the generally accepted point of view is no easy matter. In a rampantly bullish atmosphere, such as in 1928–29 or in the early part of 1937, it takes plenty of courage to be bearish. In any case, the potential margin of error in our work is large enough to sway one's opinion easily. A view contrary to the majority is unpopular, because it goes against a trend of thought that has become embedded in the minds of investors over a long period of time as stock prices move in the same direction. This makes it doubly difficult for one to muster the courage necessary to emphasize the real necessity for a basic change in investment policy. In the spring of 1937, following several years of rising prices, I felt concerned about the outlook. I was thoroughly put on the spot when one of my associates bluntly asked if I expected a bear market. My answer was: "How can I tell? Perhaps not."—prompted in considerable part by my reluctance or fear of appearing extreme and also by an abundant realization of the inadequacy and limitations of analyzing and anticipating economic and stock market trends. I believed that a conservative policy was definitely desirable, but it was indeed difficult to "burn my bridges" and go down the line with the zip and push that would have proven desirable. The same psychological obstacles have to be overcome in the midst of rampant pessimism. A contrary view seems justified on a margin of evidence that may appear pretty slim in the light of the current developments and psychology.

Fears of Stock Decline Unjustified

During the greater part of a long period of years the fears and anxiety about stock prices declining seriously are not justified. Usually the adverse developments that cause fear do not take place, or their effect on stock prices is moderate. During the last thirty years of many serious economic and political developments when stock prices went through enormous swings, serious fears about owning common stocks have been justified only about one fifth of the time.

It would have been highly desirable to own the fewest possible stocks during the various periods of time shown in the table totaling 68 months out of the 360 months, or about 19% of the period. Those inclined to regard much smaller movements in the Dow Jones Industrial Average as of great significance might add the months from May 1940 to May 1942, when the Dow Jones Industrial Average dropped 16%, and the months from September 1946 to June 1949, when the average made about the same lows but many individual stocks declined sharply. These two periods are twilight zones when a certain amount of fear was justified but when stock prices as measured by the Dow Jones Industrial Average did not suffer a serious and prolonged decline. If these periods are included, fears of a decline in stock prices were justified only about one third of the time.

Successful Management Depends on Stability

From these considerations I draw the first observation of importance. Successful investment management depends to a large extent on the emotional stability of the individual, particularly during periods of strain and stress, and on his ability to overcome the severe psychological hurdles present during crucial periods. It depends on the ability to judge cold-bloodedly new developments in their proper framework and to recognize the significance of storm signals the relatively few times that they are really important.

Second is the problem of keeping from being lost in too many details. There is a saying that "one cannot see the forest because of the trees." This idea is applicable to every human activity, and the investment field is no exception.

A well thought out investment policy formulated in ample time can easily founder because the broad essentials are blurred by petty detail considerations. The sudden emergence of new factors not anticipated assumes an unjustified importance, timidity takes the place of courage, delay takes the place of action, and opportunity is either lost or only seized halfheartedly. The confusion resulting from emphasizing minor details at the expense of a broad perspective is equally damaging when stock prices are high or low. Unexpectedly poor earnings statements, dividend omissions, strikes, a sudden drop in activity in individual industries, and unfavorable political news are examples of details that may impair the broad perspective during periods of low prices. Similar details of a favorable character often interfere with a sound policy when prices are high.

Perhaps even more important is the tendency to place an exaggerated emphasis on minor price fluctuations in the stock market. A broad buying or selling program during periods of low or high prices is often placed in jeopardy because attention is focused on short term moves of 5 or 10 points in the Industrial Average rather than on the real job of accumulating or reducing holdings during broad buying or selling areas. There is often a widespread recognition that prices are high or low as in 1928–29, in 1932–33, and in 1938 or in 1942, but even then the primary emphasis is frequently placed on minor and short term moves.

A common experience during periods when stocks should be accumulated is to place orders considerably below the market because of the reluctance to "take the bull by the horns" and buy in a market that looks sick. The result, more often than not, is that only an insignificant amount of stock is bought and that the subsequent recovery which may be very sharp leaves one with a strong feeling of having missed the boat. This feeling may easily lead to hurried purchases at much higher prices in competition with many other buyers who have gone through the same experience. Similarly, in a high market it is only too easy to place selling orders above the market so that much less stock is sold than seems called for by subsequent events.

Dow Jones Industrial Average

Date	Closing Highs	Date	Closing Lows	Subsequent Decline Not Regarded Important	Months from Important Highs to Important Lows
Oct 1919	119	Oct 1920	69	65 (June 1921)	12
Sept 1929	381	June 1932	43	—	33
Mar 1937	194	Mar 1938	99	—	12
Sept 1939	156	May 1940	114	96 (May 1942)	8
June 1946	211	Sept 1946	164	162 (June 1949)	3
				Number of months of severe declines	68

Allowance for Margin of Error

From this I draw the second important consideration: It should be taken for granted that minor swings cannot be anticipated accurately, and allowance should be made for a considerable margin of error. When prices are high and a change of policy is indicated, emphasis should be placed on selling within an ample margin, even though prices are likely to rise further. When prices are low, emphasis should be placed on buying, with the full recognition that lower prices will probably prevail. The rise in prices when selling and the decline in prices when buying should be welcomed as desirable market conditions for the proper execution of investment policy.

There are many other problems that arise from human or psychological characteristics. It is hard to resist the temptation to buy stocks when the news is good and earnings and dividends are high and the stocks have already discounted the good news. It is equally hard to keep stocks and buy more after a drop in their prices, when the outlook seems discouraging and the stocks are undervalued. It is hard also to sell a stock at a loss when it should be done because of a change in the outlook. The tendency is to let the "losses run" and to sell the stocks with profits, rather than to cut the losses short and let the "profits run." In fact, it is curious that a feeling of apprehension or fear usually accompanies the execution of any policy that proves to be sound and profitable, whereas very often the easy and comfortable action turns out to have been a mistake.

The other main category of problems of investment management includes those concerned with analytical skill, knowledge, and experience. It is well known that good quality investment management requires long and intensive training, a high degree of skill, and long experience. Investment management has acquired the status of other professions such as those of doctors and lawyers. In the last twenty years progress toward better and more extensive research and information has been outstanding, and the results in better performance on the part of the average investor seeking advice have justified the efforts made, even though there is still ample room for further improvement.

* * * * *

In conclusion, the most difficult barrier to successful investment management is psychological in character. The fear of losing capital, when prices are low and declining, and the greed for more capital gains, when prices are high and rising, are probably, more than any other factors, responsible for a poor performance. Skill, knowledge, and experience are obviously fundamental in meeting today's problems in investment management, and a realistic approach is necessary in establishing investment policies that will be consistently successful.

CAPITAL ASSET PRICES:
A THEORY OF MARKET
EQUILIBRIUM UNDER
CONDITIONS OF RISK

William F. Sharpe

In this landmark paper, appearing some 12 years after Harry Markowitz's *Portfolio Selection* article first introduced the outline of a systematic
framework for the process of investment management, Bill Sharpe provided the crucial missing element of what was shortly to become a Modern
Portfolio Theory: namely, a compelling explanation of security pricing
under the conditions of uncertainty faced by all investment managers.
Before this paper, there was no positive descriptive answer to the question,
"What *is* the relationship between present value and future prospects, taking risk into account?" After it, there was a Capital Asset Pricing Model
(CAPM)—an insight which has significantly changed both the academic
and practitioner investment worlds.

Readers are cautioned that the portions of the original article excerpted
here omit much of the detail essential to a full comprehension and appreciation of Sharpe's breakthrough. Please refer to the original for a complete exposition of his arguments and logic.

Reprinted from *The Journal of Finance*, Vol. XIX, No. 3, September 1964, 425–442. New
York, New York: American Finance Association.

I. INTRODUCTION

One of the problems which has plagued those attempting to predict the behavior of capital markets is the absence of a body of positive micro-economic theory dealing with conditions of risk. Although many useful insights can be obtained from the traditional models of investment under conditions of certainty, the pervasive influence of risk in financial transactions has forced those working in this area to adopt models of price behavior which are little more than assertions. A typical classroom explanation of the determination of capital asset prices, for example, usually begins with a careful and relatively rigorous description of the process through which individual preferences and physical relationships interact to determine an equilibrium pure interest rate. This is generally followed by the assertion that somehow a market risk-premium is also determined, with the prices of assets adjusting accordingly to account for differences in their risks.

A useful representation of the view of the capital market implied in such discussions is illustrated in Figure 1. In equilibrium, capital asset prices have adjusted so that the investor, if he follows rational procedures (primary diversification), is able to attain any desired point along a *capital market line*.[1] He may obtain a higher expected rate of return on his holdings only by incurring additional risk. In effect, the market presents him with two prices: the *price of time*, (or the pure interest rate shown by the intersection of the line with the horizontal axis) and the *price of risk*, the additional expected return per unit of risk borne (the reciprocal of the slope of the line).

At present there is no theory describing the manner in which the price of risk results from the basic influences of investor preferences, the physical attributes of capital assets, etc. Moreover, lacking such a theory, it is difficult to give any real meaning to the relationship between the price of a single asset and its risk. Through diversification, some of the risk inherit in an asset can be avoided so that its total risk is obviously not the relevant influence on its price; unfortunately, little has been said concerning the particular risk component which is relevant.

In the last ten years a number of economists have developed *normative* models dealing with asset choice under conditions of risk. Markowitz,[2] following Von Neumann and Morgenstern, developed an analysis based on the expected utility maxim and proposed a general

FIGURE 1

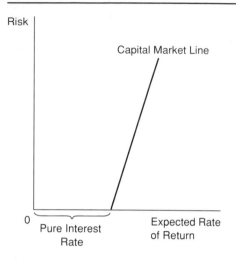

solution for the portfolio selection problem. Tobin[3] showed that under certain conditions Markowitz's model implies that the process of investment choice can be broken down into two phases: first, the choice of a unique optimum combination of risky assets, and second, a separate choice concerning the allocation of funds between such a combination and a single riskless asset. Recently, Hicks[4] has used a model similar to that proposed by Tobin to derive corresponding conclusions about individual investor behavior, dealing somewhat more explicitly with the nature of the conditions under which the process of investment choice can be dichotomized. An even more detailed discussion of this process, including a rigorous proof in the context of a choice among lotteries has been presented by Gordon and Gangolli.[5]

Although all the authors cited use virtually the same model of investor behavior,[6] none has yet attempted to extend it to construct a *market* equilibrium theory of asset prices under conditions of risk.[7] We will show that such an extension provides a theory with implications consistent with the assertions of traditional financial theory described above. Moreover, it sheds considerable light on the relationship between the price of an asset and the various components of its overall risk. For these reasons it warrants consideration as a model of the determination of capital asset prices. . . .

II. OPTIMAL INVESTMENT POLICY
FOR THE INDIVIDUAL

The Investor's Preference Function

Assume that an individual views the outcome of any investment in probabilistic terms, that is, he thinks of the possible results in terms of
some probability distribution. In assessing the desirability of a particular
investment, however, he is willing to act on the basis of only two parameters of this distribution—its expected value and standard deviation.[8]
This can be represented by a total utility function of the form:

$$U = f(E_w, \sigma_w)$$

where E_w indicates expected future wealth and σ_w the predicted standard
deviation of the possible divergence of actual future wealth from E_w.

Investors are assumed to prefer a higher expected future wealth to
a lower value, *ceteris paribus* $(dU/dE_w > 0)$. Moreover, they exhibit
risk-aversion, choosing an investment offering a lower value of σ_w to
one with a greater level, given the level of $E_w (dU/d\sigma_w < 0)$. These
assumptions imply that indifference curves relating E_w and σ_w will be
upward-sloping[9]. . . .

FIGURE 2

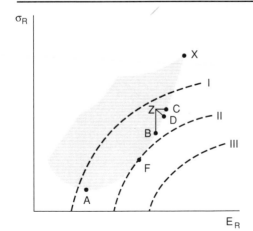

The Investment Opportunity Curve

The model of investor behavior considers the investor as choosing from a set of investment opportunities that one which maximizes his utility. Every investment plan available to him may be represented by a point in the E_R, σ_R plane. If all such plans involve some risk, the area composed of such points will have an appearance similar to that shown in Figure 2. The investor will choose from among all possible plans the one placing him on the indifference curve representing the highest level of utility (point F). The decision can be made in two stages: first, find the set of efficient investment plans and second, choose one from among this set. A plan is said to be efficient if (and only if) there is no alternative with either (1) the same E_R and a lower σ_R, (2) the same σ_R and a higher E_R or (3) a higher E_R and a lower σ_R. Thus investment Z is inefficient since investments B, C, and D (among others) dominate it. The only plans which would be chosen must lie along the lower right-hand boundary (AFBDCX)—the *investment opportunity curve*. . . .

The manner in which the investment opportunity curve is formed is relatively simple conceptually, although exact solutions are usually quite difficult.[10] One first traces curves indicating E_R, σ_R values available with simple combinations of individual assets, then considers combinations of combinations of assets. The lower right-hand boundary must be either linear or increasing at an increasing rate $(d^2\sigma_R dE_R^2 > 0)$. As suggested earlier, the complexity of the relationship between the characteristics of individual assets and the location of the investment opportunity curve makes it difficult to provide a simple rule for assessing the desirability of individual assets, since the effect of an asset on an investor's over-all investment opportunity curve depends not only on its expected rate of return (E_{Ri}) and risk (σ_{Ri}), but also on its correlations with the other available opportunities $(r_{i1}, r_{i2}, \ldots, r_{in})$. However, such a rule is implied by the equilibrium conditions for the model. . . .

III. EQUILIBRIUM IN THE CAPITAL MARKET

In order to derive conditions for equilibrium in the capital market we invoke two assumptions. First, we assume a common pure rate of interest, with all investors able to borrow or lend funds on equal terms. Second, we assume homogeneity of investor expectations:[11] investors are assumed to agree on the prospects of various investments—the expected values, standard deviations and correlation coefficients described in Part II. Needless to say, these are highly restrictive and undoubtedly unrealistic assumptions. However, since the proper test of · a theory is not the realism of its assumptions but the acceptability of its implications, and since these assumptions imply equilibrium conditions which form a major part of classical financial doctrine, it is far from clear that this formulation should be rejected—especially in view of the dearth of alternative models leading to similar results.

Under these assumptions, given some set of capital asset prices, each investor will view his alternatives in the same manner. . . .

Capital asset prices must, of course, continue to change as investors attempt to establish asset combinations until a set of prices is attained for which every asset enters at least one combination lying on the capital market line. Figure 6 illustrates such an equilibrium condition.[12] All possibilities in the shaded area can be attained with combinations of risky assets, while points lying along the line PZ can be attained by borrowing or lending at the pure rate plus an investment in some combination of risky assets. Certain possibilities (those lying along PZ from point A to point B) can be obtained in either manner. For example, the E_R, σ_R values shown by point A can be obtained solely by some combination of risky assets; alternatively, the point can be reached by a combination of lending and investing in combination C of risky assets.

It is important to recognize that in the situation shown in Figure

FIGURE 6

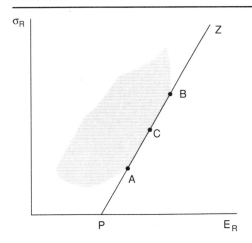

6 many alternative combinations of risky assets are efficient (i.e., lie along line PZ), and thus the theory does not imply that all investors will hold the same combination.[13] On the other hand, all such combinations must be perfectly (positively) correlated, since they lie along a linear border of the E_R, σ_R region.[14] This provides a key to the relationship between the prices of capital assets and different types of risk.

IV. THE PRICES OF CAPITAL ASSETS

We have argued that in equilibrium there will be a simple linear relationship between the unexpected return and standard deviation of return for efficient combinations of risky assets. Thus far nothing has been said about such a relationship for individual assets. Typically the E_R, σ_R values associated with single assets will lie above the capital market line, reflecting the inefficiency of undiversified holdings. Moreover, such points may be scattered throughout the feasible region, with no consistent relationship between their expected return and total risk (σ_R). However, there will be a consistent relationship between their expected returns and what might best be called *systematic risk*, as we will now show. . . .

In Figure 7 the curve *igg'* has been drawn tangent to the capital

FIGURE 7

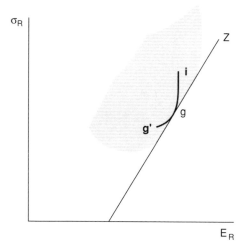

market line (PZ) at point g. This is no accident. All such curves must be tangent to the capital market line in equilibrium, since (1) they must touch it at the point representing the efficient combination and (2) they are continuous at that point.[15] Under these conditions a lack of tangency would imply that the curve intersects PZ. But then some feasible combination of assets would lie to the right of the capital market line, an obvious impossibility since the capital market line represents the efficient boundary of feasible values of E_R and σ_R.

The requirement that curves such as igg' be tangent to the capital market line can be shown to lead to a relatively simple formula which relates to the expected rate of return to various elements of risk for all assets which are included in combination g. . . . Its economic meaning can best be seen if the relationship between the return of asset i and that of combination g is viewed in a manner similar to that used in regression analysis.[16] Imagine that we were given a number of (ex post) observations of the return of the two investments. The points might plot as shown in Figure 8. The scatter of the R_i observations around their mean (which will approximate E_R) is, of course, evidence of the total risk of the asset—σ_{Ri}. But part of the scatter is due to an underlying relationship with the return on combination g shown by B_{ig}, the slope of the regression line. The response of R_i to changes in R_g (and variations in R_g itself) account for much of the variation in R_i. It

FIGURE 8

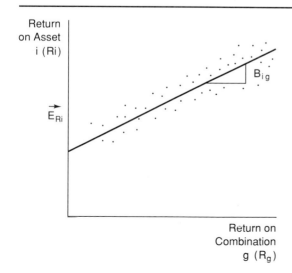

Return on Asset i (Ri)

B_{ig}

$\vec{E}_{Ri}$

Return on Combination g (R_g)

is this component of the asset's total risk which we term the *systematic* risk. The remainder, [17] being correlated with R_g, is the unsystematic component. This formulation of the relationship between R_i and R_g can be employed *ex ante* as a predictive model. B_{ig} becomes the *predicted* response of R_i to changes in R_g. Then, given σR_g (the predicted risk of R_g), the systematic portion of the predicted risk of each asset can be determined.

This interpretation allows us to state the relationship derived from the tangency of curves such as *igg′* with the capital market line in the form shown in Figure 9. All assets entering efficient combination *g* must have (predicted) B_{ig} and E_{Ri} values lying on the line *PQ*. . . . Prices will adjust so that assets which are more responsive to changes in R_g will have higher expected returns than those which are less responsive. This accords with common sense. Obviously the part of an asset's risk which is due to its correlation with the return on a combination cannot be diversified away when the asset is added to the combination. Since B_{ig} indicates the magnitude of the type of risk it should be directly related to expected return.

The relationship illustrated in Figure 9 provides a partial answer to the question posed earlier concerning the relationship between an asset's risk and its expected return. But thus far we have argued only that the relationship holds for the assets which enter some particular efficient

FIGURE 9

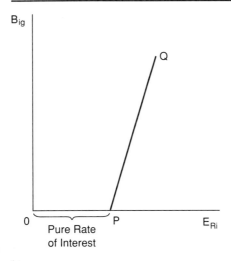

combination (*g*). Had another combination been selected, a different linear relationship would have been derived. Fortunately this limitation is easily overcome. . . . [W]e may arbitrarily select *any* one of the efficient combinations, then measure the predicted responsiveness of *every* asset's rate of return to that of the combination selected; and these coefficients will be related to the expected rates of return of the assets in exactly the manner pictured in Figure 9.

The fact that rates of return from all efficient combinations will be perfectly correlated provides the justification for arbitrarily selecting any one of them. Alternatively we may choose instead any variable perfectly correlated with the rate of return of such combinations. The vertical axis in Figure 9 would then indicate alternative levels of a coefficient measuring the sensitivity of the rate of return of a capital asset to changes in the variable chosen.

This possibility suggests both a plausible explanation for the implication that all efficient combinations will be perfectly correlated and a useful interpretation of the relationship between an individual asset's expected return and its risk. Although the theory itself implies only that rates of return from efficient combinations will be perfectly correlated, we might expect that this would be due to their common dependence on the over-all level of economic activity. If so, diversification enables the investor to escape all but the risk resulting from swings in economic activity—this type of risk remains even in efficient combinations. And, since all other types can be avoided by diversification, only the responsiveness of an asset's rate of return to the level of economic activity is relevant in assessing its risk. Prices will adjust until there is a linear relationship between the magnitude of such responsiveness and expected return. Assets which are unaffected by changes in economic activity will return the pure interest rate; those which move with economic activity will promise appropriately higher expected rates of return.

This discussion provides an answer to the second of the two questions posed in this paper. In Part III it was shown that with respect to equilibrium conditions in the capital market as a whole, the theory leads to results consistent with classical doctrine (i.e., the capital market line). We have not shown that with regard to capital assets considered individually, it also yields implications consistent with traditional concepts: it is common practice for investment counselors to accept a lower expected return from defensive securities (those which respond little to changes in the economy) than they require from aggressive securities (which exhibit significant response). As suggested earlier, the familiarity of the implications need not be considered a drawback. The provision of a logical framework for producing some of the major elements of traditional financial theory should be a useful contribution in its own right.

FOOTNOTES

1. Although some discussions are also consistent with a non-linear (but monotonic) curve.

2. Harry M. Markowitz, *Portfolio Selection, Efficient Diversification of Investments* (New York: John Wiley & Sons, Inc., 1959). The major elements of the theory first appeared in his article "Portfolio Selection," *The Journal of Finance*, XII (March 1952), 77–91.

3. James Tobin, "Liquidity Preference as Behavior Towards Risk," *The Review of Economic Studies*, XXV (February 1958), 65–86.

4. John R. Hicks, "Liquidity," *The Economic Journal*, LXXII (December 1962), 787–802.

5. M. J. Gordon and Ramesh Gangolli, "Choice Among the Scale of Play on Lottery Type Alternatives," College of Business Administration, University of Rochester, 1962. For another discussion of this relationship see W. F. Sharpe, "A Simplified Model for Portfolio Analysis," *Management Science*, Vol. 9, No. 2 (January 1963), 277–293. A related discussion can be found in F. Modigliani and M. H. Miller, "The Cost of Capital, Corporation Finance, and the Theory of Investment," *The American Economic Review*, XLVIII (June 1958), 261–297.

6. Recently Hirshleifer has suggested that the mean-variance approach used in the articles cited is best regarded as a special case of a more general formulation due to Arrow. See Hirshleifer's "Investment Decision Under Uncertainty," *Papers and Proceedings of the Seventy-Sixth Annual Meeting of the American Economic Association*, Dec. 1963, or Arrow's "Le Role des Valeurs Boursières pour la Répartition la Meilleure des Risques," *International Colloquium on Econometrics*, 1952.

7. After preparing this paper, the author learned that Mr. Jack L. Treynor, of Arthur D. Little, Inc., had independently developed a model similar in many respects to the one described here. Unfortunately Mr. Treynor's excellent work on this subject is, at present, unpublished.

8. Under certain conditions the mean-variance approach can be shown to lead to unsatisfactory predictions of behavior. Markowitz suggests that a model based on the semi-variance (the average of the squared deviations below the mean) would be preferable; in light of the formidable computational

problems, however, he bases his analysis on the variance and standard deviation.

9. While only these characteristics are required for the analyses, it is generally assumed that the curves have the property of diminishing marginal rates of substitution between E_W and σ_W, as do those in our diagrams.

10. Markowitz has shown that this is a problem in parametric quadratic programming. An efficient solution technique is described in his article, "The Optimization of a Quadratic Function Subject to Linear Constraints," *Naval Research Logistics Quarterly*, Vol. 3 (March and June 1956), 111–133. A solution method for a special case is given in the author's "A Simplified Model for Portfolio Analysis," *op. cit.*

11. A term suggested by one of the referees.

12. The area in Figure 6 representing E_R, σ_R values attained with only risky assets has been drawn at some distance from the horizontal axis for emphasis. It is likely that a more accurate representation would place it very close to the axis.

13. This statement contradicts Tobin's conclusion that there will be a unique optimal combination of risky assets. Tobin's proof of a unique optimum can be shown to be incorrect for the case of perfect correlation of efficient risky investment plans if the line connecting their E_R, σ_R points would pass through point P. In the graph on page 83 of this article (*op. cit.*) the constant-risk locus would, in this case, degenerate from a family of ellipses into one straight line parallel to the constant-return loci, thus giving multiple optima.

14. E_R, σ_R values given by combinations of any two combinations must lie within the region and cannot plot above a straight line joining the points. In this case they cannot plot below such a straight line. But since only in the case of perfect correlation they will plot along a straight line, the two combinations must be perfectly correlated. As shown in Part IV, this does not necessarily imply that the individual securities they contain are perfectly correlated.

15. Only if $r_{ig} = -1$ will the curve be discontinuous over the range in question.

16. This model has been called the diagonal model since its portfolio analysis solution can be facilitated by re-arranging the data so that the variance-covariance matrix becomes diagonal. The method is described in the author's article, cited earlier.

17. ex post, the standard error.

INVESTMENT REPORT: THE UNIVERSITY OF ROCHESTER

H. W. Tripp

H.W. "Burt" Tripp was financial Vice President and Investment Manager for the University of Rochester for many years and was responsible for much of the extraordinary investment success enjoyed by that university's endowment. Here he is reporting on 1962, an unusually difficult year for growth stock investors.

For the first time in years there is little need for an historical summary of the year just ended. The events were so dramatic that all of us can recall them only too vividly. However, for the sake of continuity of the record, it is perhaps advisable to recall some of the economic pattern of 1962. We started the year with a sense of confidence. After all, we were just coming out of the recession and on the way up in an economic sense. The stocks as measured by the Dow-Jones Industrial Average opened the year at 731.14, close to the all-time high of 734.91 recorded in December 1961. Then came the steel fiasco, an affair handled badly by both sides. The overexuberant psychology of the past was soon replaced by a growing lack of confidence in the relationship between industry and the Administration. After that, "Black Monday," and by the latter part of June the Dow-Jones Industrial Average had declined almost 200

From H.W. Tripp, *Investment Report: The University of Rochester* (Rochester, New York, 1963), 1–5, by permission of The University of Rochester.

points, or 27%. It was then that many recalled that the stock market had frequently acted as a barometer in the past, a forecaster of business. In the months following Black Monday, the New Frontier stood ready with guns loaded, ready with promises of a tax reduction aimed not at that time as a reform measure to stimulate growth but to prop up an economy which the stock market had told us was about to crash.

Later some economic calm prevailed. It became evident that institutional investors had not been heavy sellers during the panic days. Stocks in general had moved from weak hands to strong hands although even the professionals will admit that some of the strong hands were a bit shaky and perhaps lacking the strength to withstand what was coming next—the Cuban Crisis. After the crisis, the psychology changed and a sense of growing confidence was evident. At long last the United States had acted decisively. In business circles there developed a sense of hope that the Administration was not really antagonistic to business. Perhaps, as Washington spokesmen have so frequently stated, the Administration agrees that profits are essential to our economic system.

It is pertinent to recall the words of General Douglas MacArthur: "There is no such thing as security, there is only opportunity." With all of the uncertainties in 1962, many opportunities were presented in the investment markets. Events moved swiftly and in order to take advantage of these opportunities it was necessary to act decisively and courageously and at times, as President Kennedy would say, "with vigor."

In the recent past we have particularly emphasized that stocks were selling historically high in relation to earnings but that some of these prices were partially justified because of the improvement in the quality of earnings in the post-war years through growth of research, higher depreciation, a sophisticated Federal fiscal policy leading to greater economic stability, etc., etc.

Despite this improvement in the quality of earnings it is freely admitted that many common stocks were overpriced at the end of 1961. But some stocks were more overpriced than others. The growth-stock label had been freely assigned in too many instances. The near-panic conditions in May and June reflected a drastic revision of investment thinking. It seemed at times that the good and bad suffered alike. Stocks of some companies possessing strong growth characteristics sold at about the same price-earnings multiple as stocks of companies with rather dull, unimpressive prospects. Many opportunities for improving the portfolio were presented. In looking back one always wishes that more had been done. But at least we made many important constructive changes which should improve the investment list both market-wise and in an income sense.

It is becoming increasingly difficult to identify valid growth companies. In making such selections in the past the investor was aided by a background of a high post-war replacement demand, the Korean War, the economic rehabilitation of Europe, and a strong inflationary psychology. The problem of selecting growth stocks lies less in the mathematics than in the soundness of judgment used to project the growth rates. Sound judgment in turn must be based on imaginative and penetrating analysis. Although we are confident that the investment changes of the past year have strengthened our portfolio, we also recognize that the performance of some of the stocks may not live up to our expectations. We shall attempt to be alert to changing conditions and new opportunities. . . . This is the first time in fifteen years that it has been necessary to report a yearly decline in value. Perhaps the decline in market value is less than some might have expected since we have long emphasized growth stocks and quite a few market analysts state that these stocks as a class have suffered the most. On the other hand, it is gratifying to note that during 1962, forty-one of the fifty common stocks held at the year-end increased dividends. If this trend can continue we will take some satisfaction in our selection process.

* * * * *

Chart No. 1 shows the diversification of investment in general categories over the past twenty-one years. The term *Equity Fund* re quires some explanation. This fund is usually invested in somewhat special and non-seasoned securities not necessarily suitable for the regular endowment fund investments. Funds originally used to establish this fund were obtained from profits taken on securities. A study of the diversification chart will show that the percentage of common stocks held at the year-end actually increased slightly. During the year we sold common stocks with a value of $5,900,000 and purchased stocks valued at close to $12,000,000. A greater part of the funds necessary for these additional purchases came from the liquidation of bonds. We would like to be able to report that your investment officers had been astute enough to accomplish all of the sales before May 28th and the purchases subsequent to that date. Actually up to May 15th we had sold

CHART 1
Percentage Diversification of Investments at Market Value

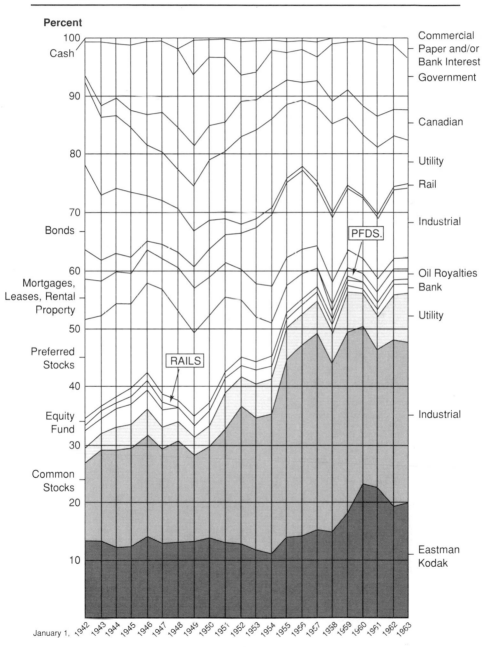

around $4,000,000 of stocks and purchased an equal amount of other stocks. After that we were heavier on the purchase side as weakness developed.

In the report submitted last year we emphasized that it was fallacious to assume that market value of a security account increased in value automatically. This thinking had become prevalent in some quarters in the post-war period. When we stated last year, "the market value of any account is subject to frequent and drastic change," we did not realize that events of 1962 would confirm this statement so dramatically. . . .While the market value of. . .[the University's] funds ended the year close to $200,000,000, or less than 4% below the all-time peak recorded January 1, 1962, at one time during 1962 the value of investments fell to $175,000,000. . . .

COORDINATING INFORMATION

Arthur Zeikel

Arthur Zeikel's writing ranges from textbook authorship to humor. Here, he applies keen insight to a problem common to all investment organizations and their people.

Proper research technique feeds upon itself, constantly improving the information flow, widening good contact relationships, improving the risk-gain relationship of portfolio decisions and, in the final analysis, creating better performance.

Scope

An efficient information system will enable analysts to detect changes among critical factors affecting an industry, group or individual company as soon as possible.

To work properly, the system must co-ordinate statistical material, library coverage, Wall Street contacts, direct industry, trade association, agency and company relationships and will include special purpose analytical techniques designed for internal use.

Information presented in a meaningful form will then be suscep-

Reprinted from *The Financial Analysts Journal*, Vol. 25, No. 2, March/April 1969, 119–123. New York, New York: Financial Analysts Federation.

tible to analysis and interpretation, thereby facilitating the comparison between new developments and original research conclusions and investment expectations.

Critical Factors

Every industry, company, and economic sector responds to a different set of business phenomena, forces and critical factors. Any sound analytical approach requires that these factors be identified, isolated and followed on a consistent basis.

Change in these elements alters the profits outlook and immediately affects investment expectations. Consequently, stock price movements will mirror these new developments long before it is generally recognized that they have taken place. Every effort must be made to interpret change swiftly and accurately. In today's market environment, the life cycle of a "new idea" is very brief, often as short as the first telephone call.

Early warning signals calling attention to a possible change may take the form of a new trend in a significant statistical indicator or a shift in the attitude of industry participants close to the point of critical action.

Critical factors are not limited to cyclical considerations nor confined to short term movements, but include slower moving basic trend changes, social and environmental developments as well as internal corporate adjustments, the adoption of new management techniques, new product introductions, changes in market share, etc.

Whatever, it is obvious the ability to recognize that a turn has occurred stems from an understanding of the fundamentals of a business and not from the gathering of functional information.

Critical factors may change over time. It is therefore necessary to constantly review a business, industry or company in terms of its customers, their needs, requirements and desires. In the long run, it is the customer who creates the business and determines its fortune.

A Special Problem

In a large fund, the element of anticipation becomes all the more paramount. Size requirements often prohibit effective action after the fact, unless the "trigger" event is signaling a major, long term trend change. Usually, however, relatively large positions must be established during the period which sets the stage for an improved operating atmosphere.

By the same token, liquidation of successful commitments must also be undertaken before the evident favorable pattern shifts—else, when demand for the issue fades, the holding develops a strong tendency to become illiquid—both emotionally and mechanically. One rarely makes the top, and then generally by accident. It's no crime to leave the buyer an opportunity to profit.

Comments on Research Technique

The responsibility of an analyst is to understand, evaluate and as much as possible, anticipate change—not collect information.

> I keep six honest serving men,
> They taught me all I knew,
> Their names are what and why and when,
> And how and where and who.
>
> –Kipling.

INVESTMENT MANAGEMENT

Effective research starts with intuitive opinions, not facts. To get the facts first is impossible.

Research can be an inefficient process; one cannot usually predict which piece of new information, fresh idea or original thought will prove productive. The object of fact finding is to narrow down the areas of uncertainty. Sound technique requires skill in excluding the unnecessary and, as quickly as possible, making some guess as to the unknown.

Therefore, the search is to ascertain those few elements which account for the greatest part of the situation—or perhaps, more severely, to isolate the one factor upon which the decision may turn. One must conquer the urge to learn everything about some new development or unexpected turn of events. A sharp distinction must be constantly made between facts needed to form a foundation for new action and those which will merely keep one more generally informed.

True effectiveness has little to do with how much "work" is actually done—but only whether a man does what is really important—and then does it well. Do first things first—and second things not at all. The alternative is to get nothing done!

In essence then one should not go more deeply into the facts than is profitable:

Knowledge Curve–Risk/Gain Possibilities

Assuming at the start nothing is known about a problem or a new question presents itself: A critical factor appears to have changed.

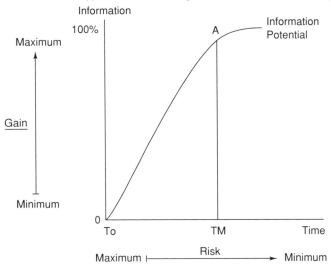

Properties of the Curve

The direction of the curve changes at point A. Up to this point, the curve rises at an increasing rate. After the point the curve increases at a diminishing rate.

What does this mean?

1. Large amounts of information can be gathered quickly; knowledge accumulates rapidly during the early stages of a research investigation.

2. The research process should not continue beyond the point when the time spent learning new facts becomes uneconomic. Beyond this point, the incremental time spent on additional research does not provide the same increment in terms of new knowledge.

New information subsequently gathered will very infrequently alter the decision already made.

3. 100% information can never be obtained no matter how much time is spent on the project.

Therefore, the goal is to make the decision as early as possible, provided the critical elements have been ascertained.

As an aside, one must realize that progress in problem solving may not be linear, and the fact-finding thinking-through process can result in temporary log jams along the road to final conclusion. This "incubation" period often requires laying the problem aside for some brief period, which then allows for the formulation of a fresh perspective. This seemingly non-productive effort should not be confused with inefficiency, as creative minds frequently require furlough from concentrated thought to be most effective.

Risk/Gain

Of greater importance, the risk/gain relationship covering portfolio action follows a similar path, and the same rules apply. As the circle of appreciation regarding a change widens, benefits from portfolio maneuvering begin to shift—with the risks increasing and the reward possibilities diminishing.

Consequently, the more time consumed in researching a project or new development, the more assured one is of the conclusions reached, the more positive one is on the course of action indicated, the less risk involved in making a poor decision—the *less profit potential inherent in the move*.

Conversely, the greater the risk in making the decision, the greater the profit potential.

With the potential derived from recognizing a change in momentum diminishing with time, it is vital that reaction to new developments be prompt and the attendant research effort concise. The desire for speed, however, is no excuse for a sloppy research. Therefore, the question of additional research must represent a balance between the fact-finding time needed to ascertain the critical elements at work and the necessity of coming to a conclusion early enough to produce a favorable risk/gain relationship, remembering, of course, that our task is not to eliminate risk but to maximize opportunities.

Fact-Finding

As to fact-finding, we must be inquisitive, taking nothing for granted, and develop initiative in gathering new information, because facts are incontrovertible—opinions are open for discussion.

Specialization is a convenience and not a virtue. It allows, among other things, the use of many talents to accomplish portfolio goals. Keep in mind that sound technique is transferable while specific information has limited application. It is not in our best interests to develop a high degree of internal technical specialization nor to operate within narrow areas of interest. We should, however, at every opportunity utilize those talents which are abundantly available in outside organizations, being careful to avoid the easy and dangerous habit of relying too heavily on the reporting of Wall Street analysts as the basis for original information. By their very nature, most analysts feel more comfortable reporting, rather than interpreting new developments; the effort and knowledge required are obviously less. Furthermore, the news is often late and usually repetitious.

It is therefore incumbent upon the staff to develop, maintain and use original contacts, people at or close to the point where the vital changes will be taking place. As to these independent information sources, friendship and personal relationships may be useful, but should not be allowed to interfere with objective fact gathering.

- Get out of the office. Visit companies, but stay away from the conventional street contacts. Check with top management to get doors open to the people most others don't get to see. Aim yourself at the heads of divisions, Research, Marketing, Sales, Production, etc. Talk to top people about their suppliers, customers and competition.
- Approach the counterpart to the subject company. Give an ear to the sub-contractor, or the raw materials supplier, or the salesman trying to unload the end product. Don't ignore the little man with the private company in the same business. He can tell you more about prices, inventories and sales than anyone else.
- *Don't limit your inquisitiveness.* Contact advertising agencies,

consultants, industry and government associations. These people usually like to talk and make known all kinds of figures. Getting acquainted with union officials isn't such a bad idea, either. Some of them give you a mouthful—once you get to know them.

- Let's not forget the reporters and editors of all the various publications. They are constantly ferreting out all kinds of tidbits for the next issue.

Emphasis must also be placed on a better utilization of available printed material. There are various, and sometimes many, publications in each industry which, if read and interpreted correctly, yield accurate accounts of industry and company developments. Many of these are probably on current library mailing lists. Insufficient use is being made of them.

Above all, keep in mind that a rising flood of written reports usually documents the end of a move, not the beginning.

Price-Earnings

Price-earning ratios are a game people play. They are not a common denominator for investment analysis or portfolio decisions. It is axiomatic that a price-earnings ratio is based on two elements—price and earnings. The price of a stock can be accurately measured, without debate, at any given time. Earnings estimates, on the other hand, are quite a different matter. Experience teaches us that earnings estimates, especially those of a longer range nature, are not particularly reliable. This is not because management will not yield the necessary information for an accurate forecast, nor because they lack the understanding of their own business. Rather, it is because earnings are the end product, the net result, the residual element of a myriad of inter-woven forces. What then is the real meaning of a price-earnings ratio?

In a sense, a price-earnings ratio measures how widely recognized— among the broad investment spectrum—are the latest expectations governing a particular company, group of similarly related stock, or the market as a whole. It also indicates the relative price leverage which will be experienced if these expectations do not materialize.

The obvious deserves some comment. It is more likely to see a favorable change develop when stocks are out of favor, earnings are depressed, price-earnings relationships are relatively low, expectations are limited, and there is no real general interest in the particular industry or stock area. The flow of written research material at this point is usually nil.

On the other hand, negative developments tend to occur when expectations are generally high, stock prices are advancing or have advanced rapidly, price-earnings ratios have been inflated and the industry or issue continues to gain new investment acceptance on an accelerated basis. Put another way, the odds seem to favor that high price-earnings stocks suffer from unexpected adverse developments and low price-earnings stocks from favorable surprises.

It is not the low multiple by itself which provides unusual opportunity nor the high evaluations that carry excessive risk. But rather that the level of investment anticipations are low on one side and high on the other. This implies that the impact of the unexpected on stock prices is obviously greater on the up side when the p/e is low, [and] greater on the down side when the p/e is high, because the balance of sentiment expects trends clearly visible to continue. New investment decisions are made, and justifiably so, when these patterns do not develop.

Which all gets back to the original point. Earnings estimates do not change in a vacuum—something happens first. It is to discover that something to which the research effort must be directed; because expansion and contraction of "price-earnings" appraisals reflects the sociology of stock ownership—following the movement of new information and its proper interpretation from the intelligent, well informed and understanding sophisticated segments, who act quickly, to the lesser informed, slower moving elements at the other end of the spectrum.

Several Recent Illustrations Come to Mind

Earlier in 1967, Westinghouse—trading between 45 and 50—did not have a friend in the world. It was considered dull, uninteresting and generally over-valued on a "price-earnings" basis.

For the previous months, the company's nuclear equipment backlog had been building steadily, new orders had been announced as received and the relative competitive position with G.E. (in this area) improved. Government and trade sources followed developments with meticulous detail. In fact, on March 15, 1967 *The Wall Street Journal* carried a feature article entitled, "Electric Utilities Order Power Plants at Record Pace, Face Six-Year Lead Time." *The New York Times*, on Sunday, July 23, 1967 provided complete statistical coverage on the situation. The article clearly pointed out, after the facts were generally well known, that Westinghouse in the first half of 1967 obtained 44% of the total nuclear business compared to 20% for all of 1966. The article also noted that new orders for the first half of this year were double the full 1966 figure.

Late in the year, with the stock up more than 40% and difficult to buy in any meaningful size, numerous reports were written calling attention to the issue as an attractive "nuclear play" based on the *unexpected* surge in nuclear plant power orders. Did anyone check with the utilities as to the equipment requirements and spending plans?

Immediately after the flood of written recommendations peaked, the stock had a sharp reaction—moving from the mid 80's to the low 60's. Not one of the authors, nor their representatives, called the turn, and neither did we. But, two very significant developments took place. One, new orders for nuclear generating equipment by the public utilities virtually stopped. The industry had stretched the delivery schedule out as far, if not further, than desirable. The trend had clearly changed.

Perhaps of equal importance, both Westinghouse and G.E. were outbid for what amounted to the industry's largest order for turbine generating equipment by a foreign company; despite the protection of a 15% import duty on the equipment. In addition to losing the sale, it clearly indicated that their competitive position in this area, which is very important to Westinghouse, had deteriorated and Brown, Boveri would now be able to develop significant market penetration at their expense.

Xerox's second quarter 1967 report is another good case in point. Results were less than expected, earnings estimates for the year (and next) were revised downward, the stock became over-priced, the price-earnings ratio suddenly became too high. And the stock went down.

If good thinking had previously decided that per unit copy usage is a critical factor in determining profits, and sound research technique had developed a method of sampling customer usage, one would not have been surprised after the fact, but would have been aware of what was actually happening. All of the reports which flowed in measured the price-earnings ratio; few mentioned usage.

Boeing, during late 1966 and through the middle of 1967, was essentially a play on the rapid backlog buildup for the new 747. Detailed coverage of every new order was reported in *The Seattle Times*, which has two full time reporters covering company developments. The stock stopped going up when additional new orders ceased to develop, and, when the concept of the "air-bus" actually became a reality, its implications were not immediately obvious. Parenthetically, earnings estimates were highest and the price-earnings ratio considered attractively low when the stock topped out.

Since then, the problem of airline overcapacity has plagued the issue, the backlog of commercial business has declined, and earnings estimates continue to be cut back as the stock sinks lower. Solution of the overcapacity problem will no doubt result in an upmove of the stock, long before analysts have had the chance to again revise earnings expectations.

Advancing lumber prices had essentially the same impact on Weyerhaeuser, which was considered very vulnerable on a price-earnings consideration late in 1966 and early in 1967. Since then, the stock has been an outstanding performer, primarily reflecting higher lumber realizations along with the market's enthusiasm for building issues. The company's first half results were well above any previous expectations. Once wood prices began to move, all the lengthy critical analysis of management's inabilities contained in our files became superfluous.

By the same token, current anticipations for future earnings growth are very high, predicated on continuation of high product prices. Lumber realizations may continue to advance, but the key to the stock will be found faster in trade publications, which carefully follow new developments, and not in the appraisal of price times estimated earnings.

A Few Fast Ones:

Control Data began acting like its old self late in 1966 and more notably in early 1967. By late March the stock had better than doubled the 1966 low. On March 20th—CDA 57—*The Wall Street Journal* carried an article documenting IBM's withdrawal from the large-scale, computer market, CDA's primary area of interest.

The stock subsequently tripled before having a setback of any serious dimension. While we were previously ignorant of this pending change, and unfortunately became overly concerned about its impact on IBM, the article noted that "Model 90 has repeatedly been rumored to be on the verge of disappearing from the line. . . ."

General Foods is one of the most diversified producers and distributors of food products in the world; but coffee items account for some 35 to 40% of total sales and probably a much higher share of profits. In the spring of 1968, after two years of extensive development and test marketing efforts, the company began going national with its new "revolutionary" coffee product, "Maxim," with outstanding results. This high priced item not only replaced some lower revenue yielding GF volume, but absorbed significant additional market share. Expenses connected with this effort had been retarding profits for some time.

Chemical stocks in the current period may prove another interesting example. Most analysts view the recent impressive market action with suspicion and question its viability. These views must be contrasted with observations which have been popping up in various trade publications over the past few weeks; of which the following is rather typical:

> . . .[T]he recent slower growth in chemical capacity combined with resurging chemical demand that is already under way should help stiffen the price situation in coming months.

Should the latter view prevail, the impact on incremental profits will be very significant.

The list is endless.

All this is not to suggest that earnings expectations, absolute or relative, are not valid bases for portfolio maneuver. However, it is not the price-earnings ratio in and of itself which causes stock to move up and down. It is rather a new set of dynamics at work, which results in "unexpected" market moves. The point of effective research is that these moves should not be "unexpected" at all.

Be Polite: Use Your Imagination

Do not waste your time on the obvious, duplicating work readily available from outside sources. Use the incoming material as a starting point for further analysis. Better still, start from your own vantage point and forget what other analysts are saying about price-earnings ratios. Whatever you do, do not spend time arguing that your point of view is right and theirs is wrong. One, they may be right. Two, it is not our function to educate those trying to provide service. Let them go to school on someone else's time.

This does not, however, imply that we should present a superior, arrogant or "all-knowing" attitude. On the contrary, the staff must make every effort to maintain an easy, appreciative and open-minded posture towards those who are conscientiously attempting to provide much needed and current information.

Broker-research contacts will often call with information already in your hands. Resist the temptation to treat these occasions in an off-handed fashion. The institutional analyst who cannot listen properly will inevitably alienate important outside contacts. Human understanding is a more important part of any relationship, and those who are receptive to new thought and easy to talk to will invariably get called first. Never let the size of our account, or the fact that we are buyers and they are sellers, go to your head. If you do, you run the obvious risk that these people will not call when they really do have something of vital value to offer.

There is more involved here than discretion and good taste—which by themselves ought to be sufficient. The proper attitude will also improve the utilization of outside research capability. In view of our needs, time pressure, and limited staff—the information exchange, like the work load, should be more or less restricted to critical new developments, supplemented by whatever additional facts are needed to document the point.

Mistakes are inherent to the business and cannot—in all honesty—be avoided. However, intelligent dedication to seeking the right questions, learning from past errors—which are often the result of judgment and not the lack of necessary information—and attempting to put change quickly into its proper perspective will significantly reduce the ratio.

In the final analysis, success is not as much a function of intelligence and ability but of personal guts—to what extent are you willing to back your own judgment, especially if it means going against the crowd.

PART 4

THE 1970s

A SPECIAL STORY

Barton M. Biggs

Barton Biggs has earned an impressive reputation among investment professionals for his wit, original thinking, and his ability to engage his many readers in the merry pursuit of ideas and reflection. Here he tells us a delightful tale.

I'm not asking, much less expecting, anyone to believe Reilly's story. It's the old magic slipper, fountain of youth thing; everybody dreams about its happening to him, but nobody really thinks it could happen, not in cold, hard daylight, in malignant New York City on that wretched Wall Street where even Cinderella or Ralph Nader would get a margin call. But it did, and Reilly told me the story.

I wouldn't say I was really a friend of Reilly's, never saw him socially or anything like that, but we had that peculiar intimacy of two guys in the same business who spent a lot of dead time together, in our case waiting on the Port Chester station platform. I can see him the way he used to be before it happened, struggling up that long flight of pock-marked cement steps to the platform, a big, beefy middle-aged man, faintly disheveled in a dark, unpressed topcoat, the shoes spotted. The face was good—strong, sturdy features arranged honestly—but the eyes, the eyes had been shot away like a long time ago and now there was nobody home most of the time.

Reprinted from *Institutional Investor*, Vol. V, No. 7, July 1971, 32–35, 64, 66–70, 72, 74, 76. New York, New York: Institutional Investor.

Those mornings Reilly moved gently, as if he had a headache, maybe a mild hangover, which was not an overwhelming surprise to anyone who had a conception of his daily martini consumption. "Got that burned-out feeling," he would say, "damn business." Now Reilly was an institutional salesman, an occupation which makes some unusual spiritual demands on one's soul (in other words, you've got to take a lot of crap), but Reilly drank two martinis at lunch, two on the train coming home, and at least two more with the "old lady" (as he called her), not for business but to "dull the pain."

He never defined to me what particular pain he was trying to assuage, but I had a pretty good idea it was related to what the industrial psychologists call "job satisfaction." George Reilly had been in institutional sales for Hudson & Company for a long time. He covered 30 of the big New York institutional accounts, and he used most of the buzz words, but none of them ever seemed to sing for him. Even 1968 and 1969 hadn't been big years for him, and now he made $20,000 a year and had to scratch for every share of it. What with negotiated commissions, the institutional business consolidating, and lots of salesmen he knew looking hard and long for jobs, he sometimes found himself awake in the night worrying about his production. Sure, he knew the big guys like Johnstone, Black and Davis, but they disdained him as a hack from a crummy wire house with third-rate research.

In fact, a good part of the time he was lucky if he even got past their dulcet-voiced secretaries or some junior analyst. The fund managers themselves were inaccessible and arrogant when they were doing well and soreheads and grouches when they were running bad. But Reilly always claimed Rhinelander of the Pinnacle Fund was the worst. Back in 1967 Pinnacle had the best record of any fund in the country, but a lot of guys said that in 1967 any maniac who would buy junk fast could make money big, and that Rhinelander wasn't really that smart, he just bought the junk faster and more indiscriminately.

Anyway, Reilly would call, and if the secretary remembered the Christmas chocolates and if the great man was in a condescending mood and had nothing better to do, Reilly would get a chance to tell him his latest stock story. And through it all, Rhinelander wouldn't say anything. Absolutely nothing. Most guys would at least kibitz or say "yeah, yeah" even if they couldn't have cared less. Not Rhinelander. He gave no playback at all; it was like talking to yourself in a vacuum. It left you feeling stupid and emasculated, but Reilly had to do it because Pinnacle gave him a little business.

Of course, the quick, young fund analysts he sometimes got shunted off on were just as bad. They acted like they already knew everything he told them and asked him obtuse Business School questions he couldn't answer as they shredded his story.

Actually, I'm pretty sure that after the fourth martini on Friday night, sitting with that white haze around him, his eyes not focusing on the blaring television, Reilly would admit to himself that the money managers and their analysts basically didn't want to hear his stories, didn't care what stocks he liked, and only bothered to listen at all because of that compulsive, gnawing money manager fear of missing something.

They thought he was just a big, dumb salesman, a loser, and he didn't blame them. Somehow he was always wrong on the market, and his stocks invariably died horrible deaths. They never failed to have something go wrong—wildcat strike, antitrust suit, unexpectedly bad earnings, or maybe the president suddenly dies. Something awful always happened.

So when Reilly bought his *Wall Street Journal* in the crush of men in the smoky, crowded Port Chester station house, it was without enthusiasm or anticipation. Some guys seem literally to devour the *Journal*; to them it is crisp and full of hope and money-making messages, but to Reilly reading it was a task, a dogged ritual of superficial scanning—all the time knowing he should be more thorough but almost not caring.

Up to now I've just been building the background and at this point the story of Reilly and *The Wall Street Journal* really begins, and I'll tell it as he told it to me that day, propped up with an oxygen tent behind him in the hospital.

Anyway, this particular morning in February, Reilly got on the usual train that looked as bedraggled as he felt and glanced at the *Journal* in his normal, desultory, distracted fashion. He read carefully only the front page, looked up a few stocks he owned, and scanned the most active list. Then he tried half-heartedly to read several new Hudson research reports on IBM and GE but instead dozed the rest of the way to New York. He usually left his *Journal* on the train, but this particular morning in his stupor, he found he still had it and stuffed it into a trash can in the station.

On the dingy subway he listened idly as two sideburned, modishly dressed young men chattered about the previous day's market.

"Fidelity must have been the seller of that 400,000-share block of GE."

"Yeah, no one else who has that much stock would dump it so hard. Most active stock and down three."

Reilly recalled seeing the block print. Something jogged his memory now. Strange, he distinctly remembered reading in the *Journal* this morning that Control Data had been the most active stock and was up 4 to 80. The company's third-quarter earnings had been in the *Journal* and had been surprisingly good. GE had been about sixth on the list and was up 1½. Odd! He'd check on it when he got to the office.

That morning he was busy with the usual trivia of phone calls, relaying the block list, tracing down a lost certificate, and getting some confirmations corrected. About noon he got an order to buy 3,000 Control Data from the Converse Fund. The stock was trading around 76 and he had bought 1,500 shares when the earnings for the third quarter came on the broad tape. Since they'd been in the *Journal* that morning, he didn't bother to flash Jack Smiley, the trader at Converse.

Abruptly Control Data began to run. The stock printed at 76 ¾, a 1,000 at 77¼, 300 at 77½, a string of singles at 78 and then 3,000 shares at 79. Smiley was on the phone now.

"Did you buy that last 1,500?"

"No, I didn't, Jack. The stock's jumped to 79 here in the last few minutes and you said to buy it around 76."

"Goddamn it, Reilly, that was before they reported third-quarter earnings up 35 per cent instead of the 10 per cent the Street was looking for. Did you see them? Why didn't you flash me?"

"I saw the earnings on the tape, Jack. I didn't flash you because they were in the *Journal* this morning."

"You're crazy, Reilly. They were not. Why do you think the stock's been running wild in the last ten minutes?"

"I'm sure I saw them in my *Journal* this morning."

"Get on the ball, Reilly. You don't know what you're talking about. What's the market in Control now?"

Reilly punched his Quotron. "79½—80. Last sale 80."

"Great, just great. The portfolio manager's all over my ass on these executions. You hacked this one bad. Cancel the damn order."

Shaken, Reilly lit a cigarette and picked up the *Journal* on the next desk. He turned to the earnings reports. No Control Data figures. Then he flipped to the Most Active List. Again no Control Data. Like the guy on the subway had said, GE was the most active. He checked another

Journal and then asked his friend Fred Zuch if he had noticed the Control Data earnings that morning in the paper.

"No, George," said Zuch, "they only came out this afternoon and they were much better than expected. You saw what they did to the stock."

"Yeah, I saw," mumbled Reilly.

By this time the market was closed, and now the tape was about to print the Most Actives. Feeling discombobulated, Reilly stared at the screen. There it was; Control Data was the most active and up 4 to 80. Reilly rubbed his eyes in a daze. He still had that headache. Damn. He was going to have to start cutting back on his martinis and begin reading the paper more carefully. It really did make a difference. Smiley from Converse had been really sore about missing that stock, and even 3,000-share orders were hard to come by these days.

But that evening on the train, his resolve was forgotten as he got into a card game and had three drinks.

The next morning he almost missed the train and barely got his paper at the station newsstand. There were no seats on the train, and standing, swaying soddenly, he glanced through the *Journal*.

Suddenly, as he looked at the Most Active List, he felt a cold shiver run up his spine. Control Data was not the most active. Natomas was and it was up 8 to 85. The second most active was Varian, down $4\frac{1}{2}$ to $30\frac{1}{4}$.

His hand shaking, Reilly turned to the market commentary column: "Natomas tacked on 8 as it announced promising shows in a deep exploratory test well offshore Java," he read, "while Varian fell on the release of very disappointing third-quarter earnings."

The train was in Grand Central Station now, and Reilly was swept out into the dimly lit platform, the *Journal* clutched damply against his body. As he entered Grand Central and the crush of commuters dissolved, he abruptly, impulsively opened the paper and turned to the stock tables again. Control Data: Open $82\frac{1}{4}$, high 83, low 78, close 78, minus 2 on the day. Now moving instinctively, almost desperately, he crammed the paper, pushing it far down into the same trash can as yesterday.

When he got to the office he was still sweating, a cold, clammy perspiration that was like the sweat of a fever, and his mouth was dry. In the subway station he had desperately wanted to buy another *Journal*, but somehow he was afraid; something restrained him. The act of buying a paper seemed enchanted, part of the spell, and he was terribly reluctant to tamper with it.

"Say Fred," he said to Zuch, "can I take a look at your *Journal*? I left mine on the train."

And, of course, it was as he had half-hoped, half-feared. The *Journal* showed Control Data as the most active and there was no mention of a Natomas discovery or Varian's disappointing earnings. Reilly handed the paper back. He felt punchy, dazed, but off somewhere in a back room of his mind it was like a bell beginning to ring insistently.

It was 9:30 now and he had to begin making his calls on the blocks Hudson & Company had indications to buy or sell. Usually he hated this job as a menial, clerk's task. Mostly he left the list of blocks with the secretary or trader; only occasionally he talked to the money manager.

This morning by chance Rhinelander came on when he called the Pinnacle Fund.

"Reilly, you seen any buyers of Mohawk?" he snapped.

"No, I haven't, but . . ." Reilly was talking very fast for fear Rhinelander would hang up, "Natomas has a discovery announcement coming today and Varian's third quarter will be down big. You better sell yours this morning."

"How do you know?"

"Well, I . . . I heard it from . . ."

"Don't waste my time, Reilly, with that know-nothing crap," Rhinelander said curtly and hung up.

Reilly could feel that tense, frozen expression he always got when someone treated him like mental dirt congealing on his face. Suddenly the confidence of knowledge surged through him, warm and utterly powerful. "Know-nothing, huh? Rhinelander will soon see who is the know-nothing."

The market was open now and on the big electronic tape in front of him Control Data opened at 82. On impulse he called Jack Smiley at Converse.

"Say, Jack, I'm sorry as hell about missing that 1,500 CDA yesterday."

"You ought to be. The portfolio manager was sore and he got chewed out—the stock opened at 82, up 2 more."

"Yeah," said Reilly, "there it goes at 82½ and a string at 83."

"And I got 5,000 more to buy with an 80 limit."

"Listen," said Reilly, "give me that 5,000 shares and I guarantee you I'll get it for you below 80 today."

"What are you talking about? Guarantee what? You're kidding?"

"I'll get the 5,000 below 80 or the firm will make good."

"Reilly, you're cracking up. You must be drinking already. That stock just broke out on the charts. It'll never see 80 again."

"I'll stop you at 78½."

"OK, OK. You got the order with an 80 limit, so it's not worth anything. Any of those partners at Hudson hear you talking like this, Reilly, and you'll be on the beach."

Control Data traded actively between 81 and 83 until around 2:30, when a large seller came in. Reilly bid 78¼ for 2,000 and his bid was hit at 3:15. He bought the last 3,000 at 78 at the close.

"Say, that was some execution, Reilly," said Smiley when he reported the last 3,000.

"Well, never follow excessive strength on a fast spike," said Reilly, astounded at how easily the words came. "I've always had a good feel for the market in hot stocks."

"Yeah, I guess you do. Well, we'll remember that."

The next morning once again his *Wall Street Journal* was for the following day. Superstitiously following the same routine, he read only the most active list and the market column. It was a dull day. Except for Motorola, the list was big blocks with little change. Then, moved by some primeval instinct, he buried the paper deep in the same trash can with the push lid.

When he called Pinnacle with his block list that morning, the secretary said Mr. Rhinelander wanted to speak with him. "Arrogant bastard," Reilly thought, "wants to speak, not talk, with me. Typical."

"Say, Reilly," Rhinelander came on, "you were sure right on the Varian earnings and that Natomas was something."

"Well, anyone analyzing the microwave and klystron tube buying patterns and Government funding shouldn't have been surprised, you know," Reilly heard himself saying with a glibness he didn't recognize.

"Yeah, I guess so." Rhinelander didn't even question his gibberish answer. "How about Natomas now?"

"Well, we have a guy on the main rig in the South China Sea who cables this friend of mine, and I'll let you know next time before they announce a discovery."

"Yeah, sure," said Rhinelander, "do that. What else do you like now?"

"I think the president of Motorola is going to make some very bullish projections at the Security Analysts lunch today, and the stock is going up big. I'd guess he's going to say their color TV division will swing over a dollar a share this year. But I see it as just a trade. I've got no feel longer term."

"Yeah, I forgot Motorola was at the Society today. Their color TV is doing that well, is it? The Street doesn't appreciate that. The stock's been dead for awhile, too. Well, let's buy 5,000."

Reilly had read that Motorola had been up over five points after the speech, but carelessly he hadn't noted the range for the day. As a result, he had been afraid of missing the execution and so had put the entire 5,000 in at the opening, got hit at 78¼ and by 11:00 the stock was 76¾ in a sloppy market.

"Great execution, Reilly," Rhinelander had snarled. "What's your hurry? Never had a 5,000-share order before?"

As a matter of fact, he hadn't had very many recently. But at two o'clock the Motorola analysts lunch broke up, and the story began printing on the broad tape. The stock began to get active and the floor flashed him there were two big buyers matching as Motorola traded at 80. At 2:30 trading was suspended, but the stock reopened at the close on 74,000 shares at 83½.

Rhinelander called about a quarter to four. "Say, Reilly, you're doing fabulously. You sure had that Motorola figured. But what do I do tomorrow, hold her or should I kick her out?"

"Let me sleep on it. I'll let you know in the morning."

"OK, doctor, OK, if you say so. You've got the hot hand, kid."

But the next morning when Reilly carefully, superstitiously following the ritual, waited until he was on the train to open his *Journal*, he found himself staring at yesterday's prices in a perfectly ordinary newspaper. Oddly, this discovery, although a shock and a letdown, was not terribly disconcerting and was almost a relief.

Reilly was neither a profound, imaginative, nor an introspective man, especially when sober, and the phenomenon that had been happening to him was so incredible to begin with, he was not particularly inclined to analyze and worry about its temporary disappearance. In a strange, fatalistic way he was quite confident his "special" *Journal* (as he now thought of it) would come again and all that was required of him was to adhere religiously to the routine. As a matter of fact, far from being unnerved or distracted, that morning Reilly read his *Journal* with unusual attention, and when Rhinelander called, calmly told him his guess was the Motorola had a little more upside in it. As it turned out, the stock did go up another couple of points over the next few days.

Well, that was the way it all started. As time went on, Reilly got his "special" *Journal* about once a week but in no regular pattern. The "special" was always tomorrow's newspaper, and Reilly made a point of never reading more than the Most Active List and the "Abreast of the Market" column. To read more, he sensed, would have been an abuse and possibly could have endangered the very existence of his "special." Why, he couldn't say. It was just a strong, spooky feeling he had.

Anyway, despite spooky feelings, through it all Reilly really was quite clever in achieving maximum exploitation of what was essentially only an occasional, one-day edge, as he was smart enough to keep his mouth shut or be noncommittal on the "off" days. Wall Street has its much-publicized short-comings, but its apparatus for identifying a "money maker," a "winner," is highly efficient. Within six months Reilly was being talked about as a "big hitter"; in a year he was known as one of the great traders and had become a recognized name on the Street.

The money managers flocked to him, and with good reason, since a chat with Reilly early in the morning on a day he had picked up his "special" could make a purchase or sale look brilliant. Lunches tended to be less rewarding and, of course, four out of five days there were no startling insights whatsoever, but the money managers were usually so mesmerized, so fascinated with the idea of having lunch with the great Reilly and then being able to say they had lunch with him, most of them never noticed they weren't getting much in the way of ideas.

Of course, Reilly padded the "off" days with liberal helpings of Irish charm and Wall Street patter. By saying nothing when he had nothing, nobody got hurt.

Once in a while someone was so uncouth as to wonder where he got his inside information, and with everyone buggy about the subject, he made sure to couch his tips in "fundamental" gibberish like "my analysis of semiconductor and integrated circuit order trends suggests Texas Instruments will report surprisingly good third-quarter earnings today," or "it seems to me world copper supplies have built up to a point where the U.S. producers' price will be cut 4 to 5 cents, which could cause severe weakness in Kennecott." He carefully avoided Act of God news events like deaths of company presidents and seldom passed on advance word of merger announcements or legal actions.

By the end of the first year, Reilly's commission production was at a $1 million annual rate, and the Converse Funds were rumored to be paying him $100,000 a year to be able to talk with him for five minutes every morning. He was a partner of Hudson & Company, of course, and he had many job offers. In fact, *The Wall Street Letter* reported he had been offered the position of portfolio manager of the Channing Special Fund, Bache had approached him on underwriting a fund for him to manage, and it was even rumored that Lazard would offer him a partnership.

Reilly's life style changed, too. Obviously, he politely deflected limousine-pool offers and continued to ride the train, but he began to dress mod like the swinging young money managers with beautifully tailored suits, $50 brightly colored shirts, and wide, but tasteful, silk ties. His sideburns were well below the middle of his ear, his hair was much longer, and he drank much less. He never called his wife "the old lady" now, and even began vaguely to talk of collecting art.

An ironic quirk of the whole thing, Reilly told me that day in the hospital, was that he never made any real money in his own account. He was in such a high tax bracket from his commission income that his accountant insisted he go exclusively for long-term capital gains. Over six months his one-day edge was relatively meaningless, and since he was, to put it politely, a less than astute investor, he never accumulated any capital.

About this point, I come into the story. I had continued to see Reilly every morning at the Port Chester station. I was aware of the spectacular improvement in his fortunes, but, obviously, I had no more idea than anyone else of the providential and mystic source of his investment advice. Although we were not confidants, I guess I was as good a business friend as Reilly had.

That June my very elderly maiden aunt was in New York Hospital with a broken hip, and since we had always been close and because she was my biggest discretionary account, I usually visited her once or twice a week. One morning in mid-June there was much talk on the commuter train that the previous day Reilly had suffered a severe heart attack and had been taken to New York Hospital.

That afternoon after visiting my aunt, I stopped by Reilly's room. He was in an oxygen tent and there was a rather grave looking private nurse in attendance. I was with him for only a few minutes and murmured the usual hearty banalities.

The next day his doctor called me at the office. Reilly, it seemed, was most insistent on seeing me again immediately.

"He's out of the oxygen tent, temporarily," the doctor said, "but I wouldn't let him have a visitor except that he's absolutely determined that you come. I want to warn you that his condition is still critical. He had some kind of shock which caused a massive seizure which could recur at any time. His heart actually stopped beating for 30 seconds, and there may have been some brain damage from the lack of oxygen."

That afternoon I found Reilly propped up in bed, looking haggard but alert. He came right to the point.

"The doctor told you my condition? Assuming I live, and for reasons I'll get to later, I'm sure I will live, I'm going to have to take it easy on the business." He paused.

"As I'll explain, I think I've got what you might call a unique franchise, and I'm proposing we go into partnership. I'll supply the stocks that are going to move, and you make the calls and handle the orders. In fact, about all I'll do is ride the train to Grand Central and talk to you afterward."

About then I thought his brain had been damaged, but then he told me the story which I have recounted. Let me say, hearing him tell it, all the while sitting there looking at him, I believed it implicitly. But don't forget it made sense to me because I had seen at close hand the virtually miraculous transformation of an affable, slightly alcoholic loser of a salesman into an uncanny short-term trader.

"So you see," Reilly was saying, "we can make it big. I get the stuff and you merchandise it. We'll make a fortune. But let me tell you what happened Tuesday which makes it even better and bigger."

Last Tuesday, it seemed, he had got a "special," but this one was different. This *Journal* was not for the next day, Wednesday; it was for the following Wednesday.

"Do you see what this means?" asked Reilly, leaning toward me, eyes intent. "Think of the moves in stocks we can catch with an edge of six trading days instead of just one. And think of the market forecasting I can do. You know I never did much with the market before when I only had the one day, but now I could be the greatest technician that ever lived."

He grinned at me. "But we'll have to tell everybody that I developed, you know, discovered a new trend oscillator with unbelievable sensitivity, plus having 29 daily indicators I chart or something kooky like that."

We, or rather Reilly, had been talking for over two hours now and for the second time a nurse came in and insisted I should depart. We shook hands, and as I was leaving I said something inane about "take care of yourself."

Suddenly Reilly was somber. "Say," he said, "I didn't go into what else that special I got last Tuesday had in it."

"Well, no, you didn't."

"There was a notice on page 35, right next to the 'Abreast of the Market' column, or else I wouldn't have seen it, dated next Tuesday, June 23, that Hudson & Company announced with deep regret the death of their beloved friend and partner, George C. Reilly."

I stared at him, horrified. He gazed back, his eyebrows arched quizzically.

"So you see," he went on, "the luckiest thing that ever happened to me, next to getting the specials of course, was to get hit with this heart attack last Tuesday. Probably the emotional shock of seeing that notice triggered the seizure, but just to be sure, I'm climbing back in that oxygen tent Monday and Tuesday and not getting out until the danger period is over. I told the doctor to be around Tuesday also. I'm not taking any chances."

I had longstanding plans to go to Boston that weekend, and when I called Monday, the nurse told me he was back in the oxygen tent again. She said it in a funny way. But Reilly had said not to worry, although I wondered how he could beat the special when all his buying in stocks didn't change the special's prices.

I called again Tuesday, but the nurse said he was still in the oxygen tent. I asked her to have the doctor call me but he never did.

I didn't sleep well Tuesday night worrying about Reilly, and I got up very early and went to the station. The newsstand had just opened and I turned to the next-to-last page and there it was, right next to "Abreast of the Market." But still, maybe it had been set in print before.

I bought a *New York Times* and on the obituary page it was there, too, with a picture. So he was definitely dead. Even with the oxygen tent and the doctor there he couldn't change the death notice in the special that had said he died on Tuesday.

You know, maybe Reilly imagined the whole thing. After all, the doctor said there had been some brain damage when his heart stopped during that first attack. If he dreamed it all up, he sure had one helluva hot streak going on his own. But the stock market is a strange thing, like an ocean, and who knows.

INVESTMENT STRATEGY

Barton M. Biggs

Barton Biggs has reached that rare level of peer recognition where the first name is enough: In conversations among investment professionals in Tokyo, London, New York, and San Francisco, he is known simply as "Barton."

This paper consists of a series of very short essays about the problems and travails of managing money. Several of them in a somewhat different form were part of an *Investment Strategy* paper we published in early 1974. I suppose it is a little presumptuous for me to lecture even in this harmless manner about investment management when many of the readers have had so much more experience managing much larger aggregations of money. However, I have for some time been interested in the trauma of money management itself and how individuals and organizations cope with the emotional problems of creative people functioning at risk.

I believe that an investment manager is complete in terms of knowledge of his profession and the business world after ten or fifteen years of managing money. In that time he has read 100,000 or so research reports and heard at least as many "stories." He has accumulated the conventional wisdom of the market and has a working knowledge of

Reprinted from Morgan Stanley & Co. Letterhead, New York, New York, January 25, 1977, with permission from Morgan Stanley & Co., Inc.

how industries function. He has had his share of winners and bloody noses, his back is permanently twisted from whipsaws, and he has gotten whatever benefit there is to get from being run up and down the market flagpole countless times.

In other words, in that time he has acquired the seminal knowledge and experience and is a seasoned veteran of the investment business. Reading another 100,000 reports, attending another thousand analyst meetings, and collecting some bruises and a limp are merely supportive input—they keep him current but do not deepen his perception or improve his performance capability. The problem is, as that old cynic George Bernard Shaw put it, "Men are wise in proportion, not to their experience, but to their capacity for experience."

And I am convinced that the only experience that counts is managing money for which you are directly accountable. Everyone else in the business, the analysts, the salesmen, the administrators, are involved only as fringe observers or commentators. They are not under fire, they are not responsible, therefore they don't sweat money. Experience in investment management is one thing you can't get for nothing; it is a hard teacher because it gives you the test first and the lesson afterwards. Or as some long-forgotten wag said: "Experience is a comb that life gives you after you lost your hair."

This paper will argue that the mature, diligent, intelligent investment manager enhances his potential for better investment performance only through greater self-understanding. This self-knowledge implies improved discipline not only of the habits of the mind and disposition but also of the portfolio. The following highly subjective thoughts reflect one individual's experience and are written with the hope they may be helpful for others.

I.

We all know that within an investment organization, communication is essential, not only because the investment managers are receiving different information from diverse sources but because, as Oliver Wendell Holmes expressed it: "Many ideas grow better when transplanted into another mind than in the one where they sprung up."

I believe that to have the investment decision makers shut into separate offices with doors that close makes the transmittal of ideas and information within the group infinitely more difficult. In my opinion, the best arrangement for a group of money managers is for all of them to sit together at desks in one large room. Immediate proximity makes communication easy and natural rather than forced. You get a phone call, read something that triggers a train of thought, and an idea appears. All you have to do to communicate it and test it is to speak. A salesman calls with important market information; you don't have to walk down the hall to tell the others, you just raise your voice.

Of course organizations with office mentalities can have meetings which help, and certainly the individuals will walk into the next office when they have something to say. . . at least sometimes. But ideas lose spontaneity and information becomes stale unless promptly transmitted. To some extent meetings can become ritualistic and structured, which in itself may discourage open expression.

This idea of the decision makers sitting together during business hours in one large room is hardly original to me. The concept goes back to the old English merchant banking houses with their "partners' room." There was a partners' room in the old J. P. Morgan & Company and the idea was that the men making decisions affected by events in a dynamic world should be in constant communication and should know everything that the other partners knew. It is interesting that in the new trust and investment headquarters of Morgan Guaranty, the investment managers sit without offices at desks in one vast magnificent room. Their research department is symbolically suspended in a balcony above them.

Obviously, there is a noise level in such a room that makes intensive reading difficult, although you find that after a while you are able to shut out extraneous conversation and concentrate. Perhaps it makes sense to have adjoining small private offices for each of the decision makers where they can have quiet and privacy if necessary. And, of course, they will have to attend meetings with outsiders elsewhere. But they should want to be in the big room as much as possible because that is where the intellectual action is.

There are also psychic benefits that may be more subtle. Managing money can be exhilarating; it can also be a lonely, introspective, depressing business. I think it helps a lot to have the extremes tempered by being with other money managers. It may sound corny, but when the market or a stock is going against you, it always seems to help to have someone to complain and commiserate with.

I worked in such a room, managing money, for eight years, and believe me, you become addicted to it.

II.

Another organizational problem with which the money manager has to contend is the deluge of reading material that descends on him daily. For the veteran investor who has read the 100,000 reports and knows the critical variables of the major industries, there is nothing to be derived from reading another long report about the structure of the paper industry unless it has some new insight. The problem is there is no way of finding this out except by reading, or at least scanning, the report. "Maintenance" information, in other words, what the next couple of quarters' earnings are going to be, has to be assimilated because you need to know what expectations are.

The other problem is that investment managers tend to become compulsive readers. Getting through a stack of reports and statements becomes an accomplishment in and of itself which is, of course, ridiculous. But I think we should all realize that in a job where there is no way to measure labor expended, there is a natural reaction towards any symbol of actually having accomplished something. And working through a pile of reports is accomplishing something. The trouble is that it may be of no benefit. The important thing, obviously, is to get something out of what you are reading.

A corollary of this is a bad habit I get into. I tend to set aside the reports and articles that I know I really want to read carefully, with the idea that I am going to go through all the "maintenance" stuff and the junk quickly and then focus on the heavyweight material. What happens, unfortunately, is that the maintenance material takes longer than it should, and I end up carrying around the good reports in my briefcase for a week or so because I simply haven't had the time to devote to them. In other words, I've processed the junk and haven't read the good reports.

I believe the only answer to this problem is to discipline yourself not to be compulsive; you don't have to look at every piece of research that is sent you. Discard the junk; ignore "maintenance." Instead, you are far better off to read a much smaller amount of good material with care and thoughtfulness. Devote the time that is needed to comprehend thoroughly what the analysis is saying. I think this is much harder than it sounds, but it represents the kind of discipline that has to be applied.

III.

The accumulated business knowledge and market experience of an investment manager are his only professional assets other than his native intelligence and perception. However, the problem is that in accumulating experience, he also acquires prejudices against industries and stocks because he has lost money in them. It is easy to develop a man-on-horseback mentality and become an investment bigot with a closed mind on many subjects.

Unless a money manager understands and compensates for this natural inclination to develop prejudices, these biases can block and impair his ability to receive and respond to new investment ideas. A money manager must remember and consider the travails of his past in making investment decisions, but he should not permit the accumulated scar tissue to block his perception. A fresh, opportunity-oriented mind, uncluttered by prejudice, is crucial for superior investing in an environment where the one constant, the one inevitability is change and industry group rotation. By definition, there can be no uninvestable industries.

I think most of us would agree that it has become a market of groups rather than a market of stocks. Charley Ellis in *Institutional Investing* documented this with a study showing that beyond the change in price due to changes in the general market level, two-thirds of the price change can be attributed to industry group factors while only one-third is directly attributable to the characteristics of the individual company. Benjamin Graham once told me that in the 1920s he had managed a hedge fund which attempted to take the market out of investing and concentrate on stock selection by owning the most "undervalued" stock and selling short the most "overvalued" in each major group. He said it hadn't worked at all because stocks tended to move both up and down as groups and there was not sufficient differentiation as to value within the groups to make his venture worthwhile.

We have analyzed the persistency of relative strength in industry groups from 1946 to 1976. . . . Many technicians assert, with their habitual utter assurance, that a strong group in any one year tends to stay strong for at least one and often two additional years. Our analysis does not corroborate this assertion. We found there was less than one chance in four (23% to be exact) that a group that was one of the ten strongest (in other words in the top 20 percentile of all groups) in one year would be one of the ten strongest in the following year and only one chance in 8 (12%) that it would repeat in the third year. Sequence was not a criteria as this would have been very rare indeed. The probability of persistent strength from one year to the next did appear to be higher than the mean when the market was moving generally upwards. A separate analysis of group strength at important turning points in the market clearly indicates an almost complete change of leadership when the market reverses direction.

Moreover, when observing the diversity of group strength in the market over the years, one has to conclude that the hackneyed old saw of "every dog has his day" has considerable veracity. An investment manager can never afford to say never. And to be honest with himself, he has to admit that a part of his automatic rejection mechanism of "I'll never buy another airline stock" or "I don't ever want to see a utility analyst again" is just impacted prejudice and pure, fat, unadulterated laziness. In fact, if I were an administrator of investment managers, I would regard comments like the above as indications of hardening of the investment arteries, and I would be inclined to think that any manager that made them was about ready for retirement to a less demanding line of work. Like running the research department.

It is certainly not easy to stay open-minded and you have to work at it and keep reminding yourself of it. Everyone has different techniques. Remember the Great Winfield in *The Money Game* who found himself unable to participate in a speculative junk market because his memory was getting in the way. He had heard all the stories before and he remembers how the stocks died when the market went down. "Now you know and I know," he says to Adam Smith, "that one day the orchestra will stop playing and the wind will rattle through the broken windowpanes, and the anticipation of this freezes us. We are too old for this market. The best players in this kind of market have not passed their twenty-ninth birthday."

The Great Winfield's very sensible solution was to go out and hire some kids to give him the fresh perspective, to get the feel, of a "kid's market." "The strength of my kids," he says, "is that they are too young to remember anything bad, and they are making so much money

they feel invincible." In another section of the same story, the Great
Winfield's kid portfolio managers are telling Adam Smith about some
swinging stocks, and he asks a question but Winfield interrupts:

> Look at the skepticism on the face of this dirty old man. . . . You can't
> make any money with questions like that. They show you're middle-
> aged, they show your generation. Show me a portfolio, I'll tell you the
> generation. The *really* old generation, the gray beards, they're the ones
> with General Motors, AT&T, Texaco, International Paper, and DuPont,
> all those stocks nobody has heard of for years. The middle-aged generation
> has IBM, Polaroid, and Xerox, and can listen to rock and roll music
> without getting angry. But life belongs to the swingers today. . . .You
> can tell the swinger stocks because they frighten all the other generations.
> Tell him, Johnny. Johnny the Kid is into the science stuff.

The point is that we've come full circle and full cycle. They buried
the kids and their science stocks, and the bear market almost killed us
middle-agers. But now we are in a new cycle, and the market marches to
the beat of a different drummer. The old generation's stocks have been
the market leaders, and basic industry, value, dividends, smokestacks
are in and high science is out. Industrial dullsville is the order of the
day. Of course, this too will change.

The total contrast between now and then is striking, and it emphasizes the flexibility of thinking and willingness to change that is required
of the successful investor. In the stock market, in investing, there is
nothing permanent except change. The investment manager should try to
cultivate a mix of healthy skepticism, open-mindedness, and willingness
to listen. It is not easy.

IV.

There is a humbling ebb and flow in the tide of investment performance
with every professional inexplicably subject to periods when he is the
"Sun King" and has a hot hand for picking "up" stocks, and to cold
spells when he is out of phase and can't do anything right. These periods
can last from a few months to several years, and the only certainty is
that whether hot or cold, they will always end. Unfortunately, there is
no boy Bernie Baruch (half market mystic, half clairvoyant economist),
who is almost always right, to lead his clients out of the investment
wilderness.

Thus, short-term performance measurements are meaningless, and it is impossible to forecast with any certainty what the relative performance of a manager will be in any given year. In fact, even a several-year span can be misleading, as a manager may be able to achieve above-average results by owning very high-risk stocks in a generally rising market (as we had in the 1960s) but be virtually wiped out in the same class of stocks in a bear market. The only true test of a money manager's ability is if he can obtain above-average results over a full cycle that includes both bull and bear markets. A great investment manager must be "a man for all seasons."

Moreover, the complete investment manager must know and believe in himself sufficiently to keep his perspective and mental composure whether he is hot or cold. Managing money in short-term, public competition with other managers is a circus that can be alternately exhilarating and obsessively depressing. This is especially true because relative performance is so quantifiable, and there can be no bad-bounce or sun-got-in-my-eyes excuses.

And he cannot let how his competition is doing overly affect his psyche. Money managers are great liars, and most talk a much better game than their numbers actually play. Back in the late 1960s, I used to talk to a guy who ran a large hedge fund and who was obviously very bright. We would talk on the phone. How was I doing? Only fair, how was he doing? Always very well. What did he own? He would read off a list of stocks, all of which I wished I owned and which were doing very well. What was he short? The stocks he mentioned invariably were doing poorly and falling sharply. When I hung up the phone, my partners and I would be discouraged by the brilliance of this inscrutable, bearded genius who owned only up stocks and was short only down ones. It was only years later when I lunched with one of his ex-associates that I learned he would sit there talking to people, taking his alleged long portfolio from the new high list of the morning newspaper and his shorts from the new lows. "Good P.R." was his rationalization.

When a manager is hot and his market feel is good, he can easily develop an arrogance and ego as big as the great outdoors, but he should preserve his humility and manners (even to brokers) and continue to treat his peers as unindicted co-conspirators—not as the intellectually unwashed. When he is cold and at the bottom of the rankings and his fans are transformed to wolves overnight, he must resist being enervated by depression and must stick to his own investment standards and style.

And since an investment manager mentally carries his portfolio with him everywhere, he must try not to take his burden of gloom home too much or let it affect his sleep. Above all, in his desperation he should not copy the latest vogue of the moment which he doesn't believe in because inevitably he will do it badly and be too late. There's nothing wrong with worrying and reexamining, but a manager must have the inner poise and toughness not to panic mentally.

In this regard, the introduction Bernard Baruch wrote to the 1932 edition of *Extraordinary Popular Delusions and the Madness of Crowds* has a comforting message to the downtrodden and persecuted investment manager.[1] In speaking of bad times, Baruch wrote:

> Although there be no scientific cure, yet, as in all primitive, unknown (and therefore diabolic) spells, there may be potent incantations. I have always thought that if in the lamentable era of the "New Economics," culminating in 1929, even in the very presence of dizzily spiralling prices, we had all continuously repeated "two and two still make four," much evil might have been averted. Similarly, even in the general moment of gloom in which this forward is written, when many begin to wonder if declines will never halt, the appropriate abracadabra may be: "They always did."

Incidentally, the first couple of chapters of this book, which describes in detail the great financial and stock market manias of the eighteenth century, are essential reading for all serious investors. Human nature and the emotions of greed and fear have not changed as civilization has become more sophisticated.

V.

With so much of investment performance and the stock selection an enigma of inconsistency, the frequent occurrence of one phenomenon has intrigued me for some years. In essence, the phenomenon is that portfolios consistently perform best in the first year of their existence.

For example, in the early 1960s when the first hedge funds were being formed, each year the fund that had started most recently would have the best record. There were even a few very wealthy investors who figured this out and would put money into each new fund. This system worked very well until the quality of the new entrants began to deteriorate drastically.

Many new mutual funds were started from 1965 to 1970. During those years, a disproportionate number of the funds in the top twenty percentile of performance were in their first year of existence. In 1968, for instance, each of the top three and nine of the top thirty funds were in their initial full year. And how often does an investment counselor find that his newest accounts have done the best?

It has been argued that motivation and size are the primary causes of this superior performance. The motivation thesis sounds plausible but is not valid. From experience, this writer can assert that investing under the intense, sleepless-night pressure of the first year of a new enterprise does not produce the clearest investment thinking anymore than big game pressure makes an athlete play his best. Excess motivation seems to make investment managers hyperactive mentally and they tend to overmanage.

As for the argument that relatively small size (no fund in my study was smaller than $10-million) is the important factor, enough computer analysis of fund rankings has been done using a series of coefficients of correlation as to assets and performance with the Spearman formula (whatever that is) to assert quite conclusively that there is little if any relation between size and performance.

So, what is the explanation of this so-called first-year performance phenomenon? Put simply, I have concluded that the investment manager who starts a year with nothing but cash and builds a fresh portfolio has a significant advantage (in spite of having to absorb the cost of getting invested) over the manager who goes into the year fully-invested. The manager with nothing but cash is forced to focus on opportunity, and buys the twenty or thirty most attractive stocks he can find. On the other hand, the fully-invested manager has stocks in his portfolios which he would not buy if he were starting fresh, but which he won't sell because they are still moderately attractive.

Furthermore, if he's like the rest of us with some of these tired, middle-aged stocks, he has unrecognized, subconscious, emotional hang-ups that block him from impartial, cold-blooded investment action like selling. They are stocks he believes in, but somehow the earnings or that "new product" haven't come through, or the market "stupidly" hasn't discovered them yet and he won't really admit he was wrong. And he worries that as soon as he gives up and sells them, the ornery, cussed things will rally. Besides, they're cheap on earnings, which is really the worst reason of all for holding a stock because usually the cheap get cheaper.

Or they may be stocks that he loves because they are "Great" companies with a capital "G" and have made him big money in the past. Investment managers, without realizing it, often personalize and become emotionally involved with stocks when the investment decision-making process should be completely intellectual and rational because, after all, they are just pieces of paper. Or as Adam Smith put it, the stock doesn't know you own it, and there's no reward or pension paid for being a faithful long-term holder.

It is these "holds" that are too cheap to sell but not attractive enough to buy that make a portfolio stale and retard performance. An investment manager will say he has to see potential for at least a 50% gain in a year and a minimum risk-reward ratio of two to one in a stock before he will buy it, yet in his list he will hold many stocks in which he will admit the present potential is only 10%–20% and the risk-reward relationship is closer to one to one. And he won't even see the incongruity of this position.

Obviously, he can improve the portfolio's performance by selling the ten and twenty percenters and putting the money into fifty percenters. Switching is hard (it's always easier to do nothing), and there's an inherent and natural resistance to it because the investment manager exposes himself to being wrong twice (i.e., the stock he sells goes up and the stock he buys goes down), but it's the only way to keep a portfolio young and vital. And after all, the word "manager" implies an active, involved role rather than a passive caretaker function. Furthermore, this writer would argue that rigorous, continual application of appreciation-potential analysis and risk-reward standards, while it maximizes the turnover in a portfolio, minimizes risk in that the relatively fully priced stocks are sold and relatively underpriced and attractive stocks are purchased. Always provided, of course, that the stock selection judgments are competent.

It is significant that Bernard Baruch and Jesse Livermore, probably the two greatest private investors of the twentieth century, made it a practice completely to liquidate their holdings every so often, take a vacation, and start over by buying a completely fresh portfolio. The pattern of reinvesting from scratch is apparent from their writings, although there is no evidence that either did this as a conscious investment strategy or on a regular, predetermined basis, but yet it became almost an instinctive pattern of their operations.

Baruch relates in *My Own Story* how after each major investment undertaking, he would sell his stocks and "shake loose from Wall Street to go off to some quiet place where I could review what I had done."[2] He would come back, he says, refreshed with new approaches and fresh investment ideas. Jesse Livermore, when he felt confused about the course of the market or sensed the need for a change, would "take in his lines and get into cash" and "go fishing or to Hot Springs."[3] On his return, he would usually buy or sell short completely new stocks.

And in a way, Gerald Loeb, with his concept of "The Ever Liquid Account" where the investor automatically sells and thus gets into cash when his stocks start going down, is creating exactly the same effect.[4] Loeb, incidentally, besides being a flourishing broker, was a canny investor with a trading orientation.

At the risk of belaboring the obvious, the point should be made again that an investment manager's performance capability is maximized by investing from a completely cash position. However, it is impractical because of the expense and market impact to even suggest that large portfolios be totally liquidated every so often in order that the manager can have the intellectual freedom and stimulation of a totally fresh approach.

However, a manager can simulate the effects and benefits of complete liquidity. Every year or eighteen months (or for that matter whenever he feels his portfolio is stale and his performance is lethargic), the investment manager must discipline himself to go off alone without any interruptions for at least a day. He must make a powerful effort to detach himself and to pretend he has sold everything, and that he has nothing but cash. Then he must invest his "cash" by constructing a new portfolio based on *that day's* prices, *current* appreciation-potential analysis, and *present* risk/reward ratios. He must do this honestly, and he must work through the entire process of building a new portfolio, segment by segment, including position sizes.

This exercise requires considerable discipline, and is certainly not as effective as the real thing since the mind is not truly unfettered from the old portfolio. But it works surprisingly well.

Then, to complete the treatment and get full benefit from "the first year performance phenomenon," the investment manager must modify his real portfolio to conform to the new list. Obviously, there will be considerable overlapping, but almost invariably this exercise will result in a significant reduction in the number of stocks owned. Professional money managers almost without exception are far better buyers than sellers of stock. This program is buying oriented and thus emphasizes the strength yet indirectly accomplishes the objective of selling.

This purging process is no panacea for poor stock selection. However, it can help a competent manager to work his way out of a slump, and it certainly compels the elimination of the limited potential old lumber and forces concentration of assets in the best stocks where the maximum opportunity is. It is a device, a technique, to help the investment manager focus his thinking which eventually should improve his relative performance.

Maybe successful investing is like riding a bicycle—either you keep moving or you fall down.

FOOTNOTES

1. Charles Mackay, *Extraordinary Popular Delusions and the Madness of Crowds* (Fraser Publishing Company, 1932).
2. Bernard Baruch, *My Own Story* (Holt, Rinehart & Winston, 1957).
3. Edwin Lefevre, *Reminiscences of a Stock Operator* (American Research Council, 1923).
4. Gerald Loeb, *The Battle for Investment Survival* (Simon & Schuster, 1938).

BERKSHIRE HATHAWAY ANNUAL REPORTS

Warren E. Buffett

Berkshire Hathaway's annual reports have provided the lectern from which Warren Buffett has presented his already well-thought-out views on investing, business, values, and management. Management's reviews of operations are always candid and usually run for a dozen delightful pages. These reports are so much in demand that the corporation reprinted several letters from back issues for the ever-increasing number of individuals who want to enroll in this correspondence course for investors.

1977 ANNUAL REPORT

Most companies define "record" earnings as a new high in earnings per share. Since businesses customarily add from year to year to their equity base, we find nothing particularly noteworthy in a management performance combining, say, a 10% increase in equity capital and a 5% increase in earnings per share. After all, even a totally dormant savings

From *Annual Reports*, (New York, 1977, 1982, 1984), 22–24, 40–42, 5–6 (respectively). Omaha, Nebraska: Warren E. Buffett.

account will produce steadily rising interest earnings each year because of compounding.

* * * * *

We get excited enough to commit a big percentage of insurance company net worth to equities only when we find (1) businesses we can understand, (2) with favorable long-term prospects, (3) operated by honest and competent people, and (4) priced very attractively. We usually can identify a small number of potential investments meeting requirements (1), (2) and (3), but (4) often prevents action. For example, in 1971 our total common stock position at Berkshire's insurance subsidiaries amounted to only $10.7 million at cost, and $11.7 million at market. There were equities of identifiably excellent companies available—but very few at interesting prices. (An irresistible footnote: in 1971, pension fund managers invested a record 122% of net funds available in equities—at full prices they couldn't buy enough of them. In 1974, after the bottom had fallen out, they committed a then record low of 21% to stocks.)

The past few years have been a different story for us. At the end of 1975 our insurance subsidiaries held common equities with a market value exactly equal to cost of $39.3 million. At the end of 1978 this position had been increased to equities (including a convertible preferred) with a cost of $129.1 million and a market value of $216.5 million. During the intervening three years we also had realized pre-tax gains from common equities of approximately $24.7 million. Therefore, our overall unrealized and realized pre-tax gains in equities for the three year period came to approximately $112 million. During this same interval the Dow-Jones Industrial Average declined from 852 to 805. It was a marvelous period for the value-oriented equity buyer.

We continue to find for our insurance portfolios small portions of really outstanding businesses that are available, through the auction pricing mechanism of security markets, at prices dramatically cheaper than the valuations inferior businesses command on negotiated sales.

This program of acquisition of small fractions of businesses (common stocks) at bargain prices, for which little enthusiasm exists, contrasts sharply with general corporate acquisition activity, for which much enthusiasm exists. It seems quite clear to us that either corporations are making very significant mistakes in purchasing entire businesses at prices prevailing in negotiated transactions and takeover bids, or that we eventually are going to make considerable sums of money buying small portions of such businesses at the greatly discounted valuations prevailing in the stock market. (A second footnote: in 1978 pension managers, a group that logically should maintain the longest of invest ment perspectives, put only 9% of net available funds into equities— breaking the record low figure set in 1974 and tied in 1977.)

We are not concerned with whether the market quickly revalues upward securities that we believe are selling at bargain prices. In fact, we prefer just the opposite since, in most years, we expect to have funds available to be a net buyer of securities. And consistent attractive purchasing is likely to prove to be of more eventual benefit to us than any selling opportunities provided by a short-term run up in stock prices to levels at which we are unwilling to continue buying.

Our policy is to concentrate holdings. We try to avoid buying a little of this or that when we are only lukewarm about the business or its price. When we are convinced as to attractiveness, we believe in buying worthwhile amounts. Despite a fancy price tag, the "easy" business may be the better route to go.

We can speak from experience, having tried the other route. Your Chairman made the decision a few years ago to purchase Waumbec Mills in Manchester, New Hampshire, thereby expanding our textile commitment. By any statistical test, the purchase price was an extraordinary bargain; we bought well below the working capital of the business and, in effect, got very substantial amounts of machinery and real estate for less than nothing. But the purchase was a mistake. While we labored mightily, new problems arose as fast as old problems were tamed.

Both our operating and investment experience cause us to conclude that "turn-arounds" seldom turn, and that the same energies and talent are much better employed in a good business purchased at a fair price than in a poor business purchased at a bargain price. Although a mistake, the Waumbec acquisition has not been a disaster. Certain portions of the operation are proving to be valuable additions to our decorator line (our strongest franchise) at New Bedford, and it's possible that we may be able to run profitably on a considerably reduced scale at Manchester. However, our original rationale did not prove out.

Since we have covered our philosophy regarding equities extensively in recent annual reports, a more extended discussion of bond investments may be appropriate for this one, particularly in light of what has happened since year-end. An extraordinary amount of money has been lost by the insurance industry in the bond area—notwithstanding the accounting convention that allows insurance companies to carry their bond investments at amortized cost, regardless of impaired market value. Actually, that very accounting convention may have contributed in a major way to the losses; had management been forced to recognize market values, its attention might have been focused much earlier on the dangers of a very long-term bond contract.

Ironically, many insurance companies have decided that a one-year auto policy is inappropriate during a time of inflation, and six-month policies have been brought in as replacements. "How," say many of the insurance managers, "can we be expected to look forward twelve months and estimate such imponderables as hospital costs, auto parts prices, etc.?" But, having decided that one year is too long a period for which to set a fixed price for insurance in an inflationary world, they then have turned around, taken the proceeds from the sale of that six-month policy, and sold the money at a fixed price for thirty or forty years.

The very long-term bond contract has been the last major fixed price contract of extended duration still regularly initiated in an inflation-ridden world. The buyer of money to be used between 1980 and 2020 has been able to obtain a firm price now for each year of its use while the buyer of auto insurance, medical services, newsprint, office space—or just about any other product or service—would be greeted with laughter if he were to request a firm price now to apply through 1985. For in virtually all other areas of commerce, parties to long-term contracts now either index prices in some manner, or insist on the right to review the situation every year or so.

A cultural lag has prevailed in the bond area. The buyers (borrowers) and middlemen (underwriters) of money hardly could be expected to raise the question of whether it all made sense, and the sellers (lenders) slept through an economic and contractual revolution.

For the last years our insurance companies have not been a net purchaser of any straight long-term bonds (those without conversion rights or other attributes offering profit possibilities). There have been some purchases in the straight bond area, of course, but they have been offset by sales or maturities. Even prior to this period, we never would buy thirty or forty-year bonds; instead we tried to concentrate in the straight bond area on shorter issues with sinking funds and on issues that seemed relatively undervalued because of bond market inefficiencies.

However, the mild degree of caution that we exercised was an improper response to the world unfolding about us. You do not adequately protect yourself by being half awake while others are sleeping. It was a mistake to buy fifteen-year bonds, and yet we did; we made an even more serious mistake in not selling them (at losses, if necessary) when our present views began to crystallize. (Naturally, those views are much clearer and definite in retrospect; it would be fair for you to ask why we weren't writing about this subject last year.)

Of course, we must hold significant amounts of bonds or other fixed dollar obligations in conjunction with our insurance operations. In the last several years our net fixed dollar commitments have been limited to the purchase of convertible bonds. We believe that the conversion options obtained, in effect, give that portion of the bond portfolio a far shorter average life than implied by the maturity in terms of the issues (i.e., at an appropriate time of our choosing, we can terminate the bond contract by conversion into stock).

This bond policy has given us significantly lower unrealized losses than those experienced by the great majority of property and casualty insurance companies. We also have been helped by our strong preference for equities in recent years that has kept our overall bond segment relatively low. Nevertheless, we are taking our lumps in bonds and feel that, in a sense, our mistakes should be viewed less charitably than the mistakes of those who went about their business unmindful of the developing problems.

* * * * *

Phil Fisher, a respected investor and author, once likened the policies of the corporation in attracting shareholders to those of a restaurant attracting potential customers. A restaurant could seek a given clientele — patrons of fast foods, elegant dining, Oriental food, etc. — and eventually obtain an appropriate group of devotees. If the job were expertly done, that clientele, pleased with the service, menu, and price level offered, would return consistently. But the restaurant could not change its character constantly and end up with a happy and stable clientele. If the business vacillated between French cuisine and take-out chicken, the result would be a revolving door of confused and dissatisfied customers.

So it is with corporations and the shareholder constituency they seek. You can't be all things to all men, simultaneously seeking different owners whose primary interests run from high current yield to long-term capital growth to stock market pyrotechnics, etc.

* * * * *

We have written in past reports about the disappointments that usually result from purchase and operation of "turn-around" businesses. Literally hundreds of turn-around possibilities in dozens of industries have been described to us over the years and, either as participants or as observers, we have tracked performance against expectations. Our conclusion is that, with few exceptions, when a management with a reputation for brilliance tackles a business with a reputation for poor fundamental economics, it is the reputation of the business that remains intact.

1982 ANNUAL REPORT

General Acquisition Behavior

As our history indicates, we are comfortable both with total ownership of businesses and with marketable securities representing small portions of businesses. We continually look for ways to employ large sums in each area. (But we try to avoid small commitments—"If something's not worth doing at all, it's not worth doing well.") Indeed, the liquidity requirements of our insurance and trading stamp businesses mandate major investments in marketable securities.

Our acquisition decisions will be aimed at maximizing real economic benefits, not at maximizing either managerial domain or reported numbers for accounting purposes. (In the long run, managements stressing accounting appearance over economic substance usually achieve little of either.)

Regardless of the impact upon immediately reportable earnings, we would rather buy 10% of Wonderful Business T at X per share than 100% of T at 2X per share. Most corporate managers prefer just the reverse, and have no shortage of stated rationales for their behavior.

However, we suspect three motivations—usually unspoken—to be, singly or in combination, the important ones in most high-premium takeovers:

1. Leaders, business or otherwise, seldom are deficient in animal spirits and often relish increased activity and challenge. At Berkshire, the corporate pulse never beats faster than when an acquisition is in prospect.

2. Most organizations, business or otherwise, measure themselves, are measured by others, and compensate their managers far more by the yardstick of size than by any other yardstick. (Ask a *Fortune 500* manager where his corporation stands on that famous list and, invariably, the number responded will be from the list ranked by size of sales; he may well not even know where his corporation places on the list *Fortune* just as faithfully compiles ranking the same 500 corporations by profitability.)

3. Many managements apparently were overexposed in impressionable childhood years to the story in which the imprisoned handsome prince is released from a toad's body by a kiss from a beautiful princess. Consequently, they are certain their managerial kiss will do wonders for the profitability of Company T(arget).

   Such optimism is essential. Absent that rosy view, why else should the shareholders of Company A(cquisitor) want to own an interest in T at the 2X takeover cost rather than at the X market price they would pay if they made direct purchases on their own?

   In other words, investors can always buy toads at the going price for toads. If investors instead bankroll princesses who wish to pay double for the right to kiss the toad, those kisses had better pack some real dynamite. We've observed many kisses but very few miracles. Nevertheless, many managerial princesses remain serenely confident about the future potency of their kisses—even after their corporate backyards are knee-deep in unresponsive toads.

In fairness, we should acknowledge that some acquisition records have been dazzling. Two major categories stand out.

The first involves companies that, through design or accident, have purchased only businesses that are particularly well adapted to an inflationary environment. Such favored business must have two characteristics: (1) an ability to increase prices rather easily (even when product demand is flat and capacity is not fully utilized) without fear of significant loss of either market share or unit volume, and (2) an ability to accommodate large dollar volume increases in business (often produced more by inflation than by real growth) with only minor additional investment in capital. Managers of ordinary ability, focusing solely on acquisition possibilities meeting these tests, have achieved excellent results in recent decades. However, very few enterprises possess both characteristics, and competition to buy those that do has now become fierce to the point of being self-defeating.

The second category involves the managerial superstars—men who can recognize that rare prince who is disguised as a toad, and who have managerial abilities that enable them to peel away the disguise. We salute such managers as Ben Heineman at Northwest Industries, Henry Singleton at Teledyne, Erwin Zaban at National Service Industries, and especially Tom Murphy at Capital Cities Communications (a real managerial "twofer," whose acquisition efforts have been properly focused in Category 1 and whose operating talents also make him a leader of Category 2). From both direct and vicarious experience, we recognize the difficulty and rarity of these executives' achievements. (So do they; these champs have made very few deals in recent years, and often have found repurchase of their own shares to be the most sensible employment of corporate capital.)

Your Chairman, unfortunately, does not qualify for Category 2. And, despite a reasonably good understanding of the economic factors compelling concentration in Category 1, our actual acquisition activity in that category has been sporadic and inadequate. Our preaching was better than our performance. (We neglected the Noah principle: predicting rain doesn't count, building arks does.)

We have tried occasionally to buy toads at bargain prices with results that have been chronicled in past reports. Clearly our kisses fell flat. We have done well with a couple of princes—but they were princes when purchased. At least our kisses didn't turn them into toads.

And, finally, we have occasionally been quite successful in purchasing fractional interests in easily identifiable princes at toad-like prices.

Berkshire Acquisition Objectives

We will continue to seek the acquisition of businesses in their entirety at prices that will make sense, even should the future of the acquired enterprise develop much along the lines of its past. We may very well pay a fairly fancy price for a Category 1 business if we are reasonably confident of what we are getting. But we will not normally pay a lot in any purchase for what we are supposed to bring to the party—for we find that we ordinarily don't bring a lot.

During 1981 we came quite close to a major purchase involving both a business and a manager we liked very much. However, the price finally demanded, considering alternative uses for the funds involved, would have left our owners worse off than before the purchase. The empire would have been larger, but the citizenry would have been poorer.

Although we had no success in 1981, from time to time in the future we will be able to purchase 100% of businesses meeting our standards. Additionally, we expect an occasional offering of a major "non-voting partnership" as discussed under the Pinkerton's heading on page 47 of this report. We welcome suggestions regarding such companies where we, as a substantial junior partner, can achieve good economic results while furthering the long-term objectives of present owners and managers.

Currently, we find values most easily obtained through the open-market purchase of fractional positions in companies with excellent business franchises and competent, honest managements. We never expect to run these companies, but we do expect to profit from them.

We expect that undistributed earnings from such companies will produce full value (subject to tax when realized) for Berkshire and its shareholders. If they don't, we have made mistakes as to either: (1) the management we have elected to join; (2) the future economics of the business; or (3) the price we have paid.

We have made plenty of such mistakes—both in the purchase of non-controlling and controlling interests in businesses. Category (2) miscalculations are the most common. Of course, it is necessary to dig deep into our history to find illustrations of such mistakes—sometimes as deep as two or three months back. For example, last year your Chairman volunteered his expert opinion on the rosy future of the aluminum business. Several minor adjustments to that opinion—now aggregating approximately 180 degrees—have since been required.

1984 ANNUAL REPORT

Nebraska Furniture Mart

Last year I introduced you to Mrs. B (Rose Blumkin) and her family. I told you they were terrific, and I understated the case. After another year of observing their remarkable talents and character, I can honestly say that I never have seen a managerial group that either functions or behaves better than the Blumkin family.

Mrs. B, Chairman of the Board, is now 91, and recently was quoted in the local newspaper as saying, "I come home to eat and sleep, and that's about it. I can't wait until it gets daylight so I can get back to the business." Mrs. B is at the store seven days a week, from opening to close, and probably makes more decisions in a day than most CEOs do in a year (better ones, too).

In May Mrs. B was granted an Honorary Doctorate in Commercial Science by New York University. (She's a "fast track" student: not one day in her life was spent in a school room prior to her receipt of the doctorate.) Previous recipients of honorary degrees in business from NYU include Clifton Garvin, Jr., CEO of Exxon Corp.; Walter Wriston, then CEO of Citicorp; Frank Cary, then CEO of IBM; Tom Murphy, then CEO of General Motors; and, most recently, Paul Volcker. (They are in good company.)

The Blumkin blood did not run thin. Louie, Mrs. B's son, and his three boys, Ron, Irv, and Steve, all contribute in full measure to NFM's amazing success. The younger generation has attended the best business school of them all—that conducted by Mrs. B and Louie—and their training is evident in their performance.

Last year NFM's net sales increased by $14.3 million, bringing the total to $115 million, all from the one store in Omaha. That is by far the largest volume produced by a single home furnishings store in the United States. In fact, the gain in sales last year was itself greater than the annual volume of many good-sized successful stores. The business achieves this success because it deserves this success. A few figures will tell you why.

In its fiscal 1984 10-K, the largest independent specialty retailer of home furnishings in the country, Levitz Furniture, described its prices as "generally lower than the prices charged by conventional furniture stores in its trading area." Levitz, in that year, operated at a gross margin of 44.4% (that is, on average, customers paid it $100 for merchandise that had cost it $55.60 to buy). The gross margin at NFM is not much more than half of that. NFM's low mark-ups are possible because of its exceptional efficiency; operating expenses (payroll, occupancy, advertising, etc.) are about 16.5% of sales versus 35.6% at Levitz.

None of this is in criticism of Levitz, which has a well-managed operation. But the NFM operation is simply extraordinary (and, remember, it all comes from a $500 investment by Mrs. B in 1937). By unparalleled efficiency and astute volume purchasing, NFM is able to earn excellent returns on capital while saving its customers at least $30 million annually from what, on average, it would cost them to buy the same merchandise at stores maintaining typical mark-ups. Such savings enable NFM to constantly widen its geographical reach and thus to enjoy growth well beyond the natural growth in the Omaha market.

I have been asked by a number of people just what secrets the Blumkins bring to their business. These are not very esoteric. All members of the family: (1) apply themselves with an enthusiasm and energy that would make Ben Franklin and Horatio Alger look like dropouts; (2) define with extraordinary realism their area of special competence and act decisively on all matters within it; (3) ignore even the most enticing propositions falling outside of that area of special competence; and, (4) unfailingly behave in a high-grade manner with everyone they deal with. (Mrs. B boils it down to "sell cheap and tell the truth.")

Our evaluation of the integrity of Mrs. B and her family was demonstrated when we purchased 90% of the business: NFM had never had an audit and we did not request one; we did not take an inventory nor verify the receivables; we did not check property titles. We gave Mrs. B a check for $55 million and she gave us her word. That made for an even exchange.

You and I are fortunate to be in partnership with the Blumkin family.

As we look at the major acquisitions that others made during 1982, our reaction is not envy, but relief that we were non-participants. For in many of these acquisitions, managerial intellect wilted in competition with managerial adrenalin. The thrill of the chase blinded the pursuers to the consequences of the catch. Pascal's observation seems apt: "It has struck me that all men's misfortunes spring from the single cause that they are unable to stay quietly in one room."

(Your Chairman left the room once too often last year and almost starred in the Acquisition Follies of 1982. In retrospect, our major accomplishment of the year was that a very large purchase to which we had firmly committed was unable to be completed for reasons totally beyond our control. Had it come off, this transaction would have consumed extraordinary amounts of time and energy, all for a most uncertain payoff. If we were to introduce graphics to this report, illustrating favorable business developments of the past year, two blank pages depicting this blown deal would be the appropriate centerfold.)

Our partial-ownership approach can be continued soundly only as long as portions of attractive businesses can be acquired at attractive prices. We need a moderately-priced stock market to assist us in this endeavor. The market, like the Lord, helps those who help themselves. But, unlike the Lord, the market does not forgive those who know not what they do. For the investor, a too-high purchase price for the stock of an excellent company can undo the effects of a subsequent decade of favorable business developments.

* * * * *

Our share issuances follow a simple basic rule: we will not issue shares unless we receive as much intrinsic business value as we give. Such a policy might seem axiomatic. Why, you might ask, would anyone issue dollar bills in exchange for fifty-cent pieces? Unfortunately, many corporate managers have been willing to do just that.

The first choice of these managers in making acquisitions may be to use cash or debt. But frequently the CEO's cravings outpace cash and credit resources (certainly mine always have). Frequently, also, these cravings occur when his own stock is selling far below intrinsic business value. This state of affairs produces a moment of truth. At that point, as Yogi Berra has said, "You can observe a lot just by watching."

For shareholders then will find which objective the management truly prefers—expansion of domain or maintenance of owners' wealth.

This annual report is read by a varied audience, and it is possible that some members of that audience may be helpful to us in our acquisition program.

We prefer:

1. large purchases (at least $5 million of after-tax earnings),
2. demonstrated consistent earning power (future projections are of little interest to us, nor are "turn-around" situations),
3. businesses earning good returns on equity while employing little or no debt,
4. management in place (we can't supply it),
5. simple businesses (if there's lots of technology, we won't understand it),
6. an offering price (we don't want to waste our time or that of the seller by talking, even preliminarily, about a transaction when price is unknown).

We will not engage in unfriendly transactions. We can promise complete confidentiality and a very fast answer as to possible interest—customarily within five minutes. Cash purchases are preferred, but we will consider the use of stock when it can be done on the basis described in the previous section.

* * * * *

In judging whether managers should retain earnings, shareholders should not simply compare total incremental earnings in recent years to total incremental capital because that relationship may be distorted by what is going on in a core business. During an inflationary period, companies with a core business characterized by extraordinary economics can use small amounts of incremental capital in that business at very high rates of return (as was discussed in last year's section on Goodwill). But, unless they are experiencing tremendous unit growth, outstanding businesses by definition generate large amounts of excess cash. If a company sinks most of this money in other businesses that earn low returns, the company's overall return on retained capital may nevertheless appear excellent because of the extraordinary returns being earned by the portion of earnings incrementally invested in the core business. The situation is analogous to a Pro-Am golf event: even if all of the amateurs are hopeless duffers, the team's best-ball score will be respectable because of the dominating skills of the professional.

Many corporations that consistently show good returns both on equity and on overall incremental capital have, indeed, employed a large portion of their retained earnings on an economically unattractive, even disastrous, basis. Their marvelous core businesses, however, whose earnings grow year after year, camouflage repeated failures in capital allocation elsewhere (usually involving high-priced acquisitions of businesses that have inherently mediocre economics). The managers at fault periodically report on the lessons they have learned from the latest disappointment. They then usually seek out future lessons. (Failure seems to go to their heads.)

* * * * *

HOW INFLATION SWINDLES
THE EQUITY INVESTOR

Warren E. Buffett

"Swindle" is a strong word. Here, Warren Buffett shows us that it is also an appropriate word when applied to the effects of inflation on a shareholder's claim against corporate earning power. "Stocks," he says, "in economic substance, are really very similar to bonds."

It is no longer a secret that stocks, like bonds, do poorly in an inflationary environment. We have been in such an environment for most of the past decade, and it has indeed been a time of troubles for stocks. But the reasons for the stock market's problems in this period are still imperfectly understood.

There is no mystery at all about the problems of bondholders in an era of inflation. When the value of the dollar deteriorates month after month, a security with income and principal payments denominated in those dollars isn't going to be a big winner. You hardly need a Ph.D. in economics to figure that one out.

It was long assumed that stocks were something else. For many years, the conventional wisdom insisted that stocks were a hedge against inflation. The proposition was rooted in the fact that stocks are not claims against dollars, as bonds are, but represent ownership of companies with productive facilities. These, investors believed, would retain their value

Reprinted from *Fortune*, Vol. XCV, No. 5, May 1977, 250–267. New York, New York: Time, Inc.

in real terms, let the politicians print money as they might.

And why didn't it turn out that way? The main reason, I believe, is that stocks, in economic substance, are really very similar to bonds.

I know that this belief will seem eccentric to many investors. They will immediately observe that the return on a bond (the coupon) is fixed, while the return on an equity investment (the company's earnings) can vary substantially from one year to another. True enough. But anyone who examines the aggregate returns that have been earned by companies during the postwar years will discover something extraordinary: the returns on equity have in fact not varied much at all.

The Coupon Is Sticky

In the first ten years after the war—the decade ending in 1955—the Dow Jones industrials had an average annual return on year-end equity of 12.8 percent. In the second decade, the figure was 10.1 percent. In the third decade it was 10.9 percent. Data for a larger universe, the Fortune 500 (whose history goes back only to the mid-1950's), indicate somewhat similar results: 11.2 percent in the decade ending in 1965, 11.8 percent in the decade through 1975. The figures for a few exceptional years have been substantially higher (the high for the 500 was 14.1 percent in 1974) or lower (9.5 percent in 1958 and 1970), but over the years, and in the aggregate, the return on book value tends to keep coming back to a level around 12 percent. It shows no signs of exceeding that level significantly in inflationary years (or in years of stable prices, for that matter).

For the moment, let's think of those companies, not as listed stocks, but as productive enterprises. Let's also assume that the owners of those enterprises had acquired them at book value. In that case, their own return would have been around 12 percent too. And because the return has been so consistent, it seems reasonable to think of it as an "equity coupon."

In the real world, of course, investors in stocks don't just buy and hold. Instead, many try to outwit their fellow investors in order to maximize their own proportions of corporate earnings. This thrashing about, obviously fruitless in aggregate, has no impact on the equity coupon but reduces the investor's portion of it, because he incurs substantial frictional costs, such as advisory fees and brokerage charges. Throw in an active options market, which adds nothing to the productivity of

American enterprise but requires a cast of thousands to man the casino, and frictional costs rise further.

Stocks Are Perpetual

It is also true that in the real world investors in stocks don't usually get to buy at book value. Sometimes they have been able to buy in below book; usually, however, they've had to pay more than book, and when that happens there is further pressure on that 12 percent. I'll talk more about these relationships later. Meanwhile, let's focus on the main point: *as inflation has increased, the return on equity capital has not.* Essentially, those who buy equities receive securities with an underlying fixed return—just like those who buy bonds.

Of course, there are some important differences between the bond and stock forms. For openers, bonds eventually come due. It may require a long wait, but eventually the bond investor gets to renegotiate the terms of his contract. If current and prospective rates of inflation make his old coupon look inadequate, he can refuse to play further unless coupons currently being offered rekindle his interest. Something of this sort has been going on in recent years.

Stocks, on the other hand, are perpetual. They have a maturity date of infinity. Investors in stocks are stuck with whatever return corporate America happens to earn. If corporate America is destined to earn 12 percent, then that is the level investors must learn to live with. As a group, stock investors can neither opt out nor renegotiate. In the aggregate, their commitment is actually increasing. Individual companies can be sold or liquidated, and corporations can repurchase their own shares; on balance, however, new equity flotations and retained earnings guarantee that the equity capital locked up in the corporate system will increase.

So, score one for the bond form. Bond coupons eventually will be renegotiated; equity "coupons" won't. It is true, of course, that for a long time a 12 percent coupon did not appear in need of a whole lot of correction.

The Bondholder Gets It in Cash

There is another major difference between the garden variety of bond and our new exotic 12 percent "equity bond" that comes to the Wall Street costume ball dressed in a stock certificate.

In the usual case, a bond investor receives his entire coupon in cash and is left to reinvest it as best he can. Our stock investor's equity coupon, in contrast, is partially retained by the company and is reinvested at whatever rates the company happens to be earning. In other words, going back to our corporate universe, part of the 12 percent earned annually is paid out in dividends and the balance is put right back into the universe to earn 12 percent also.

The Good Old Days

This characteristic of stocks—the reinvestment of part of the coupon—can be good or bad news, depending on the relative attractiveness of that 12 percent. The news was very good indeed in the 1950's and early 1960's. With bonds yielding only 3 or 4 percent, the right to reinvest automatically a portion of the equity coupon at 12 percent was of enormous value. Note that investors could not just invest their own money and get that 12 percent return. Stock prices in this period ranged far above book value, and investors were prevented by the premium prices they had to pay from directly extracting out of the underlying corporate universe whatever rate that universe was earning. You can't pay far above par for a 12 percent bond and earn 12 percent for yourself.

But on their retained earnings, investors *could* earn 12 percent. In effect, earnings retention allowed investors to buy at book value part of an enterprise that, in the economic environment then existing, was worth a great deal more than book value.

It was a situation that left very little to be said for cash dividends and a lot to be said for earnings retention. Indeed, the more money that investors thought likely to be reinvested at the 12 percent rate, the more valuable they considered their reinvestment privilege, and the more they were willing to pay for it. In the early 1960's, investors eagerly paid top-scale prices for electric utilities situated in growth areas, knowing that these companies had the ability to reinvest very large proportions of their earnings. Utilities whose operating environment dictated a larger cash payout rated lower prices.

If, during this period, a high-grade, noncallable, long-term bond with a 12 percent coupon had existed, it would have sold far above par. And if it were a bond with a further unusual characteristic—which was that most of the coupon payments could be automatically reinvested at par in similar bonds—the issue would have commanded an even greater premium. In essence, growth stocks retaining most of their earnings represented just such a security. When their reinvestment rate on the added equity capital was 12 percent while interest rates generally were around 4 percent, investors became very happy—and, of course, they paid happy prices.

Heading for the Exits

Looking back, stock investors can think of themselves in the 1946–66 period as having been ladled a truly bountiful triple dip. First, they were the beneficiaries of an underlying corporate return on equity that was far above prevailing interest rates. Second, a significant portion of that return was reinvested for them at rates that were otherwise unattainable. And third, they were afforded an escalating appraisal of underlying equity capital as the first two benefits became widely recognized. This third dip meant that, on top of the basic 12 percent or so earned by corporations on their equity capital, investors were receiving a bonus as the Dow Jones industrials increased in price from 133 percent of book value in 1946 to 220 percent in 1966. Such a marking-up process temporarily allowed investors to achieve a return that exceeded the inherent earning power of the enterprises in which they had invested.

This heaven-on-earth situation finally was "discovered" in the mid-1960's by many major investing institutions. But just as these financial elephants began trampling on one another in their rush to equities, we entered an era of accelerating inflation and higher interest rates. Quite logically, the marking-up process began to reverse itself. Rising interest rates ruthlessly reduced the value of all existing fixed-coupon investments. And as long-term corporate bond rates began moving up (eventually reaching the 10 percent area), both the equity return of 12 percent and the reinvestment "privilege" began to look different.

Stocks are quite properly thought of as riskier than bonds. While that equity coupon is more or less fixed over periods of time, it does fluctuate somewhat from year to year. Investor's attitudes about the future can be affected substantially, although frequently erroneously, by those yearly changes. Stocks are also riskier because they come equipped with infinite maturities. (Even your friendly broker wouldn't have the nerve to peddle a 100-year bond, if he had any available, as "safe.") Because of the additional risk, the natural reaction of investors is to expect an equity return that is comfortably above the bond return—and

12 percent on equity versus, say, 10 percent on bonds issued by the same corporate universe does not seem to qualify as comfortable. As the spread narrows, equity investors start looking for the exits.

But, of course, as a group they can't get out. All they can achieve is a lot of movement, substantial frictional costs, and a new, much lower level of valuation, reflecting the lessened attractiveness of the 12 percent equity coupon under inflationary conditions. Bond investors have had a succession of shocks over the past decade in the course of discovering that there is no magic attached to any given coupon level: at 6 percent, or 8 percent, or 10 percent, bonds can still collapse in price. Stock investors, who are in general not aware that they too have a "coupon," are still receiving their education on this point.

Five Ways to Improve Earnings.

Must we really view that 12 percent equity coupon as immutable? Is there any law that says the corporate return on equity capital cannot adjust itself upward in response to a permanently higher average rate of inflation?

There is no such law, of course. On the other hand, corporate America cannot increase earnings by desire or decree. To raise that return on equity, corporations would need at least one of the following: (1) an increase in turnover, i.e., in the ratio between sales and total assets employed in the business; (2) cheaper leverage; (3) more leverage; (4) lower income taxes; (5) wider operating margins on sales.

And that's it. There simply are no other ways to increase returns on common equity. Let's see what can be done with these.

We'll begin with *turnover*. The three major categories of assets we have to think about for this exercise are accounts receivable, inventories, and fixed assets such as plants and machinery.

Accounts receivable go up proportionally as sales go up, whether the increase in dollar sales is produced by more physical volume or by inflation. No room for improvement here.

With inventories, the situation is not quite so simple. Over the long term, the trend in unit inventories may be expected to follow the trend in unit sales. Over the short term, however, the physical turnover rate may bob around because of special influences—e.g., cost expectations, or bottlenecks.

The use of last-in, first-out (LIFO) inventory-valuation methods serves to increase the reported turnover rate during inflationary times. When dollar sales are rising because of inflation, inventory valuations of a LIFO company either will remain level (if unit sales are not rising) or will trail the rise in dollar sales (if unit sales are rising). In either case, dollar turnover will increase.

During the early 1970's, there was a pronounced swing by corporations toward LIFO accounting (which has the effect of lowering a company's reported earnings and tax bills). The trend now seems to have slowed. Still, the existence of a lot of LIFO companies, plus the likelihood that some others will join the crowd, ensures some further increase in the reported turnover of inventory.

The Gains Are Apt to Be Modest

In the case of fixed assets, any rise in the inflation rate, assuming it affects all products equally, will initially have the effect of increasing turnover. That is true because sales will immediately reflect the new price level, while the fixed-asset account will reflect the change only gradually, i.e., as existing assets are retired and replaced at the new prices. Obviously, the more slowly a company goes about this replacement process, the more the turnover ratio will rise. The action stops, however, when a replacement cycle is completed. Assuming a constant rate of inflation, sales and fixed assets will then begin to rise in concert at the rate of inflation.

To sum up, inflation will produce some gains in turnover ratios. Some improvement would be certain because of LIFO, and some would be possible (if inflation accelerates) because of sales rising more rapidly than fixed assets. But the gains are apt to be modest and not of a magnitude to produce substantial improvement in returns on equity capital. During the decade ending in 1975, despite generally accelerating inflation and the extensive use of LIFO accounting, the turnover ratio of the Fortune 500 went only from 1.18/1 to 1.29/1.

Cheaper leverage? Not likely. High rates of inflation generally cause borrowing to become dearer, not cheaper. Galloping rates of inflation create galloping capital needs; and lenders, as they become increasingly distrustful of long-term contracts, become more demanding. But even if there is no further rise in interest rates, leverage will be getting more expensive because the average cost of the debt now on corporate books is less than would be the cost of replacing it. And replacement will be required as the existing debt matures. Overall, then, future changes in the cost of leverage seem likely to have a mildly depressing effect on the return on equity.

More leverage? American business already has fired many, if not most, of the more-leverage bullets once available to it. Proof of that proposition can be seen in some other Fortune 500 statistics: in the twenty years ending in 1975, stockholders' equity as a percentage of total assets declined for the 500 from 63 percent to just under 50 percent. In other words, each dollar of equity capital now is leveraged much more heavily than it used to be.

What the Lenders Learned

An irony of inflation-induced financial requirements is that the highly profitable companies—generally the best credits—require relatively little debt capital. But the laggards in profitability never can get enough. Lenders understand this problem much better than they did a decade ago—and are correspondingly less willing to let capital-hungry, low-profitability enterprises leverage themselves to the sky.

Nevertheless, given inflationary conditions, many corporations seem sure in the future to turn to still more leverage as a means of shoring up equity returns. Their managements will make that move because they will need enormous amounts of capital—often merely to do the same physical volume of business—and will wish to get it without cutting dividends or making equity offerings that, because of inflation, are not apt to shape up as attractive. Their natural response will be to heap on debt, almost regardless of cost. They will tend to behave like those utility companies that argued over an eighth of a point in the 1960's and were grateful to find 12 percent debt financing in 1974.

Added debt at present interest rates, however, will do less for equity returns than did added debt at 4 percent rates in the early 1960's. There is also the problem that higher debt ratios cause credit ratings to be lowered, creating a further rise in interest costs.

So that is another way, to be added to those already discussed, in which the cost of leverage will be rising. In total, the higher costs of leverage are likely to offset the benefits of greater leverage.

Besides, there is already far more debt in corporate America than is conveyed by conventional balance sheets. Many companies have massive pension obligations geared to whatever pay levels will be in effect when present workers retire. At the low inflation rates of 1955–56, the liabilities arising from such plans were reasonably predictable. Today, nobody can really know the company's ultimate obligation. But if the inflation rate averages 7 percent in the future, a twenty-five-year-old employee who is now earning $12,000, and whose raises do no more than match increases in living costs, will be making $180,000 when he retires at sixty-five.

Of course, there is a marvelously precise figure in many annual reports each year, purporting to be the unfunded pension liability. If that figure were really believable, a corporation could simply ante up that sum, add to it the existing pension-fund assets, turn the total amount over to an insurance company, and have it assume all the corporation's present pension liabilities. In the real world, alas, it is impossible to find an insurance company willing even to listen to such a deal.

Virtually every corporate treasurer in America would recoil at the idea of issuing a "cost-of-living" bond—a noncallable obligation with coupons tied to a price index. But through the private pension system, corporate America has in fact taken on a fantastic amount of debt that is the equivalent of such a bond.

More leverage, whether through conventional debt or unbooked and indexed "pension debt," should be viewed with skepticism by shareholders. A 12 percent return from an enterprise that is debt-free is far superior to the same return achieved by a business hocked to its eyeballs. Which means that today's 12 percent equity returns may well be less valuable than the 12 percent returns of twenty years ago.

More Fun in New York

Lower corporate income taxes seem unlikely. Investors in American corporations already own what might be thought of as a Class D stock. The Class A, B, and C stocks are represented by the income-tax claims of the federal, state, and municipal governments. It is true that these "investors" have no claim on the corporation's assets; however, they get a major share of the earnings, including earnings generated by the equity buildup resulting from retention of part of the earnings owned by the Class D shareholders.

A further charming characteristic of these wonderful Class A, B, and C stocks is that their share of the corporation's earnings can be increased immediately, abundantly, and without payment by the unilateral vote of any one of the "stockholder" classes, e.g., by congressional action in the case of the Class A. To add to the fun, one of the classes will sometimes vote to increase its ownership share in the business retroactively—as companies operating in New York discovered to their dismay in 1975. Whenever the Class A, B, or C "stockholders" vote themselves a larger share of the business, the portion remaining for Class D—that's the one held by the ordinary investor—declines.

Looking ahead, it seems unwise to assume that those who control the A, B, and C shares will vote to reduce their own take over the long run. The Class D shares probably will have to struggle to hold their own.

Bad News from the FTC

The last of our five possible sources of increased returns on equity is *wider operating margins on sales*. Here is where some optimists would hope to achieve major gains. There is no proof that they are wrong. But there are only 100 cents in the sales dollar and a lot of demands on that dollar before we get down to the residual, pretax profits. The major claimants are labor, raw materials, energy, and various non-income taxes. The relative importance of these costs hardly seems likely to decline during an age of inflation.

Recent statistical evidence, furthermore, does not inspire confidence in the proposition that margins will widen in a period of inflation. In the decade ending in 1965, a period of relatively low inflation, the universe of manufacturing companies reported on quarterly by the Federal Trade Commission had an average annual pretax margin on sales of 8.6 percent. In the decade ending in 1975, the average margin was 8 percent. Margins were down, in other words, despite a very considerable increase in the inflation rate.

If business was able to base its prices on replacement costs, margins would widen in inflationary periods. But the simple fact is that most large businesses, despite a widespread belief in their market power, just don't manage to pull it off. Replacement cost accounting almost always shows that corporate earnings have declined significantly in the past decade. If such major industries as oil, steel, and aluminum really have the oligopolistic muscle imputed to them, one can only conclude that their pricing policies have been remarkably restrained.

There you have the complete lineup: five factors that can improve returns on common equity, none of which, by my analysis, are likely to take us very far in that direction in periods of high inflation. You may have emerged from this exercise more optimistic than I am. But remember, returns in the 12 percent area have been with us a long time.

The Investor's Equation

Even if you agree that the 12 percent equity coupon is more or less immutable, you still may hope to do well with it in the years ahead. It's conceivable that you will. After all, a lot of investors did well with it for a long time. But your future results will be governed by three variables: the relationship between book value and market value, the tax rate, and the inflation rate.

Let's wade through a little arithmetic about book and market value. When stocks consistently sell at book value, it's all very simple. If a stock has a book value of $100 and also an average market value of $100, 12 percent earnings by business will produce a 12 percent return for the investor (less those frictional costs, which we'll ignore for the moment). If the payout ratio is 50 percent, our investor will get $6 via dividends and a further $6 from the increase in the book value of the business, which will, of course, be reflected in the market value of his holdings.

If the stock sold at 150 percent of book value, the picture would change. The investor would receive the same $6 cash dividend, but it would now represent only a 4 percent return on his $150 cost. The book value of the business would still increase by 6 percent (to $106) and the market value of the investor's holdings, valued consistently at 150 percent of book value, would similarly increase by 6 percent (to $159). But the investor's total return, i.e., from appreciation plus dividends, would be only 10 percent versus the underlying 12 percent earned by the business.

When the investor buys in below book value, the process is reversed. For example, if the stock sells at 80 percent of book value, the same earnings and payout assumptions would yield 7.5 percent from dividends ($6 on an $80 price) and 6 percent from appreciation—a total return of 13.5 percent. In other words, you do better by buying at a discount rather than a premium, just as common sense would suggest.

During the postwar years, the market value of the Dow Jones industrials has been as low as 84 percent of book value (in 1974) and as high as 232 percent (in 1965); most of the time the ratio has been well over 100 percent. (Early this spring, it was around 110 percent.) Let's assume that in the future the ratio will be something close to 100 percent—meaning that investors in stocks could earn the full 12 percent. At least, they could earn that figure before taxes and before inflation.

7 Percent after Taxes

How large a bite might taxes take out of the 12 percent? For individual investors, it seems reasonable to assume that federal, state, and local income taxes will average perhaps 50 percent on dividends and 30 percent on capital gains. A majority of investors may have marginal rates somewhat below these, but many with larger holdings will experience substantially higher rates. Under the new tax law, as *Fortune* observed last month, a high-income investor in a heavily taxed city could have a marginal rate on capital gains as high as 56 percent. (See "The Tax Practitioners Act of 1976.")

So let's use 50 percent and 30 percent as representative for individual investors. Let's also assume, in line with recent experience, that corporations earning 12 percent on equity pay out 5 percent in cash dividends (2.5 percent after tax) and retain 7 percent, with those retained earnings producing a corresponding market-value growth (4.9 percent after the 30 percent tax). The after-tax return, then, would be 7.4 percent. Probably this should be rounded down to about 7 percent to allow for frictional costs. To push our stocks-as-disguised-bonds thesis one notch further, then, stocks might be regarded as the equivalent, for individuals, of 7 percent tax-exempt perpetual bonds.

The Number Nobody Knows

Which brings us to the crucial question—the inflation rate. No one knows the answer on this one—including the politicians, economists, and Establishment pundits, who felt, a few years back, that with slight nudges here and there unemployment and inflation rates would respond like trained seals.

But many signs seem negative for stable prices: the fact that inflation is now worldwide; the propensity of major groups in our society to utilize their electoral muscle to shift, rather than solve, economic problems; the demonstrated unwillingness to tackle even the most vital problems (e.g., energy and nuclear proliferation) if they can be postponed; and a political system that rewards legislators with reelection if their actions appear to produce short-term benefits even though their ultimate imprint will be to compound long-term pain.

Most of those in political office, quite understandably, are firmly against inflation and firmly in favor of policies producing it. (This schizophrenia hasn't caused them to lose touch with reality, however; Congressmen have made sure that *their pensions* — unlike practically all granted in the private sector — are indexed to cost-of-living changes *after* retirement.)

Discussions regarding future inflation rates usually probe the subtleties of monetary and fiscal policies. These are important variables in determining the outcome of any specific inflationary equation. But, at the source, peacetime inflation is a political problem, not an economic problem. Human behavior, not monetary behavior, is the key. And when very human politicians choose between the next election and the next generation, it's clear what usually happens.

Such broad generalizations do not produce precise numbers. However, it seems quite possible to me that inflation rates will average 7 percent in future years. I hope this forecast proves to be wrong. And it may well be. Forecasts usually tell us more of the forecaster than of the future. You are free to factor your own inflation rate into the investor's equation. But if you foresee a rate averaging 2 percent or 3 percent, you are wearing different glasses than I am.

So there we are: 12 percent before taxes and inflation; 7 percent after taxes and before inflation; and maybe zero percent after taxes and inflation. It hardly sounds like a formula that will keep all those cattle stampeding on TV.

As a common stockholder you will have more dollars, but you may have no more purchasing power. Out with Ben Franklin ("a penny saved is a penny earned") and in with Milton Friedman ("a man might as well consume his capital as invest it").

What Widows Don't Notice

The arithmetic makes it plain that inflation is a far more devastating tax than anything that has been enacted by our legislatures. The inflation tax has a fantastic ability to simply consume capital. It makes no difference to a widow with her savings in a 5 percent passbook account whether she pays 100 percent income tax on her interest income during a period of zero inflation, or pays *no* income taxes during years of 5 percent inflation. Either way, she is "taxed" in a manner that leaves her no real income whatsoever. Any money she spends comes right out of capital. She would find outrageous a 120 percent income tax, but doesn't seem to notice that 6 percent inflation is the economic equivalent.

If my inflation assumption is close to correct, disappointing results will occur not because the market falls, but in spite of the fact that the market rises. At around 920 early last month, the Dow was up fifty-five points from where it was ten years ago. But adjusted for inflation, the Dow is down almost 345 points—from 865 to 520. And about half of the earnings of the Dow had to be withheld from their owners and reinvested in order to achieve even that result.

In the next ten years, the Dow would be doubled just by a combination of the 12 percent equity coupon, a 40 percent payout ratio, and the present 110 percent ratio of market to book value. And with 7 percent inflation, investors who sold at 1800 would still be considerably worse off than they are today after paying their capital-gains taxes.

I can almost hear the reaction of some investors to these downbeat thoughts. It will be to assume that, whatever the difficulties presented by the new investment era, they will somehow contrive to turn in superior results for themselves. Their success is most unlikely. And, in aggregate, of course, impossible. If you feel you can dance in and out of securities in a way that defeats the inflation tax, I would like to be your broker—but not your partner.

Even the so-called tax-exempt investors, such as pension funds and college endowment funds, do not escape the inflation tax. If my assumption of a 7 percent inflation rate is correct, a college treasurer should regard the first 7 percent earned each year merely as a replenishment of purchasing power. Endowment funds are earning *nothing* until they have outpaced the inflation treadmill. At 7 percent inflation and, say, overall investment returns of 8 percent, these institutions, which believe they are tax-exempt, are in fact paying "income taxes" of 87½ percent.

The Social Equation

Unfortunately, the major problems from high inflation rates flow not to investors but to society as a whole. Investment income is a small portion of national income, and if per capita real income could grow at a healthy rate alongside zero real investment returns, social justice might well be advanced.

A market economy creates some lopsided payoffs to participants. The right endowment of vocal chords, anatomical structure, physical strength, or mental powers can produce enormous piles of claim checks (stocks, bonds, and other forms of capital) on future national output. Proper selection of ancestors similarly can result in lifetime supplies of such tickets upon birth. If zero real investment returns diverted a bit greater portion of the national output from such stockholders to equally worthy and hardworking citizens lacking jackpot-producing talents, it would seem unlikely to pose such an insult to an equitable world as to risk Divine Intervention.

But the potential for real improvement in the welfare of workers at the expense of affluent stockholders is not significant. Employee compensation already totals twenty-eight times the amount paid out in dividends, and a lot of those dividends now go to pension funds, nonprofit institutions such as universities, and individual stockholders who are not affluent. Under these circumstances, if we now shifted *all* dividends of wealthy stockholders into wages—something we could do only once, like killing a cow (or, if you prefer, a pig)—we would increase real wages by less than we used to obtain from one year's growth of the economy.

The Russians Understand It Too

Therefore, diminishment of the affluent, through the impact of inflation on their investments, will not even provide material *short-term* aid to those who are not affluent. Their economic well-being will rise or fall with the general effects of inflation on the economy. And those effects are not likely to be good.

Large gains in real capital, invested in modern production facilities, are required to produce large gains in economic well-being. Great labor availability, great consumer wants, and great government promises will lead to nothing but great frustration without continuous creation and employment of expensive new capital assets throughout industry. That's an equation understood by Russians as well as Rockefellers. And it's one that has been applied with stunning success in West Germany and Japan. High capital-accumulation rates have enabled those countries to achieve gains in living standards at rates far exceeding ours, even though we have enjoyed much the superior position in energy.

To understand the impact of inflation upon real capital accumulation, a little math is required. Come back for a moment to that 12 percent return on equity capital. Such earnings are stated after depreciation, which presumably will allow replacement of present productive capacity—*if* that plant and equipment can be purchased in the future at prices similar to their original cost.

The Way It Was

Let's assume that about half of earnings are paid out in dividends, leaving 6 percent of equity capital available to finance future growth. If inflation is low—say, 2 percent—a large portion of that growth can be real growth in physical output. For under these conditions, 2 percent more will have to be invested in receivables, inventories, and fixed assets next year just to duplicate this year's physical output—leaving 4 percent for investment in assets to produce more physical goods. The 2 percent finances illusory dollar growth reflecting inflation and the remaining 4 percent finances real growth. If population growth is 1 percent, the 4 percent gain in real output translates into a 3 percent gain in real per capita net income. That, very roughly, is what used to happen in our economy.

Now move the inflation rate to 7 percent and compute what is left for real growth after the financing of the mandatory inflation component. The answer is nothing—if dividend policies and leverage ratios remain unchanged. After half of the 12 percent earnings are paid out, the same 6 percent is left, but it is all conscripted to provide the added dollars needed to transact last year's physical volume of business.

Many companies, faced with no real retained earnings with which to finance physical expansion after normal dividend payments, will improvise. How, they will ask themselves, can we stop or reduce dividends without risking stockholder wrath? I have good news for them: a ready-made set of blueprints is available.

In recent years the electric-utility industry has had little or no dividend-paying capacity. Or, rather, it has had the power to pay dividends *if* investors agree to buy stock from them. In 1975 electric utilities paid common dividends of $3.3 billion and asked investors to return $3.4 billion. Of course, they mixed in a little solicit-Peter-to-pay-Paul technique so as not to acquire a Con Ed reputation. Con Ed, you will remember, was unwise enough in 1974 to simply tell its shareholders it didn't have the money to pay the dividend. Candor was rewarded with calamity in the marketplace.

The more sophisticated utility maintains—perhaps increases—the quarterly dividend and then asks shareholders (either old or new) to mail back the money. In other words, the company issues new stock. This procedure diverts massive amounts of capital to the tax collector and substantial sums to underwriters. Everyone, however, seems to remain in good spirits (particularly the underwriters).

More Joy at A.T.&T.

Encouraged by such success, some utilities have devised a further shortcut. In this case, the company declares the dividend, the shareholder pays the tax, and—presto—more shares are issued. No cash changes hands, although the IRS, spoilsport as always, persists in treating the transaction as if it had.

A.T.&T., for example, instituted a dividend-reinvestment program in 1973. This company, in fairness, must be described as very stockholder-minded, and its adoption of this program, considering the folkways of finance, must be regarded as totally understandable. But the substance of the program is out of *Alice in Wonderland*.

In 1976, A.T.&T. paid $2.3 billion in cash dividends to about 2.9 million owners of its common stock. At the end of the year, 648,000 holders (up from 601,000 the previous year) reinvested $432 million (up from $327 million) in additional shares supplied directly by the company.

Just for fun, let's assume that all A.T.&T. shareholders ultimately sign up for this program. In that case, no cash at all would be mailed to shareholders—just as when Con Ed passed a dividend. However, each of the 2.9 million owners would be notified that he should pay income taxes on his share of the retained earnings that had that year been called a "dividend." Assuming that "dividends" totaled $2.3 billion, as in 1976, and that shareholders paid an average tax of 30 percent on these, they would end up, courtesy of this marvelous plan, paying nearly $700 million to the IRS. Imagine the joy of shareholders, in such circumstances, if the directors were then to double the dividend.

The Government Will Try to Do It

We can expect to see more use of disguised payout reductions as business struggles with the problem of real capital accumulation. But throttling back shareholders somewhat will not entirely solve the problem. A combination of 7 percent inflation and 12 percent returns will reduce the stream of corporate capital available to finance real growth.

And so, as conventional private capital-accumulation methods falter under inflation, our government will increasingly attempt to influence capital flows to industry, either unsuccessfully as in England or success-fully as in Japan. The necessary cultural and historical underpinning for a Japanese-style enthusiastic partnership of government, business, and labor seems lacking here. If we are lucky, we will avoid following the English path, where all segments fight over division of the pie rather than pool their energies to enlarge it.

On balance, however, it seems likely that we will hear a great deal more as the years unfold about underinvestment, stagflation, and the failures of the private sector to fulfill needs.

YOU PAY A VERY HIGH PRICE IN THE STOCK MARKET FOR A CHEERY CONSENSUS

Warren E. Buffett

Warren Buffett is not supposed to be a "market timer" and would surely walk away from any awards ceremony trying to proclaim him one. But who could mind him writing this piece for *Forbes* in 1979, or telling *Forbes* in 1974, just before the Dow advanced 450 points in little more than a year, "I feel like an oversexed man in a harem. This is the time to start investing."

Pension fund managers continue to make investment decisions with their eyes firmly fixed on the rear-view mirror. This generals-fighting-the-last-war approach has proven costly in the past and will likely prove equally costly this time around.

Stocks now sell at levels that should produce long-term returns far superior to bonds. Yet pension managers, usually encouraged by corporate sponsors they must necessarily please ("whose bread I eat, his song I sing"), are pouring funds in record proportions into bonds.

Meanwhile, orders for stocks are being placed with an eyedropper. Parkinson—of Parkinson's law fame—might conclude that the enthusiasm of professionals for stocks varies proportionately with the recent pleasure derived from ownership. This always was the way John Q.

Reprinted from *Forbes*, Vol. 124, No. 3, August 6, 1979, 25-26, by permission of the author.

Public was expected to behave. John Q. Expert seems similarly afflict-
ed. Here's the record.

In 1972, when the Dow earned $67.11 or 11% on beginning book
value of 607, it closed the year selling at 1020 and pension managers
couldn't buy stocks fast enough. Purchases of equities in 1972 were
105% of net funds available (i.e., bonds were sold), a record except for
the 122% of the even more buoyant prior year. This two-year stampede
increased the equity portion of total pension assets from 61% to 74%—
an all-time record which coincided nicely with a record high price for
the Dow. The more investment managers paid for stocks, the better they
felt about them.

And then the market went into a tail-spin in 1973-74. Although
the Dow earned $99.04 in 1974, or 14% on beginning book value of
690, it finished the year selling at 616. A bargain? Alas, such bargain
prices produced panic rather than purchases; only 21% of net investable
funds went into equities that year, a 25-year record low. The proportion
of equities held by private noninsured pension plans fell to 54% of net
assets, a full 20-point drop from the level deemed appropriate when the
Dow was 400 points higher.

By 1976 the courage of pension managers rose in tandem with the
price level, and 56% of available funds was committed to stocks. The
Dow that year averaged close to 1000, a level then about 25% above
book value.

In 1978 stocks were valued far more reasonably, with the Dow
selling below book value most of the time. Yet a new low of 9% of net
funds was invested in equities during the year. The first quarter of 1979
continued at very close to the same level.

By these actions pension managers, in record-setting manner, are
voting for purchase of bonds—at interest rates of 9% to 10%—and
against purchase of American equities at prices aggregating book value
or less. But these same pension managers probably would concede that
those American equities, in aggregate and over the longer term, would
earn about 13% (the average in recent years) on book value. And,
overwhelmingly, the managers of their corporate sponsors would agree.

Many corporate managers, in fact, exhibit a bit of schizophrenia
regarding equities. They consider their own stocks to be screamingly
attractive. But, concomitantly, they stamp approval on pension policies
rejecting purchases of common stocks in general. And the boss, while

wearing his acquisition hat, will scorn investment in similar companies at book value. Can his own talents be so unique that he is justified both in paying 200 cents on the dollar for a business if he can get his hands on it, and in rejecting it as an unwise pension investment at 100 cents on the dollar if it must be left to be run by his companions at the Business Roundtable?

A simple Pavlovian response may be the major cause of this puzzling behavior. During the last decade stocks have produced pain—both for corporate sponsors and for the investment managers the sponsors hire. Neither group wishes to return to the scene of the accident. But the pain has not been produced because business has performed badly, but rather because stocks have underperformed business. Such underperformance cannot prevail indefinitely, any more than could the earlier overperformance of stocks versus business that lured pension money into equities at high prices.

Can better results be obtained over, say, 20 years from a group of $9\frac{1}{2}\%$ bonds of leading American companies maturing in 1999 than from a group of Dow-type equities purchased, in aggregate, at around book value and likely to earn, in aggregate, around 13% on that book value? The probabilities seem exceptionally low. The choice of equities would prove inferior only if either a major sustained decline in return on equity occurs or a ludicrously low valuation of earnings prevails at the end of the 20-year period. Should price-earnings ratios expand over the 20-year period—and that 13% return on equity be averaged—purchases made now at book value will result in better than a 13% annual return. How can bonds at only $9\frac{1}{2}\%$ be a better buy?

Think for a moment of book value of the Dow as equivalent to par, or the principal value of a bond. And think of the 13% or so expectable average rate of earnings on that book value as a sort of fluctuating coupon on the bond—a portion of which is retained to add to principal amount just like the interest return on U.S. Savings Bonds. Currently our "Dow Bond" can be purchased at a significant discount (at about 840 vs. 940 "principal amount," or book value of the Dow). That Dow Bond purchased at a discount with an average coupon of 13%—even though the coupon will fluctuate with business conditions—seems to me to be a long-term investment far superior to a conventional $9\frac{1}{2}\%$ 20-year bond purchased at par.

Of course there is no guarantee that future corporate earnings *will* average 13%. It may be that some pension managers shun stocks because they expect reported returns on equity to fall sharply in the next decade. However, I don't believe such a view is widespread.

Instead, investment managers usually set forth two major objections to the thought that stocks should not be favored over bonds. Some say earnings currently are overstated, with real earnings after replacement-value depreciation far less than those reported. Thus, they say, real 13% earnings aren't available. But that argument ignores the evidence in such investment areas as life insurance, banking, fire-casualty insurance, finance companies, service businesses, etc. In those industries replacement-value accounting would produce results virtually identical with those produced by conventional accounting. And yet, one can put together a very attractive package of large companies in those fields with an expectable return of 13% or better on book value and with a price which, in aggregate, approximates book value. Furthermore, I see no evidence that corporate managers turn their backs on 13% returns in their acquisition decisions because of replacement-value accounting considerations.

A second argument is made that there are just too many question marks about the near future; wouldn't it be better to wait until things clear up a bit? You know the prose: "Maintain buying reserves until current uncertainties are resolved," etc. Before reaching for that crutch, face up to two unpleasant facts: The future is *never* clear; you pay a very high price in the stock market for a cheery consensus. Uncertainty actually is the friend of the buyer of long-term values.

If anyone can afford to have such a long-term perspective in making investment decisions, it should be pension fund managers. While corporate managers frequently incur large obligations in order to acquire businesses at premium prices, most pension plans have very minor flow-of-funds problems. If they wish to invest for the long term—as they do in buying those 20- and 30-year bonds they now embrace—they certainly are in a position to do so. They can, and should, buy stocks with the attitude and expectations of an investor entering into a long-term partnership.

Corporate managers who duck responsibility for pension management by making easy, conventional or faddish decisions are making an expensive mistake. Pension assets probably total about one-third of overall industrial net worth and, of course, bulk far larger in the case of many specific industrial corporations. Thus poor management of those assets frequently equates to poor management of the largest single segment of the business. Soundly achieved higher returns will produce significantly greater earnings for the corporate sponsors and will also enhance the security and prospective payments available to pensioners.

Managers currently opting for lower equity ratios either have a highly negative opinion of future American business results or expect to be nimble enough to dance back into stocks at even lower levels. There may well be some period in the near future when financial markets are demoralized and much better buys are available in equities; that possibility exists at all times. But you can be sure that at such a time the future will seem neither predictable nor pleasant. Those now awaiting a "better time" for equity investing are highly likely to maintain that posture until well into the next bull market.

FOOTNOTES

1. Figures are based on the old Dow, prior to the recent substitutions. The returns would be moderately higher and the book values somewhat lower if the new Dow had been used.

THE NOT-SO-EXPERT EXPERT

David Dreman

Why are the "experts" so often wrong? David Dreman's *Contrarian Investment Strategy: The Psychology of Stock Market Success* brings Gustave LeBon's theories to our own front door and explains why we become more confident than accurate as we acquire and process increasing amounts of information.

The illusion of expert invincibility is one that most of us put behind us long ago. What had not been known until recently is that under certain conditions, *experts err predictably and often.* There is a consistency to the mistakes made by professionals in fields as diverse as psychology, engineering, and publishing. And. . . the conditions for such errors are as fertile in the stock market as anywhere.

The problem of expert failure can be traced to man's capabilities as an information processor. Just how much information he can handle effectively under varying circumstances has come under intense scrutiny in recent decades, and some of the results are striking. We will see that the vast storehouses of data about companies, industries, and the economy that current methods require the investor to comprehend may not always give him or her an extra "edge." In fact, ingesting large amounts of investment information can lead to making worse rather than better decisions. Impossible? At the end of the chapter, you'll see that the favorite stocks and industries of large groups of professional investors, chosen by exactly the methods we are questioning, fared far more poorly than the averages over an almost fifty-year period.

To outdo the market, then, we must first have a good idea of the forces that time and again victimize even the pros. Once these forces are understood, the investor can build defenses and find routes that skirt the pitfalls.

* * * * *

Just how good is man as a processor of information, and where does he run into trouble? Nobel Laureate Herbert Simon, one of the pioneers and leaders in the field, has studied both questions intensely over more than four decades. According to Simon, "Every human organism lives in an environment which generates millions of new bits of information every second, but the bottleneck of the perceptual apparatus certainly does not admit more than 1,000 bits per second, and possibly much less."[1] We react consciously to only a minute portion of the information that is thrown at us. But Simon states that even the filtering process is not a passive activity which provides a pretty reasonable representation of the real world, but "an active process involving attention to a very small part of the whole and the exclusion from the outset of all that is not within the scope of our attention."[2]

Simon notes: "The capacity of the human mind for formulating and solving complex problems is very small compared with the size of the problems whose solution is required."[3]

Researchers in many fields began to ponder whether such cognitive limitations actually existed, and if they did, how they might affect the decision-making process in their own disciplines. Could they, as Simon may suggest, result in a serious curtailment of the professional to carry out his responsibilities effectively in a complex field?

Some of the first experiments in cognitive limitation were conducted in the field of clinical psychology, which, like psychiatry, requires the practitioner to make complex diagnostic decisions if proper treatment is to be administered. One of the pioneer investigators was Paul Meehl. In the late 1940s and early 1950s, Meehl made twenty separate surveys of groups of clinical psychologists who, after thorough examinations, recommended treatment for psychotic and schizophrenic patients.[4] In each case the groups of psychologists made predictions of how they believed the patients would respond to the particular treatment they prescribed. These predictions were then compared with the average recovery rates based simply on the standard treatments in the past. Meehl expected the psychologists' diagnoses would undoubtedly improve the prescribed treatment and result in higher recovery rates. The past averages based on standard treatment would be the floor from which the effectiveness of the diagnoses could be gauged. But, in the words of one researcher, "This floor turned out to be the ceiling." The predictions of the groups of clinicians were inferior to the simple averages in eighteen out of twenty studies and as good only twice!

Further studies showed that there is no correlation between the amount of training and experience a clinical psychologist may have and his or her accuracy. One indicated rather surprisingly that psychologists were no better at interpersonal judgments than individuals with no training, and sometimes worse.[5]

Do such findings extend beyond the couch? Apparently so. A group of radiologists reading X-ray films failed to diagnose lung disease 30 percent of the time, although the symptoms were clearly evident.[6]

* * * * *

Dozens of such studies have made it clear that expert failure extends far beyond the investment scene. And the problems very often reside in man's information-processing capabilities. Current work indicates he is a serial or sequential processor of data who can handle information reliably in a linear manner—that is, he can move from one point to the next in a logical sequence. In building a model ship or a space station, there is a defined sequence of procedures. Each step, no matter how complex the particular technology, is linked to the preceding step and will be linked to the succeeding stage until completion.

However, the type of problem that proved so difficult to the professionals we just examined was quite different; here configural, or interactive, rather than linear reasoning was required for the solution. In a configural problem, the decision maker's interpretation of any single piece of information changes depending on how he evaluates many other inputs. Take the case of the security analyst: where two companies have the same trend of earnings, the emphasis placed on growth rates will be weighed quite differently depending on their respective industries and their financial strength. In addition, the assessment will be tempered by the dividend trend, the current payout ratio, profit margins, returns on capital, and the host of analytical criteria we looked at previously. The evaluation will also vary with changes in the state of the economy, in the level of interest rates, and in the companies' competitive environment. Thus, a successful investor must be adept at configural processing, integrating many diverse factors, since changes in any may require a revision of the total assessment.

Not unlike juggling, each factor weighed is another ball in the air, increasing the difficulty of the process. . . .

Curious about what results would be found in the stock market, Paul Slovic, a respected researcher in this area, devised a test to see how important configural (or interactive) reasoning actually was in the decisions of market professionals themselves. In one study thirteen stockbrokers and five graduate students in finance were given eight important financial inputs (trend of earnings per share, profit margins, outlook for near-term profits, etc.) that they considered most significant in analyzing companies. The optimum solution could only be found in a configural manner. As it turned out, configural reasoning, on average, accounted for only about 4 percent of the decisions made — results roughly equivalent to those of the radiologists and psychologists.

Moreover, the emphasis the brokers initially said they put on various inputs varied significantly from what they actually used in the experiment.[7] For example, someone considering the trend of earnings per share over time most important might actually place greater emphasis on near-term prospects. Finally, the more experienced the brokers, the less accurate the assessment of their own scales of weighting appeared to be. All in all, the evidence rather clearly indicates that most people are low-level configural processors, in or out of the marketplace.

* * * * *

In light of what we have just seen, we might ask how dependable current investment methods actually are. To answer this question, let's look more thoroughly at the manner in which a company is evaluated by fundamental analysis. Suppose, for example, an analyst decides to examine Aetna Life and Casualty. How will he go about it?

Examining the company's financial statements, one sees it is a gigantic operation. In 1977 it had revenues of $8.1 billion, $408 million in net income after taxes, 30,700 home office employees, and 24,000 agents. It writes group insurance for one out of ten workers in the country, automobile insurance for 4.8 million drivers, as well as homeowner's insurance for 1.4 million dwellings. But these are only openers: it also writes twenty-seven other major property and casualty insurance lines, many dozens of different policies in life, health, and pension areas, and it is engaged in several other, non-related ventures as well.

Since [an earlier] chapter. . . indicated that the most important determinant of value is an assessment of the company's earnings power, the analyst will probably start here. To do his job properly, he'll have to look at many dozens and possibly hundreds of inputs.

In the case of Aetna, he normally will review in some detail the recent history and prospects of each of its major lines. He may, for example, begin with the property-casualty business, which accounts for about 57 percent of Aetna's income. The company has twenty-eight important lines in this area, with the largest—automobile insurance— accounting for 40 percent of overall divisional revenues. Since the results of these lines can have a significant bearing on the overall outlook, the analyst will probably try to get as thorough a picture of each operation as he can. He may take the auto insurance segment, for example, and subdivide it into commercial and private passenger; these in turn can be split between bodily injury and property damage.

But if he is the thorough type—and most of the dying species of institutional analysts are—he will go further, possibly getting breakdowns from management on how each of these lines is faring in important states.

But we're not finished with our friend yet. In fact, his most difficult innings lie ahead. Multiplying this information by the large number of other businesses Aetna writes extends the length and perhaps tediousness of the analysis manifold. However, if tediousness were his only concern, the analyst might happily accept it. A far more serious problem is that much of the information he is able to ferret out has a high degree of uncertainty attached to it.

Facts provided to him by management as the basis for his various estimates are partial or incomplete at best and sometimes prove to be entirely incorrect. Varying amounts of information are normally available about individual lines. Obviously, no company will relate all the necessary profit and loss and claim experience data to an outsider.

The analyst may be told that the automotive property line is "up nicely" or that automobile liability is "so-so" in the year to date. If he asks how one should translate a "so-so" or an "up nicely" into a reasonable earnings estimate, more times than not he'll be met with a shrug and told it's corporate policy not to divulge the information, and once in a while he'll be told, "That's your problem."

In any case, the analyst is left on his own. He must rely on personal judgment, deciding whether "nicely" means up 10 percent or 30 percent, or "so-so" means flat or down sharply. Checks can be made with trade sources and the competition, but the information provided will also be qualitative and sometimes misleading. Thus the analyst's judgment is extremely important at every stage of the assessment.

In analyzing an insurance company, it is also important to evaluate the appropriateness of the current rate structure. Because of competition and rising inflation, there is a large element of doubt about how good rates actually are. Even company officers, who spend years in a particular division, can often be wrong in their assessments. In the 1973–74 period, for example, the insurance industry badly misjudged the consequences of rising inflation in its property-casualty business and did not increase rates sufficiently, taking enormous losses as a consequence. Yet, at the time most managements believed their rate structures were sound.

Forecasting the earnings of a large industrial company is not much easier. Often operating in hundreds of different markets, many of which produce intermediate products,[8] sometimes in up to one hundred separate countries, the analyst is bombarded with vast amounts of difficult-to-quantify information on competitive conditions, capacity utilization rates, and pricing. What will be the effect on Ford of a new compact introduced by GM or a sports car by Volkswagen? How badly will DuPont polyester operations be hurt if Celanese cuts prices on one or two grades of polyester tire cord? All pertinent information must somehow be synthesized and evaluated in order to arrive at the earnings estimate.

Earnings forecasting, then, depends on large numbers of underlying assumptions, many of which are rapidly changing and very hard to quantify, which means their accuracy is always in doubt.

In addition to the forecasting problems, the harried analyst must also assess the quality of management, the company's expansion plans, its finances, the probable dividend rate, the quality of its accounting, and dozens of other vital factors. And all estimates are contingent on general economic conditions, which means correctly gauging the level of interest rates, unemployment, inflation, industrial production, capital spending, and other important variables. Economists themselves are as often wrong as they are right in these estimates. . . .

Finally, even if the analyst could surmount all of the obstacles so far listed, he would still need to know as much about many other companies in order to determine whether the company he chose represented the best value.

The theory appears anything but undemanding on its poor adherents. The amount of information they are expected to process is staggering. And since a good part of it is qualitative and difficult to pin down, the money manager or analyst is required to use his judgment scores of times along the way. Ideally, the professional needs to have information-processing capabilities not dissimilar to those of a fairly large-scale computer. He must have a central storage file for the massive amounts of information of a political, economic, industry, market, and company nature he needs, and he must be able to update and cross-reference it as numerous new and sometimes contradictory developments occur. The Bionic Man might be capable of as much, but work in the behavioral sciences pretty clearly indicates that most human beings are not.

But the requirements of the theory do not end here. One also needs a very high level of configural, or interactive, reasoning ability in order to apply different weights to the scores of factors upon which the analysis is contingent. And we've already seen that man is simply not a good configural processor of information. The reach of conventional investment theory may very well exceed the grasp of many of us to use it properly. The method brings us well into the range of information overload. One of the things that can happen follows.

* * * * *

Under conditions of complexity and uncertainty, experts demand as much information as possible to assist them in their decision making.

Seems logical. And naturally, there is a tremendous desire for such incremental information on the Street, because investors believe that increased dosage gives them a shot at extraordinary profits.

But as I've indicated earlier, that extra "edge" may not help you. A large number of studies have shown pretty conclusively that increasing the amount of information available to an expert decision maker doesn't do much to improve his judgment[9]. . . .

The parallel between these examples and the investment scene is striking. Wall Streeters place immense faith in the detailed analysis of its experts. In-depth research houses turn out thousands upon thousands of reports, sometimes running up to a hundred pages or more and sprinkled with dozens of tables and charts. Washington listening posts have been set up to catch the slightest indications of impending changes in government policies affecting companies or industries,[10] and scores of conferences are called to provide the money manager with penetrating understanding in dozens of important areas.

The more detailed his level of knowledge, the more effective the expert is considered. A few years back, for example, a leading investment magazine related the story of an analyst so knowledgeable about Clorox that "he could recite bleach share by brand in every small town in the Southwest and tell you the production levels of Clorox's line number 2, plant number 3. But somehow, when the company began to develop massive problems, he missed the signs." As in the case of the psychologists and the experts of the racing sheets, the amount of information available had little to do with the outcome. The stock fell from a high of 53 to 11.[11]

This outcome is, unfortunately, no exception. The inferior investment results noted [earlier], as well as those that we will view next, were based on just such detailed research. To quote a disillusioned money manager several years back: "You pick the top [research] house on the Street and the second top house on the Street—they all built tremendous reputation, research-in-depth, but they killed their clients."[12] Perhaps a good point to note now is that *in-depth information does not mean in-depth profits.* . . .

I hope it is becoming apparent that these configural relationships are extremely complex. In the marketplace investors are dealing not with twenty-four or fifty-seven relevant interactions, but with an exponential number. We have already seen how experts working with far fewer inputs have proven remarkably inadequate at interactive judgments. Because these psychological findings are largely unknown on Wall Street, as elsewhere, investment experts continue to be convinced that their major problems could have been handled if only those extra few necessary facts had been available. They thus tend to overload themselves with information, which usually does not improve their decisions but only makes them more confident and more vulnerable to serious errors.

A famous market theorist of another era, Garfield Drew, saw the end result of this problem clearly. In 1941 he wrote: "In fact, simplicity or singleness of approach is a greatly underestimated factor of market success. As soon as the attempt is made to watch a multiplicity of factors even though each has some element to justify it, one is only too likely to become lost in a maze of contradictory implications . . . the various factors involved may be so conflicting that the conclusion finally drawn is no better than a snap judgment would have been."[13]

Under conditions of anxiety and uncertainty with a vast interacting information grid, the market can become a giant Rorschach test, allowing the investor to see any pattern he wishes. In fact, recent research in configural processing has shown that experts can not only analyze information incorrectly, they can also find relationships that aren't there—a phenomenon called illusionary correlation.

Trained psychologists, for example, were given background information on psychotics, and were also given drawings allegedly made by them. (These, in reality, were very carefully prepared by the experimenters.) With remarkable consistency, the psychologists saw cues in the drawings that they expected to see—muscular figures "drawn" by men worried about their masculinity, or big eyes by suspicious people. Not only were these characteristics not stressed in the drawings, in many cases they were in fact less pronounced than usual.[14] Because the psychologists focused on the anticipated aberrations, they missed important correlations actually present.[15]

The complexity of the marketplace naturally leads to an attempt to simplify and rationalize what seems at times to be unfathomable reality. Often investors notice things that are simply coincidental, and then come to believe that correlations exist when none are actually present. And if they are rewarded by the stock going up, the practice is further ingrained. The market thus provides an excellent field for illusionary correlation.

The head and shoulders formation on the chart cuts through thousands of disparate facts that the chartist believes no man can analyze. Buying growth stocks simplifies an otherwise bewildering range of investment alternatives, just as the Kondratieff wave occurring every fifty years clarifies economic activity which to many might otherwise appear to defy analysis. Such patterns, which seemed to have worked in the past, are pervasive in the marketplace. The problem is that some of the correlations are illusionary and others are chance. Trusting in them begets a high risk of error. A chartist may have summed it up appropriately: "If I hadn't made money some of the time, I would have acquired market wisdom quicker."

Now, unquestionably there are people with outstanding gifts for abstract reasoning that permit them to cut through enormously complex situations. Every field will have its Bernard Baruchs or Warren Buffetts, its Bobby Fischers or Anatol Karpovs. But these people are decidedly few. In chess, for example, there is only one grand master for every few hundred thousand or so players. And even masters or experts, while more plentiful, still represent only a small fraction of those who pursue the game regularly. It seems, then, that as in chess, the information-processing capabilities and the standards of abstract reasoning required by current investment methods are probably too complicated for the majority of us, professional and amateur alike, to use to beat the market regularly. . . .

At this point, some of you might ask whether the problems in decision making, particularly in the stock market, are being exaggerated. The answer, I think, can be found by looking at the favorite investments of market professionals over time.

What is the record? Let's start with a large international conference of institutional investors held at the New York Hilton in February 1970. Over two thousand strong, the delegates were polled for the stock they thought would show outstanding appreciation that year. The favorite choice was National Student Marketing—the highest-octane performer of the day. From a price of 120 in February, it dropped 95 percent by July of that same year. At the same conference in 1972, the airlines were selected as the industry expected to perform best for the balance of the year. Within 1 percent of their highs, the carrier stocks fell 50 percent that year in the face of a sharply rising market. The conference the following year voted them a group to avoid.

Are these simply chance results? In my earlier book, *Psychology and the Stock Market*, I included seven surveys of how the favorite stocks of groups of large numbers of professional investors had subsequently fared. In all the surveys, the choices of the professionals did worse than the market averages. And this before adding on commission charges and advisory fees.

As I indicated at the time, these were the only samples I had been able to locate. Since publication, with further digging and an excellent research assistant—Ms. Nan Miller—as well as some luck, we have unearthed a large number of additional samples—some fifty-one encompass investment advice given over the almost fifty-year period between 1928 and 1976. The surveys show the favorite stock or portfolio of groups of professional investors. The number participating ranged from twenty-five at the low end to as high as several thousand. The median was well over a hundred. Wherever possible, the subsequent performance of the professional choices was measured against the S&P 500 for the next twelve months.[16]

The results are presented in Table 5. The first column shows the time period for each set of surveys, the second the source of the survey, the third the total number of surveys conducted, and the final column the percentage of each set of surveys that outperformed the market in the next twelve months.

The findings startled me. While I believed the evidence clearly showed that experts make many mistakes, I did not think the magnitude of error was as striking or as consistent as the results make evident.

Seventeen of the studies measure the performance of five or more stocks the experts picked as their favorites. By diversifying into a number of stocks instead of just choosing one or two, the element of chance is reduced. And yet, the seventeen portfolios so chosen underperformed the market on fifteen occasions! This meant, in effect, that when you receive professional advice about stocks to buy, you would be given bad advice nine out of ten times. Throwing darts at the stock pages blindfolded or flipping a coin to decide what to buy would give you a fifty-fifty chance. Using a financial professional would reduce your odds considerably.

The other thirty-four samples did not do appreciably better. Overall, the favorite stocks and industries of large groups of money managers and analysts did worse than the market on thirty-nine of fifty-one occasions— or 77 percent of the time—as Table 5 shows.

TABLE V
Expert Forecasts of Favorite Stocks and Industries

Time Span	Source of Surveys	Total Surveys	Percent Outperforming Market in Next Year
1929–32	Cowles Surveys	3	0
1953–76	*Trusts and Estates*	21	33
1967–69	*Financial Analysts Journal*	1	0
1967–72	*California Business*	7	29
1969–73	*Institutional Investor*	7	0
1973	*Business Week*	2	50
1974	*Seminar* (Edson Gould)	2	0
1974	Callan Associates	4	0
1974–76	Mueller Surveys	4	25
Total number of surveys		51	
Percentage of professional surveys *underperforming* market			77

NOTE: Dividends excluded in all comparisons.

One of the first studies was done by Alfred Cowles,[17] among the earliest systematic students of markets, who made three separate studies measuring the forecasting record of investment advisors, large insurance companies, brokers, and bankers between 1928 and 1932. All underperformed the market.[18,19]

Another important survey is based on polls conducted by *Trusts and Estates* over a twenty-one-year period. Each year a large number of investment officers with bank trust departments (as a group, the largest institutional common-stock investors) were asked to name their three favorite industries for the next year. Table 6 gives the results for the 1953–76 period.[20] The favorite industry of most bank portfolio managers did worse than the market in fourteen of the twenty-one years, or 67 percent of the time. It's also interesting, since there are dozens of industries to choose from, that one industry—office equipment—was favored so often.

Moving on to more recent times, a number of broad surveys have

TABLE VI

Trusts and Estates: Subsequent Twelve-Month Performance of Favorite Industry

Year	Favorite Industry	Performance over the Next 12 Months	
		Industry	S&P 500
1953[a]	Electric and gas public utilities	1.0%	- 6.6%
1957	Oil	-16.0	-14.3
1958	Electronics and electric utilities	75.0	38.1
1959	Oil	- 9.7	8.5
1960	Auto and accessories	-26.6	- 3.0
1961	Office equipment and machine group	31.0	23.1
1962	Chemicals, office equipment, banks	-17.1	-11.8
1963	Electric utilities	6.9	18.9
1964	Chemicals	15.6	13.0
1965	Chemicals	4.3	9.1
1966	Oil	-10.6	-13.0
1967	Utilities	4.7	20.1
1968	Office equipment	- 0.9	7.7
1969	Office equipment	15.6	-11.4
1970	Office equipment	-17.5	0.1
1971	Building materials	5.5	10.8
1972	Retail	11.7	15.7
1973	Office equipment	-21.5	-17.4
1974	Office equipment	-37.0	-29.7
1975	Office equipment	27.7	31.5
1976	Petroleum	29.0	19.1
Percentage underperforming market		67%	

[a]No surveys conducted in 1954, 1955, and 1956.

been conducted by *Institutional Investor,* a magazine widely read by the professionals. In late 1971, for example, the magazine polled more than 150 money managers in twenty-seven states, each of whom chose the five stocks he or she believed would show the best performance the following year. Different types of money managers were surveyed, ranging from the people who ran hair-trigger performance funds to conservative bank and insurance types. The magazine indicated that although four hundred stocks were selected overall, there was a remarkable consensus regarding the top ten favorites, which were weighted toward concepts popular at the time.[21]

The top ten fizzled in a rising market, gaining only 1.3 percent in 1972, a year the averages rose 15.6 percent. For the two-year period, the favorites declined almost eight times as much as the averages. After the top ten that year, fifty runners-up were named. They did even more poorly, declining an average of 5 percent in 1972 and ten times as much as the market in the 1972–73 period.

Another survey was conducted the next year, 1973. It was a down year for the market and the S&P dropped 17.4 percent, hardly a ripple when compared with the average decline of 40.4 percent for the top ten, as shown in Table 7. . . . Twenty-seven other stocks were also selected

TABLE VII
The 1973 Top Ten

Company	Price		Percent Change	Price	Percent Change from 1/1/73
	1/1/73	12/31/73		12/31/74	
IBM	321⅝	246¾	− 23.3%	168	− 47.8%
Polaroid	126⅛	69⅞	− 44.6	18⅝	− 85.2
ITT	60¼	26⅜	− 56.2	14¾	− 75.5
Teleprompter	33¼	3⅞	− 88.3	1½	− 95.5
Eastman Kodak	148⅜	116	− 21.8	62⅞	− 57.6
Gillette	63⅞	35⅞	− 43.8	25⅜	− 60.3
McDonald's	76¼	57	− 25.2	29⅜	− 61.5
Motorola	65½	49¼	− 24.8	34⅛	− 47.9
Digital Equipment	91¾	101⅞	+ 11.0	50¾	− 44.7
Levitz Furniture	26⅞	3⅝	− 86.5	1¾	− 93.5
Average Change			− 40.4%		− 67.0%
S&P 500 (without dividends)	118.1	97.6	− 17.4%	68.6	− 41.9%

Note: All companies adjusted for stock splits.

TABLE VIII
Callan Associates Survey (12/31/74): Performance over the Next Twelve Months

Six-stock portfolio to buy	+ 20.7%
Favorite industry—drugs	+ 2.8%
Worst six stocks	+ 42.9%
Worst industry—electrical and electronics	+ 42.0%
S&P 500	+ 31.5%

for performance that year, and again they did worse than the averages. The surveys were discontinued after 1973. [22]

A final survey, conducted by Callan Associates, a West Coast consulting firm, is worth noting. Three dozen investment managers were asked at the end of 1974 to pick both their favorite six stocks and favorite industry and at the same time the six stocks and single industry they thought would do worst in the following year. Table 8 shows some rather extraordinary results. The "worst" stocks and single industry did better than the S&P, while the "best" did worse.

More recently, professionals have been reluctant to participate in such polls. When asked to name his favorites, one analyst replied tersely: "We don't make this information available free anymore."

What do we make of results such as these? The number of samples seems far too large for the outcome to be simply chance. In fact, the evidence indicates a surprisingly high level of error among professionals in choosing both individual stocks and portfolios over a period spanning almost fifty years.

Such evidence, in the first place, is incompatible with the central assumption of the efficient-market hypothesis.[23] But far more important are the practical implications of what we have just seen: the discovery of a very plausible explanation of why fundamental methods often do not work. The theory demands just too much from man as a configural reasoner and information processor. Both within and outside of markets, under conditions of information overload our mental tachometers appear to surge far above the red line. When this happens, we no longer process information reliably. Confidence rises as our input of information increases, but our decisions are not improved. And from the evidence we've seen in the stock market at least, they appear to deteriorate.

While it is true that experts may do as poorly in other complex circumstances, the market professional unfortunately works in a goldfish bowl. In no other calling that I am aware of is the outcome of decisions so easily measurable.

The high failure rate among financial professionals, at times approaching 90 percent, indicates not only that errors are made, but that under uncertain, complex conditions, there must be some systematic and predictable forces working against the unwary investor to account for such extraordinarily poor results. . .

FOOTNOTES

1. Herbert Simon, "Theories of Decision Making in Economics and Behavioral Sciences," *American Economic Review* 69 (No. 2, June 1959): 273.
2. Ibid.
3. Herbert Simon, *Models of Man: Social and Rational* (New York: Wiley, 1970).
4. P.E. Meehl, *Clinical Versus Statistical Predictions: A Theoretical Analysis and Review of the Literature* (Minneapolis: University of Minnesota Press, 1954); Robyn M. Dawes and Bernard Corrigan, "Linear Models in Decision Making," *Psychological Bulletin* 81 (No. 2, 1974): 95–106.
5. Stewart Oskamp, "Overconfidence in Case Study Judgments," *Journal of Consulting Psychology* 29 (1965): 261–265.
6. L.H. Garland, "The Problem of Observer Error," *Bulletin of the New York Academy of Medicine* 36 (1960); Hans Elias, "Three-Dimensional Structure Identified from Single Sections" *Science* 174 (December 1971): 993–1000.
7. Paul Slovic, "Analyzing the Expert Judge: A Descriptive Study of a Stockbroker's Decision Processes," *Journal of Applied Psychology* 53 (No. 4, August 1969): 225–263; P. Slovic, D. Fleissner, and W.S. Bauman, "Analyzing the Use of Information in Investment Decision Making: A Methodological Proposal," *Journal of Business* 45 (No. 2, 1972): 283–301.
8. These are the raw materials for another manufacturing process. Many plastic resins, for example, go into a thousand or more end products (ranging from carpets to tires). Estimating the outlook for the myriad of intermediate markets is an extremely difficult task.

9. Goldberg, "Simple Models."

10. Sounds impressive, but, I think, a waste of the client's money. Many times it seems the primary source of the listening post is the *New York Times*, the *Washington Post*, the *Wall Street Journal*, *Business Week*, *Time*, or *Newsweek*.

11. Reba F. White, "The Dangers of Falling in Love with a Company," *Institutional Investor*, November 1975.

12. *Wall Street Transcript*, September 23, 1974.

13. Garfield A. Drew, *New Methods of Profit in the Stock Market* (Boston: Metcalf Press, 1941).

14. The belief that all paranoid patients accentuate certain characteristics in their drawings belongs in the category of psychologists' old wives tales.

15. L. Chapman and J.P. Chapman, "Genesis of Popular but Erroneous Psychodiagnostic Observations," *Journal of Abnormal Psychology* (1967): 193–204; Chapman and Chapman, "Illusory Correlations As an Obstacle to the Use of Valid Psychodiagnostic Signs," *Journal of Abnormal Psychology* (1974): 271–280.

16. Several studies used different averages or time periods. For details see Appendix I, pages 250–253.

17. For those interested in more details of the samples, please refer to Appendix I.

18. Cowles was a formidable researcher and a possible precursor of the random walk theory, coming as he did from the bastion of that theory, the University of Chicago. One of his many tests measured all the recommendations of William Peter Hamilton, who you may remember was the editor of the *Wall Street Journal* and cooriginator of the Dow theory. Cowles plotted Hamilton's entire forecasting record between 1904 and 1929 and once again found that if someone had followed each recommendation, he would have done worse than the averages.

19. Alfred Cowles III, "Can Stock Market Forecasters Forecast?" *Econometria* 1 (1933): 309–324.

20. The first poll took place in 1953; no polls were made between 1954 and 1956.

21. "What's in the Cards for 1972?" *Institutional Investor* 6 (January 1972): 25–36.

22. The favorites are listed in *Institutional Investor*, January 1973.

23. The hypothesis states that it is impossible to beat the market because of the competition among professionals, which results in prices always being about where they should be. But just as the theory holds that even

professionals cannot outdo the market over time, it also holds that they cannot do substantially worse. After all, it is their very decision making that keeps prices at their proper level in the first place. The surveys, however, give us a different picture from the one assumed by the theorists. The massive underperformance in both up and down markets indicates that their most crucial assumption is inconsistent with a statistically significant body of evidence. Findings such as these appear to indicate that the hypothesis is built of straw.

THE LOSER'S GAME

Charles D. Ellis

Gifted, determined, ambitious professionals have come into investment management in such large numbers during the past 30 years that it may no longer be feasible for any of them to profit from the errors of all the others sufficiently often and by sufficient magnitude to beat the market averages.

Disagreeable data are streaming out of the computers of Becker Securities and Merrill Lynch and all the other performance measurement firms. Over and over and over again, these facts and figures inform us that investment managers are failing to perform. Not only are the nation's leading portfolio managers failing to produce positive absolute rates of return (after all, it's been a long, long bear market) but they are also failing to produce positive *relative* rates of return. Contrary to their oft articulated goal of outperforming the market averages, investment managers are not beating the market: The market is beating them.

Faced with information that contradicts what they believe, human beings tend to respond in one of two ways. Some will assimilate the information, changing it—as oysters cover an obnoxious grain of silica with nacre—so they can ignore the new knowledge and hold on to their former beliefs; and others will accept the validity of the new information.

Reprinted from *The Financial Analysts Journal*, Vol. 31, No. 4, July/August 1975, 19–26. New York, New York: Financial Analysts Federation.

Instead of changing the meaning of the new data to fit their old concept of reality, they adjust their perception of reality to accommodate the information and then they put it to use.

Psychologists advise us that the more important the old concept of reality is to a person - the more important it is to his sense of self-esteem and sense of inner worth—the more tenaciously he will hold on to the old concept and the more insistently he will assimilate, ignore or reject new evidence that conflicts with his old and familiar concept of the world. This behavior is particularly common among very bright people because they can so easily develop and articulate self-persuasive logic to justify the conclusions they want to keep.

For example, most institutional investment managers continue to believe, or at least say they believe, that they can and soon will again "outperform the market." They won't and they can't. And the purpose of this article is to explain why not.

My experience with very bright and articulate investment managers is that their skills at analysis and logical extrapolation are very good, often superb, but that their brilliance in extending logical extrapolation draws their own attention far away from the sometimes erroneous basic assumptions upon which their schemes are based. Major errors in reasoning and exposition are rarely found in the logical development of this analysis, but instead lie within the premise itself. This is what worried Martin Luther. It's what *The Best and the Brightest* is all about. It's what lifted LTV above $100; why the Emperor went for days without clothes; and why comedians and science fiction writers are so careful first to establish the "premise" and then quickly divert our attention from it so they can elaborate the persuasive details of developing "logic."

The investment management business (it should be a profession but is not) is built upon a simple and basic belief: Professional money managers can beat the market. That premise appears to be false.

If the premise that it is feasible to outperform the market were accepted, deciding how to go about achieving success would be a matter of straightforward logic. First, the market can be represented by an index, such as the S&P 500. Since this is a passive and public listing, the successful manager need only rearrange his bets differently from those of the S&P "shill." He can be an activist in either stock selection or market timing, or both. Since the manager will want his "bets" to be right most of the time, he will assemble a group of bright, well educated, highly motivated, hard working young people, and their collective purpose will be to beat the market by "betting against the house" with a "good batting average."

The belief that active managers can beat the market is based on two assumptions: (1) liquidity offered in the stock market is an advantage, and (2) institutional investing is a Winner's Game.

The unhappy thesis of this article can be briefly stated: Owing to important changes in the past ten years, these basic assumptions are no longer true. On the contrary, market liquidity is a *liability* rather than an *asset*, and institutional investors will, over the long term, *under*perform the market because money management has become a Loser's Game.

Before demonstrating with mathematical evidence why money management has become a Loser's Game, we should close off the one path of escape for those who will try to assimilate the facts. They may argue that this analysis is unfair because so much of the data on performance comes from bear market experience, giving an adverse bias to an evaluation of the long-term capabilities of managers who have portfolio beta's above 1.0. "Of course," they will concede with dripping innuendo, "these interesting analyses may have less to say about dynamic fund managers operating in a decent market." Perhaps, but can they present us with evidence to support their hopes? Can they shoulder the burden of proof? After many hours of discussion with protesting money managers all over America and in Canada and Europe, I have heard no new evidence or persuasive appeal from the hard judgment that follows the evidence presented below. In brief, the "problem" is not a cyclical aberration; it is a long-term secular trend.

Unfortunately, the relative performance of institutionally managed portfolios appears to be getting worse. Measuring returns from trough to trough in the market, the institutionally managed funds in the Becker sample are falling farther and farther behind the market as represented by the S&P 500 Average. It appears that the *costs* of active management are going up and that the *rewards* from active management are going down.

The basic characteristics of the environment within which institutional investors must operate have changed greatly in the past decade. The most significant change is that institutional investors have become, and will continue to be, the dominant feature of their own environment.

For the ten years ending December 31, 1974, the funds in the Becker Securities sample had a median rate of return of 0.0 per cent. The S&P total rate of return over the same period was 1.2 per cent per annum. (Within the Becker sample, the high fund's annual rate of return was 4.5 per cent, the first quartile fund's return was 1.1 per cent, the median 0.0 per cent, the third quartile −1.1 per cent and the low fund's annual rate of return −5.6 per cent.)

	S&P 500 Average	Becker Median	Institutional Shortfall
Last Three Market Cycles (9/30/62 to 12/31/74)	5.3%	4.1%	(0.8%)
Last Two Market Cycles (12/31/66 to 12/31/74)	2.1%	0.4%	(1.7%)
Last Single Market Cycle (9/30/70 to 12/31/74)	2.2%	(0.3%)	(2.5%)

Data: Becker Securities 1974 Institutional Funds Evaluation Service.

This change has impacted greatly upon all the major features of the investment field. In particular, institutional dominance has converted market liquidity from a source of *profits* to a source of *costs*, and this is the main reason behind the transformation of money management from a Winner's Game to a Loser's Game.

Before analyzing what happened to convert institutional investing from a Winner's Game to a Loser's Game, we should explore the profound difference between these two kinds of "games." In making the conceptual distinction, I will use the writings of an eminent scientist, a distinguished historian, and a renowned educator. They are, respectively, Dr. Simon Ramo of TRW; naval historian, Admiral Samuel Elliot Morrison; and professional golf instructor, Tommy Armour.

Simon Ramo identified the crucial difference between a Winner's Game and a Loser's Game in his excellent book on playing strategy, *Extraordinary Tennis for the Ordinary Tennis Player*. Over a period of many years, he observed that tennis was not *one* game but *two*. One game of tennis is played by professionals and a very few gifted amateurs; the other is played by all the rest of us.

Although players in both games use the same equipment, dress, rules and scoring, and conform to the same etiquette and customs, the basic natures of their two games are almost entirely different. After extensive scientific and statistical analysis, Dr. Ramo summed it up this way: Professionals *win* points, amateurs *lose* points. Professional tennis players stroke the ball with strong, well aimed shots, through long and often exciting rallies, until one player is able to drive the ball just beyond the reach of his opponent. Errors are seldom made by these splendid players.

Expert tennis is what I call a Winner's Game because the ultimate outcome is determined by the actions of the *winner*. Victory is due to *winning more points than the opponent wins*—not, as we shall see in a moment, simply to getting a higher score than the opponent, but getting that higher score by *winning* points.

Amateur tennis, Ramo found, is almost entirely different. Brilliant shots, long and exciting rallies, and seemingly miraculous recoveries are few and far between. On the other hand, the ball is fairly often hit into the net or out of bounds, and double faults at service are not uncommon. The amateur duffer seldom *beats* his opponent, but he beats himself all the time. The victor in this game of tennis gets a higher score than the opponent, but he gets that higher score *because his opponent is losing even more points*.

As a scientist and statistician, Dr. Ramo gathered data to test his hypothesis. And he did it in a very clever way. Instead of keeping conventional game scores—"Love," "Fifteen All," "Thirty-Fifteen," etc.—Ramo simply counted points *won* versus points *lost*. And here is what he found. In expert tennis, about 80 per cent of the points are won; in amateur tennis, about 80 per cent of the points are *lost*. In other words, professional tennis is a Winner's Game—the final outcome is determined by the activities of the winner—and amateur tennis is a Loser's Game—the final outcome is determined by the activities of the *loser*. The two games are, in their fundamental characteristic, not at all the same. They are opposites.

From this discovery of the two kinds of tennis, Dr. Ramo builds a complete strategy by which ordinary tennis players can win games, sets and matches again and again by following the simple strategem of losing less, and letting the opponent defeat himself.

Dr. Ramo explains that if you choose to win at tennis—as opposed to having a good time—the strategy for winning is to avoid mistakes.

The way to avoid mistakes is to be conservative and keep the ball in play, letting the other fellow have plenty of room in which to blunder his way to defeat, because he, being an amateur (and probably not having read Ramo's book) will play a losing game and not know it.

He will make errors. He will make too many errors. Once in a while he may hit a serve you cannot possibly handle, but much more frequently he will double fault. Occasionally, he may volley balls past you at the net, but more often than not they will sail far out of bounds. He will slam balls into the net from the front court and from the back court. His game will be a routine catalogue of gaffes, goofs and grief.

He will try to beat you by winning, but he is not good enough to overcome the many inherent adversities of the game itself. The situation does not allow him to win with an activist strategy and he will instead lose. His efforts to win more points will, unfortunately for him, only increase his error rate. As Ramo instructs us in his book, the strategy for winning in a loser's game is to lose less. Avoid trying too hard. By keeping the ball in play, give the opponent as many opportunities as possible to make mistakes and blunder his way to defeat. In brief, by losing less become the victor.

In his thoughtful treatise on military science, *Strategy and Compromise*, Admiral Morrison makes the following point: "In warfare, mistakes are inevitable. Military decisions are based on estimates of the enemy's strengths and intentions that are usually faulty, and on intelligence that is never complete and often misleading." (This sounds a great deal like the investment business.) "Other things being equal," concludes Morrison, "the side that makes the fewest strategic errors wins the war."

War, as we all know, is the ultimate Loser's Game. As General Patton said, "Let the other poor dumb bastard lose his life for his country." Golf is another Loser's Game. Tommy Armour, in his great book *How to Play Your Best Golf All the Time*, says: "The way to win is by making fewer bad shots."

Gambling in a casino where the house takes at least 20 per cent of every pot is obviously a Loser's Game. Stud poker is a Loser's Game but Night Baseball with deuces, treys and one-eyed Jacks "wild" is a Winner's Game.

Campaigning for elected office is a Loser's Game. The electorate seldom votes *for* one of the candidates but rather *against* the other candidate. Professional politicians advise their candidates: "Help the voters find a way to vote *against* the other guy, and you'll get elected."

Recent studies of professional football have found that the most effective defensive platoon members play an open, ad hoc, enterprising, risk-taking style—the proper strategy for a Winner's Game—while the best offensive players play a careful, "by the book" style that concentrates on avoiding errors and eliminating uncertainty, which is the requisite game plan for a Loser's Game. "Keep it simple," said Vincent Lombardi.

There are many other Loser's Games. Some, like institutional investing, used to be Winner's Games in the past, but have changed with the passage of time into *Loser's Games*. For example, 50 years ago, only very brave, very athletic, very strong willed young people with good eyesight had the nerve to try flying an airplane. In those glorious days, flying was a Winner's Game. But times have changed and so has flying. If you got into a 747 today, and the pilot came aboard wearing a 50-mission hat with a long, white silk scarf around his neck, you'd get off. Those people do not belong in airplanes any longer because flying an airplane today is a Loser's Game. Today, there's only one way to fly an airplane. It's simple: Don't make any mistakes.

Prize fighting starts out as a Winner's Game and becomes a Loser's Game as the fight progresses. In the first three or four rounds, a really strong puncher tries for a knockout. Thereafter, prize fighting is a gruelling contest of endurance to see who can survive the most punishment, while the other fellow gets so worn out that he literally drops to defeat.

Expert card players know that after several rounds of play, games like Gin Rummy go through a "phase change" after which discards no longer improve the relative position of the discarding player. During this latter phase, discards tend to add more strength to the opponent's hand than they remove weakness from the hand of the discarder. This changes long hands of Gin Rummy into a Loser's Game, and the correct strategy in this latter phase of the game is to evaluate discards not in terms of how much good they will do for your hand to get rid of them, but rather how much good they may do for your opponent.

Many other examples could be given, but these will suffice to make the distinction between Winner's Games and Loser's Games, to explain why the requisite player strategy is very different for the two kinds of games, and to show that the fundamental nature of a game can change and that Winner's Games can and sometimes do become Loser's Games. And that's what has happened to the Money Game.

The Money Game was a phenomenal Winner's Game in the mid-1920's when John J. Raskob, a prominent business executive, could write an article for a popular magazine with the encouraging title "Everybody Can Be Rich." The article gave a cookbook recipe that anybody could, theoretically, follow to riches beyond the dreams of avarice. The Great Crash abruptly reversed the situation, and made investing a Loser's Game for nearly two decades.

It was during these decades of the thirties and forties that preservation of capital, emphasis on the safety of bonds, and sobersided conventional wisdom came to dominance and the foundation was laid for the renaissance of the Winner's Game. The bull market of the 1950's gave dramatic and compelling evidence that the situation had changed, that big money could be made in the market. And this news attracted people who like to make big money—people who like to win.

The people who came to Wall Street in the 1960's had always been—and expected always to be—winners. They had been presidents of their high school classes, varsity team captains, and honor students. They were bright, attractive, out-going and ambitious. They were willing to work hard and take chances because our society had given them many and frequent rewards for such behavior. They had gone to Yale and the Marines and Harvard Business School. And they were quick to recognize that the big Winner's Game was being played in Wall Street.

It was a glorious, wonderful, euphoric time. It was a time when almost anybody who was smart and willing to work hard could win. And almost all of us did.

The trouble with Winner's Games is that they tend to self-destruct because they attract too much attention and too many players—all of whom want to win. (That's why gold rushes finish ugly.) But in the short run, the rushing in of more and more players seeking to win expands the apparent reward. And that's what happened in Wall Street during the 1960's. Riding the tide of a bull market, institutional investors obtained such splendid rates of return in equities that more and more money was turned over to them—particularly in mutual funds and pension funds –which fueled the continuation of their own bull market.

Institutional investing was a Winner's Game and the winners knew that by playing it faster, they would increase the rate of winnings. But in the process, a basic change occurred in the investment environment; the market came to be dominated by the institutions.

In just ten years, the market activities of the investing institutions have gone from only 30 per cent of total public transactions to a whopping 70 per cent. And that has made all the difference. No longer are the "New Breed on Wall Street" in the minority; they are now the majority. The professional money manager isn't competing any longer with amateurs who are out of touch with the market; now he competes with other experts.

It's an impressive group of competitors. There are 150 major institutional investors and another 600 small and medium sized institutions operating in the market all day, every day, in the most intensely competitive way. And in the past decade, these institutions have become more active, have developed larger in-house research staffs, and have tapped into the central source of market information and fundamental research provided by institutional brokers. Ten years ago, many institutions were still far out of the mainstream of intensive management; today such an institution, if any exists, would be a rare collector's item.

Competitively active institutional investing has resulted in sharply higher portfolio turnover. The typical equity portfolio turnover has gone from 10 to 30 per cent. As we've already seen, this acceleration in portfolio activity plus the growth in institutional assets and the shift of pension funds toward equities have increased the proportion of market transactions of institutions from 30 to 70 per cent which has, in turn, produced the basic "phase change" that has transformed portfolio activity from a source of incremental profits to a major cost, and that transformation has switched institutional investing from a Winner's Game to a Loser's Game.

The new "rules of the game" can be set out in a simple but distressing equation. The elements are these:

a. Assume equities will return an average nine per cent rate of return.[1]
b. Assume average turnover of 30 per cent per annum.
c. Assume average costs—dealer spreads plus commissions—on institutional transactions are three per cent of the principal value involved.[2]

d. Assume management and custody fees total 0.20 per cent.
e. Assume the goal of the manager is to outperform the averages by 20 per cent.

Solve for "X": $(X \cdot 9) - [30 \cdot (3 + 3)] - (0.20) = (120 \cdot 9)$

$$X = \frac{[30 \cdot (3 + 3)] + (0.20) + (120 \cdot 9)}{9}$$

$$X = \frac{1.8 + 0.20 + 10.8}{9}$$

$$X = \frac{12.8}{9}$$

$$X = 142\%$$

In plain language, the manager who intends to deliver *net* returns 20 per cent better than the market must earn a gross return before fees and transactions costs (liquidity tolls) that is more than 40 per cent better than the market. If this sounds absurd, the same equation can be solved to show that the active manager must beat the market *gross* by 22 percent just to come out even with the market *net*.

In other words, for the institutional investor to perform as well as, *but no better than*, the S&P 500, he must be sufficiently astute and skillful to "outdo" the market by 22 per cent. But how can institutional investors hope to outperform the market by such a magnitude when, in effect, they *are* the market today? Which managers are so well staffed and organized in their operations, or so prescient in their investment policies that they can honestly expect to beat the other professionals by so much on a sustained basis?

The disagreeable numbers from the performance measurement firms say there are *no* managers whose past performance promises that they will outperform the market in the future. Looking backward, the evidence is deeply disturbing: 85 per cent of professionally managed funds underperformed the S&P 500 during the past 10 years. And the median fund's rate of return was only 5.4 per cent—about 10 per cent *below* the S&P 500.

Most money managers have been losing the Money Game. And they know it, even if they cannot admit it publicly. Expectations and promises have come down substantially since the mid-1960's. Almost nobody still talks in terms of beating the market by 20 per cent compounded annually. And nobody listens to those who do.

In times like these, the burden of proof is on the person who says, "I am a winner. I can win the Money Game." Because only a sucker backs a "winner" in the Loser's Game, we have a right to expect him to explain exactly what he is going to do and why it is going to work so very well. This is not very often done in the investment management business.

Does the evidence necessarily lead to an entirely passive or index portfolio? No, it doesn't necessarily lead in that direction. Not quite. But the "null" hypothesis is hard to beat in a situation like this. At the risk of over-simplifying, the null hypothesis says there is nothing there if you cannot find statistically significant evidence of its presence. This would suggest to investment managers, "Don't do anything because when you try to do something, it is on average a mistake." And if you can't beat the market, you certainly should consider joining it. An index fund is one way. The data from the performance measurement firms show that an index fund would have outperformed most money managers.

For those who are determined to try to win the Loser's Game, however, there are a few specific things they might consider.

First, be sure you are playing your own game. Know your policies very well and play according to them all the time. Admiral Morrison, citing the *Concise Oxford Dictionary*, says: "Impose upon the enemy the time and place and conditions for fighting preferred by oneself." Simon Ramo suggests: "Give the other fellow as many opportunities as possible to make mistakes, and he will do so."

Second, keep it simple. Tommy Armour, talking about golf, says: "Play the shot you've got the greatest chance of playing well." Ramo says: "Every game boils down to doing the things you do best, and doing them over and over again." Armour again: "Simplicity, concentration, and economy of time and effort have been the distinguishing features of the great players' methods, while others lost their way to glory by wandering in a maze of details." Mies Van der Rohe, the architect, suggests, "Less is more." Why not bring turnover down as a deliberate, conscientious practice? Make fewer and perhaps better investment decisions. Simplify the professional investment management problem. Try to do a few things unusually well.

Third, concentrate on your defenses. Almost all of the information in the investment management business is oriented toward purchase decisions. The competition in making purchase decisions is too good.

It's too hard to outperform the other fellow in buying. Concentrate on selling instead. In a Winner's Game, 90 per cent of all research effort should be spent on making purchase decisions; in a Loser's Game, most researchers should spend most of their time making sell decisions. Almost all of the really big trouble that you're going to experience in the next year is in your portfolio right now; if you could reduce some of those really big problems, you might come out the winner in the Loser's Game.

Fourth, don't take it personally. Most of the people in the investment business are "winners" who have won all their lives by being bright, articulate, disciplined and willing to work hard. They are so accustomed to succeeding by trying harder and are so used to believing that failure to succeed is the failure's own fault that they may take it personally when they see that the average professionally managed fund cannot keep pace with the market any more than John Henry could beat the steam drill.

There is a class of diseases which are called "iatrogenic" meaning they are doctor-caused. The Chinese finger cage and the modern straight-jacket most tightly grip the person who struggles to break free. Ironically, the reason institutional investing has become the Loser's Game is that in the complex problem each manager is trying to solve, his efforts to find a solution—and the efforts of his many urgent competitors—have become the dominant variables. And their efforts to beat the market are no longer the most important part of the solution; they are the most important part of the problem.

FOOTNOTES

1. Use of nine per cent is for convenience only, and is an accommodation to its conventional acceptance. If time permitted, I'd prefer to justify and then use a figure of, perhaps, 12 per cent for the next decade which would reflect the market's reflection of expected inflation.

2. This estimate was made by the senior trading partner of a major institutional block trading firm. Other experts indicate this estimate may be low.

FOURTH ANNUAL INSTITUTIONAL INVESTOR'S CONFERENCE: DAVID BABSON'S PRESENTATION AND QUESTION AND ANSWER SESSION

David L. Babson

This dialogue took place in early 1971, as practitioners did some soul-searching about their 1970 investment actions and results, results which shook their own—as well as their clients'—faith in the profession. David Babson, outraged by the events that preceded the debacle, spoke directly and bluntly to the professional money managers assembled for the conference in a talk still referred to as "Too Many Freds."

DAVID BABSON'S PRESENTATION

Asking the performance investors of the late '60s what went wrong is like someone, in 1720, asking John Law what went wrong with the Mississippi Bubble.

From the transcript of the Fourth Annual Institutional Investor's Conference, March 18, 1971, reprinted by permission of Institutional Investor, Inc.

Or in 1635 asking Mynheer Vanderveer what went wrong with the Dutch Tulip Craze.

Nevertheless, this panel interests me because if we can identify what really did go wrong it may help to avoid a future speculative frenzy.

And if we are serious about getting to the bottom of what went wrong then we ought to say what really did go wrong.

So let me list a dozen things that people in our field did to set the stage for the greatest bloodbath in 40 years.

First, there was the conglomerate movement and all its fancy rhetoric about synergism and leverage. Its abuses were to the late 1960's what the public utility holding companies were to the late 1920's.

Second, too many accountants played footsie with stock-promoting managements by certifying earnings that weren't earnings at all.

Third, the "modern" corporate treasurers who looked upon their company pension funds as new-found "profit centers" and pressured their investment advisors into speculating with them.

Fourth, the investment advisors who massacred clients' portfolios because they were trying to make good on the over-promises that they had made to attract the business in the first place.

Fifth, the new breed of portfolio managers who churned their customers' holdings on the specious theory that high "turnover" was a new "secret" leading to outstanding investment performance.

Sixth, the new issue underwriters who brought out the greatest collection of low-grade junky offerings in history—some of which were created solely for the purpose of generating something to sell.

Seventh, the elements of the financial press who promoted into new investment geniuses a group of neophytes who didn't even have the first requisite for managing other people's money, namely, a sense of responsibility.

Eighth, the security salesman who peddled the items with the best "stories," or the biggest markups even though such issues were totally unsuited to their customers' needs.

Ninth, the sanctimonious partners of major investment houses who wrung their hands over all these shameful happenings while they deployed an army of untrained salesmen to forage among a group of even less informed investors.

Tenth, the mutual fund managers who tried to become millionaires overnight by using every gimmick imaginable to manufacture their own paper performance.

Eleventh, the portfolio managers who collected bonanza "incentive" fees—the "heads I win, tails you lose" kind—which made them fortunes in the bull market but turned the portfolios they managed into disasters in the bear market.

Twelfth, the security analysts who forgot about their professional ethics to become "story peddlers" and who let their institutions get taken in by a whole parade of confidence men.

These are some of the things that "went wrong." But for those who stuck to their guns, who tried to follow a progressive but realistic approach, who didn't prostitute their professional responsibilities, who didn't get seduced by conflicts of interest, who didn't get suckered into glib "concepts," nothing much really did go wrong.

At our firm we've never laid claim to being geniuses but our mutual fund, for example, is well above its peak of three years ago when I was here discussing "What's wrong with performance investing?"

So what did we learn from this list of horrors? Over the years most of the country has considered New England folks to be shrewd investment managers—and you know up our way the greatest compliment we can pay a man is not to say "He's really smart," rather it's to say "He's got a lot of common sense."

I think this sums up "what went wrong." As in earlier periods of delusion most investors tried so hard to be "smart" that they lost the "common sense" that pays off in the long run.

Thank you.

QUESTION AND ANSWER SESSION

MR. GOODMAN:

David, we were talking about decline here, in the market, managed by professionals. Do you think the decline was due to the professionals? It's an institutionally dominated market?

MR. BABSON:

Of course, it was due to the professionals. [1967–68] was the first wild market, 1967–68, when the big institutions and the people that ought to know how to manage investments got sucked into speculation. The 1969–70 bear market was due to the professionals—nobody else.

MR. *GOODMAN:*

What do you think we can do about this?

MR. *BABSON:*

Well, I think a lot of the professionals ought to get out of the business, personally.

I think that anybody who went to bed with a quarter million shares of Four Seasons Nursing Homes—

MR. *GOODMAN:*

Do you have anybody in mind?

MR. *BABSON:*

Things like Parvin Dohrmann, and Performance Systems. I have a list here.

MR. *GOODMAN:*

I'm not sure what the pain threshold of the audience is.

MR. *BABSON:*

I've got a group here of about thirty companies that were—

MR. *GOODMAN:*

Don't read them off.

MR. *BABSON:*

No.

—that were favorites among the professional money managers a couple of years ago. They were down 90 percent last July, and they are still down 83 percent, and it's obvious that—...

MR. *GOODMAN:*

Upside down, those charts would look very good.

MR. *BABSON:*

I don't think that it was a doctor out in Pocatello, Idaho, who was all loaded up with Performance Systems or Lums or Susquehanna or Unexcelled. I think the fellows who were loaded up with them were probably located in offices not far from here.

MR. *GOODMAN:*

I don't know anybody who has an office close to here.

We heard a lot of talk yesterday about self-regulation and Senator Muskie seemed to indicate that the country at large was unhappy with the investment business, and if you think a lot of people should leave the investment business, I wonder how we are going to pick which people and how do we enforce this so that the country at large won't rise in its wrath and do more harmful things to the investment business than it is doing to itself.

Does anybody want to comment?

MR. BABSON:

Well, if these smart investment managers, money managers, have got clients that are as smart as they are, the clients ought to determine whether they will stay in the business or not, I should think.

MR. GOODMAN:

That's a great belief in the free market. You could have said that about the clients going in, too. Then you think the people who were burned in investing in mutual funds would simply disappear or never come back again or fund another mutual fund, or what?

MR. BABSON:

I think an awful lot of people will avoid the stock market for a long time to come as a result of what has happened.

There was a survey in *The Wall Street Journal* a couple of weeks ago that showed a high percentage of people will never buy stocks again. And judging from what is going on in the business today, an awful lot of accounts are trying to find new managers.

* * * * *

MR. GOODMAN:

Isn't there just one mistake of yours that you could point to?

MR. BABSON:

I could find a couple if I dug hard, but not a serious one. Our problem was not 1970, or '69; it was '68. Our problem in '68 was why weren't we doing what David Meid was able to do or—

MR. GOODMAN:

There was a moment of silence there.

MR. BABSON:

—or the Freds—Fred Alger, Fred Carr, Fred Mates.

MR. GOODMAN:

I never thought of the group that way.

MR. BABSON:

They made our problems in 1968. In 1970, we didn't have any at all.

* * * * *

THE WORLD'S SMARTEST MAN SYNDROME

Bennett W. Goodspeed

Bennett Goodspeed earned a living as an investment manager and wrote "The TAO Jones Average." In this insightful article, he illustrates that the best thinking is not always done by looking at the facts.

The thriving analytical system on Wall Street is sophisticated almost beyond belief. Surprisingly, however, investment performance leaves much to be desired. Why is it that with the best guns and ammunition available, the professional portfolio managers miss the target with such frequency? If the tools are right, then it must be their wrong selection and mode of use that renders such anemic results. The World's Smartest Man Syndrome is most likely the cause of it.

In the story of The World's Smartest Man, he finds himself together with the President of the United States, a priest, and a hippie in a plane doomed to crash. On board are three parachutes, which prompts the President to take one immediately with the declaration that he owes it to the American people to survive. After his exit, the Smartest Man steps forth, claims his life an irreplaceable asset of humanity, and follows

Reprinted from *The Journal of Portfolio Management*, Vol. 3, No. 4, Summer 1978, 41–44. New York, New York: Institutional Investor, Inc.

suit. The priest looks at the hippie and says: "I have lived my life and now it is in God's hand; you take the last parachute." The hippie replies: "No sweat, Padre, we both are safe; the World's Smartest Man jumped out with my knapsack on his back!!!"

The reaction to this story is interesting. Not only do people find it funny, but they also seem to find it entirely plausible that the World's Smartest Man could be so dumb. Such a paradox is not only curious, but may have many implications for money managers. Don't we all know people that are intellectually brilliant, but lack common sense? And what kind of a portfolio manager would our World's Smartest Man make?

As a starting point in our examination of our impractical genius, several people were asked to list the characteristics of the World's Smartest Man. Interestingly, their answers could easily be classified into positive and negative categories:

A walking computer
Educated–PhD
An expert
Knows about everything
High I.Q.–Genius
More knowledgeable than you
Intellectual
Knows a great many statistics
Impractical
Has little common sense
Won't admit he's wrong
Close-minded
Absentminded; careless
Unwilling to see others' point of view
Thinks he has all the answers
Sees the trees, not the forest

A LOOK INSIDE THE BRAIN

The previous responses suggest that there is a flip side or possible liabilities to those who are exceptionally "brilliant." Since intelligence is an aspect of the human mind, it seems appropriate to look at the brain

Left Hemisphere

(Right Side of Body)
Linguistic
Particular
Mechanical/Categorical
Sequential
Rational
Intellectual
Deductive
Disciplining/Analytic
Motor

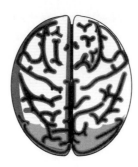

Right Hemisphere

(Left Side of Body)
Spatial/Musical
Holistic
Artistic/Symbolic
Simultaneous
Emotional
Intuitive
Inductive
Imaginative/Gestalt
Contemplative

and how it operates. Interestingly, we have two brains: a left and right hemisphere. Furthermore, each person is dominated by either one side or the other (analytical or intuitive mode preference).

As the diagram shows, our left hemisphere is analytically oriented. It reasons logically and sequentially and is the center of our speech. Like a computer, it is programmable and thus is nurtured by our highly analytical educational process. Since man has developed computers that can duplicate left-brain functions, its properties are reproductable [*sic*] and thus not unique.

Our right brain hemisphere is unique. It operates non-sequentially, is intuitive, artistic, has feelings, and is gestalt-oriented (sees the forest versus the trees). Since it is non-verbal, it communicates to us through dreams and "gut reactions." The right hemisphere blends all of our collective experience and self-programs a vast amount of input–certainly much more than we can verbally retrieve from our left brain.

A comparison of the positive qualities assigned by our sample group to the World's Smartest Man shows an interesting parallel when compared to the qualities of the left brain hemisphere. Likewise, the qualities he lacks are those of the right hemisphere. Obviously, our sample group perceives the World's Smartest Man as being so overly specialized in left hemisphere skills that he lacks right brain qualities.

Is such a specialization of the left hemisphere unusual in our society? Dr. Roger W. Sperry, a leader in split brain research, feels that it is not. "Our educational system and modern society generally discriminate against one whole half of the brain," Dr. Sperry states. He goes on to add that, "in our present school system, the attention given to the right hemisphere of the brain is minimal compared with the training lavished on the left side."

WHICH IS THE WALL STREET HEMISPHERE?

If our society is in danger of being too analytically oriented, what about Wall Street? Has the advent of sophisticated scientific research pioneered by Donaldson, Lufkin, and Jenrette some fifteen years ago been a positive influence on investments? Does "Modern Portfolio Management" make sense?

In an effort to quantify the past performance of money managers, the Becker Survey has compiled client records for the past fifteen years. Their study concludes that 87% of the managers underperformed the averages! While such a high percentage seems almost unbelievable, it is quite clear that the record of the average money manager has been disappointing.

Though little research has been done about how portfolio managers operate in their decision making roles, studies have been done that shed light on what makes top corporate managers tick. By observing many CEO's in action, Professor Henry Mintzberg of Canada's McGill University has discovered that they do not operate in the scientific manner taught at Harvard Business School. Mintzberg discovered that executive decision makers showed a dislike for written communications and for long, step-by-step tasks. They thrived on disorder, ambiguity, and frequent interruptions. In short, he discovered that they were clearly right-brain types with appropriate intuitive dominance.

In order to deal with the ambiguous inefficient side of the market, it is this author's contention that portfolio managers must have good intuitive skills such as those Mintzberg found existed in successful corporate executives. The hypothesis of this article is that the poor investment performance over the last fifteen years was primarily caused by an uneven development of skills within the investment community. While the capabilities of the left-brained, analytical skills have been given increased emphasis, the intuitive right-brained talents necessary to make effective decisions were pooh-poohed as unscientific and thus strongly stifled. In many cases, top management of investment institutions has stifled intuitive skills by requiring money managers to document every move. Thus, by waiting for empirical evidence, financial institutions force themselves into the efficient market (i.e., loser's game).

WAS THE TITANIC'S CAPTAIN SMART?

This article started with the hypothetical disaster story about the Smartest Man in the World grabbing a hippie's pajama string rather than a rip cord. We will review an actual disaster—the sinking of the Titanic —in order to gain insight about the ship's captain. History shows that the Titanic's captain was concerned about icebergs, for during the night he stationed two seamen on the bow as lookouts. A few hours before the accident, the Titanic received a telegram warning about heavy pack-ice from the Carpathian, a freighter steaming towards the Titanic. Unfortunately, this important report became lost among the many telegrams of the passengers and thus never reached the captain. Shortly thereafter, the two alert lookouts spotted the iceberg and immediately warned the captain, who promptly took proper evasive action. The captain's system was operative, but its inherent lack of lead-time resulted in one of the most famous marine disasters of all time.

The important telegram about the pack-ice did not get to the captain; thus a contributing factor in the ship's demise was an overload of information. Key information became lost within all of the passenger's incoming and outgoing messages. Likewise, portfolio managers have to constantly deal with an overload of information. Stacks of research reports on money managers' desks attest to this overload. We checked with one client who deals with this problem by keeping a plastic garbage can in his office and found that he has kept pace with the times by adding a second can.

Another factor in the disaster was the captain's preference for hard, empirical evidence (i.e., seeing an iceberg) versus soft information (clue). For example, the telegram from the Carpathian was soft information, a clue that there might be trouble ahead. The sighting of the iceberg was hard information; empirical evidence of trouble. In the case of the Titanic's captain, he had taken great pains to set up a system for handling the hard empirical evidence, while neglecting to precondition his telegraph operator to pass on any input that might give him soft clues about his ship's course. Had he reversed his informational priorities, the Titanic might well now be a Saudi Arabian hotel.

As mentioned earlier, our society and educational systems are analytically oriented. Consequently, like the captain of the Titanic, it is easy for us to prefer to rely on data or other hard, empirical information (seeing the iceberg) versus clues (the telegraph). Unfortunately, such reliance makes us vulnerable to the unexpected. Of course, it is easier to deal with certainty rather than with the unknown. Thus, it is easier to look at numbers, which are historical as they measure events after the fact, and what management has to say (the table talk of the poker game of investing) than to deal subjectively with events and with what management is *not* saying. In other words, it is easier to deal with the elements of the efficient side of the market rather than with the more mysterious inefficient side, much as it is easier to look for lost keys under a streetlight rather than in the dark area where they were dropped.

If the world were constant, without change, analytic skills would be all that was necessary for successful investing. Economic models would work perfectly, as correlations would be static and thus predictable. Unfortunately, a la Allen Toffler's *Future Shock*, not only is there change in the world, but its pace is accelerating. Consequently, there is a certain amount of skepticism about forecasting, such as John O'Leary, Deputy Secretary of Energy, who recently stated that "Most of today's trouble in the United States is because of bad forecasts."

HELPFUL HINTS

Just as forecasters have their problems with change, so do analysts. This is because initially change is numberless—the new numbers that measure the change will not be available for some time after the change has already occurred. Therefore, to deal with change, one has to rely on skills of the non-analytic or intuitive mode. Thus, a portfolio manager needs to identify change early before it can be empirically measured by everyone (before they can see the iceberg). In other words, to be effective, he must operate in the inefficient side of the market by having the courage to make decisions with only partial information. He must accept the responsibility for dealing with changing situations.

How can the portfolio/investment strategist more effectively utilize his intuitive skills so as to better recognize change? Considering the analytical dominance of Wall Street, it isn't easy.

The following suggestions may prove to be helpful.

1. Establish what mode of thought (analytic versus intuitive) best explains your brain dominance. Can you easily make investment decisions armed only with partial information, or do you tend to put off action waiting for more facts and numbers? When your logic says one thing and your gut another, what side generally wins? Just as it can be a mistake for a company to make their best salesman a manager, the duality of the brain suggests that it also can be a mistake to make your best analyst a portfolio manager (and vice versa).

2. Resist the temptation to let analysts and others make investment decisions for you. Maybe you don't have all the facts and figures they have, but probably they don't have your intuitive skills. Spend less time at meetings listening to left-brained experts and more time developing your own network of soft information.

3. Rely more on your intuition and gut feeling. Learn to develop your ability to see what is happening that is new and unique. It is important for you to transcend "Heard on the Street" to your own column better titled "Seen in the World."

4. Try to avoid being overloaded with information. Eliminate redundant input and quickly dispose of marginal input, via trash can filing.

5. Since analysts tend to talk to the same management contacts and look at similar statistics, their conclusions almost by definition will gravitate toward similarity. Therefore, it makes sense to limit one's dialogue to only a few per industry.

6. Pay more attention to what is unique than what is normal. Conversely, pay less attention to historic correlations, as a strong belief in the "conventional wisdom" can be a block to good perception.

7. Ask yourself and your analysts what *isn't* known. By so doing, you can get a better feel for the inefficient side of the market as well as the degree of uncertainty affecting the situation.

8. Spend more time looking at and reading about the economic environment and less time looking at companies. Regular

reading of the *Oil and Gas Journal* should give you a better feel for the energy situation than, say, twenty different reports on Exxon and Mobil.

9. View investing not as a science, but an art form. Constantly keep in mind that it is better to be generally correct than precisely wrong.

10. Be skeptical of management contacts. When change is affecting their business, their competitive need for secrecy will force them to restrict important information. Business is a poker game, complete with downcards, bluffing, and table talk.

The previous suggestions are only a few ways in which a portfolio manager might better focus on his responsibilities to deal with the inefficient side of the market. The objective of a portfolio manager is not to be the World's Smartest Man, but to be his opposite. Since you can add so little to the "analysis" of investments, your time is much better spent dealing with the dangers and opportunities of change that constantly lurk within the inefficient side of the market.

True, it takes courage to make decisions when only a few clues of change are available. However, one must constantly try, or else be guilty of what Marshall McLuhan refers to as mankind's tendency to "march into the future looking in the rearview mirror"—a sure way to end up playing the loser's game.

"MARGIN OF SAFETY" AS THE CENTRAL CONCEPT OF INVESTMENT

Benjamin Graham

Benjamin Graham wrote *The Intelligent Investor* for amateur investors—but most professionals read it and recommend it. This is a book, as Graham put it, of "practical counsel." Here he is explaining the "margin of safety" which was so important to his investment thesis both as to "sound" securities and to those of a carefully analyzed "margin of value over price." In a prior chapter, he admonished readers that investing was the only business in which businessmen relied on others to make profits for them, and cautioned:

> If the investor is to rely chiefly on the advice of others in handling his funds, then either he must limit himself and his advisers strictly to standard, conservative, and even unimaginative forms of investment, or he must have an unusually intimate and favorable knowledge of the person who is going to direct his funds into other channels.
>
> The truly professional investment advisers—that is, the well-established investment counsel firms, who charge substantial annual fees—are quite modest in their promises and pretensions. For the most part they place their clients' funds in standard interest- and dividend-paying securities, and they rely mainly on normal investment experience for their overall results.

In the old legend the wise men finally boiled down the history of mortal affairs into the single phrase, "This too will pass." Confronted with a like challenge to distill the secret of sound investment into three words, we venture the motto, MARGIN OF SAFETY. This is the thread that runs through all the preceding discussion of investment policy—often explicitly, sometimes in a less direct fashion. Let us try now, briefly, to trace that idea in a connected argument.

All experienced investors recognize that the margin-of-safety concept is essential to the choice of sound bonds and preferred stocks. For example, a railroad should have earned its total fixed charges better than five times (before income tax), taking a period of years, for its bonds to qualify as investment-grade issues. This *past* ability to earn in excess of interest requirements constitutes the margin of safety that is counted on to protect the investor against loss or discomfiture in the event of some *future* decline in net income. (The margin above charges may be stated in other ways—for example, in the percentage by which revenues or profits may decline before the balance after interest disappears—but the underlying idea remains the same.)

The bond investor does not expect future average earnings to work out the same as in the past; if he were sure of that, the margin demanded might be small. Nor does he rely to any controlling extent on his judgment as to whether future earnings will be materially better or poorer than in the past; if he did that, he would have to measure his margin in terms of a carefully *projected* income account, instead of emphasizing the margin shown in the past record. Here the function of the margin of safety is, in essence, that of rendering unnecessary an accurate estimate of the future. If the margin is a large one, then it is enough to assume that future earnings will not fall far below those of the past in order for an investor to feel sufficiently protected against the vicissitudes of time.

The margin of safety for bonds may be calculated, alternatively, by comparing the total value of the enterprise with the amount of debt. (A similar calculation may be made for a preferred-stock issue.) If the business owes $10 million and is fairly worth $30 million, there is room for a shrinkage of two-thirds in value—at least theoretically—before the bondholders will suffer loss. The amount of this extra value, or "cushion," above the debt may be approximated by using the average market price of the junior stock issues over a period of years. Since average stock prices are generally related to average earning power, the margin of "enterprise value" over debt and the margin of earnings over charges will in most cases yield similar results.

There are instances where a common stock may be considered sound because it enjoys a margin of safety as large as that of a good bond. This will occur, for example, when a company has outstanding only common stock that under depression conditions is selling for less than the amount of bonds that could safely be issued against its property and earning power. That was the position of a host of strongly financed industrial companies at the low price levels of 1932–33. In such instances the investor can obtain the margin of safety associated with a bond, *plus* all the chances of larger income and principal appreciation inherent in a common stock. (The only thing he lacks is the legal power to insist on dividend payments "or else"—but this is a small drawback as compared with his advantages.) Common stocks bought under such circumstances will supply an ideal, though infrequent, combination of safety and profit opportunity. As a quite recent example of this condition, let us mention . . .National Presto Industries stock, which sold for a total enterprise value of $43 million in 1972. With its $16 millions of recent earnings before taxes the company could easily have supported this amount of bonds.

In the ordinary common stock, bought for investment under normal conditions, the margin of safety lies in an expected earning power considerably above the going rate for bonds. In former editions we elucidated this point with the following figures:

> Assume in a typical case that the earning power is 9% on the price and that the bond rate is 4%; then the stockbuyer will have an average annual margin of 5% accruing in his favor. Some of the excess is paid to him in the dividend rate; even though spent by him, it enters into his overall investment result. The undistributed balance is reinvested in the business for his account. In many cases such reinvested earnings fail to add commensurately to the earning power and value of his stock. (That is why the market has a stubborn habit of valuing earnings disbursed in dividends more generously than the portion retained in the business.) But, if the picture is viewed as a whole, there is a reasonably close connection between the growth of corporate surpluses through reinvested earnings and the growth of corporate values.
>
> Over a ten-year period the typical excess of stock earning power over bond interest may aggregate 50% of the price paid. This figure is sufficient to provide a very real margin of safety—which, under favorable condi-

tions, will prevent or minimize a loss. If such a margin is present in each of a diversified list of twenty or more stocks, the probability of a favorable result under "fairly normal conditions" becomes very large. That is why the policy of investing in representative common stocks does not require high qualities of insight and foresight to work out successfully. If the purchases are made at the average level of the market over a span of years, the prices paid should carry with them assurance of an adequate margin of safety. The danger to investors lies in concentrating their purchases in the upper levels of the market, or in buying nonrepresentative common stocks that carry more than average risk of diminished earning power.

As we see it, the whole problem of common-stock investment under 1972 conditions lies in the fact that "in a typical case" the earning power is now much less than 9% on the price paid. Let us assume that by concentrating somewhat on the low-multiplier issues among the large companies a defensive investor may now acquire equities at 12 times recent earnings—i.e., with an earnings return of 8.33% on cost. He may obtain a dividend yield of about 4%, and he will have 4.33% on his cost reinvested in the business for his account. On this basis, the excess of stock earning power over bond interest over a ten-year basis would still be too small to constitute an adequate margin of safety. For that reason we feel that there are real risks now even in a diversified list of sound common stocks. The risks may be fully offset by the profit possibilities of the list; and indeed the investor may have no choice but to incur them—for otherwise he may run an even greater risk of holding only fixed claims payable in steadily depreciating dollars. Nonetheless the investor would do well to recognize, and to accept as philosophically as he can, that the old package of *good profit possibilities combined with small ultimate risk* is no longer available to him.

However, the risk of paying too high a price for good-quality stocks—while a real one—is not the chief hazard confronting the average buyer of securities. Observation over many years has taught us that the chief losses to investors come from the purchase of *low-quality* securities at times of favorable business conditions. The purchasers view the current good earnings as equivalent to "earning power" and assume that prosperity is synonymous with safety. It is in those years that bonds and preferred stocks of inferior grade can be sold to the public at a price around par, because they carry a little higher income return or a deceptively attractive conversion privilege. It is then, also, that common stocks of obscure companies can be floated at prices far above the tangible investment, on the strength of two or three years of excellent growth.

These securities do not offer an adequate margin of safety in any admissible sense of the term. Coverage of interest charges and preferred dividends must be tested over a number of years, including preferably a period of subnormal business such as in 1970–71. The same is ordinarily true of common-stock earnings if they are to qualify as indicators of earning power. Thus it follows that most of the fair-weather investments, acquired at fair-weather prices, are destined to suffer disturbing price declines when the horizon clouds over—and often sooner than that. Nor can the investor count with confidence on an eventual recovery—although this does come about in some proportion of the cases—for he has never had a real safety margin to tide him through adversity.

The philosophy of investment in growth stocks parallels in part and in part contravenes the margin-of-safety principle. The growth-stock buyer relies on an expected earning power that is greater than the average shown in the past. Thus he may be said to substitute these expected earnings for the past record in calculating his margin of safety. In investment theory there is no reason why carefully estimated future earnings should be a less reliable guide than the bare record of the past; in fact, security analysis is coming more and more to prefer a competently executed evaluation of the future. Thus the growth-stock approach may supply as dependable a margin of safety as is found in the ordinary investment—provided the calculation of the future is conservatively made, and provided it shows a satisfactory margin in relation to the price paid.

The danger in a growth-stock program lies precisely here. For such favored issues the market has a tendency to set prices that will not be adequately protected by a *conservative* projection of future earnings. (It is a basic rule of prudent investment that all estimates, when they differ from past performance, must err at least slightly on the side of understatement.) The margin of safety is always dependent on the price paid. It will be large at one price, small at some higher price, nonexistent at some still higher price. If, as we suggest, the average market level of most growth stocks is too high to provide an adequate margin of safety for the buyer, then a simple technique of diversified buying in this field may not work out satisfactorily. A special degree of foresight and judgment will be needed, in order that wise individual selections may overcome the hazards inherent in the customary market level of such issues as a whole.

The margin-of-safety idea becomes much more evident when we apply it to the field of undervalued or bargain securities. We have here, by definition, a favorable difference between price on the one hand and indicated or appraised value on the other. That difference is the safety margin. It is available for absorbing the effect of miscalculations or worse than average luck. The buyer of bargain issues places particular emphasis on the ability of the investment to withstand adverse developments. For in most such cases he has no real enthusiasm about the company's prospects. True, if the prospects are definitely bad the investor will prefer to avoid the security no matter how low the price. But the field of undervalued issues is drawn from the many concerns—perhaps a majority of the total—for which the future appears neither distinctly promising nor distinctly unpromising. If these are bought on a bargain basis, even a moderate decline in the earning power need not prevent the investment from showing satisfactory results. The margin of safety will then have served its proper purpose.

THEORY OF DIVERSIFICATION

There is a close logical connection between the concept of a safety margin and the principle of diversification. One is correlative with the other. Even with a margin in the investor's favor, an individual security may work out badly. For the margin guarantees only that he has a better chance for profit than for loss—not that loss is impossible. But as the number of such commitments is increased the more certain does it become that the aggregate of the profits will exceed the aggregate of the losses. That is the simple basis of the insurance-underwriting business.

Diversification is an established tenet of conservative investment. By accepting it so universally, investors are really demonstrating their acceptance of the margin-of-safety principle, to which diversification is the companion. This point may be made more colorful by a reference to the arithmetic of roulette. If a man bets $1 on a single number, he is paid $35 profit when he wins—but the chances are 37 to 1 that he will lose. He has a "negative margin of safety." In his case diversification is foolish. The more numbers he bets on, the smaller his chance of ending with a profit. If he regularly bets $1 on every number (including 0 and 00), he is certain to lose $2 on each turn of the wheel. But suppose the winner received $39 profit instead of $31. Then he would have a small but important margin of safety. Therefore, the more numbers he wagers on, the better his chance of gain. And he could be certain of winning $2 on every spin by simply betting $1 each on all the numbers. (Incidentally, the two examples given actually describe the respective positions of the player and proprietor of a wheel with 0 and 00.)

A CRITERION OF INVESTMENT
VERSUS SPECULATION

Since there is no single definition of investment in general acceptance, authorities have the right to define it pretty much as they please. Many of them deny that there is any useful or dependable difference between the concepts of investment and speculation. We think this skepticism is unnecessary and harmful. It is injurious because it lends encouragement to the innate leaning of many people toward the excitement and hazards of stock-market speculation. We suggest that the margin-of-safety concept may be used to advantage as the touchstone to distinguish an investment operation from a speculative one.

Probably most speculators believe they have the odds in their favor when they take their chances, and therefore they may lay claim to a safety margin in their proceedings. Each one has the feeling that the time is propitious for his purchase, or that his skill is superior to the crowd's, or that his adviser or system is trustworthy. But such claims are unconvincing. They rest on subjective judgment, unsupported by any body of favorable evidence or any conclusive line of reasoning. We greatly doubt whether the man who stakes money on his view that the market is heading up or down can ever be said to be protected by a margin of safety in any useful sense of the phrase.

By contrast, the investor's concept of the margin of safety—as developed earlier in this chapter—rests upon simple and definite arithmetical reasoning from statistical data. We believe, also, that it is well supported by practical investment experience. There is no guarantee that this fundamental quantitative approach will continue to show favorable results under the unknown conditions of the future. But, equally, there is no valid reason for pessimism on this score.

Thus, in sum, we say that to have a true investment there must be present a true margin of safety. And a true margin of safety is one that can be demonstrated by figures, by persuasive reasoning, and by reference to a body of actual experience.

EXTENSION OF THE CONCEPT OF INVESTMENT

To complete our discussion of the margin-of-safety principle we must now make a further distinction between conventional and unconventional investments. Conventional investments are appropriate for the typical portfolio. Under this heading have always come United States government issues and high-grade, dividend-paying common stocks. We have added state and municipal bonds for those who will benefit sufficiently by their tax-exempt features. Also included are first-quality corporate bonds when, as now, they can be bought to yield sufficiently more than United States savings bonds.

Unconventional investments are those that are suitable only for the enterprising investor. They cover a wide range. The broadest category is that of undervalued common stocks of secondary companies, which we recommend for purchase when they can be bought at two-thirds or less of their indicated value. Besides these, there is often a wide choice of medium-grade corporate bonds and preferred stocks when they are selling at such depressed prices as to be obtainable also at a considerable discount from their apparent value. In these cases the average investor would be inclined to call the securities speculative, because in his mind their lack of a first-quality rating is synonymous with a lack of investment merit.

It is our argument that a sufficiently low price can turn a security of mediocre quality into a sound investment opportunity—provided that the buyer is informed and experienced and that he practices adequate diversification. For, if the price is low enough to create a substantial margin of safety, the security thereby meets our criterion of investment. Our favorite supporting illustration is taken from the field of real-estate bonds. In the 1920s, billions of dollars' worth of these issues were sold at par and widely recommended as sound investments. A large proportion had so little margin of value over debt as to be in fact highly speculative in character. In the depression of the 1930s an enormous quantity of these bonds defaulted their interest, and their price collapsed—in some cases below 10 cents on the dollar. At that stage the same advisers who had recommended them at par as safe investments were rejecting them as paper of the most speculative and unattractive type. But as a matter of fact the price depreciation of about 90% made many of these securities exceedingly attractive and reasonably safe—for the true values behind them were four or five times the market quotation.

The fact that the purchase of these bonds actually resulted in what is generally called "a large speculative profit" did not prevent them from having true investment qualities at their low prices. The "speculative" profit was the purchaser's reward for having made an unusually shrewd investment. They could properly be called *investment* opportunities, since a careful analysis would have shown that the excess of value over price provided a large margin of safety. Thus the very class of "fair-weather investments" which we stated above is a chief source of serious loss to naive security buyers is likely to afford many sound profit opportunities to the sophisticated operator who may buy them later at pretty much his own price.

The whole field of "special situations" would come under our definition of investment operations, because the purchase is always predicated on a thoroughgoing analysis that promises a larger realization than the price paid. Again there are risk factors in each individual case, but these are allowed for in the calculations and absorbed in the overall results of a diversified operation.

To carry this discussion to a logical extreme, we might suggest that a defensible investment operation could be set up by buying such intangible values as are represented by a group of "common-stock option warrants" selling at historically low prices. (This example is intended as somewhat of a shocker.) The entire value of these warrants rests on the possibility that the related stocks may some day advance above the option price. At the moment they have no exercisable value. Yet, since all investment rests on reasonable future expectations, it is proper to view these warrants in terms of the mathematical chances that some future bull market will create a large increase in their indicated value and in their price. Such a study might well yield the conclusion that there is much more to be gained in such an operation than to be lost and that the chances of an ultimate profit are much better than those of an ultimate loss. If that is so, there is a safety margin present even in this unprepossessing security form. A sufficiently enterprising investor could then include an option-warrant operation in his miscellany of unconventional investments.[1]

TO SUM UP

Investment is most intelligent when it is most *businesslike*. It is amazing to see how many capable businessmen try to operate in Wall Street with complete disregard of all the sound principles through which they have gained success in their own undertakings. Yet every corporate security may best be viewed, in the first instance, as an ownership interest in, or a claim against, a specific business enterprise. And if a person sets out to make profits from security purchases and sales, he is embarking on a business venture of his own, which must be run in accordance with accepted business principles if it is to have a chance of success.

The first and most obvious of these principles is, "Know what you are doing—know your business." For the investor this means: Do not try to make "business profits" out of securities—that is, returns in excess of normal interest and dividend income—unless you know as much about security values as you would need to know about the value of merchandise that you proposed to manufacture or deal in.

A second business principle: "Do not let anyone else run your business, unless (1) you can supervise his performance with adequate care and comprehension or (2) you have unusually strong reasons for placing implicit confidence in his integrity and ability." For the investor this rule should determine the conditions under which he will permit someone else to decide what is done with his money.

A third business principle: "Do not enter upon an operation—that is, manufacturing or trading in an item—unless a reliable calculation shows that it has a fair chance to yield a reasonable profit. In particular, keep away from ventures in which you have little to gain and much to lose." For the enterprising investor this means that his operations for profit should be based not on optimism but on arithmetic. For every investor it means that when he limits his return to a small figure—as formerly, at least, in a conventional bond or preferred stock—he must demand convincing evidence that he is not risking a substantial part of his principal.

A fourth business rule is more positive: "Have the courage of your knowledge and experience. If you have formed a conclusion from the facts and if you know your judgment is sound, act on it—even though others may hesitate or differ." (You are neither right nor wrong because the crowd disagrees with you. You are right because your data and reasoning are right.)   Similarly, in the world of securities, courage becomes the supreme virtue *after* adequate knowledge and a tested judgment are at hand.

Fortunately for the typical investor, it is by no means necessary for his success that he bring these qualities to bear upon his program— *provided* he limits his ambition to his capacity and confines his activities within the safe and narrow path of standard, defensive investment. To achieve *satisfactory* investment results is easier than most people realize; to achieve *superior* results is harder than it looks.

POSTSCRIPT

We know very well two partners who spent a good part of their lives handling their own and other people's funds in Wall Street. Some hard experience taught them it was better to be safe and careful rather than to try to make all the money in the world. They established a rather unique approach to security operations, which combined good profit possibilities with sound values. They avoided anything that appeared overpriced and were rather too quick to dispose of issues that had advanced to levels they deemed no longer attractive. Their portfolio was always well diversified, with more than a hundred different issues represented. In this way they did quite well through many years of ups and down in the general market; they averaged about 20% per annum on the several millions of capital they had accepted for management, and their clients were well pleased with the results.

In the year in which the first edition of this book appeared an opportunity was offered to the partners' fund to purchase a half-interest in a growing enterprise. For some reason the industry did not have Wall Street appeal at the time and the deal had been turned down by quite a few important houses. But the pair was impressed by the company's possibilities; what was decisive for them was that the price was moderate in relation to current earnings and asset value. The partners went ahead with the acquisition, amounting in dollars to about one-fifth of their fund. They become closely identified with the new business interest, which prospered.

In fact it did so well that the price of its shares advanced to two hundred times or more the price paid for the half-interest. The advance far outstripped the actual growth in profits, and almost from the start the quotation appeared much too high in terms of the partners' own investment standards. But since they regarded the company as a sort of "family business," they continued to maintain a substantial ownership of the shares despite the spectacular price rise. A large number of participants in their funds did the same, and they became millionaires through their holding in this one enterprise, plus later-organized affiliates.

Ironically enough, the aggregate of profits accruing from this single investment-decision far exceeded the sum of all the others realized through 20 years of wide-ranging operations in the partners' specialized fields, involving much investigation, endless pondering, and countless individual decisions.

Are there morals to this story of value to the intelligent investor? An obvious one is that there are several different ways to make and keep money in Wall Street. Another, not so obvious, is that one lucky break, or one supremely shrewd decision—can we tell them apart?— may count for more than a lifetime of journeyman efforts.[2] But behind luck, or the crucial decision, there must usually exist a background of preparation and disciplined capacity. One needs to be sufficiently established and recognized so that these opportunities will knock at his particular door. One must have the means, the judgment, and the courage to take advantage of them.

Of course, we cannot promise a like spectacular experience to all intelligent investors who remain both prudent and alert through the years. We are not going to end with J. J. Raskob's slogan that we made fun of at the beginning: "Everybody can be rich." But interesting possibilities abound on the financial scene, and the intelligent and enterprising investor should be able to find both enjoyment and profit in this three-ring circus. Excitement is guaranteed.

FOOTNOTES

1. This argument is supported by Paul Hallingby, Jr., "Speculative Opportunities in Stock-Purchase Warrants," *Analysts' Journal*, third quarter 1947.

2. Veracity requires the admission that the deal almost fell through because the partners wanted assurance that the purchase price would be 100% covered by asset value. A future $300 million or more in market gain turned on, say, $50,000 of accounting items. By dumb luck they got what they insisted on.

TOWARD BRIDGING THE GAP: CAPITAL MARKET THEORY AND MONEY MANAGEMENT VIA CODIFICATION OF THE CONVENTIONAL WISDOM

Gary B. Helms

Here, perhaps, is all the Wall Street (and Main Street) wisdom you will ever need. Not only do Gary Helms' wry selections make marvelous one-liners, but in various combinations can be assembled into sentences, or even whole paragraphs full of delightfully profound (and zany) potential.

EXHIBIT 1
Conventional Wisdom Codification

Hut Number

061431–29–1	Nobody has been right three times.
123456–19–2	Turnarounds take seven years.
239561–18–3	Buy in haste, repent at leisure.
345312–17–4	The standard estimate (S.E.) for undiscovered growth companies is $1.40.

Reprinted from *The Financial Analysts Journal*, Vol. 34, No. 1, January/February 1978, 69–72. New York, New York: Financial Analysts Federation.

EXHIBIT I (continued)
Conventional Wisdom Codification

Hut Number

743216–14–2	The standard estimate for turnarounds is $2, $4 and $6.
664278–12–1	The standard estimate for sleeping giants is $8 in earning power.
432854–10–3	Blood is thicker than water, but then so is orange juice.
454180–16–5	Sell the stock when the company announces a new corporate headquarters.
209413–62–4	Sell the stock when the CEO doesn't return your call.
395610–33–5	Sell the stock when it runs off the top (or bottom) of the chart.
561234–17–6	When everybody likes a stock, it *must* go down; when nobody likes a stock, it *may* go up.
611456–14–7	Blondes have more fun because they're easier to find in the dark.
654213–22–8	If you take a starving dog and make him sleek and prosperous, he will not bite you; this is the principal difference between man and dog.
169812–44–5	No tree grows to the sky.
624318–98–2	Sell your losers and let your runners run.
247914–43–7	Never say never.
223546–68–3	Never say die.
375463–28–9	Never confuse brilliance with a bull market.
454189–52–4	More stocks double than go to zero.
302178–11–6	The market is a random walk up a 9.3 per cent grade.
821466–71–2	If anybody really knew, they wouldn't tell you.
971684–33–7	Take two aspirin *before* retiring.
513621–89–5	New York is more provincial than the provinces.
986624–64–8	He jests at scars who never felt a wound.
779945–15–4	A watched pot never boils.
439755–11–2	There are no cabs when it's raining.
446210–77–4	$E = MC^2$.
384159–92–7	The best thing about money management is that it's indoor work with no heavy lifting.
272451–79–9	All generalizations are false, including this one.
698132–24–2	A stock well bought is a stock half sold.
048651–58–9	It's a long, long time from May to December, but no longer long enough for a long-term capital gain.
235725–93–6	In a bull market, be bullish.
437981–73–2	Water seeks its level.
756336–45–8	The bottom is always 10 per cent below your worst case expectation.
479142–46–7	If you buy a suit with two pairs of pants, you'll burn a hole in the coat.
318940–63–2	There are no customers' yachts.
714652–53–4	Never knock late with nine or 10.

EXHIBIT I (continued)
Conventional Wisdom Codification

Hut Number

643175–37–5	There's no free lunch in Wall Street, nor a decent cheeseburger at any price.
437591–22–8	Nothing is more deleterious to portfolio performance than a mediocre analyst or a mediocre secretary.
012644–73–6	Risk is what's left over after the bad news hits.
951483–29–1	Money can't be managed within the letter of the law.
126351–30–3	The first word in analyst is anal.
813794–05–9	Open-faced sandwiches fall jelly side down.
343320–49–1	OTB processes a ticket cheaper than Don Weeden.
725541–61–8	If you know what's going on, you don't have to know what's going on to know what's going on.
214463–23–1	All growth is temporary.
858439–26–5	Candy's dandy but liquor's quicker.
313579–40–3	A bright and energetic guy can make all the mistakes in this business in five years, but fools and sluggards can take a lifetime.
663611–39–5	Stars tend to twinkle a lot.
223459–51–2	If you need to get out of town in the worst way, call Eastern.
592243–55–3	The race isn't necessarily to the swift, but that's the way to bet it.
517980–24–2	Beauty is only skin deep, but in many cases, that's deep enough.
758423–51–3	You only need two research sources on a stock if one is a bull and one is a bear.
644432–34–9	An outstanding portfolio always contains an outstanding stock.
597632–39–9	Analysts write long research reports when they don't have time to write short ones.
125459–40–1	Nobody is smarter than the guy who gave you your last winner.
368921–41–3	Not to decide is to decide.
454425–49–8	Shut up when a trader enters the room.
953174–36–4	The budget will not be balanced in your lifetime.
663611–39–5	There's never been a good Super Bowl.
223459–51–2	Economics is what economists do.
592243–55–3	You never understand a stock until you're long (or short).
517980–24–2	There are no holds.
758423–51–3	You can't kiss all the girls.
644432–34–9	Some stocks will beat you every time.
579134–35–6	Go with pitching in a short series.
597632–39–9	Bulls make money and bears make money, but pigs get swine flu.
125459–49–1	Money makes the mare go.
368921–41–3	Money matters.
365455–53–6	Beauty is in the eye of the beholder.
145641–75–9	If you play too tight, the ante will eat you up.

EXHIBIT I (continued)
Conventional Wisdom Codification

Hut Number

641777–72–3	Hot research shops burn out in $5\frac{1}{2}$ years.
456891–63–1	Never answer the phone call of an analyst, but allow him to leave word.
232150–27–2	The best telephone message is "Ask him to call me before the close."
451678–33–3	This business is getting more complicated.
378123–54–8	None of the old rules work any more, but then they never did.
315489–53–1	Never throw good money after bad.
363276–45–7	Never dip into capital.
981204–50–6	Washington is a city of Northern charm and Southern efficiency.
324857–15–9	Someone will always have a better record.
234445–85–4	Ten doubles will make one million dollars out of one thousand.
513792–63–8	A lot of things aren't worth knowing.
798366–77–2	A penny saved will depreciate rapidly.
301259–36–6	Half of your portfolio is cyclic, but you don't know which half.
554211–63–5	You will never be the first to hear.
521598–14–3	Cyclic stocks should be bought when their multiples are high and sold when their multiples are low.
771234–59–4	Growth will bail you out—if you live long enough.
815657–44–7	It is better to be number 1 and down 10 per cent than number 200 and up 10 per cent.
717543–60–8	Never look back; something might be gaining on you.
614855–10–1	Never eat at a place called Mom's or play poker with a man called Doc.
227655–84–5	Trust everybody but cut the cards.
471352–35–6	You will lose most 50-50 bets.
321029–30–3	There is no such thing as inside information.
673956–64–1	The millennium will have come when the Found column is as long as the Lost.
680551–85–9	Calories do count.
732540–87–7	Sell at the opening, buy at the close.
610555–83–9	You can only buy for growth, yield or assets.
454545–61–8	You can make a silk purse out of a sow's ear, but it's not worth the effort.
699877–35–6	Mass follows class.
754100–28–3	Nobody knows what you're going through.
666300–45–1	Don't hold research meetings on Friday afternoons or Monday mornings.
554010–59–4	Successful money managers have brains, nerve and luck.
239624–71–9	Living well is the best revenge.
245988–47–5	Every time a trade is made, somebody was wrong.
494847–40–9	Two things cause a stock to move—the expected and the unexpected.

EXHIBIT I (continued)
Conventional Wisdom Codification

Hut Number

525546–29–6	The market is a discounting mechanism.
689529–15–5	A cynic knows the price of everything and the value of nothing.
889444–27–3	Don't apologize for acting on your instincts if you've spent years developing them.
655931–29–6	Nature abhors a vacuum.
334455–55–4	Opportunity knocks but once.
411123–79–1	Money could be managed with a *Wall Street Journal* and a 12-year Cycligraph if it weren't other people's money.
608954–74–2	It's not what you make—it's what you don't pay in taxes.
495049–81–4	A money manager without a client is not a money manager at all.
499975–30–6	What's good for G.M. is good for the country.
987464–51–9	You can always get sober but you can't get smart.
877212–67–4	Money management is 10 per cent inspiration and 90 per cent perspiration.
254773–38–2	You really should cut your list.
657124–33–5	There are no atheists in foxholes nor conservatives when the subsidies are being passed out.
543890–15–8	The new high list will do better in the subsequent six months than the new low list will.
115599–86–4	Ralph Nader is unsafe at any speed.
445010–75–3	You drink too much coffee.
511105–32–5	Anyone who wants to give youth a greater say hasn't been to a rock concert lately.
452890–36–7	Shift into neutral when idling.
293949–28–6	Sell down to your sleep point.
675680–84–4	The stock doesn't know you own it.
161514–74–8	Shake well before using.
474930–64–3	Make sure that seatbacks and tray tables are in their full upright position.
321998–25–7	When two people in an organization think exactly alike, one of them is redundant.
698754–13–3	You can't spend relative performance.
764333–19–1	The trouble with managing money is that everybody once made a successful investment.
288443–47–7	Eagles don't flock.
379204–56–6	Sell when the research file gets full.
223965–63–8	Drive for show, putt for dough.
413172–33–2	Own West Coast companies in bull markets, Boston companies in bear.
582155–26–5	Don't ask your legal counsel if but how.
729360–75–8	Be long term but watch the ticks.
496370–18–4	Small money is easier to manage than big money only if you own the same stocks.

EXHIBIT I (continued)
Conventional Wisdom Codification

Hut Number

217341–17–3	Beware of your colleague who doesn't seem busy.
208911–11–1	Wherever the American city is going, Newark will get there first.
451352–25–4	It's easy to be a brilliant manager if you control $1/_{250}$ of the land mass of the continental U.S.
252321–35–1	There is more than one way to skin a cat, and six ways to roll a seven.
334372–42–6	Too many cooks spoil the broth.
553466–45–7	You can't trust a newly-rich management or anyone in investor relations.
531723–38–1	A portfolio that goes down 50 per cent and comes back 50 percent is still down 25 per cent.
451425–27–3	There are only 17 really great companies in the U.S.
828381–54–3	Never average down.
651789–37–4	There are no one-decision stocks.
789554–40–1	A good relationship means never having to say you're sorry.
398765–75–4	Rudyard Kipling said it all.
675493–62–5	John Maynard Keynes said it all.
547270–39–4	Bernard Baruch said it all.
459697–34–7	Howard Cosell really said it all.
749760–51–3	All really great money management organizations have had three partners.
929259–41–5	If you had it to do over, you'd do the same.
471124–87–8	A group of men thinks like a single woman.
555952–92–9	A manager is only truly evaluated on his first and last days with a firm.
393043–94–5	Fewer poor investment decisions are made in February than any other month.
663042–75–4	Working long hours is a sign of insecurity.
926956–93–6	Two plus two equals four.
406527–82–7	Never own it if the corporate title includes the words Universal, Global, or Intergalactic.
315067–94–7	There are many millionaires in Wall Street, not all of whom started out as multimillionaires.
743796–69–4	Babe Ruth once led the league in strikeouts.
457567–89–3	Price wars get worse than you think.
645982–31–4	Every wheat crop is given up on seven times before it is harvested.
796854–32–6	The market will fluctuate.
894105–04–3	About half the people in your shop are pulling their weight.
183327–13–5	Miss at least one meeting a day.
153123–25–2	If you have a great thought and write it down, it will look stupid 10 hours later.
556441–28–1	Get caught bluffing once a night.

EXHIBIT I (continued)
Conventional Wisdom Codification

Hut Number

153123–25–2	There are no greater fools.
543387–43–4	You might be right about where the market or a stock is going, but you can't possibly predict where it will go after that.
452253–15–4	You can be 200 per cent wrong when you switch.
111367–26–1	Talk is cheap, but so is paper.
371143–79–2	A guy who likes a stock but doesn't own it has no right to an opinion.
785431–68–8	You'll never know who your friends are until you've had two bad years in a row.
271143–92–6	Bad as it is, there are some people who'd like your job.
857063–92–7	War is diplomacy carried out by other means.
746996–37–6	The difference between the productivity of the American truck driver and the Chinese coolie is the truck.
562551–28–5	Money management is a cottage industry.
665402–97–3	If a white lie will save 45 minutes of useless conversation, tell it.
474344–88–2	Lighters run out of fluid the second day of a three-day trip.
191333–46–7	Slow down when going through a small town.
331457–89–6	W. C. Fields would really rather be in Philadelphia.
752999–12–3	Waste time only with people you like.
346039–47–4	One peek is worth two finesses.
277693–32–7	There are no defensive stocks.
448086–57–6	When everybody indexes, the 500 stocks will remain unchanged relative to each other.
961457–98–6	If you can figure out who will get the cash inflow in a cycle, you've got that cycle beaten.
523501–11–5	He who knows not and knows that he knows not is a wise man.
357010–54–4	A good portfolio manager never asks a question unless he knows the answer.
851098–34–5	A guy who has all the answers doesn't even understand the questions.
321432–19–8	To err is human, to hedge divine.
545150–80–7	The best defense is a good offense.
486212–77–4	The trouble with the stock market is not that it is controlled by mathematical factors, or that it is controlled by non-mathematical factors, but that it is controlled by nearly mathematical factors.
915475–79–9	The trouble with this generation of analysts is that they never lived through a bull market.
603779–99–4	The trouble with economists is that they never met a payroll.
393455–75–5	The trouble with statistical analysis is that the first seven kings of England named Henry had an average of 1.3 wives.
418940–59–4	Recognition of an idea is more important than the origination thereof.

EXHIBIT I (continued)
Conventional Wisdom Codification

Hut Number

247459–80–6	A statesman is a dead politician.
797321–11–4	Nobody can see his own backswing.
551925–98–6	All the news that fits, they print.
133445–72–7	Chicken Little was right.
428911–62–0	Malthus was right.
757462–31–5	Archimedes was right (re: leverage).
624651–02–5	If the industry leader is overvalued, don't buy the dogs.
246395–17–5	Always take out your bait after a triple.
014052–72–8	Always follow through high to a full extension.
273521–24–6	There will always be a two-tier market.
030201–52–4	There will always be an England.
685218–39–5	You can always tell a Harvard man, but you can't tell him much.
203222–71–5	Newton was the first technician.
164590–32–5	The dogs come late and sit near the bar.
865422–14–6	The truth will set you free, but Scotch isn't bad either.
029103–30–3	Price is a fundamental—it's the only thing you know for sure about a stock.
725611–73–9	The pen is mightier than the pencil.
012064–77–2	Don't bet a sure thing unless you can afford to lose.
834371–55–4	If Shakespeare lived today, he'd be writing copy for Doyle, Dane.
221543–41–6	If Shakespeare lived today, he'd have his own rock group.
356212–63–7	Pressure is playing a $10 Nassau with strangers and only $7 to your name.
723429–26–4	The wife is not necessarily the last to know.
828182–31–4	More people have read Sylvia Porter than Paul Samuelson.
623197–42–9	The public will come back.
515942–61–7	You don't really understand IBM unless you've owned SDS and Amdahl.
948261–37–2	The difference between plagiarism and research is that research utilizes more than one source.
674193–62–7	Buy on the rumor, sell on the news.
617852–29–2	Buy when you can't find a bull.
869516–36–5	Options aren't new, since Esau sold one and had the position called away.
626849–38–2	There is no Santa Claus.
717399–26–4	Time is money.
412856–51–7	The Garden wouldn't hold all the guys who claim to be at the Ranger games.
825182–42–5	If the idea is right, eighths and quarters won't matter.
386716–73–4	The most consistently profitable extractive industry is dentistry.
823182–51–4	Chart breakouts don't count if your own buying does it.
765317–42–8	Whoever has the gold makes the rules.

EXHIBIT I (continued)
Conventional Wisdom Codification

Hut Number

015428–64–3	The Eskimos have 17 words to describe different kinds of snow, and there isn't an FAF chapter within miles.
625614–57–8	Middle age is when you are doing more things for the last time, and fewer things for the first time.
715372–42–3	If God had meant money managers to fly coach, he'd have given them narrower posteriors.
629033–27–4	The first wheel was square.

INTEREST
ON INTEREST

Sidney Homer
Martin L. Leibowitz

The great importance of "Interest on Interest" was not recognized sufficiently in 1972 when Sidney Homer and Martin Leibowitz published *Inside
the Yield Book*. Subsequent instruction in the lesson over the next 15 years
was both extensive and intensive. The main idea is clearly presented in
the first chapter from that book.

The recent high level of bond yields and the uncertainty whether yields
will be high in the years ahead emphasizes the importance of interest-
on-interest, that is to say, the rate at which receipts from coupons
can be reinvested in the future. An original investment compounds
automatically at the purchase yield only until the funds are paid back in
the form of coupons and finally of principal. However, some investors
mistakenly expect that a bond purchased at a given yield will always
produce that rate as a realized compound yield over the whole life of the
bond. If future reinvestment rates during the life of the bond are less
than the purchase yield, then the realized compound yield for the whole

life of the bond will be less than the purchase yield; if future rates are higher than the purchase yield, then the realized compound yield will be more than the purchase yield.

LONG-TERM PAR BONDS

For most long-term bonds, the interest-on-interest is a surprisingly important part of the total compounded return to the bondholder: typically over half.

Table 1 shows that for an 8% 10-year bond bought at 100 to yield 8% the total return over the twenty-year period may vary from $1,600 per $1,000 invested (4.84%) to $4,832 (9.01%) depending upon whether the interest-on-interest is 0% (interest spent—in a financially non-productive way—as coupons are paid) or 10%. When the reinvestment rate is also 8%, the coupons over the twenty years will total $1,600 per $1,000 invested and the interest on this interest will total $2,201 or 58% of the total return of $3,801. If the rate of interest-on-interest is 6%, the interest-on-interest will decline to $1,416, and the total return to $3,016 per $1,000 invested, bringing the total realized compound yield to the purchaser down from the original 8% to 7.07%. On the other hand, if the rate of interest-on-interest rises to 10%, interest-on-interest will rise

TABLE 1
An 8% Non-Callable 20-Year Bond Bought at 100 to Yield 8%

Interest-on-Interest						Total
Reinvest-ment Rate	% of Total Return	Amount	Coupon Income	Discount	Total Return	Realized Compound Yield
0%	0%	$ 0	$1,600	0	$1,600	4.84%
5	41	1,096	1,600	0	2,696	6.64
6	47	1,416	1,600	0	3,016	7.07
7	53	1,782	1,600	0	3,382	7.53
8*	58*	2,201*	1,600*	0	3,801*	8.00*
9	63	2,681	1,600	0	4,281	8.50
10	67	3,232	1,600	0	4,832	9.01

*Yield from Yield Book.

to $3,232 and total return to $4,832 per $1,000 invested bringing the total realized compound yield to the purchaser up to 9.01%.

It follows that a present purchaser of a long-term 8% non-callable bond at 100 is by no means assured of a realized yield of 8% for the life of his investment if by yield is meant interest compounded on the entire original investment for the entire life of the bond: it might turn out to be 6.64% or 9.01% or more or less, depending on the future trend of bond yields. The uncertainty is entirely confined to the compounding factor. In terms of simple interest, the investor is sure to get 8% from this 8% bond, i.e., $80 a year per $1,000 if the bond is not called or defaulted.

THE YIELD BOOK

The Yield Book serves the essential function of providing a uniform basis for comparing the market values of bonds having different coupons, maturities, dollar prices and, consequently, different cash flows over their life. To achieve this uniformity, the Yield Book in essence refers every dollar of every bond's cash flow to the standard of an initial investment allowed to accumulate compound interest semiannually at the Yield Book rate until it is paid off in the form of coupon or principal. For example, suppose one has two 20-year bonds, one with a coupon of 8% and the other with a 4% coupon, both priced "to yield 8%." This 8% figure can be taken to mean that both bonds are equivalent to the standard of an 8% semiannually compounded investment, which would realize a return of $3,801 per $1,000 invested over the twenty-year period.

It is not so well known that to obtain this objective it is necessary that the bonds' coupon income be reinvested so as to gather "interest-on-interest" at a rate exactly equal to the yield-to-maturity itself. The two 8% yield-to-maturity bonds in the above example would realize the standardized 8% return of $3,801 per $1,000 invested only if each and every coupon were itself reinvested at an exact 8% rate. If the coupons cannot be reinvested at the Yield Book rate, then the realized compound yield over the bond's life of the dollars originally invested may vary widely from the Yield Book figure. For this reason, when facing future periods involving possible major swings in yield levels, it becomes vitally important to distinguish between the yield-to-maturity (as stated in the Yield Book) and the realized compound yield that will actually be obtained if the bond is held to maturity.

SIMPLE INTEREST VS. COMPOUND INTEREST

Many investors, like university endowment funds and foundations and private investors, simply collect and spend their coupons. They tend to ignore the variability of compound interest. Others, like pension funds, accumulate interest receipts, merge them with principal and reinvest them; these are vitally affected by the future rate of interest and ordinarily cannot, when they invest, obtain any assurance as to just what their total return will be.[1]

MATURITY

As maturity is reduced, the importance of interest-on-interest declines sharply. This is illustrated by Table 2 which shows that for a 1-year 8% bond at 100, interest-on-interest will account for only 2% of total return, while for a 40-year 8% bond it will account for 86% of total return. The uncertainty can be said to be basic only for longer maturities.

It is obvious, however, that shorter maturities, while reducing or

TABLE 2
Effect of Maturity on the Importance of Interest-on-Interest (Assuming Reinvestment at Yield Rate)

	% of Total Return Represented by Interest-on-Interest	
Maturity	8% Bonds Bought at 100 to Yield 8%	4% Bonds Bought at 100 to Yield 4%
1 Year	2%	1%
5 Years	17	9
10 Years	33	18
20 Years	58	34
30 Years	75	47
40 Years	86	59

almost eliminating the uncertainty of the rate of interest-on-interest do not solve the problems of maintaining future income. Indeed, the uncertainty is larger with shorter term bonds because in the reinvestment of shorts at maturity the coupon, in addition to the compounding factor, is uncertain. Thus, the old rule will usually hold: if future rates are to rise, shorts bought now will be better than longs; if rates decline, longs will be better than shorts.

LONG-TERM DISCOUNT BONDS

Table 3 shows the same calculation for a deep discount bond, a 20-year 4% bond selling at about 60⅜ to yield 8%. The top panel shows

TABLE 3
A 4% 20-Year Bond Bought at 60.414 to Yield 8%

Reinvest- ment Rate	Interest-on-Interest		Coupon Income	Discount	Total Return	Total Realized Compound Yield
	% of Total Return	Amount				
A: Per Bond						
0%	0%	$ 0	$ 800	$396	$1,196	5.53%
5	31	548	800	396	1,744	6.90
6	37	708	800	396	1,904	7.25
7	43	891	800	396	2,087	7.61
8*	48*	1,100*	800*	396*	2,296*	8.00*
9	53	1,341	800	396	2,536	8.41
10	57	1,616	800	396	2,812	8.85
B: Per $1,000 Invested						
0%	0%	$ 0	$1,325	$655	$1,980	5.53%
5	31	907	1,325	655	2,877	6.90
6	37	1,172	1,325	655	3,152	7.25
7	43	1,474	1,325	655	3,454	7.61
8*	48*	1,820*	1,325*	655*	3,800*	8.00*
9	53	2,218	1,325	655	4,198	8.41
10	57	2,674	1,325	655	4,654	8.85

*Yield from Yield Book.

total return in dollars from one bond, and the bottom panel translates the same figures on the basis of each $1,000 invested, so that the returns can be compared with the 20-year 8% bond in Table 1. Here we find that the variation of total return based on changes in interest-on-interest is also large, but not as large as in the case of the par bonds. This is because the discount (eventual capital gain) is a fixed component of total return that does not vary with future interest rates. When coupon income is a smaller proportion of total return, interest-on-interest must also be a smaller portion of total return. The difference, however, between the par bond and the discount bond is not so large as to provide an absolute guide for selection. If interest-on-interest varies, between 6% and 10%, the total realized compound yield of the 8% bond will vary between 7.07% and 9.01%, while that of the 4% bond will vary between 7.25% and 8.85%. At lower future rates, the 4% bond will yield more than the 8% bond because the fixed discount substitutes for some variable interest; at higher future rates the 8% bond will yield more than the 4% bond because interest-on-interest is a larger component of total return and there is no discount.

Another way of viewing this effect is to compare the different Yield Book values giving rise to the same realized compound yield under the same reinvestment assumption. For example, the 8% par bond (Table 1) with coupons reinvested at 6% results in a realized compound yield of 7.07%. To obtain this same realized compound yield of 7.07% under the same reinvestment assumption (6%), the 4% coupon bond (Table 3) would have to be priced to yield 7.70% by the Yield Book. In other words, one could "give up" as much as 30 basis points in yield at cost, and the 4% discount bond would still prove to be as good a buy from the standpoint of realized compound yield. This comparison would, of course, not be valid in case of stable or rising interest rates.

LONG-TERM BONDS AT LOWER YIELDS

These considerations show that long-term bonds bought a few years ago at yields of 4% to 5% are actually permitting the purchasers to receive a much higher compound yield than the expected rate if the purchasers have been reinvesting their coupons. This is because those lower yields at cost assumed future reinvestment rates of 4% to 5% while their coupons have recently been reinvested at rates as high as 8% to 9%.

TABLE 4
A 4% Non-Callable 20-Year Bond Bought at 100 to Yield 4%

	Interest-on-Interest					Total
Reinvest- ment Rate	% of Total Return	Amount	Coupon Income	Discount	Total Return	Realized Compound Yield
0%	0%	$ 0	$800	0	$ 800	2.96%
1	9	83	800	0	883	3.19
2	18	178	800	0	978	3.44
3	26	285	800	0	1,085	3.71
4	34*	408*	800*	0	1,208*	4.00*
5	41	548	800	0	1,348	4.31
6	47	708	800	0	1,508	4.65
7	53	891	800	0	1,691	5.01
8	58	1,100	800	0	1,901	5.40
9	63	1,341	800	0	2,141	5.80
10	67	1,616	800	0	2,416	6.24

* Yield from Yield Book.

Table 4 . . .is comparable to Table 1 except that the original investment
is in a 4% bond at 100 to yield 4%. Discount rates are tabulated
all the way from 0 to 10%. It will be seen that the proportion of
total return depending on interest-on-interest is exactly the same as
that of the 8% bond in Table 1 if the reinvestment rates are the same
while, of course, the total returns and yields are very much less.

TIMING OF RATE CHANGES

In all of the previous tables, the future rate of interest-on-interest is
stated as one figure which might seem like an average for the twenty-
year period, but it is not: It is an artificially fixed rate of reinvestment for
all coupons from first to last at the indicated rate assumed by the tables.
In real life, rates vary widely from year to year, and a simple average
would be fallacious because of the time factor. A low reinvestment
rate a year or two after investment followed by higher rates would
bring much bigger total interest-on-interest than an early period of high
rates followed by low rates. This is because the high reinvestment rate
later would earn much more interest from the larger accumulation of

funds being reinvested. Thus, the maximum income benefit to today's purchaser would accrue from a rapid rise in interest rates soon after his purchase and thereafter sustained high rates. This, of course, is just the opposite to his profits or losses from principal fluctuations.

INVESTMENT IMPLICATIONS

1. The purchaser of long-term bonds who plans to compound his return has not achieved a certainty as to just what his total compounded realized yield will be even if the bonds are non-callable. The area of doubt is perhaps a yield range of 2%.

2. Conversely, the purchaser of non-callable long-term bonds who plans to spend his income can count on a predetermined rate of return provided only that the bonds remain in good standing.

3. For the compounding investor who expects interest rates to average lower over a long period of years than at time of purchase, there is a structural advantage in discount bonds over par bonds because that part of his return represented by the discount is fixed and cannot decline with interest rates. This advantage is supplementary to other advantages such as superior call protection and (for taxpayers) a lower tax rate. However, these advantages are often offset when discount bonds yield substantially less than high coupon bonds.

4. Conversely, for those who expect high or higher interest rates in the years ahead but who are constrained to stay with long-term bonds, there is a structural advantage in par or premium bonds because their total return will rise more rapidly with rising rates. Also, they usually yield more at time of purchase.

5. Short-term bonds provide much greater certainty of the compounded rate of return than do long-term bonds, but only for limited periods corresponding to the short-term maturities. Thereafter, because their entire principal amount must be reinvested at the then prevailing rates, the area of uncertainty is very much larger than in the case of long-term bonds.

FOOTNOTES

1. It would be possible to design a bond issue that would guarantee a rate of compound interest by paying coupons in debt rather than in cash, but it has rarely if ever been done. Savings bonds do provide guaranteed compound interest.

HOW TO INVEST IN
PROBLEM COMPANIES

Winthrop Knowlton
John L. Furth

Winthrop Knowlton and John Furth were primarily interested in successful
investment in growth stocks when they wrote *Shaking the Money Tree*,
but this chapter on investing in "value" stocks is too good to miss.

The great majority of publicly owned companies in the United States are
in some kind of trouble. Some of them—whose problems are temporary
and can be solved—represent excellent value. Others do not.

As already indicated (hopefully not to the point of reader ex-
haustion), it takes a special combination of managerial, technical, and
marketing skills for a company to rise above the general battle, to create
and dominate large, new markets that provide continually handsome
returns for shareholders. (In recent years approximately sixty companies
have accounted for close to half of all domestic corporate profits. Eight
companies have accounted for nearly a quarter of the total.)

Nevertheless, there is money to be made in problem companies.
There is a place for them in a portfolio.

As an investor in a problem company, *your* problem is to distinguish between those concerns that have a genuine recovery potential and those in which present difficulties will persist. Most businessmen—including company presidents—must be optimistic about their company's future. How else can they summon the energy to go to the office every day and to devote more time to their careers than to any other aspect of their lives? This optimism, this "can do" approach, is one of the important reasons that we have a trillion-dollar economy. But as an investor you must beware of false managerial hopes sometimes buttressed, alas, by the superficial and naive judgments of investment advisers and brokers.

Keep the following investment principles in mind when considering a commitment in a problem company:

1. Every investment in a problem or value company (as opposed to a growth company) requires *two* decisions: when to *buy* and when to *sell*. Rarely does this kind of company turn into the kind of success story we have been describing, the kind of money tree you can hold and shake for a decade or more.

2. Patience may be even more necessary for the owner of a problem company than of a growth stock. Admittedly, the growth stocks we discuss in this book by and large sell at high price-earnings ratios and provide low dividends. It may take some time before you realize sizable appreciation. However, the problems of problem companies have a way of lingering, almost always postponing rewards longer than one anticipates. "The way out of trouble," according to E. W. Howe, "is never as simple as the way in."

Let us list ten key problems confronting what may euphemistically be described as "nongrowth" companies.

1. *Cyclical problems*. The difficulties of the business cycle affect the great bulk of American companies. Each time the economy slumps, a staggering array of mining and manufacturing concerns—steel, auto, machine tool, paper, housing, chemical companies, etc.—suffer the slings and arrows of idle capacity and price weakness. Earnings drop and dividends are jeopardized.

2. *Regulatory problems*. Utilities, railroads, airlines, banks, insurance companies, broadcasters, investment banking and brokerage firms and others are subject to regulation. Sometimes this creates a degree of certainty; more often, uncertainty. One can never tell, for example, whether rate increases will be granted, route structures changed, or mergers permitted. Long lags may persist between the adjustment of revenues to rising costs. One's political antennae have to be sharply tuned.

3. *Labor problems.* Only about 17 million, or 18 to 19 percent of our domestic work force of 85 million people, are unionized. Such labor unions have penetrated deeply into a number of basic industries: steel and automobiles, for example. On the whole, managements have not done a good job in standing up to unionized labor because they have believed the increased wages and fringe benefits could be passed on to customers in the form of higher prices. A company with high direct labor costs and strongly entrenched unions faces the recurring difficulties of strikes and strike threats. Both distort earnings patterns. Costs increase faster than productivity, and if prices are raised to offset these higher costs, the company usually runs into the next problem.

4. *Import problems.* Find a company with a serious labor problem and you are likely to find an import problem as well. High domestic labor costs have been a prominent factor in the generation of foreign competition in steel, autos, aluminum, chemicals, textiles, and glass, to specify a few areas. There are also American corporations that have been sluggish about keeping their products up to date—insufficiently attuned to consumer styles, needs, and pocketbooks—who have been clobbered by alert Japanese and Western European competitors. This brings us to still another problem.

5. *Obsolescence.* Some companies ride on successful products too long. Then new competition arrives, taking advantage of patent expirations, improved research, or more effective marketing. Such competition destroys the original leader's position of strength. (We will later discuss one such problem company to illustrate the difficulties and opportunities involved in betting on a comeback.)

6. *Technological problems.* We refer here not to the company suffering from product obsolescence but to those experiencing difficulty in converting a new technology into profitable, mass-produced products. Occasionally a concern shifts from one kind of manufacturing process to another and cannot smoothly bring the new line on-stream. New chemical plants, oil refineries, paper mills, and large printing presses are cases in point.

7. *Ecological and environmental problems.* Of all the problems we list, this one is the newest and hardest to evaluate. The environmental problem is having an impact on virtually the whole economy. It has delayed transportation of oil and gas from Alaska, arousing emotions and disturbing corporate earnings patterns. It affects the construction of coal-mining facilities. It hastens the obsolescence of paper mills. It increases the cost of automobiles. More importantly, it casts real doubt on the future growth rates of a number of basic industries. In view of our environmental problems, *can we really consume 50 to 100 percent more electricity per capita in the United States ten years from now, as the electric utilities insist?*

8. *Nationalization problems.* Any company with substantial assets overseas—particularly in less-developed nations—lives with the possibility that such assets will be expropriated. Witness the recent experiences of Kennecott and Anaconda in Chile, or the growing success of the Arab oil-producing nations in obtaining a higher share of profits from oil production, and their demands for an equity position.

9. *Financial problems.* This is a problem in and of itself but tends also to be the end result of all the other difficulties we enumerate. It manifests itself, ultimately, in the form of inadequate cash balances. Borrowing power is exhausted. Convertible securities and warrants adorn the balance sheet like Christmas tree ornaments—bright but empty. Dividends on the company's common stock are omitted, and a low price-earnings ratio makes it difficult, if not impossible, to raise additional equity capital. If the company is short of cash simply because it has allowed its accounts receivable and inventory to get out of hand, the financial problem in question can often be corrected. But the fact that a company does not have these assets under control tells you something about its management.

10. *Management problems.* Depressed enough? If not, hang on. If a company has a *nonmanagerial* problem of sufficient severity, the quality of its management may be irrelevant. Take Kennecott Copper. Let's assume it has the best management in the world. The company's large Chilean mines have been expropriated. Its merger with Peabody Coal is being contested by the Justice Department. The future of its new and proposed Southwestern coal and copper mining facilities is clouded by environmental complications. Its domestic copper-mining and fabricating business is beset by problems of low-grade ore bodies and competition from newer materials. How can a management with all the dedication and intelligence in the world make a situation with these underlying fundamentals attractive to you as an investor *relative to* other investment opportunities?

In a number of other cases, however, *management itself is the problem.* And this is almost always *top* management. In most situations the man at the top, and the associates he selects, still make virtually all the difference.

Telltale signs of management weakness include, but should not be restricted to, the following:

- an aging top executive
- nepotism[1]
- luxurious executive facilities
- a record of overly optimistic forecasts
- high executive turnover
- too many footnotes to the company financial statements
- lack of clearly defined corporate objectives

We submit that if you test the companies we have described as "successful" in the preceding chapters of this book, *you will find that in an overwhelming number of cases they have none of these problems*. We urge you to measure any other companies you are considering for investment against the list of ten problems to determine whether they are successful or not.

Assuming, as a result of this exercise, that you discover the company in question is a problem company, and you want to consider investing in it on that basis, then proceed as follows:

1. *Define the problems.*   Are they external and thus out of management control? Or are they internal, depending more on new capital expenditure programs, extensive research efforts, or new marketing programs? Ask yourself and your adviser why the company is in this position and, depending on your answer, how realistic it is to expect it to extricate itself in the near future.

2. *Do not invest in a company with too many problems.*   Especially avoid companies that have to cope both with external (say, import) difficulties and with internal weaknesses (lousy management). Many times the two go hand in hand. Sometimes there's a real opportunity when they do *not* go hand in hand.

3. *Avoid companies with a serious financial problem.*   Solutions to most of the other difficulties we have described require money—as well as people and time. If a company has borrowed all the money it reasonably can, if it must raise additional common stock at 5 times earnings, and if it can pay no dividend while you wait, our advice is to look elsewhere. What Henry Crown may wish to accomplish personally at General Dynamics (in his second round) or what the Rockefellers may once have been willing to risk on Chrysler or Eastern Airlines is almost certainly not for you.

4. *Avoid companies with management problems.* Life is too short, and there are too many good managements, to risk handing your money over to a bunch of second-raters. The other side of this coin is: *Keep your eye out for situations in which there has been an important, constructive management change at the top.* But in these situations look carefully at the old problems the new management will have to solve and do not be impatient. We know of virtually no situations in which a new management in the last decade has turned a problem company around in less than three years. You may have to wait even longer. But if you can double your money in, say, five years, the wait may be worth it.

5. *Find companies that reward you while you wait.* You should be rewarded by a generous dividend return while awaiting new and improved industry conditions, more effective management, or some combination of the two, to take hold.

6. *Ask yourself whether a less problematical company in a particular industry would not do as well or nearly as well as the particular company you are considering.* Do you, for example, want to "go all the way" and buy Pan American World Airways, a problem company par excellence, or would you be better advised to invest in TWA? A favorable change in industry conditions will help both, but it may not help Pan Am enough.

In concluding, let's take a brief look at one company that illustrates, *in principle*, the kinds of risks that may be worth taking in that portion of your portfolio devoted to "turnaround" situations. The company is Smith, Kline & French Laboratories.

SKF's management admits that it rode far too long on its successes of the 1950s and 1960s as the developer, patenter, and marketer of Thorazene and a host of other tranquilizers. For years the company as a whole was overstaffed and its research efforts superficial, undermanned, and inadequately funded.

As Thorazene patents expired, and as the Justice Department and the Food & Drug Administration restricted the sale of amphetamines, and as no compensating new products materialized, SKF stock, which had commanded a premium price-earnings ratio, plunged from a high of 86$^{3}/_{4}$ in 1965 to a low of 36 in 1969. The value now given in relation to other drug companies is dramatically illustrated in the [table below and the table on page 587.]

Under the supervision of a new president, Tom Rauch, in his late forties, the company began several years ago to plan for the next two decades. Management recognized that it would take many years to rebuild the company from the ground up and determined to do so carefully and unflamboyantly. It has increased its commitment to pharmaceutical research. It has embarked on a program of building its lines of proprietary consumer products, which it hopes will ultimately represent 50 percent of its net income. In an unusual statement of corporate objectives, management stated that the company's goal is "to attain annual earnings increases of 10% or more. We realize, however, that in the next few years a more modest target is required as we continue to invest in projects for the long run."

Here, then, is a sound industry environment (the best companies in the drug industry do very well indeed); a management that candidly recognizes past mistakes and is moving to correct them (but is not promising the moon in the process); a stock price which is still skeptical about the future; and a dividend return which, if not spectacular, is somewhat better than average and is well protected.

Smith, Kline & French vs. Other Drug Industry Securities—Comparative Analysis

	Market Value in Millions of Dollars*	Net Sales per Share[+]	Net Sales per Dollar of Market Value[+]	Net Earnings Before Taxes as % of Sales[+]
Smith, Kline & French	$ 838	$23.70	$0.41	23
Eli Lilly	3,871	8.70	0.15	25
Merck	4,520	20.51	0.17	29
Warner-Lambert	3,058	32.77	0.41	15
Upjohn	1,071	27.02	0.37	19
G. D. Searle	1,086[†]	13.50	0.19	16

*Based on shares outstanding at year end 1970, stock prices as of 12/31/71.
[+]Based on 1970 results.
[†]Assuming full dilution of Cumulative Convertible Preferred Stock.

Drug Industry—Comparative Analysis

	Current Price 12/31/71	Earnings per Share†				Price-Earnings Ratio			Current Indicated Dividend	Current Yield–%
		1969	1970	1971*	1972*	1970	1971*	1972*		
Smith, Kline & French	57	$2.81	$3.01	$3.01	$3.35	19.0X	18.5X	17.1X	$2.00	3.5
Eli Lilly	57	1.26	1.40	1.35	1.65	40.6	42.1	34.5	0.70	1.2
Merck	124	2.80	3.11	3.45	3.95	39.9	35.9	31.4	2.20	1.8
Warner-Lambert	80	2.39	2.57	2.80	3.05	31.0	28.5	26.1	1.30	1.6
Upjohn	73	2.54	2.56	2.65	3.00	28.4	27.5	24.3	1.60	2.2
G.D. Searle	74	2.08	2.32	2.60	2.80	31.8	28.4	26.3	1.30	1.8

*Estimated

†All earnings-per-share figures are based on the Faulkner, Dawkins & Sullivan Universe, "Comparative Summary of Earnings and Market Performance," October 29, 1971.

These are a few of the ingredients required to make a rewarding investment in a problem company. Whether this problem company proves rewarding or not remains to be seen.

FOOTNOTE

1. There are exceptions to every rule, and several of the successful companies we describe in this book have been run by one family for several generations.

YOU NEED MORE
THAN NUMBERS TO
MEASURE PERFORMANCE

Robert G. Kirby

Robert Kirby has been one of Capital Group's lead portfolio managers for two decades, a member of the faculty at Stanford Business School for a semester, and a racer of Porsches for the better part of a lifetime. He keeps showing up in the "one shot" sessions of our profession, easing wisdom and good humor into the fray.

It is often said in this business that there's no such thing as a free lunch. There's also no such thing as a long-term plan. That's true because most long-term plans won't survive short-term fluctuations. I think many money managers have found out over the last few years that no matter what kind of an institution you work for, it's run by people who make steel, or hamburgers, or run religious organizations, or whatever. They do not really have the experience to anticipate the fluctuations that occur in equity prices. Therefore, whether the institution is the Ford Foundation or the Topeka YMCA, when you encounter a '73 or '74, you're in deep grease unless you've got a plan strong enough to survive

From a paper given at a seminar sponsored by the Institute of Chartered Financial Analysts and the Financial Analysts Research Foundation, Chicago, Illinois, April 2, 1976, by permission of the author.

on a short-term basis. I'm sure that all the colleges McGeorge Bundy talked to in 1971 thought they had long-term objectives, but the long-term plans couldn't survive short-term fluctuations.

I am really optimistic, at this point in time, about not only [the] money management business, but even the performance measurement business. I think the pendulum is coming back again toward the point of rationality in money management. Companies that went from one trustee and one money manager to maybe one or two dozen are discovering that they have found a way of insuring eternal mediocrity and are moving back toward five or six managers or whatever makes sense within a structured investment policy employing a spread of defined "styles."

Performance measurement is one of those basically good ideas that somehow got totally out of control. In many, many cases, the intense application of performance measurement techniques has actually served to impede the purpose it is supposed to serve—namely, the achievement of a satisfactory rate of return on invested capital. Among the really negative side effects of the performance measurement movement as it has evolved over the past ten years are:

1. It has fostered the notion that it is possible to evaluate a money management organization over a period of two or three years—whereas money management really takes at least five and probably ten years or more to appraise properly.

2. It has tried to quantify and to formulize, in a manner acceptable to the almighty computer, a function that is only partially susceptible to quantitative evaluation and requires a substantial subjective appraisal to arrive at a meaningful conclusion.

3. It has to take most of the blame for creating the cult of market timing.

Actually, I'm really a strong advocate of careful performance measurement. I just quarrel with some of the systems that are in use and with many of the ways in which the data are used.

One of the great weaknesses of modern performance measurement is that it often attempts to draw useful and meaningful conclusions based solely on quantitative data covering a relatively short period of time. One or two years of solely quantitative data will rarely help anyone arrive at any useful conclusion or a meaningful evaluation of a money manager. Yet, this is what performance measurers often attempt to do.

At the other extreme, I will freely admit that if the time interval covered by the data is 15 or 20 years, there would be no reason to use qualitative measures at all. That observation is probably also true if the time interval is ten years or, perhaps, even as short as five years. *Ultimately*, one has to succeed as a money manager to produce an investment return on the capital under one's supervision that is satisfactory from an absolute and a relative standpoint. Numbers alone will lead eventually to the right answer if the time interval is long enough—but it rarely is.

To gain some perspective on my complaints, let's see if we can find something that good money management organizations seem to have in common. Many qualified money managers are around. It seems to me that the outstanding characteristic the best ones all have in common is a well-defined investment philosophy that has proven to be successful over an extended period of time, such as 20 or 30 years. Most of these organizations stick closely to this investment philosophy, pretty much through thick and thin. The things that change, often violently and quickly, are the fads and fashions of the market place. These organizations know that from time to time the stock market is going to make them look a great deal smarter than they really are and at other times a great deal dumber than they really are. Most good investment managers are rational; the stock market is not.

The short-term vagaries—the excessive swings and the sudden changing fads that occur in the stock market in the short run—are primarily the product of a great many full-time, well-informed, aggressive investors all trying to outperform the investment universe on a month-to-month and quarter-to-quarter basis! The good investment management firms are not playing this game and are attempting to make long-term investment decisions consistent with a well-defined philosophy. The market itself really represents nothing more than a pendulum that swings back and forth through the median line of rationality. It spends very little time at the point of rationality and most of the time on one side or the other.

I won't state that short-term, quantitative performance data are totally useless. On the contrary, such data are often quite useful as an *inverse* indicator. If I were looking for an outside money manager to manage my company's pension or profit sharing fund, I would go through a procedure something like the following: I would first look for an organization that had been around for awhile and that had produced good, long-term performance records with a variety of portfolios. I would make sure that the individuals in the organization were experienced and talented. I would determine that the good, long-term record was the result of a consistent application of a clear investment philosophy. I would satisfy myself that the organization provided an environment in which it was rewarding to work so that good people would stay. Then, after I had identified the organizations that met all these specifications, I would hire the one who, for the past two years, had had the *worst* record. And I don't say this the slightest bit facetiously.

Short-term investment performance data are a far better inverse indicator of what to expect in the immediate future than anything else. The past 10 or 15 years in the investment management business covers a long series of unfortunate disappointments where money managers have achieved spectacular results over two or three years with $50 to $100 million under management, only to bomb out over the subsequent two or three years with $500 million or a billion dollars under management. But it wasn't entirely the fault of the money managers. Responsibility for these recurring disasters rests with all those naive souls who believed that some guy with a red hot, couple-year record has suddenly solved the secret to it all and can apply the same magic formula to an unlimited amount of money or an infinite time horizon.

I have in my file one absolutely classic example that someday maybe I'll make into a Harvard Business School case study. It concerns a corporation who hired us in 1970 to manage its pension fund. We replaced a large bank and took over a classic portfolio of Eastman Kodak, Procter & Gamble, Xerox, Johnson & Johnson, and the like. Late in 1971, we concluded those stocks were getting too high priced, and we methodically sold them off and reinvested the proceeds in sounder values offering lower P/E ratios, higher yields, and greater asset protection. Needless to say, in the months that followed, the "fully valued" stocks that we had sold off took off like rockets, while the sound, basic values that we bought lagged the market substantially. At long last, as we reached the middle of 1973, the client could stand it no longer. He called us one day to say that our services were no longer required.

By some vagary of the complex accounting system of. . .[the custodian] bank, we continued to get daily transaction sheets on the portfolio after our investment management services were terminated. These transaction reports came in for about five weeks, and I watched in horror as the portfolio reverted to its original 1970 composition, but with a little more emphasis on the "new" growth stocks such as Avon and Disney. Let me give you a few of the grisly details, ten purchases and ten sales:

	BUYS		SELLS
Avon	125	Exxon	49
Baxter Lab.	47	American Telephone	51
Disney	78	Internat'l Paper	35
Johnson & Johnson	115	Bethlehem Steel	27
Xerox	156	Phelps Dodge	42
Warner-Lambert	49	Kerr-McGee	59
Burroughs	115	Connecticut General	45
Schlumberger	101	Union Oil	37
Coca-Cola	142	Amax	31
Procter & Gamble	103	Heinz	21

I have never been able to develop enough morbid curiosity to figure out the costs of this management change. However, since eventually most [of the] BUYS went down a lot and most of the SELLS went up a lot, I suspect the shift came pretty close to turning potential dollar bills into four-bit pieces. When applied to a $25 million corporate pension fund, the differential becomes a bit staggering. This case is a horrifying example of the cost of drawing fixed conclusions from two or three years of quantitative performance data.

For some reason that I never will understand, it seems that almost no one involved in investment management and performance measurement has ever studied the history of the several large portfolios, with published data available, that have had outstanding records over periods of 25 or 30 years or more. Almost without exception, no matter how good the overall long-term record has been, the performance includes a couple of intervals of from one and one-half to three years where the results were terrible.

Somehow, there seems to be no broad awareness of this plain fact of life. If even the best money management firm must periodically hit a year-or-two-performance-air-pocket, and if institutional clients, aided by performance measurers, are going to hire and fire money managers based on a couple of years of quantitative data, I think we have just succeeded in turning our so-called profession into a modified form of Russian roulette.

I am sure you recognize that here and there I have exaggerated a bit for a dramatic effect. Most institutional clients don't actually fire you after two years of poor performance, but they do begin to have more frequent and more lengthy review sessions with more performance measurers present. I won't make any direct comparisons of such sessions to the Spanish Inquisition, but I will say that the process certainly does not help the manager stick by that time-tried, clear investment philosophy that produced a good long-term record that got him hired in the first place.

But the plain fact is—at least in many cases—that the application of performance measurement techniques has served to put the most pressure on a money manager to change his approach just when he should not—and the greatest pressure not to change just when he should.

Performance measurement systems have frequently created an incredibly intense pressure for short-term, relative performance when what both we and our clients are actually seeking is long-term, absolute performance. All managers are besieged with monthly and quarterly relative performance rankings that compare each with the other, with all sorts of indexes, and with almost any other number that can be carried out to two or three decimal places. We money managers wouldn't be human if our palms didn't get a bit sweaty or our hearts didn't skip a beat when we find we've just dropped from third to fifth in the rankings for the month of March.

It is this kind of pressure, plus the terrible bear market of 1973–74, that has created a cult of the market timer. After all, what is the easiest way to get quick, relative performance and improve your position in the rankings? The answer is simple. Just figure out when the market is going to take its next sharp drop and then get out of common stocks before the dip occurs. If a manager is two-thirds in cash during a 15 percent drop in the market, he can gain almost 10 percentage points of relative performance on his fully invested competitors. Ten percentage points of relative performance is the kind of thing that takes three or four years to obtain through old fashioned, sound research and careful stock selection.

Perhaps, as you can tell from the tone of my remarks, I regard market timing as the investment management business' answer to the Tooth Fairy. In my opinion, there is no such thing as market timing—or, to put it another way, it is just plain impossible to predict interim swings in stock prices with any degree of accuracy or consistency.

No money manager can perform successfully in all kinds of markets. There *is* no man for all seasons. Sure, some guys had the big growth stocks at the right time, and other guys who [*sic*] had the little growth stocks at the right time; some guys had the basic industries at the right time, and other guys had all cash at the right time. But the research that I have done on the subject would indicate that for the most part they were all different guys!

Stop and think for a minute. The stock market was made so that it can only go one of two ways—up or down. Therefore, during any month or quarter or year, it is a mathematical probability that of all the people out there willing to list themselves in the Yellow Pages as investment advisors, half are going to be right in their forecasts. And if you take the lunatic fringe of the half that is going to be right, they are going to be spectacularly right. As long as lots of investors out there in Wonderland still continue to believe that those who are spectacularly right during some dramatic upward or downward move in stock prices are right as a result of diligence, skill, and hard work, and can, therefore, do a series of repeat performance[s], then the Tooth Fairy will live forever.

The only way to produce superior results over time is to do a better job of research and a better job of security selection. If you go back and look at those big portfolios with the long-term records of superior performance, you won't find any of them that got there through so-called "market timing."

Well, I guess I have said it about as many ways as I can: First, two or three years of quantitative performance data tell you almost nothing; second, too many performance measurement systems currently in use ignore this basic truth. However, I also want to state very plainly that two or three years' experience with a money manager will not prevent you from reaching some useful and significant conclusions about that manager. But in my judgment, to be useful those conclusions have to be based almost totally on qualitative performance data—not on numbers.

In many ways, choosing a money manager is a little bit like choosing a wife. The honeymoon is almost always good, because each party anticipates an idyllic relationship and tends to ignore evidence to the contrary. There is usually a slightly tense period six to twelve months out as each party becomes aware that the other has at least a few imperfections. As a little more time goes by, it begins to get easier and easier to identify a bad relationship that isn't going to succeed. Both bad marriages and bad money managers *can* be identified with considerable conviction in just a couple of years. However, good marriages and good money managers can often take a much longer time to appreciate.

To what extent is the performance measurement problem further abused by emphasizing a portfolio manager's performance relative to his competitors, rather than in relation to the investment objectives of the client? I think that is a measure none of us can escape. But a big problem of this business is that of some half dozen relevant variables that can be used to measure portfolio management, we emphasize one way too much and completely ignore a couple of others. Unless somebody develops a better index than those we commonly use, the S&P 500 or the Dow Jones Industrial Average, we are always going to be looking at distorted relative performance results. You go through one period, such as '71, '72, and '73, where almost no one can beat the S&P 500. Then you hit another like '65, '66, '67 where my ten-year old daughter could easily beat the S&P 500. In the latter period, we were all so entranced with how we did relative to the S&P 500, we forgot we were lucky and thought we were smart. That's why we got roughed up so terribly in the subsequent years. Performance measurement is like trying to measure a distance from where you are to some place else when you are on a moving platform. The overall environment often makes it either easy or impossible to beat the capitalization-weighted index that is your bogey. You almost have to relate your performance to the other money managers, or to the same portfolio with the same set of policies and the same ground rules. Again, I go back to the fact that you can't draw any conclusions if you are looking at two or three years of data, but once you get long-term data on a group of managers, you may decide that even though you've got eight managers, that the worst of the eight is still doing fine. The only real problem is if you over-emphasize comparing a group of portfolio managers. If you are lucky enough to pick the best eight in the country, you're not going to achieve anything by replacing the eighth one.

I'm reminded of another joke that is typical of how, in this crazy business, we try to deceive ourselves. It concerns a guy who was a plumber and had saved some money. His brother-in-law, Marvin, was a retail broker for a stock exchange firm. Marvin had been handling the plumber's portfolio for several years. Finally in 1974, the plumber came in and said, "Marvin, I've got to talk to you about my investment program. I've reviewed the whole thing and as I look back, we bought Electronic Data Systems in 1970, Equity Funding in 1971, Levitz in 1972, Mattel in 1973, and Coastal States Gas in 1974. Really, I find this whole program very disappointing. We've got to do something, and I suggest that we salvage the residual value of my stocks, and reinvest the money in bonds." Then Marvin said, "Sure Harry, that's fine for you, but what do I know about bonds?"

I have sometimes been asked just what would make me fire a money manager if I were a corporate pension fund administrator. The first answer would always, of course, be a long-term underperformance of a clearly stated and reasonable set of investment objectives. However, what the questioner really means is what would make me fire a money manager in the short run.

In my opinion, the only valid causes for dismissal in the short run are entirely qualitative. They might go something as follows:

1. If the manager's portfolio composition changed substantially and often.
2. If the manager suddenly moved from a maximum equity position to 60% or 70% in cash—or vice versa—without extraordinary justification.
3. If the manager's portfolio turnover consistently averaged toward 100%.
4. If frequent and significant changes occurred in the people involved in the manager's investment decision-making structure.
5. If the selection of individual securities in the fund involved a risk, volatility, or a quality inconsistent with the long-term objectives of the portfolio.
6. If the portfolio manager assigned to my account changed frequently.

As you can tell from these statements, I still believe that *investment* management is a real business and not some new art form.

I have been asked, "Do you measure your performance on individual accounts in terms of average annual compounded growth, standard deviation of returns, beta, alpha, or a correlation of returns?" My reply is, "I don't even know what most of these terms mean."

If money management is a business, then the people who know the most about macroeconomics and the industries and companies they invest in will make the best decisions. If you believe that money management is some kind of intuitive, black magic sort of thing, then you should look for a witch doctor or a gypsy. If you believe that money management is some kind of a fashion contest in which the critical factor is to identify the next fad, you should go look for a social psychologist or a politician. But with these last two approaches, you do the measurement—not me.

Maybe herein lies the problem of most performance measurement. Many performance measure[r]s don't think investment management is a business. I'll allow for the possibility that they may be right, but I'm too much of a Calvinist to believe it. Good investment results take hard work and a willingness to accept a risk if it's a reasonable one.

HORIZON ANNUITY: LINKING THE GROWTH AND PAYOUT PHASES OF LONG-TERM BOND PORTFOLIOS

Martin L. Leibowitz

Martin Leibowitz has a knack for reminding us of things we know but have conveniently ignored. Trees don't grow to the sky, and pension funds don't enjoy a net accumulation of contributions and income forever. What happens at the point of conversion, when the accumulation phase ends, and the payout phase begins? How can we plan for it? What do we need to remember?

Many institutions, including pension funds, have a two-phase life cycle. During the first phase, the fund grows and compounds. Sooner or later, however, the fund converts from the compounding phase into the second, payout phase.

The dollars accumulated in the compounding phase depend on the rate at which income can be reinvested. Once a fund has passed the conversion horizon, however, it is not so much the dollars accumulated in the compounding phase that counts, but their power to generate income. The latter depends critically on the level of interest rates

By Martin L. Leibowitz, Managing Director of Salomon Brothers, Inc. Reprinted from *The Financial Analysts Journal*, Vol. 35, No. 3, May/June 1979, 2–8. New York, New York: Financial Analysts Federation. Copyright 1976 by Salomon Brothers Inc.

prevailing beyond the horizon. When reinvestment rates during the compounding phase and beyond the conversion horizon are linked, the level of payout the fund can sustain (the so-called "horizon annuity") becomes very sensitive to the joint rate.

The author develops a simplified model of a two-phase investment fund that permits him to examine the implications of this sensitivity. The model shows that the best passive defense against a secular downtrend in reinvestment rates is a truly long-term portfolio protected against excessive exposure to call. Unfortunately, the best long-term portfolio will often have an extremely volatile short-term performance. The growing popularity of short-term performance measurement has made it difficult for many managers to gear their portfolio structure entirely to long-term objectives.

The very expression "fixed income security" conveys a warm feeling of stability. A high-grade bond may not be exciting, but at least it should provide the promised level of nominal dollar payments.

Unfortunately, this is an uncertain world. For many long-term investment purposes, the fixed income portfolio can only offer relative, not absolute, comfort, even in nominal dollar terms. This is especially true for funds whose "life cycles" take the form of a growth phase followed by a long-term payout phase.

Consider an example at the personal level. Suppose a 45-year-old investor has accumulated $50,000, which he puts into a fixed income portfolio with the hope that it will provide a supplemental source of retirement income. On the basis of an 8.5 per cent interest rate, the investor estimates that his $50,000 investment, with interest compounded, will grow to $264,000 by the time he retires at age 65. With this money, he plans to buy an annuity that will provide annual payments of almost $27,700 over the next 20 years.

Rather impressive, even if we have neglected taxes! Can the calculation really be correct? Aside from the neglect of taxes, it is.

Of course, there is the tacit assumption that interest rates will remain constant at 8.5 per cent. What happens if interest rates drop to five per cent? In that case, our investor's retirement income would decline to $10,700 per year, less than 39 per cent of his original estimate.

In principle, of course, he can "lock in" some of today's 8.5 per cent rate by buying a portfolio of long-term bonds. But if he buys a $50,000 portfolio of 40-year, 8.5 per cent par bonds, and rates then drop to five per cent (i.e., if all coupon payments and annuity purchases take place at five per cent), his annual retirement income level will drop to $17,000—well below his original estimate of $27,700. Moreover, if his 40-year bonds contain the typical call feature, they will almost surely be refunded in the fifth year. In that case, even with full reinvestment of the call premium, his future income level will fall to $12,900.

Obviously, our investor faces surprisingly large variations in his retirement income, and virtually all of the variation can be traced to changes in the reinvestment rate. He can minimize his risk, however, by focusing on achieving a long-term maturity structure that is carefully balanced against excessive call vulnerability.

TWO-PHASE FUNDS

The above example provides a very simple illustration of a two-phase fund. During the first phase, annual contributions to the portfolio exceed disbursements, and all investment income is reinvested. The fund grows and compounds. This growth continues until some point at which the portfolio "converts" into a second phase characterized by disbursements exceeding contributions. During this second, "payout," phase, the portfolio is no longer a full compounder. Some or all of its investment income is being paid out.

Many institutional portfolios, including pension funds, have a similar two-phase life cycle. Initially, they enjoy a long period of growth through retention and reinvestment of investment income, as well as through the flow of net new contributions to the fund. Since this growth phase usually continues for many years, it has become conventional to view these funds as essentially perpetually growing entities. However, in most cases, planned annual payouts eventually increase to the point where they surpass the fund's income and contribution flows. At this point, the fund shifts into a payout phase.

The transition from growth to payout phase represents a fundamental change in the fund's investment character. The value of the fund during the compounding phase depends on the yields to maturity of the fund's current holdings and on the reinvestment rate during the compounding phase. It is natural for the portfolio manager to focus on rate of return during the long-term horizon that coincides with the fund's compounding phase. The reinvestment rate over this horizon will be critical in determining the fund's value at the point at which it converts into a payout phase. But, once the fund has passed into the payout phase, it is not so much the magnitude of the accumulated dollars that counts, but their power to generate income. The level of annuity income they can support during the payout phase depends entirely on the level of interest rates prevailing at the fund's conversion horizon.

On the other hand, it is not unreasonable to assume some linkage between the reinvestment conditions of the compounding phase and the interest rate structure at the fund's point of conversion. For example, when a portfolio manager assumes a six per cent average reinvestment rate over the next 20 years, he clearly envisions a major secular downtrend in rates. Thus his assumption for reinvestment rates during the horizon period has strong implications for his expectations for the interest rate that will prevail at the horizon. The investor who assumes a six per cent reinvestment rate will also probably expect interest rates to be around six per cent (or lower) in the 20th year. An investor exploring a 10 per cent reinvestment rate over the next 20 years presumably thinks in terms of a 10 per cent interest rate prevailing in the 20th year.

Any such linkage will greatly reinforce the impact of the reinvestment assumption on a given investment strategy. For example, a full coupon bond maturing at the conversion horizon will produce considerably fewer accumulated dollars of return under a six per cent reinvestment assumption than under a 10 per cent reinvestment assumption. Moreover, these dollars could then presumably generate only a six per cent yield rate during the payout phase. Under these linked six per cent assumptions, the fund's total projected payout would be far less than the payout expected under a 10 per cent rate assumption. Thus the fund's ability to fulfill its ultimate promise—to provide a certain level of absolute income during the payout period—will depend heavily on the investor's reinvestment rate assumption and long-term investment strategy.

THE HORIZON ANNUITY MODEL

To examine the implications of the investment strategy and reinvestment rate assumption of the compounding period for the ability of the fund to fulfill its promises during the payout period, we developed a highly simplified model of a two-phase investment fund. Our fund consists of one specified fixed-income investment, such as a 20-year, 8.5 per cent bond. All relevant interest rates move suddenly to the level of the specified reinvestment rate and the resultant flat yield curve persists throughout both the compounding and payout phases.

During the compounding phase, all coupon payments and maturing principal of the fund are reinvested at the specified rate level. At the end of the compounding phase (i.e., at the conversion horizon), all the dollars accumulated in the fund are used to purchase a level annuity that will span the fund's payout phase. The cost of the annuity is based upon an interest rate that is the same as the initial reinvestment rate, and the annual annuity payments are designed to exhaust the fund's resources completely by the end of the payout phase.[1]

To determine whether the fund is fulfilling its payout obligations, we use as a convenient yardstick of its productivity during this phase the magnitude of the annual annuity payments. Dividing this amount by the fund's beginning market value provides the number of dollars that can be paid out annually during the payout phase for each dollar initially invested. We refer to this measure, expressed as a percentage, as the fund's "horizon annuity."

Table I illustrates the life cycle of one such two-phase fund. Here we assume that $100 million dollars is completely invested in 20-year, 8.5 per cent par bonds, and that the reinvestment rate is six per cent. During the first 20 years—the compounding phase—the fund has no payouts, and all coupon receipts are reinvested at the assumed rate. The compounded income derived from this reinvestment process is shown in the "Interest on Interest" column.

At the end of the compounding phase, the total accumulated value in the fund—$420.45 million—is used to purchase a 20-year, six per cent annuity. At this rate, the annuity will provide for 40 semiannual payments of $18.19 million. As with any annuity, this payout level exceeds the interest receipts, so the fund's principal erodes. By our definition, this erosion is scheduled so that the principal is completely exhausted at the end of the 20th year of the payout phase.

In this example, the *annual* payment during the payout phase is $36.38 million (twice the semiannual payment of $18.19). Since the fund's initial investment was $100 million, the annual payout per initial dollar invested is $0.3638 ($36.38 million divided by $100 million). Expressed as a percentage of each initial dollar invested, the fund's horizon annuity is 36.38 per cent.

TABLE I

The Horizon Annuity Concept—Cash Flow Schedule of $100 Million Portfolio Consisting of 20-Year, 8.5 Per Cent Par Bonds

20-Year Compounding Phase with Reinvestment at Six Percent

Semiannual Period Ending After	Principal	Interest on Principal	Interest on Interest	Total Fund Value Before Payouts	Payouts	Total Fund Value After Payouts
0.5 Years	$100.00 MM	$ 4.25 MM	$0 MM	$104.25 MM	0	$104.25 MM
1.0	100.00	4.25	0.13	108.63	0	108.63
1.5	100.00	4.25	0.26	113.14	0	113.14
2.0	100.00	4.25	0.39	117.78	0	117.78
.	.	.	.	.	.	.
19.0	100.00	4.25	8.44	393.92	0	393.92
19.5	100.00	4.25	8.82	406.99	0	406.99
20.0	100.00	4.25	9.21	420.45	0	420.45

Conversion into 20-Year Full Payout Phase Through Purchase of a Six Per Cent, 20-Year Annuity Paying $36.38 Million Annually

20.5 Years	$420.45 MM	$12.61 MM	0	$433.06 MM	$18.19 MM	$414.87 MM
21.0	414.87	12.45	0	427.32	18.19	409.13
21.5	409.13	12.27	0	421.41	18.19	403.22
22.0	403.22	12.10	0	415.31	18.19	397.12
.	.	.	.	.	.	.
39.0	51.46	1.54	0	53.00	18.19	34.81
39.5	34.81	1.04	0	35.85	18.19	17.66
40.0	17.66	0.53	0	18.19	18.19	0

Table II demonstrates what happens to the same fund's future value (its value at the conversion horizon) and horizon annuity when we assume different reinvestment rates. Obviously, the reinvestment assumption will have a strong effect upon the fund's future value. Moving from a reinvestment rate of five per cent to one of 10 per cent increases the fund's future value by 58 per cent—from $386.46 million to $613.38 million. The reinvestment rate's effect can also be seen in the fund's total value through compounded reinvestment—over the compounding phase. This increases from 6.88 per cent to 9.28 per cent as we move from a reinvestment rate of five per cent to one of 10 per cent. But a change in the reinvestment rate assumption will have an even more profound effect on the fund's horizon annuity. With a change in the rate assumption from five to 10 per cent, the horizon annuity increases by over 132 per cent—from 30.79 to 71.49 per cent! The horizon annuity's

TABLE II

Sensitivity of Future Value and Horizon Annuity to Reinvestment Rate—$100 Million Portfolio Consisting of 20-Year, 8.5 Percent Par Bonds

	20-Year Compounding Phase with Fund Then Converting into a 20-Year Payout Phase		
Reinvestment Rate	Total Future Value of Fund at 20-Year Conversion Horizon	Realized Compound Yield over First 20 Years	Horizon Annuity Over Next 20 Years of Payout Phase
5%	$386.46 MM	6.88%	30.79%
6	420.45	7.31	36.38
7	459.33	7.77	43.02
8	503.86	8.25	50.91
9	554.86	8.75	60.31
10	613.38	9.28	71.49

sensitivity to reinvestment rate is a result of the direct linkage between the reinvestment rate and the annuity purchase rate.

THE SAVINGS ACCOUNT ANALOGY

The first column of Table III, labeled "cash," shows the horizon annuity values provided by savings accounts with various guaranteed interest rates. For example, suppose $100 were placed in a savings account that guaranteed five per cent interest (semiannual payments). If all interest payments were allowed to remain in the account and compounded for the next 20 years, then exactly $21.39 could be withdrawn every year (in two semiannual installments) over the subsequent 20 years, leaving the account totally empty by the end of the 40th year. This corresponds to the horizon annuity of 21.39 per cent for a "cash" portfolio under a five per cent reinvestment assumption. By using Table III to explore a range of "savings account" reinvestment rates, one can assess the impact of uncertainty regarding reinvestment rates on the value of the horizon annuity.

The savings account approach can also be enlarged to explain the horizon annuity concept for bond portfolios of various maturities. The last four columns of the table show what horizon annuities the investor can expect if, instead of placing his money in the savings account

TABLE III

Horizon Annuities of 8.5 Percent Par Bonds With Different Maturities

20-Year Compounding Phase With Fund
Then Converting Into a 20-Year Payout Phase

	1	2	3	4	5
Reinvestment Rate	Cash	Five-Year Maturity	10-Year Maturity	20-Year Maturity	40-Year Maturity*
5%	21.39%	24.67%	27.23%	30.79%	34.29%
6	28.22	31.23	33.47	36.38	38.88
7	37.08	39.39	41.03	43.02	44.52
8	48.51	49.50	50.16	50.91	51.42
8.5	55.41	55.41	55.41	55.41	55.41
9	63.22	61.96	61.16	60.31	59.81
10	82.06	77.30	74.39	71.49	69.99

*At 20-year conversion horizon, all bonds are assumed priced to yield the reinvestment rate.

initially, he purchases 8.5 per cent par bonds of various maturity and, at the end of 20 years, reinvests the accumulated coupon payments and principal in a savings account that offers a guaranteed interest rate equal to the given reinvestment rate.

Suppose the investor had the one-time opportunity to buy a 20-year, 8.5 per cent bond at par. If he puts his $100 into this bond, instead of into the savings account, he will receive a higher level of interest payments over the bond's life. Now assume he places all these coupon payments, along with the $100 principal repayment, in a five per cent savings account. As a result of the first 20 years of higher return, the portfolio's horizon annuity is boosted to 30.79 per cent, as Table III shows.

For bond investments with maturities of less than 20 years, of course, we must make some determination regarding the reinvestment of the principal payments for the remainder of the 20-year compounding phase. For purposes of simplicity, it is convenient to treat all maturing principal payments as being rolled over at the given reinvestment rate. This treatment is consistent with our basic assumption of a sudden and permanent move to a flat yield curve.

Table III shows a range of horizon annuities dependent, not only upon the assumed reinvestment rate, but upon bond maturities. For a

20-year maturity, the various reinvestment rates yield the same horizon annuities depicted in Table II; these range from 30.79 per cent, assuming a five per cent reinvestment rate, to 71.49 per cent, assuming a 10 per cent rate. But the same selection of reinvestment rates yields a broader range of horizon annuities for a portfolio invested in 10-year maturities; in this case the bottom end of the scale is down to 27.23 per cent and the top up to 74.39 per cent. And the range for a cash portfolio (Column 1) widens considerably more—from 21.39 to 82.06 per cent. Thus, as the initial maturity of the invested portfolio becomes shorter, future reinvestment rates play an increasing role in determining the fund's asset and annuity values.

It is apparent from Table III that longer maturity portfolios provide some protection against lower reinvestment rate assumptions. At a five per cent reinvestment rate, a cash portfolio would compound like a five per cent savings account, providing a horizon annuity of only 21.39 per cent. On the other hand, a 10-year, 8.5 per cent bond would provide a higher interest rate on the original principal for the first 10 years, and this would eventually lead to an improved horizon annuity of 27.23 per cent. The longer one can hold on to the higher return through longer maturity, the higher will be the annuity over the payout phase. If the investor purchases a 20-year, 8.5 per cent bond, the horizon annuity grows to 30.79 per cent, assuming a five per cent reinvestment rate.

On the other hand, the effect of portfolio maturity is surprisingly small in comparison to the impact of the reinvestment rate assumption. A guaranteed, six per cent savings account provides a horizon annuity of 28.22 per cent—almost as much as a 20-year, 8.5 per cent bond subject to reinvestment and annuity purchase at five per cent. Furthermore, the advantage in holding a longer maturity portfolio decreases as assumed reinvestment rates rise. When the reinvestment rate equals the purchase yield of the par bonds, all monies end up being compounded at the same rate—8.5 per cent. Consequently, it makes no difference whether the initial portfolio consists of cash or of five, 10 or 20-year bonds; the horizon annuity will be 55.41 per cent for all.

As the reinvestment rate rises above this point, the advantage shifts to shorter maturity portfolios. At a 10 per cent reinvestment rate, a cash portfolio will generate a horizon annuity of 82.06 per cent. An 8.5 per cent bond of any maturity would naturally lead to a lower horizon annuity. Table III shows that an initial purchase of a 20-year, 8.5 per cent par bond would produce a horizon annuity of only 71.49 per cent.

Maturities beyond the conversion horizon—40-year bonds, in Table III—form a special case. So far, our basic model has assumed that all fund assets are liquidated at the conversion horizon (20 years) and the proceeds used to purchase an annuity covering the payout phase. To accommodate longer maturity bonds, we have to specify a technique for determining their market value at the end of 20 years. We have used the simplest solution–equating the yield to maturity of outstanding bonds with the assumed reinvestment rate. This is again in keeping with our assumption of a flat yield curve.

Table III shows that the extension to 40-year maturities provides a relatively modest shift in the horizon annuity. In most cases, extending the maturity from 10 to 20 years has a greater impact on the horizon annuity than extending it from 20 to 40 years.

DISCOUNT BONDS AND PREMIUM BONDS

Up to this point, the discussion has centered on par bonds. However, a bond's coupon rate is an important determinant of its sensitivity to changing reinvestment rates. As shown in *Inside the Yield Book*, the future value of a zero-coupon pure discount is totally insensitive to reinvestment rates.[2] However, since our model links the annuity purchase rate to the reinvestment assumption, the horizon annuity of even zero-coupon bonds will exhibit some sensitivity to reinvestment rates. The future values, hence horizon annuities, of higher coupon bonds become more and more dependent upon the reinvestment rate, the higher their coupon rate.

Table IV shows for various reinvestment rate assumptions the horizon annuity values corresponding to the various coupon rates of 20-year bonds priced to a conventional yield to maturity of 8.5 per cent. The zero-coupon, pure discount bond has the smallest range of horizon annuity values—from 42.11 to 61.61 per cent. By contrast, the horizon annuities of a premium bond with a 10 per cent coupon range from 30.46 to 71.78 per cent, depending on the reinvestment rate. For purposes of comparison, the table also shows the corresponding values for a cash portfolio.

Because discount bonds are relatively less sensitive than par bonds, they are better able to preserve a promised higher return in the face of

TABLE IV

Horizon Annuities of Discount and Premium Bonds

	20-Year Compounding Phase with Fund Then Converting into a 20-Year Payout Phase					
	1	*2*	*3*	*4*	*5*	*6*
	Coupon Rate on 20-Year Bonds Priced to Yield 8.5 Percent					
Reinvestment Rate%	*Cash%*	*0%*	*4%*	*7%*	*8.5%*	*10%*
5%	21.39%	42.11%	32.77%	31.23%	30.79%	30.46%
6	28.22	45.73	38.02	36.75	36.38	36.11
7	37.08	49.50	44.15	43.27	43.02	42.83
8	48.51	53.41	51.35	51.01	50.91	50.84
8.5	55.41	55.41	55.41	55.41	55.41	55.41
9	63.22	57.45	59.80	60.20	60.31	60.39
10	82.06	61.61	69.75	71.11	71.49	71.78

lower reinvestment conditions. Thus, even at a five per cent reinvestment rate, the zero-coupon bond provides a horizon annuity of 42.11 per cent; this exceeds the horizon annuity of a savings account with a guaranteed interest rate of 7.5 per cent. Unfortunately, as one moves toward bonds with more realistic coupon levels, this advantage deteriorates rapidly.

FUND PLANNING AND HORIZON ANNUITY

Managers developing an overall fund plan often select a relatively low rate of return value—one which they believe to have a high probability of being exceeded by the portfolio's actual long-term return—to serve as a measure of the minimum long-term investment return.

This rate of return assumption becomes the yardstick by which they match asset requirements against expected future liabilities and, as such, plays a critical role in determining the funding procedure for the portfolio. It becomes deeply embedded in virtually all the fund's long-term planning and investment strategy.

There is a connection between our horizon annuity concept and this target rate of return. Suppose, for example, that a $100 million fund is established with a single lump sum contribution—i.e., there will be no future contributions. For the first 20 years, the fund has no liability requirements. Over the second 20 years, it must pay out $37.08 million each year. After 40 years, it has no residual liabilities and can be extinguished. The fund manager has targeted a reinvestment return of seven per cent.

This case corresponds to our two-phase, $100 million portfolio with a 20-year compounding phase and a 20-year payout phase. By consulting Table III, we see that a constant seven per cent compounding and annuity purchase rate will produce exactly the required $37.08 million annuity during the payout phase. If the seven per cent rate can be assured, then the fund's initial $100 million of assets will just meet its scheduled liabilities.

If interest rates were at the 8.5 per cent level, one might expect the fund to realize the minimum seven per cent level of return easily. However, it is really the fund's horizon annuity that matters. As Table III illustrates, any secular downtrend in interest rates could prevent the fund from achieving the required horizon annuity of 37.08 per cent. For example, if reinvestment rates declined to six per cent, then the portfolio would have to be invested in bonds with maturities exceeding 20 years in order to provide the needed horizon annuity.

Given a clear-cut minimum target, it can be useful to express the various outcomes as percentages of this target level. For example, under a reinvestment assumption of six per cent, a 20-year portfolio of 8.5 per cent par bonds would achieve only 98 per cent of the fund's minimum target. Table V translates the horizon annuity values of Table III into "fulfillment percentages."

Since the fixed income portion of a fund is often viewed as playing a special risk-avoidance role, serving as an "anchor to windward," fulfilling minimum objectives is far more important to the bond portfolio than generating returns above any expected levels. Table V shows that a secular downtrend in rates can threaten the fulfillment of minimum horizon annuity objectives.

Ironically, higher interest rates pose no such threat. Of course, our model assumes that the portfolio manager does not attempt to anticipate rate movements. The only sale of bonds occurs at the conversion horizon; consequently, price changes become important only if bonds have maturities longer than the conversion horizon. For example, the

TABLE V

Fulfillment Percentages—Horizon Annuities of 8.5 Percent Par Bonds with Different Maturities as Percentage of Fund's Minimum Target (Based on a Seven Percent Return Objective)

	20-Year Compounding Phase with Fund Then Converting into a 20-Year Payout Phase				
	1	*2*	*3*	*4*	*5*
Reinvestment Rate	*Cash*	*Five-Year Maturity*	*10-Year Maturity*	*20-Year Maturity*	*40-Year Maturity**
5%	58%	66%	73%	83%	92%
6	76	84	90	98	105
7	100	106	111	116	120
8	131	133	135	137	139
8.5	149	149	149	149	149
9	171	167	165	163	161
10	221	208	201	193	189

*At 20-year conversion horizon, all bonds are assumed priced to yield the reinvestment rate.

40-year, 8.5 per cent bonds in Table III would have a remaining life of 20 years at the conversion horizon. At this point, under a 10 per cent reinvestment assumption, these bonds would be sold at a price of $87.13, corresponding to a 10 per cent yield to maturity. In this case, the higher level of reinvestment and annuity purchase would more than compensate for the principal loss.

For our simple two-phase fund, lower interest rates pose a far greater long-term problem than higher interest rates. This threat is further exacerbated by the problem of call vulnerability. In a declining interest rate environment, there is a growing probability of refunding calls.[3]

Table VI shows the potential impact of call vulnerability for two different cases of call protection—(1) the bond becomes refundable in the fifth year at a call price of 107 and (2) the bond becomes refundable in the 10th year at a call price of 104.

A call is assumed to take place only if it would lead to lower horizon annuity values. For the rate levels depicted in Table VI, this means that refunding calls would occur only in the case of reinvestment

TABLE VI

Horizon Annuity Values Under Different Degrees of Call Vulnerability—
$100 Million Portfolio Consisting of 20-Year 8.5 Percent Par Bonds
(Fund's Minimum Target Based on a Seven Percent Return Objective)

20-Year Compounding Phase with Fund
Then Converting into a 20-Year Payout Phase

Reinvestment Rate	Without Call		Callable in Five Years at 107		Callable in 10 Years at 104	
	Horizon Annuity	*Fulfillment Percentage*	*Horizon Annuity*	*Fulfillment Percentage*	*Horizon Annuity*	*Fulfillment Percentage*
5%	30.79%	83%	25.84%	70%	27.75%	75%
6	36.38	98	32.71	88	34.10	92
7	43.02	116	41.23	111	41.78	113
8*	50.91	137	50.91	137	50.91	137
8.5*	55.41	149	55.41	149	55.41	149
9*	60.31	163	60.31	163	60.31	163
10*	71.49	193	71.49	193	71.49	193

*Call not exercised at these levels.

assumptions below eight per cent. The full proceeds from the call—the par value plus the call premium—would be rolled over at the specified reinvestment rate. Thus under a six per cent rate assumption, a call in the fifth year at 107 would lower the horizon annuity from 36.38 per cent to 32.71 per cent. If the fund's minimum return objective were seven per cent, then the call would mean a decline in the portfolio's fulfillment percentage from 98 to 88 per cent.

Unfortunately, call vulnerability hurts most just when every increment of return is needed to cover the fund's minimum objectives.

INVESTMENT IMPLICATIONS

Our examples have used a series of highly simplifying assumptions—e.g., lump sum funding, no future contributions, nominal dollar liabilities falling into an annuity pattern, a future of flat yield curves, a passive portfolio process, a linkage making the annuity purchase rate exactly equal to the reinvestment rate. Obviously further development is needed before the horizon annuity concept can become a reasonably good representation of actual pension funds. However, even the simplistic analysis presented here shows that two-phase funds have a special vulnerability to interest rate movements. A secular decline in rates can pose a significant problem for such a fund's payout phase, even when current market rates appear to exceed comfortably the fund's planning rate.

The best *passive* defense against these problems lies in a truly long-term portfolio balanced against excessive exposure to call. Of course, an actively managed fund will depart from this long-term defensive "baseline" in order to take advantage of various market opportunities. The incremental return anticipated from such activity should perhaps be gauged relative to the risk it introduces.

Aside from the pursuit of market opportunities, there are a variety of reasons why a portfolio manager may find it necessary or desirable to depart from a portfolio structure patterned solely upon long-term objectives. For one thing, even long-term portfolios tend to have a high level of short-term price volatility. (In fact, it can be demonstrated that the most volatile bond over short horizons will theoretically provide the best protection against declining rates over long horizons.) A long-term maturity structure with an implied high degree of volatility may not fit the practical considerations and constraints of actual fund management.

In particular, the growing popularity of performance measurement has tended to focus managers' attention toward increasingly short-term results. If carried to extremes, performance pressures could lead to dangerous overemphasis of the short term. Evaluation would be more balanced if measurement of the fund's short-term performance were expressed in terms of its contribution to long-term goals.

FOOTNOTES

1. For clarity, returns and investment measures are expressed solely in terms of nominal dollars, even though inflation effects are clearly a critical factor in any comprehensive evaluation.

2. Sidney Homer and Martin L. Leibowitz, *Inside the Yield Book* (Englewood Cliffs, NJ: Prentice-Hall, 1972).

3. See Martin L. Leibowitz, *Call Vulnerability: A New Fact in the Bond Market* (New York, NY: Salomon Brothers, September 23, 1976).

THE SYSTEMS APPROACH

William T. Morris

William Morris was Chairman of Industrial Engineering at Ohio State University, where he wrote *How To Get Rich Slowly But Almost Surely* before moving to Katmandu, Nepal, as Chief of the U.S. Educational Mission in 1979. Morris explains, in an informal style, how the investor interacts with the market, often to his own disadvantage.

You and the market as an interactive system. Things the market does to you without your realizing it. Solving the "everybody makes money" puzzle. What to look for when you look at yourself. What character do you play? What's your style?

THE EVIDENCE

The most useful, yet most sadly neglected, data about the market is the data which tells us what happens to people when they actually put their money on the line. There are differences, interesting and useful differences, between:

From William T. Morris, *How To Get Rich Slowly But Almost Surely* (Reston, Virginia, 1973), by permission of Reston Publishing Company, Inc. Prentice-Hall, Inc.

- Reading a book about the market and actually doing what it suggests.
- Listening to "good, sound advice" and actually following it.
- Firmly resolving to follow a financial plan and resisting the frequent and strong temptations to forget it.
- Learning from simulated, make-believe market operations and learning from real operations involving one's own funds.
- Knowing it's sensible to sell at highs and actually bringing one's self to do it when everybody else thinks there's no end in sight.
- Planning to buy at lows and actually putting your money down when everyone is highly pessimistic about the market ever coming back.
- Seeing the great logic of sometimes taking a loss and actually telling your broker to sell out a losing position.
- Behaving like a pro and behaving like an amateur in your financial operations.

There are still other kinds of evidence around which can be very useful if we devote a little effort to making useful sense of it.

- Successful brokers seem almost more interested in the emotions and attitudes of their customers than in the market itself.
- In a recent study of 8,782 commodity speculators over a nine-month period, it turned out that 75 percent of them showed a net loss.
- The primary reason for this result was a reluctance to close out a losing position.
- Psychologists have persistently shown that pressures, anxieties, tensions, and fears seriously degrade our skills as decision makers.

This evidence begins to make a little sense if we go at it from the viewpoint of modern systems analysis. To do this, we need to alter our usual level of observation. Instead of studying the market and trying to understand its almost infinitely complex behavior, we need to examine ourselves and the market as interacting components of a single system. Instead of exclusive[ly] trying to understand what we can do to the market, we need to add to our concern the things the market can do to us. To become sensitive to the effects the market may have on us and the ways these effects, in turn, influence our financial operations, is to see a system in which the parts act on and react to one another. This, our basic hypothesis, is likely to be far more helpful to our ultimate financial performance than exclusively studying the stock tables and earnings reports.

To act in this manner will require a degree of self-perception and self-awareness which is far from usual for most of us. It suggests that the really productive kind of research is not more testing of the random walk hypothesis. What is more likely to make a difference in one's financial operations is research on one's own plans, attitudes, and emotions. This, it begins to appear, may be the real secret of consistent financial effectiveness. It may be *the* essential prerequisite to getting rich slowly with a very high probability of success. It is almost surely the key to understanding why most people do not get rich at all.

Seeing yourself and the market as influencing each other is the real clue to getting the most out of your GRQ [Get Rich Quickly] experiments. As interesting as you will find the progress of your commitments, what may be of even greater long-term interest is your own progress through the GRQ experiment. As you look at your experiment and, indeed, as you look at all your financial operations, see if you can detect some of the ways the market is influencing you: For example:

> How do you feel when you've experienced a sudden large loss or large gain? Does the emotional impact show up in the way you deal with your job, your family, or the next financial decision you make? Does it affect your attitude toward your family budget? Toward taking your spouse out for dinner? Toward the kids' next request?

> Are the funds you're using all you have on which to retire, educate the children, or meet a major emergency? Does the fear and tension associated from the possibility of wiping out your financial future bring you to a high state of nervousness or panic when the market drops sharply?

> Are you holding some things that went down a long time ago and stayed there, hoping that one of these days you'll be able to get even and get out?

> Are you losing sleep over your financial operations? Are you a worrier? Do you call your broker frequently and read everything you can get your hands on, searching for fragments which tend to confirm your judgment and restore a little of your confidence?

> Do you feel that you should be in the market all the time? Can you stay out for awhile, or are you too afraid of missing a rise?

Do you get upset by the stories of people who have made a killing?

When your holdings are up, everybody is feeling great, and stock market news begins to appear on the front page, do you decide that we're in for a whole new era of prosperity, that it's easy to make lots of money, that there's no end in sight, and that the best thing to do is hold and buy more?

When the market goes down and everyone is discouraged, do you avoid buying anything, promise yourself you'll quit the market forever if you can only get out even, and feel like a personal failure has occurred?

When you buy a stock, are you certain that it will go up? When it goes down, do you feel that you've made a mistake?

Do you honestly have a clear idea of what your past financial performance has been, or is there a lot you really are not too interested in remembering? . . .

Is your program of financial operations kind of random, hit-or-miss, or "flexible"? Does it get a lot more of your attention when the market is going up than when it's going down?

Could you say that you have a systematic plan or approach to the market? Have you written it down? Could you say honestly that you've pretty well stuck to your plan for several years? . . .

This is more than enough to give you the idea. Try developing your own hypothesis about what the market may be doing to you. Once you get sensitive to the possibilities, you'll see yourself reacting in all sorts of interesting ways. . . .

RESOLVING A BASIC DILEMMA

. . .You may be of the opinion that professionals don't make much money and you may be right. I'm convinced, however, that generally speaking they make more than most of us and that none of them seems to have a consistently better approach in the long run than any of their colleagues. All of this strikes me as a kind of dilemma. It seems to say that what the professionals have is something besides their system, their approach, and their basic theories of the market. These are not simple questions and it is idle to suppose otherwise. Yet, some measure of understanding may emerge from a simply stated principle.

Getting deliberately rich or achieving consistent financial performance is at least as much a psychological problem as it is a logical problem.

The real function of a stock market system or theory is to lead us toward a set of more or less reasonable operating rules which will protect us from ourselves. Left alone to suffer all the emotional impacts of the market on our decision making abilities, we are almost sure to do things which are self-defeating. We hang on too long to a losing position, rush almost blindly into risky speculations, change our objectives frequently, get greedy and try for more and more, or get discouraged and give up. Left alone, we seem prone to decisions which we later come to regret, because when our emotions subside we can see that they didn't make much sense as a consistent and sensible approach to the market. This contrariness of emotional behavior, its inconsistency with good market performance, seems to me to be the top candidate for explaining why "the small investor always gets taken." The function which can be served by almost any reasonable set of operating rules is to keep us insulated from the psychological pressures which the market generates. These psychological pressures seem to have the peculiar effect of making us do things which can only result in a very low level of market performance. The unaided investor, the investor without some consistent approach, just doesn't seem to have a long run chance.

Here, it seems to me, we are very close to understanding how there can be professionals who get consistent performance with many different approaches to the market. There are in fact many different market theories which can perform *the* essential function of supporting and encouraging systematic, unemotional financial operations. An approach to the market may be technical, fundamental, or involve almost any reasonably coherent set of ideas. It need not be complex, subtle, or novel. It simply needs to make some minimal degree of sense to the person using it, and it has to be *followed*. In this sense there seem to be lots of good approaches and probably very, very few outstanding ones. Some may be a little better than others at forecasting the movements of the market, but many of them seem able to perform the function of insulating us from our own emotional natures, of helping us avoid our naturally counterproductive market behavior. . . .

To look at ourselves as components of a system in which we do things in the market and it does things to us is to focus on the real difficulty of the GRS [Get Rich Slowly] hypothesis. It is probably relatively easy to design a simple GRS program which, *if followed*, has a very high probability of making one rich. The probability of following a plan over the necessarily extended period of time is unhappily quite small for most of us. It is significantly more important to devote our energies to increasing this probability, than to devote them to learning more about the market. There is a greater return from efforts aimed at understanding our own lack of poise, our own impatience, our own emotionally tainted thinking, than there is from an equal effort devoted to reading research reports from one's broker.

The thing which most distinguishes the amateur from the professional in financial operations is, simply, self-awareness. The secret of the professional, I'm now convinced, is the discovery that they can dramatically increase their chances of success by watching themselves even more carefully than they watch the market. The thing about the pros is not so much the specific knowledge of investment opportunities they have, but the fact that they know enough about themselves to protect themselves from themselves.

* * * * *

THE ROY NEUBERGER
ALMANAC

Roy R. Neuberger

Roy Neuberger has been successfully—and enthusiastically—investing and trading for two or three times as many years as some of the profession's current leaders have been in business. Here are some of his beliefs and observations.

I have set down in random fashion on the pages that follow a variety of thoughts, ideas, and loose principles which have served me well. In my last forty-four years of buying and selling securities, I have used these tools to my advantage. If you gain useful knowledge in the pursuit of profit as well as enjoyment from these comments, I shall be more than content.

Rule #1: *Be flexible*. My philosophy has necessarily changed from time to time because of events and because of mistakes. My views change as economic, political, and technological changes occur both on and now off our planet. It is imperative that you be willing to change your thoughts to meet new conditions.

Rule #2: *Take your temperament into account*. Recognize whether

From Roy Neuberger, *The Roy Neuberger Almanac* [New York, New York, (original edition published 1977, revised edition copyright©1988 Roy R. Neuberger)], 1–14, by permission of the author.

you are by nature very speculative or just the opposite: Fearful—timid of taking risks. But in any event—

Rule #3: *Be broad gauged.* Diversify your investments, make sure that some of your principal is kept safe, and try to increase your income as well as your capital.

Rule #4: *Always remember there are many ways to skin a cat!* Ben Graham did it by understanding basic values, Ben Smith did it by knowing when and how to sell short, T. Rowe Price appreciated the importance of the growth of new industries (like mobile homes); each was successful in his own way. But to be successful, remember to

Rule #5: *Be skeptical.* To repeat a few well-worn useful phrases:

A. Dig For Yourself.
B. Be From Missouri.
C. There's a sucker born every minute. (Compliments of P. T. Barnum).

A FEW THOUGHTS ABOUT TIMING

By timing, I mean when is it a good time to get in the market: to buy; and when is it a good time to get out, stay out—that is: to sell. Timing may not be everything but it's an awful lot. The best long-term investment can look terrible for years ahead if you buy at the wrong time. And sometimes you can make money in highly speculative stocks by buying at the right moment. The very best security analysts can do well without following market trends but it's a lot easier to work with them.

A speculator or investor is often successful because he is willing to commit large sums on the buy side when the market is very weak and he gets a lot of securities for his money. On the opposite side he creates his eventual buying power by having the guts to sell in the very strong markets where you sell comparatively few securities for high prices and get large sums. That's a very simple principle. I've used the word "guts," but it's really more a matter of sticking to a common sense viewpoint.

Timing is partly intuitive, partly contrary, and requires independence in thinking. Over U.S. financial history there have been a host of both bull and bear markets. Often the uptrend occurs during a business cycle downtrend and declines come in periods of full prosperity. Paul Samuelson wrote "The stock market has forecast eight of the last three recessions." True enough, and intuition then becomes temporarily as important as analytic security knowledge.

Remember, too, that timing is delicate, sometimes exquisite. To go short the right stock at the wrong time (on the way up) may be horrendously expensive—ask those who went short Litton, Teleprompter, Levitz Furniture, Memorex, and many others rightly but too soon. I knew a man once who lost his shirt selling short in the summer of 1929: he didn't have the reserves to hold out until autumn.

Bull markets tend to be longer than bear markets and prices tend to go up more slowly or erratically than they go down. Bear markets tend to be shorter, more severe, more intense. But the market does have certain fairly consistent habits. Rarely do the market and business rise concurrently for more than six months. Rarely do they decline together longer than six months. Therefore, I believe the sensible investor will concentrate his buying at a time when the market has been very weak while business has been very strong. If the market and business had been strong together, I would be much less optimistic about the market.

INTEREST RATES AND THE MONEY SUPPLY

Of all the tools for market trend predicting, no single tool is more important than the trend of interest rates. In addition to the trend, there is the difference in yield between stocks and bonds to worry about. When bond interest remained low for many years, public utility stocks (as in the 1950s) were very attractive compared to bond returns. But now high yielding bonds compete with equities for investment money. Usually when both short-term *and* long-term rates start rising, they tell the stock investor one story: Run For The Hills.

But how do you tell which way interest rates are going to go? It's become popular to watch the money supply, and I think it's possible that the market sometimes makes a mistake in being bearish because of a big money supply. This big money supply may cause short-term interest rates to go up because the Federal Reserve lifts rates to hold the money supply in check. But where is this money going to go? It can be used in business, but if business is sluggish the money will probably search for another outlet. Among the possible outlets are the bond market and the stock market. Of course, if interest rates are very high, the bond market may out-compete the stock market for that money.

PSYCHOLOGY

Don't underrate the importance of psychology in the stock market. When people buy they are more anxious to buy than the seller, and vice versa. So many things go into the buy or sell decision besides economic statistics or security analysis. A bad (or good) buy or sell decision may be made merely because of a headache.

Some people try to guess what the crowd will do, believing they can be swept along in a favorable current. But this is dangerous. The crowd may be very late in acting. Suppose it's an institutional crowd. Sometimes they over-influence each other and are the victims of their own habits.

Personally, I like to be contrary. When things look awful, I become optimistic. When the crowd and the world looks most rosy, I like to be a seller, perhaps prematurely, but usually profitably.

Ancient Wall Street Cliche: The bulls make money, the bears make money, but what happens to the pigs?

SOME FORGOTTEN CONCEPTS

Asset Values

In the 1960s, investors paid less attention to real assets than they did early in the 20th century. By real assets, I mean the value of the plant and equipment and cash behind each share. But now that the affluent society concept is fading fast and the energy crunch is coming in strong, investors are becoming more interested again in real assets. So companies with lots of extra oil and gas reserves, real estate, unused coal and copper mines, great stands of forests, these and other assets are again being given a substantial plus in appraising a stock's worth. And why not? The last few years have seen enormous price appreciation in other tangibles: antique furniture, ancient art, modern art, gold, diamonds, jewelry, and real estate. So if a company owns a lot of real property of one sort or another, it has to be a reason for wanting to own the stock. To be sure, in the long run these assets have to be connected with a company's earning power and, therefore, tied into its ultimate worth.

Dividends

In recent years most institutional investors pay too little attention to the actual dividends paid out. Paradoxically, individual investors concerned with maximizing their income often make the size of the dividend too important a consideration. For years the big growth stocks have zoomed while paying two percent; on the other hand, utility stocks have had a very hard time since the early 1960s even though the dividends may have been 4% back then and 7 to 8% right now. Dividends are an important plus because, if the company's dividend is safe, it helps put a floor on the price.

Incidentally, you should check into a company's payout policy. If it pays out 90% of its earnings, beware. It's usually a real danger signal of a dividend cut ahead. If it pays out 10%, vice versa. An average company would pay out 40 to 60% of earnings as dividends; most utility companies are more generous.

"Growth" Stocks and Price-Earnings Multiples

In the 1920s, a prime market influence was a book by Edgar Smith called "Common Stocks for Long Term Investment". It was a brilliant and important book. Mr. Smith's main point was to advocate the benefit to corporate growth of the application of retained earnings and depreciation. Thus capital appreciates. The book was perhaps influential in changing accepted multiples of 10 times earnings to higher multiples of 20 to 30 times earnings.

But people have often paid too much for assumed persistent growth, only to find out that a general economic decline, an act of war, or a series of government controls will change either the appraisal of the growth rate or change the growth rate itself. Rarely can securities be valued correctly at over 15 times earnings, because rarely is there any clear prospect that a company's earnings will grow sufficiently in the future to make it worth that price. We know that there are exceptions, but they account for perhaps 1% of the cases. So the odds are against you when you pay a very high multiple.

What is a "growth stock"? One intelligent growth stock adherent thinks it's a company discovered in an early stage of its potential. Often the label stays with it after it's become mature. The growth has slowed, but people or institutions continue to buy it because their imagination doesn't go beyond the obvious.

In any case, there is no magic to the phrase "growth stock." The word "growth" describes what we are all trying to do. Long before the phrase became popular, investors and speculators were trying to foresee which companies in the future were going to fare well in earnings, gross business, reputation, and so forth. Everyone hopes to unearth a company that produces a new article that will become commonly used. The trick is to discover those companies before you have to pay too big a price for them in terms of the earnings multiple.

Sometimes, after a price decline, some companies need to be rediscovered. The stocks that were the rage and sold at very high multiples in the late sixties and early seventies came down drastically in price after that period. In the best cases, the problem was not with the companies but with the price of the stocks, and at some point several of the stocks became attractive again. These were companies that had stood the test of time; they were much better than the average big company, and their growth rates were much better and more sustained. A multiple of between 10 and 15 on an outstanding company is acceptable to me even if there are many stocks selling between 6 and 10. There may be acceptable values in both groups.

Of course, deciding what represents good value is a matter of judgment. Sometimes you can get a better grasp on values by looking at aggregates. You should always be summing up the total market value of a company. I remember that at one point in the late seventies, IBM was selling at 40 billion dollars. Since the total corporate wealth of the U.S. was estimated at $900 billion, IBM's $40 billion was a very big figure, but IBM was a very special company. On the other hand, in 1961, when IBM was much smaller, there was a period of months when the company was selling in the market for $16 billion, but the figure at that time worked out to 80 times earnings. That was too high, and in 1962 the price dropped by 50 percent. Or take the case of Avon Products, which in 1972 was selling in the market for $8 billion when it was earning about $125 million, or 64 times earnings. That also turned out to be too high.

The "One Decision Concept"

This means buying but not selling. There is only "one decision" namely when to buy. Some brilliant investors have used one-decision concepts and have been successful. But the odds are so much against your being right that I think that very few people should use this concept. The institutions made this a successful formula for several years and indeed created a cult concept for a certain number of stocks. The tax laws helped to institutionalize the practice; why sell if the governments (federal, state, city) took more and more of the profits? But this approach assumes that a company goes only one way, and we have seen that it can and does backfire.

Calendar Comments

Mark Twain covered the calendar with wise stock comments. He said: "October is one of the peculiarly dangerous months to speculate in stocks. The others are July, January, September, April, November, May, March, June, December, August, and February. "

Are there stocks for the seasons? Should toy stocks be bought in late summer for fall Christmas hopes? Should retail stores be? Should beer stocks be bought in the spring if you anticipate a hot summer? I doubt it. To borrow a title from a great play, I prefer a stock for all seasons.

Four Seasons

Almanacs deal with events in man's calendar. The seasons, even with their infinite minor variations one year to next, are really repetitive milestones in time's passage. Some people, noting how stock market behavior is often repetitive, try to find some correlation to the seasons.

Many people assume or hope the market will be dull in summer so that vacations can be taken without care. Some years summer's the time to be around as with the price freeze in '70 or throughout the summer of 1929.

In the autumn there is often the expectation of a business activity increase consonant with the fall-style weather but sometimes fall surprises are hurricanes—also a fall phenomenon.

Then comes bleak winter and everyone thinks the world is cold; but there is the hope of the New Year. A bad winter means more salt and fuel are used; a bad winter may mean more skiing and resort business.

Our greatest hopes are always in springtime. The world is new again as fresh rainfall and new plants usher in the daylight saving days. The ants scurry outside their nests and the birds are on the wing. In Wall Street it's a time for judging agricultural developments: Will the world need more fertilizer? Tractors? Hybrid seed? But in reality such decisions can be made at any time; it's unnecessary to invest by the calendar. Just realize there are real opportunities at all times for the adventuresome investor and that the joys of living and investing are enhanced by the variability of the seasons.

Watching the Kettle Boil

A sizable part of the Wall Street community has in recent years developed an obsession. It appears to be over-zealous in finding out what is happening minute by minute to corporate earnings. The fever has spread as well to corporation executives who appear to worry excessively over reported quarter-to-quarter earnings. The greatest game among a number of research firms seems to be to find out the next quarter's earnings, before someone else does. This focus on short-term earnings appears to be losing the point of the significance of longer term trends in earnings. Corporations often must make current expenditures, with an effect on current earnings, to build for the future. If the goal of immediate reported earnings gains becomes dominant it could become detrimental to a company's future. Gains in earnings should be the result of long-term strategies, excellence in management, good exploitation of opportunities and so on. If these things fall in place properly, short-term earnings should not be of major importance.

Another trouble with overattention to each quarter is the upset when a favorite stubs its toe. Then the unexpected causes a stock price drop which can be both precipitous and shocking.

Fads

There seem always to have been fads in Wall Street. For some reason or other the move in Stutz Bearcat autos was a fad in the 1920s. Conglomerates were a fad in the 1960s when reported earnings were often helped by some athletic bookkeeping. In any case, the criteria for purchase of any substantial amount of stock should remain on solid grounds: 1–good products, 2–a necessary product, 3–an honest management, 4–honest reporting. The investment can always be helped by a bit of luck, but fads come and go. Beware.

Falling in Love

One should fall in love with ideas, with people, or with idealism based on the possibilities that exist in this adventuresome world. In my book, the last thing to fall in love with is a particular security. It is after all just a sheet of paper indicating a part ownership in a corporation and its use is purely mercenary. The fact that a number of people have been extremely fortunate in the past by falling in love with something that went their way is not necessarily the proof it will always be that way. Stay in love with a security until the security gets overvalued, then let somebody else fall in love.

SOME THOUGHTS ON TECHNIQUES

Losses

I must admit to being wrong perhaps about 20% of the time over a long period which totals to an awful lot of losses. However, it was the 80% that mattered. The goal was to be a bit like Ty Cobb rather than Babe Ruth. Since an important factor in investing is the matter of judgment this will inevitably be unfortunate at times. One needs to recognize as quickly as possible an error in judgment. One rule is to take a loss pretty habitually at approximately 10%. The technique I have practiced is to take a profit occasionally on something that has gone up to a price over what was expected and simultaneously to take losses wherever misjudgment seems evident. This creates a reservoir of buying power that can be used to make fresh judgments on what are the best values in the market at that time. The mistake of many is to make one decision and to get locked into that position. Perhaps half of those "one-decision ideas" work out favorably to those who have carried the stocks for a long period to avoid taxes. Others don't work out. The buyers have become stubborn and kept them too long with large losses. All in all, the essence of taking losses, which is ultimately a question of character, is to acknowledge when one is wrong.

Profits

This is the name of the game. Something that goes your way, and where your judgment or your luck is helping to improve your fortunes, usually requires patience in holding. These are the types of securities where it is advisable to restrain one's greed in taking an accomplished fact. One should only recognize "Don't count your chickens before they are hatched."

When a particular security starts to sell above a reasonable intrinsic value, say 50% above purchase price, your only problem in selling is one of taxes. That is a good time to take profits even if it is short of the top of the market. Mr. Bernard Baruch was an advocate of buying a bit too soon and selling a bit too soon. His fame has endured.

Being Right

If any investor were right all of the time he would have accumulated a considerable portion of the world's wealth. Obviously this is a possibility but in actuality it has never happened except among liars. There are billionaires (some temporary) who have owned a large part of a corporation that in their lifetime has grown to immense size and success. This formula for investment is not one I am trying to advocate. I can add, however, that up to age 65, I consistently reinvested profits in my own business to satisfactory advantage.

Non-Importance of Breaking Even

I have referred above to an often successful method of taking losses semiautomatically at the 10% level. The use of the money elsewhere has usually been more fruitful than in maintaining the mistaken position. I have, on the other hand, often seen the person who has stubbornly stuck to his position, increasing his potential loss and waiting many years to break even in the stock. On the other hand, there also exists the investor who, after showing paper losses and then on having the opportunity to break even, eagerly gets out without trying to reappraise the current situation. Nine times out of ten, the security was then a buy rather than a sell.

If one is to learn from these particular situations the lesson is that the market does not know about these individual transactions. There is no magic to the price *you* paid for a security and one must learn the hard way the antics of evaluation and re-evaluation.

Hedging

I would not recommend this procedure or being short some stock and long others at the same time for more than a very small percentage of private individuals. One has to have a stubborn, perverse and patient attitude in selling short securities that are too high in one's eyes. But, if it is done methodically and continuously, it is an excellent method to help in the accumulation of capital and education. Here are the advantages: 1. It gives one more patience to hold on to undervalued long positions, as a good purchase at low prices often requires infinite patience. 2. It makes one less concerned with the psychology of fear that dominates the market from time to time, as it permits you to have an "anchor to windward." Even if things go down—you benefit.

I would prefer not to make too much of this philosophy. In remembrances of things past, however, it stood me in good stead in late September of 1929. My portfolio was down about 12% and I had an uneasy feeling about the market and conditions in general. Those were days of 10% margin and I studied the lists carefully for a stock that was overvalued in my opinion and which I could sell short as a hedge. I came across RCA at about $100 per share. It had recently split 5 for 1 and appeared over valued. There were no dividends, little income, a low net worth and a weak financial position. Its only bullish aspect was hope for the future age of radio. I sold short a dollar value of this stock equal to the dollar value of my long portfolio. It proved to be a timely and profitable move. The bear market that occurred in 1930–32 made it imperative to sell short if you wanted to make a profit. The habit has become somewhat ingrained in me by now, although it is quite possible to do well without it.

Investment Balance

Only a small portion of the population have all their money in the so-called "market" although there are over 20 million investors. Investors range from those with 10% or less of their wealth invested in securities to over 100% of their wealth. I think personal temperament is a very important factor in how much to invest. When interest rates are very high, perhaps a considerable portion of the average person's position should be in bonds. Many years ago, one could compound annually in the bond market only at around 5%. I had reasonable preference for risk-taking and tried to compound at 10–15% or more. This is hard for most entities to attain. To do this requires a large segment of common stock risk at a time of deep pessimism in the market and a search for companies whose products are necessary for the ongoing economy.

Returning to balance, however, one must be flexible. I know someone who has only recently contemplated buying the first bond he ever owned in 50 years. He has done very well without them in the past.

It is better to do some hard work and to do your own choosing rather than to take tips. However, a tip from a brilliant man is like a word to the wise and one should scrutinize that kind of idea. If a second person unrelated to the first should mention the same security, it is time to really dig in. But if one is following the other, do as I said before— beware. Don't play follow the leader.

Physical Condition

One of the best ways to be a good investor is to be in good physical condition. And by good physical condition, I also mean good mental condition. Early to bed and early to rise is perhaps too ideal. To drink in moderation is perhaps better than not to drink at all and to eat in moderation is certainly better than not to eat at all. In any case, to walk at least one hour a day, either by yourself or with someone else, is a good way to improve your market ideas. Walking is better than running; you can't work out an idea running.

General Philosophy

Over a period of time the market seems to have long waves of advances lasting about two years; it has waves of declines lasting a shorter period, perhaps one half the period of the upswing. During the down cycle, there is extreme irregularity in most individual securities affording institutions and people great opportunities for enhancement of wealth. If one is not too fearful in bad times and not too optimistic in good times; if one accepts a small loss because of poor judgment; if one is willing to pay the taxes because of enormous gains when securities become overvalued, then one can generally gain by investing in so-called Wall Street, which now stretches across the country.

THE NEW ERA
FOR INVESTORS

T. Rowe Price, Jr.

In the years after his initial essays on investment policy, one of several perceptive concepts developed by T. Rowe Price related to inflation's erosion of the purchasing power of money. In this 1970 piece, he introduces the notion of a New Era for investors—offering vast new opportunities, but requiring new investment policies to cope with "far more difficult" circumstances arising from anticipated pervasive inflation.

INTRODUCTION

This article, "The New Era For Investors," is a resume of a series of five bulletins written from 1964 to 1966 about social, political, and economic trends which would cause a new environment for investors after 1965. It is updated and a revision of an earlier article which was published in September, 1969.

An era may be of long or short duration covering a period of a few years or many years. For the investor it may cover years of economic

From T. Rowe Price, Jr., *The New Era For Investors* (Baltimore, Maryland, 1970), 3–22, by permission of T. Rowe Price Investment Services.

depression, such as the 1930s, or years of great prosperity such as the 1950s and 1960s. It may be a span of peace or war economy. It may be an age of great industry change due to new inventions.

The successful investor should be looking forward and trying to anticipate changing eras ahead of the crowd. This requires both foresight and patience. The timing of the change is of great importance but often difficult to identify because the change is gradual and irregular like the waves in a changing tide. It requires patience because of temporary periods of deflation and changes in the business cycles which obscure the major trends that are taking place. It is better to be too early than too late in recognizing the passing of one era and the waning of old investment favorites, and the advent of a new era affording new opportunities for the investor.

ERA OF GREAT PROSPERITY

The boom of the 1920s was followed by the great depression of the 1930s and World War II. From 1930 to 1946, a period of 16 years, building and construction of peacetime facilities and the production of durable goods for the consumer in the United States were sharply below normal demands. During World War II the foreign countries involved in the War experienced the greatest destruction of property in history. Many years were required for the reconstruction of the destroyed properties of these nations and the replacement of worldwide shortages in consumer and durable goods.

At the end of World War II the United States was the richest nation in the world. We held most of the gold. Many of our plants which were built during the War were modern, and hundreds of millions of dollars had been spent on research and development . . .we possessed both the wealth and the know-how. We then proceeded to give and lend money to other nations and we taught them the American way of becoming prosperous. In so doing, these nations became our greatest competitors in world markets.

From 1946 to 1965, a period of 19 years, we experienced the greatest period of prosperity in history. There were many reasons:

1. We had become the wealthiest nation in the world and had suffered little or no destruction within our country.

2. The underproduction in the United States during the 1930–1946 period needed to be made up.
3. We were providing much of the aid needed for the reconstruction of the war devastated countries of Europe and Japan, where consumer and durable goods had to be replenished.
4. The population explosion created further demands for goods and services.
5. Built-in supports and anti-depression legislation cushioned the effect of cyclical business recessions.
6. A great number of new industries emerged as a result of advanced technologies developed during the War years.
7. The Korean War, which started in 1950, further stimulated the economy by requiring increased production of war materials before the shortages of peacetime goods created by World War II had been replenished.
8. The escalation of the Vietnam War accelerated and prolonged the boom.

By the middle of the 1960s the foreign nations had fully recovered financially and economically. They no longer felt the need to pull together under the leadership of the United States to protect themselves from their No. 1 enemy—Russia and her satellites. A long period of cooperation which we designated as internationalism was gradually being replaced by feelings of self-sufficiency and independence. This was illustrated by France's stated desire to become the leading nation of Europe. *The spirit of unity, harmony and togetherness, which prevailed during the early post-war years, was replaced by friction and lack of cooperation, and a trend toward isolationism which we designated as nationalism. This trend was unfavorable for the welfare of the western world. Unity had created strength; lack of unity fostered weakness. No real leadership in world affairs developed in either the United States or Europe. This trend toward nationalism and disintegration continues today.*

Too much prosperity within a short period of time among the majority of the United States citizens, demands of the poor and underprivileged for an increased share in the wealth, rivalry among various groups such as labor unions, business enterprises, and speculators to get a larger share of the wealth have led to friction and disunity among the people of this country. *Congress has put politics ahead of statesmanship and the welfare of the nation.*

THE NEW ERA

The prolonged period of prosperity created and fostered the problems which led to the new era for investors, starting in the mid-1960s. It is a change from the period of great prosperity following World War II, when social, political, and economic conditions were generally favorable for the investor, to another period when accelerated inflation, more socialization of basic industries, and increased competition, both domestic and foreign, will increase the risk of loss and decrease the opportunity for profit. *In the new era it will be far more difficult to invest successfully, and a different investment policy will be required.*

Investment eras are the result of far more than pure economic factors. They can be traced back to the social and political trends that are responsible for the economic condition.[1] A study of these trends shows how the new investment era differs from our previous investment era of great prosperity.

Six areas of concern helped to signal the change. These concerns and their relation to investment policies were detailed in five bulletins on economic trends written between February, 1964 and November, 1966. They dealt with these subjects: (1) The rapid deterioration of our nation as a leader in the non-communist world; (2) The absence of leadership in the other capitalistic nations; (3) A probable change for the worse in our favorable balance of trade; (4) Rising debt, particularly consumer debt which had reached dangerous levels that could cause real trouble once the business cycle turned down and disposable income declined; (5) Rising interest rates in foreign countries which could soon force us to follow suit in order to prevent our deficit balance-of-payments from reaching dangerous proportions and a new run on our gold supply; (6) Racial trouble at home.

The Serious Problems of the Nation Have Become Worse

Yesterday's areas of concern have become today's realities.

Leadership in the capitalistic or non-communist nations is still lacking. [The President] . . . is making an effort to fill the void, but it is too soon to determine whether he will be successful.

Our entering the civil war in Vietnam was a colossal mistake and there is no prospect of a satisfactory ending.

Our adverse balance of international trade has worsened. Our balance-of-payments deficit has increased. Our gold reserves are inadequate to meet the claims of other nations.

Total debt in this country—Federal, State and Local, consumer, mortgage, corporate and miscellaneous—has increased from $400,000,000,000 in 1945, to an estimated $1,700,000,000,000 in 1969.

Interest rates are the highest in the past century, and liquidity of our financial institutions and many of our commercial and industrial corporations is critically low.

Our racial and other dissenting group problems remain unsolved. The racial uprising has spread to a revolt against the "Establishment" by other than the minority groups based on color. There is spreading discontent among youth of all classes of society who are demanding more rights to determine their status in a society. Youth insists on greater power and a greater voice in society and politics. Fifty percent of the population of the country is under 28 years of age. Many of these young people have little understanding and appreciation of the fundamentals that have made this country great. If a business recession occurs and unemployment increases materially, these social problems will become even more serious.

Inflation has escalated and appears to be out of control.

Accelerated Inflation—The No. 1 Problem

Can our Government control inflation? It seems doubtful for a number of reasons. The Full Employment Act of 1946 requires the Government to provide full employment even if it inflates our economy. *We can not have full employment without continued inflation.*

The minimum wage law forces periodic raises in wages per hour. This escalation of wages not only forces costs of labor upward, but it prevents many workers who are willing to work for less than the minimum wage from getting a job. The untrained and the inexperienced, especially youth, can not obtain jobs because their productivity is too low to make their employment economically justified. The number of unemployed and the cost of providing for them are increased, thus fomenting further social unrest.

In a socialistic, or welfare state, the Government provides compensation for all. As the cost of living rises, minimum compensation escalates.

Since 1934 our population has been indoctrinated with the belief that a little inflation is good for everyone. It causes a continuous rise in wages and provides consumers with more money to spend. Inflation, once started and accepted by the masses as the best way of life, is bound to accelerate. Wages and prices keep pushing each other up and up. As wages rise, prices rise, and the increase in wages is offset by higher and higher prices. This forces the cost of living upward and erodes the purchasing power of the dollar.

When the Government endeavors to provide full employment, to fight costly foreign wars, to do the many things required under the objectives of the Great Society and the Welfare State, and fails to balance its budget year after year, even during periods of great prosperity, there is only one outcome. *Even the richest nation in the world can not continue to spend more than it collects without going broke.* It is only a matter of time. Its bills must be paid, and the only way to do so is to print more paper dollars backed by nothing but other paper money, such as SDR (Special Drawing Rights) which are referred to as "paper gold."

The Government has spent, invested, and given away more money than it has taken in during all but two years since 1949. The accumulated deficit in the nation's balance-of-payments totals more than $44 billion in this period. In the year 1969 the net outflow was $7 billion.

Uncontrolled inflation seems unavoidable as long as full employment and perpetual prosperity are a goal of the nation. Historically, uncontrolled inflation has always led to a boom and bust. There seems little likelihood that current inflation will do otherwise. There is no turning back once it gets out of control. *After the boom comes the bust and a serious business depression. A serious business depression will create social revolution and confiscation of property of the "haves" by the "have nots." Thus, the destruction of the wealth of those who have created and accumulated wealth takes place by taxation, devaluation of the paper currency, and confiscation of property.*

Historic Background of Inflation

The *Consumer Price Index*, prepared by the Department of Labor, is the best yardstick we have to measure the changes in the cost of living. The following table shows the changes which have taken place during the past

Periods of War & Peace	Consumer Price Index	% Change	Annual Compound Rate of Change
World War I 1914–1920 (6 yrs.)	1914 = 35.0 1920 = 69.8	+ 99.4%	+ 12.2%
Peace 1920–1941 (21 yrs.)	1920 = 69.8 1941 = 51.3	− 26.5%	− 1.5%
World War II 1941–1947 (6 yrs.)	1941 = 51.3 1947 = 77.8	+ 51.7%	+ 7.2%
Peace 1947–1950 (3 yrs.)	1947 = 77.8 1950 = 83.8	+ 7.7%	+ 2.5%
Korean War 1950–1956 (6 yrs.)	1950 = 83.8 1956 = 94.7	+ 13.0%	+ 2.1%
Peace 1956–1965 (9 yrs.)	1956 = 94.7 1965 = 109.9	+ 16.1%	+ 1.7%
Vietnam War 1965–1969 (4 yrs.)	1965 = 109.9 1969 = 127.7	+ 16.2%	+ 3.8%

55 years, which include four wars: World War I, World War II, the Korean War, and the Vietnam War to date. The 55 years [1914–1969] have been divided into seven periods to show the rate of inflation during years of war and peace. The war periods include approximately two post-war years when inflation accelerated after the removal of war taxes and price controls.

The rise in the cost of living for the 55 years was 264.9%, or an annual compound rate of increase of 2.4%. Most of this increase took place during the war periods, particularly World Wars I and II. The first peace period of 21 years included the great depression, during which the Consumer Price Index declined to a low of 45.1 in 1933. For the total 21 years leading up to World War II, the Price Index declined 26.5%, or an annual compound rate of decline of 1.5%.

Historically, all wars are inflationary. Prior to World War II, all war inflations were followed by periods of depression with a decline in business activity and in the cost of living.

During the second World War period we had price controls which held inflation in check, and the annual compound rate of increase was only 7.2%.

During the period of peace, 1947 to 1950, the annual compound rate of increase in the index was 2.5%. During the Korean War, the rate of increase averaged 2.1%. During the subsequent peace period, 1956–1965, the Consumer Price Index increased an annual compound rate of only 1.7%.

From 1947 to 1965, when this country experienced the greatest prosperity in its history, the cost of living increased at an annual compound rate of only 1.9%. From 1966 to date, inflation has accelerated, as the following figures indicate:

Annual Figures	% Increase	12 Mos. End.	% Increase
1966–1967	2.8	Dec. 1969	6.1
1967–1968	4.2	Jan. 1970	6.2
1968–1969	5.4	Feb. 1970	6.3

It is apparent that the Government's efforts to decelerate inflation have not succeeded to date.

In the opinion of the author, the masses who elect the Chief Executive and members of Congress will not support any government in the near future which puts the control of inflation ahead of full employment and continued prosperity.

Other Developments Which Have Necessitated a Change in Investment Policy

Inflationary Trends in the U.S. and Foreign Countries

It is generally believed that the U.S. dollar is the strongest currency in the world. It is accepted as a medium of exchange. Inflation in other capitalistic countries is currently taking place. Inflationary trends in the U.S. and foreign nations not only have an influence on each other, but also a very important bearing on:

a. Our adverse balance of trade
b. Our balance-of-payments deficits
c. Future demands on our gold reserves

The following table shows that, during the 1960–1965 period, the cost of living in foreign countries rose much faster than in the United States. The export price index in the U.S. increased only slightly more than the export price index in foreign countries. The second period (1965–1969) shows that the cost of living in the United States increased faster than in foreign countries, and that the export price index increased nearly four times as much as the foreign export price index.

	Rise in Cost of Living		Export Price Index	
	1960–1965	1965–1969	1960–1965	1965–1969
United States	+ 6.8%	+ 18.3%	+ 5.1%	+ 15.4%
Foreign	+ 23.6%	+ 15.5%	+ 3.6%	+ 3.9%

During recent years, imports of goods and services have been increasing faster than exports of goods and services. The following table illustrates total exports (in millions of dollars) and total imports from 1964 to 1969, and the increasing ratio of imports to exports over the period.

	Total Exports	Total Imports	Ratio of Imports
	(Millions of dollars)		to Exports
1965	39,399	32,278	.819
1966	43,360	38,081	.878
1967	46,188	41,011	.888
1968	50,594	48,078	.950
1969	55,387	53,314	.963

During the 1965–1969 period, when the cost of living and export prices rose faster in the United States than in foreign countries, we experienced an adverse balance-of-trade. This was a contributing factor to our balance-of-payments deficit and a run on our gold supply.

Escalating costs of production in terms of goods and labor have greatly restricted corporate profits within our country. This factor has induced U.S. corporations to establish operations in foreign countries where costs in terms of goods and labor are far less, and where they can, therefore, better compete in world markets. Because of these lower costs, foreign subsidiaries of American corporations can sell their products at lower prices to other foreign countries and to the United States. This increases U.S. imports, restricts our nation's exports, and limits the market for our nation's production within our own country. The consequences of this trend have been obvious in the plight of the domestic textile and shoe industries which suffer the effects of the marketing of equal or superior products produced in foreign countries at lower prices than prices at which domestic products may be sold at reasonable profit. This is true of other import products, such as automobiles, steel, machine tools, photographic equipment, radios, TV's, and household appliances.

The adverse effects of the increased foreign competition on our nation's industry have been to create excess U.S. plant capacity, reduce domestic employment opportunities, and force U.S. producers to lower prices to meet foreign competition. The magnitude of excess plant capacity is indicated by operating rates, which are down from 90.8% four years ago to below 80% currently.

As a defensive measure, American corporations have established many new foreign plants, thus increasing competition with existing American plants, and thereby further increasing our imports from foreign countries.

Taxes Set New Records in 1969

The acceleration of the Vietnam War and increased expenditures for the Great Society and the Welfare State greatly increased the Federal Government's deficit. This necessitated an increase in Federal taxes in 1969. Subsequently, the 10% annual Surtax was reduced to 5% for the first half of 1970 and supposedly will be eliminated in the second half.

While Federal income taxes are currently being reduced, taxes in most other areas are increasing at an alarming rate, as illustrated by the following:

1. State sales tax levies, the largest tax source of State government, totaled $14.2 billion in 1969, an increase of 19.4% over the previous year, while retail sales showed an increase of only 3.6% in the same period.

2. State corporate net income taxes showed the largest percentage gain in fiscal 1969, climbing 28.7% to $3.2 billion, while corporate pre-tax profits showed a gain of only 2.9% in the same period.
3. Revenue from individual income taxes accounted for $8.9 billion of State tax collections, up 19.3% from fiscal 1968, while personal income rose only 8.6% in the same period.
4. The $31.9 billion in State and local property taxes, most of which go to local governments, increased 9.6% over 1968.

Labor Gets an Increasing Share of the Corporate Pie

The three contestants which have shared in corporate income are (1) *labor*—in terms of compensation to employees; (2) *government*—in terms of corporate taxes, and (3) *stockholders*—in terms of corporate profits after taxes.

The following table shows that employees' compensation and corporate taxes have been increasing much faster than corporate profits during recent years:

	% Increase 1960–65	Annual Compound Increase	% Increase 1965–69	Annual Compound Increase
Employees' Compensation	33.9	6.0	43.3	9.4
Corporate Taxes	36.1	6.4	38.3	8.4
Corporate Profits (after taxes)	74.2	11.7	8.6	2.1

The annual compound rate of increase in employees' compensation from 1960–1965 versus 1965–1969 has gone up from 6.0% to 9.4%, while the annual rate of increase in corporate profit had dropped from 11.7% to 2.1%.

Are Common Stocks a Hedge Against Accelerated Inflation?

It is well known that bonds, mortgages and other fixed income obligations do not provide a hedge against inflation. Historically, common stocks, as measured by the various stock indices, have, in terms of market value and dividends, increased faster than the rise in the cost of living. However,

	12/31/65	12/31/69	% Change
Dow Jones Ind. Avg.	969.26	800.36	−17.4%
S&P "500"	92.43	92.06	− 0.4%
Consumer Price Index	111.0	131.3	+18.3%

during the past four years, a period of accelerated inflation, the Dow Jones Industrial Average and Standard and Poor's "500" stocks have not kept pace with the rise in the cost of living. [See table on p. 646.]

In the future, it is doubtful that the majority of common stocks will afford the investor adequate protection.

More Socialization of Industry

Socialization of an industry can be said to be taking place when the Government undertakes to (1) regulate wages, hours, and working conditions for employees, (2) prescribe prices and rates, and (3) restrict earnings to a specified rate on the invested capital. As a result, management is required to do more and more for employees and the public at the expense of stockholders who are the owners of the business. This is a handicap to management and usually lessens flexibility of operations and reduces earnings potential.

Industries most affected by socialization have certain characteristics in common. In general, they are those which furnish what are considered the necessities of life—basic foods, shelter, public transportation, communications, water, heat, light, and social benefits covering the broad fields of health, education, and insurance against fire, casualty, sickness, injury, and old age.

New steps toward further socialization of industry are taking place. As illustrations:

1. The Government is pressuring basic industries to train and employ unskilled people from the hard core unemployables.
2. Banks and other financial institutions are experiencing additional regulations as to deposits, loans, and interest rates, and are receiving increasing competition from various government financial agencies.
3. Automobile and tire manufacturers will be forced by the Government to provide greater protection against injury and air pollution.

4. Power plants, factories, and refineries are being required to spend vast sums of money to prevent air and water pollution in order to provide better living conditions for society.
5. Laws have been passed which place more restrictive standards on the merchandising of food, beverages, and packaged goods.

Socialism tends to discourage individual initiative and enterprise and lessens the motivation of potential entrepreneurs to devote their money and talent to organizing industry. If the promise of free enterprise and its rewards is in doubt, the incentive to create industry and assume the risks is weakened and, therefore, quality investment opportunities are lessened. The investor must be more and more alert to the changes influencing profit opportunities in the future.

Our social, political, and economic environment has changed and will continue to change. *We are now in a new era where the investor is faced with the greatest risks in a lifetime.* There is no safe investment. All securities possess varying degrees of risk. Change is the investor's only certainty. A constant vigil is necessary if success in the future is to be attained.

INVESTMENT POLICY FOR THE NEW ERA

Early in 1966 our bulletin, "Change—The Investor's Only Certainty in 1966," listed the following four areas for investment:

1. Electronic data processing, business and office equipment, and the broad field of electronics which reduce labor costs.
2. Cosmetics, toiletries, companies which benefit from leisure time activities and the growing educational and welfare fields.
3. Small businesses with high rates of earnings growth.
4. Natural resources companies which own land, minerals including gold and silver, timber, oil and gas, and other basic commodities needed by industry, which can be produced and marketed profitably during the period of rising prices, rising labor costs, and a dollar with depreciating purchasing power.

The author's current program provides for three groups of stocks: (1) Consumer and Service; (2) Science and Technology; and (3) Natural Resources. Groups (1) and (2) feature growth stocks including many of the past favorites. It is believed that growth stocks continue to be among the best mediums for investment. However, it seems likely that there will be a very limited number of blue chip premier growth stocks with an annual rate of earnings growth of more than 10%. Therefore, the increasing demand from institutional investors will greatly exceed the supply. Consequently, these stocks may be expected to command even higher premiums (price-earnings ratio) in the future than in the past. It is expected that they will be overpriced in relation to their intrinsic worth most of the time. They should be purchased only when they are available at reasonable price-earnings ratios.

Most of the popular growth stocks of the past with an annual compound earnings growth of 5% to 10% will now become less desirable for long-term investment for two reasons: (1) As basic industries become more and more socialized, operating costs will increase faster than prices for services and products, and the rate of earnings growth will shrink. (2) As inflation accelerates, investments in some of the growth stocks with slower rates of earnings growth may not provide the hedge necessary to offset the decline in the purchasing power of the dollar.

Interest rates will also have a bearing on earnings growth. If high rates of interest prevail, as would be expected during accelerated inflation, earnings per share may decline instead of increase for those companies which have to borrow money to provide for expansion and pay a rate of interest above the rate of return they receive on their invested capital. Public utilities, including telephone companies that earn 5% to 7½% on their capital and have to pay 8% to 9½% for borrowed money, will have great difficulty in qualifying as growth stocks. The same goes for industrial enterprises. When interest rates on borrowed capital (bonds and bank loans) were 3% to 5% and the return on invested capital ranged from 5% upward, common stockholders benefited because the difference between the cost of borrowing money and the company's return on this invested capital increased the earnings available for common stocks. The reverse is true when interest rates on borrowed capital increase and are higher than the return on invested capital.

The *Consumer and Service* group consists predominantly of stable growth stocks which are subject to only minor fluctuations in earnings during the ups and downs of a business cycle. It includes stocks of small companies with high rates of earnings growth, as well as seasoned, blue chip growth stocks.

The *Science and Technology* group, which includes both stable and cyclical stocks of companies operating in the areas of electronic data processing, business and office equipment, and the broad field of electronic products which reduce labor costs, should also be featured in the investor's portfolio in the new era.

Natural Resources: The major change recommended during the new era for investors is the inclusion of natural resources and real estate companies.

The basic reason for their attractiveness during this new investment era is that the supply of many of these natural resources is physically limited, and the need and demand for many of them are increasing at a more rapid rate than population and many other social and economic measures. As an example—changing life styles are making the planned community, with internal space allocated for recreation and sports, more and more attractive. Such communities require more land and space per family unit than the dense residential communities that have been added as supplements to existing metropolitan centers.

In the area of minerals, demand for many is rising at a far more rapid rate than population. Per family accumulation of equipment and other hard goods is increasing rapidly. When this per family increase is placed on top of anticipated population increases, it can be readily seen that the tonnage of basic materials needed will increase at a far more rapid rate than the increase in the Federal Reserve Board's index of industrial products and Gross National Product in terms of constant dollars.

The investor should include in his portfolio shares in business enterprises owning tangible property that will increase in value as fast or faster than the rise in the cost of living. Real estate is a good example. Real estate investments include both developed and undeveloped property. Developed real estate includes homes, commercial and industrial buildings, and property which will increase in price because of the rising rentals and increase in asset values. Undeveloped real estate is land which should be strategically located and for which there will be a future demand for development.

Natural resources include forest products, oil, gas, coal, metals such as iron, copper, nickel, molybdenum, and many other commodities for which there will be increasing demand. Throughout history, precious metals, such as gold and silver, have been a haven for people with wealth desiring protection from the ravages of run-away inflation of paper currencies.

Therefore, it is important that investors own stocks of gold and silver mining companies.

Many of the natural resources stocks, particularly the metals, will be subject to wide fluctuations in market value. This is due to the changing supply-demand situation. There will be periods when excess supply of the metal forces prices downward and other periods when shortages force prices upward. For example, silver bullion dropped from a high of $2.56 per ounce in 1968, to a low of $1.53 per ounce in the summer of 1969. The market prices of silver stocks reflected these changes by sharp advances and equally sharp declines. Because of the volatility of these metal stocks, it will be necessary to make more frequent shifts from one group to another to take advantage of the profit opportunities.

Performance Is the Best Proof

Management of a model portfolio since January, 1966 is the best test of the soundness of the recommended policy and strategy in this new era. This model portfolio is in addition to a Growth Stock Portfolio which has served as a model since 1934. The following figures compare the results of a $10,000 investment in each of these two model portfolios from January, 1966 through December 31, 1969, with Dow Jones Industrial Average, Standard and Poor's "500," and the Consumer Price Index which measures the cost of living:

	12/31/65	12/31/69	% Change
Model Inflation Portfolio	$10,000	$21,485	+ 114.9
Model Growth Stock Portfolio	10,000	14,345	+ 43.5
Dow Jones Industrial Average	10,000	8,257	− 17.4
Standard & Poor's "500"	10,000	9,960	− 0.4
Consumer Price Index	111.0	131.3	+ 18.3

The above table shows that during the four years ended December 31, 1969, the stock averages did not keep pace with the rise in the cost of living (Consumer Price Index). The Model Growth Stock Portfolio, which is predominantly invested in blue chip growth stocks, rose more than twice as much as the cost of living. The increase in the unit value of the model

Inflation Portfolio was 114.9%, or more than 6 times the 18.3% increase in the Consumer Price Index.

The Model Inflation Portfolio was approximately 64% invested in Natural Resources and Real Estate. The balance was in Consumer and Service, Science and Technology, and cash.

The investment program and portfolio strategy recommended for the new era for investors have proven to be a most successful hedge against inflation to date.

FOOTNOTES

1. Discussed in "Change—The Investor's Only Certainty" under the caption of "The Rise of the Masses to Power and Influence."

HOW MR. WOMACK
MADE A KILLING

John Train

John Train's thoughtful and wise writings on investments and investment managers are both instruction and pleasure. Here is one of his many tales worth telling.

Everybody who finally learns how to make money in the stock market learns in his own way.

I like this tale of his own personal enlightenment sent in by reader Melvid Hogan, of Houston:

> Right after I was discharged from the Army at the close of World War II and went into the drilling-rig building business, on the side (and at first as a hobby) I began buying and selling stocks. At the end of each year I always had a net loss. I tried every approach I would read or hear about: technical, fundamental and combinations of all these . . .but somehow I always ended up with a loss.
>
> It may sound impossible that even a blind man would have lost money in the rally of 1958—but *I* did. In my in-and-out trading and smart switches I lost a lot of money.
>
> But one day in 1961 when, discouraged and frustrated, I was in the Merrill Lynch office in Houston, a senior account executive sitting at a front desk whom I knew observed the frown on my face that he had been seeing for so many years and motioned me over to his desk.

Reprinted by permission of *Forbes* Magazine, Vol. 122, No. 7, October 2, 1978. New York, New York: © Forbes, Inc., 1978.

"Would you like to see a man," he asked wearily, "who has never lost money in the stock market?"

The broker looked up at me, waiting.

"Never had a loss?" I stammered.

"Never had a loss on balance," the broker drawled, "and I have handled his account for near 40 years." Then the broker gestured to a hulking man dressed in overalls who was sitting among the crowd of tape watchers.

"If you want to meet him, you'd better hurry," the broker advised. "He only comes in here once every few years except when he's buying. He always hangs around a few minutes to gawk at the tape. He's a rice farmer and hog raiser from down at Baytown."

I worked my way through the crowd to find a seat by the stranger in overalls. I introduced myself, talked about rice farming and duck hunting for a while (I am an avid duck hunter) and gradually worked the subject around to stocks.

The stranger, to my surprise, was happy to talk about stocks. He pulled a sheet of paper from his pocket with his list of stocks scrawled in pencil on it that he had just finished selling and let me look at it.

I couldn't believe my eyes! The man had made over 50 long-term capital-gain profits on the whole group. One stock in the group of 30 stocks had been shot off the board, but others had gone up 100%, 200%, and even 500%.

He explained his technique, which was the ultimate in simplicity. When during a bear market he would read in the papers that the market was down to new lows and the experts were predicting that it was sure to drop another 200 points in the Dow, the farmer would look through a Standard & Poor's Stock Guide and select around 30 stocks that had fallen in price below $10—solid, profit-making, unheard-of companies (pecan growers, home furnishings, etc.) and paid dividends. He would come to Houston and buy a $25,000 "package" of them.

And then, one, two, three or four years later, when the stock market was bubbling and the prophets were talking about the Dow hitting 1500, he would come to town and sell his whole package. It was as simple as that.

During the subsequent years as I cultivated Mr. Womack (and hunted ducks on his rice fields) until his death last year, I learned much of his investing philosophy.

He equated buying stocks with buying a truckload of pigs. The lower he could buy the pigs, when the pork market was depressed, the more profit he would make when the next seller's market would come along. He claimed that he would rather buy stocks under such conditions than pigs because pigs did not pay a dividend. You must feed pigs.

He took "a farming" approach to the stock market in general. In rice farming, there is a planting season and a harvesting season; in his stock purchases and sales he strictly observed the seasons.

Mr. Womack never seemed to buy stock at its bottom or sell it at its top. He seemed happy to buy or sell in the bottom or top range of its fluctuations. He had no regard whatsoever for the cliché—Never Send Good Money After Bad—when he was buying. For example, when the bottom fell out of the bottom of the market of 1970, he added another $25,000 to his previous bargain price positions and made a virtual killing on the whole package.

I suppose that a modern stock market technician could have found a lot of alphas, betas, contrary opinions and other theories in Mr. Womack's simple approach to buying and selling stocks. But none I know put the emphasis on "buy price" that he did.

I realize that many things determine if a stock is a wise buy. But I have learned that during a depressed stock market, if you can get a cost position in a stock's bottom price range it will forgive a multitude of misjudgments later.

During a market rise, you can sell too soon and make a profit, sell at the top and make a very good profit, or sell on the way down and still make a profit. So, with so many profit probabilities in your favor, the best cost price possible is worth waiting for.

Knowing this is always comforting during a depressed market, when a "chartist" looks at you with alarm after you buy on his latest "sell signal."

In sum, Mr. Womack didn't make anything complicated out of the stock market. He taught me that you can't be buying stocks every day, week or month of the year and make a profit, any more than you could plant rice every day, week or month and make a crop. He changed my investing lifestyle and I have made a profit ever since.

THE TRUSTEES' DILEMMA

John Train

In one of the many short pieces that John Train has written with charm and insight about investing and investors, he addresses here a serious concern of all who advise individual investors.

A widow was left a substantial amount of money by her husband when he died. The income went to her for life, with the capital to be divided among their three children after her death.

Her late husband had been a successful New York businessman, and the family had two large houses: one in Greenwich, Conn. and one on Cape Cod, where they went in summer. The children liked coming to the Greenwich place on weekends and spending long periods on Cape Cod in summer, so she kept both. As a result, the widow found herself living at the limit of her resources.

At her annual meetings with her trustees, the problem was aired frankly. How could she maintain the houses and keep up roughly the same standard of living as before, with her husband's considerable salary no longer available? Each year it was decided to sell some growth stocks with low yields and move into bonds or high-yielding equities to maintain the needed income, and hope that all would be well.

Reprinted by permission of *Forbes* magazine, Vol. 124, No. 1, July 9, 1979. New York, New York: © Forbes Inc., 1979.

So the trust portfolio eventually became roughly half fixed-income securities and half high-dividend stocks, notably utilities and the like.

Unfortunately, however, the investment objective was impossible on its face. At a time when costs are rising 10% a year, income has to rise 12% to 15%, as the tax bracket rises, in order to stay even in real terms.

Now, very few income stocks increase their dividends at anything like 15% a year; and, of course, bond payments don't increase at all.

After some ten years of a princely existence, the widow's buying power in real terms was about 40% of what it had been just after her husband died. The old trustees, friends of her husband, stepped down, and new ones with a more austere and realistic attitude came in. They were dismayed at what they saw. She had to sell both her houses and move into a smaller one, where it was a strain to have any of her children for weekends, since they now had families of their own and came in groups of four or five.

She has many years of life ahead of her, which she will spend in straitened circumstances. If she had cut back right away and adopted a realistic investment policy, she could have been comfortable for her lifetime.

Furthermore, in the future, when the grandchildren come into the inheritance, they will have a justifiable complaint against the old trustees, if they're still around. They can't make out a case at law, but it seems to me that they can certainly make one in common sense and morality. By investing flat out for income at a time of hyperinflation, the trustees knowingly dissipated the corpus of the testator's estate, and thus did violence to his stated wishes and gypped the remaindermen. When the grandchildren ask what happened to their inheritance, their elders will have to explain that it was essentially blown on high living. In fact, the widow herself also has a valid complaint. The original trustees, old business friends of her husband, were paid to give her the benefit of their realism and experience. Why didn't they look ahead and set her on a sustainable course?

This quandary afflicts most trustees of generation-skipping trusts today. I observe that many trusts are now invested about half in equities and half in fixed-income instruments, with the income beneficiary consuming the distribution from both sections of the trust.

However, in real terms, bond income these days is simply a return of capital: The buying power of the bond is declining at much the same rate that the interest is being paid out (faster, for municipals).

The "rule of 72" tells you how fast money doubles at compound interest. It's the interest rate divided into 72.

But the rule also works in reverse. Money loses half its real value in the number of years that the inflation rate goes into 72. Thus, in a time of 10% inflation the half-life of money is seven years. So in 20 years of 10% inflation, the bonds in a portfolio may well have been cut in half three times, or be worth in real terms one-eighth of what they were at the outset. In other words, the bond component will essentially be all gone.

What, in this situation, is the prudent and ethical thing for the trustees to do?

There seem to be two reasonable procedures for a trust to follow: (1) Hold some Treasury bills or similar instruments as a reserve, but wait for a good buying point to put most of the portfolio in solid stocks whose income will rise at least as fast as inflation; or (2) If a lot of the portfolio is in bonds, don't distribute all the income. Alternatively, if there are a lot of bonds, buy some stocks with strong growth but little or no income, such as Crown Cork, Capital Cities, American International Group, Schlumberger or Tektronix, to offset the illusory income from the bond portfolio.

At the moment, good stocks with inflation-resistant characteristics can be bought to yield roughly 4% to 5%. That, therefore, is the *maximum* that can ordinarily be distributed from any trust to an income beneficiary, if capital is to be preserved.

To get an income beneficiary with limited means used to living on a return of 7% to 8% would seem to me to be a grave mistake, and is likely to be disastrous in the end.

In discussing with clients how much they can live on, I have to explain that if their life expectancy is 20 years or more, they cannot logically hold bonds unless they reinvest *all* the income, and *even then* they will be unable to maintain the real value of the capital.

I would appreciate comments from professional trustees on this issue. It's a problem that requires airing.

COMMENTS FROM ACROSS THE YEARS

Peter H. Vermilye

Peter Vermilye has been a senior investment officer at the Morgan Bank, State Street Research, Alliance Capital Management, Citibank, and Endowment Management & Research. Throughout his career he has been a charismatic "investor's investor," respectfully listened to by all practitioners. Here are a few of his insightful comments from across the years.

1970

The star system is dead, the system where you get geniuses that go their own way, sitting in hermetically sealed ivory towers. We also think that the committee decision method—where you have 15 part-time ill-informed investment people arriving at the least common denominator, with approved lists and so on—is not valid. So far as our fund management is concerned, we have interacting teams, fairly informal, fairly unstructured.

From Peter H. Vermilye, selected articles and reports (Boston, Massachusetts, 1970, 1973, 1980, 1981, 1982), by permission of the author.

1973

Investment management is a profession; like law and medicine it requires discipline, complete integrity, a lifetime of continuing learning and a diversity of talent. It is part science and part art; only the best practitioners create significant and lasting value. Mediocrity begets failure.

The investment process is organic. It distills and refines an infinite stream of information. It requires accurate interpretations of fundamental developments and orderly implementation of action. It seeks to determine the reasons for the success or failure of the few companies which lead in creating change. The process begins with superior understanding; it ends with sound judgment.

Simplistic or one-dimensional investment approaches alone may work occasionally when used expertly, but they are not sufficient in today's rapidly changing complex economy and volatile markets. To satisfy the specific needs of individual clients, a professional investment firm needs strategic portfolio planning, experts in the economic, political and industry environments, competent equity and fixed income managers, researchers in growth stocks and basic industries—and a lot more.

1980

With regard to the current depressed stock market: we have lived through at least 10 of these bear markets over the last 40 years and more, and we have learned that you lose only if you sell out near the bottom. Tragic histories are recorded of the trust companies, investment managers and plan sponsors that have done exactly that—permitted themselves to be stampeded out of positions as markets decline.

Markets recover. Bear markets provide superb opportunities to establish and increase positions in dynamic companies. At present, the market has focused its attention on the negatives of high interest rates, a sluggish economy and declining earnings estimates. Inevitably, it will turn to focus on the positives of abating inflation, the business-oriented Reagan administration and the economic recovery on the other side of the valley. No one can predict exactly the depth and duration of this recession and this bear market—but we do know they will end. Recovery will occur. We believe that at some point in the future, we will look back at this current period and see it as a time of major investment opportunity.

1981

On the Need for Professionalism

We work in an investment world of enormous and increasing complexity. It is a configuration of the interwoven forces of economics, politics, geopolitics, technology and business. It is characterized by a continuous explosion of information, and accelerating rates of change in all its elements; by global interdependence of economies, and industrial rivalries among nations. Within this *gestalt*, and forming one of its components, is the intensified competition for investment performance among thousands of institutions and millions of individuals.

For investment managers to excel in such an environment, they must become more professional than ever before — professional in the higher sense.

This higher professionalism means to us exercising the strictest discipline on our demand for quality and value in the investments we buy and hold. It means recognizing the limits of our knowledge and understanding, and investing within those limits; selecting types of assets in line with values and opportunities, while insisting on minimum risk; calibrating the economic winds and their impact on investments, but recognizing that the winds will shift — always unpredictably. It means not chasing fashions, but being prepared to invest against them when they have gone too far; not paying for speculative futures; avoiding the frenetic short term performance game — yet achieving superior results in most years and over time.

1982

The most difficult problem that we all have is guiding strong, talented egos without cramping them, teaching a talented person to see his limitations. It's hardest to teach them when they're riding high. That's when it is most dangerous, when you are both most vulnerable. The most important lesson I try to teach them is to know when they know and when they don't. It takes a lot of hard knocks to learn that, but that's the essence of successful investing.

ON THE THREAT OF CHANGE

Arthur Zeikel

Arthur Zeikel, President of Merrill Lynch Asset Management and co-author of the leading textbook, *Investment Analysis and Portfolio Management*, is a regular and thoughtful observer of the investing scene. Here, he leads us to an answer to the question, "Why are so many of us wrong so much of the time?"

Why are so many of us wrong so much of the time? Surely, one reason is that we accommodate change poorly. More for emotional than logical reasons, we tend to base our expectations on the status quo. All too often, our expectations fail to materialize. John Maynard Keynes put it this way: "The facts of the existing situation enter, in a sense disproportionately, into the formation of our long-term expectations: our usual practice being to take the existing situation and to project it into a future modified only to the extent that we have more or less definite reasons for expecting a change."[1]

We compound the problem by tending to become overly protective of our own judgments. Not because they are right, or even likely to be right, but because they are ours. This in turn leads to an unwillingness

Reprinted from *The Financial Analysts Journal*, Vol. 31, No. 6, November/December 1975, 3–7. New York, New York: Financial Analysts Federation.

to accept new information for what it's worth. Frequently, it's worth a great deal, and our reluctance to consider new information with an open mind makes it harder to recognize the flaws in our old operating premise. Instead, we tend to develop a "defensive" interpretation of new developments, and this cripples our capacity for making good judgments about the future.

Investors, portfolio managers and the like have even more than the normal problems to contend with. For one thing, they are continuously forced to deal with change. Their principal task is, or should be, building an accurate concept of the future, a task fraught with uncertainty. For another, the myriad opinions available at any time, usually from reliable sources, inevitably include those embracing ideas whose time has passed.

THE HUMAN SIDE OF ERROR

Most of us harbor an almost natural, instinctive resistance to change. We find it much more comfortable to deal with past certainties, no matter how unpleasant, than contemplate the unknowns of the future. To this extent we try to preserve the present for as long as possible. As a result, our primary response to change is reactive, not anticipatory. Something has to happen first, before we are willing to respond. That is why, as Peter Bernstein recently noted, "Single events may prompt investors to resolve indecision and act—but the fundamental environment has to be such that people are looking for a reason to act positively."[2] Humphrey Neill suggests that "sudden events quickly crystallize opinion."[3]

Indecision has probably cost investors more than bad judgment. It is hard for people who reach a decision after careful analysis of their information to change their minds easily—or quickly. Thus we go, according to Claude Rosenberg, ". . .to the greatest extremes to support original judgments—even after they have been proved incorrect."[4] Rather than keeping a free and open mind we set our opinions too firmly, thereby preventing an explanation of information contrary to our expectations.

People's responses reflect their insecurities and desires for self-protection. Fear of being wrong, for example, influences the way people react to new information. We have to learn how to be wrong more gracefully and to accept errors of judgment, particularly in forecasting, as normal—in fact, inevitable. Only then can our orientation towards that aspect of reality that is change be more adequate. Rather than practicing the "human tendency to rationalize mistakes,"[5] we will be better able to accept change for what it is: "the disparity between the course of events and our expectation or our hopes and fears."[6] It has to be recognized, and accepted, that change is not an implicit criticism of our personal investment in the status quo, but rather an inevitable part of reality. On the other hand, it usually requires some fresh thinking and, very often, a new response.

To be sure, most of us would rather react to than initiate a new point of view. In dealing with this very problem, Thomas Kuhn accurately points out in *The Structure of Scientific Revolutions* that "the man who embraces a new paradigm at an early stage must often do so in defiance of the evidence provided by problem-solving. He must, that is, have faith that the new paradigm will succeed with the many large problems that confront it, knowing only that the older paradigm has failed with a few. A decision of that kind can only be made on faith."[7]

Many investors get "nickeled and dimed" into penury by failing to appreciate that the first loss is not only the best, but usually the smallest. They must learn to avoid defensive rationalization of their past bad judgments. When things change, they change, and it is better to recognize it, by admitting error and shifting, than fighting reality until conventional opinion converges on the new view and sweeps the old one away. A good rule to practice is that, once a pattern of expectation is accepted and taken for granted, its reasonableness should be questioned all the more: Circumstances change faster than is commonly recognized.

Many of us have encountered the "no" orientation. To some extent, it exists in all of us and, unfortunately, can even permeate an entire organization or decision-making process. It is an attitude that inclines us, when faced with a new set of circumstances, to respond negatively: It cannot be done, we cannot do it on time, it won't work, it is illegal, etc. (Rarely is it *wrong*, which requires the differentiation from right, hence conviction.) Such response reflects an unwillingness to accept change, risk and challenge. All of us, according to Basil and Cook, have difficulty accepting unconventional ideas or changes that we do not understand or are ill-prepared to accept.[8] We generally hear what we want to, and not what we should be listening for.

INFORMATION MANAGEMENT
AND IDEA RECOGNITION

Most of us conduct the search for new information, i.e., research, in much the same manner. In every discipline, professional judgments regarding the future implications of new information tend toward unanimity; Kuhn reminds us that, "What a man sees depends upon what he looks at and also what his previous visual conceptual experience has taught him."[9] Take Wall Street, for example: Members of the investment community, despite a diversity of opinions, prejudices and exposure, have undergone roughly similar educational and professional training. In the process they have absorbed the same body of literature and technique, reflected upon the same history, and are drawn to many of the same lessons of the past.

In recent years the concentration of research activity, combined with extensive publicity as to who is "first team" and who is not, has increased the tendency toward unanimity. Today, the general information base for most major participants is very similar, and in some cases exactly the same. The focus is on the same key analysts, the same important firms, the same economic and business conditions and consultants, the same conference attendance, much the same business problems, the same fears, and so on. All of which seems to be producing pretty much the same results. In part this tendency can be attributed to the way the Street is organized. But it is also the result of laziness and a lack of intellectual curiosity, not to mention an unwillingness to stand alone against the crowd. (More recently, minority and unconventional opinion, supported by innovative research investigation, has gained some popularity—probably because conventionally accepted ideas no longer accommodate current circumstances.)

The function of efficient research is to understand, evaluate and, as much as possible, anticipate change—not to collect data. The following observations are directed towards providing a better understanding and accommodation of change. Although it cannot be avoided, the unexpected can at least be incorporated into the decision-making process.

It must be recognized that research can be an inefficient process; one cannot usually predict which piece of new information, fresh idea or original thought will prove productive. The object of fact finding is to narrow down the areas of uncertainty. Sound technique requires skill in excluding the unnecessary and, as quickly as possible, making some guess as to the unknown.

The search is to ascertain those few elements that are critical — in the extreme, to isolate the one factor upon which the decision may turn. One must conquer the urge to learn everything about some new development or unexpected turn of events. One must distinguish between facts needed to form a foundation for new action and those that merely serve to keep one better informed.

But what is the nature of information? Ed Glaser defines information as "the effective communication of something known to the sender but new to the receiver."[10] Servan Schreiber considers information a valuable raw material to be detected, extracted and, above all, utilized carefully because errors in handling it can mean disaster.[11]

Information has another characteristic that is often too little appreciated: It is a perishable commodity. The life cycle of new ideas steadily grows shorter. Change must be placed into its proper perspective much more quickly than heretofore. New developments are usually recognized, appreciated and acted upon by a few. The new trend enjoys progressively wider recognition until it finally becomes the conventional wisdom, when it is extrapolated beyond its reasonable horizon. *The First National City Bank Monthly Economic Letter* recently noted: "The temptation to extrapolate events of the recent past into the indefinite future is strong, but it will lead to the wrong conclusion if the fundamental conditions that created these events are changing rapidly and significantly."[12] The point is, they usually are.

We must also recognize that, all too frequently, too much information is transmitted. It has been estimated that roughly four per cent of available literature produces 60 per cent of the pertinent information. According to Clausewitz, interpreters of change need a certain power of discrimination that only knowledge of men and affairs can give. He further noted, some 150 years ago, that the law of probability must be a guide and that most reports are false, the timidity of men acting as a multiplier of lies and untruths.[13]

THE PRICE OF GROWTH

Information, once received, has to be interpreted effectively if it is to be of any real value — a significant problem for most organizations.

The problem is to get the right information to the right people at the right time. The structure of most organizations complicates this task by introducing a variety of lags, filters, and road blocks to the decision-making process. Frequently, new and important information enters the organization at the wrong point, only to be passed from hand to hand, refined, modified, and interpreted before reaching the ultimate decision-maker.

John Hackett warns us that "new information should as much as possible be directly received by the decision-makers, not filtered through others who have a vested interest in preserving the status quo or protecting their own decision by defending past judgments. . . . The larger the organization becomes and the further removed senior management is from actual operations the less valid its interpretation of data becomes. . . . The decision-making environment must create the appropriate atmosphere for encouraging skepticism and doubt, and controversy, thus preventing an illusion of invulnerability."[14]

An effective information management system must ascertain, first of all, the needs of the decision-making apparatus—needs that vary with the size and objective of the organization. It must be compatible with the personalities and abilities of the people involved. A well-formed information system, however, can go far beyond providing the organization with a continuous, flexible flow of knowledge; it can determine the very structure of the organization.

Because the time horizon for effective response has been shortened, decision-making responsibility should be located as close as possible to those receiving new information with potentially critical impact. A short line of communication between the receipt of new information and the ultimate decision—both in terms of people and time—is a necessity.

Contrast this with the way most organizations actually operate, especially after they have grown substantially. Size is often used as an excuse for resisting change. Hackett points out that "As an organization expands its size and complexity it requires increased uniformity in its activities and decision-making process. At some point in the growth cycle the need for rejuvenation becomes a major deterrent to the creativity and innovation that may have accounted for much of its success."[15]

By the same token, as the scope of their responsibilities expands, individuals tend to develop a "rejective" attitude towards change. Hackett again: "As corporate executives begin to sense that their capacity to interpret events correctly is diminishing, they tend to adopt management systems that resist the changes necessary to maintain the vitality and growth of their companies."[16] They would do better if they considered conditions likely to foster change realistically, rather than seeking the comfort of their own previous judgments.

NEWS AND THE MARKET

There is, according to Klein and Prestbo, "a flow to the news, and when it is pronounced the market as a whole moves with it. There is a flow to the news regarding individual issues and companies, and the stocks involved tend to move with it."[17]

There is also, according to Walter F. Stone, a cycle of investor psychology. Bull markets, Stone notes, "develop out of periods of great pessimism. They begin when the vast majority of investors are convinced that the market will continue to go down. Conversely, bear market declines come out of periods of great optimism and speculation. They start when the vast majority of investors are convinced that the market will continue to go up."[18]

Peter Bernstein adds: "If things look good, and prices are falling, you are already late, as you will also be late if things look bad and prices are rising."[19] Keynes reminds us, "The professional investor is forced to concern himself with the anticipation of impending changes, in the news or in the atmosphere, of the kind by which experience shows that the mass psychology of the market is most influenced."[20]

To my own way of thinking, there are trends in events, but the trends are not endless.[21] And the greater the belief in the persistence of a trend, the less likely it is to persist. Consequently, decision makers must learn not to make too heavy an investment in the configuration of discernible trends. The comfort seemingly afforded by extrapolating existing conditions too far into the future is hazardous. According to Peter Bernstein, "Momentum causes things to run further and longer than we anticipate. The very familiarity of a force in motion reduces our ability to see when it is losing its momentum. Indeed, that is why extrapolating the present into the future so frequently turns out to be the genesis of an embarrassing forecast."[22]

It is obviously difficult to assess accurately exactly what stage an idea is passing through, and harder still to have complete confidence that future events will not, in fact, reinforce the recent past. But there is a stage at which someone else's old idea carries excessive risk if it is pursued as our own new thought. The question is one of attitude and probabilities, not precise analysis. We never know for sure at which stage an idea is when we encounter it for the first time.

THE LONG-TERM FORECAST

Long-term forecasts, particularly those in the dismal realm of economics, have historically been unreliable. The reason behind the failure of events to mirror expectations is often less obvious than it should be. Otto Eckstein offers one explanation: "[The] future order of society can never be foreseen, for it is the product of social inventions not yet made."[23] Barbara Tuchman suggests: "The doomsayers work by extrapolation: they take a trend and extend it, forgetting that the doom factor, sooner or later, generates a coping mechanism . . .you cannot extrapolate any series in which the human element intrudes: history, that is the human narrative, never follows and will always fool, the scientific curve."[24]

Economics and sociology are not the only disciplines subject to poor forecasting; inaccuracy prevails in other areas as well. In "The Phaeton Ride" Forrest McDonald tells us that "The United States patent office, which Congress had seriously considered shutting down in the 1830's on the ground that everything had been invented, issued four times as many patents in the 1860's as it had previously issued in its entire seventy years of existence, and in each of the next two decades the number of patents doubled again."[25]

It is reported that Admiral William Leahy sent a note to President Truman in 1945 giving his opinion on the prospects of the atomic bomb as, "That is the biggest fool thing we have ever done. The bomb will never go off, and I speak as an expert in explosives." There are of course many other illustrations, some funny, some serious, that document the same important point. The one that best covers our current situation can be found in an October 10, 1847 editorial in *Harpers Magazine*, which assessed our future as follows: "It is a gloomy moment in the history of our country. Not in the lifetime of most men has there been so much grave and deep apprehension; never has the future seemed so incalculable as at this time. The domestic economic situation is in chaos. Our dollar is weak throughout the world. Prices are so high as to be utterly impossible. The political cauldron seethes and bubbles with uncertainty. Russia hangs, as usual, like a cloud, dark and silent, upon the horizon. It is a solemn moment. Of our troubles no man can see the end."

FOOTNOTES

1. John Maynard Keynes, *The General Theory of Employment, Interest, and Money* (New York: Harcourt, Brace & Co., 1935), p. 148.
2. Peter L. Bernstein, "A Green Light for Stocks?" *New York Times*, Feb. 2, 1975.
3. Humphrey B. Neill, *The Ruminator* (Caldwell, Idaho: The Caxton Printers, Ltd., 1975), p. 18.
4. Claude N. Rosenberg, Jr., *Psycho-Cybernetics and the Stock Market* (New York: Playboy Press, 1971), p. 77.
5. *Ibid.*, p. 76.
6. Geoffrey Vickers, *Freedom in a Rocking Boat* (Middlesex, England: Penguin Books, Ltd., 1970), p. 123.
7. Thomas S. Kuhn, *The Structure of Scientific Revolutions* (Chicago: University of Chicago Press, 1962), p. 158.
8. Douglas C. Basil and Curtis W. Cook, *The Management of Change* (New York: McGraw-Hill, 1974), p. 112.
9. Kuhn, p. 113.
10. Edward Glaser, *Information Technology* (New York: The Conference Board, 1972), p. 23.
11. Jean Louis and Servan Schreiber, *The Power to Inform* (New York: McGraw-Hill, 1974, p. 189.
12. *The First National City Bank Monthly Economic Letter* (May 1975), p. 1.
13. Karl Von Clausewitz, *On War* (New York: Penguin, 1969), p. 162.
14. John T. Hackett, "Drawbacks of Continuing Corporate Growth," *Harvard Business Review* (January–February 1974), p. 7.
15. *Ibid.*
16. *Ibid.*
17. Frederick C. Klein and John A. Prestbo, *News and the Market* (Chicago: Henry Regency Company, 1974), p. 219.

18. Walter F. Stone, "Stock Market Forecasting: Using Technical Analysis to Measure Investor Psychology," *Trusts and Estates*, Vol. III (January 1972), p. 47.

19. Bernstein, "Can You Forecast The Stock Market?" *Challenge*, The Magazine of Economic Affairs (March–April 1973), pp. 13–19.

20. Keynes, p. 155.

21. Arthur Zeikel, "The Random Walk and Murphy's Law," *The Journal of Portfolio Management* (Fall 1974).

22. Bernstein, "Forecasts Will Be Wrong," *New York Times*, Oct. 21, 1973.

23. Otto Eckstein, "Will Capitalism Survive In the United States?" *Business and Society Review* (Summer 1974), pp. 5–7.

24. Barbara Tuchman, "History of Mirrors," *Atlantic Monthly* (September 1973), pp. 39–46.

25. Forrest McDonald, "The Phaeton Ride," *The Crisis of American Success* (New York: Doubleday, 1974), p. 27.

PART 5

THE 1980s

CAN PROFESSIONAL INVESTORS BEAT THE MARKET?

Richard A. Brealey

Richard Brealey's light, lucid language gives a clarity of expression that almost masks the depth of his expert knowledge of investment technology. This chapter from *An Introduction to Risk and Return from Common Stocks* raises one of the central contemporary questions.

In an efficient market, prices reflect all available information. We saw . . .[earlier] that there is considerable evidence that stock prices at least reflect the information contained in past prices. This weak form of efficiency implies that technical analysis is an unprofitable activity.

[Previously] we saw that stock prices also impound other kinds of publicly available information. This "semi-strong" form of efficiency implies that it is impossible to earn consistently superior profits simply by a study of readily available information, such as the latest dividend or earnings or the president's annual statement.

In practice few professional analysts confine their attention to such basic items of information. The important remaining issue, therefore, is whether stock prices reflect not only publicly available information but any additional information that results from the tireless inquiries

From Richard A. Brealey, *An Introduction to Risk and Return from Common Stocks*, 2nd ed. (Cambridge, Massachusetts, 1983), 53–62, by permission of The MIT Press. Copyright 1983 by The Massachusetts Institute of Technology.

of professional security analysts. This would constitute a strong form of efficiency. It would indicate that no investor, however skilled, could earn superior profits other than by chance. Investment in such a market would be neither more nor less than a fair game.

Nobody believes literally in this strong form of the efficient market theory. The interesting question is how closely actual markets approximate such a visionary ideal.

PERFORMANCE OF PROFESSIONALLY MANAGED PORTFOLIOS

In a perfectly efficient market no portfolio manager could achieve consistently superior performance. Let us look therefore at some studies of whether professional managers can beat the market.

The classic study of investment performance examined the record of 115 mutual funds between 1955 and 1964.[1] The return on these funds depended not only on the ability of the manager to pick stocks but on the fund's volatility. Some of the mutual funds were invested in stable income stocks, which tended to maintain their value in bear markets but to lag in bull markets. Other mutual funds were invested in volatile growth stocks, which often had high returns in bull markets but performed badly in bear markets. Therefore, in order to measure the skill of each fund manager, it was necessary to abstract from the effect on the fund of general market movements. In order to do this, the return on the fund was compared with the return on an equally volatile package of the market index and risk-free debt.[2] Since the fund and the package had the same volatility, any consistent superiority in the fund's return should be due to the manager's skill in picking stocks.

In the case of the 115 mutual funds, the return before management expenses was on average 0.1 percent a year less than the return on an equally volatile package of the market index and risk-free debt. In other words, any gain from picking stocks was slightly more than offset by the transaction costs. Of course, some funds performed better than the average and others performed worse, but these differences were no greater than one would expect as a result of chance. There was no sign that *any* manager was able to achieve consistently superior performance.

Because mutual funds are so much in the public eye, they have been a popular object of performance studies. But other institutions do not seem to have performed any better. For example, the average abnormal returns before expenses on 1,200 portfolios managed by banks, insurance companies, investment counselors, and mutual funds (1968–1977) were −1.6, −1.1, −1.6, and −1.4 percent, respectively.[3] It is clear that mutual funds were not alone in failing to beat the market.

We should not claim too much precision for these studies of fund performance. We cannot be sure whether professional managers are likely to make very small percentage gains or (as it appears) very small percentage losses. We also cannot be sure whether there are any consistent differences between managers. Despite these cautions, it is clear from studies of fund performance that professional managers work in a very competitive environment and do not make large profits at the expense of the hapless amateur. It is equally clear that most of the differences between the performance of individual funds are the result of chance. These important conclusions are a warning against high ambition.

STOCK RECOMMENDATIONS AND FORECASTS

While the performance record of investment managers is exactly what we should expect in an efficient market, it remains possible that analysts do have some power to forecast security prices. For example, it could be that managers ignore the advice of their analysts or act on it too late. Or perhaps their orders to buy or sell a stock forewarn other investors that the stock is mispriced. Or perhaps the purchases and sales are too small in value to add much to the performance of the total portfolio. Therefore, before we conclude that stock prices do indeed reflect all available information, we should look at the profitability of analysts' recommendations and forecasts.

One of the most extensive sources of analysts' recommendations is the *Wall Street Journal* column "Heard on the Street." This column generally reports the opinions of several analysts about the same stock. For example, during 1970 and 1971 there were 785 occasions on which the column reported a unanimous recommendation to buy or sell stock. Figure 3.1 shows the relative performance of these stocks in the days surrounding publication.[4] Notice that when the stock is recommended for purchase, the price rises by about 1 percent on the publication day, whereas when it is recommended for sale, the price falls by about 2 percent. Although these price movements are scarcely dramatic, they do

FIGURE 3.1
The Relative Performance of Purchase and Sell Recommendations.
From P. L. Davies and M. Canes, "Stock Prices and the Publication of
Second-Hand Information," *Journal of Business* **51 (1978): 43–56**

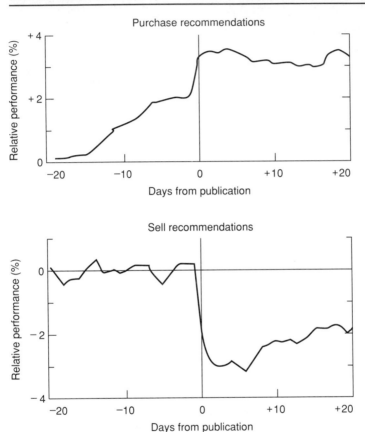

suggest that the analysts' forecasts have some modest value. As you can see from table 3.1, other studies of published investment advice point to a similar conclusion.

In addition to analyzing recommendations, it is also useful to examine the accuracy of analysts' forecasts. If the market is perfectly efficient and all information is impounded in the stock price, there should be no relationship between the forecast and actual returns. If it is not efficient and professional analysts do have superior information, there should be a positive correlation between the forecast and actual returns.

TABLE 3.1

Findings from Studies of Published Investment Advice

Author	Publication Date	Number of Advisory Services	Number of Recommen-dations	Percentage Return on Prepublication Price		
				Publication Day	After One Week	Longer Term
Cowles (14)	1933	45	7,500			−1.4
Cowles (15)	1944	11	6,904			0.2
Ferber (18)	1958	4	345	0.5	1.1	
Ruff (21)	1963	1	31		4.0	
Colker (13)	1963	1	1,054			3.6
Stoffels (12)	1966	3	264	0.7	1.5	
Cheney (12)	1969	4				2.0
Diefenbach (17)	1972	24	1,209			2.7
Black (11)	1973	1	500			10.0
Logue and Tuttle (20)	1973	6	304			3.0
Groth et al. (19)	1979	1	6,014			2.6
Stanley et al. (22)	1981	1	4,461		0.7	
Bjerring et al. (10)	1982	1	80–92	1.5	1.2	

In June 1971 one financial institution analyzed the medium-term prospects for 250 stocks.[5] Each stock was rated on a scale of 1 to 5 in terms of its prospective performance relative to the rest of its industry. Thus the 15 stocks that the analysts placed in rank 1 were expected to perform worst; the 61 stocks that they placed in rank 2 were expected to offer somewhat below-average performance; and so on. Six months later the same stocks were again rated from 1 to 5 on the basis of their actual performance relative to their industry. Thus the 15 worst performers were placed in rank 1, the 61 next worst performers were assigned rank 2, and so on. If the analysts were perfect forecasters, there should have been an exact correspondence between the forecast rank and the actual rank; if they had no forecasting ability, the correlation between the two sets of ranks should have been zero. In fact the correlation was 0.17, which suggests that the analysts had a small but significant degree of forecasting skill.

In a similar exercise sixteen investment firms provided ratings between 1972 and 1974 for about 150 stocks.[6] Over the subsequent four to seven months the correlation between the forecast and actual ranks averaged 0.16.

Finally, the same techniques have been used to assess the quality of investment advisory services.[7] Thus between 1973 and 1976 there was an average correlation of 0.07 between the Value Line stock rating and the actual outcome six months later, and there was an average correlation of 0.14 between Wells Fargo's stock rating and the actual outcome.

These direct studies of forecasting skill are somewhat more encouraging. They suggest that while the analysts' forecasts can explain only a small proportion of what subsequently happens, there is at least some relationship between the two. If this is so, the delicate problem is to translate such forecasts into superior portfolio performance. Unless the portfolio manager is aware of the amount of information in the analysts' forecasts, he is liable either to pass up profitable opportunities or to overreact and fritter away the gains in excessive transaction costs. Even if the manager does know exactly how much he should buy or sell on the strength of the forecasts, he still faces the difficulty of doing so without signaling his views to other investors.

IMPLICATIONS OF THE EFFICIENT MARKET THEORY

In the United States there are about 25 million common stock investors. Many of these may be inactive and others may be foolish, but there also undoubtedly exist many others who are both energetic and well informed. Given this competition, it would be surprising if important, available information went unnoticed for long.

It is this picture of a large number of investors competing to achieve similar ends that has prompted the suggestion that for the majority of the participants investment is a fair game. If this is indeed the case, you can easily match the performance of the average stockholder, but you need considerable skill to do better than this. Some investment institutions have, therefore, given up the attempt to obtain superior performance and have invested passively in a broad and representative sample of stocks. Although such a policy guarantees average performance at minimum cost, it would be stretching both theory and empirical evidence to insist that this is the only sensible portfolio strategy. If institutions must pay to obtain information, they will require some prospective reward before investing in security analysis. Moreover, although the studies of fund performance do not indicate that security analysis pays for itself in terms of portfolio performance, we have seen that there is slightly more encouraging evidence that professional security analysts have some forecasting ability.

If an institution is going to obtain superior performance, it will not be with the sole aid of public information, whether that information is the earnings record, management's most recent statement, or a brokerage firm's circular. Hence it is not sufficient to employ average analysts to do average things. One author has compared security analysis to a fairground game in which each player guesses the number of beans in a jar and wins only if his guess is better than the average of all other guesses.[8] This average guess represents the combined information of all the other players. So, if you wish to win such a game, you not only need to know more than any other single player, you need to know more than *all* other players.

Even though other players in the fairground game may individually make large errors, these errors will tend to cancel out as long as they are unrelated. Therefore, your only effective chance to win is if you notice that all the players are making the same mistake. When you play the security analysis game, you face a similar problem. As long as the stock price incorporates the information available to all other investors, you are unlikely to come up with a better assessment of the stock's worth simply by being more careful and more diligent. Your only chance of winning is to detect instances in which all analysts are relying on similar incorrect information sources.

If security analysis is to be effective, the organizational structure must encourage analysts to concentrate their attention on areas where they have a comparative advantage and focus on stocks where there is some chance of misvaluation. Neither condition is likely to be met if each analyst is compelled to comment at frequent intervals on a large number of securities.

These then are the primary conditions for superior investment performance. Yet it is important to bear in mind that in an efficient market the investment return is likely to depend far more on the risk that the fund assumes and more on its tax liability than on the accuracy of the analysts' forecasts. Thus the realization that markets are efficient has led institutions to focus more closely on the crucial aspects of risk and tax management.

FOOTNOTES

1. See Jensen, M.C. "The Performance of Mutual Funds in the Period 1945–1964." *Journal of Finance* 23 (May 1968):389–416.
2. The rationale for measuring performance in this way is described in chapter 11.
3. See Bogle, J.C., and Twardowski, J.M. "Institutional Investment Performance Compared: Banks, Investment Counselors, Insurance Companies, and Mutual Funds." *Financial Analysts Journal* 36 (January-February 1980):33–41.
4. See Davies, P. L. and Canes, M. "Stock Prices and the Publication of Second-Hand Information." *Journal of Business* 51 (1978):43–56.
5. See Ambachtsheer, K. P. "Portfolio Theory and the Security Analyst." *Financial Analysts Journal* 28 (November-December 1972):53–57.
6. See Ambachtsheer, K. P. "Profit Potential in an 'Almost Efficient' Market." *Journal of Portfolio Management* 1 (Fall 1974):84–87.
7. See Ambachtsheer K. P., and Farrell, J. L. "Can Active Management Add Value?" *Financial Analysts Journal* 35 (November-December 1979):39–48.
8. The bean jar analogy was suggested by Treynor.

THE PARADOX

Charles D. Ellis

The curious emphasis of investment managers on manipulating portfolios rather than on investment counseling is questioned in this essay. If policy guidance from the client is lacking, is it not the manager's duty to either obtain it or supply it?

A PARADOX IS HAUNTING INVESTMENT MANAGEMENT

The paradox is that funds with very long-term purposes are being managed to meet short-term objectives that may be neither feasible nor important. And they are *not* being managed to achieve long-term objectives that are both feasible and worthwhile.

The unimportant and difficult task to which most investment managers devote most of their time with little or no success is trying to "beat the market." Realistically—without taking above-average market risk—to outperform the equity market by even one half of 1 percent *consistently* would be a great success which almost no sizable investment managers have achieved for very long.

The truly important but not very difficult task to which investment managers and their clients could and should devote themselves involves

From Charles D. Ellis, *Investment Policy* (Homewood, Illinois, 1985), 21–28, by permission of Dow Jones-Irwin.

four steps: (1) understanding the client's needs, (2) defining realistic investment objectives that can meet the client's needs, (3) establishing the right asset mix for each particular portfolio, and (4) developing well-reasoned, sensible investment policies designed to achieve the client's realistic and specified long-term investment objectives. In this work, success can be easily achieved.

For example, if the long-term average rate of return on bonds is 8 percent, and the return from investments in common stocks is 16 percent—because there must be a higher long-term rate of return on stocks to convince investors to accept the risk of equity investing—then shifting just 5 percent of the portfolio's assets from bonds to stocks and keeping it there would, over time, increase the portfolio's average annual rate of return by $^4/_{10}$ of 1 percent (8×5 percent $= 0.40$ percent).

Shifting the asset mix of a 60 percent equity/40 percent fixed income portfolio to 65:35 is not a major proposition, but . . . consistently beating the market rate of return by 40 basis points a year through superior stock selection would be a substantial achievement.

Very few institutional investors have been able to achieve and sustain such superior results.

It is ironic that a change of even such modest magnitude in the basic asset allocation decision can capture an improvement in total return significantly greater than the elusive increment sought in the beat the market syndrome.

Clearly, if the asset mix truly appropriate to the client's objectives justified an even more substantial emphasis [on] equities–70:30, or 80:20, or 90:10, or even 100:0—the incremental rate of return, on average, over the 60:40 portfolio would be even greater: 0.8 percent annually at 70:30 increasing to 1.6 percent annually at 80:20 and 3.2 percent average annually at 100 percent. Virtually no substantial investment manager can hope to beat the market by such magnitudes.

Of course, these calculations are mechanical. They present averages ignoring the fact that actual returns in individual years come in an impressive, even intimidating, distribution around these averages.

The crucial question is not simply whether long-term returns on common stocks would exceed returns on bonds or bills *if* the investor held on through the many startling gyrations of the market.

The crucial question is whether the investor will, in fact, hold on. The problem is not in the market, but in ourselves, our perceptions, and our reactions to our perceptions. This is why it is so important for each client to develop a realistic knowledge of his own and/or his organization's tolerance for market fluctuations and his long-term investment objectives, and to develop a realistic understanding of investing and of capital markets. The more you know about yourself as an investor and the more you understand investment management and the securities markets, the more you will know what asset mix is really right for your portfolios, and the more likely you will be able to sustain your commitment for the long term.

In investment management, the real opportunity to achieve superior results is not in scrambling to outperform the market, but in establishing *and adhering to* appropriate investment policies over the long term—policies that position the portfolio to benefit from riding with the main long-term forces in the market. Investment policy, wisely formulated by realistic and well-informed clients with a long-term perspective and clearly defined objectives, is the foundation upon which portfolios should be constructed and managed over time and through market cycles.

In reality, very few investors have developed such investment policies. And because they have not, most investment managers are left to manage their clients' portfolios without knowing their clients' real objectives and without the discipline of explicit agreement on this mission as investment managers. *This is the client's fault.*

As a result of not knowing enough about the particular facts and values of their different clients, investment managers typically manage all funds in virtually the same way and with very nearly the same asset mix, even in such extraordinarily different kinds of employee benefit funds as pension funds and profit sharing funds.

The profound differences between the functions and needs of pension plans and profit sharing plans make them striking examples of a disconcertingly standardized approach to the most important investment decision: the asset mix. So far as the total sum received by each individual is concerned, profit sharing plans terminate entirely on the day he or she retires or leaves; thus the fund has a series of absolute and predictable end points.

This risk of "end period dominance" calls for an investment policy that avoids major fluctuations in market value.[1] Pension plans, on the other hand, are virtually perpetual investment vehicles, funded to provide a stream of annuity payments to plan participants over a very long and highly predictable period; they can easily accept quite substantial market fluctuations during the long "interim" period.

That the investments of pension funds and profit sharing plans are not, in fact, differentiated on even such a powerful and basic dimension as the stock-bond ratio leads to the sobering conclusion that while investment policy conforming to the client's particular investment objectives may be honored in theory, it is little used in practice.

The differences in employees benefit plans can be substantial, but these differences will only matter if corporate executives vigorously represent the special characteristics of their company and their plan when basic investment policies are being formulated or reviewed.

It is hardly conceivable that senior corporate management would routinely delegate full operating responsibility for comparable millions of dollars[2] to regular operating divisional executives—let alone a manager not directly supervised by top management—with only such broad guidelines or instructions as: "Try to do better than average," or "You're the experts, see what you can do for us."

The real question is not whether portfolio managers are constructing portfolios to match the goals and objectives of each specific client. (The uninspiring reality is that they do not.) The relevant question is: Who is responsible for bringing about the requisite change? The pragmatic answer is that the responsibility is not going to be fulfilled by investment managers. It will be left to the client. Clients can and should accept this responsibility.

Clients can do more for their portfolio's long-term rates of return by developing and sustaining wise long-range policies that commit the portfolio to an appropriate structure of investments than can be done by the most skillful manipulation of the individual holdings within the portfolio.

In brief, clients should subordinate portfolio operations to investment policy, and should assert their responsibility for leadership in policy formation. This is not an investment problem that should be left to portfolio managers—no matter how skilled and conscientious they are—any more than, as Clemenceau observed, war should be left to the generals. It is the client's problem, and while responsibility for it can be abdicated, it really cannot be delegated.

Only the client will know enough to speak with relevance and credibility to such important characteristics as the amount, timing, and certainty of flows *out* of the fund. Only the client knows his own or his organization's tolerance for changes in market prices—particularly at market extremes where it really matters—because it is at such stress periods when investment policies seem least certain and the pressure for change is most strong. For individual investors, only they will know their overall financial and investment situation—their earning power, their ability to save, their obligations for children's educational expenses, or how they feel about investments.

Corporate executives will know their pension plan's actuarial assumptions and how close to reality these assumptions really are; the company's tolerance for intrusions upon its quarter-to-quarter and year-to-year progression of reported earnings by a sudden need to fund a deficit in plan assets caused by an abrupt drop in market value of pension assets; the company's evolving philosophy of employee benefits and how benefit programs might be changed; the company's likeliness to increase benefits to retired plan participants to protect their purchasing power from the corrosion of inflation; and the tolerance of interim market fluctuations among staff, senior executives, and the board of directors. The "risk tolerance" of a corporate pension plan sponsor is not just the risk tolerance of the pension staff or even the senior financial officer: It is the risk tolerance of a majority of the board of directors at the moment of most severe market adversity.

Here are six important questions each client should think through, and then explain his own answers to the investment manager. (Investment managers would be wise to urge their clients to do this kind of "homework.")

First, what are the real risks of an adverse outcome, particularly in the short run? Unacceptable risks should never be taken. For example, it would not make sense to invest all of a high school senior's college tuition savings in the stock market because if the market went down, the student might not be able to pay the tuition bill. If the student's parents have been fortunate enough to win the "money game" so far, they can keep it that way simply by not continuing to play.

Second, what are the probable emotional reactions of clients to an adverse experience? As the axiom goes, some investors care about *eating* well and some care about *sleeping* well. The portfolio manager should know and stay well within the client's informed tolerance for interim fluctuations in portfolio value. The emphasis on *informed tolerance* is deliberate. Avoidance of market risk does have a real "opportunity cost," and the client should be fully informed of the opportunity cost of each level of market risk *not* taken.

Third, how knowledgeable about investments and markets are

clients? Investing does not always make sense. Sometimes it seems almost perversely counterintuitive. Lack of knowledge tends to make investors too cautious during bear markets and too confident in bull markets—sometimes at considerable cost. Managers should be careful *not* to assume their clients will be more sophisticated than they really are.

Portfolio managers can help their clients by explaining the way capital markets behave—and misbehave—and clients can help educate themselves.

The client who is very well informed about the investment environment will know what to expect. This client will be able to take in stride those disruptive experiences that may cause other less informed investors to overreact to either unusually favorable or unusually adverse market experience.

Fourth, what other capital or income resources does the client have and how important is the particular portfolio to the client's *overall* financial position? For example, pension funds sponsored by large and prosperous corporations can reasonably accept greater market risk than can a college endowment, which may have difficulty raising capital to replenish losses. A retired widow usually cannot accept as much risk as can her alma mater.

Fifth, are any legal restrictions imposed on investment policy? Many endowment funds have restrictions that can be significant, particularly when they specify how income is to be defined or spent, or both.[3]

Sixth, are there any unanticipated consequences of interim fluctuations in portfolio value that might affect policy? A frequently cited example is the risk in a pension fund of being obliged to augment contributions if the portfolio's market value drops below a "trigger" level built into the actuaries' calculations of current contributions.[4]

Each of these possible concerns should be rigorously examined to ascertain how much deviation from the normally optimal investment policy—broad diversification at a moderately above average market risk—is truly warranted. Understanding and using these insights into the specific realities of the particular client's situation and objectives is the basis upon which wise investment policies can be developed for each different portfolio.

In pursuing the goal of developing and using wise investment policies, we must recognize that most *institutional* funds such as pensions and endowments are *unowned* money: They do not really belong to anyone. There is no individual who can or would say "This is my money. *This* is what I want you to do with it. Or else." There are, in other words, no principals.

Second, we should recognize that those who are "at the controls" are usually only representatives of an organization and subject to after-the-fact criticism by powerful Monday-morning quarterbacks. These representatives have clear economic incentives to protect their careers: "It may not be my money, but it is my job."

Third, the careers of these institutional representatives seldom hinge on the work they do in setting investment policy or managing investment managers. Most have other more important functions, and almost all will hold their present responsibilities for only a few years. They are *not* long-term players.

In such circumstances, what pattern of behavior would we expect of these representatives? Clearly they will be defensive in the "minimax," and will make their decisions with reference to a relatively short time period, say three to five years. They will not seek to optimize, they will seek the most acceptable near-term balance between desires for superior returns and avoidance of unusual or unorthodox positions. And above all, they will avoid any unnecessarily distressing risk to their own careers!

What are investment managers doing? The very same thing. They want to keep their accounts. They are understandably cautious. They are compromising with a defensive tilt, seeking "not to lose" over a three-to-five-year horizon.

Observers of the paradox that haunts investment management say it is unrealistic to expect investment managers to risk strained client relationships by insisting on a well-conceived and carefully articulated investment policy with explicit objectives when their clients seem uninterested in going through the discipline.

For that, we must look not to the agents but to the principals. But in institutional investment management there *are* no principals. And if there often are no agents willing to act like principals, then we can be sure that the paradox will remain for a long time.

Escape from the paradox depends upon clients asserting their role as experts on their own needs and resources, and insisting on appropriate investment goals and policies.

FOOTNOTES

1. Profit sharing plans can easily be designed to minimize this problem. In more and more companies, each plan participant has a separate account in which the asset mix can be adapted to the risk preferences of the individual and can be changed over time to reflect the worker's changing circumstances: all in growth stocks when young, shifting to a conservative balanced portfolio toward retirement, and so forth.

2. At some companies, pension fund assets are larger than the sponsoring corporation's net worth.

3. As William Carey and Craig Bright advocate in their fine study, *The Law and the Lore of Endowment [Funds]*, restrictions should be carefully examined because they may not be as confining as they might initially appear.

4. Actuarial calculations have an apparent precision that Fellows of the Society of Actuaries would be among the first to caution are based on estimates and judgments.

THE FOLLY OF STOCK MARKET TIMING

Robert H. Jeffrey

Robert Jeffrey is a serious—but never too serious—student of investing who strives always to develop a depth of understanding that will suit his engineer's standards of what works, and why. Here he reports on one of his studies.

Many readers of this magazine, either as senior executives or as members of governing boards or both, have been responsible at one time or another for overseeing on a part-time basis the management of money for the benefit of others—in pension funds, endowment funds, trust funds, and charitable foundations. While no definitive published survey on the long-term investment performance of such funds exists (in contrast to the performance of the money managers, on whom there is a plethora of data), my observation of a large number of trusteed funds over the years suggests that many and probably most have underperformed on a long-term basis the market as measured by, say, the *Standard & Poor's* "500."

One explanation for these seemingly substandard results is simply that many fund owners deem a total commitment to equities inappropriate because of high current income needs, future cash requirements, or concerns about volatility. Because equities (for good theoretical reasons) have generated higher long-term returns than bonds and cash equivalents, a portfolio that is required to have less than 100% of its assets in equities is therefore likely to fall short of the long-term return from the S&P 500.

But if we look at only those segments of portfolios designated by their governing authorities, either officially or on a de facto basis, as being available for equities, we still generally find their long-term results to be inferior to the "unmanaged" S&P. Since these funds have typically retained professional investment managers to produce better results than could be obtained from a passive equity index fund, what explains this poorer performance? The academics tell us that, because the stock market is efficient, the fees paid to managers, plus the trading costs from their activity, more than offset their ability to beat the market by buying undervalued and selling overvalued stocks. While this argument has more validity than is generally recognized and should properly lead to greater use of index funds, I believe there is another explanation for substandard performance.

This is the propensity of many managers to engage in so-called market timing, that is, moving assets back and forth between equities and cash equivalents (e.g., 90-day Treasury bills) often at what prove to be the worst possible times.

In this article I will:

Introduce empirical evidence suggesting that the risks inherent in market timing are much greater than most governing executives, directors, and trustees realize and are disproportionate to the incremental rewards to be gained from it.

Maintain that, without a clear and often-articulated policy from the governing authority that either prohibits or strictly limits market timing, this activity tends to go on to one degree or another (often unnoticed) to the likely long-term detriment of its fund, because the career time horizons of the employees or agent-managers who are responsible for the fund are usually much shorter than the time horizon of the fund itself.

Propose that successful market timing necessitates a "contrarian" view of the market. Since such a view by definition is usually at odds with the conventional wisdom of governing authorities at any given time, it follows that market-timing strategies are probably best employed by individuals (using their own money) and not by committees, which is the typical form of governance in overseeing the management of other people's money.

RISK VS. REWARD

To illustrate how market timing affects portfolio risk and reward, I have used a quarterly timing strategy for the 1975-1982 period and have assumed for simplicity that the portfolio manager has but two investment modes, an S&P 500 index fund and 90-day Treasury bills, the so-called riskless investment. The dotted line in *Exhibit I* represents the actual growth over 32 quarters, relative to Treasury bills, of a dollar put into the S&P 500 on January 1, 1975, with dividends reinvested. By December 31, 1982, this continuous investment in the S&P 500 would have produced $1.56 in real terms, or a compound annual return of 5.7% more than T-bills.

Because the T-bill return has more or less corresponded to the inflation rate (at least until quite recently), we can say that with the S&P 500 as a proxy, the dotted line represents the real return from equities. The flat line across the middle of the chart represents the real return from T-bills—by definition, zero.

The upper solid line on the chart depicts the maximum achievable real return had a market timer foreseen at the beginning of each quarter whether the S&P 500 return would be positive or negative relative to T-bills for that quarter, and invested accordingly. In periods when the S&P real return is positive, the upper solid line moves up exactly parallel with the S&P line; in years when the S&P real return is negative, the upper solid line moves sideways in parallel with the flat T-bill line. The upper solid line therefore shows the best real return, $3.75, or 18% a year, which could theoretically have been achieved in the 1975–1982 period with the perfect market timing on a quarterly basis and with no transaction costs.

The drop at the end of the upper solid line reflects the effect of accumulated transaction or trading costs associated with a timing strategy, including commissions and the abstruse—but nonetheless very real—impact on prices of simply being a buyer or a seller in the market. Such costs, which I have assumed to be 1%, are incurred each time the portfolio is shifted into or out of equities. Since perfect quarterly

EXHIBIT I

Maximum Impact of Market Timing on S&P 500 Real Return* 1975–1982, Using Quarterly Intervals

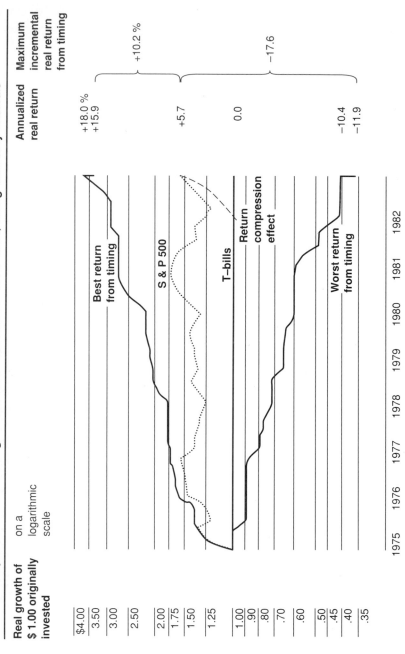

*Real return = S + P total return ÷ T-bill total return.

Data Source (1975-1981): Roger C. Iblootson and Rex A. Sinquefield *Stocks, Bonds, Bills, and Inflation,* 1982 edition (Charlottesville, Va.: Financial Analysts Research Foundation, 1982) Author derived data for 1982.

timing in the eight-year period would have required 14 such shifts, the compound cumulative effect of transaction costs would be to reduce the ending portfolio value by about 13%, to $3.26, and the real return to +15.9% per year.

(A 1% assumption for transaction costs, incidentally, may be too high for very large funds with professional management but too low for most small funds. In any case transaction costs, including commissions and the larger but unseen effect of market impact, are significant and become more so as the use of market timing increases the number of transactions.)

The lower solid line in *Exhibit I* depicts the reverse timing phenomenon of being out of equities and into T-bills in all years in which the relative S&P return was positive and into equities when it was negative. In this worst-case scenario and after giving effect to transaction costs, the original dollar invested would have shrunk in these eight years to 36 cents in real terms, or to a compound annual return of -11.9%.

The most important message in *Exhibit I* appears on the right-hand side, where we see the maximum incremental real returns from following a timing strategy instead of passively investing full-time in the S&P 500. The appeal of market timing is obviously the possibility of achieving results falling along or approaching the upper solid line. With perfect implementation, timing would have produced 10.2% more real return per year than being fully invested in the S&P.

This is the good news; the bad news is that with totally imperfect timing, the real return per year would be 17.6% less!

Because the human mind does not deal well with comparisons of compound percentage growth rates over long periods of time, it is useful to look at the widths of the brackets defining the incremental returns on the right-hand side of the chart. The worst-case incremental return bracket is about twice as wide as the best-case bracket, which simply means that, absent some special forecasting ability, the maximum potential loss from quarterly market timing during this period was twice as large as the potential gain. (See the Appendix for the mathematical confirmation of this nearly 2:1 loss-gain relationship.)

From 1975 through 1982, the market timer was clearly climbing a very steep hill relative to his buy-and-hold cousin. If 1983 data were appended to the 1975–1982 results, the hill would become even steeper; the incremental return ratio would increase from 1.98 to 2.18. (The inclusion of 1983 data, incidentally, would have no material effect on other calculations in this article.)

On the short dashed line labeled "return compression effect," *Exhibit I* shows the degree to which the overall positive real return from the S&P depended on "being present" in equities during the few periods when real equity returns were high. This compression line is plotted backward, beginning at the point where the S&P line ends on the right and moving left and downward as the positive effect of the best quarter for the S&P, the second-best quarter, and so on are removed sequentially from the overall S&P return. For simplicity the plotting of the line ends where it crosses the T-bill line.

The "missed" best quarters comprising the return compression effect were, in descending order of real return, the first quarter of 1975, the last quarter of 1982, and the second quarter of 1975. Since these three quarters closely followed periods in which the performance of stocks was substantially negative, a good many market-timing investors had probably left the party just when the equity music began playing the loudest.

The point of including the return compression effect line on the chart is simply to illustrate how many (or rather, how few—in this case 9%) of the best quarters for the S&P 500 actually make up its entire positive real return for the eight years. As *Exhibit I* shows, the investor who was so intimidated by the market collapses of 1973–1974 and 1981–1982 that he missed the "bull quarters" of early 1975 and late 1982 would have been just as well off to be in T-bills throughout the 32 quarters! The rationale for being a full-time equity investor is not that there are more positive real return periods than negative ones in most time frames, but rather that most of the "positive action" is compressed into just a few periods, which (perversely but understandably) tend to follow particularly adverse times for stocks. To put it another way, Wall Street traffic lights don't have many yellow lenses—only red and green.

Looking at Longer Periods

Since 1975–1982 was obviously a good period for real returns from equities, the reader may reasonably ask if this unbalanced risk-reward phenomenon from market timing holds true in other time frames as well. *Exhibit II* includes data from six other periods, including the full 57 years from 1926 through 1982, using annual and quarterly timing intervals. The exhibit also includes 1965–1974, which was the worst ten-year period for real returns from equities for periods beginning with 1926.

The real return from the S&P 500 over the full 1926–1982 span was +6% per year, which means that a dollar invested would have grown in real value to $28. Using annual timing intervals (cited here because the quarterly ending values are so extreme), the best case from timing would have produced a handsome $670 real return (+12.1% per year), whereas the worst case would have left only 2 cents (−6.4% per year) of the original $1. The ratio of the worst-case to the best-case incremental return is 2.23, meaning that the maximum downside risk from timing was more than twice as great as the maximum upside reward. In virtually all respects, the analysis of the 57-year period supports the conclusions drawn from the shorter 1975–1982 analysis.

In the case of 1965–1974, the next-to-last period in *Exhibit II*, when annual real equity returns were negative (−4%), the worst case-best case incremental return ratio does indeed shift to less than 1.0 (.77 for annual timing and .70 for quarterly), meaning that the upside reward from timing was somewhat greater than the downside risk. But consider the following:

- We are still confronted with a worst-case real dollar return possibility of ending with only 35 cents or 24 cents (depending on the timing interval) of the original dollar invested (column m of *Exhibit II*).
- Since 1926 only 10 (out of 48) ten-year spans have had negative S&P real returns (which in most cases were fairly nominal).
- Last, and most important, how does one find a timing manager who can foresee returns ten years hence? Since the worst case-best case incremental return ratios are clearly unfavorable for a market-timing strategy in all of the more frequent positive return time frames (column n), and since in all of these positive cases the real S&P returns were compressed into a very small percentage of the periods (column p), my conviction that you can't be successful as a part-time equity investor remains statistically intact.

If You Are Mostly Right. . .

While in some timing strategies the originator's genius may offer better odds for success than the 50-50 chances in a coin-flipping exercise, the portfolio owner would still be well advised to calculate, if only for reference purposes, what the odds would be if the coin were evenly

EXHIBIT II
Maximum Impact of Market Timing on S&P 500 Real Returns for Seven Periods, 1926–1982

Time Frame	Timing interval	Number of intervals	Switches*		Annualized nominal return		Annualized Real Return		
			Number	Percent	S&P 500	T-bills	S&P 500	Best timing†	Worst timing†
a	b	c	d	e	f	g	h	i	j
1926–1982	Years	57	28	49%	9.3%	3.1%	6.0%	12.1%	− 6.4%
	Quarters	228	89	39	9.3	3.1	6.0	19.3	−13.9
1926–1945	Years	20	8	40	7.1	1.1	6.0	15.5	− 9.0
	Quarters	80	29	36	7.1	1.1	6.0	28.6	−19.9
1946–1982	Years	37	20	54	10.6	4.3	6.0	10.3	− 4.9
	Quarters	148	60	41	10.6	4.3	6.0	14.6	−10.4
1960–1982	Years	23	13	57	7.9	6.0	1.8	7.6	− 6.4
	Quarters	92	37	40	7.9	6.0	1.8	12.8	−12.6
1970–1982	Years	13	7	54	7.9	7.6	0.3	7.3	− 7.6
	Quarters	52	23	44	7.9	7.6	0.3	13.7	−14.9
1965–1974	Years	10	5	50	1.2	5.4	4.0	4.4	− 9.9
	Quarters	40	16	40	1.2	5.4	4.0	10.9	−13.1
1975–1982	Years	8	4	50	14.9	8.7	5.7	9.5	− 4.4
	Quarters	32	14	44	14.9	8.7	5.7	15.9	−11.9

*The number of points between intervals at which the S&P 500 real return changes from positive to negative, and vice versa.
†"Best timing" assumes being in the S&P 500 during all intervals when the real return is positive and in T-bills during all other intervals. "Worst timing" assumes the converse.

EXHIBIT II (continued)
Maximum Impact of Market Timing on S&P 500 Real Returns for Seven Periods, 1926–1982

Time Frame	Timing interval	Ending real value of $1 invested		Worst timing †	Worst-best ratio‡	Number of best intervals comprising real S&P return§	
		S&P 500	Best timing †			Number	Percent
a	b	k	l	m	n	o	p
1926–1982	Years	$28.00	$ 669.73	$ .02	2.23	10	18%
	Quarters	28.00	23,468.55	.00	1.76	14	6
1926–1945	Years	3.22	17.93	.15	1.78	3	15
	Quarters	3.22	153.87	.01	1.45	2	3
1946–1982	Years	8.71	37.72	.16	2.74	8	22
	Quarters	8.71	152.52	.02	2.18	18	12
1960–1982	Years	1.51	5.35	.22	1.53	2	9
	Quarters	1.51	15.84	.05	1.49	3	3
1970–1982	Years	1.04	2.51	.36	1.20	0	3
	Quarters	1.04	5.32	.12	1.31	0	C
1965–1974	Years	.67	1.54	.35	0.77	NA	NA
	Quarters	.67	2.81	.24	0.70	NA	NA
1975–1982	Years	1.56	2.06	.70	2.89	2	25
	Quarters	1.56	3.26	.36	1.98	3	9

*The number of points between intervals at which the S&P 500 real return changes from positive to negative, and vice versa.

† "Best timing" assumes being in the S&P 500 during all intervals when the real return is positive and in T-bills during all other intervals. "Worst timing" assumes the converse.

‡Compares the worst-case incremental return from market timing with the best-case incremental return. (See the Appendix for details.)

§Were only these best S&P 500 real return intervals removed from the overall return for the time frame, the overall real return would be 0%, that is, the T-bill return.

balanced. Consider the 1975–1982 period again (the last in *Exhibit II*). The attraction of employing an annual timing strategy in lieu of staying full-time in the S&P is the prospect of raising the annual real return over eight years from +5.7% to as much as +9.5% and the real dollars from $1.56 to $2.06.

But the natural odds of attaining this maximum return, which is to say the chances of being correctly in or out of equities in each of the eight annual periods, are only 4 out of 1,000! (That is, $.5^8 = .004$.) The natural odds of achieving the maximum return of +15.9% per year, using quarterly timing intervals during 1975–1982, are so small that the answer must be expressed in scientific notation.

But a portfolio owner might reasonably protest, "I'm not that greedy. I'd settle for my market timer being right, say, three-quarters of the time." Unfortunately, once we leave the convenient parameters of being totally right or totally wrong, the timing probability problem becomes much more complex.

Since each period's return exerts different leverage on the return for the overall time frame, the owner's statement can only be answered by posing a question: "In which three-quarters of the periods will your timer be right?" Will he err just in those periods when the S&P's real return is only marginally different from the T-bill return, which would result in only a modest reduction of the overall best case result? Or might he miss the best years for the S&P and be fully invested in the worst?

The "tilted football" in *Exhibit III*, covering 1926–1982 on an annual timing basis, graphically illustrates these two extreme paths of market-timing results that connect the ultimate points of being totally right (at the top left) and totally wrong (at the lower right). The slope of the upper best-case curve, tracing the depressing effect on cumulative wealth, falls gradually at the top but becomes steeper as the timing accuracy rate diminishes. Exactly the reverse phenomenon applies to the lower worst-case curve, where the downward slope (and the effect on cumulative wealth) is steepest at the beginning and flattens at the end.

Notice also that the area of the timing "football" above the S&P 500 line is dramatically smaller than the area below that line. This difference simply illustrates once again that the incremental rewards from market timing are vastly less than the incremental risks, even when the analysis parameters are adjusted to reflect more than the extreme situation.

Exhibit IV is an explosion of the area in *Exhibit III* lying between the 75% and 50% timing accuracy lines. These outer limits reflect the wishes of our hypothetical portfolio owner and the judgment of statisticians (and most academics), who tell us that 50% accuracy is about all we should expect from timing. The numbers next to the vertical lines are the worst-case to best-case incremental return ratios that I have previously discussed.

An examination of the left side of *Exhibit IV* tells us that *if* one could engage a market timer who could *guarantee* that he could correctly

EXHIBIT III
Impact of Market Timing Accuracy on Real Returns
1926–1982, Using Annual Intervals

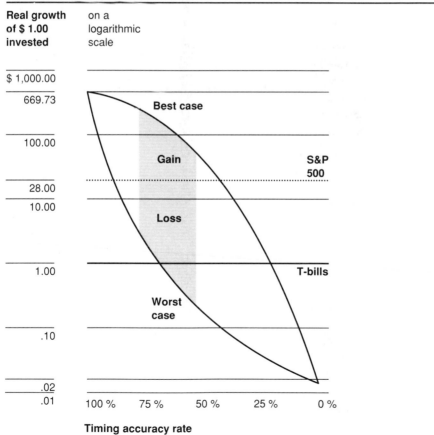

anticipate whether the real return from the S&P would be positive or negative 75% of the time, one would probably be advised to retain his services. With 75% accuracy, the "worst case" real return on $1.00 invested over the full 1926–82 period using annual timing would be $4.36 or + 2.6% per year, which would occur were the timer wrong on the 25% most significant periods, i.e. those years with the highest and lowest real S&P returns. While $4.36 does not compare well with the $28.00 (+ 6.0% per year) real return from the S&P, it is nonetheless significantly positive relative to T-bills. Furthermore, were the timer clever or fortunate enough to be wrong only on the 25% least significant periods (i.e. those years with S&P real returns, either positive or negative, closest to 0.0%), the strategy would generate a very handsome $371.80 or + 10.9% per year. Given the fact that, one, the "worst case" real return in this case is still positive, and two, that the "worst:best" ratio of the incremental returns is .72 (meaning that the "risk" potential is only 72% of the "reward" potential), a "being right three-quarters of the time" market timing strategy might seem to be appealing. The problem, of course, is that no market timer can *guarantee* in advance a minimum accuracy rate nor in which periods he will err.

The risk-reward trade-off changes markedly if the timer's accuracy should slip from being right three-quarters of the time to just two-thirds of the time, which, most would agree, would still be a very impressive accuracy rate. While the worst-case real return for 1926–1982, with 67% accuracy, is still nominally positive at $1.33 (+ .5% per year), and while the best-case return is still an attractive $227.28 (+ 10% per year), the worst-best ratio increases to 1.45, meaning that the downside risk of being right even two-thirds of the time is nearly 50% greater than the upside reward.

If we look at the theoretically probable "fifty-fifty" accuracy rate for 1926–1982 on the right-hand side of *Exhibit IV*, the risk-reward trade-off becomes obviously unacceptable. Here the $1 originally invested shrinks to 29 cents (−2.1% per year) in real terms in the worst case and grows to only $62.81 (+ 7.5% per year) in the best case, producing a disastrous worst-best ratio of 5.56. Said another way, if the theoreticians are correct about the inefficacy of market timing (that is, it will generally be accurate only 50% of the time), the probable outcome is a best-case real dollar return only about two times greater than what would come from continuous investment in the S&P, while the worst case produces about 100 times less!

EXHIBIT IV
Impact of 75%–50% Market Timing Accuracy on Real Returns
1926–1982, Using Annual Intervals

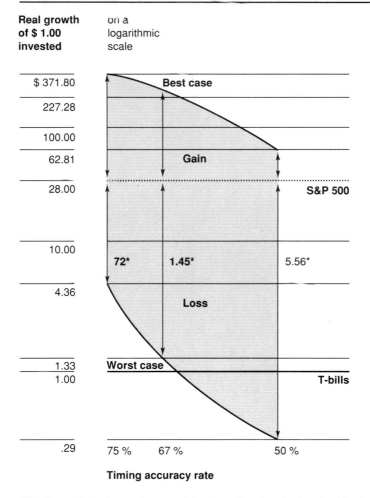

| Real growth of $ 1.00 invested | on a logarithmic scale |

*Worst-case to best-case incremental return ratios, i.e., the length of the loss vector relative to the corresponding gain vector.

The point of these charts and statistics is simply to emphasize that a market-timing strategist has tremendous natural odds to overcome, and that these odds increase geometrically with the length of the time frame and with the frequency of the timing interval. There is probably no situation where caveat emptor is more apropos for the portfolio owner than in interviewing prospective timing managers.

PORTFOLIO OWNER'S ROLE

While taking advice on important matters in informal settings is probably a bad idea, the fact remains that a great many money managers are hired and investment strategies implicitly adopted because some respected director, trustee, or senior executive "heard just the other day about this guy who's had a fantastic record." Advice of this sort should be (and all too often is not) subjected to the following test, especially if the alleged genius is a market timer.

Is the performance record indeed genuine, and has it been accumulated over a time frame that more or less corresponds with the portfolio owner's own future time horizon? As the diagrams suggest, it takes only a very few wrong decisions to deflate a market timer's record to the point where it is no better than that of those dull folk who just sit with their equities, and this may be just the "good news" half of the story.

Because the natural long-term odds vis-a-vis market timing are clearly stacked in favor of the house, extensive use of timing strategies should be confined to managing one's own money and not that of others. For individuals with the proper temperament and with sufficient discretionary financial resources, market timing can be fun and perhaps rewarding. But since neither having fun nor incurring disproportionate risks falls within the scope of the "prudent man's" job description, trustees, directors, and senior executives having responsibility for overseeing the management of money for others should forbid or at least narrowly restrict their employees' and agents' market-timing activities.

The need for such a policy becomes more apparent when we consider that employees and agents have a natural tendency to engage in market timing. Take the case of typical in-house, full-time pension executives. With a few notable exceptions (mainly in very large companies), such persons are one of two sorts—young, upwardly mobile executives who hope to receive their next promotions within a few years or older employees whose careers have peaked and who are beginning to think in terms of postretirement security. Both sets of employees are very conscious of the possibility of failure. The same may be said of retained managers or agents, whose own cash flows obviously depend on retaining their accounts.

If the environment in which an employee or an agent operates is such that he might even infer that his superior or client would view a 20% or a 30% portfolio value drop over one or two years as a personal failure, he will be tempted to water down the portfolio with cash. While this dilution usually amounts to only 10% to 50% of the asset pool and thus does not expose the full portfolio to the unbalanced risk-reward parameters that I have outlined, the shift nonetheless constitutes market timing and adds to the assumed risk.

Using "closet timing," the employee (or agent) may well retain his job (or account) and perhaps even receive a promotion (or additional funds) if the performance numbers fall more or less right for several years in a row. But in the long run the portfolio owner will be the eventual loser, for he will inevitably miss at least a part of the rare vintage performance periods for equity that constitute most of the reward for being an equity investor.

Timers as Contrarians

Portfolio owners should recognize that a successful timing strategy depends on buying stocks when the prevailing view is that they should be sold, and vice versa. While following this contrarian approach is unquestionably the explanation for the success that some market timers have presumably enjoyed, can anyone expect subordinate employees and agents, with their short time horizons, to paddle their career canoes upstream against this consensus current if their superiors or clients are part of the consensus?

To change metaphors, the most telling argument against market timing is the problem of employing a strategy that, to be successful, requires the "hired chauffeur" to spend most of his time driving on what seems to be the wrong side of the road just when the opposing traffic is the heaviest. Such driving, if done at all, demands a great deal of courage and steady nerves on the part of both the chauffeur and his owner-passenger and is thus probably best done by the owner himself in his own automobile, alone. The problem is, of course, that most portfolio owners do not know how to drive, and so they must employ chauffeurs, to whom they unfortunately tend to give backseat driver advice, usually at the worst possible times and with disastrous consequences.

To minimize the counterproductive effect of this natural difference in the time horizon of the true portfolio owner—which is often infinity, as mortals perceive infinity—and of the hired hands, a thorough examination of risk must be undertaken. And by risk I mean the volatility of portfolio returns. As many writers have noted, there is a direct link between the length of an owner's time horizon and his ability to cope with volatility. I have also suggested elsewhere that risk is really the "likelihood of having insufficient cash with which to make essential payments" and that every owner has his own unique payment requirements.[1]

To synchronize the risk perceptions of the chauffeur and the owner-passenger, we must ascertain how much volatility can be tolerated in the given situation and invest accordingly. If we can't be full-time equity investors with all our money—because of current income requirements, future cash needs, constituent attitudes, or legal constraints—how far in this direction can we go? If the answer is 90% or 60% or 25%, this money should be fully committed to equities. And both the owner overseers and the hired employees and agents should be made to understand that the volatility from this segment of the portfolio is a statistic with no meaningful consequence. Given this fact, there is no need to dampen volatility by attempts to time the market, with its resulting diminution of long-term returns.

As Charles Ellis asserts so well, "The priority objective in investment management is to control risk."[2] But risk can be controlled only after it has been locally defined and its pertinence quantified. These tasks are solely the responsibility of the portfolio owner. This process, however, takes thought, thought takes time, and time is something that part-time overseers almost by definition have too little of. Thus, they usually delegate the risk control function to employees and agents, who understandably have their own agendas.

When market-timing strategies go wrong, the managers and employees are generally blamed. But the blame should lie with the persons who have the ultimate responsibility for setting policy. It is usually the absence of such policies that leads to the folly of stock market timing.

APPENDIX: BEST CASE-WORST CASE RATIOS

The worst case-best case incremental ratios, which are the principal basis for my conclusions about the inefficacy of market timing, are derived by using logarithms, which measure relative change or growth. By using logarithmic scales on the vertical axes of the three charts in the article, one can make the lengths of the brackets, or vectors, indicate the relative upside reward and downside risk from market timing versus being full-time in the S&P 500. The mathematical confirmation of the 2:1 relationship of the worst-case to best-case incremental return brackets in *Exhibit I* is as follows (where $ = ending value of the $1 originally invested):

$$-(\text{Ln worst case \$} - \text{Ln S\&P\$})/(\text{Ln best case \$} - \text{Ln S\&P\$}) =$$
$$-(\text{Ln }.36 - \text{Ln }1.56)/(\text{Ln }3.26 - \text{Ln }1.56) =$$
$$-(-1.022 - .445)/(1.182 - .445) = 1.98$$

The preceding minus sign in the equation is included simply to prevent confusing the reader with a negative ratio result, which would always be the case since "worst case $" is always less than the initial $1 investment and logarithms of values less than 1 are always negative.

FOOTNOTES

1. See my article, "A New Paradigm for Portfolio Risk," *Journal of Portfolio Management*, to be published in Fall 1984.
2. Charles D. Ellis, "Setting Investment Objectives," in *Investment Manager's Handbook*, ed. Sumner N. Levine (Homewood, Ill.: Dow Jones-Irwin, 1980), p. 66.

THE COFFEE CAN PORTFOLIO

Robert G. Kirby

Robert Kirby's easy charm and "down-home" humor—and a great lesson
for investors—flow gently but surely from this wise and engaging reflection.

During recent years, there has been a gradual but steady increase in the
use of index funds by institutional investors. This disturbs me, because I
believe that superior investment research and management can produce
consistently above-average results. Even beyond that point, however, I
am also bothered by the wide, unquestioning acceptance of a form of
indexing that appears to be seriously flawed. Nevertheless, despite these
complaints, I do not disagree out of hand with those who adopt indexed
investment programs.

We all know that, *in the aggregate*, professional money managers
do not produce a return superior to that of a broadly based, unmanaged
portfolio. We ignore the data that show that a few money managers have
done consistently better, and a few others have done consistently worse.
This means that we should not be surprised when an investor who has
been a client of a poor money manager decides that he would be better
off with an index fund. To beat the market is not easy. In addition to a

Reprinted from *The Journal of Portfolio Management*, Vol. 10, No. 1, Fall 1984, 76–79. New
York, New York: Institutional Investor, Inc.

good investment manager, the investor needs perspective, patience, and courage—qualities that do not abound in today's intensely competitive world. For many investors, institutional and individual, an index fund may well be the best kind of common stock investment program.

WHY INDEX? AND WHY NOT?

Perhaps I have a suspicious and cynical mind. Each surge in the popularity of index funds seems to follow a period during which the S&P 500 has been an excellent performer. Most index funds are not set up to avoid inferior performance; their purpose is to secure superior performance—just as when an investor hires a new investment manager with a great recent record. These are the wrong reasons.

Other investors adopt index funds for the right reasons. They believe that (1) the market is efficient in pricing assets so that it is virtually impossible to achieve consistently superior returns, and 2) the underperformance of professional money managers is the result of futile transaction costs. I disagree with these assumptions, but they support a position that is logical and makes sense. The question that completely perplexes me is why, with this sensible and logical approach to equity investing, these people then choose to replicate the Standard & Poor's 500, which (1) is in reality actively managed, and (2) does not represent the market?

WHEN IS PASSIVE ACTIVE?

In case you're shocked, let's examine these two statements. First, on the point of active management, maybe you can accuse me of splitting hairs, because turnover in the S&P 500 is small in comparison to that of most "active" money managers. Even modest activity, however, if it occurs year after year, produces a substantial cumulative change in the portfolio. In the past 10 years, Standard & Poor's has made several hundred changes, both eliminations and additions, in their portfolio, and these changes have created transaction costs for holders of S&P 500 index funds. Further, the changes are not the result of a formula that produces a consistent, predictable kind of alteration: They represent individual judgments of the Standard & Poor's staff, based on a combination of research and intuition, just as old-fashioned, active portfolio managers do it. Yet many people who are well aware that the S&P 500 is a faulty index are unwilling to go to the trouble to re-educate the investors whom they represent. But assume you are a brave and responsible fiduciary. What should you do?

In my opinion, you have two alternatives. Which you choose depends on your reasons for pursuing an index fund to begin with. Do you believe that the market is efficient and you want to adopt a program that replicates the market, because that's the best you can do? Or, do you believe that traditional, active portfolio management incurs such high transaction costs that even the best money managers are unlikely to produce superior investment returns consistently? These are different reasons.

If you believe that a market return is the best an investor can hope for, you should pursue an investment program that will replicate the market, which is best represented by the Wilshire 5000 Stock Index. Clearly, it is impractical to use the actual Wilshire 5000. Such a program would drive both the computer and the trading department bonkers. The last 1000, or so, stocks in the index barely qualify as publicly owned and have about the same marketability as a 1961 Edsel. On the other hand, a tailor-made "Wilshire 1000" would represent 87% of the Wilshire 5000 and should be an acceptable proxy for "everything out there," providing true market results.

WHEN IS ACTIVE PASSIVE?

But, if you have decided that the greatest detriment to superior investment returns is transaction costs, then I have a novel solution. For many years, I have been intrigued with an idea that I call the "Coffee Can" portfolio. I suspect that this notion is not likely to be popular among investment managers, because, if widely adopted, it might radically change the structure of our industry and might substantially diminish the number of souls able to sustain opulent life-styles through the money management profession.

The Coffee Can portfolio concept harkens back to the Old West, when people put their valuable possessions in a coffee can and kept it under the mattress. That coffee can involved no transaction costs, administrative costs, or any other costs. The success of the program depended entirely on the wisdom and foresight used to select the objects to be placed in the coffee can to begin with.

As you might guess, I didn't write this article to suggest a better way for Efficient Market folks to improve their approach to passive investing. Rather, it is to provide help for investors who are concerned about the bit taken out of total investment returns by high and rising transaction costs. This problem has grown in recent years, as the focus on month-to-month and quarter-to-quarter investment returns has intensified. This pressure has been reflected in shorter decision time horizons by money managers and higher turnover.

If transaction costs are one of the main deterrents to superior long-term investment results—a point of view I embrace—why not have your passive portfolio represent the best possible portfolio, rather than a changing list of 500 stocks selected by Standard & Poor's? I suggest that you find the best investment research organization you can and ask them to select a diversified portfolio of stocks with the knowledge that the portfolio will not be re-evaluated or re-examined for a period of at least 10 years.

Having looked at a great number of portfolios over 30 years, I believe that about the maximum premium return that a money manager can expect to achieve in relation to an index such as the S&P 500 would be three percentage points in annual compound rate of return. I am aware that some money managers have exceeded this premium substantially for a 5-year period and some have exceeded it for a 10-year period, but most of these records have qualifying circumstances— usually involving a relatively small amount of capital under management by a few individuals during the early years. Any money management organization with a large amount of capital under management will find it difficult to reach that three percentage point premium over the S&P 500 for any time period in excess of 10 years. In my judgment, this result would be close to a Becker first percentile performance. I am sure that I would be turning clients away from my door in 10 years if I could attain only a two percentage point advantage.

Compare these hoped-for premium rates of return to current trans-action costs in most institutional portfolios. Admittedly, it is difficult to measure transaction costs. Actual commissions paid are probably a minor fraction of the total.

Although I cannot prove this, I believe there are many money managers in today's world who produce transaction costs that reach, or exceed, 2% of those assets per year. A. G. Becker data for the past five years show a *median* turnover in institutional portfolios of 74%. One half of the funds did more! In many cases, current transaction costs are running somewhere close to the hoped-for 2% return premium above a passive portfolio. It is fascinating to realize that you could virtually double the premium return that active management is in existence to obtain—if you could eliminate the transaction costs.

What kind of results would good money managers produce without all that activity? The answer lies in another question: Are we traders, or are we really investors? Most good money managers are probably investors deep down inside. But quotrons and news services, and computers that churn out daily investment results make them act like traders. They start with sound research that identifies attractive companies in promising industries on a longer-term time horizon. Then, they trade those stocks two or three times a year based on month-to-month news developments and rumors of all shapes and sizes.

THE HOW AND THE WHY OF BETTER
PASSIVE PERFORMANCE

The notion that a "Coffee Can" portfolio can outperform an actively managed portfolio selected by the same investment management organization (at least over some particular time horizon) is not without a basis in logic. The basis is really simple. Take the example of constructing a new common stock portfolio of $100 million. The average, orthodox, professional money manager would build a portfolio of something like fifty $2 million commitments, each representing 2% of the fund. If that portfolio were then buried and forgotten for a while, several obvious conditions would apply. First, the most that could be lost in any one holding would be 2% of the fund. Second, the most that the portfolio could gain from any one holding would be unlimited. After all, there would be no one to apply the concepts of diversification and too much exposure to a given company, or a given industry.

The Coffee Can idea first occurred to me in the middle 1950s when I worked for a large, investment counsel organization, most of whose clients were individuals. We always told our clients that we were in the business of preserving capital, not creating capital. If you wanted to get a lot richer than you already were, then you should hire someone else. We were there to preserve, in real terms, the client's estate and the standard of living that it provided.

And, indeed, we were. The investment counsel business, as it is traditionally practiced, and probably as it should be practiced, is a simple process of making sure that clients never have so much risk exposure that their capital or standard of living can be impaired by some specific negative surprise. In other words, as your most successful investments grow in value, you make partial sales and transfer the capital involved to your less successful investments that have gotten cheaper. The process results in a stream of capital being transferred from the most dynamic companies, which usually appear somewhat overvalued, to the least dynamic companies, which usually appear somewhat undervalued.

The potential impact of this process was brought home to me dramatically as the result of an experience with one woman client. Her husband, a lawyer, handled her financial affairs and was our primary contact. I had worked with the client for about ten years, when her husband suddenly died. She inherited his estate and called us to say that she would be adding his securities to the portfolio under our management. When we received the list of assets, I was amused to find that he had secretly been piggy-backing our recommendations for his wife's portfolio. Then, when I looked at the total value of the estate, I was also shocked. The husband had applied a small twist of his own to our advice: He paid no attention whatsoever to the sale recommendations. He simply put about $5,000 in every purchase recommendation. Then he would toss the certificate in his safe-deposit box and forget it.

Needless to say, he had an odd-looking portfolio. He owned a number of small holdings with values of less than $2,000. He had several large holdings with values in excess of $100,000. There was one jumbo holding worth over $800,000 that exceeded the total value of his wife's portfolio and came from a small commitment in a company called Haloid; this later turned out to be a zillion shares of Xerox.

THE TROUBLE IN MANAGEMENTLAND

Admittedly, there is a difference between the way we managed individual portfolios 20 or 25 years ago and the way that institutional funds are managed today. While today's methods are different, I am not at all sure that they are a whole lot better. We are still doing many of the same things today for institutions that we did for individuals years ago.

The primary difference is that we make our decisions on a much shorter time horizon. The old concept of averaging down has faded, to a fair degree, because that is hardly the way to get next month's market winners. On the other hand, most of us are faster than Wyatt Earp ever dreamed of being when it comes to taking a profit. The concept of being a long-term partner in a sound and growing business enterprise seems as far away as the Stone Age.

I believe there are two reasons why so many institutional clients are disappointed by their money managers, and why so many money managers are hired and fired every month. First, money managers have created expectations that far exceed their abilities. Second, they have encouraged the measurement of results on a short time horizon that is a far greater reflection of luck than skill.

The plain fact is that the professional money management fraternity of more than 2,000 firms has produced a ho-hum aggregate result over the years. That is hardly surprising. We usually produce high turnover. Many money managers generate commissions each year that substantially exceed 1% of their assets under management. Thus, for example, firms that manage $1 billion produce $15–$20 million in commissions—a result that is totally incompatible with the word "investment."

The higher investment returns that should be the logical product of superior research analysis are dissipated in trading activity. That classic question, "Where are the customers' yachts?" is alive and well. We're making the brokers rich! That is one point on which the advocates of both passive and active portfolio management can agree. This problem occurs precisely because few money managers are willing to make a long-term decision.

INVESTING THE RIGHT WAY: INVEST!

As a money manager, I have frequently looked at an investment decision that I felt had a high probability of success on a three-year horizon, but about which I had many doubts on a six-month time horizon. Institutional investing, as it is structured today, simply makes it more difficult to make a high-conviction, long-term decision than to make a low conviction, short-term decision. The rewards of short-term results substantially superior to the market, and the penalties of short-term results well below the market, are awesome. The only investment management organizations willing to take an extreme position are those with little to lose. Prudent investment management is really a sophisticated and complex system of hedging risks. The "go-for-it" philosophy may be a laudable personal approach, but it has no place in professional money management.

Nevertheless, the biggest earners in today's world are not rock musicians or professional athletes. Our system accords the highest earnings to money managers. I know perhaps a half a dozen people whose earned incomes exceed $2 million per year. All of them are money managers.

The rewards of establishing a successful, new investment management organization over the past five years have been mind-boggling. This success requires achieving something I would call "orbital velocity." You escape the force of gravity. Once you have achieved "orbital velocity," it doesn't matter what happens from then on.

To reach that exalted state, money managers have to produce an investment result that will get them in the top decile of the A. G. Becker universe on a three-year time horizon. Fortunately, it does not matter how much money is under management while this record is achieved. Then, a couple of skilled marketing guys will need about six months to raise between $500 million and $1 billion in new accounts. Because of the brilliant 3-year record, the money manager will ask for and receive a premium fee of perhaps .6% or more.

This is "orbital velocity." The firm has a revenue stream of between $3 million and $6 million per year, of which perhaps 70%-80% goes through to the bottomline, pre-tax. No matter how bad the performance may be in the future, at least four to five years will have to pass before they lose all those new clients. During that time, anywhere from $10 million to $30 million in revenues will cycle through the investment management firm, regardless of how they manage the clients' money. The firm's fixed costs are nominal. Even if the endeavor is a total flop, the principal or principals end up set for life.

Obviously, you don't achieve that top 10% of the A. G. Becker universe on a three-year time horizon without going out on the proverbial limb. A high R^2 is not going to do the job. The investment management organizations willing to take the required extreme positions are likely to be those with very little to lose. It is easy to see why turnover is up and speculation has replaced investment. Who wouldn't like to make two mil. a year?

Our business needs to encourage *investing*, both for our benefit and for the benefit of our clients. Though a bit gimmicky, the Coffee Can portfolio would serve this end. But I admit that I quake at the thought that someone will one day walk into my office and say, "Okay, Kirby, I read about your wild idea. I would like a Coffee Can portfolio for $100 million. What will you charge?" It's at that point that I have a concern about getting punched in the mouth. I really believe that if I were willing to accept the assignment for a $2 million fee, the client would be getting the bargain of the century. I am also fairly certain that if I quoted the price, I would get a split lip.

The Coffee Can portfolio concept has two problems. First, who is going to buy a product, the value of which will take 10 years to evaluate? A decade is likely to exceed the career horizons of most corporate executives and pension fund administrators, to say nothing of most money managers. Second, who will pay the large fee, up front, that is necessary to support a mature, first-class investment research organization needed to select a superior 10-year portfolio? You can hardly assemble a group of proven professionals for a one-shot project, no matter what the compensation. Further, even outstanding individuals do not constitute an effective management organization until they have had experience working together as a team.

TRENDS IN BOND PORTFOLIO MANAGEMENT

Martin L. Leibowitz

The "Baseline Portfolio" is now generally accepted as the most useful standard against which to evaluate the performance of a bond portfolio manager. Here, Martin Leibowitz explains the concept with the profound erudition and clarity that have become our normal expectations from him.

THE YARDSTICK OF TOTAL RETURN

Many of the problems confronting today's bond portfolio manager can be traced to the sole reliance upon total return comparisons over short-term periods. Total return measurements do provide a useful yardstick of the extent to which the portfolio manager took advantage of general market opportunities during the measurement period. But this is only one factor in the complex process of portfolio management. A fundamental problem seems to arise when a single yardstick—total return measurement over short-term periods—is taken as the sole yardstick for all management activity.

From *The Investment Manager's Handbook*, Sumner N. Levine, ed. (Homewood, Illinois, 1980), 496–506, by permission of Dow Jones-Irwin.

This concentration on the single yardstick of total return can force dangerously simplistic comparisons among portfolios that may actually differ widely in function and purpose. In fact, the same level of achieved return may represent a very satisfactory result for one portfolio while having quite dismal implications for another portfolio with a different set of goals.

Moreover, even with a given portfolio, an over-emphasis on short-term return can lead to conflicts with the long-term goals of the fund. For example, it could lead the portfolio manager into concentrating his activity on catching short-term swings in interest rates. In turn, this excessive rate anticipation could lead to a frequent series of major portfolio shifts, thereby introducing considerable timing risk into the overall management process. The resulting volatility risk might be in direct contradiction to the original purpose of placing the funds into a fixed-income portfolio in the first place. This is just one instance of how an exclusive focus on maximization of total return over short periods can violate a fund's policy constraints and cause deviations from the fund's true long term objectives.

These problems are particularly acute for fixed-income portfolios because of certain distinctive characteristics of the bond market. Much of the institutional investment in bonds is motivated by long-term, risk-avoidance purposes. These long-term purposes typically overshadow any specific requirements for total return over short-term periods.

Thus, the ideal solution would be to find some concrete way of relating the returns achieved over short-term measurement periods to the fund's long-term goal.

We believe that such goal-oriented management is indeed possible through application of a technique which we call "The Baseline Portfolio." This technique combines the modern total return approach with a "back-to-the-fundamentals" concept reminiscent of the pre-1970s style of bond portfolio management.

THE BASELINE PORTFOLIO

In theory, the portfolio management process can be viewed as consisting of the four major steps shown in Figure 9. The first step is to identify the long-term objectives of the fund. The second step commences with

FIGURE 9
Overview of the Portfolio Management Process

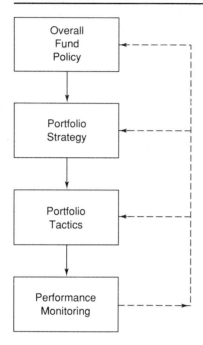

the manager's judgments regarding market prospects. At this point, the manager must make the broad decisions that relate to portfolio strategy, *i.e.*, to determining the portfolio's maturity structure. The Rate and Yield Curve Anticipation efforts would fall into this category of "strategy" decisions. Once this has been done, the third step consists of deciding upon the detailed portfolio tactics to be employed. These consist of selecting specific sectors to take advantage of perceived market opportunities. Sector and Substitution Swap activity would lie in this area of "tactical" decisions. The fourth step then consists of a continuing performance monitoring (in the most general sense) to ensure that the portfolio objectives are being fulfilled.

The first step is far more difficult than generally believed. It is no simple matter to identify a full set of portfolio objectives and then to define these objectives in a useful way. Such efforts tend to lead to either a frustratingly vague description of the objectives or an impossibly long

FIGURE 10
Portfolio Objectives

Maximum Long Term Nominal Return
Maximum Long Term Real Return
Maximum Prescribed Liability Schedule
Reserve Against Uncertain Liabilities
Earnings Contribution
Earnings Management
Tax Liability Management
Liquidity Warehouse
Stability of Principal
Stability of Income Over Time
Facilitate Corporate Flexibility
Corporate Compliance
Aura of Balance and Prudence

---

collection of goals which mix the minor considerations in with the major ones.

For example, Figure 10 illustrates a partial list of the many objectives that could be ascribed to fixed-income portfolios. Moreover, any set of objectives are closely intertwined with an associated set of risk factors. (In this connection, risk is being defined in a far broader sense than the single volatility measure which has become traditional in many modern analyses. In the sense used here, risk entails all those potential events that could interfere with the portfolio being able to fulfill its long-term objectives.) When there are a large number of potential objectives and associated risk factors, it is no easy task to generate concrete guidelines for portfolio managers.

The purpose of the "Baseline Portfolio" is to provide a practical procedure for articulating the fund's long-term objectives in a concrete and useful fashion. The underlying idea is to take advantage of the relatively well-defined sector structure of the fixed-income market.

An important characteristic of the bond market is the structural clarity of its asset classes. This clarity enables the return/risk relationships among the different market sectors to be relatively well-defined, especially over longer term horizons. The longer term motivation of investors and the market's structural clarity obviously fit hand-in-glove, allowing for the identification of market sectors that are particularly well suited for serving the specific goals of a given fund. By selecting market sectors to match the fund's objectives and associated risk factors, one should be able to develop a portfolio structure which best suits the fund's long-term goals (Figure 11). This is called the fund's "Baseline Portfolio"[1].

Since the Baseline Portfolio structure should be determined primarily by long-range considerations, it should be relatively independent of

FIGURE 11
The Theoretical Baseline Portfolio

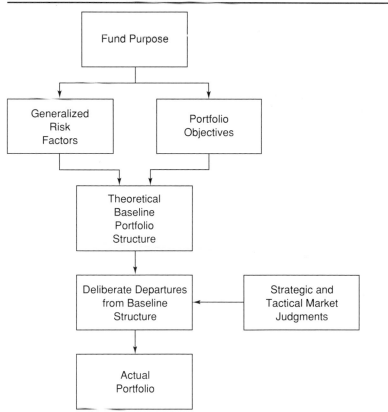

the active manager's day-to-day market judgments. Thus, the Baseline Portfolio could be defined as the most balanced possible fulfillment of all of the fund's complex objectives and goals in the absence of an active market-related management activity. In other words, the Baseline is that passive portfolio which carries the "least risk" relative to the fund's long-term goals.

MANAGEMENT ACTIVITY RELATIVE TO THE BASELINE PORTFOLIO

From the vantage point of the Baseline Portfolio, one purpose of investment management is to take advantage of market opportunities. Active management can then be viewed as a series of strategic and tactical judgments such as those shown in Figure 12. These judgments would lead to market-motivated departures from the Baseline Portfolio in an effort to achieve improved portfolio results. The resulting portfolio improvements—as well as the incremental risks incurred in achieving them—should theoretically be measured against the yardstick of the Baseline Portfolio itself.

The portfolio manager, in selecting his actual portfolio, clearly incurs an incremental risk in departing from the Baseline Portfolio. By so doing, he seeks an incremental return above and beyond what could be achieved with the Baseline Portfolio. Therefore, the benchmark for measuring the portfolio's return is the return that could have been achieved by simply holding the "Baseline Portfolio", *i.e.*, the Baseline's return becomes the natural "bogey" for the actual portfolio. In essence, the Baseline constitutes a sort of total return index customized to the fund's individual goals. To the extent that the achieved return exceeds the Baseline return, to that extent the portfolio manager has added to the achievement of the portfolio goals as denominated in the currency of the Baseline Portfolio itself.

Evaluating Proposed Departures from the Baseline

The Baseline Portfolio can serve prospective as well as retrospective functions. At the beginning of each investment period, the Baseline can help the portfolio manager to gauge—in a quantitative, objective fashion—the incremental risk incurred relative to these same goals.

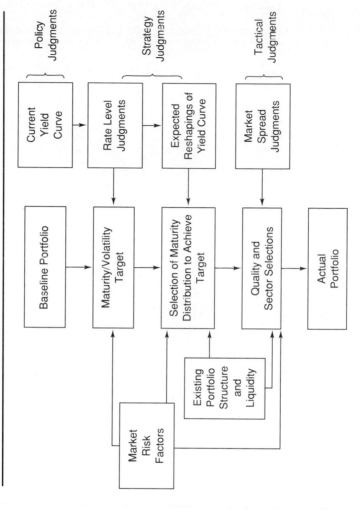

FIGURE 12
Active Bond Portfolio Management

FIGURE 13
Dependence of Incremental Returns upon Direction of Market Movement

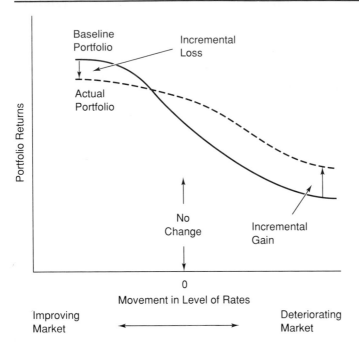

This prospective application of the Baseline Portfolio may be the most important one of all.

Figure 13 illustrates how a manager can compare his actual portfolio's return profile to that of the Baseline. Here the projected returns from the two portfolios are plotted across a range of potential movements in the overall level of interest rates. These "return vectors"[2] clearly show the nature of the tradeoffs involved in the departure from the Baseline. The actual portfolio is considerably more defensive than the Baseline — as long as the market stays at the same level or deteriorates (*i.e.*, rises in yield level), the actual portfolio will outperform the Baseline. There will be a loss relative to the Baseline only under improving market conditions (*i.e.*, declining yields). The choice of the actual portfolio suggests that the manager has a rather pessimistic outlook on the market, or that he feels that incremental performance is more important in dreary markets.

Another way of exploring this risk-return tradeoff is for the manager to assign probabilities to the different rate movements. The expected returns (*i.e.*, the probability-weighted average returns) can then be plot-

FIGURE 14
Market-Motivated Departures from the Baseline Portfolio

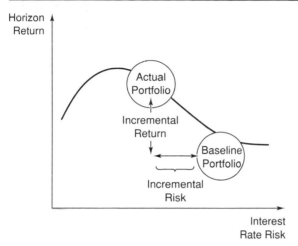

ted as shown in Figure 14. The horizontal axis in Figure 14 represents some measure of portfolio "aggressiveness"—*i.e.*, "interest rate risk."

As noted earlier, the maturity structure is the most important decision made by an active portfolio manager. By varying the maturity structure, he can control the amount of "interest rate risk" contained in his portfolio. Various proxies for the "interest rate risk" of a portfolio have been proposed—average maturity, historical variability, percentage price volatility, Macaulay's duration, Horizon Volatility, Proportional Volatility.[3] However, for any of these measures, the Baseline can be viewed as the reference point. To the extent that the active manager departs from this Baseline level of interest rate risk, to that extent he risks falling below the Baseline's performance.

This holds true for departures in both directions. In the case of Figure 14, the manager is making a "defensive departure" from the Baseline's risk level. By choosing a portfolio with less interest rate sensitivity than the Baseline, the manager hopes to obtain a sizeable improvement in incremental returns, given his basically pessimistic outlook. However, he is exposing his portfolio to a considerable shortfall in return relative to the Baseline in the event that his pessimistic view fails to materialize.

One should take note of the apparent paradox in the situation portrayed in Figure 14. The greatest risk here is the prospect of a stronger-than-expected downward move in interest rates. This action would normally be viewed as an "improving market." However, in this case, such a "market improvement" would lead to underperformance relative to the Baseline Portfolio, and hence would constitute the gravest threat to the fund's progress towards its long-term goals.

Figure 14 thus shows how a manager can gauge his incremental interest rate risk relative to the Baseline and, by implication, measure his more generalized risk relative to long-term goals. There may be some controversy regarding what constitutes a satisfactory measure of interest rate risk. However, there is no disagreement that a greater level of risk consciousness needs to be introduced into the management process. Once any such volatility measure has been selected, the procedure implied in Figures 13 or 14 can be quantified, thereby providing the manager (and the sponsor) with a concrete, numerical indication of the incremental risk associated with a prospective portfolio strategy.

SOURCES OF RETURN

This approach can be further refined by combining it with an analysis of the component sources of prospective return. The first part of this article described four main categories of bond portfolio activity—Pure Yield Pick-Up, Substitution Swap, Sector Spread Swaps, and Rate Anticipation. A given portfolio structure will typically embed (intentionally or otherwise) some degree of each activity. By "parsing out" the components of bond return, one can associate each category of management activity with its corresponding contribution to the return-risk characteristics of the overall portfolio. One such technique identifies 8 component sources of return:

1. yield curve accumulation
2. sector spread accumulation
3. rolling yield effect
4. revaluation in sector spread
5. market shifts
6. yield curve reshaping
7. sector response to yield curve changes
8. specific issue spread action beyond that of the associated sector.

Another way of analyzing these return components is in terms of the kind of risks they represent. Thus, the combination of the first three components is simply the sector's Rolling Yield.[4] This Rolling Yield return is fairly well assured for sectors whose quality is not in doubt. In contrast, the Revaluation Return reflects a spread judgment that the sector is undervalued. There may be considerable risk surrounding any such projected Revaluation.

The next three components of return all depend on the magnitude of the overall market movement, the resulting yield curve reshaping, and the sector spread response. It is useful to combine these three volatility factors into a measure of the sector's "Total Market Volatility."

Figure 15 provides a graphic representation of the relationships

FIGURE 15
Sector Returns for a Range of Market Shifts

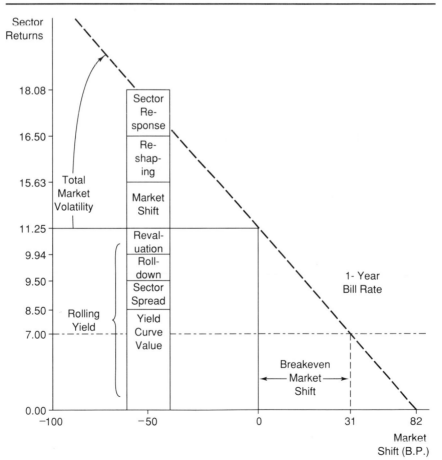

among these different return components and risk categories. A detailed explanation of this approach is contained in a study entitled *Sources of Return in Corporate Bond Portfolios*.[5]

These classification techniques have been developed to assist the investment manager in organizing and quantifying the many market judgments that are embedded in his portfolio structure. The classification process also highlights the nature of the different risks incurred, as well as the differences in their portfolio impact over varying investment horizons. By analyzing the marketplace in terms of this same classification system, the manager may be better able to construct a portfolio having a desired set of characteristics. This classification procedure could also prove helpful in more precisely identifying the manager's motivation behind an intended departure from a goal-oriented Baseline Portfolio.

COMMUNICATION BETWEEN
SPONSOR AND MANAGER

The Baseline Portfolio approach can facilitate the communication process between sponsor and manager.

At the outset, the Baseline Portfolio should itself be the result of discussions between the fund's sponsor and the manager. In these initial discussions, the sponsor must try to convey his sense of the fund's purpose, to define his overall objectives and their relative priorities, and to identify and delimit the risk factors that concern him. On the other hand, the manager contributes his knowledge of the behavioral characteristics of the various asset classes, along with his belief as to how they will function in the context of different portfolio structures. (At this point, the manager should try to put aside his perceptions of immediate market value, and concentrate on the general long-term characteristics of the various market sectors.)

In all too many instances, this interchange tends to remain at a rather fuzzy level of generality, with both parties espousing the obviously desirable "Nirvana points," *e.g.*, maximum return with minimum risk, highest yield without sacrifice of quality, minimum volatility with greatest stability of income, etc. If the discussion of goals ends at this point, then neither party has communicated his sense of the appropriate tradeoffs. In a rather fundamental sense, no real understanding has been achieved.

However, a joint determination to specify a Baseline Portfolio can drive these discussions down to the concrete level. It will force the difficult choices to be made—and made *jointly* by both sponsor and manager. The sponsor must articulate the subtle priorities that can organize his many objectives, and he must develop a clear-cut structure by relating these priorities—with the manager's help—to choices between specific market sectors. The manager must rise above his active orientation to define the most balanced, passive portfolio structure matching his client's needs. In this fashion, both parties are able to merge and consolidate their different points of view. In essence, by specifying a Baseline Portfolio, they have come to agree on a practical, passive alternative to active management.

As with any real process of communication, these interactions may prove painful and arduous at the outset. However, once defined, the Baseline can prove a mutual vantage point for interpreting the actual returns achieved over time. The all-too-common on-going confusion between conflicting short-term results and long-term goals will be reduced. Because of the sponsor's role in defining the Baseline, the manager will no longer find himself quite so vulnerable to criticism for the many portfolio effects that are (in reality) mandated by the nature of the fund. In particular, having the Baseline as a "baseline" may considerably reduce artificial pressures on a manager with regard to high volatility, yield give-ups, particularly high or low quality postures, having the portfolio balanced away from the general market structure, or for deviations from the performance returns achieved by general market indices or theoretical peer groups.

Moreover, by concentrating the objective-setting in an initial phase shared with the sponsor, the Baseline approach should allow the investment manager to focus more clearly on his day-by-day market activities in the fund's behalf. At the same time, the fund sponsor will achieve the security of knowing that his long term risk/return objectives are not being inadvertently compromised in the pursuit of short term performance.

FOOTNOTES

1. *Goal-Oriented Bond Portfolio Management: The "Baseline" Method for Relating Short-Term Performance to Long-Term Goals,* Martin L. Leibowitz, Salomon Brothers, May 15, 1978 (Now Chapter 1, in Total Return Management, Salomon Brothers, 1979).

2. *Portfolio Returns and Scenario Analysis,* Martin L. Leibowitz, Salomon Brothers, March 20, 1978 (Now Chapter 5 in *Total Return Management,* Salomon Brothers, 1979).

3. *The Risk Dimension,* Martin L. Leibowitz, Salomon Brothers, October 5, 1977 (Now Chapter 4, in *Total Return Management,* Salomon Brothers, 1979).

4. *The Rolling Yield,* Martin L. Leibowitz, Salomon Brothers, April 21, 1977 (Now Chapter 2, in *Total Return Management,* Salomon Brothers, 1979).

5. *Source of Return in Corporate Bond Portfolios,* Martin L. Leibowitz, Salomon Brothers, August 3, 1978 (Now Chapter 6, in *Total Return Management,* Salomon Brothers, 1979).

A BACKWARD GLANCE
O'ER TRAVELLED ROADS

Herman Liss

Herman Liss was the Dean of bond portfolio managers for more than two decades prior to this reminiscence presented as a talk at the 1980 Financial Analysts Federation annual conference.

My assignment is to provide a retrospective view of the opportunities that have existed over the years in senior securities. In this backward glance o'er travelled roads, I draw comfort from a quotation on the frontispiece of Graham Greene's autobiography: "Only robbers and gypsies say that one must never return where one has been."

A NOTE ON FORECASTS

At the outset, I wish to make it clear that I shall have little to say about interest rate forecasts and the structuring of maturities. Two of the most skillful leaders in forecasting interest rates have made their views loud

Reprinted with permission from the *Financial Analysts Journal*, Vol. 38, No. 2, March/April 1982, 55–59. New York, New York: Financial Analysts Federation.

and clear without equivocation and without alternative views. They are the envy of the professionals in this field.

I would suspect that these eminent economists would agree—or would they?—that management of portfolios, senior securities or equities begins when forecasting ends. Without elaborating on each of the reasons why I arrive at this conclusion, herewith are a few observations.

In the management of security portfolios that have no likely short-term demands in excess of cash flow, it is imprudent (in my judgment) to rely completely on one forecast. Rather, management should weigh a primary and a series of alternative forecasts of the level of interest rates. It is beyond the perception of even the most successful proponents of only one projection to be able to cope with myriad likely and unexpected events. I doubt whether successful corporations, in projecting cost of funds for new projects with a long life factor, would rely on only one forecast, especially if there are competing projects with different break-even levels.

In recent years, short money market paper has been about the only safe port against the rumble and thunder in the senior securities market. Of all sectors, money market rates are the most volatile and, in this sense, the most speculative for investors who do not have to maintain capital stability on, say, a year to year basis or even somewhat longer. When money market rates are sky high and higher than longer paper, they are indeed comparable to a very attractive rental without a lease. What institutions with liabilities with distant calls for payment can live without a lease? If I misjudge my projected cash income, and if my expenditures remain unchanged, I can move out of my house, pare down my other expenses and seek to balance my account. Can institutions do this—move out of their buildings and possibly slash other expenditures?

Forecasting as practiced by the eminent leaders is concerned solely with a single or a series of continuous single numbers, sometimes with a cap on the future level, and at other times without a cap on the risk side. Under certain conditions, I find this singularly barren. Here is one excessively simple reason: When the yield from a long-term bond increases from, say, eight to nine percent, from nine to 10 percent, from 10 to 11 percent and so on, the risk element at each higher level begins to diminish, as reflected in rates of return.

To illustrate, if bond yields move from eight to nine percent, the annual total return for, say, a three-year holding period would be 5.4

percent, whereas in moving from 12 to 13 percent, the comparable figure would be 10.4 percent, and from 14 to 15 percent, the annual return would be 12.7 percent. These rates of return reflect two simple mathematical factors. First, a one percentage point increase in yields starting at eight percent involves a larger price decline than one starting at 14 percent. Second, the contribution of an eight percent coupon to the total rate of return is obviously substantially less than the contribution of a 14 percent coupon to the total rate of return. Yet this simple computation has not been factored into forecasts that I speak of, as far as I'm aware.

MANAGING A BOND PORTFOLIO

I will now turn to a number of areas that can make an occasional contribution to the management of a bond portfolio. The first is the shape of yield profiles, variously described as positive, negative, flat, humped or of varying combinations.

Yield Curve Profiles

In August 1966, it was possible to observe that the pitch of the Treasury yield curve was sharply out of line with corporate and municipal profiles. While the pitch of the municipal profile is normally different from the Treasury or corporate yield profiles, something was amiss in the Treasury profile in mid-August 1966.

Extensive testing of a variety of possible yield profiles in stronger and weaker bond markets and for different time spans identified the seven-year Treasury—the $4^1/_4$, 1974, yielding about 54 basis points more than long Treasuries—to be outstandingly attractive relative to long Treasuries.

The potential for marked price appreciation that even the seven-year 1974 maturity shared with much longer Treasuries was due to the considerable "discount" at which the 1974 maturities sold, combined with the probability that this "discount" would disappear in a lower yield market and might even turn into a "premium," and that the years to maturity were sufficiently long to bring about a sizable price advance with lower yields. Furthermore, the 1974 maturities had the increasing potential for a comparatively better performance if yields were to remain unchanged for an indefinite period, or to continue to increase.

By May 1967, interest rates were considerably lower throughout the yield profile, and the negative yield profile was replaced by the traditional positive profile in keeping with a confident bond market. These lower yields provided a test of one of the challenges to a shift out of the long-term bond market nine months earlier. How would a seven-year bond stand up against a long-term issue in a strong bond market? It did exceedingly well.

The explanation for this seeming anomaly is to be found in (1) the substantial negative yield profile being succeeded by a positive one and (2) the seven years to maturity being sufficiently long, in combination with the change in the profile, to bring about a sizable price advance. Both possibilities were considered in our analysis. Two other possibilities were also weighed—if yields remained unchanged for an indefinite period and if yields increased. In the first case, the 65 basis point higher yield from the seven-year bond was obviously an advantage. The second case had its ultimate test when the $4^{1}/_{4}$, 1974 matured at 100 in May of that year, when long-term issues were weak.

In the winter of 1976, a reverse situation was observed. Then medium-term governments commanded an excessive "premium," which we identify as the premium for maturity preference.

Foreign Currency Bonds

Another area of potential contribution is foreign currency bonds. I will limit my remarks to the Canadian currency. For over 20 years, investors have been able to purchase Canadian government bonds payable in Canadian currency, moving in and out as values changed relative to U.S. dollar obligations. From 1976 to 1980 alone, an investor could have had four round trips to his advantage relative to an investment in comparable long U.S. government bonds.

On technical grounds, we place considerable weight on the size of the yield differential from Canadian pay securities over comparable U.S. pay issues, and on the outlook for the Canadian dollar, as we perceive it. In recent years, transactions into and out of Canadian pay issues have been sparked more by a significant change in the yield differential than by changes in the currency rate, although both enter into our decision. To facilitate our appraisals, we construct a variety of matrices to identify risk and opportunity under a postulated range of yield differentials over U.S. pay issues and currency rates.

Railroads

Among the most rewarding perceptions that a student of relative values could have held occurred in 1968, when it was possible to perceive that railroads rich with natural resources might consider dividing their pool of assets into two distinct operations—(1) natural resources and (2) railroad operations. A number of managements were becoming aware that less than adequate attention was being paid to the development of their non-rail assets. Certainly, there was an enormous need to do so, given the scant rate of return from rail operations alone. While this possibility was there to see, Union Pacific presented a unique situation.

This company's four percent preferred stock was entitled to one vote per share, the same as the common with three times as many shares outstanding. The articles governing the preferred stock were unique. Its preference as to dividends was stated, as was to be expected. There was, however, no provision regarding its liquidating value; further, the issue was non-callable. Its aggregate market value was only a slight percentage of the equity at market, hence whatever action the company deemed desirable would not significantly affect the estimated market value of the equity.

If Union Pacific were to divide its operations between natural resources and rail activities through formation of two or more separate subsidiaries, how would Union Pacific handle the unique situation of its preferred stock? An investor in the company's preferred had to make three judgments: Would the company consider a realignment of operations? How would the company treat the preferred holder who might claim parity with the common in a recapitalization? Could the preferred stand on its own on a relative value basis, with yields in line with the general run of preferreds, regardless of these possible developments?

Rather than risk litigation, Union Pacific took two actions. It purchased the four percent issue in the open market and then eliminated the balance through an attractive exchange offer.

Convertibles

For over 40 years, convertible securities have provided, on occasion, uncommon opportunities to share in the growth prospects of equities with varying degrees of risk, and infrequently, with only a nominally greater risk than a comparable quality, non-convertible senior security. Our approach to the use of these securities is as varied as their essential differences.

They are viewed in a variety of ways, depending on the quality of the credit, the price risk relative to non-convertible issues of comparable quality, the conversion premium, the prospects for the equity and, in some instances, their yield comparison. It is our appraisal of these factors, when quality standards are met, that determines whether to invest in a convertible security in lieu of a non-convertible senior security, or in lieu of holding the company's common stock directly. Within this broad approach and in cooperation with our equity analysts, we have developed a number of refinements in the use of convertibles in competition with other forms of securities.

Looking back at the record, I am still at a loss to account for the occasional opportunity to acquire convertible bonds and preferreds of good to satisfactory quality at only a scant premium relative to investment value but with a long-term call on an equity. I know of no writer of options who sells a call on a general market equity, not for 60 or 90 days, but for years, at a nominal price. These two markets are obviously not always on speaking terms.

THE BOND/EQUITY EQUATION

With some temerity, I turn to equities. Possibly more than any challenging ideas I have espoused, my views on the relation of equities to bonds in 1968 and 1969 (and in a number of subsequent years, notably in January 1975) stand out, in my judgment, as my most rewarding contributions to an understanding of relative values.

Under the title *Total Money Management*, Sidney Homer, formerly a general partner in Salomon Brothers and an earlier associate of mine, observed in 1973:

> It is often said that the medical profession has too many specialists and too few generalists. Surely this is even more true of investment management. I am a bond man; perhaps you are a stock man, or an oil stock man, or a bank stock man, or a mortgage man. Where are the generalists?
>
> There are of course top managers who seem to control overall invest-

ment policy, but look closely: this one has a stock market background, this one came up from the bond department. Of course, there always have been a few real generalists, wise men with long and balanced experience and a worldwide view of investment basics.

I hope I am not being too immodest if I lay claim to being somewhat of a generalist. In any event, it was in that role that I like to think my firm asked me to debate the issue of equities versus bonds in 1968.

In this debate, I took the position that the market for equities had confused the source and the repetitive meaning of the surge in equity prices over the preceding 20 years. The major impetus for this rise was the dramatic increase in the earnings multiplier, not outsized earnings growth.

At the end of 1949, the earnings multiplier for the S&P 425 industrials was 6.8 times. Five years later it rose to 13, to 20 in 1958, to 22 in 1961 and ended in 1968 at 18 times.

At the end of 1949, when the Dow yielded 6.4 percent, quality corporate bonds yielded 2.7 percent and five-year Treasuries 1.4 percent. Clearly, the then discount on equities compared to an investment in bonds was untenable, assuming only modest earnings growth and dividend payout over a period of years.

By the time of my involvement in the challenge of equities versus bonds, the market had seemingly more than corrected the excessively low valuation of equities and excessively high valuation of senior securities in the immediate postwar period. Yields on equities were down below four percent, corporate bond yields were above eight percent, and five-year Treasuries in excess of seven percent. At the end of 1968, the Dow was 944.

Time is not available to discuss the maze of statistics I compiled nor the arguments I marshalled to buttress my view. I took special pleasure repeating former Prime Minister Macmillan's historic phrase after a visit to Africa: "A new wind is blowing." And I added, "Who hears, who listens and who understands."

Also, it was in June of 1968 that Robert Metz of the *New York Times* reported in his column, The Market Place, "A Bank Decides Bonds Won't Do":

> In the sumptuous offices of _____ a quiet revolution is going on that would shock the founders of this, one of the nation's oldest banks.
> For the bank, regarded as one of the nation's most astute in the manage-

ment of investments, has passed the word around that bonds—the ordinary fixed-interest kind that have delighted the coupon-clipping set on Park Avenue for generations—are completely out. And he was talking about the fixed-interest portion of the bank's money management activities.

"We haven't bought a straight corporate bond since last August," is the way the executive vice president put it yesterday.

Sound imprudent? Quite the contrary. He thinks that a good way to get clobbered these days is to be in the bond market.

A straight-line projection of earnings growth, dividend payout and multiplier over a 25-year period was used by the bank to justify an investment in utility stocks rather than in bonds. Could these trends be reasonably extrapolated? Surely if bond yields were to rise significantly, wouldn't this risk affect earnings, dividend payout and the earnings multiplier?

Subsequently I wrote a paper titled, "The Earnings Multiplier Has No Life of Its Own." I challenged the simplistic concept of justifying, at any one date, the level of equities by comparing the then earnings multiplier with an average prevailing over a specified period of years, generally the most recent five or 10 years. What a meaningless comparison, unless attention is paid to the differences, now and then, in the rates of return on corporate equity and total capitalization, on earnings growth, calculated properly, on dividend-paying capacity, on bond yields, on the state of social and political health, domestically and abroad, and on prospects for inflation.

Finally, just a quick glance on my views in January 1975 when the Dow industrial average reached 600. It was my opinion, expressed in a position paper, that 600 was an attractive level. This was not, needless to say, an innovative view, merely a view contrary to general market sentiment. What I think had more than common merit at that time was the concept I used to appraise the inner meaning of the equity averages.

I stressed that the risk of selling equities then was not that of foregoing the oft-quoted nine percent return from equities over a period of years, but rather foregoing the front end of a future rally. The nine percent historical return, I noted, was made up of three parts—the front end in any cyclical rise (say as much as 40 percent or so), the middle part (a modest rise) and the end movement (which could be a decline of sizable proportions). It was these three segments that produced the nine percent rate of return. As equities move from unrelieved pessimism, this appraisal proved to have validity.

CONCLUSION

To summarize, innovative ideas and perception of uncommon values are the end result of:

experience,

independence of thought,

intense interest,

ability to hear voices only faintly heard by others and

a modicum of artistry.

With these virtues you will experience the "spirit of delight," to borrow a phrase from Virginia Woolf.

THE TIME TESTED MAXIMS OF THE TEMPLETON TOUCH

William Proctor

John Templeton–with deep faith, a drive for excellence, and a habit of goal setting–has achieved a remarkable record in investment management. Here are his maxims for investors.

These are the twenty-two key guiding principles that Templeton says have enabled him to become one of the world's greatest living investors. These points are expressed in his own words, and they serve as a kind of summary statement of the Templeton Touch. Some of these have been discussed in depth in previous pages; others are relatively new nuggets of wisdom; all are maxims that the savviest investors should keep in mind as they decide where to place their money.

1. For all long-term investors, there is only one objective– "maximum total real return after taxes."
2. Achieving a good record takes much study and work, and is a lot harder than most people think.

3. It is impossible to produce a superior performance unless you do something different from the majority.
4. The time of maximum pessimism is the best time to buy, and the time of maximum optimism is the best time to sell.
5. To put "Maxim 4" in somewhat different terms, in the stock market the only way to get a bargain is to buy what most investors are selling.
6. To buy when others are despondently selling and to sell when others are greedily buying requires the greatest fortitude, even while offering the greatest reward.
7. Bear markets have always been temporary. Share prices turn upward from one to twelve months before the bottom of the business cycle.
8. If a particular industry or type of security becomes popular with investors, that popularity will always prove temporary and, when lost, won't return for many years.
9. In the long run, the stock market indexes fluctuate around the long-term upward trend of earnings per share.
10. In free-enterprise nations, the earnings on stock market indexes fluctuate around the replacement book value of the shares of the index.
11. If you buy the same securities as other people, you will have the same results as other people.
12. The time to buy a stock is when the short-term owners have finished their selling, and the time to sell a stock is often when short-term owners have finished their buying.
13. Share prices fluctuate much more widely than values. Therefore, index funds will never produce the best total return performance.
14. Too many investors focus on "outlook" and "trend." Therefore, more profit is made by focusing on value.
15. If you search worldwide, you will find more bargains and better bargains than by studying only one nation. Also, you gain the safety of diversification.
16. The fluctuation of share prices is roughly proportional to the square root of the price.
17. The time to sell an asset is when you have found a much better bargain to replace it.

18. When any method for selecting stocks becomes popular, then switch to unpopular methods. As has been suggested in "Maxim 3," too many investors can spoil any share-selection method or any market-timing formula.
19. Never adopt permanently any type of asset or any selection method. Try to stay flexible, open-minded and skeptical. Long-term top results are achieved only by changing from popular to unpopular the types of securities you favor and your methods of selection.
20. The skill factor in selection is largest for the common-stock part of your investments.
21. The best performance is produced by a person, not a committee.
22. If you begin with prayer, you can think more clearly and make fewer stupid mistakes.

If you own one stock and are considering switching to a second, the second stock should be at least 50 percent more valuable than the first one for the switch to be worthwhile.

* * * * *

WORLDWIDE INVESTING

John Templeton

John Templeton gave this talk at the 1984 Financial Analysts Federation annual conference. He began his career as a "statistician" with Fenner and Beane, at one dollar an hour, 47 years earlier, and studied at night school, where his teacher was Ben Graham.

Today let's talk about a growth industry. Because investing worldwide is a growth industry. Direct investing across national borders probably will grow; but the great growth industry is portfolio investing, partly because it is more welcome politically in the host nations.

Nineteen nations now have stock markets with securities listed on each of those exchanges exceeding $10 billion in market value. All over the world people want to own more American stocks and last year foreign buying reached 10% of the volume on the New York Stock Exchange. Also, enthusiasm is growing in America for foreign stocks. About 800 foreign stocks are now continuously traded in America. Large pension funds and endowments are hiring more and more advisers to help them invest abroad.

Increasingly brokers are opening foreign offices and buying foreign stocks. Investment counselors are doing the same. Financial journals are publishing more and more information, news and ideas on foreign

From the transcript of an address given at the Annual Conference of the Financial Analysts Federation, May 2, 1984, reprinted by permission of John Templeton.

stocks. Mutual funds to facilitate cross-border investing are springing up by the dozens. Banks have begun to set up master trusts for worldwide safekeeping of foreign securities. As you well know, societies of security analysts have been founded abroad with more than 1000 analysts each in Canada, England and Japan, and smaller groups in 20 other nations.

If some of you want to participate in this growth industry of world-wide investing, a good way to begin is to study the differences between nations. Learn the different tax rates and concepts of taxable income for both corporations and individuals. Learn the customs and attitudes of investors in each nation and the different restrictions on foreigners. Also the peculiar accounting methods and diverse regulations of business, as well as the exchange controls, present and probable. Then to begin your security analysis, of course, you will need the sources of information from foreign security analysts, investment journals, visits with management, etc. Naturally this is a lot of work but it does pay off in better investment results.

Worldwide investing provides many benefits for investors:

- If you search for bargains worldwide you may find more bargains and also better bargains.
- Even more important is that you will reduce the risk. When your nation suffers a bear market, you will suffer less if your investments are diversified among many markets.
- Investing worldwide teaches you what can happen in your own nation. For example, American analysts know what can happen when inflation reaches 20% a year. But it does open your eyes to study share prices in a nation where inflation is 100% a year like Mexico or Israel, or 400% a year as in Argentina. For example, you will learn that rising bond yields do not always cause lower share prices . . . sometimes yields on bonds or deposits can rise to more than 5 times the yield on common stocks.
- Opportunities are revealed by seeing how different the popular investment theories can be in different nations and in different cycles. As an example, for the same industry, at the same time, price earnings ratios can be sky high in one nation and low in another nation. In America today there is a popular theory that

price earnings ratios must remain low because bond yields are high, but already now price earnings ratios have reached 29 in Japan and 26 in Singapore . . . and even some brokers here in America are enthusiastically recommending to their clients buying certain stocks at 29 times earnings when they could buy American bonds, high quality, to yield 14%. So if it can happen in other nations it might happen in America, too.

- The most successful way to benefit from differences in various nations is not to hire a local adviser in each of five or more major nations, but instead to hire one worldwide adviser who is given freedom to shift assets from nation to nation wherever the best bargains are found at different times.

Some of you may want to know where in the world to invest right now.

The common sense answer is to buy wherever you find the best bargains. Of course the outlook for future growth is very different in different nations and growth prospects are a big part of finding bargains. Common sense reveals quite clearly which nations are likely to enjoy increasing prosperity. Prosperity is apt to flow to that nation which has these following blessings:

Less government ownership.

Less government regulation.

Less quarrelsome unions.

Lower taxes.

Higher research budgets.

People who are honest and reliable.

People who are far-sighted, rather than short-sighted.

Higher rates of saving. (For example, the Japanese now save more than twice as much as Americans from each dollar earned.)

Such growth incentives predominate in the East Asia markets and that is why in the past 20 years the market value of shares traded on those exchanges grew from 13% to 92% of the total market value for 12 European exchanges.

Good judgment is a basic requirement for success in security analysis. In predicting the future no group does better than security analysts. Politicians may prosper from promises and salesmanship, but security analysts must be far-sighted and deal in factors and common sense.

Security analysts are a civilizing influence on business practices. They enquire and expose. Security analysis accelerates progress in productive methods and truth in accounting. Your first duty as security analysts is to produce for your clients superior total real returns, net after tax. But also, security analysts can and do help all people worldwide to enjoy more prosperity, peace and brotherhood.

Worldwide investing is a force for understanding and cooperation between peoples and nations. Worldwide investing helped poor nations grow rich. Security analysts can be missionaries for people's capitalism and can gain happiness from helping people worldwide to attain more prosperity, peace, and brotherly love.

Now, what is the shape of the future? As long as freedom lives, the future is glorious.

When I was born in Franklin County, Tennessee, the uniform wage for unskilled men was 10 cents an hour. Now the average for factory workers is $9.00. Even after adjusting for inflation, the increase is more than 10 fold. The federal budget in nominal dollars is now almost 300 times as great as at the peak of prosperity in 1929. In my lifetime real consumption per person worldwide–that is, the standard of living in real goods–has more than quadrupled.

A landmark for freedom was the publication 208 years ago of Adam Smith's great work called "An Inquiry into the Nature and Causes of the Wealth of Nations." The necktie I wear today, bearing the likeness of Adam Smith, is supplied by the Philadelphia Society to commemorate that great liberation. In 208 years of relative freedom, the yearly output of goods and services worldwide has increased more than a hundred fold. This is a hundred fold increase in real goods and services consumed, net after eliminating inflation.

Before Adam Smith less than 1000 corporations existed on earth, but now corporations are being created at the rate of 4000 every business day. In the days of Adam Smith, 85% of the people were needed on the farms, but now less than 4% on the farms in America produce a surplus of food.

Our children and grandchildren now being born will enjoy even more progress than we. For many reasons progress may not only continue but may also accelerate. To try to foresee the future let us begin by mentioning a few of the changes which have already occurred in just my lifetime.

When I was born 71 years ago the highest salaried person in my county was paid less than $2,000 a year. The federal debt was only one billion dollars.

- *In 1912, Americans had:*

    No income tax . . . no Federal Reserve

    No Financial Analysts Federation . . . no financial analysts

    No investment counsellors . . . no mutual funds

    No vitamins . . . no refrigerators

    No radios . . . no transcontinental telephones . . . no traffic lights

    No plastics . . . no man-made fibres . . . and no fluorescent lights

- *Much later after the great 1929 boom, Americans still had:*

    No Social Security . . . no unemployment insurance

    No Securities and Exchange Commission

    No capital gains tax . . . no inheritance tax

    No air mail . . . no airlines

    No antibiotics . . . no nylon . . . no frozen foods

    No television . . . no transistors

    No lasers . . . and no nuclear energy

Who could have imagined back then the variety of new blessings in my lifetime and who can imagine now the even greater new blessings in store for our children and our grandchildren?

At the peak of the 1929 boom the federal budget was only $3 billion. Now GNP per person is 30 times what it was 50 years ago; and in the next 50 years it may grow 30 fold again, from $15,000 now to $450,000 per year per person.

In the latest 50 years, each $1 invested in the average of all American stocks grew to more than $100 if dividends were re-invested. Fifty years from now, maybe each $1 invested back in 1934 will have grown to 100 times $100. If 100 times $100 seems too much to expect, then calculate the results which may be possible if you are wise enough in your stock selections to exceed the market average by 5% yearly. If you assume that the next 50 years will be the same as the last, and if you re-invest dividends, and if your results have been and continue to be 5% a year better than the market average, then each $1 invested 50 years ago may 50 years from now have grown to 950 times $950. . . that's more than $900,000.

––––––––––––

Now, as I conclude, let me speculate about the future.

We now enjoy prosperity greater than ever dreamed of before this century. Will these trends continue in the future? If we are able to preserve and enhance freedom, these trends may continue and accelerate. We may expect more rapid change and wider fluctuations. Life will be full of adventure and opportunity and never dull or routine.

In America alone this year over $100 billion will be dedicated to research and development. More in one year in one nation than the total research for all the world's history before I was born. Awesome new blessings are visible also in health, entertainment, spiritual growth and charity. In America alone over $50 billion will be donated to churches and charities this year. Each year the generous and voluntary giving by Americans alone exceeds the total income of all the world's people in any year before Adam Smith.

We should be overwhelmingly grateful to have been born in this century. The slow progress of prehistoric ages is over, and centuries of human enterprise are now miraculously bursting forth into flower. The evolution of human knowledge is accelerating, and we are reaping the fruits of generations of scientific thought: only 60 years ago astronomers became convinced that the universe is 100 billion times larger than previously thought. More than half of the scientists who ever lived are alive today. More than half of the discoveries of the natural sciences have been made in this century. More than half of the goods produced since the earth was born have been produced in the two centuries since Adam Smith. Over half of the books ever written were written in the last half-century. More new books are published each month than were written in the entire historical period before the birth of Columbus.

Discovery and invention have not stopped or even slowed down. Who can imagine what will be discovered if research continues to accelerate. Each discovery reveals new mysteries. The more we learn, the more we realize how ignorant we were in the past and how much there still is to discover.

If you do not fall down on your knees each day, with overwhelming gratitude for your blessings—your multiplying multitudes of blessings— then *you* just have not yet *seen* the big picture.

YOUR OWN
BEST INTEREST

Andrew Tobias

Andrew Tobias has written several wonderful, lucid books on investing, including *The Only Investment Guide You'll Ever Need*, and on business. In this excerpt from "Your Own Best Interest," he explains the marvels of compound interest.

If you could be any financial concept in the world, which one would you be? Inflation? Hedging? Disintermediating? (Sorry; "rich" is an adjective, not a concept. You've got to pick a concept.) If you were smart, you'd pick compound interest. It never fails to dazzle.

Today, for example, I bought $200,000 worth of zero-coupon municipal bonds. Zero coupon means they pay no interest. Municipal means I pay no taxes. (Why taxes should be a consideration at all when no interest is paid I shall explain momentarily.) All these bonds offer is the promise that on January 1, 2014, they will be redeemed at full face value: $1000. I bought 200 such little promises.

Now, even a fine-arts major knows that $1000 well into the next century is worth something less than $1000 in cash today. (A bird in the hand, and all that.) But how much less?

I called my broker, a man of surpassing charm and experience, who does things the old-fashioned way. "Buy me two hundred of these New Hampshire zeros of 2014," I said. I love to talk like that.

Reprinted from *Playboy*, Vol. 30, No. 3, March 1983, 119, 160–162. Reprinted by permission of Sterling Lord Literistic, Inc. Copyright ©1983.

"At what price?" he asked, his quill pen at the ready.

"They're quoted two and five eighths," I told him.

"What do you mean?" he asked.

"I mean they're quoted two and five eighths," I explained.

"What do you *mean*?" he asked.

When a bond is quoted at par (100), that means it's selling for 100 cents on the dollar—its full $1000 face value. When it's quoted at 55, that means it is selling for 55 cents on the dollar. Eventually, it will be redeemed at full face value—$1000—but right now, if you tried to get rid of it, $550 is all you would get. And when a bond is quoted at two and five eighths, that means it is selling for two and five eighths cents on the dollar, or $26.25 a bond. Not a lot of money.

"I mean," I said, "that each bond costs twenty-six dollars and twenty-five cents."

"That can't be right," said my broker. "It must be two sixty-two fifty." The old decimal-point trick. Not $26.25—$262.50.

"Hunh-unh," I explained again, "twenty-six twenty-five."

"You mean," he said, "that for every twenty-six dollars you pay now, you get a thousand dollars in thirty-one years?"

"Now you've got it."

"Wait," he said, "That can't be right."

But it is. And I bought them—$200,000 worth for $5300. It is the so-called magic of compound interest. It astonished us as children (*Ripley's Believe It or Not!*); it astonishes us today.

I called to tell a young investment-banker friend about these bonds. He holds two Harvard degrees and earned a bonus last year of $73,000. Money is his business. I asked how much he thought it would take to build up $200,000 in after-tax money by 2014.

"You want me to figure it out for you or just guess?" he said.

"Just guess," I said.

"Three thousand a year?"

"No, fifty-three hundred once."

"That can't be right," he said, reaching for his calculator. "What rate of return is that?"

"Twelve percent a year, compounded."

"It is!" he said, a moment later, marveling at the cherry-cough-syrup display of his pocket calculator.

———

It was Homer who said that $1000 invested at a mere eight percent for 400 years would mount to 23 quadrillion dollars—$5,000,000 for every human on earth. (And you can't see any reason to save?) But, he said, the first 100 years are the hardest. (This was Sidney Homer, not Homer Homer—A *History of Interest Rates*. Outstanding.)

What invariably happens is that long before the first 100 years are up, someone with access to the cache loses patience. The money burns a hole in his pocket. Or through his nose.

Doubtless that would have been true of the Correa fortune, too, had Domingos Faustino Correa not cut everyone out of his will for 100 years. That was in 1873, in Brazil. You could have gotten very tired waiting, but if you can establish that you are one of that misanthrope's 4000-odd legitimate heirs, you may now have some money coming to you. Since 1873, Correa's estate has grown to an estimated 12 billion dollars.

Benjamin Franklin had much the same idea, only with higher purpose. Inventive to the end, he left £1000 each to Boston and Philadelphia. The cities were to lend the money, at interest, to worthy apprentices. Then, after a century, they were to employ part of the fortune Franklin envisioned to construct some public work, while continuing to invest the rest.

One hundred ninety-two years later, when last I checked, Boston's fund exceeded $3,000,000, even after having been drained to build Franklin Union, and was being lent at interest to medical school students. Philadelphia's fund was smaller, but it, too, had been put to good use. All this from an initial stake of £2000!

And then there was the king who held a chess tournament among the peasants—I may have this story a little wrong, but the point holds— and asked the winner what he wanted as his prize. The peasant, in apparent humility, asked only that a single kernel of wheat be placed for him on the first square of his chessboard, two kernels on the second, four on the third—and so forth. The king fell for it and had to import grain from Argentina for the next 700 years. Eighteen and a half million trillion kernels, or enough, if each kernel is a quarter inch long (which it may not be; I've never seen wheat in its pre-English-muffin form), to stretch to the sun and back 391,320 times.

That was nothing more than one kernel's compounding at 100 percent per square for 64 squares. It is vaguely akin to the situation with our national debt.

Just as the peasant could fool the king, so are we peasants now and again fooled. For decades, for example, one of the most basic deceptions in the sale of life insurance has been what is called the net-cost comparison.

Without sitting you down at the kitchen table and walking you through the whole thing (it being difficult to sit and walk simultaneously), suffice it to say that whole-life insurance, seemingly expensive, could be shown by the insurance professional to cost *nothing*. For after 20 or 30 years, the accumulated cash value and dividends could exceed all the premiums you had paid in!

The only thing this comparison ignores is the time value of money — the fact that all those premiums, had they been accruing interest on *your* behalf, might have been worth far more than the amount with which the life-insurance company was willing to credit you.

"Do you realize," I have been asked angrily by life-insurance salesmen, "that we have policies now that can be paid up after just eight or nine years?" They ask it as if the companies were doing an incredible, unappreciated, magnanimous thing, when, of course, the *reason* no additional premiums are due after the first eight or nine years is simply that the excess charged in those years is enough, when compounded at today's extraordinary interest rates, to fund the policy forever after. There is no magic here, no magnanimity, merely the workings of compound interest.

It is remarkable how many people, while they certainly know such terms as interest and return on investment, fail fully to understand them.

Say you borrowed $1000 from a friend and paid it back at the rate of $100 a month for a year. What rate of interest would that be?

A lot of bright people will answer 20 percent. After all, you borrowed $1000 and paid back $1200, so what else could it be? *Forty* percent?

No. More.

If you'd had use of the full $1000 for a year, then $200 would, indeed, have constituted 20 percent interest. But you had full use of it for only the first month, at the end of which you began paying it back. By the end of the tenth month, far from having use of $1000, you no longer had use of *any* of the money. So you were paying $200 in the last two months of the year for the right to have used an average of $550 for each of the first ten. That comes to a bit more than a 41.25 percent effective rate of interest. (Trust me.)

Because this sort of thing is complicated, there are truth-in-lending laws requiring creditors to show, in bold type, what they're really charging for money. (Well, they show nominal rates, not effective rates, but it's close enough.). . .Unfortunately, no similar disclosure law applies to life insurance.

* * * * *

IF FREUD WERE A
PORTFOLIO MANAGER

Byron R. Wien

Byron R. Wien writes on investment strategy for Morgan Stanley. Previously, he spent two decades as a portfolio manager at two investment counsel firms.

A few weeks ago I was in Vienna to meet with some Austrian portfolio managers. I had a free hour before lunch and used it to go over to the stately apartment house at 19, Berggasse where Sigmund Freud lived and worked for almost half a century. A part of the great psychoanalyst's former apartment is open to the public as a kind of museum, and the original waiting-room furniture and the general feel of the place are still there, but the famous couch, his writing desk, and his large, high-quality collection of antiquities are now in London where Freud moved in 1938 to escape the Nazis. The examination room and study walls have photo enlargements of the original furnishings, so one can stand there and envision what it must have been like to be in the presence of the man whose insights had such a profound effect on the way we understand ourselves as well as on the literature of much of the last century.

Reprinted from Morgan Stanley Letterhead, New York, New York, July 7, 1986, with permission of the author and Morgan Stanley and Co.

In the stillness of the study, I began to think about Freud's combining his speculations about human psychology with his clinical observations. He accomplished much because he successfully anticipated the next step in his developing theories, and he did that by analyzing everything that had gone before very carefully. This is the antithesis of the way portfolio managers approach their work. Although the investment business makes extensive use of computer-generated information about stocks, groups, portfolios, performance, risk, the economy, and the market, very little of that data-crunching power is directed toward the analysis of past decisions. I think most of us have developed patterns of mistake-making, which, if analyzed carefully, would lead to better performance in the future. Instead, portfolio managers tend to assume that poor decisions are random events in an ever-changing environment. They reason that, since circumstances in the future will never be the same as they were in the past, they are not likely to repeat previous mistakes. Future misjudgments, they think, will come from faulty responses to new phenomena. In an effort to encourage investment professionals to determine their error patterns, I have gathered the data and analyzed my own follies, and I have decided to let at least some of my weaknesses hang out. Perhaps this will inspire you to collect the information on your own decisions over the past several years to see if there aren't some errors that you could make less frequently in the future.

Here are some of the recurring investment mistakes. Perhaps you will hear some familiar chimes ringing.

Selling too early. All of us do this once in a while. I tend to fall into the trap in attempting to fine tune the portfolio. Last year, I thought the drug, food, and media groups were overextended and it made sense to cut back somewhat. I had concluded that the economy was weak and therefore continued to be bullish on disinflation stocks generally, and these stable growers were the leaders of that concept. So here was a case where what I thought was profit-taking prudence was in conflict with my core investment concept. It is true that you never lose money taking a profit, but you can lose precious performance points. Make sure you're not making a change to look busy.

The turnaround with the heart of gold. For years I have been a sucker for laggard groups and stocks that have an outside chance of making it big. Many of us have a contrarian streak in us that results from the conviction that in America good things happen to the frail.

When I was a child, I often dreamed of hitting home runs after being the last picked for a softball game. I was frequently the last picked but hit few homers. Why can't I remember how hard it is to turn around a major company in the competitive international business environment that exists today?

Overstaying a winner. I have had a lot of good stock ideas in my career or, more accurately, I have recognized quite a few solid opportunities when analysts have shown them to me. I have also held more than a few round-trip tickets on some very good stocks, because I have assumed that what has treated me well in the past would continue to do so in the future. More often than not, this happens because I become complacent about my knowledge of the fundamentals. Sometimes portfolio managers become so thirsty for new ideas that they don't properly maintain their knowledge of the developments taking place in the companies they have held for a long time.

Underestimating the seriousness of a problem. As Dennis Sherva has said about emerging growth stocks, "The first bad quarter is rarely the last." More often than not, it seems, the right response to a negative surprise is to sell and keep an eye on the situation from the sidelines. We can all come up with exceptions like Digital Equipment, which snapped back after the troubling September 1983 quarter, but, with smaller companies, a disappointment usually results from a set of conditions that will take time to repair and other stockholders may not have your patience. Sometimes the first day's plunge after a negative announcement is followed by a brief recovery, but if you're going to stay around for things to really improve, you'd better have plenty of other good stocks and very tolerant clients.

Freud said that "Psychoanalysis warns us to abandon the unfruitful factors of fate and has taught us regularly to discover the cause of neurosis." By studying printouts of all of your decisions over the past market cycle, I think you will uncover patterns that will enable you to improve the quality of your judgments in the future. Better yet, have one of your colleagues look over the printout and give you his analysis of your recurring transgressions. Try it. It may not help, but, as my grandmother used to say, "It couldn't hurt."

THERE ARE ONLY THREE WAYS TO GET RICH
THEM THAT'S GOT GETS
STAYING RICH IS FAR MORE IMPORTANT THAN GETTING RICH

Fred J. Young

Fred Young was a key member of the Trust Department of the Harris Bank and continues to inform and entertain with talks and a book having the encouraging title, *How to Get Rich and Stay Rich*. Here are some excerpts.

THERE ARE ONLY THREE WAYS TO GET RICH

1. Inherit it. If you can see that you are going to inherit it, then you have it made. You can skip to the part of this book about staying rich. Someone else has already made the sacrifice of spending less than they earned to create this wealth for you. You should be grateful. You

From Fred J. Young, *How to Get Rich and Stay Rich* (Hollywood, Florida, 1983), 31–32, 41, 43–44, 83, 113–114, by permission of Frederick Fell Publishers, Inc.

didn't have anything to do about it; your ancestry is completely beyond your control. You are fortunate indeed.

2. Marry it. This is an area in which you do have some control. This is something you can work on, but you have to get started on it before you get involved with some poor person. This can be quite a project, and I have seen both men and women work this approach to wealth quite effectively. I see nothing wrong with it. I grew up in an area and at a time when most people, boys and girls, firmly believed that the Good Lord made someone especially for them. Growing up for these young people was largely a search for their "intended." Well, if your intended, when you find him or her, happens to have a lot of money, you should graciously accept the situation. Don't fight it.

3. If you are not going to inherit it, and you have already blown the chance for wealth through marriage, then you have only one chance left to get rich. You spend less than you earn and invest the difference in something that you think will increase in value and make you rich.

What should you invest in? Most rich people I know got rich from investments in one or more of the following:

a. Real estate
b. Own their own business
c. Common stocks
d. Savings accounts (thanks to the magic of compound interest rates)

* * * * *

Good Luck

Any time you have a choice between good luck and good judgment, you should take good luck. Good luck, by definition, denotes success. Good judgment can still go wrong.

* * * * *

Courage

A very important ingredient of successful stock investing is courage. The courage to buy when others are selling; the courage to buy when stocks are hitting new lows; the courage to buy when the economy looks bad; courage to buy at the bottom. If you look back over the years, you will note that the times when the gloom was the thickest invariably turned out to have been the best times to buy stocks.

But most people like to buy when everything is rosy and stocks are hitting new highs. That takes no courage. There is a great tendency to think that stocks will continue doing whatever it is they have been doing. If they have been going up, they will continue going up forever, think the masses. If they are hitting new lows, they will continue hitting new lows forever. Maybe they will continue declining a while longer after you buy them, but you are not likely to be able to know when the bottom has been reached. So your best bet is to pick a level you are willing to pay and proceed with part of your investment funds. If they go lower, you can buy more at even better prices. If they turn and go up, then you will make a profit on what you have.

* * * * *

THEM THAT'S GOT GETS

This is a term I heard my father use over and over when I was a kid growing up in East Tennessee. I thought he originated it, but I learned later that this was not the case at all. Jesus Christ used this term, 2,000 years ago. Matthew 25:29 says, "For unto everyone that hath shall be given." Everytime I read this I think to myself how right He was. Yet I find it presumptuous of me to be emphasizing that Christ was right. It reminds me of the well known story of British Field Marshall Montgomery who gained fame with his success in North Africa in World War II. The story goes that at one time he was addressing his troops and said, "Now as Christ said in the Sermon on the Mountain, . . . and I might add that He was right." That is the way I feel when I find myself pointing out that Christ was right when He said, "For unto everyone that hath shall be given."

Your first $1,000 is hard to get. If you put it in the bank and let it draw interest, your second $1,000 will be a little bit easier to get, but not very much easier. Your first $10,000 is hard to get. The second

$10,000 is a little easier. Your first $100,000 is hard to get, your second $100,000 a lot easier. Your first $1,000,000 is very hard to get. Your second $1,000,000 is a snap.

* * * * *

STAYING RICH IS FAR MORE IMPORTANT THAN GETTING RICH

Once you have made yourself rich, for gosh sakes don't lose it. The inconvenience of going from rich to poor is greater than most people can tolerate. That is the reason they tend to destroy themselves. It is an unusual person who can gracefully make the transition from riches to poverty or even from being rich to modest circumstances. . . .

How do you stay rich once you get rich? Don't hesitate to seek professional help. Staying rich usually requires an entirely different approach from that of getting rich. Lots of people know how to make money, but are not gifted at all in the art of preserving it. Frequently, the risk that was involved in making you rich is the same risk that can make you poor again.

* * * * *